ADVANCED AUDITING

Fundamentals
of EDP and
Statistical Audit Technology

Miklos A. Vasarhelyi

AT&T Bell Laboratories
Columbia University

Thomas W. Lin

University of Southern California

ADDISON-WESLEY PUBLISHING COMPANY

Reading, Massachusetts • Menlo Park, California • New York
Don Mills, Ontario • Wokingham, England • Amsterdam
Bonn • Sydney • Singapore • Tokyo • Madrid • San Juan

Muirhead Library
Michigan Christian College
Rochester, Michigan

Library of Congress Cataloging-in-Publication Data

Vasarhelyi, Miklos A.
　　Advanced Auditing.

　　Bibliography: p.
　　Includes Index.
　　1. Auditing. I. Lin, W. Thomas. II. Title.
HF5667.V34　　1988　　657'.45　　86-17232
ISBN 0-201-05328-4

Many of the designations used by manufacturers and sellers to distinguish their products are claimed as trademarks. Where those designations appear in this book, and Addison-Wesley was aware of a trademark claim, the designations have been printed in initial caps or all caps.

Additional Credits:

The following material is reprinted courtesy of the American Institute of Certified Public Accountants, Inc.

Page 164, 166, 436 — Copyright © 1980
Page 165, 230, 397 — Copyright © 1974
Page 165, 201, 202, 229, 397— Copyright © 1976
Page 165, 201 — Copyright © 1977
Page 165, 200, 230 — Copyright © 1979
Page 166, 435 — Copyright © 1982
Page 166, 202, 436 — Copyright © 1985
Page 200 — Copyright © 1971
Page 200, 396, 397 — Copyright © 1981
Page 201 — Copyright © 1972
Page 202, 397, 398 — Copyright © 1978
Page 202, 230, 436, 437 — Copyright © 1984

Page 229 — Copyright © 1969
Page 229, 437 — Copyright © 1983
Page 230, 398 — Copyright © 1973
Page 230, 396, 397 — Copyright © 1975
Page 435 — Copyright © 1986

The following material is reprinted courtesy of The Institute of Internal Auditors, Inc.

Page 321 — Copyright © 1976
Page 321 — Copyright © 1979
Page 321 — Copyright © 1981
Page 321, 322 — Copyright © 1982
Page 322 — Copyright © 1978
Page 322 — Copyright © 1980

ABCDEFGHIJ-DO-898

Preface

The field of auditing is changing radically. First, the advent of computers, their widespread use, and their developing sophistication of applications have pioneered considerable changes in audit procedure requirements.

Second, the Foreign Corrupt Practices Act of 1977, emphasizing internal controls, has intensified the concern of management and rule formulating bodies about the auditor's role in internal controls.

Third, the increasingly competitive nature of the auditing profession which is struggling with price competition, increased regulations, client resistance to cost increase, inflation, and an anachronistic structure of employee development and utilization has brought about real process automation needs.

Finally, the expansion of internal audit and audit committee functions in corporations has created major concerns for accounting educators regarding the focus of audit education. In response to these needs, many universities have dramatically changed their accounting curricula to include a framework of accounting and auditing for the 1980s. These curricula changes prompted the creation of special EDP audit courses, the expansion of accounting curricula to five-year programs, and the inclusion of an increased number of required courses related to EDP. This text attempts to service this changing market by introducing progressive topics.

Aimed at preparing the future breed of highly technical and forward thinking auditors, *Advanced Auditing: Fundamentals of EDP and Statistical Audit Technology* is a useful complement or sequel to traditional audit texts. This book includes not only the emphasis on the audit of particular features of DP systems, but also an emphasis on new issues such as sampling, internal control evaluation, utilization of time-series techniques in analytical reviews, and audit planning.

Therefore, the key objectives of this book are as follows:

1. To complement the preparation of future auditors;
2. To supply not only current audit tools, but also future tools;
3. To provide a realistic illustration of EDP audit in the field;
4. To avoid misleading pedagogical oversimplification; and
5. To furnish experiential learning in relation to GAS.

Advanced Auditing is oriented toward courses in the new five-year accounting programs, advanced auditing and computer auditing courses, graduate level auditing courses, and a wide range of educational modules practiced at CPA firms and internal audit departments. For in-house training of external and internal auditors, this book should be enhanced with actual cases and auditing standards from within the organization.

Advanced Auditing is divided into four main parts. The first section, Chapters 1–6, provides a common foundation for the ensuing parts of the book. The reader with a strong computer background may want to skip Chapters 2 and 3. The reader with a solid accounting background may skim through Chapters 4 and 5. Chapter 4, however, presents a systematic overview of the audit process.

The second part presents EDP audit issues. Chapter 7 introduces Generalized Audit Softwares as an audit tool, Chapter 8 describes DP oriented controls, and Chapters 9–11 conclude this section by describing audit procedures for DP Centers, Applications and System Development.

The third section, Chapters 12–16, covers statistical audit technology. Chapter 12 surveys risk assessment and analytical review, and in the remaining chapters statistical sampling is divided into basic concepts in sampling, attribute sampling, variable sampling, and dollar unit sampling.

Finally, Chapters 17–20 discuss current issues in auditing, including advanced DP systems and audits, the EDP auditor career, and a framework for the evolution of the audit process.

The book's appendix uses the TREAT system (Vasarhelyi and Lin, 1979) to represent generalized audit softwares and also to provide rich examples of audits in different areas of business data processing. The system is used only as an illustration of the use of GAS and this illustration is easily transported to any other type of generalized audit software. Upon request, the TREAT system may be obtained gratuitously from the authors.

The authors would like to acknowledge the work of Professor Walter O. Baggett of Manhattan College, who prepared most of the end-of-chapter exercises and helped with many valuable and insightful suggestions. We also appreciate the help of Professors Da-Hsien Bao and Luis Carlos Duclos in the development of the TREAT materials and the financial support of the Touche Ross Foundation in funding the TREAT project. The assistance of Professor C.J. McNair and the suggestions of Professors Michael

Ginzberg, D.H. Bao, James Lampe, Theodore J. Mock, Richard Savich, Gordon Shillinglaw, B.N. Srinidhi, as well as of Messrs. Carl Pabst, Keagle Davis, Donald Wood and Henry Korff of Touche Ross and Co. were of great value to the final product. The authors are particularly thankful for the thoughtful comments of Mr. John Lainhart of the Department of Transportation. Finally, we acknowledge the research assistance of Ms. Barbara Williams, Evelyn Faillace, Desiree Kim, Sandra Ayee, Georgiana Hsu and Viola Fong.

New York, NY   M.A.V

Los Angeles, CA   T.W.L

To our families,

Marina, Miklos, and Elizabeth

Angela, Bill, and Margaret

for their patience and understanding in this long project.

Contents

Chapter 1

Data Processing and Auditing

1.1 INTRODUCTION

Computers have evolved from *technological aids* that perform voluminous and repetitive tasks to everyday tools that pervade our lives. Today, many important professional tasks require a certain degree of human–computer interaction. Doctors make use of computer billing, computer-aided diagnosis, and computer-generated laboratory results. Lawyers search legal databases for precedents, use word processors for preparing most types of legal documents, and manage their practices with computerized accounting routines. Accountants work with computerized information systems in many of their analytical, reporting and attestation duties.

We begin by presenting an overview of electronic data processing (EDP) developments that have affected organizations and therefore accounting and auditing systems. In the next section, we briefly describe traditional and modern computer systems. We then discuss the functional evolution of computer-based systems as they mature in an organization. In the following section, we conceptualize management information systems (MIS). We conclude by examining the role of auditing in the context of evolutionary technology.

LEARNING OBJECTIVES

By the time you complete this chapter, you should be able to:

1. Describe the role of computers in the modern organization.
2. Identify five types of modern computer systems.
3. Describe four stages of EDP growth in terms of initiation, contagion, control, and maturation.
4. Define *management information system.*
5. Describe the evolutionary audit pattern from auditing manual systems to file systems, database systems, and microcomputer systems.

1.2 THE ROLE OF COMPUTERS IN ORGANIZATIONS

Computers were initially used in business for the labor-intensive and repetitive clerical tasks in accounting. In this role computer applications often involved the general ledger, accounts payable, and accounts receivable functions. Consequently, computer centers historically were placed under the jurisdiction of the finance department jurisdiction. We can still see evidence of this organizational approach: many computer centers still report to the corporate vice-president for finance or the corporate controller. An emerging pattern is the creation of the position of corporate MIS vice-president, with responsibilities for data processing and the management of the information resource. Today, the influence of data processing in organizations is pervasive. Typically, organizations spend from 1 to 3 percent of sales on activities related to data processing, with the percentage climbing every year.

In the 1960s and 1970s, data processing activities tended to be concentrated around corporate mainframe computers. Most large processing applications were performed on a batch basis and delivered on voluminous paper printouts. During the late 1970s and into the 1980s, the advent of cost-effective minicomputers and the increased reliability of data communications spurred reexamination of EDP policies. Many organizations started to disperse parts of their data processing activities. The advent of microcomputers and the emergence of workstations will further this change in the approach to data processing. It seems likely that certain bulk applications will continue to be processed as large mainframe operations, whereas many analytical processes will be switched to microprocessors. Most large organizations still face a major backlog in software development for mainframe systems, but organizations are increasingly resorting to micro-based local systems as both interim and longer term software solutions.

Figure 1.1 shows a general outline of traditional and modern corporate data processing structures. Modern systems include substantial added functional responsibilities, including increased data custody and security, communications support, word processing support, and the like. The systems described in Figure 1.1 symbolically represent the evolution from a centralized batch-oriented data processing system to the hybrid structures, found today in many large organizations. The highly structured *data flow* of sequential job processing gave way to systems that support both batch and online processing, while also linking computers of different sizes and functions.

The function of *data custody*, formerly either at the mainframe site (computer readable) or at a user site (source documents), evolved substantially to function-related, dispersed processing custody. Data are now kept at different sites and in different forms for the convenience of data

Figure 1.1   Data Processing Structures: (a) Traditional; (b) Modern

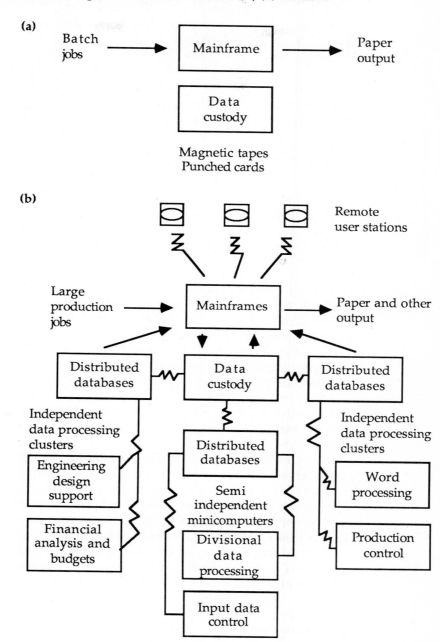

processing users. *Data processing* is performed at three levels: (1) mainframe for large application and integration support; (2) minicomputer for cluster support and divisional operations; and (3) microcomputer for self-contained or analytical functions.

These enhanced features of data processing systems theoretically expand the domain of auditor concern. Studies of overall data processing costs indicate that more than 20 percent of total expenditures fall outside the formal data processing budget. These costs include the costs of hardware, telephone lines, word processing equipment, consultants, remote input/output devices, and the like. A survey by Datamation[1] generated responses from 642 organizations that indicated a mean expenditure of $291,000 for computer-related items over and above the DP budget. The role (and consequently the level of concern) of the auditor is closely related to the type of data processing system used.

1.3 TYPES OF EDP SYSTEMS

Traditionally, computer systems were divided into (1) business systems and (2) scientific systems. The first were typically limited by input/output (I/O), while the latter were processing bound. That is, the throughput of business systems was constrained mainly by limitations on the ability to input and output data, while that of scientific computing was constrained mainly by processing capability.

Modern computer systems may be classified in five classes:

1. *Business systems,* which are oriented primarily to performing operational business functions such as accounting, billing, mailing, and the like.
2. *Scientific systems,* which are oriented to performing research-related functions. These computer systems may be a university computer center, a system to support research conducted by a business (such as computer systems at AT&T's Bell Laboratories), or systems directed at gathering scientific data.
3. *Production systems,* which are directed at supporting manufacturing processes such as job-shop management systems, production-line control systems, inventory control systems, nurse-station support systems, and the like.
4. *Decision support systems,* which are oriented to supporting management decisions. The features of these systems overlap with those of the first category but differ in that the emphasis is on decision support not operations; on ad hoc reports, not regular reports; and on active use as opposed to passive use.[2]

5. *Other systems*, which include a wide variety of systems that perform various types of tasks and do not fall neatly into one of the other categories. Among these systems are the many entertainment-oriented computer systems that have proliferated since the advent of the microcomputer.

Most computer systems based on a mainframe encompass some features of each type of system. These definitions are mainly for conceptual purposes and should be thought of as the *main* function of a computer system. For example, Columbia University's IBM 4341 systems are oriented primarily toward academic research (scientific system). However, some game and business software is also available for public use.

We discuss business systems in Chapter 3. Their most common characteristics are intense data orientation and repetitive data processing. In their most traditional form, business systems are composed of:

1. Data screening programs.
2. Transaction files.
3. Master files.
4. Master file update programs.
5. File management programs.
6. Report programs.

1.4 THE STAGES OF EDP GROWTH

Data processing in organizations does not evolve in a purely technological way. The extent of computer use has much to do with the evolution and maturity of a data processing system. Typically, the major obstacles to effective corporate data processing are managerial and behavioral rather than technical. The absorption of technological processes into day-to-day management and work-force routines is frequently a major barrier to advances in data processing.

Nolan[3] discusses the stages of EDP growth, relating data processing and information system evolution to four key factors: (1) nature of DP planning and control; (2) involvement of top management; (3) cost allocation routines; and (4) types of applications. These four factors indicate the stage that data processing has reached in an organization. We present the following classification as a modification of Nolan's work, taking into consideration more recent technological developments and their implications for audit work.

Figure 1.2   Profile of an Evolving EDP System

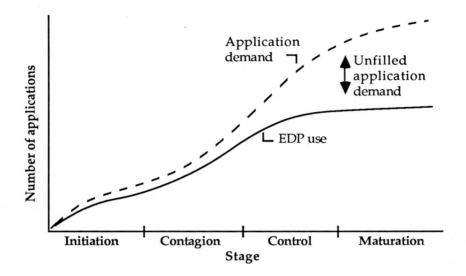

Figure 1.2 shows our view of a typical profile of application demand and EDP use during the evolution of a data processing system, and Table 1.1 includes several typical EDP applications that can be found in each of the four stages.

INITIATION STAGE

During the *initiation stage,* an organization decides to utilize computers either by acquiring its own equipment or by contracting for computer services. That is, the organization may purchase a microcomputer or decide to automate a process such as payroll by obtaining the services of a third party—for example, a company such as ADP.[4] In the 1960s initiation could have involved a reasonably large firm that was starting to use data processing. Currently, it is highly unusual for a medium-sized company (say, more than 200 employees) not to have a number of computer-based applications in place.

Computer initiation involves top management study and approval but leads to limited top management involvement; computer management is usually delegated to technical staff. The company typically puts into place systematic and formal data gathering, data entry edit, and data correction procedures. Personnel has to be retrained for computer related skills such as coding, key entry, and error screening. At this stage

Table 1.1   Typical EDP Applications

Initiation	Contagion
Payroll	Cash flow
Accounts receivable	General ledger
Accounts payable	Budgeting
Billing	Capital budgeting
	Forecasting
	Personnel records
	Order processing
	Sales
	Inventory controls

Control	Maturation
Purchasing controls	Simulation models
Scheduling	Planning models
Database integration	On-line systems for personnel, client
Expenditure controls	support, data entry at the source
Computer cost allocations	Application regrouping

substantial behavioral resistance to data processing, particularly at the
lower operational levels, may be encountered. Recently, however,
initiation has taken a very different direction. Many companies have
started using EDP by acquiring microcomputers for word processing or self-
contained applications and have then expanded progressively into other
operational uses.

When organizations begin to use EDP, they typically allocate most of
the costs to some type of general corporate overhead. For example, microcomputers are often buried in departmental budgets under items such as
supplies or miscellaneous equipment. Allocating these costs to overhead
leads to poor cost-benefit decisions and widespread development of unrelated applications. Managers who are provided with "free data processing" are not forced to evaluate on an incremental basis the costs of EDP
versus savings in labor costs and improvements in service quality.
Conversely, EDP cost allocation to overhead tends to motivate managers to
use EDP because they perceive it as a free resource, which is being paid by
someone else.

Auditors find systems in the initiation stage simple to audit; there are
no major barriers to auditability. In addition, the number of applications
that may materially affect financial statements is limited. However,
systems at the initiation stage will have poor (if any) controls. This condition should lead the external auditor to increase reliance on substantive

testing and internal auditors to work on increasing the number and quality of internal controls.

CONTAGION STAGE

When an organization moves to the *contagion stage,* numerous applications blossom throughout its departments and many are implemented on an unplanned, ad-hoc basis. The climate in the organization now favors new computer applications and experimentation. Top management is even less involved in EDP management because incremental applications do not involve major capital disbursements. Management is unfamiliar with and somewhat frightened by most computer-related decisions. Without direct charges for data processing costs, little consideration is given to cost-benefit tradeoffs in expanding EDP systems. This failure leads to capricious adoption of applications that do not pay for themselves either in labor economies or in service and information improvements.

Organizations that expand their EDP systems in the micro age face a series of decisions about the utilization of microcomputers in the crucial area of information preparation. Often, microcomputers are used for tasks that should instead be performed on time-shared systems. Lack of integration leads to the repeated gathering and processing of the same information. At this stage an organization must resolve often difficult compatibility problems because the system grew without proper consideration of efficiency, integration, and standards. Often, different makes of microcomputers, incompatible software, and abandoned applications are found.

At this stage the multiplicity of applications creates increased audit exposure and the potential for material accounting error. The auditor will find a worse control climate even though the technical complexity of the system and applications remains stable. Organizations that rely heavily on microcomputer processing present a special set of auditing problems, which we discuss in Chapter 18.

CONTROL STAGE

The cost explosion and the chaos that result from uncontrolled data processing application growth now become a substantial concern to management. It feels cost pressures, and that processes are out of control. Consequently, management inhibits the proliferation of new applications, assumes control of priorities, establishes professional management for data processing, and sets up a formalized management control system for EDP.

At the *control stage* we often observe changes in data processing management; techniques that seemed to work before, now fail; and homegrown data processing managers seem unable to handle formalized planning, tight controls, and limitation of activities. The number of central data processing projects actually decreases, and, system documentation, data quality, and accounting controls are emphasized. The method of accounting for data processing costs changes. A *partial cost allocation* philosophy is adopted, whereby mature data processing subentities pay their costs fully and others get preferential treatment.

With the compression of formally authorized computer projects, the demand for unfilled applications accumulates, which can create lead times of several years for large software projects. Organizations often set up steering committees as a coping mechanism to guide the data processing effort, increase the emphasis on project control, improve system documentation, and start the integration of applications into databases. Francl et al.[5] suggest the use of zero base budgeting (ZBB) to deal with this problem. *Zero base budgeting* is a method that requires managers to set up for yearly review decision packages that contain their current and proposed activities. At budget time these packages are ranked, and choices are made that may drastically realign activities.

The advent of microcomputers has opened up EDP alternatives for divisional managers. Faced with the frustrating prospect of having to wait years for systems they deemed essential, these managers can resort to homegrown micro-based systems. This approach is similar to the contagion stage and can lead to proliferation of microcomputers that, in the long run, can become a serious problem for the organization.

At this stage auditors rely more on internal controls and evaluate them more closely. The auditing emphasis shifts to interim work, system evaluation, and compliance testing. The increased integration of EDP applications poses a larger set of conceptual problems and technical challenges for the auditor. Finally, the advent of independent microcomputers creates a new series of exposures that, fortunately, are usually limited in scope.

MATURATION STAGE

Nolan describes three additional stages (integration, data administration, and maturity), which we combine into one, the *maturation stage*. At this stage we find: (1) data processing systems that are increasingly integrated to allow for database system communicating or that contain data from different functional areas; (2) fully allocated cost responsibilities; (3) the elevation of MIS direction to the vice-presidential level, with full authority and responsibility for custody of the information resource; and

(4) substantial maturity in the selection of applications, with a keen view toward implied benefits versus costs.

Mature systems present new concerns to the auditor. The basic set of controls is usually reasonable and may be relied on, but the use of advanced technology increases the difficulty of comprehending conceptually the large-scale, integrated applications. Advanced auditing techniques must be brought to bear on these systems.

A CAUTIONARY NOTE

The four main stages in the evolution of an EDP system represent the maturing of an organization's information processing, computer use, and management information system. However, we must add a note of caution. The elements of organizations change at different rates, and certain functional areas may be much further ahead in implementing EDP applications than others. A company involved in on-line customer-related operations (such as seat reservations) may still use primitive data gathering and payroll processing procedures. In addition, the type and age of computer equipment may be a poor indicator of EDP system maturity. The organization's culture, particularly as expressed by management's attitude toward technological advance, may have a much greater influence on data processing maturation.

1.5 MANAGEMENT INFORMATION SYSTEMS

The advent of computers also helped to focus attention on the information needs of the organization. From the one-person venture to the multinational firm, management processes encompass a vision of the future (planning), records of past actions (accounting), and decisions about the present.

These time-oriented elements are linked by information. Most of the events that are relevant to an organization can be measured and recorded. The actual measurement and recording of events, however, represents only a small fraction of all potentially measurable and recordable events related to the organization. The items that are recorded constitute *data*. Data prepared in a useful form and relevant to decision making is called *information*.

Figure 1.3   A Management Information System

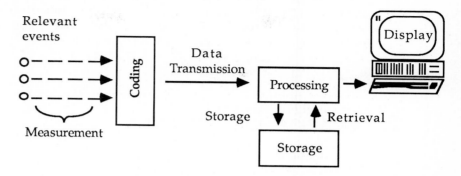

A *management information system* (MIS) is a set of procedures used to gather data, code it in meaningful form, transmit it, process it into information, and store, retrieve, and display the results of processing. This view of an MIS is shown in Figure 1.3.

Modern management information systems (MIS) incorporate (1) data processing systems (applications), (2) decision support modules, (3) in some recent instances expert systems, and (4) other supplementary functions.

In a modern organization the MIS function has in its background the operational functions required to support functionally day-to-day operations. The data processing (DP) applications perform such basic functions as payroll, accounts receivable, accounts payable, inventory management, and the like. The operational functions serve as the foundation to accumulate basic corporate information to be placed in corporate databases.

Decision support system (DSS) modules are tailored to specific decision settings, allow for ad hoc query, are flexible in use, and frequently link independent or semiautonomous data processing systems for the preparation of analytical information.

Expert systems (ES), still infrequent in practice, incorporate expertise into software dedicated to a particular function. These elements replace decision makers to a limited extent, instead of exclusively supplying decision support information. The line of differentiation is a fine one, typically the technology used in the construction of a particular element of an MIS. Most traditional DP and DSS systems have algorithms in their software to deal with specific situations. ES will use fifth generation languages (such as PROLOG), will specifically draw on the expertise of specialists, and will have inference rules, and may choose between alternatives based on some set of objectives.

Finally, other elements are emerging in a corporate MIS. Organizations now typically incorporate to DP, DSS and ES functions some office automation (OA) features such as electronic mail, word processing, teleconferencing, and desktop publishing. These communications and word-based functions enhance and link separate parts of the corporate MIS. Another element of importance in modern systems is the use of external databases in the support of many of its functions. Brokers use stock-quote systems, doctors use hotlines for vital organ availability and new technical information, analysts use accounting data databases, and so on.

1.6 AUDITING AND EVOLUTIONARY TECHNOLOGICAL ENVIRONMENT

This textbook is oriented toward the auditing of computer-based systems and focuses on the discussion of advanced auditing technology. In the preceding sections of this chapter, we presented the general role of data processing systems, the evolutionary stages of EDP implementation, and management information. In this section we trace the same evolutionary pattern but from the perspective of different types of audits. As today's business environment becomes more complex, the threat to data integrity and accuracy increases. Additional study of auditing is needed for numerous reasons. For example: (1) virtually all audits are based on financial statements that are generated in whole or in part by EDP; (2) the auditing environment is an increasingly competitive and maturing industry; and (3) there is an increasing level of litigation against auditors.

All three of the above major trends indicate that every auditor must have more than a minimal understanding of EDP and statistical concepts. It becomes apparent that auditors need above-average expertise in order to make auditing efficient and sufficiently objective to support independent audit decisions as well as the final audit reports.

We could identify and describe many different types of audits, but we will define only the most basic ones and then concentrate on the evolution of the verification and attestation process. There are four major types of audits.

1. *Financial audit* (or outside audit) is the process whereby an outside, unrelated party examines the records and information systems of an organization and attests to the fairness of its financial representations. This type of audit is usually performed by an external licensed CPA issuing an independent auditor's opinion. It may also sometimes be performed by an internal auditor as a support of the external audit function (to reduce audit fees) or to extend the levels of assurance provided by the attestation.

2. *Internal audit* is the process whereby a unit within an organization verifies the integrity and accuracy of organizational in-

formation processing and reporting on a continuous or repetitive basis. The internal audit by definition is done by someone within the organization. It is sometimes an audit of financial information and sometimes an audit of nonfinancial organizational information. It is typically for the purpose of reporting to management on efficiencies, internal controls, or potential improvements.

3. *Operational audit* is the process of examining the effectiveness and/or efficiency of performance of an organization in meeting its objectives. The operational audit can be done by external or internal auditors but currently is most commonly done by governmental auditors such as the GAO. There is an emerging trend in internal audit organizations to increase the emphasis on the performance of operational (and management) audits.

4. *Tax audit* is the process related to the examination of an organization's economic activities for the purpose of assessing the fairness of its taxation. These audits are performed by the IRS or other tax entities on individuals or corporations with typical emphasis on tax payments not accuracy in financial reporting.

Other types of statutory audits would be mandated public audits of public school systems and municipalities to see whether they comply with their statutes and objectives.

All these processes deal with the measurement of economic activity and require evaluation and the exercise of judgment. Typically the audit process involves activity planning, process (economic flow) measurement, and accumulated quantity (level) validation.

Table 1.2 shows the relative emphases of the different types of audits. While the financial (external) audit stresses attestation within materiality bounds, the internal audit is more concerned with internal control and fraud. The operational audit stresses efficiency and effectiveness, whereas the tax audit is directed to the tax obligations of the organization. We discuss the specific steps for financial and internal auditing in Chapter 4. Here we will briefly discuss the scope of problems that technology presents to the auditor, along with some opportunities and specific terminology.

Accounting systems were devised to measure business activity, control stewardship, and provide for checks and balances on business activity. Auditors were added to the system to provide independent verification of an organization's financial operations, as part of its checks and balances. Figure 1.4 illustrates the increasingly complex system of verification that auditors face because of evolutionary EDP technology.

Table 1.2   Relative Emphases of Different Types of Audits

Type of audit	Internal Control	Materiality	Fraud	Verification	Taxation	Attestation	Independence	System Effectiveness
Financial	M	M	M	I	S	M	M	S
Internal	M	I	M	I	S	S	I	I
Operational	S	S	I	I	S	S	I	M
Fiscal	S	S	I	M	M	S	I	S

M = Major variables.
I   = Intermediate variables.
S   = Small-impact variables.

AUDITING MANUAL SYSTEMS

Traditionally, an auditor examining the books of an organization would find sequentially numbered pages with transactions written in indelible ink and carefully annotated. This system provided readable records, unchangeable data, and a direct trace to some type of *source document.* At the same time, the way that an organization processed its information could be traced to persons performing those functions and preparing the documents. The records and documents were physically transported and were stored as visible and readable accounting records.

AUDITING TRADITIONAL FILE SYSTEMS

With the advent of computers (Figure 1.4a) the auditing task became more complicated. First, the use of computers required the reading of source documents and their transcription (through key punching) to a computer readable medium (such as punched cards). This operation was of concern to auditors (attestors) because transcription increases the number of errors by adding data preparation errors to raw data errors. Controls were developed (batch totals, check digits, key verification) to decrease the number of transcription errors and allow logical verification to the quality of the

Figure 1.4   The Auditor's Dilemma

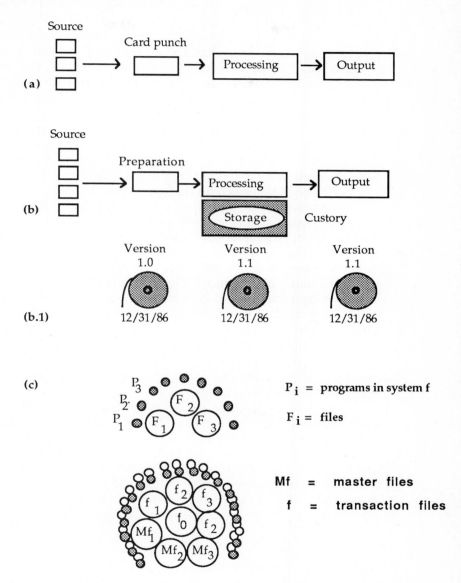

source data. The auditor could read punched cards and trace them to directly generated output listings that could be arithmetically verified.

However, the introduction of magnetic tape (Figure 1.4b.1) created a medium that *could not* be read directly by the auditor and allowed modification without leaving a trace. To cope with this problem system designers created data safeguards. First, data tapes were physically safeguarded to prevent unauthorized access and to avoid misplacement. Second, certain totals were printed out at the initial processing stage, matched against source documents, and examined for integrity throughout processing. During this stage the auditor lost the ability to trace data changes directly, as well as the ability to examine the data visually. Auditors had to start relying on third parties to read the data or had to acquire computer skills themselves to manipulate data directly. Many auditors developed computer software to facilitate and generalize verification processes. An additional difficulty arose with regard to year-end adjustments. In traditional systems these adjustments were booked formally and could be easily examined by the auditor. However, computerized systems often present several versions of book-close data on tapes that were produced at different stages of the closing process.

Each of these systems, called *file systems*,[6] was typically restricted to one major application (such as payroll) and involved a series of programs that performed related tasks. Most systems tended to be driven by transaction files (controlled by transaction totals), and updating was performed by means of a master file. One complication that auditors faced was that these independent file systems often contained substantial duplicate data, but these data were not necessarily identical because they had been generated from different sources and measured on the basis of different standards or criteria. Auditors quickly learned that tapes must be carefully controlled and monitored. Some of the data redundancies served as valuable cross-checks and assisted in reconciliation. However, the systems also presented greater complexity in processing logic, which was quite difficult to verify manually.

The EDP audit software packages developed for data examination became valuable tools for numerically replicating the logical processes by parallel simulation. These software packages also became useful for performing some of the rather tedious and labor-intensive tasks required in audits. Client files could be used to generate computer-printed confirmation letters; simple programs could be used for file footing (totaling); programs could also be used for extension; and multiple forms manually filed could be used to verify source documents against computer records.

AUDITING DATABASE SYSTEMS

With the development of databases (Figure 1.4c), EDP systems became substantially more complex. A layer of software comprising the database management system (DBMS) was added on top of the data and between the auditor and the application. Not only were the data invisible, but it was now also nearly impossible (if not meaningless) to identify the physical location of data. On the other hand, DBMSs came with improved access methods and security and decreased (controlled) data redundancy.

Database systems are typically associated with data communication, whereby users can access the data remotely at their discretion and without any physical access restriction with the exception of logical passwords and certain types of hardware protection. These systems also allow auditors remote access to systems and on-line monitoring of processes. Auditors are progressively coping better with this type of more advanced system.

AUDITING MICROCOMPUTER SYSTEMS

Microcomputers were formerly a minor part of information systems but now pose new problems for auditors. Data access terminals were connected to mainframes, were physically identifiable, and stored data only if designed to do so—they could also be carefully monitored. Microcomputers violate most of these conditions. On the other hand, these devices provide powerful on-site tools for the auditor[7] and are changing the nature of the audit process.

These developments have left the auditor without directly visible data, traceable changes, traceable transactions, and directly verifiable computations. Furthermore modern data processing systems, in which transactions often are recorded without paper (such as automatic teller machines) are changing the nature of source documents. Clearly, the absence of source documents with more and more accounting transactions recorded as they occur, is now becoming a general trend. This latest step in the evolution of EDP systems poses new and greater challenges to systems designers and auditors.

LOOKING AHEAD

While these technological advances have greatly affected the nature of information systems that auditors examine, some technological developments are also coming to the aid of auditors. Understanding of the audit process (see Chapter 4, audit concepts and process), data processing technology (see Chapter 2, EDP concepts; Chapter 3, business systems; Chapter 17, advanced EDP concepts) helps in giving the reader adequate technical background. Major developments in sampling theory and auditing sampling practices (see Chapters 13–16) allow for more effective data examination; more experience with and improved comprehension of internal controls allow for better interim examination (see Chapters 5, 6, and 8–11) of information systems. Advanced auditing techniques (see Chapter 12, analytical review and Chapter 20, evolution of the audit process) help in the early detection of potental problems. Finally, the raw power of computers and computer readability of some source documents allow for 100 percent examination of certain items (see Chapter 7, generalized audit software, and Chapter 18, audit of advanced systems).

1.7 Summary

In this chapter we described generally the role of computers in the modern organization. The five categories of modern computer systems are business, scientific, production, decision support, and other systems.

The use of computers has much to do with the evolution and maturity of the data processing systems in organizations. We examined the four stages in the evolution of EDP systems: initiation, contagion, control, and maturation. We discussed briefly data processing in the context of a management information system.

There are four major types of audits: financial, internal, operational, and tax. The same evolutionary pattern observed in EDP systems is relevant to auditing, that is, the evolution from auditing manual systems to file systems, to database systems, and to hybrid mainframe–microcomputer systems.

Questions

1. What were some of the first applications of EDP in business organizations, and why were these applications chosen?
2. From these earliest applications, how have EDP applications evolved?
3. What are some of the factors that have led to changes in EDP applications?
4. What have the changes in technology and applications done to the data processing function in organizations?
5. What are the five categories of modern EDP systems and their characteristics?
6. What are some of the factors that have affected the evolution of computer use in organizations?
7. Identify and describe the four stages of the evolution of computer usage.

8. What is the relationship between data and information and how does this lead to the concept of management information systems?
9. Define the characteristics of each of the following types of audits: financial, internal, operational, and fiscal.
10. How has the evolution of the computer affected the work of auditors?
11. What are the critical problems posed to auditors by the advent of large-scale database management systems?
12. How do microcomputers differ from mainframes in terms of auditability, security, and use in corporate systems?

Problems

1. Locate someone at your college or university who has been on campus and in contact with computers since they were first installed. Ask that person to describe his or her experience with these computers and compare it with the evolution of EDP systems described in this chapter. Also try to locate someone in industry (alumnus, alumna, parent, or friend) who has had a similar experience.
2. How do you think the attitude toward the computer on the part of management that has been using the computer since the 1960s would vary from that of management that is just starting to use the computer?
3. How do you think the evolution of computer use varies between scientific and business users? What do you think might be some of the differences among various types of industries?
4. Based on what you have read in this chapter, what are the main effects of computer use on the auditor? Are these effects all related to changes in technology?
5. Do you think that the evolutionary process described for business systems will be accompanied by a corresponding evolution in the audit process? Why or why not?
6. Describe the evolution of the audit process presented in Section 1.6 for two of the four types of audits. For example, explain how the introduction of magnetic tape affected fiscal and operational auditing.
7. Many universities and business entities are currently connected into computer networks for the purpose of data access, data communication, remote computer access and the like. Describe, based on the type of reasoning presented in this chapter, particularly Section 1.6, the increased challenge faced by auditors due to this development.
8. Place yourself in the position of the administrative support person at a public accounting firm and describe the key economic events, coding, data transmission, storage, retrieval, processing, and display of in

formation relevant to monitor auditor work hours. Describe other information and connected processes that involve the scope of the administrative management information system in question.

Notes

1. Verity, John W., "1985 DP Budget Survey," *Datamation*, March 15, 1985, pp. 74–78.

2. See Keen, P. G., and Scott-Morton, M. S., *Decision Support Systems: An Organizational Perspective.* Reading, Mass.: Addison-Wesley, 1978.

3. Nolan, R. L., "Managing the Crises in Data Processing," *Harvard Business Review*, March–April 1979, pp. 115–126.

4. ADP is a company that specializes in providing third-party data processing services. In its traditional mode of operation, data sheets are picked up by a courier, the data is processed, and the output is returned to the customer.

5. Francl, T. J., Lin, W. T., and Vasarhelyi, M. A., *Planning, Budgeting, and Control for Data Processing.* New York: Van Nostrand Reinhold, 1984.

6. Nolan, R. L., "Computer Databases: The Future Is Now," *Harvard Business Review*, September–October 1973, pp. 98–114.

7. Vasarhelyi, M. A., "Audit Automation: Online Technology and Auditing," *The CPA Journal*, April 1985, pp. 10–17.

Chapter 2

An Overview of EDP

2.1 INTRODUCTION

In this chapter we introduce you to the fundamental concepts of electronic data processing and the aspects of EDP that are of importance and interest to the auditor. Our intent is to give you a basic understanding of computerized data processing systems without becoming enmeshed in the details of systems analysis, computer programming, and computer operations. This foundation will allow you to identify and apply proper procedures to the audit of computerized accounting information systems.

LEARNING OBJECTIVES

By the time you complete this chapter, you should be able to:

1. Describe basic EDP concepts.
2. Identify the stages of computer hardware development.
3. Describe major computer hardware elements and configurations.
4. Describe different types of computer software.
5. Discuss current data management issues.
6. Explain different types of computer operating environments.
7. Discuss the importance of personnel in EDP.
8. Describe effective EDP organization and management.

2.2 SOME BASIC EDP CONCEPTS

Early efforts in electronic data processing related to the electromechanic machines used in the Manhattan Project, which led to the development of the first atomic bomb in the 1940s. At the same time, scientists at several universities were involved in the development of "calculating devices." The noted scientist, John Von Neumann, laid out the logical design and key concepts of digital computers that remained in effect for nearly 40 years.[1]

Table 2.1   Decimal and Binary Numbers

Decimal Representation	Binary Representation
0	0
1	1
2	10
3	11
4	100
5	101
.	.
.	.
.	.
16	10000

The first data processing devices performed basic arithmetic operations in preset sequences. These devices (as well as today's computers) stored information (either data or instructions) in what is called a *binary storage mode;* that is, numbers are represented by 1's and 0's, as shown in Table 2.1. For example, the number 2 in the decimal system is the number 10 in the binary system; a 4 in the decimal system becomes 100 in the binary system; and an 8 in the decimal system becomes 1000 in the binary system.

Information for these processing machines was one of two types: (1) instructions (or programs) that represented sequences of operations to be performed by the machine; or (2) data that were processed by these machines in accordance with the stored sequences of instructions (programs). A machine command may have looked like:

10000 01 111

This series of numbers and spaces would have been interpreted as an instruction to (1) retrieve the content of memory location 10000 (binary 10000 = decimal 16); (2) add it to the content of location 111 (binary 111 = decimal 7); and (3) place the results in register A (operation code 01). This type of instruction was later changed to a decimal system type of instruction:

16 01 7

which, in turn, was improved by the use of mnemonic operators, or:

16 AD 7.

This simple series of changes illustrates the first steps in the evolutionary process that led to simpler and more compact forms of programming and to the higher level languages discussed in later sections of this chapter.[2]

Figure 2.1   Evolution of Computer Hardware Configurations: (a) Early Computers; (b) Second Generation; (c) Third Generation; (d) Fourth Generation; (e) Fifth Generation; (f) Future Systems

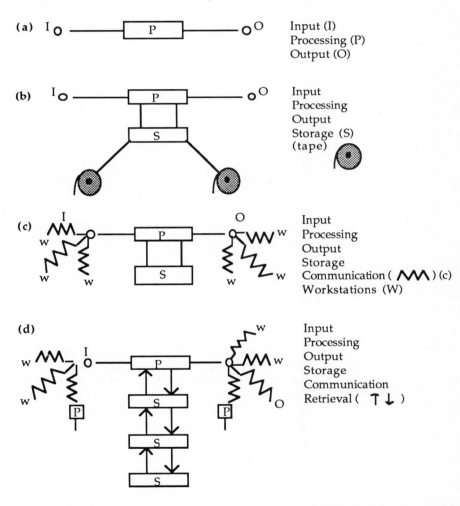

(continued on next page)

Figure 2.1   Evolution of Computer Hardware Configurations (continued)

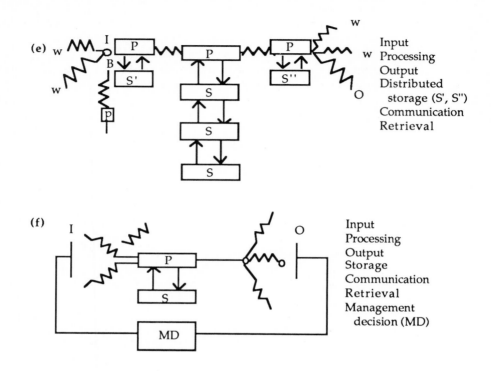

(e)

Input
Processing
Output
Distributed
   storage (S', S'')
Communication
Retrieval

(f)

Input
Processing
Output
Storage
Communication
Retrieval
Management
   decision (MD)

2.3 THE STAGES OF COMPUTER HARDWARE DEVELOPMENT

The evolution of computer hardware is shown in Figure 2.1. In the 1950s, the early computers were designed basically to decrease the time and complexity of repeated calculations. In essence they were calculators with very primitive input and output devices. The machine's main switching elements were vacuum tubes.

Early in the 1960s, the second generation of computers was developed. These computers featured transistors or magnetic cores and magnetic storage devices (such as magnetic tape units), which allowed the storage of substantial amounts of data in sequential form. This improvement led to considerably greater use of EDP because it shifted the emphasis from facilitating calculations to the storage and processing of business records. Second-generation IBM equipment (such as the 7094) was oriented toward business processing and allowed for the utilization of a limited number of compilers.

Late in the 1960s, the concepts of time-sharing and communication were introduced by the third generation of computers. Not only could these computers be used as processing and data storage devices, but also as communicators, linking diverse units, data files, and individuals in an organization. This generation of computers represented a greatly expanded EDP system and changed the way many users accessed EDP systems. Instead of the *batch* approach, whereby each application waited its turn in a queue, the new *time-sharing* approach gave users the impression of immediate, direct, and unique access to EDP equipment. Workstations (initially "dumb terminals") were found at the end of communications links.

Late in the 1970s and early in the 1980s, the fourth generation of computers enhanced the concept of information as an organizational resource. Computer hardware developments such as mass storage devices and dramatically reduced costs for main memory storage allowed computers to be used not only in a storage mode but also for data management and integration. This generation of hardware allowed the development of large databases linking the main elements of specific corporate applications.

The fifth generation of computers emerged in the mid-1980s. It can be described as an *information archipelago*,[3] in which large and small computer hardware configurations interact to support an information system. The proliferation of microcomputers and the availability of substantially less expensive peripheral memories allowed for intelligence and data distribution along more rational lines. In general, this allows for data collection at the location of economic events and installation of decision-support databases at the location of data use. In this generation of hardware, workstations typically have independent communication, data storage and processing capabilities.

Future generations of EDP systems will distribute some of the "intelligent" functions of data systems, serve as organizational communication networks, and perform "aid-to-action" management decision functions in organizations. To facilitate these developments, less expensive and faster access memories, substantially enhanced microcomputer processing capabilities, a multitude of special processor-type hardware (such as LISP[4] machines), and new I/O interfaces (such as voice) will emerge.

2.4 COMPUTER HARDWARE CONFIGURATIONS

Figure 2.2 shows a generalized computer hardware configuration for a large (mainframe) EDP system. It is based on an actual large IBM configuration, which is also connected to other systems. Figure 2.2 will serve as the basis for the following discussion on the elements of computer hardware configurations and their functions.

Figure 2.2   A Large System Hardware Configuration

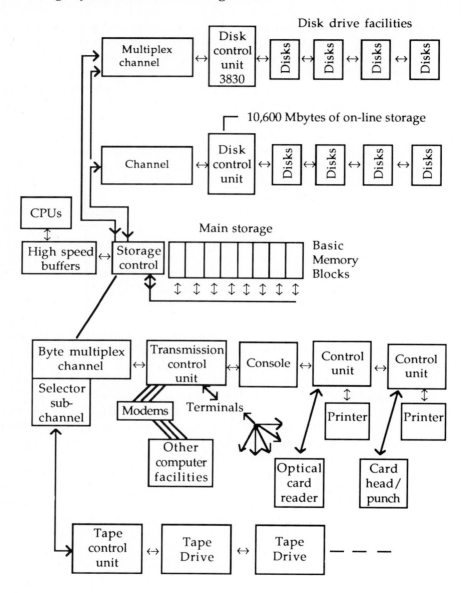

Modern systems may be composed of one or more *central processing units* (CPUs), which serve as the main calculating unit of the machine. The entire EDP system is geared toward supplying the CPU(s) with processing functions. A well-balanced system minimizes CPU wait time by optimizing computer processing time. In other words, the system operates to keep the CPU(s) as busy as possible most of the time.

A second element of major importance in the mainframe is the *main memory* or *core storage,* where all programs, part of the operating system, and frequently used functions are stored. The main memory serves as temporary storage for programs or instructions that are to be executed by the CPU. Core storage permits very rapid access but is also very expensive and may affect throughput efficiency considerably. These limitations led to the development of "virtual" or "multiprogrammed" computers, which we discuss later in this chapter.

Data channels serve as routing devices for the flow of information, which is controlled by the operating system and the CPU. The data rates of these devices indicate the channel capacity of each of these units (that is, their ability to conduct data). Channels of larger capacity are used to connect magnetic disk units or higher data intensity units, whereas less intense data flows—such as those generated by card readers, magnetic tape units, and terminals—are connected by channels of smaller capacity.

The communication links between computers (synchronous lines) or with remote terminals (more or less "intelligent," asynchronous lines) are another crucial component of the mainframe. They usually have less capacity because they are normally connected to and depend on the quality and availability of public switching telephone lines or leased lines. Usually the slower the access time of a device, the lower is the cost of data storage on that device. Table 2.2 displays typical access times for some storage devices.

Traditional systems use tape devices as means of storage, and they are usually adequate for storing bulk data sequentially. A magnetic tape (2400 feet) storing data at 6250 bpi (bits per in.) could theoretically hold 2400 x 6250 x 1218 bits of information, or 22.5 million (megabytes) characters (at 8 bits per byte and 1 byte per character). Considering that a tape costs about $15.00, the cost per byte stored is very low.

On the other hand, the slow speed of retrieval of specific information from tapes makes tape storage undesirable for frequently accessed and immediately needed data. In on-line systems, magnetic disk drives provide much faster (and higher cost) access times. An interesting compromise is the use of mass storage devices where data is stored on tape cylinders and brought into disk drives mechanically. An emerging form of storage is the usage of WORM (write once read many) laser disk technologies where a credit card sized storage device may store as much as 400 megabytes of information.

In summary, the *mainframe* includes (1) The CPU(s); (2) main memory (or core) storage; (3) high-speed buffers and storage control units; and (4) communication channels. In addition to these essential elements, there is a wide variety of *peripheral* equipment: (1) magnetic tape devices; (2)

Table 2.2   Storage Device Access Times

Device	Access Time*
Fixed head disk	Milliseconds
Core	Tens to hundreds of nanoseconds
Movable arm disk	Tens of milliseconds
Magnetic tape	Seconds to minutes

*   1 millisecond = 0.001 second.
    1 nanosecond = 0.000000001 second.

magnetic disk devices (with fixed or movable heads); (3) card reader and card punch units; (4) printers; (5) transmission control units (for both synchronous and asynchronous communications); and (6) computer terminals (operator's console(s), hardcopy units, and video displays). The auditor must be able to clearly distinguish the functions, appearance, and main features of hardware elements, particularly magnetic tape units, disks, and the operator's console and logs.

Data processing professionals usually classify computers as mainframes, minicomputers, and microcomputers. Mainframe computers are large computers, such as the IBM 3390 and 4000 series, which offer comprehensive data processing, storage, and output capabilities. Minicomputers, such as HP 3000, VAX 11, IBM 4370, and IBM 36, are disk-based computers about the size of a refrigerator and have multiple keyboards, display screens, a printer, and magnetic tape storage devices. Microcomputers, such as the IBM/PC and Macintosh, are desk-sized and have a microprocessor, a single keyboard and display screen, a printer, and diskette drive(s).

2.5 TYPES OF COMPUTER SOFTWARE

As we mentioned in the preceding section, two main types of information are stored in the computer: programs (or sets of commands) and data. Computer programs in general are referred to as *software*. In this section we discuss the most common types of programs used in EDP installations.

Software is an essential part of all major computer systems. Considerable thought goes into determining which system features are to be incorporated into hardware and which are to be left to software. The interchangeability of features in modern systems has been furthered by the development of firmware features, which basically entail read-only-memories (ROM) with software burned on them. Computer software is requiring an increasingly larger portion of total EDP budgets and is rapidly becoming the most important element of EDP systems. The five main categories of software are:

1. Operating Systems.
2. Compilers and interpreters.
3. Utilities.
4. Application software.
5. Specialized software.

OPERATING SYSTEMS

An operating system is the "package of software that controls the machine." It is supplied with the data processing equipment and performs most of the administrative functions for the equipment. A standard operating system will (1) control and keep occupied most system peripherals; (2) administer the sequence of operations (and interrupts) of the EDP system; (3) control and administer the location of all pieces of information within the system including jobs (programs) to be processed, jobs being processed, and jobs already processed; (4) account and bill for all utilization of the equipment; (5) maintain records on the characteristics of equipment utilization; (6) control access and user priorities in the system; and (7) perform a multitude of other functions for the system. Operating systems are extremely complex, and installations of medium-to-large size require a specialized staff, called "system programmers," to deal with its intricacies. Among the most common operating systems for mainframes are IBM's OS, VS, and MVS; DEC's TOPS-20, and RSTS; Burrough's MVT; CDC's KRONOS; and AT&T's UNIX. Among the most common operating systems for microcomputers are the popular CPM, DOS, and UNIX.

Table 2.3 presents a comparison of some of the interactive operating system commands from the more popular operating systems. Many of these operating system commands are considered as *utilities* in a traditional batch system. Typically, these utilities were part of the job control language (JCL) and constituted one or two job-header cards. Under DOS, a copy command might entail:

copy a:aud10.mss c:aud10x.mss

Table 2.3   Examples of Operating System Commands

DOS (IBM/PC)	UNIX (AT&T UNIX PC)	TOPS-20 (DEC-20)	Function
copy	cp	copy	Copies a data set
ren	mv	rename	Renames a data set
dir	ls	dir	Lists the directory
N/A	exit	logoff	To logout
erase	rm	era	Deletes a dataset
format	N/A	N/A	Formats a disk for use
print	lp	print	Prints a dataset
type	cat	type	Lists a dataset

which can be read as "copy from the floppy disk device (a:) to the hard disk device (c:) a file named aud10.mss and name it aud10x.mss.

In 1969, Bell Laboratories withdrew from the multiuser interactive system (MULTICS) project at MIT, and Ken Thompson at the Bell Lab began tinkering with a DEC PDP-7 minicomputer reject. He attempted to create an operating system that could support the coordinated efforts of a team of programmers in a programming research environment. This system was also to provide a document preparation aid for the lab's patent organization.[5] An early version of the UNIX System, using a PDP 11/20, was eventually delivered to the Bell Labs Patent Organization in 1971.

COMPILERS AND INTERPRETERS

Communication between users and machines started with the change from direct binary coding to the use of decimal mnemonic symbols. Unfortunately, computer hardware will obey only binary-type commands (machine language), so a device must be used to translate the binary–mnemonic form into machine language. At first this was accomplished by simple conversion programs. Soon after the introduction of EDP, programmers realized that many of their commands would be repeated in clusters over and over again. This repetition made possible the development of highly summarized command protocols that brought considerable efficiency to computer programming. These protocols are called high-level languages, and they helped to revolutionize EDP. Low-level languages, such as the decimal mnemonic example presented earlier in this chapter (which may be called an assembler language), generate one machine-language command per programmed command. High-level languages (such as FORTRAN, ALGOL, PL/1) allow for much higher ratios (1:10 or 1:50) of programmed commands to machine-language command.

Figure 2.3   Compilers and Interpreters

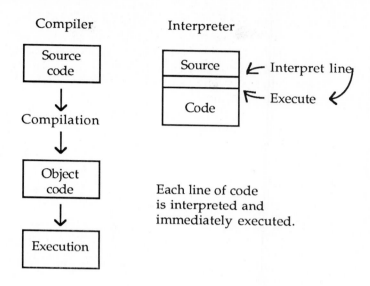

The software used to translate the high-level language used by the programmer into machine language is called a *compiler.* If a programmer writes a program in a high-level language such as FORTRAN, this program is called the *source code.* When this program is read by computer it is translated into machine language by the source code compiler. The translated code is called the *object code.* Therefore, in order to use a program written in high-level language, its code will have to be compiled before the program can be executed. Upon completion of the program development process, most computer installations maintain working programs in object code to avoid the extra cost of compilation each time the program is used. Figure 2.3 shows the main features of this process.

Higher level software (such as BASIC and APL) accompanied the introduction of time-sharing. These softwares are called interpreters (incremental compilers) and replace direct compiling. Such software will interpret one line, execute it, and then proceed to the next line instead of translating (compiling) the entire program before execution.

In 1973, Dennis Ritchie rewrote the UNIX System in the C programming language, which is a general-purpose, programming language that he had developed.[6] This improvement freed the system from the original PDP 11 machine architecture and made it more easily adaptable to a wide range of systems. This transportability and conformatibility feature allowed development of a wide range of UNIX-based products.

During the 1970s and 1980s, we have witnessed the development of numerous computer languages, many of which have special features and problem orientations. However, by far the most common language being used in business systems is COBOL, followed by IBM's RPG. All other languages account for a very small portion of business applications and are of less interest to auditors. The concepts of source and object code, however, are important to auditors. Programmers typically tinker with source code and then compile an application. Therefore separate custody of programs in object code and in source code ensures a certain degree of program integrity in an EDP facility.

UTILITIES

Utilities are software used in EDP installations to carry out commonly required data management and organization tasks. In larger IBM installations, the operating system obeys specialized job control language (JCL). Utilities interact with the system to perform simple tasks, such as copying and transferring data from medium to media (disk to tape, tape to tape, card to disk), listing data sets, sorting records (probably the most important utility), and the like. These utilities are usually supplied with the mainframe, but some software vendors provide improved utilities to EDP installations. A popular software package is called SYNCSORT, and its developers claim that its utilization offers considerable savings (say, 20 percent of CPU time) compared to the standard IBM sort procedure.

The rapidly evolving microcomputer world added new dimensions to computer utilities. Microcomputer utilities include: (1) backup protection for software (such as COPY II PC); (2) special printing fonts (Software Fonts, Fancy Font); (3) floppy disk directory covers, notepad, calculator, and calendar (Borland International's Sidekick); (4) increasing disk access times (PCSG's Lightning); and (5) mainframe access (IBM's Emulation Adapters).

As operating systems evolve many utilities get incorporated into the set of common functions. Consequently, interactive operating systems already have copy, rename, and other former utilities in their basic command sets.

APPLICATION SOFTWARE

Application software performs important business data processing functions, including payroll; general ledger; accounts payable; accounts receivable; property, plant, and equipment; inventory control, and order entry. In Chapter 3 we will follow the evolution of a typical EDP application as part of the data processing of an organization.

The general approach at computer centers is to customize programs to meet their specific needs and objectives. Although this approach is widespread, there is an increasing tendency on the part of computer centers to purchase ready-made or semifinished (such as Cullinet) software packages in order to avoid development costs. Such purchases will probably become more common in the future, when software development and maintenance costs become the major part of EDP budgets and when hardware costs become a constant or even declining percentage of EDP costs.

Complete sets of application software are available for systems such as IBM's system 38, from the manufacturer—at a price. If these systems are purchased, their cost may exceed that of the hardware. The microcomputer revolution opened the door for small-business computer applications. Integrated accounting packages typically include a series of different applications that can be purchased as modules or as an integrated set. The BPI Business Series[7] offers a variety of modules, including:

1. Inventory control.
2. Time accounting.
3. General accounting.
4. Accounts receivable.
5. Accounts payable.
6. Payroll.
7. Personal accounting.

Such software packages allow the computerization of small-business applications and the structuring of important parts of a new business at the outset along preset lines. While large businesses usually hesitate to fully adopt an accounting package, small businesses will readily adopt the software and its suggested forms, controls, and procedures.

SPECIALIZED SOFTWARE

A considerable amount of specialized software has been developed to perform supplementary operating system tasks or to supplement available compilers with expanded features, such as simulation, statistical analysis, auditing, and text editing.

Specialized software typically includes the following seven types:

1. *Simulation*—to provide languages for continuous (such as DYNAMO) or discrete (such as SPSS, SYMSCRIPT, and SIMULA) simulation.
2. *Statistical analyses*—to aid in research and other numerical analysis functions (such as SPSS, BMD, IDA, SAS, and SAS/PC). A subset of these may be the generalized audit softwares discussed later in the book (such as STRATA and Audex).

3. *Report generators*—to extract particular reports rapidly and efficiently from files (such as MARK-IV, RPG, and Personal Pearl).

4. *Database systems*—to administer corporate databases [such as IMS, TOTAL, ADABAS, DBase III (Ashton-Tate), and Knowledgeman (MDBS)].

5. *Data communication*—to help control and manage data communications (such as CICS, Enviro, DL/1, Kermit, and Scan).

6. *Spreadsheets*—to provide computational and analytical aid to managers in the form of a matrix layout (such as Lotus 1-2-3, Multiplan, and Visicalc).

7. *Other operating system additions*—to improve system security and system library administration, to analyze system hardware and software utilization and the like.

The line separating different classifications of software is a faint one. Software previously considered to be the utility type has been incorporated into operating systems. Spreadsheet menus look more and more like programming languages. Dbase III includes a full-fledged applications-oriented language and some accounting applications. Lotus 1-2-3 not only offers spreadsheet features but also includes database and graphics features. Consequently, software classifications should be used only for convenience in identifying different broad types of software, not as fixed definitions.

2.6 DATA AND DATA MANAGEMENT

In Section 2.1, we introduced binary numbers as storage representations of logical elements, but the *byte* is used as the main character storage unit in many modern computer systems. A byte usually contains 8 bits, allowing the representation of 2^8 different elements or *characters.* Therefore the basic character set allows for the representation of all decimals, letters, and a multitude of different special purpose (control) characters.

A typical business file is composed of *fields,* which consist of several bytes. For example, a field may be 30 characters (bytes) long and allow for the storage of someone's name. A *record* typically contains several fields that are related to one particular logical unit (employee, inventory item type, customer). A group of interrelated records constitutes a *file.* The general relationship of these data elements is illustrated in Figure 2.4. (A set of interrelated files with some common denominator(s) is called a *database,* the structure, organization, and management of which we discuss in Chapter 17.)

Figure 2.4 The Relationship of Basic Data Elements: (a) BitsDatabase; (b) Example of a Record and File

(a)

8 bits	→	1 byte (character)
Several bytes	→	1 field
Multiple fields	→	1 record
Multiple records	→	1 file
Several files	→	1 database

(b)

Name	Address	Employee Number	Salary	
30 characters	60 characters	8 bytes	8 bytes	Record
Chatsky, P. T. Boris, D. G. Hsu, G. A. Shapiro, J. D.	233 W. 58th St., NY NY 10037 20 Astor Pl, NY NY 10022 160 E. 116th St., NY NY 10027 200 Oak Ave., Clifton, NJ 07973	0247 0240 1407 1536	75000 50000 45300 56000	Employee file content (partial)

Recall that in Chapter 1 we discussed the evolution of systems from "file systems" to "integrated databases." In the early days of EDP, data were gathered at different locations and hand carried to a centralized data processing center, where they were converted into computer-readable form and processed. Some custody of raw data was dispersed, but custody of processed data was centralized. Data were coded either at the location of origin or at a central pool. Resolution of data discrepancies typically required consultation between personnel at the processing center and at the location of origin. With the ever-decreasing cost of on-line storage per byte and the increased reliance (and reliability) of data transmission, managers started to disperse more data functions throughout the organization.

The continuing evolution of EDP technology increasingly merges source documents and their magnetic form by creating paperless transactions that have to be edited intensively at the creation stage. In addition, the use of databases and remote access terminals tends to keep data close to the location of its use. For example, airline databases, which were completely centralized in their early stages, are now slowly evolving into hub-oriented data storage with inquiries automatically communicated to the appropriate hub database. New forms of macro-database organization, management technology, and management processes raise questions of *data custody* that are important to auditors. However, data custody issues must be considered in the context of the specific operating environment of a computer facility.

2.7 TYPES OF OPERATING ENVIRONMENTS

In recent years several improvements have been made in system environments. Early systems tended to operate in a single program and single CPU environment. A program was loaded into the main memory and processed sequentially to completion. This approach resulted in substantial under-utilization of the CPU. Most of the time it would be waiting for data requests from relatively slow units such as disks and magnetic tapes.

This waste of time and its high cost led to the development of memory partitioning and multiprogramming. In these environments several programs are brought into the main memory. The first program is processed until a data request or another scheduled application interrupts. When this happens data is retrieved from the data storage unit while the next program is being processed. This process continues until the cycle is completed and the system resumes processing the first program. When a program has been run, the system unloads it from the main memory and brings in another program to be processed. These improved processes enabled larger systems to operate with greatly increased CPU utilization and efficiency.

At about the same time that these developments took place, the idea of time-sharing was introduced. *Time-sharing* permits users to connect to the EDP installation through terminals and to converse with the system as if it were totally theirs. The slow speed of these terminals and of the human–machine interaction (relative to CPU speed) allowed a large number of users to be served by one computer and, most likely, by only one of its main core regions. More recently, systems having more than one CPU were developed. They are called multiprocessors. They functioned like multiprogrammed machines except that they allowed programs to utilize CPUs interchangeable, contingent on availability.

Finally, limitations of main memory size led to the development of virtual systems. *Virtual systems* allow programs to be segmented into pages or sectors. They are brought one by one into memory regions for processing, while the other pages or segments remain in their disk location. This approach resolves a series of memory-limitation problems. Unfortunately, it adds considerable overhead to a system because the segment-management task is very cumbersome. Figure 2.5 summarizes in graphic form the different types of operating environments described so far.

Figure 2.5 Computer Operating Environments: (a) Batch Processing of a Single Program; (b) Multiprogram of Batch Sequences; (c) Time-sharing Multiprogramming; (d) Time-sharing Multiprocessing; (e) Time-sharing Virtual Systems.

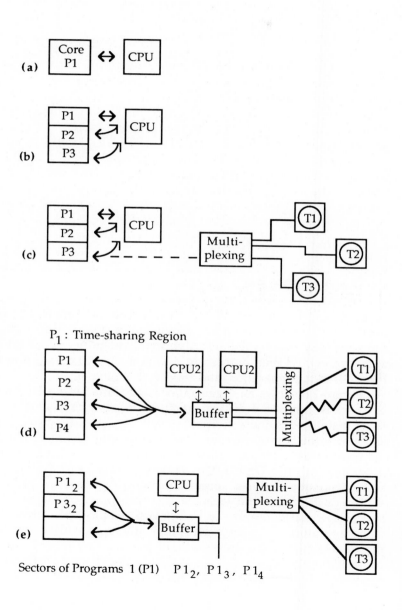

The emergence of microcomputers also brought changes in operating environments. Word processing systems are now typically placed in one of three arrangements:

1. *Independent,* when most of the work is self-contained.
2. *Clustered,* when a group of users benefits from shared files.
3. *Networked,* when file-sharing and electronic mailing of files are used extensively.

The use of self-contained, totally independent microcomputers is rapidly disappearing. Many microcomputer configurations include modems and often serve as communication devices. The AT&T UNIX/PC (3B/1) allows multiuser simultaneous access and UNIX-to-UNIX communication and has a built-in full-fledged telephone management system. Some of the same general features are offered by the IBM PC/AT's XENIX (a version of the UNIX operating system), which allows for multiple access and UNIX-like commands. The emerging technology seems to be moving toward a multiprocessing-multiprogramming (multitasking) environment, with microcomputer control of operating systems, including decisions about which function is performed at what level.

2.8 EDP ORGANIZATION AND MANAGEMENT

As in most functional areas of an organization the competency and motivation of EDP personnel is a key factor in effective performance. The EDP function may be divided into five main categories: (1) data processing management; (2) data processing development; (3) data processing operations; (4) data preparation; and (5) data custody.

Figure 2.6 shows an organization chart for a large EDP installation. It is basically composed of two functions: development, and operations. In large installations the activities in each area are directed by a manager and performed by numerous professional and technical personnel. The manager of development provides guidance to the heads of analysis and programming units who, in turn, supervise systems analysts, programmers, special function analysts, special function programmers, and other highly skilled professional and technical personnel. The manager of operations supervises a large number of less-skilled technical personnel, such as machine operators, data-entry staff, and others, in addition to higher level personnel, such as database and data communication managers and data controllers. In Chapter 8, we examine in detail some of the issues in and solutions to EDP-center control problems.

Figure 2.6   Typical Organization of an EDP Center

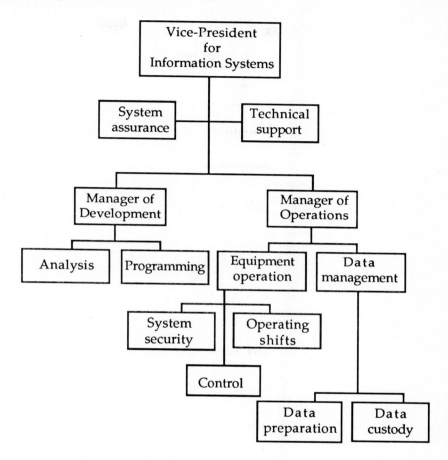

Microcomputers raised many new concerns for EDP management. In an attempt to head off potential problems, personnel of many—but by no means all—EDP facilities have assumed important roles in microcomputer consulting, standardization, and guidance in their organizations. Three anecdotes illustrate this point:

• A major New York-based insurance company developed an insurance-broker management system and acquired thousands of IBM PCs, which it resold at cost to its agents. This strategy allowed for improved broker management and substantial standardization of equipment.

Figure 2.7   The Expanded EDP-Center Organization

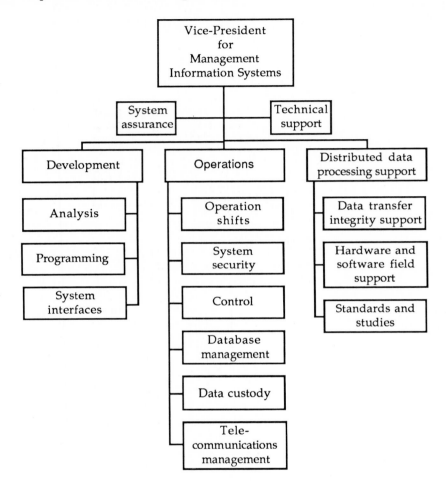

- A Big-Eight CPA firm acquired thousands of microcomputers and distributed them among the technical staff of its offices nationwide without a specific application plan. The approach taken was to let basic spreadsheets and database use flourish into natural grassroots applications.
- An aerospace company became extremely concerned about the proliferation of computers at its different facilities. A self-proclaimed centralized data processing unit found more than 300 minicomputers and microcomputers of different makes—and serving different purposes—that were performing EDP-type

functions. The group's response was to create and provide data processing consulting services, which included issuing guidelines for the future acquisition and use of minicomputers and microcomputers.

The problems related to EDP personnel management are similar to those found in any other functional area. Training, however, deserves special attention because data processing is a rapidly changing field of an extremely technical nature. The auditor should pay particular attention to the competency and training of the client's staff because they have crucial internal control implications. In addition to a concern for competency and training, the auditor should be especially concerned with several other organizational factors. Most of these factors are discussed in detail in subsequent chapters, but a few deserve mention here.

Obviously, not all the functions and supervisory levels shown in Figure 2.6 will exist in smaller systems. Small EDP operations often perform myriad data processing functions without any significant division of duties among personnel—and, in fact, may even be one-person operations. In any case, whether the system is large or small, issues related to the separation of data processing operations and management, relationships between data processing operations and users, and data processing budgets and controls are of major importance and will occupy a substantial portion of the auditor's time.

Figure 2.7 displays an expanded view of the MIS function, incorporating the additional functions that technological advances are creating. A third major branch of facility management is needed to support local operations. Development of microcomputer applications is performed in a hybrid manner, partly by the development unit (particularly the interface group) and partly at the site where the equipment is located. This type of structure does not adhere strictly to the chain of command and scalar principles of organization design but does recognize the realities that modern data processing organizations face.

2.9 Summary

In this chapter we presented an overview of the key concepts necessary for auditor comprehension of electronic data processing (EDP). We limited the discussion to concepts that are applicable to all types of EDP systems and described generally the characteristics of management information systems that are affected by an evolving technology. We identified the six stages of computer hardware development, described major hardware configurations and types of software, discussed the evolution of data custody, and concluded by presenting the key factors affecting EDP environments, organization, and management.

Data processing units face substantial control and management problems. Most of these problems, however, are analogous to those confronting management in general and should not present unusual situations for auditors. However, there is a problem of terminology and translation. Auditors must learn EDP terminology and the issues facing data processing facilities.

Questions

1. Why may a computer be called a stored-instruction information processing device?
2. Describe the prominent features of the first, second, third, and fourth generations of computers.
3. What is the relationship between the CPU and main memory?
4. Define the computer operating system and describe some of its major functions.
5. Describe the relationship between high-level programming languages, compilers, and machine language. Relate this relationship to the concepts of source code and object code.
6. How does specialized computer software vary from high-level languages and operating systems?
7. Why are multiuser and time-sharing systems useful?
8. What are some of the key features of an EDP organization?
9. What are the differences between multiprogramming and multiprocessing?
10. Theoretically, how many characters can be stored on a 1200 foot tape recorded at 1600 bpi (bits per inch)?

Problems

1. What are some of the forces that have led to the proliferation of computer languages? Operating systems?
2. If you were asked to write a computer program for accounts payable, how would you decide whether to write it in COBOL, BASIC, or some other computer language?
3. What type of an operating system would you choose for a computer installation? Could you choose one? Why?

4. What effect might the work performed by an EDP center have on its organizational structure?

5. Find some historical references to the development of the earliest computer. Compare the problems faced to those encountered by current system developers, as reported in the current data processing literature.

Notes

1. Von Neumann, J., "First Draft of a Report on EDVAC." Unpublished paper, June 1945; printed in Rondell, B. (Ed.), *The Origins of Digital Computers—Selected Papers.* Springer-Verlag, 1975.

2. A rich and captivating description of the evolution of computing thought is presented in Fishman, K. D., *The Computer Establishment.* New York: Harper & Row, 1981.

3. McKenney, J. L., and McFarlan, F. W., "The Information Archipelago—Maps and Bridges," *Harvard Business Review*, September–October 1982, pp. 109–119.

4. LISP is a list-processing-oriented language whose basic elements are objects manipulated as an entity. This language, originally developed in the 1960s for text manipulation, is very popular for artificial intelligence (AI) and expert systems applications. LISP machines are special computers to perform these applications.

5. Christian, Koan, *The UNIX Operating System.* New York: John Wiley & Sons, 1983.

6. Kernighan, B. W., and Ritchie, D. M., *The C Programming Language.* Englewood Cliffs, N.J.: Prentice-Hall, 1978.

7. Produced by BPI Systems, Inc., 3423 Guadalupe, Austin, TX 78705.

Additional References

Alter, Steven L., "How Effective Managers Use Information Systems," *Harvard Business Review*, November–December 1976, pp. 97–104.

Burch, John G., F. R. Strater, and G. Grudnitski, *Information Systems: Theory and Practice,* 2nd ed. New York: John Wiley & Sons, 1979.

Benton, John B., "Electronic Funds Transfer: Pitfalls and Payoffs," *Harvard Business Review*, July–August 1977, pp. 16–35.

Davis, Gordon B., *Management Information Systems: Conceptual Foundations, Structure, and Development.* New York: McGraw-Hill, 1974.

McFarlan, F. Warren, James L. McKenney, and Philip Pyburn, "The Information Archipelago—Plotting a Course," *Harvard Business Review*, January–February 1983, pp. 145–156.

McFarlan, F. Warren, and James L. McKenney, "The Information Archipelago—Governing the New World," *Harvard Business Review*, July–August 1983, pp. 91–99.

Moscove, Stephen A., and Mark G. Simkin, *Accounting Information Systems: Concepts and Practice for Effective Decision Making,* 2nd ed. New York: John Wiley & Sons, 1984.

Poppel, Harvey L., "Who Needs the Office of the Future?" *Harvard Business Review*, November–December 1982, pp. 146–155.

Chapter 3

Business Systems

3.1 INTRODUCTION

In this chapter we examine the main features of computer-based business information systems, show typical computer applications in business, and present transportable concepts that are applicable to a variety of business firms. We begin with the identification of common characteristics and major components of business systems. In the following section we use a payroll system to illustrate these major components. The next section describes the systems life-cycle concept and its four major phases. The final two sections describe a sales/accounts receivable system and a purchase and inventory system.

LEARNING OBJECTIVES

By the time you complete this chapter, you should be able to:

1. Identify the major components of a business system.
2. Use a payroll system to illustrate the major components of a computer-based business system.
3. Explain the business life-cycle concept.
4. Describe the major tasks undertaken during the four major phases of the system life cycle.
5. Explain the steps involved in setting up a computer-based accounts receivable system.
6. Describe a minicomputer-based purchase and inventory system.

3.2 COMPONENTS OF BUSINESS SYSTEMS

The most common characteristics of business systems is their intensive data orientation. Students in business schools extensively manipulate small data files, whereas actual business records tend to be massive and their manipulation is held to a minimum. Students therefore often have difficulty in comprehending the nature and extent of computer utilization in business. In their most traditional form, the major components of a computerized business system are:

1. A data screening program (edit), which collects data from a standardized input format, screens them for range, validity and other features, and posts the data to transaction files.
2. Transaction files, which contain one record per transaction. Transaction files include sales, purchases, cash receipts, and cash payments files and are used for updating master files.
3. Master files, which contain ongoing balances of particular accounts, histories of these accounts, background data on the accounts (that is, data not needed for transaction processing), and other accounts-related data. Master files are maintained for customers, employees, vendors, inventory items, and the like.
4. Master file update programs, which capture data from transaction files, match the data by a common key (say, account number) with a master file, and update the master file. Updating programs often utilize logical checks on transactional data, such as comparing transaction data with average balances, to perform additional data screening functions. These update programs often tabulate summaries of the changes at the end of execution.
5. File management programs, which administer the master files by adding new accounts, purging dormant accounts, correcting data errors, and the like.
6. Report programs, which retrieve preselected data from files and prepare the needed management information.

Typical business systems may include marketing systems, logistics systems, human resource systems, and accounting systems. Accounting systems may encompass (1) sales/accounts receivable systems; (2) purchase and inventory systems; (3) general ledger systems; and (4) others.[1]

3.3 A PAYROLL SYSTEM

Figure 3.1 depicts a typical business system: a simplified version of a payroll system having all the components described in the preceding section. This system is for a monthly payroll; the procedures for semimonthly, biweekly, and weekly payrolls would be the same, although the amount of payroll preparation work would be greater. In this system the master file (MF) is created and administered separately from daily transaction files. Typical modifications (updating) of the MF reflect the hiring

Figure 3.1 A Simplified Payroll System

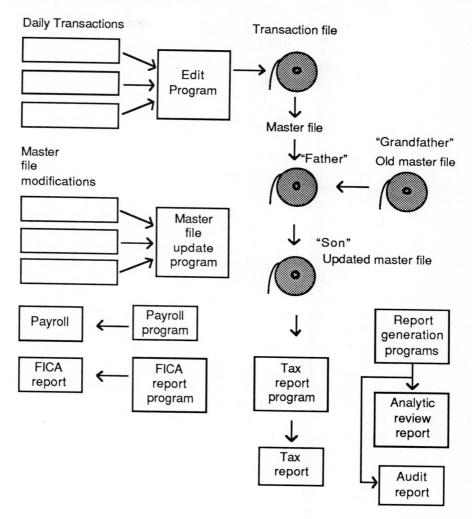

of new employees, wage-rate changes, employee dismissal, and other events outside normal monthly occurrences, such as overtime, vacations, and the like. This type of system will continue paying a salaried employee until termination and will not pay an hourly employee unless there is a transaction record indicating hours worked. This type of file system requires close monitoring because no monthly initiation is required for a payment. Without this monitoring an employee could go on being paid after dismissal or death.

Figure 3.2 shows the original source documents that provide transactional data. These documents are transported as a part of a batch (with a batch header) to the data conversion point. There, the data are entered into the system by either direct key-to-disk or key-to-tape methods (which include limited data screening), or by being punched onto cards and then processed through the transaction edit program. Many modern business systems use a word processor with a display screen, on which an image of the form being processed appears, to enter data into the system.

Figure 3.2(a) shows the form used to record the amount of overtime worked by salaried employees for the month. The total at the bottom of the form is entered manually at the originating department for batch verification purposes. If more than one form is used, each form has its own total. The name field is used to verify employee numbers.

Figure 3.2(b) shows the form used to record the hours worked by hourly employees. The actual wage rate is controlled by the allowable wage range in the MF. Additionally, in this department, part-time students work on different tasks at different times of the year for different wages. Again, each form used carries its own total, and the name field is used to verify employee numbers.

Employee numbers are issued consecutively to employees as they are hired. The employee number contains six digits, five of which represent the number itself; the sixth serves as a verifying digit. For example, Tereza Aczel is issued employee number 01230 when she is employed. The number becomes 012303 because the verification algorithm selected requires the sum of digits to be a multiple of 9 ($0 + 1 + 2 + 3 + 0 = 6 + 3 = 9$). The sixth digit, called a *check digit*, is a control technique to detect invalid employee numbers.

Figure 3.3 shows the master file change form, which (1) enters a new employee; (2) withdraws an employee; (3) changes the status of an employee; and/or (4) changes some other data about an employee. Different levels of file change require specific authorization by departmental and/or personnel office representatives. Data preparers are given a specimen of authorizing signatures and will punch in the code for those signatures that appear on the form. Corporate approval procedures, as prescribed in internal control procedures, are coded into the software and any changes require approvals.

This system allows for separate file and record maintenance and two levels of editing. Transaction files are stored sequentially in the order processed and have to be sorted prior to being merged with either the existing or updated MF.

Files are sorted frequently in business systems. Most records are maintained in some type of sequence, such as by ascending order of employee number. Then transaction sorts are required for updating files or other data access purposes. Modern database systems substantially decrease the need for data sorting because of their design, structure, and features.

Figure 3.2 Transaction Forms: (a) Overtime Record for Salaried Employees; (b) Record of Hours Worked for Hourly Employees; (c) Punched Cards Representing Batching

(a)

Department of Student Records Monthly Payroll			
Employee Name	Overtime Hours Worked	Employee Number	Observations
Total	▢▢▢		

(b)

Department of Student Records Monthly Payroll				
Employee Name	Employee Number	Hours Worked	Pay Rate	Observations
Total	▢▢			

(continued on next page)

Figure 3.2   Transaction Forms (continued)

(c)

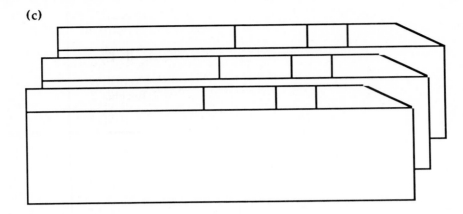

3.4 THE SYSTEM LIFE CYCLE

Each computer-based business system has a *system life cycle* consisting of distinct phases. The four main phases, shown in Figure 3.4, are:

- System analysis and definition.
- System design.
- System implementation.
- System evaluation.

SYSTEM ANALYSIS AND DEFINITION

In order to illustrate Figure 3.4, we will discuss the design and implementation of a payroll system at the PITL Corporation. The company has been in business for 10 years and currently has 100 employees. Its payroll has been prepared by an outside accounting firm for the last five years, but recently this arrangement has not been satisfactory. The owner (and chief executive officer) of PITL has decided to design and implement an in-house payroll system on its IBM 34 mainframe. Lisa Baumol, the data processing manager, who is also the data processing analyst, programmer, operator, and data converter, sees this as her great opportunity. She identifies the

Figure 3.3   Master File Change Form

MASTER FILE CHANGE FORM
Personnel System

Originating Department: ☐☐☐☐☐☐ (Number)

Fill in all Available Data

Event: Admission ☐   Deletion ☐   Status change ☐

Employee Number: ☐☐☐☐☐☐ (Leave blank if new employee)

Employee Name:
    (Last)
    (Middle)
    (First)

Employee Address:
    (Street & no.)
    (Apt. No.)
    (City or town)
    (State, ZIP)

Social Security Number: ☐☐☐-☐☐-☐☐☐☐

Employee's Signature   Date
_____   _____

Fill in Only New Data or Data to be Changed

Date of Birth: ☐☐-☐☐-☐☐

Marital Status: Married ☐   Single ☐   Divorced ☐

Sex: Male ☐   Female ☐

Base Salary: ☐☐☐☐☐☐☐☐

Union Affiliation:
(Enter initials or leave blank)

Work Category:

Number of Exemptions:

Approvals

Department Head: _____ ☐

Supervisor: _____ ☐

Personnel: _____ ☐

Figure 3.4   System Life-Cycle Phases

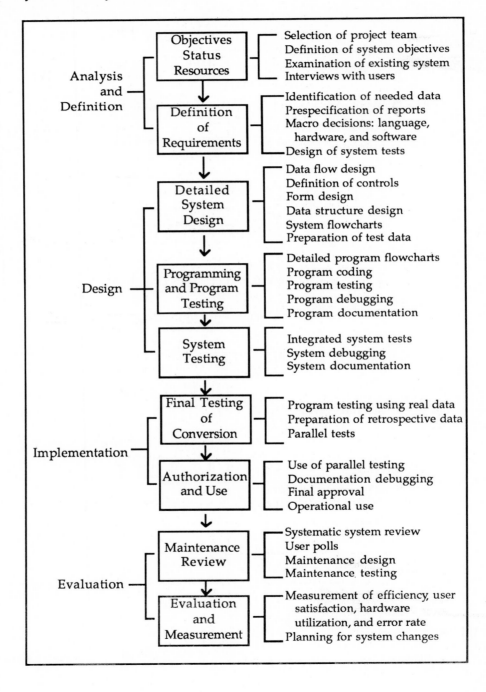

phases of the system life cycle and the activities required in each phase and then proceeds to work on the system.

She examines the literature and asks for bids on the cost of preprogrammed payroll systems. Following discussions with the owner and the personnel manager, she lists the main characteristics of the proposed system:

1. A system that will handle all current personnel transactions and reports and payroll preparation.
2. A system that can be integrated into the planned corporate management information system in the future.
3. A system that will be modular in nature to allow for expansion of the company and for changes in product lines.
4. That system development and implementation not take more than six months.

She then meets with department heads and departmental personnel involved in data preparation and data preparation and statutory requirements. During these interviews, she gathers information that will help her to assess:

- Type and frequency of changes to the MF.
- Volume of data involved.
- Types of reports needed.
- Analytical information needed.
- Availability of historical data.
- Statutory requirements and governmental regulations.

Next, the owner establishes a project team of Lisa Baumol, the personnel manager, the head of production, and a personnel clerk. In addition, he asks an outside auditor to participate in the process as a consultant.

Lisa continues her efforts by preparing flowcharts of existing procedures. These flowcharts include lists of data currently being collected and used and who is performing these tasks; she also jots down ideas on how these procedures can be changed. She and the other members of the project team then make preliminary decisions about computer language (COBOL, for consistency with other PITL applications), hardware (the IBM/34), and software (floppy disks to store data). In addition, they design forms and extensively discuss how to prespecify the ways of performing necessary program and system tests.

SYSTEM DESIGN

Throughout the system-design phase, Lisa works by herself, consulting as necessary other team members, the consultant, and a representative of IBM. The steps in the systems design phase involve:

1. Designing data flows and defining controls in consultation with outside auditors.
2. Designing the detailed forms and data screens to be used.
3. Designing data structures and developing criteria for inclusions, deletions, aggregation, and retention.
4. Designing system flowcharts.
5. Designing detailed program flowcharts.
6. Coding the COBOL programs.
7. Program testing and debugging.
8. Program documentation.

The testing of each program is followed by system tests. These tests are necessary because data flows, records, programs, and data structures often do not perform correctly as a system, in spite of trouble-free, debugged program tests. Only after these problems are cleared up can system documentation be completed.

SYSTEM IMPLEMENTATION

Lisa Baumol is aware that the implementation phase will be the real test of the system. The project team explains and discusses the need for and advantages of the system with key people in the company in order to gain their understanding and support. Preparation of retrospective data involves a substantial data search and results in the realization that existing records are both incomplete and inadequate. In general, the new system will not be able to rely on past data so much as on the data it generates. Extra help is obtained for the parallel testing of the old and new systems. Discrepancies are reconciled and the transition from manual to automated processes, and vice-versa, are rehearsed. The parallel test of PITL's payroll lasts two months, at which time the personnel manager is satisfied with the system's reliability. The project team reviews the system reports and user reactions regarding the quality of data being obtained and gives the system its final approval.

After the system has been in use for 15 months the personnel manager requests some patches and additional reports to solve several minor problems. After he discusses the matter with the owner, his request is granted, and the project team is reestablished. Now, however, many steps in the process are performed summarily. Lisa is aware of the shortcomings of maintenance updating without documentation and insists that the outside

Figure 3.5   A Sales/Accounts Receivable System

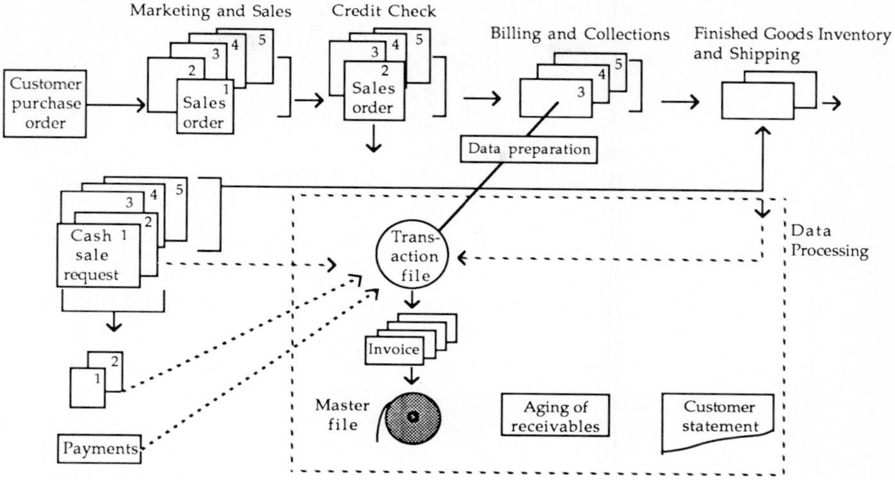

auditor review both the maintenance design and documentation before she makes the changes operational.

SYSTEM EVALUATION

A CPA firm is then engaged to conduct a system review to measure its effectiveness. After completing this review, the CPA firm praises the quality of the existing system and suggests several minor expansions and enhancements, reinforcing the owner's confidence in the system and in Lisa Baumol.

3.5 A SALES/ACCOUNTS RECEIVABLE SYSTEM

We now turn to a somewhat more intricate system: management of a sales/accounts receivable cycle. Figure 3.5 describes the general document flow for the system, which provides for two types of sales: (1) customer purchase orders (PO); and (2) cash sales. Sales are recorded on different-colored sales order (SO) forms, depending on the type of sale. An SO is created after verification of inventory availability and concurrently reserves the required quantity of the items ordered. Copies of the SO first go through a credit check; if credit is approved, copies of the SO are sent to billing and collection. There, an invoice is prepared, and the shipping order is issued. The shipping department dispatches the items and verifies that the shipment has been made. Customer statements and various management reports are produced periodically. Let's take a closer look at the steps in this process.

When a purchase order comes in from a customer, an order clerk in marketing and sales prepares a five-part pink sales order (SO). (If this were a cash purchase, an identical blue form would be prepared.) The sales order is prepared only if on-line inventory records indicate an adequate supply of the desired items. The clerk keys a reservation of the quantity ordered into the on-line inventory control system, files one copy of the SO, and sends four copies to credit check.

At credit check the name of the company placing the order is matched against the master credit files and the master sales file. By using a credit algorithm and/or information from the master files about the customer, the credit clerk approves or rejects the sale. If the sale is approved, one copy of the SO is filed along with any credit annotations. The three remaining copies of the SO are sent to billing and collections.

Billing and collections is responsible for the management of accounts receivable and cash sales information. One copy of the SO is keypunched and entered into the transaction control file. This on-line file edits the transaction and verifies controlled fields. An invoice is prepared and forwarded to the warehouse along with two copies of the SO; these documents constitute the shipping order. The transaction file is executed daily in a batch mode against the master accounts receivable file. Subordinate transactions are checked against inventory, and entries are posted to a cash reconciliation account. The transaction records also note payments received on outstanding invoices and cash payments.

Monthly customer statements showing the level and age of outstanding receivables are generated. In addition, management reports are prepared that list (1) the age of each receivable; (2) predicted cash flow; (3) exception reports on problem accounts; and (4) sales-commission payment analyses by salespersons. Sales commission data (net of returns) are issued in report form and sorted on magnetic tapes that serve as transaction input for the payroll program.

The shipping department dispatches goods to the customer. The shipping transaction is entered into the on-line inventory control file, expunging the reservation made by the marketing and sales clerk. Inventory is counted and the inventory control file is updated periodically.

3.6 A PURCHASING AND INVENTORY SYSTEM

The sales/accounts receivable management system that we discussed in the preceding section interfaces with the purchasing and inventory management system. Figure 3.6 represents an integrated system for departmental purchasing from the company's warehouse (central stores), company purchasing from outside vendors, and maintaining an adequate stock of inventory. This system is designed to minimize paperwork and is based on the use of a time-shared minicomputer with remote access terminals.

In this instance, the various departments of the company request needed items through the corporate acquisition system. The actual cost of these purchases is charged against the authorized departmental budgets by means of an estimated appropriation and later adjustments are made to reflect the actual cost. Department managers must query the inventory master file for item availability and then enter the order in the form of a purchase order (PO).

Purchase orders are received either from an ordering department or from inventory management as automatic reorder instructions or management requests. Orders are entered through a terminal and create pending transactions. Items that are stocked in the warehouse are delivered to the department. If an unusual item is being ordered, a precise specification for the item must be submitted. A technical review of item specification is usually performed by purchasing or by a third party. Upon approval, a request for bids is sent to vendors on an approved list or, if necessary, other sources are sought out.

Corporate procurement rules allow for certain acquisitions without eliciting bids, but these acquisitions require approval from purchasing and top management. Approvals are entered through a terminal and followed up by a distribution listing.

On the bid due date, all bids are opened and coded into the purchasing system. A rating of vendor reliability is obtained from the approved-vendor file. A purchasing agent examines the bids, matches them with vendor reliability, and selects the lowest and best bid. This choice is matched to the appropriate POs, which are updated. A purchase voucher is automatically issued to the vendor selected. The inventory file and the payables master file are updated.

When the items are received at the warehouse, an entry is made in the payables master file and the inventory file. Any adjustments are posted to these files and the vendor is notified. Departments that placed orders for the item are informed of its receipt by electronic mail.

The payables system organizes the outstanding obligations, ages them, sorts them by vendor and prepares a schedule of payments. Charges to the budgets of the ordering departments are entered at this point as offsets against the balance in the appropriate budget category.

Figure 3.6   A Purchasing and Inventory System.

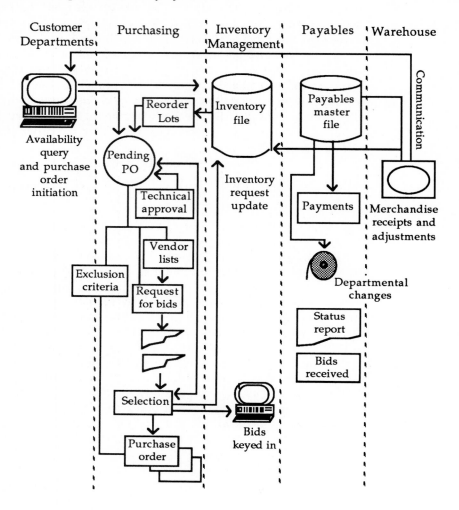

3.7 Summary

In this chapter we examined the main features of traditional computer-based business systems. The most common characteristic of business systems is their intense data orientation. The major components of computer-based business systems include a data screening program, transaction files, master files, master file update programs, file management programs, and report programs.

Common to business systems and their design is the concept of a system life cycle. The four major phases in a system life cycle are system analysis and definition, system design, system implementation, and system evaluation.

Typical accounting systems include a sales/accounts receivable system, purchasing and inventory system, payroll system, and general ledger system. We used a simple payroll system, a sales/accounts receivable system, and a purchasing and inventory system to illustrate the components of and some of the procedures used in computer-based business systems.

Questions

1. What are the six components of a business system?
2. Using the examples provided in the text, describe some of the typical files found in business systems.
3. What are some of the ways that files are typically updated?
4. What are the phases of a system life cycle, and why is the life-cycle concept helpful in understanding systems?
5. What are some of the factors that typically must be considered before a computer-based system can be designed?
6. What are the major features of the sales/accounts receivable and purchasing and inventory systems described in this chapter?
7. How do systems designed for batch processing vary from systems designed for on-line processing?
8. In the description of Lisa Baumol's work in developing a payroll system, what were the managerial parts of her job? Technical aspects?
9. Besides talking to users, how else might the information required to design a system be collected?
10. When does the evaluation of an EDP system stop?

Problems

1. Review Lisa Baumol's activities in designing a payroll system. Which activities seem more intense than others? Do you think that the emphasis on the different phases of system development will vary from project to project? Why? Why not?

2. Using the sales/accounts receivable and purchasing and inventory systems described in this chapter, prepare preliminary systems designs in terms of the major components of business systems.

3. In designing and implementing a computer-based business system, how much "political savvy" as opposed to technical expertise is called for? As a data processing manager, how would you surmount internal political problems?

4. From what you have read, what skills must a systems designer have? How do those skills compare to those traditionally developed through accounting education?

5. Based on the many skills demonstrated by Lisa Baumol during the development of the payroll system, how might the same tasks be divided up among members of a project team?

6. Design a system to manage and control the usage of ATM (Automatic Teller Machines) for a small bank. You may make any assumptions you need to make the design simpler. Remember that ATMs were one of the first on-line applications to come into fashion. Assume that the ATMs to be used are microcomputers constantly connected to the bank's mainframe and keeping a log of all transactions performed. It is standard, in this type of application, that two bank employees daily open the ATM and reconcile the machine's record with the deposits in the box as well as money dispensed and recorded withdrawals. For increased learning you may want to go to your local bank and find out as much as you can on the operations of their ATMs.

Notes

1. If you do not have enough background on business systems, you can refer to accounting information systems textbooks, such as those by Li (1983), Moscove and Simkin (1984), Cushing (1982), Leitch and Davis (1983), Wilkinson (1986), and Wu (1983).

2. Adapted from "AICPA Guidelines for Development and Implementation of Computer-Based Applications Systems," *Management Advisory Services Guideline Series Number 4*. New York: American Institute of Certified Public Accountants, 1976.

Additional References

Cushing, Barry E., *Accounting Information Systems and Business Organizations*, 3rd ed. Reading, Mass.: Addison-Wesley, 1982.

Leitch, Robert A., and K. Roscoe Davis, *Accounting Information Systems.* Englewood Cliffs, N.J.: Prentice-Hall, 1983.

Li, David H., *Accounting Information Systems: A Control Emphasis.* Homewood, Ill.: Richard D. Irwin, 1983.

Moscove, Stephen A., and Mark G. Simkin, *Accounting Information Systems: Concepts and Practice in Effective Decision Making*, 2nd ed. New York: John Wiley & Sons, 1984.

Nash, John F., and Martin B. Roberts, *Accounting Information Systems.* New York: Macmillan, 1984.

Page, John, and Paul Hooper, *Accounting and Information Systems*, 2nd ed. Reston, Va.: Reston Publishing Company, 1982.

Robinson, Leonard A., James R. Davis, and C. Wayne Alderman, *Accounting Information Systems: A Cycle Approach*. New York: Harper & Row, 1982.

Wilkinson, Joseph W., *Accounting and Information Systems*, 2nd ed. New York: John Wiley & Sons, 1986.

Wu, Frederick H., *Accounting Information Systems: Theory and Practice.* New York: McGraw-Hill, 1983.

Chapter 4

Audit Concepts

4.1 INTRODUCTION

In this chapter we introduce the key concepts and approaches of the audit process. Because we oriented this book toward the more technical aspects of auditing, we present only a summary of the conceptual framework. Specifically, we cover definitions, audit steps, hypothesis testing, and an overview of auditing data processing systems. You should read this chapter in conjunction with a review of the content of a traditional introductory auditing text.

LEARNING OBJECTIVES

By the time you complete this chapter, you should be able to:

1. Describe the organizational system and the search for evidence in support of organizational reporting.
2. Identify standard-setting bodies and professional associations in the audit field.
3. Describe key steps in the audit process.
4. Identify some specific audit philosophies.
5. Explain a systemic view of auditing.
6. Briefly describe the audit of EDP systems.

4.2 THE SEARCH FOR EVIDENCE

Typically, the audit process is discussed in terms of established procedures and professional standards that are applied in a moral and legal context. At times, this traditional orientation is detrimental to an understanding of the intrinsic nature of the audit process and the correct interpretation of evidence. Rigid standards and procedures may also hamper the development of new ideas and approaches that can result from research based on sound theoretical models.

We prefer to view the audit process as a continuing search for evidence, based on the application of a mixture of concepts from basic research, the scientific method, and the practicalities of business operations. Such an approach serves to illuminate the nature and characteristics of the audit process and audit evidence. Many research scholars and some practitioners believe that this approach will increasingly be taken to resolve problems that have proven intractable to the traditional procedures and standards approach.

Table 4.1 shows a summary of the features of an organization as an economic entity and the audit process as the means of measuring, aggregating, and evaluating the set of economic events related directly to the organization being audited. Churchman discussed the main features of a system along five main dimensions: (1) objectives; (2) elements; (3) resources; (4) environment; and (5) management.[1] Thus, if we compare the organization and the audit process in Table 4.1 as systems, it is clear that the audit process as a system is much different from the organization as a system. For example, if we view the internal audit function as an organizational subsystem, its objectives are very different from those of the organization as a whole. And, if we view the audit firm instead of the audit process as a system, we again have an organizational system. Consequently, auditing objectives, standards, and independence differentiate a profit-making enterprise from an audit-oriented system.

ECONOMIC EVENTS OCCURRENCE STAGE

Let's extend the same systemic view of the organization to that shown in Figure 4.1. Economic events are discussed at three main stages: occurrence of economic events, their measurement, and their aggregation into accounting levels. Stage 1 includes the organizational system's environment, particularly the economic events that occur. The organizational system being considered (a for-profit business or a not-for-profit organization) actually is a subsystem of its total environment. Many economic events occur in that environment that may not be relevant to the organization; other events affect the system but are not relevant for accounting and auditing purposes; and others are directly related to the system and their effects have to be measured. The selection of relevant data, that is, the items to be measured, is an important decision, which is often performed by systems analysts who know a great deal about economic events, their relevance to the nature of the system, and methods of measuring them.

Table 4.1   The Organization and the Audit Process as Systems

Feature	Organization	Audit Process
Objectives	Profit, service, self-preservation	Attestation, measurement, and evaluation
Elements	Individuals, physical facilities, and business entities	Audit personnel, organizational record-keeping and reporting methods
Resources	Human, capital, and physical resources	Audit personnel and audit technology
Environment	Economic environment	Generally accepted accounting principles, generally accepted auditing standards, and Securities and Exchange Commission regulations
Management	Corporate management	Audit partner or internal audit management

The relationship of *economic events* and accounting measures is important to an understanding of major accounting and auditing issues. The environment and the system are separated by a *system boundary*, which provides a useful definition of an entity for accounting and auditing purposes. Thus, when analyzing a system, an analyst has to define boundaries and attributes carefully. The importance of boundary definition is illustrated by our earlier comparison of the audit-process system and the audit-firm system.

Figure 4.1   Economic Events and the Organizational System

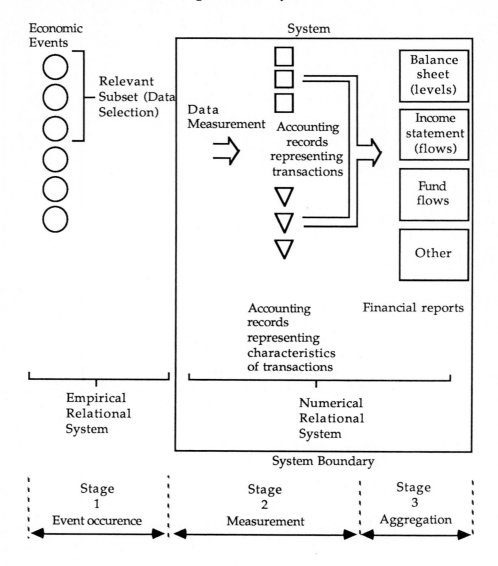

Let's look at the situation that a stockbroker faces as an example. Environmental data that can be used to support the broker's decisions include trade information, portfolio information, potential client lists, market information, news items, and the like. Obviously the amount of information available on all stocks and potential clients far exceeds the broker's ability to store and process it, requiring the broker to preselect certain types of information for scrutiny. In addition, information usually costs something, even though, on an incremental basis, it may cost very little. And, despite the wide range of information actually evaluated by the broker, many relevant events may not be monitored or cannot be measured. Among such events are decisions affecting international events, ecological versus economic choices, and moods and behaviors of clients.

Actually, a large majority of relevant environmental economic events are not measured, and the few events that are monitored seldom generate transactions that are worth recording and divulging. Experience may provide general guidelines about what to record and not to record at different stages of the system's life. The systems analyst and users who jointly design a corporate information system have to make these choices.

MEASUREMENT STAGE

Related specifically to accounting events, a minimum set of information must be recorded, recoverable, and traceable. When accounting-related events occur, they are measured and recorded in terms of a *transaction* (stage 2). For example, when a customer decides to place an order, no record is created until the order is actually received. After a record has been created, its form and content change as the order is processed. The record initially represents someone's intention to purchase goods from the system. Later, it represents a production order or an order to withdraw stock from inventory. Still later, it represents the delivery of goods to the customer and the accrual of an obligation by the customer. Finally, when the customer has satisfied the obligation, the record loses its active status as a direct generator of activity and becomes a historical record.

Modern information and accounting systems generate a multitude of papers (or EDP entries) that relate to the different elements of a particular transaction. Typically, the transaction is assigned and carries a unique *transaction number* throughout its life. The transaction number is posted to each of the forms of the record generated and serves as the transaction identifier. This multiplicity of representations of the original transaction record is an unavoidable complication of business systems. A one-to-one relationship between a transaction and a register is feasible but would probably entail major delays in the commercial operations of the system. The existence of multiple documents that relate to the different operations or procedures needed to complete a transaction is clearly an audit problem. Auditors must evaluate the controls on the number of transactions flowing through a system (population controls) to avoid violations of the integrity of the flow (documents added, subtracted, or changed).

Figure 4.1 also indicates that transactions have qualitative characteristics. Thus transactions not only have event-related attributes, but they also have attributes that are intrinsic or are added during the process.

Let's assume that the organizational system is a major publishing house that supplies the college textbook market. A particular bookstore orders 50 copies of a particular textbook. The order is transmitted by letter and recorded in the company's books by transcription onto proper sales forms; transaction information is transcribed both from the order (such as customer name, item, quantity, and amount) and from company records (such as item number, customer number, priority, and shipping date). This transaction is then routed to the credit department where its qualitative characteristics are changed either by approval of the customer's order or by the requirement for prepayment. Other qualitative characteristics and quantitative characteristics may be changed throughout the processing of the order to reflect changes in the unit price, addition of shipping costs, detection of the availability of a new edition, inventory stock limitations, and the like. Typically, these steps relate to a set of records for one transaction. In most instances, a listing of sales is not adequate for financial reports. Sales must be aggregated, processed, and adjusted prior to use in financial reporting. We do not show this intermediate posting stage in Figure 4.1 but do examine it later in this chapter.

REPORTING STAGE

Stage 3 in Figure 4.1 represents the various financial reports that are prepared by the organization. The accounts in these reports can be grouped into two major types: *levels* and *flows*. Quantities represent the accumulation of flows over time and can be measured directly. For example, the balance sheet measures the level of an entity's assets and liabilities on a particular date. The value (level) of a particular inventory at any particular time corresponds to the physical quantities of goods on hand multiplied by their respective unit prices. The auditor can actually examine these physical quantities and assess the adequacy of attributed unit prices. These prices must reflect one of the general measurement rules, such as historical cost under first in, first out (FIFO) or last in, first out (LIFO).

Other measurements of levels can be related to physical evidence, such as cash and marketable securities. On the liabilities side, there is documentary evidence of obligations incurred that, accumulated, comprise liabilities. Other levels, such as goodwill and paid-in-capital in surplus, do not actually correspond to the accumulation of physical or documentary units but have to be recognized nonetheless.

Table 4.2   Economic Events and Organizational System: an Illustration

Economic Events	Transactions	Financial Reports

Purchase of
  assets
  materials
  services
	Generation of
	  depreciation
	  cost assignments
	  goodwill
	  personnel records
		Levels
		  Balance sheet
		  Accounts receivable balance
		  Accounts payable balance
		  Integrity of records

Sale of goods	Generation of
	  credit records
	  cash records
	  inventory flow
	  records
		
		Flows
		  Income statement
		  Funds flow

Flows pose different problems. Typically, the management of flows relates to the day-to-day operations of a business. Time and resource constraints prevent the auditor from reviewing these transactions as they occur. Thus the auditor must evaluate the reliability of the system used to record the transactions in order to assess their accuracy. Flows are usually recorded in some type of transactional source document and accumulated in a subsidiary ledger. Totals from this subsidiary ledger represent the measurement of accumulated flows and are converted into trial balances and financial reports.

Table 4.2 presents further details of the three levels shown in Figure 4.1. These three stages are extremely useful for understanding the role of information in an organization, as well as the method, positioning, and role of auditing in the corporate management process. They separate the processes into their essential characteristics of: economic event, recorded transaction or aggregation. Economic events, such as sales and purchases (stage 1), including contractual obligations, are measured and recorded. They are then classified (stage 2) and their transactional characteristics defined. This step is often followed by transcription to a specialized account in which temporary balances can be maintained. Translating this process into levels and flows, we have unit transactions (with a certain level that corresponds to the dollar amount of each transaction) flowing through the system into temporary accounts where levels are computed and maintained. These subtotals are temporary levels at any specific time. At predetermined dates (such as the closing of the fiscal year) they are closed and converted first to trial-balances and then to financial reports (stage 3).

RELATIONAL SYSTEMS

We can define the relationships among actual events as the *empirical relational system*. We can characterize the relationships among the measurements of relevant events as the *numerical relational system*. Ideally, event relationships will be reflected in numerical relationships. In addition, we also expect that no numerical relationships (such as accumulations into individual credit balances) exist that do not have event relationship counterparts. The audit process examines flows through *interim work* and *internal control evaluation*, whereas it examines levels at *year-end* through *substantive testing*.

4.3 DEFINITIONS

The audit process is concerned with *verification* and *attestation*. Its aim is to verify whether the client's *financial reports are fairly stated in accordance with generally accepted accounting principles* (GAAP) and to attest to this finding by issuing an *opinion* that the finding is unqualified or qualified; if qualified, the auditor presents the qualifying features of the finding.

Historically, organizations with distributed ownership tended to prepare a set of reports to show the financial well-being of the entity. These reports were viewed by the owners (shareholders or partners) as a form of control over management. These *financial statements* slowly began to be used for other purposes, such as financial evaluation first by loan officers, then by potential outside investors, and, finally, by governmental regulatory bodies.

Over a period of years, the reporting practices used for financial statements emerged as a series of generally accepted procedures. The term *general acceptance* became very important when groups responsible for codifying accounting rules started to issue them as standards for verification purposes by auditors.

MATERIALITY

The auditor's objective is to determine whether the financial statements *fairly* represent the economic well-being of the entity, using *generally accepted auditing standards* (GAAS). Measurement theory indicates that there are no perfect measures.[2] Actually, measurements are as accurate as the precision of the measuring instrument and tend to improve in accuracy as additional resources are applied. Unfortunately, there is a point of diminishing returns. At some point the amount and advantages of increased accuracy do not justify further expenditures. Therefore there is an intrinsic level of error in any measurement, and the auditor has to establish, mainly on the basis of judgment, what constitutes fair representation. In other words, the auditor must decide on a level of error that is acceptable in the financial statements he or she is auditing. This level, or threshold, of error is called *materiality.* Accountants have been struggling for decades to define a specific threshold of materiality, but no generally accepted standards have emerged.

The current audit standard requires the auditor to "consider" materiality and audit risk during the planning stage of an audit and when evaluating the adequacy of evidence. Most authorities interpret this to mean that materiality is established at the beginning of an audit and then reevaluated at the end of the audit. However, the standard sets no concrete criteria for determining materiality.

A rule of thumb often used by accountants is that allowable error can be 5–10 percent of average net income from operations. Because income is a highly volatile number, a percentage of sales or total assets would probably make more sense. In an attempt to deal with the true complexity of this concept Peat, Marwick, Mitchell has recently been using a materiality threshold that is defined as a function of assets or revenues.[3] In addition, the auditor's sample sizes and control reliance procedures will also relate to the threshold of materiality selected.

GOING CONCERN

Another important concept for the audit profession is that of the *going concern.* This concept states that the entity being audited is a viable concern and that in the normal course of events it is not expected to fail. This concept is essential to the valuation of a business based on historical value, following the traditional accounting model. If a firm is not a going concern, its assets should not be valued by its historical cost (net of depletion) but by its realization value (exit value).

INTERNAL CONTROLS

Management of organizational systems involves four main types of activities: planning, management decisions, implementation, and control. An organization's *internal controls* monitor actual performance operations and the degree to which they are conducted in accordance with corporate policies. The process of control entails comparing actual performance (as measured by accounting) with preset standards (established by plans, procedures, or objectives); discrepancies trigger decisions and action.

Verification of the effectiveness of an organization's internal controls requires the auditor to describe and evaluate them and test accounting and other procedures for compliance.

4.4 SETTING ACCOUNTING AND AUDITING STANDARDS

In the United States the auditing profession is traditionally viewed as part of the accounting profession. Following in the tradition of other professions, it is self-regulating; that is, it sets most of its own rules, enforces them and disciplines members for infractions.

The American Institute of Certified Public Accountants (AICPA) is the oldest professional accounting organization in the United States. It initially undertook the task of setting both accounting and auditing standards. Accounting principles and standards were originally promulgated by one of its senior technical committees, the Accounting Principles Board (APB). Because of a number of controversies surrounding the impartiality of board members, an independent Financial Accounting Standards Board (FASB) was established. It is a privately funded organization and sets accounting standards for private business in the United States.

Auditing standards continue to be set by the AICPA through the Auditing Standards Board. In 1917, the AICPA produced a document on balance-sheet auditing from which auditing standards have evolved. Appendix 4.A contains a 1973 review of the evolution of audit standards to the issuance of the first Statement on Auditing Standards (SAS); SASs constitute the most important part of the Generally Accepted Auditing Standards (GAAS).

Certain functions of the Auditing Standards Board were changed recently by the establishment of the Accounting and Review Services Committee. This committee is generally empowered to authorize the issuance of opinions by certified public accountants (CPAs) that provide a level of assurance less than those provided by GAAS audits. Similarly, actions by other AICPA committees appear to permit accountants to issue reports that provide varying levels of assurance in such areas as taxation and projected financial statements.

Other significant AICPA functions include enforcement of standards of ethics; preparation and grading of the uniform CPA examination, which controls entry into the public practice of accounting; generating continuing education programs; setting standards of practice for management advisory and taxation services; and maintaining relations with governmental bodies and other professions.

The Securities and Exchange Commission (SEC) is a federal agency that was created by the Securities Acts of 1933 and 1934 to police the activities of the capital markets. Companies whose stock is publicly traded and brokers who handle stock transactions come under its jurisdiction. Over the years the SEC has increasingly taken the lead in seeking additional disclosures in financial statements. Through its Accounting Series Releases (ASRs), it has prompted action by the FASB on many issues and has imposed a series of additional disclosure requirements on publicly traded corporations.

The Financial Accounting Standards Board (FASB) is a privately funded entity established to set accounting standards for private business in the U.S. It replaced the Accounting Principles Board that was initially set up by the AICPA. Unlike the SEC, the FASB has no charter or direct enforcement power. Its rules are interpreted and enforced by independent public accountants who examine the records of public and private entities. The resulting auditor's opinion attests to the adequacy of an entity's financial statements in terms of generally accepted accounting principles. Publicly traded companies must provide this annual audit opinion or the SEC will exert its enforcement powers. Certain accounting practices, even if cleared by independent accountants, can be questioned by the SEC. These disagreements over what constitutes proper disclosure often raise "emerging issues" to be considered by the FASB when issuing new or revised standards.

Many other organizations exert great influence over accounting and auditing practice, including the Financial Executives Institute (FEI), the Institute of Internal Auditors (IIA), the American Accounting Association (AAA), and the National Association of Accountants (NAA). Substantial differences in disclosure are found in financial statements in various industries. The FASB has recently dealt with some of these differences, such as in the motion picture and oil and gas industries, but many are still to be examined and evaluated. Meanwhile, a set of *preferable accounting principles* guides financial disclosures.[4]

4.5 KEY STEPS IN THE AUDIT PROCESS

The auditor's task can be compared to that of the scientist. The auditor searches for the true financial health of an organization by applying a set of rules (GAAS), as the scientist would apply the scientific method. The auditor uses induction and environmental scanning to formulate hypotheses about the business to be audited and formulates a detailed plan of action to test these hypotheses. Data are gathered and analyzed to test the hypotheses. Finally, the auditor's statement of opinion becomes the record of the research findings.

Figure 4.2   The Audit Process

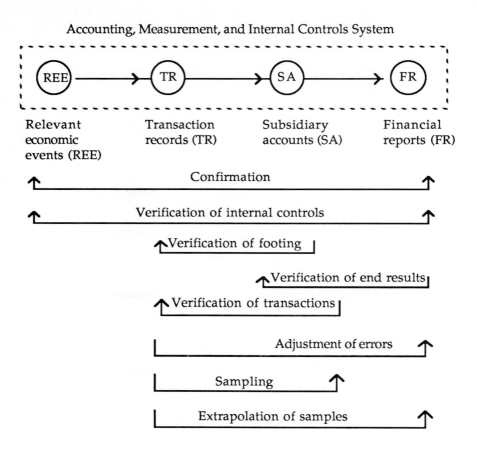

The audit process endeavors to verify the fairness of financial statements. This process of measurement and "search for the truth" requires substantial formalization and conformance to standards and procedures defined by the standard setting boards.

Most major audit firms establish their specific procedures for performing an audit, in accordance with generally accepted audit standards. The steps presented in this section summarize the key aspects of the audit process. These steps are not necessarily performed sequentially; actually, there can be a substantial degree of interaction among them.

Figure 4.2 shows an overview of the audit process. Note that we have added the intermediate step of posting transactions to subsidiary accounts to the three components of Figure 4.1. We also reoriented Figure 4.1 to emphasize the auditing process rather than the data gathering and recording process of the organization. Recall that only a small, selected subset of economic events that occur require recording. However, it is essential that *all* of the events in each type selected be recorded. For example, it is essential in large organizations that sales be formally recorded. If all are not recorded, the total sales of the firm will be understated and the financial statement may be materially incorrect. Fraud involving cash sales occurs when salespersons make a sale but do not record it, and the inventory shortage is explained away as shrinkage.

Table 4.3   The Audit Steps

Step	Major Activities
Feasibility study	Environmental scanning Task definition Establish objectives
Engagement planning	Audit planning Risk assessment Benefit and cost assessment Analytical review
Evaluation of internal controls	Documentation examination and document flow assessment Analysis of internal control questionnaires Flowchart and narrative description preparation
Proof of compliance with internal controls	Compliance sampling Sample-result evaluation
Proof of details (substantive testing)	Detail sampling and testing Analytical review Statistical extrapolation
Attestation	Final judgment formulation Opinion Management letters

After a transaction has been recorded, it may be incorrectly tran-scribed, altered, incorrectly posted, or improperly aggregated. These possibilities require population controls, as well as integrity controls. The auditor enters an organization and works back against the flow of transactions, from the financial statements back to the original economic events. The auditor's task is to verify that the financial statements are materially free from error at minimal effort and cost. The verification and attestation steps and the major activities associated with them are described in Table 4.3.

FEASIBILITY STUDY

In this section we concentrate on the public accountant's role in auditing and audit objectives and procedures. The auditor should be aware of the wide range of audit objectives and emphasis that he or she may encounter. Different types of auditing represent different challenges. Thus the first step in preparing for an audit is to define the type of client and establish audit objectives. Auditors who perform external audits for publicly traded companies are well informed about the objectives, needs, and minimal requirements for a comprehensive audit. Internal, operational, and tax audits present different sets of possibilities and objectives. For example, a congressionally mandated audit of a particular government agency to be performed by the U.S. General Accounting Office (GAO) will be very different in nature and scope than a cash audit of the sales store at the Metropolitan Museum of Art.

An auditor faces two basic situations in practice: (1) a new client; and (2) a repeat engagement. An audit feasibility study is required for each new engagement. While an auditor examines the auditability of a prospective client from a number of different technical standpoints, he or she also examines whether undertaking the engagement makes sense from the auditor's standpoint. Two key questions have to be asked: (1) Is the system auditable? (2) Should we do the audit?

With respect to the first question, a not-for-profit organization may collect all its money from donations made by people walking along the street. The organization may be auditable from the standpoint of expense accountability, but verifying whether the revenues declared represent the total actually collected may be impossible. For example, it was found that one such organization diverted undeclared revenues to political action prior to accounting for revenues. Another instance of difficulty, if not impossible auditability, occurs when management frequently overrides internal controls or engages in fraudulent practices. These instances make reliance on internal controls impossible and the definition of relevant economic events infeasible.

As for the second question, a particular auditor or audit firm may decline to audit a system for a number of different reasons. The benefits versus the cost may not be positive. Often, firms invited to submit a proposal for a municipal audit, will not participate because of the lack of local facilities or the small amount of the audit fee. Also the lack of specialized staff, the size of the engagement, or the year-end date make certain engagements undesirable. A conflict of interest, where related parties are employed by the auditor and the client or related economic interests, can prevent an auditor from taking an engagement. After the feasibility study has been completed, an engagement letter is issued specifying the terms, scope, and other issues related to the engagement.

ENGAGEMENT PLANNING

In recent years added emphasis has been given to the importance of engagement planning. The final product of this step is the definition of the audit plan including tasks to be performed, personnel to be used, areas to be stressed, assessment of audit risk, areas to be audited, audit scheduling, and personnel scheduling. Analytical review is now frequently used in engagement planning, as it has been in the past in other steps in the audit process. In essence, analytical review involves the examination of financial reports of an entity (or of a lower level of aggregation) through analytical means to detect, *a priori*, the areas of major exposure or extended risk. Audit planners use the results of analytical review when they establish audit steps and decide on audit emphasis. Many authorities stress planning as a continuous process, whereby each new piece of evidence affects subsequent audit steps.

EVALUATION OF INTERNAL CONTROLS

The Foreign Corrupt Practices Act of 1977[5] (FCPA) was enacted during a traumatic period in American history. The impeachment proceedings initiated against President Nixon and extensive revelations about improper practices abroad by such major U.S. corporations as Lockheed, IT&T, and Bendix led to the need for restrictive legislation. The title, FCPA, is something of a misnomer: While the act makes bribing foreign officials an illegal practice, its main impact is on the internal controls of corporations.

The act made top management responsible for weaknesses in internal controls and personally liable in civil and criminal litigation. This legislation quickly focused attention on many issues related to internal control and, consequently on audit committees, the independence of the internal audit function, the proper use of external auditors, and potential conflicts of interest of directors. As with most legislation of this type, the initial reaction and shock were greater than the act's immediate consequences; there have been few actual instances of FCPA-based litigation to date. The AICPA considered the possibility of requiring external auditors to issue an opinion on internal controls but later dropped the issue. However, the long-range effects of the act will probably be noteworthy.

In the evaluation of internal controls, the auditor examines the *prescribed* system of internal controls, that is, the system that should be working if the company follows to the letter its own control rules. Evaluation activities include:

- Careful examination of all existing documentation (rules, methods, and procedures) and assessment of document flows.
- Preparation and distribution of internal control questionnaires (ICQs) and analysis of responses.
- Preparation of flowcharts and narrative descriptions that serve to consolidate the information obtained and the auditor's observations. These materials are often used later to document working papers.

The ICQ, a valuable and commonly used analytic tool, is often based on the auditor's experience and logical thinking and (increasingly) on legal precedent or weaknesses found in other audits. The questionnaire is usually divided into sections that reflect the main corporate transaction cycles and asks questions about how the system is supposed to work. Figure 4.3 shows a questionnaire developed for a noncomputerized accounting system. Typically, the questions can be answered Yes, No, or N/A (not applicable), where a Yes denotes a control and a No denotes no control. The lack of a particular control does not necessarily signify a weakness in controls. However, some audit firms (such as Deloitte, Haskins & Sells) use preset overlays to identify critical combinations of controls that must be in place. Such questionnaires are slowly being computerized, with built-in automatic checks for critical combinations of controls.

COMPLIANCE WITH INTERNAL CONTROLS

After the system of internal controls has been identified, the auditor has to exercise some judgment regarding the system's adequacy. If the system is adequate and can be relied on, the auditor must then evaluate compliance with system rules and procedures. The auditor uses compliance testing, which involves the examination of particular controls and an evaluation of the degree to which the rules are being followed, for this purpose. For example, the auditor may examine vouchers for the existence of two independent signatures, review files for reconciliation of sequential numbers,

Figure 4.3   An Internal Control Questionnaire. Part I

Control SET Illustration — The Questionnaire

PURCHASES AND TRADE PAYABLES	Check (✔) Which
	Yes No

PURCHASING AND RECEIVING

PURCHASES AUTHORIZED BY (Describe the source and scope of authority and the documentation of other means of indicating general and specific authorizations) ....
....

PURCHASE ORDERS PREPARED BY (Indicate any persons who check or test this operation) ....
....

PURCHASE ORDERS APPROVED BY ....
....

RECEIVING RECORDS PREPARED BY (Describe records briefly. Indicate any persons who check, test, or otherwise approve this operation) ....
....

VENDOR INVOICES CHECKED BY ....
....

BLANK PURCHASE ORDER FORMS IN CUSTODY OF (Indicate applicable controls)............
....

1. Are purchases of goods and services so authorized that persons who approve and execute transactions can determine whether:
   a. The authorization was issued by persons acting within the scope of their authority? ....
   b. The conditions specified or implied in the authorization have been satisfied? .... ___ ___
2. Are purchase orders (or equivalent documents such as contracts or bids) approved for conformity with general or specific authorization as to vendor, goods or services ordered, prices, and other terms and specifications for all significant purchases of :
   a. Goods? ....
   b. Services (excluding utilities and similar routine services)?.................................... ___ ___
3. Are receiving records prepared for equivalent documents such as invoices, packing slips, bills of lading, or freight bills checked or adequately tested for all significant receipts of:
   a. Goods?...
   b. Services? .... ___ ___
4. Are vendor invoices checked or adequately tested and approved as to:
   a. Conformity with authorized prices, terms, and specifications? ....
   b. Receipt and acceptance of goods or services? ....
   c. Extensions and footings of individual items and related recapitulations? ....
   d. Coding or account distribution?... ___ ___
5. Are there procedures to monitor and control (by deduction from vouchers or otherwise) returned purchases, claims for adjustment, returnable containers, and other items chargeable to vendors (describe briefly)? .... ___ ___
6. Is the supply of blank purchase-order forms accessible only to the custodian and to those who prepare purchase orders? .... ___ ___

RECORDING PURCHASES

INITIAL PURCHASES RECORDS PREPARED BY (Include persons who—in circumstances permitting alteration, insertion or suppression—prepare or handle media from which records are prepared. If copies of vouchers are not used for this purpose, describe records briefly. Indicate any persons who check, test, or otherwise approve this operation. Describe supporting documents that are required by payment) ....
....

OTHER PURCHASES RECORDS PREPARED BY (Describe each record briefly. Indicate any persons who check or test this operation)
    Intermediate Records ....
    Final Records ....

PURCHASES RECORDS FOOTED BY (Indicate any persons who check or test this operation):
    Initial Records ....
    Intermediate Records ....
    Final Records ....

Source: By permission from the Deloitte, Haskins & Sells AUDITSCOPE manual.

(continued on next page)

Figure 4.3   An Internal Control Questionnaire. Part II (continued)

Control SET Illustration — The Questionnaire

PURCHASES AND TRADE PAYABLES (Continued)	Check (✔) Which
	Yes No

RECORDING PURCHASES (Concluded)

7. Is the preparation of initial purchases records performed by, or adequately tested by persons who do not also:
   - a. Prepare all supporting documents required for payment? ...... ___ ___
   - b. Sign checks (whether single or dual signatures are required)? ...... ___ ___
   - c. Handle signed checks? ...... ___ ___
   - d. Handle cash receipts after initial recording? ...... ___ ___
   - e. Have sole custody of other tangible assets? ...... ___ ___

8. Is the preparation of intermediate and final purchases records performed by, or adequately tested by persons who do not also:
   - a. Prepare all supporting documents required for payment of vouchers? ...... ___ ___
   - b. Issue checks singly? ...... ___ ___
   - c. Handle signed checks? ...... ___ ___
   - d. Handle cash receipts after initial recording? ...... ___ ___
   - e. Have sole custody of other tangible assets *and* maintain related subsidiary records or prepare the reconciliation to the general ledger? ...... ___ ___

9. Are the footings of initial, intermediate and final purchases record performed by, or adequately tested by persons who do not also:
   - a. Prepare all supporting documents required for payment of vouchers? ...... ___ ___
   - b. Issue checks singly? ...... ___ ___
   - c. Handle signed checks? ...... ___ ___
   - d. Handle cash receipts after initial recording? ...... ___ ___
   - e. Have sole custody of other tangible assets *and* maintain related subsidiary records or prepare the reconciliation to the general ledger? ...... ___ ___

10. Are there procedures for determining that purchases and returned purchases and other items chargeable to vendors are recorded at the amounts and in the accounting periods in which transactions are executed (describe briefly)
    - a. At year end? ...... ___ ___
    - b. At interim dates? ...... ___ ___

MAINTAINING TRADE-PAYABLES RECORDS

SUBSIDIARY RECORDS OF TRADE PAYABLES MAINTAINED BY (Include person who—in circumstances permitting alteration, insertion, or suppression—prepare or handle posting media or any preceding records. Describe such subsidiary records and related posting media briefly) ......
......

SUBSIDIARY RECORDS OF TRADE PAYABLES RECONCILES WITH GENERAL LEDGER ACCOUNTS BY
   Trial Balance Prepared By ....
   Reconciliation Prepared By (Include persons who foot the trial balances used in the reconciliation, and indicate frequency of reconciliation. Indicate any persons who check or test this operation) ......
VENDOR STATEMENTS, PAYMENT REQUESTS AND INQUIRIES AS TO VENDOR BALANCES CHECKED OR HANDLED BY (Indicate reasons for any such handling)
......

11. Are the subsidiary records of trade payables maintained by persons who do not also:
    - a. Prepare all supporting documents required for payment of vouchers? ...... ___ ___
    - b. Issue checks singly? ...... ___ ___
    - c. Handle signed checks? ...... ___ ___
    - d. Handle cash receipts after initial recording? ...... ___ ___
    - e. Have sole custody of other tangible assets? ...... ___ ___

12. Are recorded disbursements matched individually or adequately tested with initial credits in the subsidiary records, *and* the balances of individual vendor accounts computed or adequately tested, by persons who do not also:
    - a. Prepare all supporting documents required for payment of vouchers? ...... ___ ___
    - b. Issue checks singly? ...... ___ ___
    - c. Handle signed checks? ...... ___ ___
    - d. Handle cash receipts after initial recording? ...... ___ ___
    - e. Have sole custody of other tangible assets?

(continued on next page)

Figure 4.3   An Internal Control Questionnaire. Part III (continued)

Control SET Illustration — The Questionnaire

PURCHASES AND TRADE PAYABLES (Continued)	Check (✔) Which
	Yes No

MAINTAINING TRADE-PAYABLES RECORDS (Concluded)

13. Is the trial balance of the subsidiary records of trade payables prepared by persons who do not also:
   a. Prepare all supporting documents required for payment of vouchers? ....
   b. Issue checks singly? ....
   c. Handle signed checks? ....
   d. Handle cash receipts after initial recording? ....
   e. Have sole custody of other tangible assets?

14. Are subsidiary records of trade payables reconciled with general ledger accounts (including adequate investigation of reconciling items) promptly at least once a month *and* is the reconciliation performed by, or adequately tested by, persons who do not also:
   a. Prepare all supporting documents required for payment of vouchers? ....
   b. Issue checks singly? ....
   c. Handle signed checks? ....
   d. Handle cash receipts after initial recording? ....
   e. Have sole custody of other tangible assets? ....

15. Are vendor statements, payment requests, and inquiries as to vendor balances checked to the trial balances used in reconciling subsidiary records of trade payables with general ledger accounts and any differences investigated by, *and* such statements, requests and inquiries handled only by, persons who do not also:
   a. Prepare all supporting documents required for payment of vouchers? ....
   b. Issue checks singly? ....
   c. Handle signed checks? ....
   d. Handle cash receipts after initial recording? ....
   e. Have sole custody of other tangible assets?

OTHER PROCEDURES

16. Are required documents supporting paid initial purchases selected from initial cash-disbursements records *and* checked or adequately tested subsequently by internal auditors or other persons who do not also (if so, explain briefly):
   a. Prepare all supporting documents required for payment of vouchers? ....
   b. Issue checks singly? ....
   c. Handle signed checks? ....
   d. Have sole custody of other tangible assets? ....

17. Are unfilled purchase orders, purchase contracts, and other purchase commitments reviewed for possible losses *and* are appropriate provisions recorded as necessary (describe briefly):
   a. At year end? ....
   b. At interim dates? ....

18. Is the foregoing information considered adequate as the basis for an evaluation of internal accounting control—in that there are (explain negative answers briefly, and indicate conclusions as to their effect)
   a. No significant additional control procedures that mitigate any weaknesses indicated above? ....
   b. No adverse factors that impair any controls indicated above? ....

and verify checking accounts for bank reconciliations. Compliance testing usually is performed on a sample of documents identified by compliance sampling methods or as a dual test that examines compliance and substantive qualities at the same time.

SUBSTANTIVE TESTING

If the internal system of controls is adequate and is being complied with, the auditor may rely on it and decrease the extent of substantive sampling. If the system cannot be relied on, or can only be relied on to a limited extent because of lack of compliance, poor design, or other reasons, an increased amount of substantive sampling will be required. Some CPA-firm procedures require auditor evaluation of the degree of reliability of a particular internal control system and, consequently, its effect on the substantive sample. Figure 4.4 shows the effect of reliance on internal controls relative to substantive testing.

Substantive testing involves the examination of records and their actual validation. Records are drawn by sampling methods, verified for accuracy, footed and extrapolated to the general sample to verify the validity of balances. Records are checked against source documents to verify transcribed data validity and are then *confirmed* by means of mailed queries to third parties. These queries may be positive (where a response is expected) or negative (where a response is expected only if a discrepancy is found). Figure 4.5 illustrates the format and nature of confirmations.[6]

In 1981, a study was conducted to examine the effectiveness of different formats and wording of confirmations, as well as use of the U.S. mail to verify addresses and the actual existence of a particular third party.[7] The results were very favorable, showing outstanding reliability on the part of the U.S. Postal Service and a greater effectiveness for certain types of confirmations.

ATTESTATION

The last step in the audit process is the attestation by the auditor. By issuing an unqualified opinion, the auditor is stating that no material errors were found and that the entity audited was in compliance with GAAP. Figure 4.6 is an example of an unqualified opinion for Pizza Time Theater, Inc. It is a standard two-paragraph opinion, in which the first paragraph is the scope and the second paragraph is the opinion. A one-paragraph version of the unqualified opinion is also often used.

Figure 4.4   Effect of Reliance on Internal Controls on Substantive Testing

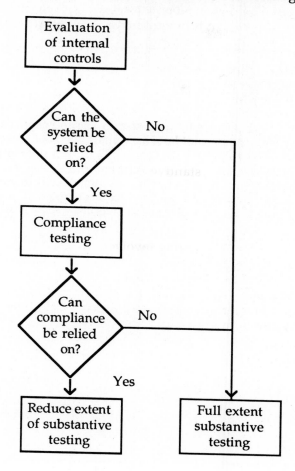

Figure 4.7 shows a second type of opinion: a subject-to (or qualified) opinion. It reflects the audit firm's uncertainty about whether the Chrysler Corporation in 1981 met the test for a going concern.

Finally, Figure 4.8 is an example of an infrequent adverse opinion. It shows the audit firm's disagreement with disclosure practices or the quality of numbers exhibited by the Manhattan Life Insurance Company in 1975.

The attestation step is the outcome of a long process of gathering data, interpreting evidence, and making decisions about subsystems, adjustments, and aggregation. Auditors are required to attest within a materiality threshold on a deterministic basis. Auditors cannot issue probabilistic

Figure 4.5   Examples of Confirmation Requests: (a) Positive Confirmation Request; (b) Negative Confirmation Request

(a)

Postler Rubber Artifacts
347 Grant Road
Wading River, NY 11792

   This request is being sent to you to enable our independent auditors to confirm the correctness of our records. It is not a request for payment.
   Our records on <u>December 31, 19X1</u> showed an amount of $20,274.23 receivable from you. Please confirm whether this agrees with your records on that date by signing and returning this form directly to our auditors. A self-addressed, stamped envelope is enclosed for this purpose. If you find any difference please report details directly to our auditors in the space provided below.

<u>Desiree Kim</u>
Controller

The above amount is correct [ ].
The above amount is incorrect for the
following reasons:

Postler Rubber Artifacts

By: _____

Conf. No. 6

(continued on next page)

opinions despite the fact that many of the subentities of the audit process may be judged stochastically. The final audit judgment is a composite of the outcomes of a series of initial decisions about scope, the result of audit procedures, and informal decision that aggregates influence and attestation rules. The decisions are made at the following points in the audit process:

- *Planning*—decisions about effort allocation and area choice.
- *Internal control evaluation*—judgments about adequacy of management information system design.

Figure 4.5   Examples of Confirmation Requests (continued)

(b)

Please examine this monthly statement carefully
and advise our auditors

Kim and Hsu
Certified Public Accountants

as to any exceptions.

A self-addressed, stamped envelope is enclosed for
your convenience.
THIS IS NOT A REQUEST FOR PAYMENT

- *Compliance testing*—based on sampling plans and error occurrences, determinations of reliance on internal controls and substantive sample-size selection.
- *Evidence of substantive testing*—based on sampling and analytic review results, aggregation into judgment on parts of the system.
- *Final judgments on opinions to be issued*—inferences and aggregation of partial judgments, some qualitative, some quantitative.

4.6 SOME SPECIFIC AUDIT PHILOSOPHIES

A number of different audit philosophies exist among the many large and small firms in the field. The firm of Deloitte, Haskins & Sells, for instance, tends to have a highly formalized system termed *AUDITSCOPE*, in which auditors are carefully guided through a step-by-step process. This philosophy increases consistency between different audit situations and attempts to decrease reliance on auditor judgment. Other firms such as Coopers & Lybrand have tended to emphasize auditor judgment decreasing the relative emphasis of other evidence such as statistical sampling. Recent developments at the AICPA and at this firm seem to indicate a present trend toward more extensive use of statistical sampling. Touche

Figure 4.6   An Unqualified Opinion

Auditors' Report

The Board of Directors
Pizza Time Theater, Inc.:

We have examined the balance
sheets of Pizza Time Theater, Inc. as
of December 27, 1981 and December
28, 1980 and the related statements of
operations, shareholders' equity and
changes in financial position for the
years then ended. Our examinations
were made in accordance with generally accepted auditing standards, and
accordingly included such tests of the
accounting records and such other
auditing procedures as we considered
necessary in the circumstances. The
financial statements for the year
ended December 30, 1979 were
examined by other auditors whose
report dated February 22, 1980
expressed an unqualified opinion on
those statements.

In our opinion, the aforementioned
financial statements present fairly the
financial position of Pizza Time
Theater, Inc. at December 27, 1981 and
December 28, 1980 and the results of
its operations and the changes in its
financial position for the years then
ended in conformity with generally
accepted accounting principles
consistently applied during the period
subsequent to the change, with which
we concur, made as of the beginning
of fiscal 1980, in the method of
recognizing territorial development
fee income as described in the notes to
the financial statements.

San Jose, California
February 4, 1982

Figure 4.7   A Qualified Opinion

Accountants' Report

**Shareholders and Board of Directors
Chrysler Corporation
Detroit, Michigan**

We have examined the accompanying consolidated balance sheet of Chrysler Corporation and consolidated subsidiaries at December 31, 1981 and 1980, and the related consolidated statements of operations and changes in financial position for each of the three years in the period ended December 31, 1981. Our examinations were made in accordance with generally accepted auditing standards and, accordingly, included such tests of the accounting records and such other auditing procedures as we considered necessary in the circumstances.

The financial statements referred to above have been prepared using generally accepted accounting principles applicable to a going concern which contemplate the realization of assets and the satisfaction of liabilities in the normal course of business. The Corporation incurred substantial losses in 1979, 1980 and 1981. The continuation of the Corporation as a going concern is dependent upon a return to sustained profitable operations and, if needed, availability of additional financing. The Corporation has been able to fund its losses primarily through federally guaranteed loans, concessions from its lenders, employees and suppliers, and the sale of assets. Through restructuring of its operations, the Corporation has reduced fixed costs significantly, but its ability to achieve sustained profitability will be affected by many factors (Note 2) some of which are beyond its control. The deterioration in the Corporation's financial condition has diminished its ability to absorb future losses which, if

(continued on next page)

Figure 4.7   A Qualified Opinion (continued)

incurred, could adversely affect its ability to continue as a going concern. Additionally, the Corporation is continuing negotiations for an industrial cooperation agreement with Peugeot S.A. (see Note 6), and accordingly continues to value its 14% ownership in Peugeot as a long-term investment. However, the carrying value of the Peugeot stock may require adjustment if the nature of this investment changes.

In our report dated February 27, 1981, we did not express an opinion as to whether the 1979 and 1980 financial statements of the Corporation were presented fairly because in view of the uncertainties and the ongoing restructuring described therein, we were unable to determine whether or not the use in those statements of generally accepted accounting principles applicable to a going concern was appropriate. Although there continues to be uncertainty regarding the Corporation's going concern status, the business and financial progress made by the Corporation in 1981 has reduced the need for ongoing restructuring. Consequently, we are now in a position to render an opinion on the 1979 and 1980 financial statements subject to the going concern uncertainties described above.

In our opinion, subject to the effects of such adjustments, if any, which might have been required had the outcome of the uncertainties regarding the Corporation's going concern status and its investment in Peugeot been known, the accompanying financial statements present fairly the financial position of Chrysler Corporation and consolidated subsidiaries at December 31, 1981 and 1980 and the results of their operations and changes in their financial position for each of the three years in the period ended December 31, 1981 in conformity with generally accepted accounting principles applied on a consistent basis, except for the changes, with which we concur, in the capitalization of interest in 1980 and in depreciation methods in 1981.

TOUCHE ROSS & CO.
Certified Public Accountants

February 24, 1982, Detroit, Michigan

Figure 4.8   An Adverse Opinion

Auditors' Report	To the Board of Directors and Shareholders of the Manhattan Life Insurance Company:

We have examined the balance sheet (statutory basis) of the Manhattan Life Insurance Company as of December 31, 1975, and the related statements (statutory basis) of income, surplus, and changes in financial position for the year then ended. Our examination was made in accordance with generally accepted auditing standards and, accordingly, included such tests of the accounting records and such other auditing procedures as we considered necessary in the circumstances. We previously examined and reported upon the financial statements for 1974.

The company presents its financial statements in conformity with accounting practices prescribed or permitted by the Insurance Department of the State of New York. The effects on the accompanying financial statements of the variances between such practices and generally accepted accounting principles are described in Note 10.

It is our opinion that, because of the materiality of the effects of the differences between generally accepted accounting principles and the accounting practices referred to in the preceding paragraph, the aforementioned financial statements do not present fairly the financial position of the Manhattan Life Insurance Company at December 31, 1975 and 1974, or the results of its operations or changes in its financial position for the years then ended, in conformity with generally accepted accounting principles. It is our opinion, however, that the supplementary data included in Note 10 present fairly surplus at December 31, 1975 and 1974, and net income for the years then ended, in conformity with generally accepted accounting principles applied on a consistent basis. Also in our opinion, the accompanying statutory financial statements present fairly the financial position of the Manhattan Life Insurance Company at December 31, 1975 and 1974, and results of its operations and changes in its financial position for the years then ended, in conformity with accounting practices prescribed or permitted by the Insurance Department of the State of New York which, except for the change in computing policy reserves as described in Note 12 to the financial statements, have been applied on a consistent basis.

COOPERS & LYBRAND
New York, New York
March 8, 1976

Ross & Co. has implemented an approach called *TRAP* (Touche Ross Audit Approach), which relies heavily on a systemic view of the audit process and deductive thinking. This approach is substantially different from the highly procedural method being used by firms like Arthur Andersen & Co.

An interesting study by Cushing and Loebbecke[8] examined and compared the approaches used by different firms. All the Big Eight and several other firms participated in the study. Responses indicated that most large firms evaluate and place some reliance on the internal controls of clients. In addition, about half the large firms have preprinted ICQs, and the others use guidelines and criteria for evaluation of internal controls. Flowcharting is a tool that is also used quite often; some firms make it a requirement, while others either recommend or allow its use. A small number of firms also use a risk matrix for evaluating internal controls. Of 13 large firms, Loebbecke and Cushing found that five require the use of statistical sampling, three expressed a preference for its use, three allow the use of both statistical and nonstatistical sampling methods, and one uses exclusively nonstatistical sampling methods.

The other side of the coin is presented by the results of an earlier study by Mautz et al. sponsored by FEI.[9] Among its many findings were that:

- Managers find control to be an integral part of their jobs.
- Managers resent the implications and certain provisions of the FCPA and view them as irrational or uneconomical.
- A wide range of reaction has followed enactment of the FCPA, ranging from major changes to the assumption that the corporation's current system satisfies the act's provisions.
- Some of the theoretical distinctions in the act are difficult for managers to grasp.
- The aspect that most troubles executives in relation to internal controls is the increased reliance on computers for operational effectiveness.

4.7 A SYSTEMIC VIEW OF AUDITING

In Section 4.2, we presented the relationships in an organization. Economic events are measured, recorded, and then summarized into financial statements. Figure 4.2 related these three stages to various aspects of the audit process. However, in the search for evidence, the auditor is concerned with testing of one main hypothesis:

H0: There is no material error in the financial statements as presented.

In addition, the auditor uses two secondary hypotheses to help in the testing of the main hypothesis:

H1: The internal control system is reliable, consistent, and produces accurate data.

H2: The aggregation of details as stated in the financial statements is materially correct.

Ideally, the results of testing H1 and H2 will be unambiguous and will lead the auditor to the final opinion by either supporting or rejecting the main hypothesis. However, if the testing of these two hypotheses leads to ambiguous results, the auditor is faced with a problem. For example, if H1 is rejected and H2 is accepted, an unqualified option would result; however, if H1 is supported and H2 failed to be rejected, a qualified or adverse opinion would result. Additionally, *materiality* is hard to define operationally because it is closely related to the desired reliability of the auditor's tests.

The following analytic statements were developed by Warren[10] to describe the relationships between the secondary hypotheses:

$$R = 1 - (1 - C)(1 - D)$$

$$(4.1)$$

where

C = Reliance assigned to internal controls and other factors.
D = Reliance assigned to substantive tests of details.
R = Desired combined reliance.

An additional secondary hypothesis can be added to the testing of the main hypothesis:

H3: The analytic review does not present materially biased patterns.

This hypothesis can be integrated into the reliability formula as:

$$R = 1 - (1 - C)(1 - A)(1 - D)$$

$$(4.2)$$

where

A = Reliance assigned to analytical review.

Equations (4.1) and (4.2) linearly aggregate the statistical results of three different testing schemes. The individual factors can be analyzed one by one and/or combined into an overall reliability factor. The latter approach (combining individual factors) can be stated in an even more general form:

$$R = 1 - (1 - C)^{\alpha}(1 - A)^{\beta}(1 - D)^{\gamma}$$

$$(4.3)$$

where α, β, and γ are exponential weighting parameters greater than or equal to zero.

Equation (4.1) combines two reliance measures, which can be developed from sampling procedures. The first element, C, is largely subjective and is introduced at the design evaluation stage, whereas the second element, D, is more objective, especially when considered independently. Unavoidably, the combination of two such measures of such a different nature will lead to divergence in the formulation of a final opinion.

This method used to formulate reliability estimates is of major importance in the audit process. The model presented in Equation (4.3) leads to a better understanding of the overall process and the interaction of evidence gathered during the different audit stages. We did not stress the actual use of analytic review in this chapter; rather, we discussed it briefly in terms of its contribution to audit planning. However, as the preceding analytic models show, it is an important element in the overall assessment of system reliability.

The assignment of the weights, x, y, and z and the role of human bias in estimating C (and possibly A) involve key human information processing questions that still need further research. It is important to note, however, that the decision theory approach used in estimating D should be integrated into the human information processing model for the formulation of the test of the main hypothesis.

4.8 AUDITING DATA PROCESSING SYSTEMS

The advent of computers created major concerns for auditors who had to change the way in which they approached and performed audits. Computers not only changed the nature of corporate information systems, but they also provided facilities to aid in the audit process. Four major changes in information systems occurred:

1. Data became illegible without the computer's help.
2. Data could be changed without leaving a trail.

3. Procedures (programs) are difficult to read.
4. Many reports are prepared from the same data. Which is the original?

The increased use of EDP in business also caused auditors to recognize that:

- Reliance can be placed on repetitive processing.
- The concept of the separation of duties is different.
- Retracing the path of a particular transaction is difficult, if not impossible, in some systems.

Early EDP auditing efforts produced three different approaches to the relationship between computers and auditing:

1. *Audit around the computer,* using manual methods to audit the system with primary emphasis on manual reconciliation of input data and output reports.
2. *Audit with the computer,* stressing the use of data processing as an audit tool.
3. *Audit through the computer,* placing emphasis on the examination of computer processes and procedures with or without using computers for this purpose.

Auditors initially used computers in an ad hoc manner by writing specific programs, in any language of their choice, to facilitate their own tasks. Typical of this period was the writing of programs to prepare confirmations from the client's master files or to foot large files. These specific applications soon evolved into major repetitive efforts, culminating in the development of generalized audit software by most of the major audit firms. With the discovery of major EDP-related fraud, such as that at Equity Funding (see Chapter 6), attention was drawn to the audit of EDP processes and facilities. Mair, Wood and Davis[11] divide EDP audit and control into three major areas:

1. Audit and control of the information processing facility.
2. Audit and control of software development.
3. Audit and control of applications.

The accounting profession responded to the dramatic changes resulting from the use of EDP systems by issuing Statement of Auditing Standards No. 3 (SAS No. 3). This SAS has been amended by SAS No. 48 and supplemented by a number of AICPA audit guides. They require auditors to make a preliminary review of a client's EDP system to determine whether the use of computers to process information can materially affect the financial statements. This preliminary review should (1) determine system data flows; and (2) examine the volume, type, and amount of transactions. If the auditor concludes that the system may materially affect the financial statements, a detailed review of the system is required.

The essence of the evolution from manual to automated information processing systems is that the audit process was substantially affected, had to undergo change, and must continue to change. Even more dramatic changes in the nature of audits are being required by technological advances such as microprocessors, distributed data processing, databases, and telecommunications. We will address these issues, trends, techniques, and difficulties in greater detail in later chapters.

4.9 Summary

Auditing is a process of verification and attestation that assesses the fairness of the client's financial statements. An organization's information processing system selects, measures, and records relevant information. This information is transmitted, transcribed, summarized, and interpreted in various ways as it progresses through the system.

Accounts in financial reports can be classified as flows and levels. The audit procedures used to verify them, in general, are different. The evaluation of internal controls is oriented toward assurances concerning the control of data flows, whereas year-end and other aggregation work is oriented toward the valuation of levels.

The audit process can be divided into the following steps: feasibility study, engagement planning, evaluation of internal controls, compliance testing, substantive testing, and attestation. Each step was described and discussed; examples of unqualified, qualified, and adverse auditors' opinions were presented; and different audit philosophies were summarized.

The advent and increasing use of EDP has led to major changes in the scope of audits and the ways in which they are performed. The professional organizations that set audit standards and the larger audit firms are continuing to address these changes through revised standards and procedures.

Questions

1. What are the main features of a system?
2. What are GAAP and GAAS and where do they come from?
3. What is the importance of the concept of levels and flows in financial statements?
4. Describe the relationships among empirical relational systems, numerical relational systems, and the recording of accounting transactions.
5. Describe each of the following accounting organizations:
   AICPA
   FASB
   NAA
   AAA
   FEI
   IIA
6. Why does an auditor perform a feasibility study?
7. What is the difference between compliance testing and substantive testing? Give some examples of each.
8. What do the elements in the formula

$$R = 1 - (1 - C)(1 - A)(1 - D)$$

mean and what does this formula represent?
9. What are the major changes in auditing caused by the computer?
10. How have advances in computer technology affected the auditor's choice to either audit through or around the computer?

Problems

1. The AICPA was at one time the AIA. A number of histories of the accounting profession describe this change. Find some of the reasons for the change.
2. The transfer of responsibility for setting accounting standards from the AICPA to the FASB was caused by a number of historical events. Find these causes. Do you think that the same thing could happen to GAAS? If so, how and why?
3. How concerned with economic theory should an auditor be? Why?

4. Review the current text of auditing standards on planning and super-vision and describe some of the changes that appear to have taken place in them in recent years.

5. Try to assign weights to the elements R, C, A, and D in the audit-risk hypothesis formula. What variables might an auditor try to estimate from testing procedures?

Notes

1. Churchman, C. W., *The Systems Approach.* New York: Dell, 1968.

2. Mock, Theodore Jay, *Measurement and Accounting Information Criteria*, Research Monograph Vol. 13, Sarasota, Fla.: American Accounting Association, 1976.

3. Elliot defines the materiality gauge "G" as G = (1.6) (the greater of assets or revenues)$^{2/3}$ in R. K. Elliot, "Unique Audit Methods: Peat Marwick International," *Auditing: A Journal of Theory and Practice*, Spring 1983, pp. 1–12.

4. Miller, Martin A., *Preferable Accounting Principles.* New York: Harcourt Brace Jovanovich, 1980.

5. The Foreign Corrupt Practices Act of 1977 amended the Securities Exchange Act of 1934.

6. From the Deloitte, Haskins & Sells *AUDITSCOPE* system.

7. Ashton, R. H., and Hylas, R. E., "Increasing Confirmation Response Rates," *Auditing: A Journal of Practice & Theory*, Summer 1981, pp. 12–22.

8. Cushing, B. E., and Loebbecke, J. K., "Comparison of Audit Methodologies of Large Accounting Funds," University of Utah, 1983. Forthcoming as an Accounting Research Monograph of the American Accounting Association.

9. Mautz, Robert K., et al., *Internal Control in U.S. Corporations: The State of the Art.* New York: Financial Executive Research Foundation, 1980.

10. Warren, C., "Statistical Technique for Analytical Review—A Decision," *Journal of Accounting Research* (Suppl.) *13*, 1975.

11. Mair, William C., Wood, Donald R., and Davis, Keagle W., *Computer Control and Audit.* Altamonte Springs, Fla.: The Institute of Internal Auditors, 1978.

Additional References

Arens, Alvin A., and James K. Loebbecke, *Auditing: An Integrated Approach.* Englewood Cliffs, N.J.: Prentice-Hall, 1976.

Mautz, Robert K., Alan G. Merten, and Dennis G. Severance, *Senior Management Control of Computer-Based Information Systems,* N.J.: Financial Executives Research Foundation, New York 1983.

Robertson, Jack C., *Auditing.* Plano, Texas: Business Publications Inc., 1979.

Appendix 4.A   HISTORICAL BACKGROUND OF AUDIT STANDARDS*

A.1 THE "BULLETINS" OF 1917, 1918, 1929, and 1936

In 1917, the American Institute of Certified Public Accountants, then known as the American Institute of Accountants, at the request of the Federal Trade Commission, prepared "a memorandum on balance-sheet audits," which the Commission approved and transmitted to the Federal Reserve Board.

The Federal Reserve Board, after giving the memorandum its provisional endorsement, published it in the Federal Reserve Bulletin of April 1917; reprints were widely disseminated for the consideration of "banks, bankers, banking associations; merchants, manufacturers, and associations of manufacturers; auditors, accountants, and associations of accountants" in pamphlet form with the title of "Uniform Accounting: a Tentative Proposal Submitted by the Federal Reserve Board."

In 1918, it was reissued under the same sponsorship, with a new title— "Approved Methods for the Preparation of Balance-Sheet Statements." There was practically no change from 1917 except that, as indicated by the respective titles and corresponding change in the preface, instead of the objective of "an uniform system of accounting to be adopted by manufacturing and merchandising concerns," the new objective was "the preparation of balance-sheet statements" for the same businesses.

In 1929 a special committee of the American Institute undertook revision of the earlier pamphlet in the light of the experience of the past

---

* *From* AICPA Professional Standards, U.S. Auditing Standards, Section AU.

decade; again under the auspices of the Federal Reserve Board, the revised pamphlet was issued in 1929 as "Verification of Financial Statements."

.

.

.

Between 1932 and 1934 there was correspondence, dealing with the accounting and auditing matters, between the Institute's special committee on cooperation with stock exchanges and the committee on stock list of the New York Stock Exchange. The views expressed were an important development in the recognition of the position of accountancy in finance and business. The series of letters was published in 1934 under the title Audits of Corporate Accounts.

In 1936 a committee of the Institute prepared and published a further revision of the earlier pamphlets under the title of "Examination of Financial Statements by Independent Public Accountants." The Institute availed itself of the views of persons outside the ranks of the profession whose opinions would be helpful, but the authority behind and responsibility for the publication of the pamphlet rested wholly with the institute as the authoritative representative of a profession that had by that time become well established in the business community.

In the 1936 revision, aside from the very briefly noted "Modifications of Program for Larger or Smaller Companies," the detailed procedures were restrictively stated to be an "outline of examination of financial statements of a small or moderate size company." Moreover, the nature and extent of such examinations were based on the purpose of the examination, the required detail to be reported on, the type of business, and, most important of all, the system of internal control; variations in the extent of the examination were specifically related to "the size of the organization and the personnel employed" and were said to be "essentially a matter of judgement which must be exercised by the accountant."

.

.

.

A.2 STATEMENTS ON AUDITING PROCEDURE

The Committee on Auditing Procedure had its beginning on January 30, 1939, when the executive committee of the Institute authorized the appointment of a small committee "to examine into auditing procedure and other related questions in the light of recent public discussion."

On May 9 of that year, the report "Extensions of Auditing Procedure" of this special committee was adopted by the Council of the Institute and authority given for its publication and distribution, and in the same year the bylaws were amended to create a standing Committee on Auditing Procedure.

In 1941, the executive committee authorized the issuance to Institute members, in pamphlet form, of the "Statements on Auditing Procedure," prepared by the Committee on Auditing Procedure, previously published only in *The Journal of Accountancy*.

The "Statements of Auditing Procedure" were designed to guide the independent auditor in the exercise of this judgment in the application of auditing procedures. In no sense were they intended to take the place of auditing textbooks; by their very nature textbooks must deal in a general way with the description of procedures and refinement of detail rather than the variety of circumstances encountered in practice that require the independent auditor to exercise his judgment.

Largely to meet this need, the Institute began the series of Statements on Auditing Procedure. The first of these presented the report on the original special committee, as modified and approved, at the Institute's annual meeting on September 19, 1939, and issued under the title of "Extensions of Auditing Procedure."

.

.

.

The "Codification of Statements on Auditing Procedure" was issued by the Committee on Auditing Procedure in 1951 to consolidate the features of the first 24 pronouncements which were of continuing usefulness.

When the Securities and Exchange Commission adopted the requirement that a representation on compliance with generally accepted auditing standards be included in the independent auditor's report on financial statements filed with the Commission, it became apparent that a pronouncement was needed to define these standards. Accordingly, the Committee undertook a special study of auditing standards (as distinguished from auditing procedures) and submitted a report that was published in October 1947 under the title "Tentative Statement of Auditing Standards—Their Generally Accepted Significance and Scope." The recommendations of this brochure ceased to be tentative, when at the September 1948 meeting, the membership of the Institute approved the summarized statement of auditing standards.

In 1964 the "tentative" brochure was replaced by the booklet *Generally Accepted Auditing Standards—Their Significance and Scope,* which was issued as a special report of the Committee on Auditing Procedure. This pronouncement also gave recognition to the approval of Statement on Auditing Procedure No. 23 (Revised), "Clarification of Accountant's Report when Opinion Is Omitted" (1949) and the issuance of the "Codification" (1951).

Statement on Auditing Procedure No. 33 was issued in 1963 as a consolidation of, and a replacement for, the following pronouncements of the Committee on Auditing Procedure: Internal Control (1949), Generally Accepted Auditing Standards (1954), Codification of Statements on Auditing Procedure (1951), and Statements on Auditing Procedure Nos. 25–32, which were issued between 1951 and 1963. Statement No. 33 was a codification of earlier Committee pronouncements which the Committee believed to be of continuing interest to the independent auditor.

A.3 STATEMENTS ON AUDITING STANDARDS

After issuance of Statement on Auditing Procedure No. 33, 21 additional Statements on Auditing Procedure, Nos. 34 to 54, were issued by the Committee on Auditing Procedure. In November 1972, these pronouncements were codified in Statement on Auditing Standards No. 1, Codification of Auditing Standards and Procedures. Also, in 1972, the name of the Committee was changed to the Auditing Standards Executive Committee to recognize its role as the AICPA's senior technical committee charged with interpreting generally accepted auditing standards.

The Auditing Standards Executive Committee issued 22 additional statements through No. 23. These statements were incorporated in the AICPA's loose leaf service, Professional Standards, as issued. The loose leaf service began in 1974 and is administered by the AICPA staff. It provides a continuous codification of Statements on Auditing Standards.

A.4 THE AUDITING STANDARDS BOARD

As a result of the recommendations of the Commission on Auditors' Responsibilities, an independent study group appointed by the AICPA, a special committee was formed to study the structure of the AICPA's auditing standard-setting activity. In May 1978, the AICPA Council adopted the recommendations of that committee to restructure the Committee. Accordingly, in October 1978 the Auditing Standards Board was formed as the successor to prior senior technical committees on auditing matters.

Chapter 5

Internal Controls

Abscond, v.i., To "move in a mysterious way,"
commonly with the property of another.

Spring beckons! All things to the call respond; the
trees are leaving and cashiers abscond.

*Ambrose Bierce**

5.1 INTRODUCTION

In this chapter we introduce the nature of controls used by organizations, types of exposures and losses, the impact of computers on internal controls, types of computer controls, and evaluation of internal controls for computerized systems.

LEARNING OBJECTIVES

By the time you complete this chapter, you should be able to:

1. Identify the nature and importance of controls in both profit-making and nonprofit organizations.
2. Explain major types of exposures that lead to organization losses.
3. Describe the structure of controls, reasonable assurance, and internal accounting controls.
4. Identify different classifications of computer controls.
5. Describe the use of taxonomies of internal controls and errors.

---

* From Ambrose Bierce, *The Devil's Dictionary.* New York: Dover Publications, 1958.

5.2 THE NATURE OF CONTROLS

Controls are essential to the effective performance of organizational systems: They safeguard assets and monitor implementation of policies and procedures. In pursuit of their objectives, organizations plan, act, and control. When *planning*, organizations consider alternative courses of action, select an appropriate one, and quantify it using forecasts and budgets. When *acting* organizations implement their plans, adjusting them as necessary to reflect changing conditions. When *controlling*, organizations compare actual performance with planned performance and measure the amount of *variance*, which may lead to corrective actions.

Controls are management tools, which do not directly add to assets and corporate profits. However, they are essential to the work of modern enterprises and to the avoidance of substantial misdirection and loss. Controls must always be considered in terms of benefits versus costs, as well as within the statutory context of safeguarding assets.

Organizations continually face the risk of losing their assets and records. An organization assumes these risks in order to achieve desired objectives, whether they are to earn profits, to provide not-for-profit services, or simply to survive as a viable enterprise. Management must assess the risk of events such as deliberate fraudulent actions by individuals inside or outside the organization, accidental record-keeping errors, or the failure of marketing, financial, or production plans to meet expectations. Management then has the responsibility to minimize the chances for such events to occur and to limit their impact on the organization when they do occur by instituting a system of internal controls.

> The system of controlling and reporting on enterprise activity includes policies, procedures, and the means of monitoring compliance with them. Collectively, these policies and procedures are designated as internal controls because they operate within an enterprise as a means of reducing its unintentional exposure to business, financial and accounting risks. Before a system of internal controls can be designed, or an existing system evaluated, management must know something about the kinds of risk that exist in a particular organization, assess their significance, and determine which ones can be avoided.[1]

As we mentioned in Chapter 4, the Foreign Corrupt Practices Act of 1977 and the increased use of EDP in organizations have focused greater attention on management's responsibility to establish and maintain adequate systems of internal accounting controls. The act requires organizations to maintain a system of internal accounting controls in order to provide reasonable assurances that:

1. transactions are executed in accordance with management's general or specific authorization;
2. transactions are recorded as necessary (I) to permit preparation of financial statements in conformity with generally accepted accounting principles or any other criteria applicable to such statements, and (II) to maintain accountability for assets;
3. access to assets is permitted only in accordance with management's general or specific authorization; and
4. the recorded accountability for assets is compared with the existing assets at reasonable intervals and appropriate action is taken with respect to any differences.

These statutory requirements were incorporated verbatim into Paragraph 27 of AICPA's SAS No. 1 as the revised definition of internal accounting control. This definition replaces the wording codified in SAS No. 1, which had previously replaced the traditional 1948 definition of internal control:

> Internal control comprises the plan of organization and all of the coordinate methods and measures adopted within a business to safeguard its assets, check the accuracy and reliability of its accounting data, promote operational efficiency, and encourage adherence to prescribed managerial policies.[2]

The statement then goes on to delineate two types of controls: internal accounting controls and administrative or operational controls. *Internal accounting controls* encompass the plan of the organization, procedures and records concerned with safeguarding its assets and the reliability of financial records. These are concerned with transaction authorization and the accuracy of the accounting system in cataloging, recording, and reporting the financial transactions of the organization. In contrast, *administrative or operational controls* encompass the plan of organization and records that are concerned with the decision processes leading to management's authorization of transactions. Such authorization is a management function directly associated with the responsibility for achieving the objectives of the organization and is the starting point for establishing accounting control of transactions.[3] These two types of controls, then, are interdependent; neither exists in isolation from the other, and the integrity of one directly affects that of the other.

In addition, SAS No. 1 and its amendment by SAS No. 48 state that the ". . . essential characteristics of internal accounting controls include": (AICPA, 1986, Secs. 320.29 to 320.49)

- Personnel (competence and integrity)
- Segregation of functions (independence of assignment functions)
- Execution of transactions (authorization, scope of authority, accuracy)
- Recording of transactions (correct amounts, period)
- Access to assets (limited to authorized personnel)
- Comparison of recorded accountability with assets. (comparing records with actual counts)[4]

Table 5.1 shows the five dimensions of the internal control process within an organization. The cycles are simply subsystems of the internal control system, as defined by the auditor. The objectives determine the type of function being performed. The department or function is a component to be determined in the systems design stage. Finally, numerous types of internal control procedures and errors can be identified.

Table 5.1   The Five Dimensions of the Internal Control Process with Examples

Cycles	Objectives	Department or Function	Internal Control Procedures	Types of Events or Irregularities
I. Treasury	A. Authorization	1. Order Entry	a) Segregation of Duties	i. Lack of Approval
II. Purchasing	B. Accounting	2. Shipping	b) Physical Assets Restriction	ii. Bad Total
III. Payroll	B1. Transaction Processing	3. Billing	c) Direct Supervision	iii. Incorrect Posting
IV. Conversion	B2. Classification	4. Credit and Collection	d) Indirect Supervision	iv. Incorrect Amount
V. Revenue	B3. Substantiation	5. Maintenance of Receivables Records etc.	e) Periodic Compliance Audit	v. Unauthorized Adjustment
VI. Financial Reporting	C. Safeguarding		f) Backups	vi. Missing Transaction
			g) Insurance and Fidelity	vii. Duplicate Transaction
			h) Bonds	viii. Missing Assets etc.
			i) Sales, etc.	
			j) Batch Totals	
			k) Controlled Custody	
			l) Prenumbering	
			m) Physical Counts	
			n) Order Entry	
			o) Job Description etc.	

5.3 TYPES OF EXPOSURE

Since the purpose of internal controls is to reduce the risk of loss, organizations must first identify the types of loss to which they are exposed and the consequences of such losses if they do occur. Only then can internal control systems be properly designed and implemented. The major occurrences that can lead to organizational losses are:

- erroneous record keeping;
- unacceptable accounting;
- business interruption;
- erroneous management decisions;
- fraud and embezzlement;
- statutory sanctions;
- excessive costs or lost revenues;
- loss or destruction of assets; and
- competitive disadvantage.[5]

Erroneous record keeping can be defined as the recording of financial transactions in a manner that is contrary to the established accounting policies of the organization. The resulting errors can involve the amount, timing, or classification of specific transactions. Such errors can adversely affect the integrity of financial reports by reducing their accuracy and reliability. Uncovering material errors of this type is one of the major objectives of the substantive testing phase of an audit. The entry of $10,000.00 for a $100,000.00 transaction represents this type of error.

Unacceptable accounting is closely related to erroneous record keeping, which, again, is the cause of the problem. However, rather than violating organizational policies, it devotes non-compliance to generally accepted accounting principles. These errors can lead to further problems for the entity if they represent statutory or legal violations. The noncapitalization of a substantial sales-type lease or the capitalization of R&D in most cases is unacceptable accounting.

Business interruptions can be temporary or permanent and often result from physical damage to the facilities or other assets of the organization. The losses faced from such interruptions are a function of the cause and severity of the interruption. In many cases, major losses represent an insurable risk for the firm, and should be treated as such by management. Fire, flood damage, snow days, and failure to receive raw materials as scheduled can cause business interruptions.

Erroneous management decisions are among the most serious risks facing an organization. They are also among the least controllable because the very people who control the system commit these errors; it is unlikely that a formal reporting and control system would readily identify or bring these errors to management's attention. Therefore, unless erroneous decisions are self-evident, they are unlikely to be controllable. Such decisions may result from misleading or incomplete information, errors in judgment, or incompetence. The key, then, is to act to remove the source of the error by improving the reliability of the information system and, if necessary, replacing the decision-maker. A bank that decides to expand its portfolio of foreign loans must have accurate and timely information in order to monitor this strategic decision and closely examine loan performance and curb overall loan losses.

Fraud and embezzlement are serious concerns for any organization and its control system, especially in an EDP environment. Because of their importance, we cover this type of exposure more fully in a separate chapter. Discrepancies may result from either errors or irregularities, the latter accounting for only a small percentage of the total discrepancies that cause losses.

Statutory sanctions are the penalties, both monetary and operationally restrictive, that judicial or regulatory authorities can impose on an organization. The system of internal controls should be designed to prevent violation of or noncompliance with the statutes and regulations that are relevant to the organization's activities. Applicable statutes include the Clean Air Act, antitrust legislation, labor-relations laws, Occupational Safety and Health Act, and wage and hours laws.

Excessive costs include any expense incurred by the organization that could have been avoided if those responsible had exercised reasonable caution or restraint. Closely related to this risk is that of loss of revenues that were stolen, not collected, or spent when they should not have been. Systems of authorization and procedures for recording transactions are two ways to protect against such losses. Recent cost overruns in arms procurement have been claimed to be avoidable by proper oversight of the U.S. Department of Defense.

Loss or destruction of assets reflects unintentional financial and/or physical damage to assets or claims against those assets. These losses can result from poor security or be caused by errors and/or omissions in record keeping. Additionally, the increased reliance on EDP and mass data storage has increased the exposure to loss through destruction of an organization's information system components. Backup and duplicate access/retrieval systems have been designed to decrease the magnitude of this risk.

Competitive disadvantage refers to the inability of an organization to remain effectively abreast of the demands of the marketplace or to respond to competitive challenges. This inability cuts into revenues and threatens the firm's viability as a going concern. Firms or even entire industries may lobby for regulatory protection (such as tariffs or import quotas) when they perceive themselves to be at a competitive disadvantage in relation to foreign suppliers.

Management therefore sets up a system of internal controls to reduce the risk of loss associated with these types of exposures. The value of the control system in this context is a function of its ability to reduce losses relative to the costs incurred to initiate and maintain it. Losses can be reduced if the control system either decreases the probability that the loss will occur or minimizes the amount of the loss if it should occur.

Controls reduce potential losses by acting on the causes of loss. The auditor's task here is to evaluate how well the internal control system is meeting this objective. Such a task is performed through evaluation of the design of the internal control system and testing of compliance with the system. This overall evaluation must be based on an adequate understanding of the organization's control environment.

5.4 THE CONTROL ENVIRONMENT

> *Some accountants believe that the internal accounting control environment established by management has a significant impact on the selection and effectiveness of a company's accounting control procedures and techniques.*[6]

The AICPA's definition of an internal control environment includes the company's organizational structure, the competence and integrity of its personnel, and the manner and extent of managerial delegation of authority and responsibility. These are qualitative features of the internal structure it employs to deal with environmental uncertainty. While these areas are subject to control by management through its choice of formal hierarchies, employees, and markets, the type and extent of internal control is highly constrained by the historical operations of the company, its culture, and the external forces with which it must contend.

Some factors considered by the AICPA to be part of the organization's control environment reflect specific areas that management can control through policies and procedural choices. These areas are (1) the use of budgets and financial reports as a means of formulating and communicating the company's objectives, plans, and operations; (2) the use of organizational checks and balances to separate incompatible activities and provide for supervision by higher levels of management; and (3) the extent and methods of data processing used by the company. In particular, the degree of control exercised by management over the development and maintenance of the EDP system is crucial.

Figure 5.1 illustrates the structure of the control environment. The total control environment consists of environmental and activities controls.

Figure 5.1   Structure of the Control Environment

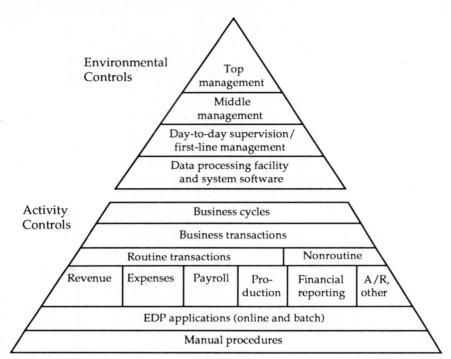

Source: Adapted from Keagle W. Davis, Luis Minuelle, and Donald R. Wood, "EDP Internal Control Requirements and Evaluations as a Part of Systems Development Standards." Presented at the 8th International Conference of the EDP Auditors Association, June 16–18, 1980.

5.5 THE INTERNAL CONTROL SYSTEM

From the perspective of forming an opinion on economic reports, the system of internal control represents a condition of the client that can significantly affect the risk of material error or omission in financial reports. In forming an opinion, then, the auditor's essential internal control related activities are (1) learn and document those components that could affect the reports, (2) evaluate the apparent quality of the internal controls to assist in planning the collection of audit evidence, and (3) on a highly integrated and sequential basis continually reevaluate the internal controls as a part of error assessment decisions up to and including the final opinion and reporting decision.[7]

Although an accounting system is a necessary element of internal controls, the total system consists of much more, as shown in Fig. 5.1. A good system of internal controls contains elements that have little or no relationship to accounting activities.[8] Recall that the entire system encompasses both administrative, or operational, controls and internal accounting controls. The basic objective of these two types of controls is the same: to decrease the total risks faced by the organization. They work together but differ in method and level of application.

As we pointed out in Section 5.2, SAS No. 1 states that internal accounting controls should be designed to provide reasonable assurance that transactions are properly authorized and executed, transactions are recorded to permit preparation of adequate financial statements and maintain accountability for assets, access to assets is restricted, and all assets controlled by the organization are properly accounted for. The concept of reasonable assurance recognizes that the costs of internal controls should not exceed the benefits derived from them.[9] The expected benefits, as noted previously, are decreased losses and corporate business risk. The expected costs relate to the resources dedicated to setting up and maintaining the system of controls. The actual determination of these costs and benefits, though, is largely subjective because of the limited measurability of certain costs and benefits.

Based on the objectives of the system, internal controls can be classified as preventive, detective, and corrective. *Preventive* controls operate as early in the transaction processing cycle as possible, in order to prevent errors from actually occurring. *Detective* controls identify errors that have occurred and reduce their frequency. Finally, *corrective* controls ensure that detected errors are properly corrected.

The extent of control that an organization achieves results from the interactive and compensatory nature of the various types of controls and the specific controls it establishes. Figure 5.2 shows a generalized control system. Suppose control 1 to be procedures for reconciling batch totals; control 2, the separation of duties; control 3, clear lines of authority and responsibility and precise job descriptions; and control 4, direct supervision of activities. Controls 2 and 3 will be effective against collusion but control 1 will be ineffective in this dimension. On the other hand, in the case of errors in transaction amounts, identification numbers, or posting to accounts, control 1 may prove to be effective but the others ineffective. These differences lead to the following conclusions:

Figure 5.2   A Generalized System of Controls.

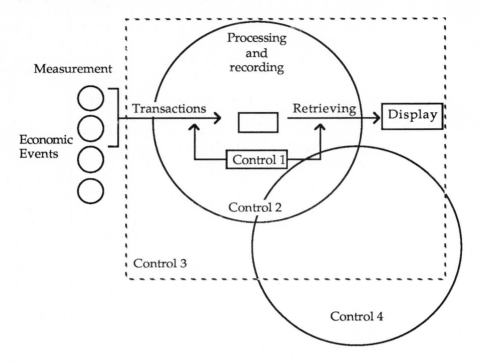

1. Each type of control will have a potentially different effect on each type of error.
2. Each transaction will be subjected to different sets of controls and may generate a multiplicity of errors of identical and/or different types.
3. Each set of controls may have different effects on different errors.
4. The finer the focus of a control on a particular error type, the more likely it is to be ineffective in relation to other errors.
5. The combination of controls may have additive, counteractive, multiplicative, or neutral effects on particular error types.[10]

Conclusion 5 raises the issue of combination controls and its effects. Most organizational processes are at least partially subjected to more than one control. A particular activity may only be controlled by direct supervision, indirect reviews and control totals. Some controls may also deal with related and/or complementary issues. Figure 5.3 shows conceptualized forms of control relationships. These control relationships may

Figure 5.3   Conceptualized Control Relationships: (a) Sequential Controls;
(b) Parallel Controls; (c) Independent Controls (Venn Diagram);
(d) Overlapping Controls; (e) Redundant Controls (Different Boundaries).

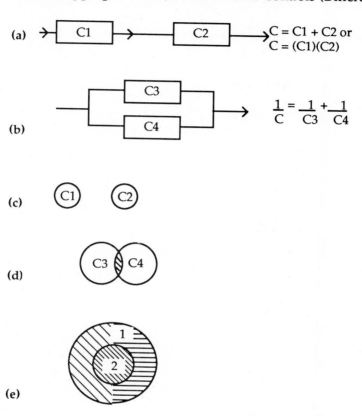

Source: Miklos A. Vasarhelyi, "A Taxonomization of Internal Controls
and Errors for Audit Research." In D. Nichols and H. Stettler (Eds.), *Proceedings* of the 1980 Touche Ross/University of Kansas Symposium on Auditing Problems, Lawrence, Kansas, 1980.

serve to facilitate the comprehension of the effect of multiple controls
upon a particular system.

Another way to view internal controls is as classic engineering, systems, and, to an extent, management literature define them. From this
perspective, a true control is an independent feedback mechanism that
compares outputs to inputs. When there is a departure from the expected
outputs, the reasons are identified, and corrective action is taken. Thus
control involves segregation of duties and independent checks on perfor-

mance. However, certain qualitative aspects of internal control, such as competent and trustworthy personnel, physical security, and adequate records do not fit into this perception of a true control. Instead, they appear to be factors that increase the reliability of the system.

Concepts of reliability engineering have been used by some academic authors[11] to mathematically compute the resulting reliability from component reliabilities. This method, though not yet applicable in practice, provides some insight into the complex issue of control measurement and aggregation. It points out the potential effect of adding and subtracting controls from a system.

Internal control as defined in accounting literature can be viewed as a three-level structure. At the lowest level is a basic set of records and procedures that permit the recording of transactions. At the next level is the performance of functions related to transaction recording and reporting and the safeguarding of assets. The highest level is independent checks on performance. To be completely independent, the comparison of actual to anticipated results must be based on a feedback network that is separate from the system. This type of true control normally occurs only in restricted accounting subsystems, although certain managers who are aware of the anticipated performance of the organization may question financial statements that do not measure up to their expectations.

While the engineering control model has not to date been widely accepted as a powerful method of assessing internal control, it does help explain some of the differences in terminology between accounting and other disciplines. Furthermore, it provides a methodology of quantification that may in the future be developed into a much needed improvement in accuracy in a field that is currently very qualitative.

5.6 INTERNAL CONTROL AND THE COMPUTER

Computers and their related support equipment have not in any significant way altered established accounting theory as it relates to the kind of data to be collected or the manner in which such data should be organized for reporting purposes. But the computer has substantially altered the methods by which that theory is put into practice.[12]

The widespread use of electronic data processing has led to changes in the nature of accounting controls, prompting further formalization of controls and increased scrutiny. Manual systems had allowed for informal controls based on the user's ability to recognize error patterns in the data; the examination of processing consistency and adequacy of supervision were emphasized. With the emergence of automated systems, the emphasis shifted to system design and integrity because consistency was virtually ensured.

These developments led major CPA firms to modify many of their procedures and the AICPA and other standard-setting bodies, such as the SEC, to promulgate statements of position and proposed rules. One such statement that had far-reaching implications for the EDP auditor was issuance of the original SAS No. 3. It described the "effects of the use of EDP on the various characteristics of accounting control and on an auditor's study and evaluation thereof . . ." and provided "a framework for the development of further guidance concerning auditing procedures in examining financial statements of entities that use EDP in accounting applications."

Replacement of SAS No. 3 by SAS No. 48 enlarged its impact by integrating the auditor's consideration of EDP into the auditing standards on planning and supervision, analytical review procedure, internal control, and the nature of sufficient competent evidence.

Jancura and Lilly have stated that the introduction of EDP into organizations had several other implications besides changing the manual nature of transaction control. Electronic data processing equipment required that the recording and processing of data be concentrated in departments other than those from which the data originated. Integrated information systems eliminated independent records that previously provided sources of comparative data. Computerization also substantially reduced the time available for the review of transactions before their entry into accounting records. As a result, in poorly controlled systems the opportunity for discovering errors before they affected operations had been reduced or even eliminated, especially in the case of real-time systems.[13] Each of these changes has increased the importance of internal control system integrity. Tables 5.2 and 5.3 present control techniques for batch and on-line processing, respectively. Comparison of entries in these tables shows clearly the evolution in the nature of controls owing to advances in technology.

Computer-based accounting systems add special emphasis to three of the basic auditing standards contained in SAS No. 1: technical training adequacy and auditor proficiency; the study and evaluation of internal control; and the collection of evidence in substantiating audit conclusions. One of the most intractable problems associated with EDP systems is the lack of segregation of duties and responsibility. To compensate for this deficiency, Hoard proposed that personnel in different work areas report to different supervisors.[14]

In SAS No. 3, the AICPA divided controls into general and application controls. The former relate to all EDP activities, while the latter refer to control of specific accounting tasks. To quote from the standard:

Table 5.2   Control Techniques for Batch Processing

Control Category	Technique	Function
Input preparation	Segregation of duties	To prevent a person from having access to both a resource and the records for control of that resource To limit an individual to only one interface with the system To prevent a person from both initiating and authorizing To prevent a person from being able to both convert and control
	Batch controls established close to the point of input preparation	To prevent the introduction of unauthorized input To prevent the loss of data
	Verification of authorization	To prevent unauthorized input or update
Programmed processing	Validation routines	To verify all significant data fields for existence, reasonableness, and compatability
	Batch totaling	To verify that all transactions have been entered To preclude duplicate input transactions To verify that the totals of significant fields in the input transaction agree with predetermined totals
	Error rejection	To prevent erroneous transactions from updating the master file
	Reasonableness checks	To check for high/low balances before updating master file To detect unusual or unreasonable conditions encountered during processing

(continued)

Table 5.2   Control Techniques for Batch Processing (continued)

Output and error correction	Reconciliation	To detect the loss of data during processing To identify the introduction of unauthorized input during processing To take summary information and trace it back to the original source document and vice versa
	Retention	To comply with legal, accounting, and management requirements
	Distribution	To ensure that output is returned only to person indicated by output
	Assignment of accountability for error correction	To ensure that all errors are corrected in a timely manner To delegate responsibilty for correction of transactions that have multiple sources

General controls comprise (a) the plan of organization and operation of the EDP activity, (b) the procedures for documenting, reviewing, testing and approving systems or programs and changes thereto, (c) controls built into the equipment by the manufacturer (commonly referred to as "hardware controls"), (d) controls over access to equipment and data files, and (e) other data and procedural controls affecting overall EDP operations.

Application controls relate to specific tasks performed by EDP. Their function is to provide reasonable assurance that the recording, processing and reporting of data are performed.[15]

General controls can be divided into six categories: (1) organization; (2) operations; (3) documentation; (4) system development and programming; (5) hardware and systems software; and (6) access and library. *Application controls* can be divided into three categories: (1) input; (2) processing; and (3) output.

The concept of *compensating controls* was introduced for the first time in an EDP context in SAS No. 3: "In a computer-based accounting system, the possibilities for accounting control are so great that it is possible to maintain one or more controls that effectively compensate for the lack of an otherwise important control."[16] Hence, computerization allows for in

Table 5.3   On-line Control Techniques at Order Entry Point

Technique	Function
Operator terminal transactions, IDs	To control and limit access/updating of data To segregate responsibility To implement policy constraints To help establish accountability To provide evidence of attempts to avoid security safeguards
Message sequencing	To protect against message loss
Program-generated batch controls	To ensure against garbled data To protect against message loss
Edit and feedback	To provide for data integrity To provide for error correction during data entry To promote prompt recognition of incorrectly entered data
System message log	To provide mechanism to evaluate transaction status in system at time of failure To provide capability to recreate and reprocess unprotected transactions To provide audit trail of messages processed
Database file control	To promote prompt recognition of out-of-balance condition To ensure run-to-run file balancing To provide trail to isolate occurrence of file imbalance condition
Copying	To provide capability to recover database
Update record	To provide capability to recover database To provide audit trail of transactions

expensive redundancy in data collection and processing controls. This redundancy helps to decrease the extent of control required to maintain transaction integrity in an EDP system.

Figure 5.4 represents another approach to classifying computer controls. Management controls are found in the outer layers of the diagram. Their purpose is to attempt to ensure that the development, implementa

Figure 5.4   The Computer Control Framework

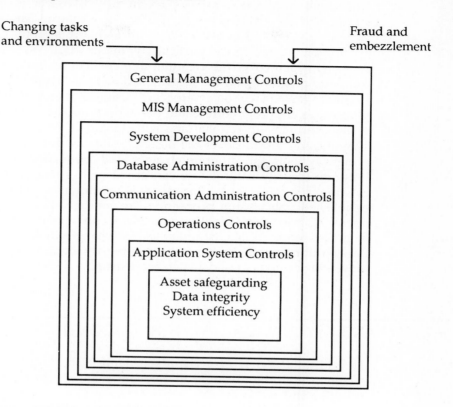

Source: Adapted from Ron Weber, *EDP Auditing: Conceptual Foundations and Practice.* New York: McGraw–Hill, 1982, p. 25.

tion, and operation of the information system proceeds in an orderly, controlled manner. Top management determines the long-term objectives of the EDP system, makes policy decisions about how the EDP capability will be used in the organization, and ensures that the facilities are well-managed. EDP management itself has overall planning and control responsibility for computer facility activities. System development management is responsible for designing, implementing, and maintaining systems of applications. Programming management is charged with the programming of individual applications, maintaining these applications, and providing general software support. Database administration controls the use of the organization's database and applications systems library. Finally, operations management controls the daily activities of the EDP facilities, including transaction flows and hardware maintenance.[17]

Application controls, on the other hand, attempt to ensure that "individual application systems safeguard EDP assets, maintain data integrity, and process data effectively."[18] These controls can be exercised at various stages of transaction flow through the system. One aspect of application controls that is particularly unique to EDP systems is integrity controls, which cover the creation, implementation, security, and use of computer programs and the security of data files. As noted by Johnson and Jaenicke, implementation controls are designed to ensure that appropriate procedures are programmed into the various applications, both when the system becomes operational and subsequently when changes are made. They include controls over the design, testing, and initial operational use of new systems and program changes, and the related documentation.[19] Program security controls are concerned with unauthorized changes to existing programs and procedures. Operations controls ensure that established policies and procedures are consistently adhered to by EDP operating personnel. Finally, data file security controls limit access to data files to guard against unauthorized changes or use of the organization's information. Each of these integrity controls is important in preventing computer fraud and embezzlement.

5.7 EDP AND EVALUATION OF INTERNAL CONTROLS

An auditor's review of a client's system of accounting control should encompass all significant and relevant manual, mechanical, and EDP activities and the interrelationship between EDP and user departments. The review should comprehend both the control procedures related to transactions from origination or source to recording in the accounting records and the control procedures related to recorded accountability for assets.

The objectives of the auditor's review of accounting control within EDP are similar to those for manual and mechanical processing. The review is an information-gathering process that depends on knowledgeable inquiries directed to client personnel, observation of job assignments and operating procedures, and reference to available documentation related to accounting control.

Neither an internal control system nor a review of that system can achieve ultimate perfection. Not only do cost/benefit relationships affect the design and review of a control system, but there are inherent limitations that must be recognized in considering both the system and its evaluation.[20]

Keeping these thoughts in mind, the purpose of evaluating internal controls is to determine whether the actual error rate experienced by the system exceeds the allowable rate determined by management. Therefore the focus of the evaluation procedure is the detection of transaction flows that exhibit an unacceptably high error rate. The evaluator does not specify the acceptable rate, but rather analyzes the system to discover whether it is operating as management planned.

As provided in SAS No. 3: "The preliminary phase of an auditor's review should be designed to provide an understanding of the flow of transactions through the accounting system, the extent to which EDP is used in each significant accounting application, and the basic structure of accounting control."[21] Such understanding is ordinarily obtained through inquiry, involving the study of procedures manuals and interviews with EDP personnel and users of the system.

If the auditor decides to rely on the system of internal controls, he or she must perform sufficient tests of compliance to establish a reasonable degree of assurance that the system is being used and is operating as planned.[22] Hence the audit plan consists of forming a judgment on the adequacy of the internal control system as designed and then using compliance tests to determine whether the controls are being adhered to. This information allows the auditor to determine the degree of reliance that can be placed on the control system and, subsequently, the amount of substantive testing he or she will need to perform before reaching an audit opinion.

Johnson and Jaenicke have presented a basic framework for evaluating the internal control system. It consists of the following steps:

1. Obtain and record an understanding of the internal accounting control procedures established for each transaction type.
2. Understanding of the system as recorded in flowcharts is confirmed by means of a transactions review. Namely, the documentation for one transaction of each type is followed through the accounting system and the flowchart is modified if necessary.
3. Evaluate the system to determine whether there are any inherent control weaknesses. Internal control questionnaires are one means of obtaining the necessary information.
4. Assess control weaknesses to determine whether they are potentially significant.
5. Assess controls that are in place to determine whether they are operating effectively.
6. Report to senior management on internal control weaknesses.[23]

In order to make the report to senior management meaningful, Johnson and Jaenicke go on to suggest, the internal control weaknesses identified during the evaluation process be ranked in order of importance under the following loss criteria. (1) possible consequences of the internal control weaknesses (such as the misappropriation of assets, deliberate or accidental accounting errors, or decreased operating efficiency); (2) possible exposure to adverse consequences; (3) chance of adverse consequences actually occurring; (4) likelihood of timely detection of misappropriation and errors; (5) qualitative attributes of the control weakness; (6) the relationship to traditional materiality criterion; and (7) the effect of weaknesses in integrity controls on the programmed procedures or data elements at risk.[24]

The EDP Auditor's Foundation has proposed the following four major objectives for EDP-based internal control for the 1980s. Pursuing these objectives and strategies should aid the EDP auditor in maintaining the quality of the audit process in a computerized system.

- Management has the ultimate responsibility for systems control. Therefore management must have appropriate comprehension and understanding of controls and where they can break down.
- Users have a nonnegotiable responsibility for the controls of their own systems. Clear definition of user controls and user understanding of those controls are essential to overall systems control.
- Short- and long-term planning and budgeting within a properly designed organization structure is itself a key internal control. Without it, the entity will not be able to recognize, accept, or manage the changes that are and will take place within the entity.
- An appropriate systems methodology, which requires active management and user participation and which results in a documented structure of systems control, is essential to managing and maintaining the structure of control and to auditability.

The point is . . . proper controls will reduce errors and omissions, please top management and make auditing easier and more accountable.[25]

CLASSIFICATION OF CONTROLS AND ERRORS

The use of categories, or a *taxonomy*, of controls can aid in ranking control system weakness and can simplify the difficult task of evaluation. One such taxonomy of controls is:

1. Authorization controls
2. Validity controls
3. Population and transfer controls

4. Process controls
5. Coverage controls
   (a) Segregation of duties
   (b) Supervision
   (c) Rules and procedures
   (d) Insurance
6. Access controls
7. Audit (ex post facto) controls
8. Compliance with GAAP controls

Authorization controls prevent the occurrence of exchanges, allocations, or valuations that are not in accordance with company policy (such as requiring a credit check before a credit sale is completed). *Validity controls* are used to verify the validity of transactions through the reasonableness of its content (such as range) and intrinsic characteristic (such as ID number, check digit computation). *Population and transfer controls* are used to assure integrity of populations where no transactions are added, subtracted or changed in transit. *Process controls* ensure accuracy when data has changed form through aggregation or disaggregation, changed content through processing, or changed mode of presentation through different formats of presentation and timing (such as calculation of depreciation controls and footings).

Coverage controls are applicable to one particular process or set of transactions. Segregation of duties ensures that certain activities or responsibilities within a sequence are assigned to separate individuals (such as custody versus record keeping for an asset; activity versus control over that activity, as in sales/credit approval; and interrelated activities, as in credit/approval/bad debt write-offs). Collusion among employees is needed to override these controls. Supervision controls refer to the supervision by a superior of a task being performed. It does not imply specific authorizations or approvals. Rules and procedures refer to the formalization and documentation of control steps. Insurance controls relate to the expenditure of resources to counterbalance potential losses related to a particular event.

Access controls ensure that limitations are placed on access to physical or informational assets in the system (such as computer-access passwords). *Audit controls* serve ex post facto to find errors and irregularities in controls and accounting data (such as visual checks for authorization on a sample basis). *Compliance with GAAP controls* covers procedures used to verify whether transactions are being recorded and processed in accordance with current accounting rules.

Appendix 5.A shows a taxonomy of controls using the preceding categories and drawn from several publications. Appendix 5.B presents another way to classify different types of controls. In addition, a taxonomy of er-

rors can prove useful in evaluating internal controls. The following classification scheme summarizes the taxonomy of errors in Appendix 5.C.

1. Procedural errors (violations or lack of internal controls)
2. Computation errors (errors in the numerical processing of trans-
    actions)
3. Accounting errors (incorrect accounting transactions)
4. Integrity errors (addition or deletion of unauthorized transac-
    tions or duplication of authorized transactions)
5. Timing errors (transactions recorded at the wrong time)
6. GAAP errors (transactions not measured in accordance with
    proper accounting practice)
7. Irregularities (fraudulent and deliberately false transactions)
8. Legal errors (transactions or events that violate legal con-
    straints)

An almost infinite number of combinations of alternative internal control procedures may be used in the attempt to avoid, decrease or eliminate
an equally large number of errors of different types. In order to simplify
the evaluation of systems of internal controls, we can use taxonomies to reduce the number of internal control procedures and error types. These simpler sets that classify control and errors into one of their eight categories
can lead to smaller groups of alternative combinations of errors and controls for modeling and evaluating the internal control system and related
risk exposure.

5.8 Summary

In this chapter we dealt with the concepts of internal control, exposure to
risk of loss, evaluation of controls, and the unique features of internal controls in an EDP system. Throughout, we emphasized that an adequate control system is essential to viable organization, ensuring that objectives are
pursued in an effective and legal manner.

Computer controls were divided into two main categories: general controls and application controls. The first were subdivided into: organization, operation, documentation, system development and programming,
hardware and system software, and access and library controls. The latter
were divided into input, processing, and output controls. Furthermore we
classified controls and errors into eight categories each which allow for
easier comprehension and description of internal control systems.

Questions

1. Why are controls necessary in organizations?
2. What is the relationship of the Foreign Corrupt Practices Act to internal controls?
3. Auditing Standards define what two major classes of internal controls?
4. What four major assurances do internal controls provide?
5. What are the five dimensions of errors that internal controls are designed to prevent?
6. *Control environment* refers to what aspects of internal controls?
7. How may controls be viewed as complementary or additive?
8. How does accounting internal control compare to the control concepts of engineering and general systems theory?
9. How has the computer affected the auditor's approach to internal control?
10. What steps must be taken to assess internal controls in an EDP-based system?
11. What are some of the ways that controls can be evaluated in a computer-based system?
12. Describe and cite examples of the eight major types of controls and the eight major types of errors.

Problems

1. Obtain a copy of the Foreign Corrupt Practices Act of 1977, (Public Law 95-213) and review the accounting and corrupt practices sections.
2. Review the internal control tables of this chapter (Tables 5.2 and 5.3) and questionnaire from their text (Fig. 4.3) and from other sources and determine how well they fit the taxonomies provided in Appendixes 5.A, 5.B, and 5.C.
3. List the primary similarities and differences in the methods used to review internal controls in a manual and in an EDP accounting system.
4. If you were the CEO or the member of an audit committee of a large corporation, what steps might you take to ensure a strong control?
5. Small businesses often do not have enough employees to permit extensive segregation of duties. What measures can such entities take to provide adequate internal control?
6. Identify a microcomputer accounting software that is being used in a small business. Read its manual with care and review all suggested

application controls. List types of errors that may be found. Rate the suggested system in terms of the quality of those controls. Classify those controls and errors into the general taxonomies described in the Appendices 5.A, 5.B, and 5.C.

7. Review the system you identified in question 6 as it is implemented in the business in question. Identify controls being used, controls added, and actual errors typically encountered in the operation. Describe your findings and recommendations in the form of a "management report."

Notes

1. Johnson, Kenneth P., and Jaenicke, Henry R., *Evaluating Internal Control: Concepts, Guidelines, Procedures, Documentation.* New York: John Wiley & Sons, 1980, p. 2.

2. Statement on Auditing Standards No. 1, Paragraph 320.08, AICPA, 1973.

3. Ibid., Paragraph 320.27.

4. Ibid., Paragraphs 320.30 and 320.36–320.48.

5. Mair, William C., Wood, Donald R., and Davis, Keagle W., *Computer Control & Audit,* 2nd ed. The Institute of Internal Auditors, Inc., Altamonte Springs, Fl: 1978, pp. 11–12.

6. Johnson and Jaenicke, p. 22.

7. Felix, Jr., William L., and Niles, Marcia S., "Research on Internal Control Evaluation." Unpublished working paper, University of Washington, Seattle, April 1982, p. 1.

8. Johnson and Jaenicke, p. 5.

9. SAS No. 1, Paragraph 320.32.

10. Vasarhelyi, Miklos A., "A Taxonomization of Internal Controls and Errors for Audit Research." in Nichols and Stettler (Eds.), *Proceedings of the 1980 Touche Rose/University of Kansas Symposium on Auditing Problems,* Lawrence, Kansas, 1980, p. 45.

11. See Barry E. Cushing, "A Mathematical Approach to the Analysis and Design of Internal Control Systems," *Accounting Review,* Vol. 49, 1974 (pp. 24–41) or William O. Stratton, "Accounting Systems: The Reliability Approach to Internal Control Evolution," *Decision Sciences,* Vol. 12, 1981 (pp. 51–67).

12. Jancura, Elise G., and Lilly, Fred L., "SAS No. 3 and the Evaluation of Internal Control," *The Journal of Accountancy,* March 1977, p. 69.

13. Ibid.

14. Hoard, Bruce, "Impact of Poor Controls on Auditing Decried," *Computerworld,* June 23, 1980, p. 14.

15. SAS No. 1. Paragraphs 321.07 and 321.08, 1974.

16. Jancura and Lilly, p. 72.

17. Weber, Ron, *EDP Auditing: Conceptual Foundations and Practice.* New York: McGraw-Hill, 1982, p. 26.

18. Ibid.

19. Johnson and Jaenicke, p. 45.

20. Ibid., p. 61.

21. SAS No. 3.

22. Jancura and Lilly, p. 73.

23. Johnson and Jaenicke, p. 60.

24. Ibid.

25. Hoard, p. 44.

Additional References

AICPA, AU Section 321, "The Effects of EDP on the Auditor's Study and Evaluation of Internal Control," *AICPA Professional Standards,* December 1974.

AICPA, AU Section 640, "Reports on Internal Control," *AICPA Professional Standards,* November 1972.

AICPA, "The Auditor's Study and Evaluation of Internal Control in EDP Systems," New York, 1977.

Bariff, Martin L., "A Study of EDP Auditor's Evaluations of Internal Control Systems." Unpublished working paper, The Wharton School, University of Pennsylvania, Philadelphia, January 1979.

Davenport, Phillip N., "Controls: An Auditing Perspective," *EDPAF Session Report,* Houston, March 9, 1977.

Davis, Keagle W., Luis Minuelle, and Donald R. Wood, "EDP Internal Control Requirements and Evaluations as a Part of Systems Development Standards." Presented at the 8th International Conference of the EDP Auditors Association, June 16–18, 1980.

GAO, "Evaluating Internal Controls in Computer-Based Systems: Audit Guide," document #AFMD-81-76, U.S. General Accounting Office, Gaithersburg, Maryland, June 1981.

Appendix 5.A *A TAXONOMY OF INTERNAL CONTROLS*

I. Authorization Controls
1. Approval of master file maintenance reports
2. Proper procedures of authorization
3. Advance approval required for customer returns
4. Written authority required for removing assets from premises

II. Validity Controls
5. Control over unused and voided billing forms
6. Approved list of suppliers
7. Preprinted official order forms
8. Matching invoice to receipt
9. Goods counted and inspected before acceptance
10. Unmatched receiving reports and invoices investigated

III. Population and Transfer Controls
11. Unissued checks numerically accounted for
12. Batch totals
13. Prenumbering
14. Accounting for prenumbering
15. Records maintained of costs incurred under product warranty
16. Verification and validation of data entered in EDP system
17. Scanning data for reasonableness before entry
18. Reconciliation of interface amounts exiting one system and entering another
19. Check of algorithms
20. Transmission verification techniques
21. Written requisitions and purchase orders with multiple copies

IV. Process Controls
22. Reconciliation of balances (subsidiary to general ledgers)
23. Transaction-by-transaction balancing
24. Depreciation calculations independently checked for accuracy and reasonableness
25. Calculations independently checked for accuracy and overall reasonableness (capitalization and amortization)

V. Coverage Controls
V (a) Segregation
26. Segregation of duties
    (a) operational responsibilities/financial record keeping
    (b) custody of assets/accounting for assets
    (c) authorization of transactions/custody of assets
    (d) within the accounting function
27. Segregation and rotation of input and processing duties

28. Separate areas maintained for receiving, storage, and shipping functions
29. Each cash fund assigned to one individual, independent of others
30. Monthly statements sent to all customers
31. Complaints (about monthly statements) handled independently of cashier or accounts receivable bookkeeper
32. Delinquent accounts handled independent of cashier

V (b) Supervision
33. Employee performance reviews
34. Direct supervision
35. Indirect supervision
36. Physical storage methods reviewed to spot inventory deterioration
37. Interest expense regularly posted (fluctuations investigated)
38. Operational planning

V (c) Rules and Procedures
39. Competitive bidding
40. Clearly defined processing and exception procedures
41. Competent and trustworthy personnel
42. Adequate documents and records
43. Established cutoff procedures
44. Chart of accounts and accounting procedures manual
45. Procedure for reflecting necessary general ledger corrections
46. Continuing education programs
47. Formal policy for capitalization and amortization
48. Flowcharts of control system
49. Prompt processing of billings and credits
50. Each day's receipts deposited intact that day
51. Paid notes canceled and retained
52. Organization charts
53. Job descriptions

V (d) Insurance
54. Insurance and fidelity bonds
55. Backups (for master files)
56. Retention of source documents, tape and disc files

VI. Access Controls
57. Dual signatures required for access to securities and adjustments on a timely basis
58. Physical access restriction
59. Safes and other locked enclosures to protect assets from people and physical hazards
60. Controlled custody
61. Password procedures in EDP system

62. Movement of inventory subject to verification by the area assuming responsibility for it
63. ID tags or serial numbers affixed to assets
64. Guards and/or alarm system used
65. Employees identified by badge or card
66. Unissued checks locked up

VII. Audit Controls

67. Regression analysis for forecasting expected activity level
68. Physical counts
69. Internal auditing
70. Variance analysis
71. Periodic compliance audit
72. Intercompany accounts balanced regularly

VIII. Compliances with GAAP Controls

73. Assignment of responsibility and establishment of procedures for accumulation of notes to financial statements including a review
74. Revenues recognized on long-term projects based on engineering function
75. Formal policies for assigning lives and depreciation method
76. Allowances for depreciation regularly reviewed for adequacy
77. Leases reviewed for classification as capital or operating
78. Intercompany profits eliminated
79. Periodic analysis of intangible assets; review for loss in value
80. Formal policies for identifying, reporting permanent and timing differences
81. Timing differences allocated between current and noncurrent
82. Warranty reserve regularly reviewed for adequacy
83. Estimated costs to complete long-term contracts regularly reviewed

IX. Management Controls

84. Appropriate cost system in use (job versus process versus standard versus direct code)
85. Compliance with loan covenants and lease agreements monitored
86. Current intercompany accounts zeroed out regularly
87. Investments previously written off, or fully reserved, regularly reviewed for possible realization
88. Selling and administration expenses under budgetary control
89. Employees handling receipts bonded

Appendix 5.B AN ALTERNATIVE TAXONOMY OF CONTROLS

A. Organizational Controls
2, 3, 6, 10, 15, 26, 27, 28, 29, 30, 31, 32, 33, 37, 39, 40, 41, 42, 43, 44, 45, 46, 47, 48, 50, 52, 53, 73

B. Repetition and Matching Type Controls
8, 9, 11, 12, 13, 14, 18, 22, 24, 25, 68, 72, 76

C. Authorization and Supervision Controls
1, 4, 34, 35, 57, 62

D. Physical Controls
7, 21, 51, 55, 56, 58, 59, 60, 61, 63, 64, 65, 66

E. Audit Controls
48, 67, 69, 70, 71

F. Economic Compensation Controls
54, 89

G. Process Controls
16, 17, 19, 20, 23

H. GAAP Compliance Controls
75, 75, 77, 78, 79, 80, 81, 82, 83

Appendix 5.C A TAXONOMY OF ERRORS

I. Procedural Errors
1. Lack of approval
5. Unauthorized adjustment
11. Goods shipped to bad credit risk
17. Assets unnecessarily exposed to unauthorized use
25. Unauthorized services performed
27. Lack of communication between departments (purchase versus production depts) resulting in overstocking of useless materials

II. Computation Errors
2. Bad total
32. Miscalculation of depreciation
39. Miscalculation of contingent lease payments

III. Accounting Errors
3. Incorrect posting
19. Sales discounts not recognized, or recognized when they should not be
23. Misapplication of overhead
29. Sales misclassified
35. Misclassification of long- or short-term debt

IV. Integrity Errors

4. Incorrect amount
6. Missing transaction
7. Duplicate transaction
8. Missing assets
9. Sales recorded but goods not shipped
10. Goods shipped but not invoiced
13. Inflated payroll
14. Misappropriation of funds (cash received posted at lower amounts or not at all)
22. Accepting shipments of unauthorized quality/quantity
24. Fictitious employees
38. Capital leases not recorded/operating leases recorded
42. Dividends paid to wrong parties/wrong amounts
45. Investment losses not monitored
46. Goodwill, patents, other intangibles carried in excess of value
49. Investment losses not reflected in accounting records

V. Timing Errors
12. Sales recorded in wrong period
16. Conditions affecting accounting valuations not recognized on a timely basis
43. Profits recognized prematurely on intercompany sales
47. Intangibles remain on books after disposal or expiration
48. Tax liability expense not reflected in accounting records

VI. GAAP Errors
25. Nonconformity to GAAP
26. Computation of LIFO inventory does not meet IRS regulations

VII. Irregularities
18. Defalcation and fraud
33. Kickbacks
36. Pledged assets not disclosed
44. Management conceals permanently impaired value of investment (uncollectibility of intercompany receivable)

VIII. Legal Errors
37. Violation of restrictive covenants resulting in default
40. Unauthorized sale of shares (violates option terms)
41. Unauthorized stock options exercised (violates option terms)

IX. Miscellaneous Management Errors
20. Financial reports do not fairly represent them
21. Receiving or producing poor quality assets
30. Idle assets not identified
31. Undetected deterioration of property
34. Company becomes obligated for debts at unfavorable terms.

Chapter 6

Computer-Related Crime

This boat that we just built is just fine—
And don't you try to tell us it's not.
The sides and the back are divine—
It's the bottom I guess we forgot . . . .

Shel Silverstein[*]

6.1 INTRODUCTION

Silverstein's poem depicts reality for many companies that have been victimized by crime involving the use of computers. Although advanced data processing hardware and physical safeguards for computer facilities are now commonplace, far too few companies have upgraded their internal control systems to meet the changing demands brought on by the increased reliance on electronic data processing.

The major cause of EDP-related business losses is unintentional error and security violations. These are random events that are usually discovered and remedied and account for approximately 95 percent of all data discrepancies. The second largest cause of losses is insider malfeasance, which encompasses the remaining 5 percent of data discrepancies and represents fraudulent entries of a purposeful nonrandom nature. We are concerned with this 5 percent in this chapter in which we deal with the topic of computer-related crime and, particularly, the definition, characteristics, and control of computer fraud.

[*]From Shel Silverstein, "Homemade Boat," in *Where the Sidewalk Ends.* New York: Harper & Row, 1974, p. 12.

LEARNING OBJECTIVES

By the time you complete this chapter, you should be able to:

1. Describe the nature of computer fraud.
2. Identify the six main groups from which those responsible for the majority of computer crimes come.
3. Describe the threats represented by computer crime and methods used.
4. Identify famous cases of computer fraud and describe their outcomes.
5. Recognize red flags of fraud and propose ways to control computer fraud.
6. Understand the meaning of management fraud.

6.2 NATURE AND EXTENT OF EDP-RELATED CRIME

Computer-related crime is any illegal act in which *knowledge of computer technology* plays a role in commission of the crime. The computer itself is involved in either an active or a passive role. The losses involved in computer crime far outweigh losses resulting from many other types of crime. The average loss from a bank robbery is $3200, and the average loss from an act of simple fraud is approximately $23,000. These amounts seem trivial compared to the average loss of $500,000 from a computer-related crime.[1]

Most experts feel that a high percentage of all computer crimes go undetected. The main causes of this low detection rate are the complexity of the system, the lack of proper auditing techniques to deal with EDP systems, poor internal controls, and the pervasive opinion among auditors that detection of computer fraud is management's responsibility. Thus computer-related crime—and computer fraud, in particular—pose a growing menace to organizations that depend on EDP in their daily operations.

COMPUTER FRAUD

Fraud is an intentional act designed to deceive or mislead another party. In legal terms there are two classes of fraud: actual and constructive. *Actual fraud* occurs when someone causes harm to another party because that party relied on an intentionally misrepresented material fact. *Constructive fraud,* on the other hand, differs from actual fraud in that the act is unconnected to purposive behavior designed to result in personal gain for the perpetrator; that is, it is not deliberate.

Computer fraud itself is defined as any defalcation, or embezzlement, accomplished by tampering with computer programs, data files, operations, equipment, and/or media, which results in losses to the organization whose computer system was manipulated.[2]

Of the instances of computer fraud that are detected, only 15 percent are reported to law-enforcement authorities. Most of those making disclosures are financial institutions that are legally required to report all irregularities. Data processing crime has been characterized by many as the rape of a business. This analogy goes a long way in explaining the low rate of reporting and prosecution in computer fraud cases. Most organizations fear the public panic or embarrassment that such disclosures can cause—and the subsequent effects on their credibility and reputations. Additionally, the current lack of a unified law to deal with those who commit data processing crimes often results in light sentences and/or fines and further frustration for the victims of computer fraud.

COMPUTER INVOLVEMENT

To date, computers have been involved in EDP-related crime as objects, subjects, instruments, and symbols.[3] As *objects* of crime, computers and/or their contents have been subjected to unauthorized use, and, in some cases, computers and the facilities that support them have been physically destroyed. Computers are the *subjects* of crime when computerized assets are stolen. Such crimes take place within the computer, and so they become the sites of criminal acts. Complex crimes may require use of computers to carry them out or keep track of their details, in which case computers are *instruments* of the crime. Finally, computers become *symbols* in support of crime when they are used in schemes that involve deception based on computerized data in reports.

When an organization moves toward the extensive use of EDP for its accounting and management systems, it encounters the real dangers of computer fraud. In the early transition stage, responsibilities and functions tend to be concentrated in the data processing department. This increases the probability of fraud and error, as a small group of people retain control over the integrity of the entire system.

COMPUTER CRIMINALS

The computerized system is never more vulnerable than in the hands of those who feed and care for it[4] because the most sensitive and vulnerable part of the system is at the person/machine interface. The type of person who actually commits computer crimes, most experts believe, is the same type of person who committed crimes against organizations—and for many of the same reasons—before the advent of the computer.

People from six main groups are responsible for the majority of computer crimes. The first group, dissatisfied employees, usually feels justified in taking revenge on the organization. Their acts are usually destructive and thus have the potential for causing large losses. The second group includes those employees who feel challenged to "beat the system." The challenge to their ingenuity has caused more than a few programmers to gain access into a system by breaking its codes and routines. Losses are usually minimal, but the devices used often open the way for others to enter the system and cause damage and other types of losses.

Employees in personal trouble (gambling debts, sexual misadventures) often commit or are forced to commit EDP crimes involving the theft of assets and/or information. Such losses are potentially large if the employee involved holds a position of authority, with control over various aspects of the system's integrity. Dissatisfied customers represent the fourth main group. The crimes committed by people from this group usually involve the destruction of physical assets and large losses.

The last two groups that produce EDP criminals are the politically motivated and the habitual criminal. The actions of the former are usually destructive and often entail blackmail of the organization's employees or the data center itself. The motive of the latter is personal gain, which results in very little physical destruction but in significant financial losses.[5]

Most computer security systems are designed to deny physical access to outsiders. The types of groups that spawn computer criminals, though, indicate that the most serious threats come from insiders. The inanimate nature of the computer can lull employees and management into laxness regarding internal control and computer security. Criminal intent and actions do not lie with the machines, but rather with those who know how to operate and maintain them. Data integrity is the crucial issue and the primary cause of losses from EDP crimes is the breakdown of internal controls. Information is the asset, and it is essential for the organization to safeguard this fundamental asset.[6]

TYPES OF THREATS TO EDP SYSTEMS

Threats to information processed by the computer fall into four general types. The first type of threat is that of physical damage or even destruction of equipment, data, or programs. The second type of threat involves transactional acts, such as imposturing or piggybacking. *Imposturing* means assuming the identity and privileges of another person in order to gain access to information or initiate unauthorized transactions. *Piggybacking,* on the other hand, is the unauthorized second use of a still-open terminal that another person had properly used to access the system. Electronic threats, the third type, include both wiretapping and electronic hardware modification, which can be used to produce the same results as software tampering: unauthorized access, faulty information, or tainted output. The final type of threat is that of software tampering, initiated by the programmer.[7]

METHODS OF DATA MANIPULATION

For each of the types of threats to EDP systems to become reality, access to a computerized system and its processes is required. When access into the system is gained, the EDP criminal can use a wide assortment of data manipulations. Some of the most common are:

1. *Salami technique,* which involves rounding off the odd fractions left in bank accounts after interest calculations have been made. These few mils are then diverted into another account. The manipulation entails a software modification for which there is an infinite number of derivations.
2. *Trojan horse,* in which access is gained by placing an unauthorized program within an authorized program. Locating the faulty code is very difficult. Trojan horses often include a "logic time bomb," or program that can order the computer to execute instructions sometime in the future and then erase all evidence of the illegal access.
3. *Asynchronous attack,* which uses the asynchronous nature of most computer operating systems to command parallel execution of two programs while only recording one continuous run in its operating log.
4. *Trapdoor,* which takes advantage of the breaks in code that often appear in programs during their developmental stages. If these holes are not removed during final editing, whether by error, faulty design logic, or intent, future access and changes are possible. These trapdoors can be used to hide instructions to the system so that not even the operating system is aware of the manipulations.
5. *Data diddling,* which is the most common type of EDP crime and involves the physical alteration or addition to data input or output records.

The vast majority of computer crimes involve data diddling. People who possess very little technical knowledge of the operating system or of programming can alter input and output records. Each type of manipulation attacks the integrity of the data entered, processed, or released from the system. The system itself is no more responsible than the paper on which a fraudulent balance sheet is printed. Only through improved internal controls can these types of data manipulations be detected and prevented.

6.3 SELECTED CASES OF COMPUTER FRAUD

Unlike pilferage, in which each action requires stealth and involves the risk of detection, a properly carried out computer aided swindle can be repeated with ease. And, unlike the pencil-pushing embezzler whose growing number of fraudulent entries tends to increase the likelihood of their being noticed, a conscientious electronic thief may operate for an indefinite period with practically no risk of detection.[8]

Some computer crimes can be committed in milliseconds. This introduces a new time frame of criminal activity. Similarly, the geographic scale has changed. The criminal no longer has to be present when the crime is committed. These changes in: geographic scale, increased concentration of resources, nature of technology and the diffusion of this computer technology underlie the ease with which fraud can be committed in computerized systems. Thus conditions inherent in the EDP mechanism itself partially explain why fraud can be as prevalent in computerized systems as in a manual system.

SUSCEPTIBILITY OF FRAUD

The chief characteristic of computerized systems that makes them susceptible to fraud is concentration of people and resources. A large number of processing steps are combined into a small number of programs as manual systems are automated. This concentration, coupled with the speed of processing, results in a loss of data integrity. Whereas in the manual system each clerk exercised some form of control over the process, EDP involves relatively little physical handling and verification of data manipulations.

Another unique feature of EDP is that records are "invisible." Data is stored on magnetic tapes, disks, or some other medium and is therefore hard to verify. Detection of errors and fraudulent entries is difficult from the data records themselves. Instead, reports and programmed controls must be relied on for the detection of irregularities.

Moreover, computers are programmed to print out only certain items. Therefore many of the data manipulations and processing steps never appear on printed reports. A related problem is that, as we noted earlier, controls can be stored within computer programs, which transfer the review process from people to the computer itself. Not only are irregularities unnoticed by operators, the programs themselves can be changed without detection. Trojan horses, trapdoors, and other manipulations can be used to alter what the computer records on its operating log and what it transmits to its operators and users.

These problems, which are unique to EDP systems, can be compounded by the lack of stringent internal controls. By limiting access to the computer room and the computer itself, by establishing tests of reasonableness, and by maintaining proper access codes and other built-in controls, management can meet the new challenges to the integrity of the organization's information resource.

FAMOUS FRAUD CASES

Now that we have identified ways that computer fraud can be committed, let's briefly review some of the more famous cases of detected (and reported) computer fraud.

Equity Funding. This EDP crime was uncovered in 1973, but not before $27.25 million had been embezzled. The top management of this insurance holding company used computers to create phony insurance policies, which were later sold to reinsurers. Of total company assets, $143.4 million were found to be fictitious, an estimated 19 percent the direct result of computer fraud. This fraud was a pure case of data diddling by management.

Union Dime. In 1973, a teller employed by this bank was caught in another form of data diddling. Money was skimmed from new large accounts by making a simple computerized correction entry. The teller was caught after police raided a bookie he frequented and questioned the source of his betting money (over $30,000 per week). The total loss to Union Dime was in excess of $1.2 million.

Security Pacific. In this 1978 case, the perpetrator was an outside consultant who bluffed his way into the bank's wireroom, where he found the electronic funds transfer codes openly displayed on a bulletin board. Later, posing as a branch manager, he called from a public telephone and used the code to transfer money to a Swiss bank account. He was apprehended only after bragging openly about the crime to a group of friends. The total loss to Security Pacific from the imposturing was $10.3 million.

Morgan Guaranty. In 1980, this New York bank accepted a bogus telex from the Central Bank of Nigeria. Some $21 million in funds were electronically routed to three different banks. When an attempt was made to wire the funds to a new $50 account in Santa Ana, California, the transfer was refused. This trivial transaction attempt led to the uncovering of the fraud, with no loss to Morgan Guaranty.

Wells Fargo. Between 1979 and 1981, an operations officer used the bank's computerized interbranch account settlement process to withdraw funds from a different branch. Fraudulent credits were generated to cover the withdrawals. The total loss was $21.3 million.

414's. This Milwaukee-based group of "hackers" was finally stopped in 1983 when one member penetrated the medical records data system at Sloan-Kettering Institute in New York. No losses were discovered, but the group also successfully accessed several systems at government facilities at Los Alamos and other sites. This new wave of computer crime presents the greatest challenge to organizations for maintaining data security while providing easy access routines for authorized users.

6.4 CONTROL OF COMPUTER FRAUD

Many reasons are given by management for their inattention to internal controls, including haphazard design of a system, complexity of programs, reliance on data processing professionals and auditors to point out weaknesses, and the fact that overall, EDP expenditures represent an insignificant portion of the total budget. However, no explanation can provide comfort or restore losses to an organization when it has been victimized by computer fraud. The answer lies in increased awareness of the warning signals of computer fraud and better internal controls.

RED FLAGS OF FRAUD

In 1978, the AICPA's standing committee on methods, perpetration, and detection of fraud compiled a list of fraud's major warning signals. Then, in 1980, Elliot and Willingham identified the forces that influence a person's decision to commit fraud: (1) situational pressures; (2) opportunity to commit fraud; and (3) personal factors, such as personal honesty.[9] The decision to commit fraud is based on the interaction of these forces. A person with a high level of personal honesty and no real opportunity or pressure to commit fraud will probably not do so. Management cannot control personal values and can only partially control the job-related aspect of situational

Table 6.1   Red Flags of Fraud

Situational Pressure Flags	
Personal	Company

Financial Pressures
  Heavy personal debts
  Severe illness in family
  Inadequate income and/or living
    beyond means
  Extensive stock market speculation
    that creates indebtedness
  Loan shark involvement
  Excessive gambling
 	
Revenge Motives
  Perceived inequities (such as under-
    paid, poor job assignment)
  Resentment of superiors
  Frustration, usually with job
	Financial Pressures
	  Unfavorable economic conditions
	    within the industry
	  Heavy investment or losses
	  Excess capacity
	  Severe obsolescence
	  Extremely high debt
	  Unusually heavy competition
	  Profit squeeze
	  Progressive deterioration of earnings
	  Success of company dependent on
	    one or two products, customers, or
	    transactions
	  Unusually high profits with a cash
	    shortage
	  Unmarketable collateral
	  Fear of merger
	  Significant litigation, especially
	    between management and share-
	    holders

(continued on next page)

Excerpted from Robert K. Elliot and John J. Willingham, *Management Fraud: Detection and Deterrence.* New York: Petrocelli Books, 1980.

pressure. Therefore the primary management question is whether sufficient controls can be instituted to effectively decrease the opportunity for fraud, thereby lessening the possibility that the other two forces can prevail.

Table 6.1   Red Flags of Fraud (continued)

Opportunity Flags	
Personal	Company

Personally Developed Opportunities
  Very familiar with operations
  In position of trust
  Close association with cohorts,
    suppliers, and other key people
  Work environment that fosters and/
    or creates opportunities
  Employees not informed about rules
    and discipline of fraud perpetrators
  Rapid turnover of key employees
    (quit or fired)
  No annual vacations required of
    executives
  No rotation or transfer of key
    employees
  Dominant top management
  No attention paid to details
  No viable outlets for dissatisfaction
    and grievances
  Lack of personnel evaluations
  Dishonest management and/or
    environment
  No requirement for executive
    disclosures and examinations
	Nature of the Firm
	  Allows transactions between related
	    parties
	  Complex business structure
	  No effective internal auditing staff
	  An extremely large or decentralized
	    firm
	  A highly computerized firm
	  Inexperienced people in key positions
	
	Relationship with Outside Parties
	  Uses several different auditing firms
	  Reluctance to give auditors needed
	    data
	  Changes auditors often
	  Hires an auditor who lacks expertise
	  Consistently brings unexpected
	    information to the auditor's attention
	  Changes legal counsel often
	  Uses several different banks, none of
	    which can see the entire picture
	
	Accounting Practices
	  Large and unusual year-end transac-
	    tions
	  Many adjusting entries required at the
	    time of the audit
	  Poor internal control system or control
	    procedure enforcement
	  Unduly liberal accounting practices
	  Poor accounting records
	  Inadequate staffing of accounting
	    department

(continued on next page)

Table 6.1   Red Flags of Fraud (continued)

Personal Flags	
Personality Traits	Social Characteristics

A lack of personal honesty
No well-defined code of personal
  ethics
A "wheeler-dealer," who enjoys
  feelings of power, influence, social
  status, and excitement associated
  with rapid financial transactions
  involving large sums of money
Neurotic, manic-depressive, or
  emotionally unstable
Arrogant or egocentric
Sociopathic personality
Low or threatened self-esteem
Intrigued by the personal challenge of
  subverting a system of controls
	Criminal history
	Questionable asssociates
	No or poor references

The list of *red flags* presented in Table 6.1 indicate a company's vulnerability to fraud or the likelihood of corporate malfeasance. For example, a careful examination of the Equity Funding case previously mentioned revealed the presence of 37 of these red flags. Careful attention to the problem areas identified by these warning signals can help management to avoid fraud. Management and auditors alike can use these red flags as a form of checklist to detect situations in which the potential for fraud exists. By decreasing the opportunities for fraud and increasing the probability of detection through better internal controls, exposure to losses from computer fraud can be reduced.

WAYS TO CONTROL COMPUTER FRAUD

As an organization increases its reliance on sophisticated data processing equipment and techniques, it must alter its control policies and procedures to ensure data integrity and provide clear audit trails. As Figure 6.1 indicates, two types of internal controls are applicable to EDP systems: general controls and application controls. General controls relate to all EDP activities. Application controls relate to controls that are specific to a particular application. For example, a payroll system may undergo a series of edits relative to payee name and address that are applicable nei-

Figure 6.1   Internal Control Relationships

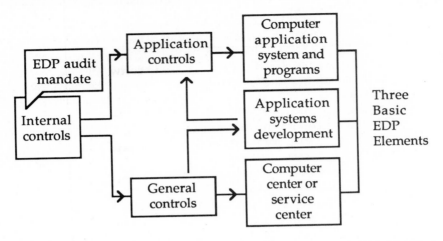

ther to other applications nor to the data processing facility. Internal controls are not only valuable in the context of fraud prevention and detection, but are also crucial to guaranteeing the integrity of the entire accounting system.

The responsibility for internal control tends to be fragmented in most organizations, opening the way for errors and fraud. Controls usually are established piecemeal to meet evolving needs at various stages of manual and computer processing without ever being evaluated in the context of overall control objectives or the operation of the total EDP system.

The three most common control shortcomings are (1) the assumption by personnel in the user department that control of data processing is the sole function and responsibility of the EDP department; (2) the failure to keep duties such as data input and control segregated; and (3) the failure to restrict a user access to data after it has entered the EDP system. These shortcomings can be overcome through system control, which is one of the best investments a company can make; it produces a continuous payback in data integrity, while making overall operations more efficient.

Overall System Security. Security of an EDP system involves deterrence, prevention, detection, recovery, and protection of data files. If also requires the understanding and support of top management and the formulation of well-defined control policies. The trade-off for increased security is less system availability, flexibility, and generality, so all security decisions should be examined within the framework of system objectives, user needs, and data vulnerability. Henkel has emphasized that "management must evaluate not only the processors and programs, but the users and all the procedures that make up a system when it comes to creating a workable security system."[10]

Specific Types of Security Measures. The protection of the information stored and processed in an EDP system requires effective physical, personnel, procedural, computer hardware and software, and communications security measures. Although they are very important, physical security measures are often overdone at the expense of internal controls. Physical security measures are often easier to define, implement, and maintain than the measures needed to ensure the integrity of data. The latter involve segregation of duties, restriction of access privileges, and tight control and authorization procedures for altering existing programs or creating new ones. Recall that the greatest potential risk of fraud involves unauthorized access to and manipulation of data files.

Top management should assign to middle and first-line managers the responsibility for internal controls and security in their respective areas. Computer system security can be coordinated through a staff position established to aid first-line managers in their control efforts and encourage feedback on the effects of these efforts. The staff person can then relate these effects to management's objectives. Whenever significant systems changes are made, security should be reviewed and updated as necessary to ensure that adequate control features are maintained.

Hiring and other personnel practices should be designed to ensure that employees in a position of trust warrant that trust. Key employees should attend periodic briefings on security policies, procedures, and problems.

Security software that restricts users access to only those files they are authorized to use is available. All access attempts are recorded according to the time, place, and employee who initiates them. This process employs the computer's capabilities to protect the data it stores. Other software packages allow even an inexperienced auditor to verify the processing and data integrity of an EDP system.

Encryption uses hardware devices to scramble data during transmission to and from computer terminals. Only a computer with a matching device can decipher the incoming message, which decreases the risk of data manipulation by outside sources.

Finally, all computerized systems should have backup computerized data files. These files allow for the reconstruction of the current status of a company's data. This is done by restoring master files as of a certain date and then applying ensuing transactions up to the current level.

Reporting of Fraud and Punishment. All of these precautions have little meaning if instances of computer fraud go unreported, unpunished, and unpublicized. Organizations must take firm action to protect the integrity of their data, which includes the punishment of those who commit computer fraud. Many legislators see the need for upgrading the penalties associated with the various forms of computer fraud, but laws do not curtail behavior—action does.

6.5 MANAGEMENT FRAUD

Management fraud is deliberate fraud committed by management with the intent of deceiving and injuring investors and creditors through materially misleading financial statements. Management here refers to those who are high enough in the organization to have the power to override accounting controls.[11]

Under this definition, management fraud is confined to financial statement manipulations. Management can commit many other purposive or accident errors or omissions that could potentially defraud customers, employees and others, but this category looks only at faulty information to investors and creditors. If management intentionally misapplies accounting methods to produce misleading results, records fictitious transactions regarding assets or revenues, or enters transactions without warrant (i.e. no economic change has occurred), management fraud has been committed. The Equity Funding case that was noted previously falls into this category of computer and business crimes, perpetrated by management.

The red flags denoted earlier provide the auditor with a set of tools to aid in the detection of management fraud. While the auditor's responsibility for detection here is restricted to those actions that could normally be expected to be discovered by the application of generally accepted auditing practices, the need to maintain the integrity of the attestation process requires increased auditor involvement in detecting management fraud.

In 1986 the National Commission on Fraudulent Financial Reporting (the "Treadway" commission) commissioned a study of lawsuits against auditors to examine issues related to management fraud. Among 456 lawsuits against auditors, spanning the period from 1960 through 1985, they found that:[12]

> Management fraud was present in about one-half of the cases
> The auditor was sued in only about 20 percent of those cases among
> which, over one-half also involved management fraud.

With the evolution of technology, and increasing computerization of financial systems, the issues of computer-related management fraud are going to assume increasing importance in the eyes of auditors, stockholders, and regulatory officials.

6.6 Summary

In this chapter we examined computer-related crime, with particular emphasis on computer fraud. The advent of the Foreign Corrupt Practices Act has forced management to accept legal responsibility for its accounting and internal control systems. Additionally, recent court decisions have underlined the auditor's role in detecting and reporting areas where the risk of computer fraud and other computer-related crime is high. The legal and moral imperatives noted throughout this chapter indicate that more resources must be committed to stopping computer fraud. Furthermore, the natural reluctance by corporations to divulge and prosecute computer crime is a serious problem. Legislation will be necessary that equates computer with non-computer crime as well as requires businesses to disclose its occurrence.

Systems management and accounting controls that interweave with systems security and system auditability functions, will provide management with the type of control necessary to oversee the entire information flow in an organization. Management must use the knowledge gained in observing these flows to design responsibility and performance evaluation measures that motivate line managers toward meeting the objectives of system security and control. Information is a valuable asset that must be adequately protected and controlled.

> . . . it does not follow that (management) fraud should be detained by any means or at any price. Society may be unwilling to devote the resources necessary to eradicate it, and deciding what level . . . is tolerable is a matter of assessing the relative costs of detection and deterrence . . . One cannot put a dollar value on the desire for a more ethical society.[13]

Questions

1. In legal terms, what are the two kinds of fraud? Define and distinguish between them.
2. How is loss from computer fraud different from losses that result from other kinds of computer-related crime?
3. What are the six main groups from which people who commit computer crimes come? Why is it generally felt people commit these crimes?
4. What are the four general areas of threat to EDP systems?

5. Describe the following computer-fraud techniques and identify the EDP areas they threaten.
   Salami technique
   Trojan horse
   Asynchronous attack
   Trapdoor
   Data diddling
6. What are the time, geographic, and concentration of resources problems that make computer fraud difficult to prevent and detect?
7. What are some of the red flags of computer fraud and how can they be helpful in detecting fraud?
8. How do internal controls help prevent fraud? Do they provide any other benefits?
9. How does management fraud differ from other kinds of fraud?
10. What was the general impact of the Foreign Corrupt Practices Act on management's attitude toward fraud?

Problems

1. What kinds of problems are caused when computer fraud is not prosecuted? If you were a company president would you follow such a policy?
2. If you were a data processing manager, which of your employees would you consider to be potentially the most damaging in terms of committing fraud? How would you answer this question if you had to further break the fraud into the potential dollar loss to your company, that is, small, medium, or large?
3. Do you believe that the size of fraud losses presented in this chapter is stated accurately? See if you can locate more recent ones and determine how they were estimated.
4. Besides the value of actual assets stolen, how do you think you might estimate the value of lost time and inconvenience caused by computer fraud? How might such figures be used in a risk analysis?
5. How much do you think effective internal control represents computer-fraud prevention and how much does it represent good management generally?
6. Identify three episodes of computer fraud from the popular press and try to establish if they could be considered management fraud, the techniques used, and the types of controls that failed or were not present.

Notes

1. Paul, Lois, "Exec Warns Computer Crime Already Here," *Computerworld*, July 6, 1981, p. 25.
2. Allen, Brandt, "The Biggest Computer Frauds: Lessons for CPA's," *Journal of Accountancy*, May 1977, pp. 52–62.
3. *Computer Crime—Computer Justice*, U.S. Department of Justice pamphlet. Washington, D.C.: SRI International, 1979, p. 4.
4. "The Head in the Sand Caper: A Question of Vulnerability," *Datamation*, September 1979, pp. 70–71.
5. Pantages, Angeline, "Sophisticated Crime," *Dun's Review*, August 1979, p. 88.
6. Paul, Lois, p. 25.
7. "The Head in the Sand Caper," p. 71.
8. Jones, G. Hunter, "DP Error and Fraud—What You Can Do about It," *Price Waterhouse Review*, 1976, p. 5.
9. Elliot, Robert K., and Willingham, John J., *Management Fraud: Detection and Deterrence*. New York: Petrocelli Books, 1980, p. 221.
10. Henkel, Tom, "New Tech Seen Threatening Security," *Computerworld*, December 22, 1980, p. 21.
11. Elliot and Willingham, p. 5.
12. The chairman of the "National Commission on Fraudulent Financial Reporting," James Treadway made a speech before the AICPA Annual Meeting on October 21, 1986 describing the commissioner's initial findings. The study of litigation against independent auditors was: Zoe-Vanna Palmrose, "Litigation and Independent Auditors: the Role of Business Failures and Management Fraud," working paper, School of Business Administration, University of California, Berkeley.
13. Elliot and Willingham, p. 3.

Additional References

AICPA, "Report on the Activities of the Special Investigations Committee of the SEC Practice Section of the AICPA Division for CPA firms." AICPA, New York, 1985.

De Gouw, Chris, "Data Processing Crimes," *EDPACS*, January 1978.

Fine, Leonard, "The Total Computer Security Concept and Security Policy," *EDPACS*, November 1982.

Moscove, Stephen Allen, "Is Computer Fraud a Fact of Business Life?" *National Public Accountant*, August 1978, pp. 16–22.

Murray, William H., "Good Security Practices," *EDPACS*, October 1980.

"New Wave Computer Crime," *Newsweek*, August 29, 1983.

Perry, William E., and Henry C. Warner, "Systems Auditability: Friend or Foe?" *Journal of Accountancy*, February 1978, pp. 52–60.

Roberts, Ray, "Internal Controls: It's Not Only the Auditor's Headache," *Data Management*, July 1979, pp. 19–21, 49.

"Spreading Danger of Computer Crime," *Business Week*, April 20, 1981, pp. 86–92.

Srinivasen, C. A., and Paul E. Dascher, "Computer System Security and Auditing Implications," *National Public Accountant*, January 1978, pp. 20–24.

Weber, Ron, "Accounting and EDP," *Journal of Accountancy*, 1983.

Chapter 7

Generalized Audit Software

7.1 INTRODUCTION

Auditors have used the computer primarily to test information processing systems or internal control procedures (compliance testing); to test the details of transactions and balances (substantive testing); and as a tool to help perform certain mechanical audit duties (such as using spreadsheets for trial balances). In the 1960s, large accounting firms, vendors, and researchers developed computer software designed specifically to help the auditor do these tasks and thereby perform audits *with* the computer. Audit software development and refinement continued during the 1970s and, in 1979, AICPA defined *generalized audit software* (GAS) as

> A computer program, or a series of computer programs, specifically designed to perform certain audit-related data processing functions. These functions include reading computer files, selecting desired information, performing calculations, and printing reports in a format specified by the auditor.[1]

Generalized audit software can be used by the auditor to conduct compliance testing (sample selection and analysis) but is particularly applicable to substantive testing (footings and extensions, audit data comparison, and confirmations). Generalized audit software is the most frequently used computer-aided audit tool, and its use requires the auditor to have minimal data processing skills and knowledge.

We begin this chapter by presenting GAS objectives, functions and uses. We then describe a specific GAS application called the TREAT system. Next, we discuss the use of microcomputer software as GAS. Finally, we present the advantages and disadvantages of GAS and criteria for selecting specific applications of GAS for use in conducting an audit.

LEARNING OBJECTIVES

By the time you complete this chapter, you should be able to:

1. Define and give examples of generalized audit software.
2. Discuss the objectives, functions, and uses of generalized audit software.
3. Describe the purpose and use of the TREAT system.
4. Explain how to use a microcomputer software as GAS in performing audit tasks.
5. Identify the major advantages and disadvantages of GAS.
6. Identify selection criteria for specific GAS applications.

7.2 GAS OBJECTIVES, FUNCTIONS, AND USES

A large number and wide variety of GAS applications have been developed and are being used. The majority, however, were based on the same objectives and have many common functional characteristics.

OBJECTIVES

The objectives of generalized audit software are to:

1. Provide the auditor easy access to data and information generated by a variety of computer systems and stored in computer-readable formats.
2. Provide the auditor with the means of dealing effectively with large quantities of data.
3. Provide computer-based audit independence and lessen the auditor's dependence on client EDP personnel.
4. Increase the range of analytic techniques, such as sampling and confirmation, available to auditors.
5. Enhance the auditor's understanding of the client's EDP system and operations.
6. Produce economical and high-quality audits.

FUNCTIONS

Based on those objectives, generalized audit software commonly perform the following functions. That is, they:

1. *Create,* by reading the client's data file and storing it in the auditor's work file.
2. *Search and retrieve,* by selecting only those records from the file that meet predetermined criteria.
3. *Calculate,* by performing mathematical computations and logical operations on fields of information within records.
4. *Summarize,* by combining similar records, based on a specific field or total amounts, for all records within a given sequence.
5. *Sample select,* by selecting randomly a statistical sample of records.
6. *Sort,* by arranging records in ascending or descending sequence.
7. *Merge, compare, or update,* by combining or comparing two files with an option to print either matched or unmatched records or insert information from one file into another.
8. *Total or subtotal,* by computing and printing the grand total as well as subtotals.
9. *Print or punch,* by printing or punching output, with the report format determined by the user.
10. *Perform miscellaneous functions,* such as providing statistical measures (mean, standard deviation, range), printing confirmations, printing diagnostic flowcharts, and the like.

USES

The functions commonly performed by generalized audit software allow the auditor to use GAS to accomplish five basic types of audit tasks:

1. *Examination of files for quality.* Examples of this task are (a) reviewing accounts receivable balances for amounts over the credit limit; (b) reviewing inventory quantities for negative balances; (c) reviewing payroll files for terminated employees; and (d) listing and reviewing all accounts receivable that are missing credit information.
2. *Recalculations and extensions.* Examples of this task are (a) extending inventory prices and quantities; (b) recalculating interest; (c) recalculating the accuracy of sales discounts; and (d) recalculating net pay of employees.
3. *Audit data comparison.* Examples of this task are (a) comparing the changes in accounts receivable balances between two dates with the sales and cash receipts in transaction files; (b) comparing current and prior period inventory files to review obsolete or slow-moving items; (c) comparing the pay rates in the payroll master file with those in the payroll transaction

file; (d) comparing inventory quantity test counts with perpetual records; and (e) comparing confirmation of returns to initial requests.

4. *Audit sample selection analysis and printing.* Examples of this task are (a) accounts receivable and accounts payable confirmations; (b) selecting inventory items for observation; (c) printing fixed asset additions for vouching; and (d) printing dates of selected items for cutoff tests.

5. *Summarizing of resequencing data.* Examples of this task are (a) footing the accounts receivable file and summarizing the file according to audit location; (b) testing accounts receivable aging; (c) summarizing inventory turnover statistics for obsolescence analysis; and (d) totaling and resequencing inventory items by location to facilitate inventory physical observations.

The auditor can use GAS to run compliance tests of computer files by performing tasks 1 and 4. For example, in an accounts receivable audit, the auditor can use a sample selection routine to calculate the sample size, select the sample, and evaluate sample results. The auditor can then use GAS to print dates of selected transactions for cutoff tests and to examine records for quality, such as listing all accounts receivable that are missing credit information.

For substantive testing of computer files, the auditor can use GAS to perform all five of the basic types of audit tasks. For example, in an inventory audit, the auditor can use a sample selection routine to calculate the sample size, select the inventory sample, and evaluate sample results. The auditor can then use GAS to recalculate the extension of inventory items, compare current and prior period inventory files to review obsolete or slow-moving items, total and resequence inventory items by location to facilitate physical observations, compare inventory quantity test counts with perpetual records, and review inventory quantities for negative and unreasonably large balances.

In addition to accounts receivable and inventory applications, generalized audit software has been used successfully to audit cash receipts and disbursements; payroll; sales; payables; and property, plant, and equipment. For an audit of cash receipts and disbursements, the auditor can select cash transaction sample for compliance or substantive testing. The auditor can also use GAS to print and foot cash receipts and cash disbursement journals; to test for unusually large receipts, unusual classifications, or unusual allowances or discounts; and to compare checks cashed with checks issued.

In a payroll audit, the auditor can select and print sample terminations and new employees in the audit period. The auditor can also use GAS to print and foot payroll register; to determine the accuracy of employees' net pay computations; and to merge the payroll transaction files with the payroll master files for testing unusual payrate, gross pay, and hours worked.

In a sales audit, the auditor can select and test sample sales transactions for unusually large amounts. The auditor can also use GAS to print and foot sales journal; to compare sales records to accounts receivable file; to test for missing or duplicate invoice numbers; and to analyze sales by product line, region, customer, etc.

In the audit of payables, the auditor can select and test records with past-due and debit balance. The auditor can also use GAS to foot accounts receivable file; to compare creditor statements with accounts payable file; and to review unusual master file data such as sudden large transactions for an inactive supplier.

In the audit of property, plant, and equipment, the auditor can select sample for testing additions and retirements. The auditor can also use GAS to calculate depreciation; to test accuracy of footings and extensions; and to classify items according to location and asset type.

Generalized audit software packages are available from a number of vendors and public accounting firms. Appendix 7.A identifies and describes several GAS packages developed by accounting firms. Three useful analyses of GAS are available in the works by Will,[2] Adams and Mullarkey,[3] and Perry.[4]

7.3 TERMINAL RELATED EDUCATIONAL AUDIT TOOL (TREAT)

The authors developed the Terminal Related Educational Audit Tool (TREAT) in 1978 under a grant from the Touche Ross Foundation as part of its program of sponsoring educational research in accounting. This system emulates the STRATA auditing software package and thereby provides a realistic method of learning for the student. The TREAT system provides on-line, question-and-answer interaction between the student and the computer as the student first develops and then executes computer audit programs. The system enables both the student and the instructor who have little or no computer experience to rapidly develop skills in computer auditing. Table 7.1 lists the specific steps and topics involved in learning about GAS systems and how to use them, including the TREAT system.

Table 7.1   Learning About and How to Use GAS

Step	Topic
1: Problem description and specification	Nature of audit problems Documentation of data processing files General application flowcharts Additional investigation questions
2: Problem solution flowcharts	Symbolic problem solution descriptions Programming logic flowcharts Audit programming logic
3: Language description	GAS language features Specific programming language features Power of data processing
4: Preparation of coding sheets	Specific syntaxes Nature of data processing files Rigidities and limitations of programming languages
5: Hands-on terminal interation	Debugging techniques Logical "honesty" Time estimates Ad hoc problem exploration
6: Debriefing	Nature of the total experience What to expect in "real life"

MAIN COMPONENTS AND FUNCTIONS

The TREAT system is composed of four micromodules (modes of operation):

1. *Definition mode*—to define STRATA-type functions and edit them at entry.
2. *Execution mode*—to execute TREAT programs and allow suspended execution in case of nonfatal error.

3. *List mode*—to provide an annotated listing of TREAT programs for debugging and documentation purposes (similar to STRATA's diagnostic).
4. *Modification mode*—to redefine pages or lines of TREAT code.

The key functions of the system are the same as those of other GAS applications, which we presented in Section 7.2. Figure 7.1 shows a symbolic representation of the TREAT system. More detailed descriptions of TREAT are contained in two works by Vasarhelyi and Lin.[5,6]

APPLICATION PROCEDURE

There are four major steps in using TREAT: TREAT system familiarization, audit planning, TREAT application program development, and execution and analysis of results.

The students start with learning TREAT system and its key functions such as auditor file definition, mathematical functions, sampling functions, sorting function, summarization function, and report generation function. They then proceed with audit planning, including audit objective identification, report specification, and setting up criteria for result evaluation.

A typical TREAT application program development includes designing a general application flowchart and detailed logic flowchart, filling out TREAT function specification sheets, and entering program definition from specification sheets into the computer.

After the program has been entered into the computer through Definition Mode, students can use List Mode to prepare a list of the program and evaluate it. If errors are found in the program listing, students can use Modification Mode to fix the mistakes and then use Execution Mode to execute the program to generate reports. The students finish the audit project with the analysis of results to achieve audit objectives.

TREAT CASES

The TREAT learning system utilizes three cases. The inventory case requires the calculation of cost extensions, the preparation of reports for use when taking physical inventory, and an exception report for unit costs. The property, plant, and equipment case requires slightly more computation involving depreciation data. Finally, the accounts receivable case is even more complex, requiring the aging of receivables, summarization of transactions, and application of payments. An extension of the accounts receivable case illustrates the updating of the master file by transaction

Figure 7.1   Symbolic Representation of TREAT System

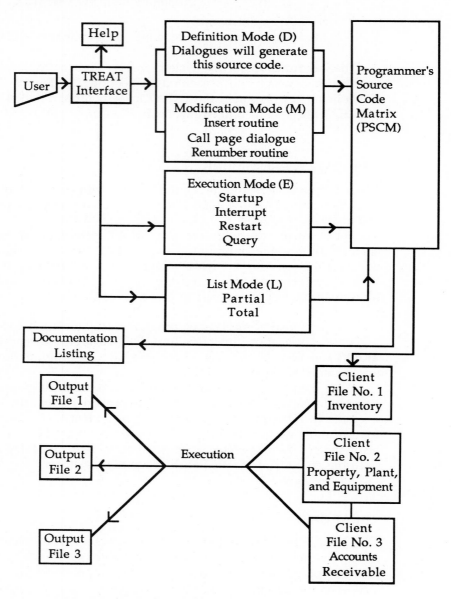

(Adapted from Vasarhelyi and Lin, 1985, p. 84.)

files. A more extensive description of the TREAT system is presented in Appendix I at the end of this textbook. It is followed by the inventory case (Appendix II), property, plant, and equipment case (Appendix III); the accounts receivable case (Appendix IV); and the accounts receivable case extension (Appendix V).

ADVANTAGES AND DISADVANTAGES

The major advantages of the TREAT system are that it:

1. Helps the student to better understand the underlying concepts and use of GAS.
2. Is flexible enough to allow the user to apply it to many different audit situations.
3. Allows fast, easy program debugging and error correction.
4. Allows use of a computer auditing package at remote audit sites.
5. Is easy to understand and does not require extensive computer programming knowledge.
6. Has an intricate error detection and correction subsystem with immediate error feedback.

The major disadvantages of using TREAT are that it:

1. Is written in a special programming language called APL. In order to use TREAT, the student must have access to a computer system that includes an APL compiler.
2. Is accessed through a terminal. The student must have adequate terminal availability.
3. Is stored in mainframe computer disk storage. Some disk space must be made available for both software system and student program storage.

7.4 MICROCOMPUTER-BASED GAS

Many organizations, both large and small, now use microcomputers in their operations. Auditors can also use microcomputers to increase audit efficiency and productivity and improve generally the audit process.[7] Specifically, auditors can use a microcomputer database management system called dBASE III[8] as a GAS to perform four of the audit tasks mentioned in Section 7.2: (1) data examination; (2) data manipulation and comparison; (3) sample selection; and (4) data summary and analysis.

As a relational database system, dBASE III, allows information to be stored in two-dimensional tables called "files" and to be accessed by the user based on any desired relationship such as employee-department relationship in payroll application. For auditors, this feature makes the system easier to understand and is flexible in reorganizing data for different audit objectives. Another important feature is that the auditor can develop his or her own criteria and then use dBASE III to examine records based on those criteria and identify records that are exceptions to the criteria. The system also has a query command, which allows the auditor to request information, and a report generator.

Some typical audit applications that an auditor can perform using dBASE III are:

1. Select and print all accounts receivable that are missing credit limit information.
2. Select and print a sample of customers for confirmation.
3. Select and print all accounts receivable having balances in excess of the credit limit.
4. Identify and print inventory records with negative quantity on hand.
5. Recalculate depreciation expenses, employee net pay, and similar quantities.
6. Extend inventory costs and quantities.
7. Compare quantities in the perpetual inventory records with those from inventory test counts.
8. Compare the balances in the accounts receivable subsidiary ledgers with the totals of open invoices.
9. Resequence fixed assets records by locations to facilitate inventory physical observation.
10. Prepare the aging of accounts receivable report.
11. Select and print high-dollar inventory items for observation.
12. Print all current year's additional fixed assets for vouching.

Appendix 7.B presents four examples of audit applications using dBASE III as GAS.

7.5 ADVANTAGES, DISADVANTAGES, AND RESULTS

ADVANTAGES

The use of GAS packages has numerous audit advantages. First, generalized audit software is usually user-oriented, which allows the auditor who does not have a detailed understanding of the hardware and software to use the computer. This advantage also allows the auditor greater independence from his client's personnel, especially from those in the data processing department.

The auditor can do more in less time because GAS reduces the amount of time required to perform mundane audit tasks. For example, the auditor can quickly select a sample from a large number of inventory accounts, which would be fairly time-consuming if done manually. The auditor can then use the time save to make additional analyses, thereby extending the scope of the audit.

The use of GAS to access a variety of records interchangeably, rather than developing a special program for each application, and to test a variety of files saves time and money. It is also much quicker and less expensive than performing the same work manually.

It is possible to increase the reliability of certain aspects of an audit through the use of GAS. For example, rather than relying on test footing of the client's payables trial balance, the auditor can use GAS to foot the entire payables file. Finally, GAS allows the auditor to control totally the programs used. If the auditor's firm develops GAS, it can embody that firm's auditing approach, such as its working paper requirements and its statistical sampling plan.

RESULTS

Generalized audit software permits the auditor to examine and evaluate vast quantities of data and numbers of transactions quickly and efficiently. Let's look at some practical results of applying generalized audit software.[9] Some of these results would not have been possible without GAS; others would have been impractical in terms of the amount of personnel and time required had the audits been conducted manually.

Purchasing. In an automatic reordering system, the auditors discovered that certain parts were still being ordered, although the company was no longer manufacturing the product for which the parts had been needed. The auditor made this discovery by extracting a list of all inventory items that showed no withdrawals for three months. The system had been programmed to automatically order $190,000 of this particular part at fixed time intervals.

Banking. The auditors recomputed monthly service charges on customer checking accounts. They discovered that the bank was undercharging customers a total of $48,000 per month.

Inventory. The auditors discovered that 23 percent of the items carried in the inventory master file were no longer manufactured by the company. The company was able to reduce the size of its files by purging them of these items.

Department Store Billing. The auditors extracted all accounts more than 150 days old, sorted them by date, and listed them. They discovered that 80 percent of these accounts were suspense accounts that were uncollectible and that, as a result, accounts receivable were being overstated. Further analysis detected numerous cases of fraud, loose credit practices, and inadequate procedures for error correction.

Telephone Billing. The auditors for a company obtained a magnetic tape of toll billings from the telephone company. The auditors sorted the toll calls by the number called. They then extracted toll calls on the bases of predetermined dollar values, volume of calls made to a particular number, and calls made after normal working hours. The auditors found that 13 percent of the calls were made after normal working hours, 13 percent of the calls were for nonbusiness purposes, and 1 percent of the calls were made by unauthorized personnel. The company was able to use the auditors' suggestions to control its telephone expense.

Government Agency. Audit tests indicated that more than 50 percent of the agency's requisitions for spare parts were for amounts of less than $25.00. Since the cost of processing each requisition exceeded this amount, each transaction cost more than the part. New methods of handling requisitions for spare parts were devised and resulted in significant savings.

DISADVANTAGES

There are three main disadvantages of using GAS, which have a direct bearing on whether an auditor can use it in a given audit situation. First, GAS is not available for all types of hardware; hardware and file constraints can limit the types of software used with the system. Second, some types of file layout or organization cannot be accessed or read by GAS; in particular, certain database management systems cannot be processed. Finally, GAS is typically written for ease of implementation by the user without regard to the efficient use of computer hardware and processing capabilities; thus its use can be more time-consuming and expensive in certain situations than the use of software developed for specific audit applications.

7.6 SELECTION CRITERIA

With a wide variety of generalized audit software to choose from, an auditor contemplating the use of GAS will need to evaluate the alternatives available. Unfortunately, no one software package can be rated as the best in terms of applicability, effectiveness, and cost. Adams and Mullarkey suggest that answers to the following questions can be used as a means of determining which software package is best.[10]

1. What computer audit applications will be processed?
2. What computer resources are available?
3. What data media must be processed?
4. What level of data processing expertise is available?
5. What training is required?
6. How available is the package and what kind of back-up or support is provided?

Obviously, the auditor must first ask whether the audit offers an opportunity for effective use of the computer. If not, there is no reason to become involved in selecting a package. When the auditor has concluded that a computer audit application is appropriate, hardware considerations are vital. Whether the auditor has a computer, can obtain machine time from the client, or wants to use a service bureau, the package must be one that can be processed by the particular equipment involved. Next, the auditor must evaluate the data to be processed in terms of the media used by the client to record the data. If the records are on a disk pack, the package selected must be able to handle disk.

The auditor also has to evaluate realistically the availability of personnel knowledgeable about auditing with the computer in order to achieve a balance between flexibility and ease of use. After determining the level of expertise that is available, the auditor must try to match it with the extent and depth of the training required to use a particular package. After the possible choices have been narrowed, the auditor should obtain from the software developers a more detailed description of training requirements and methods available for those packages still under consideration.

In evaluating any package, the auditor must be concerned with the availability of and level of support for software. Thus the auditor must determine how long it will take to obtain the software, what it will cost, and what types of supporting services are supplied by the vendor.

By going through this process, the auditor can at least narrow the choices, if not arrive at a clear-cut decision. Because of the different types of assessments involved, the decision ultimately will be a judgment decision by the auditor.

Wasserman recommends the following similar criteria for selection of GAS:

1. Does the package operate directly on your files, or do the files have to be converted or reconditioned?
2. Does the package operate in your operating environment (core size, operating system, partitioned storage, and the like)?
3. Is the package efficient with respect to auditor preparation time and computer processing time?
4. Are the editing routines comprehensive enough to ensure complete and accurate processing?
5. If more than one computer center is to be audited, is the system portable?
6. Is the package largely self-documenting? (By retaining the original instructions, do you have a clear record of what was processed?)
7. Is there a user's group to provide for the sharing of audit information?
8. Does the vendor provide package maintenance? For what period of time?
9. What is the quality of the vendor's documentation?
10. Will the vendor provide a list of all its users? What is the vendor's reputation?
11. What is the quality of the training and installation program provided by the vendor?[11]

7.7 Summary

Generalized audit software is a set of computer programs specifically designed to perform a number of data processing functions such as reading computer files, selecting desired information, performing calculations, and printing reports in a user specified format. It is an audit tool to help the auditor perform a large number of tasks involving vast amounts of data of different varieties quickly and accurately. Generalized audit software has been successfully applied to the audit of inventory; accounts receivable; property, plant, and equipment; cash receipts and disbursements; payroll; sales; and payables transactions. It can be used to examine records for quality, completeness, consistency, and correctness. It also performs the functions of computation, comparison, selection, printing, sorting, and summarization.

We described one GAS educational tool, called TREAT, that we developed. We also briefly described the uses of dBASE III as a microcomputer-based GAS. We presented the major advantages and disadvantages of using GAS. Since no one GAS is best for all situations, we listed and discussed selection criteria that can be used as guidelines for GAS selection.

Questions

1. What is generalized audit software?
2. Identify the objectives of the generalized audit software.
3. What are some of the more important functions GAS can perform?
4. What are some of the basic audit tasks that the auditor can use the generalized audit software program to perform?
5. How might you use GAS in each of the following audit areas?
    (i) Cash receipts and disbursements
    (ii) Payroll
    (iii) Sales
    (iv) Payables
6. List some of the GAS developed by CPA firms.
7. Briefly describe the main components and functions of the TREAT system.
8. What are the typical steps a student would follow in the design and implementation of an application in TREAT system?
9. How might microcomputer software such as dBASE III be used to perform computer audits?
10. What are the advantages and disadvantages of using GAS?
11. What are the selection criteria for choosing a GAS package for an auditing organization?
12. In each of two sets of selection criteria presented, how many of the questions are hardware related and how many are personnel and client related?

Problems

1. What are the most important criteria for selecting GAS? Why should we make the selection decision?
2. What questions would you ask of a client if you were thinking about using GAS on their audit?
3. Why do the largest CPA firms develop their own GAS? Do you think this was efficient?
4. What might be some of the obstacles in using GAS? How about training audit personnel?
5. How much of an improvement over systems utilities and high- level programming and database languages do you think GAS really is?
6. Find a specialized audit software package and list those functions included in the package that are not available in a generalized audit software package.
7. Select a generalized audit software package and try to find information that describes the advantages and limitations of the package.
8. After determining that computer controls are valid, Hastings is reviewing the sales system for Rosco Corporation in order to determine how a computerized audit program may be used to assist in performing tests of Rosco's sales records.

   Rosco sells crude oil from one central location. All orders are received by mail and indicate the pre-assigned customer identification number, desired quantity, proposed delivery date, method of payment and shipping terms. Since price fluctuates daily, orders do not indicate a price. Price sheets are printed daily and details are stored in a permanent disk file. The details of orders are also maintained in a permanent disk file.

   Each morning the shipping clerk receives a computer printout which indicates details of customers' orders to be shipped that day. After the orders have been shipped, the shipping details are inputted in the computer which simultaneously updates the sales journal, perpetual inventory records, accounts receivable, and sales accounts.

   The details of all transactions, as well as daily updates, are maintained on disks which are available for use by Hastings in the performance of the audit.

   Required:
   a. How may a computerized audit program be used by Hastings to perform substantive tests of Rosco's sales records in their machine readable form? *Do not discuss accounts receivable and inventory.*

b. After having performed these tests with the assistance of the computer, what other auditing procedures should Hastings perform in order to complete the examination of Rosco's sales records?

(AICPA adapted)

9. *Multiple Choice Questions from Professional Examinations*

(1) An auditor would be least likely to use a generalized computer audit program for which of the following tasks?

  (i) Selecting and printing accounts receivable confirmations.

  (ii) Listing accounts receivable confirmation exceptions for examination.

  (iii) Comparing accounts receivable subsidiary files to the general ledger.

  (iv) Investigating exceptions to accounts receivable confirmations.

(2) The primary purpose of a generalized computer audit program is to allow the auditor to

  (i) Use the client's employees to perform routine audit checks of the electronic data-processing records that otherwise would be done by the auditor's staff accountants.

  (ii) Test the logic of computer programs used in the client's electronic data-processing systems.

  (iii) Select larger samples from the client's electronic data-processing records than would otherwise be selected without the generalized program.

  (iv) Independently process client electronic data-processing records.

(3) An auditor can use generalized computer audit program to verify the accuracy of

  (i) Data-processing controls.

  (ii) Accounting estimates.

  (iii) Totals and subtotals.

  (iv) Account classification.

(4) The purpose of using generalized computer programs is to test and analyze a client's computer

  (i) Systems.

  (ii) Equipment.

  (iii) Records.

  (iv) Processing logic.

(5) A primary advantage of using generalized audit packages in the audit of an advanced EDP system is that it enables the auditor to

       (i) Substantiate the accuracy of the computer.

      (ii) Utilize the speed and accuracy of the computer.

    (iii) Verify the performance of machine operations that leave visible evidence of occurrence.

    (iv) Gather and store large quantities of supportive evidential matter in machine-readable form.

(6) Which of the following is an advantage of generalized computer audit packages?

       (i) They are all written in one identical computer language.

      (ii) They can be used for audits of clients that use differing EDP equipment and file formats.

    (iii) They have reduced the need for the auditor to study input controls for EDP-related procedures.

    (iv) Their use can be substituted for a relatively large part of the required compliance testing.

(7) Which of the following is true of generalized audit software packages?

       (i) They can be used only in auditing on-line computer systems.

      (ii) They can be used on any computer without modification.

    (iii) They each have their own characteristics which the auditor must carefully consider before using in a given audit situation.

    (iv) They enable the auditor to perform all manual compliance test procedures less expensively.

(8) The most important function of generalized audit software is the capability to

       (i) Access information stored on computer files.

      (ii) Select a sample of items for testing.

    (iii) Evaluate sample test results.

    (iv) Test the accuracy of the client's calculations.

(AICPA adapted)

Notes

1. American Institute of Certified Public Accountants, *Computer Assisted Audit Techniques.* New York: AICPA, 1979, p. 12.

2. Will, H. J., "Computer Based Auditing—Part 2," *Canadian Chartered Accountant*, March 1971, pp. 32–34. The author analyzed 11 software packages developed by CPA firms and 4 by vendors.

3. Adams, D. L., and Mullarkey, J. F., "A Survey of Audit Software," *The Journal of Accountancy*, September 1972, pp. 39–66. The authors analyzed 10 software packages developed by CPA firms and 6 by vendors.

4. Perry, William E., *Auditing News*, March 1977, pp. 1–10. The author evaluated 5 software packages developed by CPA firms and 10 by vendors.

5. Vasarhelyi, Miklos A., and Lin, W. Thomas, *TREAT: Terminal Related Educational Audit Tool.* New York: Touche Ross Foundation, 1979.

6. Vasarhelyi, Miklos A., and Lin, W. Thomas, "EDP Auditing Instruction Using an Interactive Generalized Audit Software," *Journal of Accounting Education*, Fall 1985, pp. 79–89.

7. For a generic introduction to microcomputer-based database software, see Vasarhelyi, M. A., and Loebbecke, J., *Microcomputer Applications to Business Problems*, Homewood, Illinois: R. D. Irwin, 1986.

8. The dBASE III system is a product of Ashton-Tate. For a detailed description of dBASE III and its uses, see *dBASE III User Manual.* Culver City, Calif.: Ashton-Tate, 1984. See, also, Grudnitski, Gary, "Generalized Audit Software Capabilities for Microcomputers." In J. Sardinas (Ed.), *Proceedings of 1984 EDP Audit Symposium*, University of Massachusetts at Amherst, 1984. Grudnitski discussed potential use of dBASE II as a way to implement the use of GAS. dBASE II is the predecessor of dBASE III. One can easily change dBASE II programs and files into dBASE III programs and files.

9. Wasserman, J., "Selecting a Computer Audit Package," *The Journal of Accountancy*, April 1974, p. 34.

10. Adams and Mullarkey, pp. 48–49.

11. Wasserman, p. 32.

Additional References

Henitz, Michael J., "What Internal Auditors Should Know About Selecting Audit Software," *Bank Administration*, December 1981, pp. 27–35.

How to Acquire and Use Generalized Audit Software. Altamonte Springs, Fla.: Institute of Internal Auditors, 1979.

Perry, William E., "Software Analysis for Internal Auditing," *Advanced Technology Newsletter*, Institute of Internal Auditors, 1981, pp. 12–16.

Perry, William E., and Donald L. Adams, "Use of Computer Audit Practice," *EDPACS*, Vol. VI, No. 5, November 1978, pp. 1–18.

Pleier, Joseph R., "Computer-Assisted Auditing," *The EDP Auditor*, Vol. 2, 1984, pp. 13–20.

Appendix 7.A GAS SYSTEMS DEVELOPED BY ACCOUNTING FIRMS

Most of the Big-Eight accounting firms have developed their own audit software. We selected eight of the systems and present a brief description of each in the sections. These descriptions were taken from the firm's own publications or articles about the systems that appeared in other publications.

A.1 AUDEX

AUDEX, an acronym for Audit Extract, was developed by Arthur Andersen. Its basic functions are: to extract data from a variety of computer files and to process that data into formats best suited to the needs of each audit. Specifically, AUDEX is a library of computer routines that can be linked together to perform the desired audit procedures. The functional capabilities of AUDEX include: select, extract, sort, merge, match, accumulate, summarize, sample, format, calculate, sequence check, and print.[1]

A.2 AUDITAPE

AUDITAPE was the first GAS available to the accounting profession. It was developed by Deloitte, Haskins & Sells in 1965. AUDITAPE is a system for extracting significant data from the computer and manipulating it to satisfy a particular job at hand. It was designed for use by independent auditors, to provide ready access to detail they must test, review, and analyze, and it is useful to internal auditors for the same purposes. It has also proven to have a variety of uses for providing management information, particularly where it is needed on a timely but nonrecurring basis.[2]

A.3 AUDIPAK

AUDIPAK was developed by Coopers & Lybrand. It is a "package" of COBOL programs, SCAN and RELATE, designed to operate on any computer having a COBOL compiler. The input to AUDIPAK's SCAN is a data file maintained on any media. The RELATE program will accept two data files. The output from AUDIPAK will be audit reports in a variety of formats, and a file on any media. AUDIPAK can: (a) Multiply the amounts in two data fields within a record; (b) Accumulate totals of items and amounts, or extended values of records processed and of any records selected; (c) Accumulate subtotals; (d) Calculate the mean of the population and of the samples selected; (e) Match data in records found on different files and print the results; (f) "By-pass" specific records; (g) Select a sample of records or subtotals—the selection may be systematic, or both; (h) "Age" input records or subtotals into four categories.[3]

A.4 AUDITRONIC

AUDITRONIC was developed by Ernst & Whinney. It is a system that allows the auditor to perform tests on EDP files by modifying existing programs to perform audit tests. It was designed to be used by an auditor without an extensive EDP background. . . . The programs on the disk pack are task-oriented. This means that they will, for example, calculate, sort, merge, summarize, print, and select.[4]

A.5 AYAMS

AYAMS, the AY Audit/Management System, was developed by Arthur Young. It is an information retrieval system with extended analytical testing and reporting capabilities. The system consists of a set of computer programs that can be used with virtually complete independence of any of the client's programs. Essentially all that is needed are compatible computer hardware and the client data files from which inquiries are to be made.[5]

A.6 CFA

The Computer File Analyzer (CFA) was developed by Price Waterhouse. It is designed for use by non-EDP personnel to provide them with an independent means of creating computer programs to perform a wide range of information retrieval and report-generating functions. The system provides the user with an easy-to-learn, English-like, coding language allowing the user to create and implement computer programs . . . to perform record selection, computations, and report generation.[6]

A.7 STRATA

STRATA, or System by Touche Ross for Audit Technical Assistance, is a system that can access information from existing files, and then perform a wide range of data processing functions on the accessed data. These functions include sorts, summarization, updates, calculations, file generation, and report printing. STRATA is designed for use by non-programmers who have a general understanding of automated data processing.[7]

A.8 SYSTEM 2190

System 2190 was developed by Peat Marwick Mitchell. It is an auditing language for audit functions performed on client magnetic tape files. The auditor flowcharts and programs in System 2190 language and the program is edited, compiled and executed in one of four original data centers.[8]

A.9 COMMENTS

Most of these software systems are mainframe computer and minicomputer applications. The programming languages are COBOL and Basic Assembly Language. Most of these systems are designed for use by auditors in batch processing. However, they also run on time-shared facilities and can handle some databases. The required training time for auditors is generally less than a week, usually averaging 3-5 days.

Notes

1. Fortson, M.H., and Delves, E. L., "AUDEX: Computer Audit Extract System," *The Arthur Andersen Chronicle*, December 1969, pp. 16–18.

2. Stringer, K. M., and Rowe, W. E., "AUDITAPE: A New Tool for Auditor and Manager," *The Federal Accountant*, June 1968, pp. 64–68.

3. Coopers & Lybrand, *AUDITPAK–A Preview*, 1969.

4. Ernst & Ernst, *Staff Accountants Reading and Case Studies Manual*, 1975.

5. Moore, M. R., and Yocum, R. H., "The AY Audit/Management System: An Information Tool for Auditors and Managers," *Computer Auditing in the Seventies*, Arthur Young, 1970, p. 29.

6. Price Waterhouse & Co., *Systems Manual*, 1975.

7. Touche Ross & Co., *IBM OS STRATA Reference Manual*, July 1978.

8. Harlan, Jr., S. D., and Donahue, T. J., "A Generalized Computer Audit System: SYSTEM 2190," *World*, Peat Marwick Mitchell, Fall 1970, p. 3.

Appendix 7.B USING dBASE III AS GAS

In this appendix we present four examples of audit applications using dBASE III as GAS: data examination, data manipulation, sample selection, and data summary and analysis.

B.1 DATA EXAMINATION

One audit task is to examine the client's data for quality. For example, the auditor can list all accounts receivable having a balance in excess of the credit limit by using the accounts receivable file ACCTREC shown in Figure 7.B.1. The auditor can write dBASE III Program 7.B.1 to achieve the audit. The auditor then uses the following command to execute the program and print the output shown in Figure 7.B.2.

.DO OVERLIMI.CMD

Figure 7.B.1   Data Structure of Accounts Receivable File.

```
STRUCTURE FOR FILE: ACCTREC.DBF
NUMBER OF RECORDS: 00020
DATE OF LAST UPDATE: 12/31/86
PRIMARY USE DATABASE
FLD     NAME        TYPE   WIDTH  DEC
001     ACCTNO      C      005
002     CUSTOMER    C      025
003     ADDRESS     C      025
004     CITYSTATE   C      020
005     ZIP         C      005
006     RATING      C      001
007     CRLIMIT     N      006
008     AGE_0_30    N      009    002
009     AGE_31_60   N      009    002
010     AGE_61_90   N      009    002
011     AGE_91      N      009    002
012     BALANCE     N      009    002
013     AGENT       C      002
** TOTAL **                00134
```

Program 7.B.1

```
MODIFY COMMAND OVERLIMI.CMD
USE ACCTREC
SET PRINT ON
?"                        BALANCES IN EXCESS OF CREDIT LIMIT"
?
?
?"ACCT  #          CUSTOMER NAME      LIMIT          BALANCE"
?"_____          _____      ____          _____"
?
DO WHILE .NOT. EOF
IF BALANCE > CRLIMIT
?
DISPLAY OFF ACCTNO,"        ", CUSTOMER, CRLIMIT,"        ",BALANCE
ENDIF
SKIP
ENDDO
SET PRINT OFF
```

Figure 7.B.2   Balances in Excess of Credit Limit

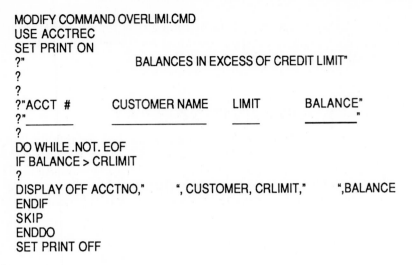

ACCT #	CUSTOMER NAME	LIMIT	BALANCE
00002	May Wang	$5000	$ 5300.00
00004	Vivian Chu	1000	1545.00
00007	Chain Company	8000	9700.00
00010	Ball Company	1000	2500.00
00012	Barry & Co.	5000	5500.00
00013	Randon Company	2000	2400.00
00014	Kleen Enterprises	0	2000.00
00015	Quality Co.	1000	1600.00
00016	Double Corporation	8000	10650.00
00018	Hank's Company	0	500.00
00019	Sparkle Corp.	2000	3300.00

B.2 DATA MANIPULATION

Our next audit task is to test the client's calculations. For example, the auditor can use the inventory file name INVENTOR shown in Figure 7.B.3 and write dBASE III Program 7.B.2 to extend inventory cost and quantities. The auditor then uses the following command to execute the program and print the output shown in Figure 7.B.4.

```
.DO INVEXTNS.CMD
```

Figure 7.B.3   Data Structure of Inventory File

```
STRUCTURE FOR FILE: INVENTOR.DBF
NUMBER OF RECORDS: 00020
DATE OF LAST UPDATE: 12/31/86
PRIMARY USE DATABASE
FLD      NAME          TYPE   WIDTH  DEC
001      TICKETNO      C      006
002      TEAMNO        C      003
003      PARTNUM       C      005
004      DESCRIPT      C      025
005      ENDINV        N      008    002
006      STDCOST       N      005    002
** TOTAL **                  00052
```

Program 7.B.2

```
MODIFY COMMAND INVEXTNS.CMD
USE INVENTOR
SET PRINT ON
?
?"          INVENTORY EXTENSIONS"
?
?"PART #          DESCRIPTION    QTY_YREND      STD COST        VALUE"
?"_____          _____    _____      _____        _____"
?
STORE 0 TO SUM
DO WHILE .NOT. EOF
STORE ENDINV*STDCOST TO VALUE
STORE VALUE + SUM TO SUM
? PARTNUM, DESCRIPT, ENDINV,"      $", STDCOST,:      $", VALUE
?
SKIP
ENDDO
?
?"TOTAL INVENTORY VALUE: $", SUM
SET PRINT OFF
```

Figure 7.B.4   Inventory Extensions

PART #	DESCRIPTION	QTY_YREND	STD COST	VALUE
10012	Product Y	1,800	$0.40	$ 720.00
10009	Product K	0	0.30	0.00
10015	Product O	8,500	0.25	2,125.00
10001	Product A	1,000	1.20	1,200.00
10011	Product T	300	0.50	150.00
10005	Product H	1,000	0.30	300.00
10019	Product Z	1,300	0.50	650.00
10013	Product R	500	0.30	150.00
10014	Product L	0	0.45	0.00
10010	Product G	13,000	0.10	1,300.00
10008	Product D	0	0.25	0.00
10003	Product B	200	0.50	100.00
10023	Product U	21,000	0.30	6,300.00
10017	Product E	0	0.15	0.00
10018	Product Q	700	0.30	210.00
10021	Product I	4,900	0.80	3,920.00
10020	Product X	0	0.60	0.00
10006	Product C	300	1.00	300.00
10008	Product D	700	0.25	175.00
10022	Product P	9,000	0.10	900.00

TOTAL INVENTORY VALUE: $ 18,500.00

B.3 SAMPLE SELECTION

A third audit task is to select samples for further testing. For example, the auditor can write dBASE III Program 7.B.3 to select inventory items that have an extended value of more than $1000 for observation. The auditor then uses the following command to execute the program and print the output shown in Figure 7.B.5.

.DO HIGHINV.CMD

Program 7.B.3

```
MODIFY COMMAND HIGHINV.CMD
USE INVENTOR
SET PRINT ON
?
?"                    INVENTORY OVER $1,000"
?
?"PART #        DESCRIPTION    QTY    STDCOST        AMOUNT"
?"_____        _____    ___    _____        _____"
?
```

(continued on next page)

Program 7.B.3 (continued)

```
DO WHILE .NOT. EOF
STORE ENDINV*STDCOST TO AMOUNT
IF AMOUNT > 1000
?
? PARTNUM, DESCRIPT, ENDINV," $", STDCOST," $", AMOUNT
ENDIF
SKIP
ENDDO
SET PRINT OFF
```

Figure 7.B.5   Inventory Value of More Than $1,000

PART #	DESCRIPTION	QTY_YREND	STDCOST	VALUE
10015	Product O	8,500	0.25	2,125.00
10001	Product A	1,000	1.20	1,200.00
10010	Product G	13,000	0.10	1,300.00
10023	Product U	21,000	0.30	6,300.00
10021	Product I	4,900	0.80	3,920.00

B.4 DATA SUMMARY AND ANALYSIS

Our fourth audit task is to summarize and analyze data. For example, the auditor can write dBASE III Program 7.B.4 to summarize the aging of accounts receivable by agents. The auditor then uses the following command to execute the program and print the output as shown in Figure 7.B.6.

.DO AGENT. CMD

Program 7.B.4

```
MODIFY COMMAND AGENT.CMD
USE ACCTREC
SET PRINT ON
INDEX ON AGENT TO ACCTRECA
USE ACCTREC INDEX ACCTRECA
?
?"AGING SUMMARY OF ACCTS.RECVBLE.BY COLLECTION AGENTS"
?
?"AGENT    0 - 30      31 - 60      61 - 90      OVER 90      BALANCE"
?"_____    _____      _____      _____      _____      _____"
?
```

(continued on next page)

Program 7.B.4   (continued)

```
DO WHILE .NOT. EOF
STORE AGENT TO XAGENT
STORE 0 TO SUM1
STORE 0 TO SUM2
STORE 0 TO SUM3
STORE 0 TO SUM4
STORE 0 TO SUM5
DO WHILE .NOT. EOF .AND. AGENT = XAGENT
STORE (AGE_0_30 + SUM1) TO SUM1
STORE (AGE_31_60 + SUM2) TO SUM2
STORE (AGE_61_90 + SUM3) TO SUM3
STORE (AGE_91 + SUM4) TO SUM4
STORE (BALANCE + SUM5) TO SUM5
SKIP
ENDDO
DISPLAY OFF XAGENT, SUM1, SUM2, SUM3, SUM4, SUM5
?
ENDDO
SET PRINT OFF
```

Figure 7.B.6   Aging Summary of Accounts Receivable by Agents

AGENT	0–30	31–60	61–90	91–XX	BALANCE
01	$2,400.00	$860.00	$0.00	$100.00	$3,360.00
02	9,700.00	8,400.00	8,800.00	100.00	22,600.00
03	3,500.00	2,200.00	0.00	0.00	5,700.00
0 4	8,800.00	1,100.00	4,000.00	800.00	12,700.00
05	8,900.00	10,200.00	2,700.00	2,545.00	22,995.00

B.5 OTHER TASKS

The auditor can also use dBASE III to perform other tasks, such as comparing data in order to ascertain consistency between items or to verify that certain conditions have been met. For example, the quantities in the perpetual inventory records may be compared with those from inventory test counts. Finally, dBASE III can be used to print accounts receivable confirmation request forms and envelopes.

Chapter 8

General Controls

8.1 INTRODUCTION

The typical EDP facility performs three general functions: operations, systems development, and applications. The internal controls that govern all EDP-center operations and systems development are called *general controls.* The controls related to specific computer applications are called *application controls.*

In this chapter we present and discuss general controls in terms of four control areas: organization and operations controls, hardware and software controls, access controls, and data and procedural controls.[1] Table 8.1 shows these four control areas and types of control that are applicable to each area. In Chapters 9, 10, and 11, we discuss computer application controls, auditing EDP-center and application systems, and controls for and auditing systems development, respectively.

LEARNING OBJECTIVES

By the time you complete this chapter, you should be able to:

1. Identify and describe the four major areas of EDP-center controls.
2. Describe organization and operations controls.
3. Describe hardware and software controls.
4. Describe access controls.
5. Describe data and procedural controls.

8.2 ORGANIZATION AND OPERATIONS CONTROLS

Basic to many control procedures are effective organization and operations controls for the EDP center (or department). The type of organization and

Table 8.1   EDP-Center Control Structure

Control Area	Control Type
Organization and operations	Segregation of EDP-department and users functions
	Authorization of transactions
	Segregation of functions within the EDP department
	Personnel
	Planning, budget, and user billing systems
Hardware and software	Vendor provided recording, investigation, and recovery from hardware errors
	Equipment maintenance
	Formal procedures for changes in systems and application software
Access	Limitations on physical access to computer operations area and hardware
	Program documentation
	Data files and programs
	On-line facilities
Data and procedures	Control group
	Files and database
	Standard procedures
	Physical security
	Insurance
	Internal audit

the scope of controls can vary with the size and nature of the EDP facility, but the necessity for and objectives of such controls are the same for all EDP facilities.

SEGREGATION OF EDP-DEPARTMENT USER FUNCTIONS

To the extent possible, the same segregation of functions provided in nonEDP systems should be maintained in computerized systems. Thus the EDP department should have no responsibility for initiation and authorization of transactions, initial recording of transactions, custody of assets other than computer equipment and supplies, changes to master files and transaction files, and error corrections (unless the errors originate within the EDP department).

Since the EDP department is heavily involved in the processing of transactions, it should not initiate or authorize transactions except for the purchase of EDP supplies and services.[2] The EDP department often maintains accounting records related to non-EDP assets such as cash, securities, and notes receivable. Consequently, it should not have direct physical control of such assets. Employees who initiate or process transactions, especially master file changes, can perpetuate errors or irregularities unless there is third-party control or review. Thus if EDP-department personnel are assigned to and are responsible for processing transactions within user departments, other personnel should independently check this work, or duties should be rotated so that others periodically perform these duties.

In certain situations, it may not be practical to separate the EDP department completely from transaction initiation, transaction authorization, and custody of assets. For example, a computerized inventory control system may automatically initiate purchase orders based on predetermined inventory reorder points, requiring the use of compensating controls outside the EDP department (such as periodic review by the purchasing department).

The EDP department should report to a senior manager who is independent of EDP-user departments. Organizational independence of the EDP department from user departments creates a framework in which user controls may be applied independently of data processing controls. At the same time it allows the EDP department to maintain objectivity and independence from user departments. An EDP steering committee should be organized to establish objectives, determine priorities, set policy, and approve controls for the organization's EDP functions. The Committee members should represent different functions or areas of the organization and be drawn from middle or top management.[3]

AUTHORIZATION OF TRANSACTIONS

Management should be sure that all transactions processed by the EDP system are authorized. This assurance requires that managerial responsibility be clearly assigned both for the initiation and execution of transactions and for the review of the computer processing of transactions to ensure that unauthorized activity is detected.

The organization should maintain a current list of all individuals authorized to submit transactions to the computer system, identifying the type and amount of transactions that each individual is authorized to approve. All transactions not produced by the EDP system, including master file changes, should be reviewed and approved by the appropriate authority before they are submitted for computer processing. A list of all master file changes, indicating both the *before* and *after* status of each change, should be returned for review either to the initiator or to an independent reviewer. To ensure that only authorized data is processed, input documents should bear evidence of authorization and should be reviewed by the person responsible for evidence control. However, programmed controls can be considered an appropriate form of review.

The detection of unauthorized transactions requires the review of transaction activity logs or exception reports by personnel not directly involved in the computer processing activity, such as the internal auditor. Again, programmed controls may be used to test the validity of the transactions. In many situations, a comparison of output with properly authorized input may prove to be an effective control.

SEGREGATION OF FUNCTIONS WITHIN THE EDP DEPARTMENT

Segregation of duties is fundamental to internal control. Many irregularities related to data and programs go undetected (at least for awhile) because one employee's work is never checked by another. The two major purposes of segregating functions within an EDP department are (1) to ensure that staff personnel do not perform incompatible duties; and (2) to ensure that the duties of one person provide a check over those performed by another.

Thus, within an EDP department, the following functions should be segregated: (1) systems and programming; (2) computer operations; (3) input/output control and scheduling; and (4) library maintenance. The structures of small, medium, and large EDP organizations are shown in Figures 8.1, 8.2, and 8.3, respectively. Systems design and programming should be separated from computer operations, so that no one person will have the opportunity to both write or revise a program and run the program with live data. The systems analysts and programmers know the details of program logic, record layouts, and file structures; they should not also have access to or be allowed to make changes in the live data being processed. Similarly, computer operators, who usually have access to live data, should not have access to or an intimate knowledge of detailed program documentation, or be allowed to modify programs.

Operators or data entry personnel should not be allowed to correct erroneous source input data. Programmers should not be allowed to access live computer programs or data files (programs or data used for production runs). If such access is considered necessary for technical reasons, it should

Figure 8.1   Organization of a Small EDP Department

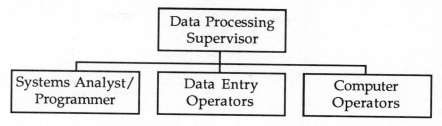

Figure 8.2   Organization of a Medium-Sized EDP Department

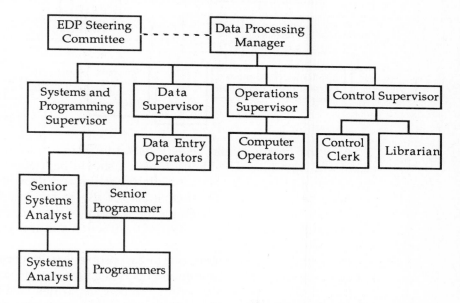

be supervised. Tests of program revisions should be run by computer operators or, remotely, by programmers using software for program testing and specially developed test data.

Systems analysts, programmers, and computer operators should not have access to input/output controls, such as batch control totals or master file field totals. A control group should be established as an independent unit within the EDP department. Control functions would be performed independently of EDP operations. The control group would test the efficiency and effectiveness of all aspects of the system, receive data from user departments, check transactions for proper authorization, verify or establish user batch controls, schedule work to be processed, reconcile input and output, and distribute output to authorized personnel.

Figure 8.3   Organization of a Large EDP Department

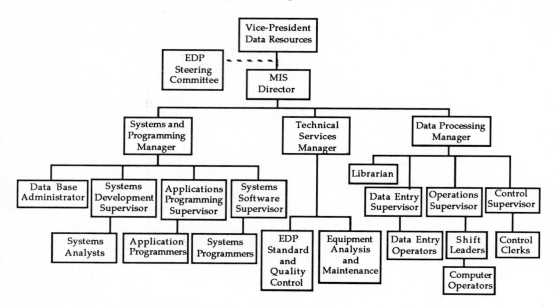

A *central library* should be established to maintain security over programs and data files. The library function should be independent of both operations and programming. All the programs and data files should be available only to authorized personnel for use in processing scheduled work. The library must provide for the security of the programs and data files, including security from physical destruction and loss of the file data stored on various media.

In small EDP departments, one or two people usually perform a combination of systems, programming, and operating functions. In such situations, the lack of division of duties within the EDP department should normally be compensated for by increased management supervision of EDP activities; increased review and control of all computer input documents and output reports by user departments, use of passwords to protect menus, programs, and data files; after-processing managerial approval; and review of transaction logs by the EDP manager and users.

PERSONNEL CONTROLS

The human element dominates the newspaper stories about computer crime. (See Chapter 6.) One of the most sensitive and important resources in an organization is EDP personnel. Therefore personnel controls are crucial. They include (1) job descriptions; (2) selection and training; (3) supervision and evaluation; and (4) rotation, vacation, and bonding.

Job descriptions identify responsibilities and duties of a position, required qualifications, and the relationship of the position to other positions in the organization. Because separation of duties is essential to adequate control, job descriptions should clearly reflect a division of responsibilities among positions. For example, the job descriptions for systems analysts and programmers should state specifically that they are expected to program and make changes in existing programs. Those of operators and data entry personnel, however, would not and might even include a prohibition of these duties. The job descriptions, policies and procedures manuals, and EDP organization chart should be kept up to date.

The organization should have formal policies and procedures and specific criteria for the selection of qualified personnel. The criteria may include integrity, trustworthiness, experience, and technical skill and be subject to a reference check, which is a relatively inexpensive personnel control. Prospective employees for particularly responsible and sensitive positions should be subject to security investigation. After employment, such employees should be subject to periodic security investigations. On-the-job training and continued education are very important in the EDP field owing to the rapid evolution in EDP technology. Refresher seminars on confidentiality, security, and controls should be held periodically. Employees should be cross-trained to provide backup capabilities for all important jobs.

To ensure that personnel adhere to standard operating procedures and to minimize the risk of errors or irregularities (particularly where employees have been cross-trained) adequate supervision and review of EDP operations is essential. Employee job performance should be formally and periodically evaluated in relation to job descriptions to ensure that personnel continue to perform competently and reliably. In order to avoid accusations of unfairness, management must fully inform the employee about the criteria used for evaluation.

There should be periods during which the normal duties of data processing personnel, especially programmers and computer terminal operators, are reassigned. Duties can be rotated by rotating either personnel or the scheduled run times of applications among shifts. Duty rotation can be combined with vacations, during which time one person's duties are performed by another. Finally, all key EDP employees should be bonded.

PLANNING, BUDGET, AND USER BILLING SYSTEMS

Data processing management is responsible for planning for adequate provision of EDP facilities, equipment, software, and personnel. The EDP department's long-range, strategic planning should be tied to the organization's strategic plan. The EDP department's annual budget should be an integral part of the organization's budget preparation and control process.

A formal reporting method must be used to identify and evaluate deviations from planned application processing. This control contributes to the reasonable assurance that the computer is not being used for unauthorized processing. Users should be charged for service provided on a basis that includes only those actual costs over which the user has an influence. That is, typical responsibility accounting techniques should be applied to user billing. Software packages for charge-out systems are available and are called job-accounting packages. The following criteria should be used to select the best job-accounting package: accountability for total costs, equitability of charges, simplicity of charging algorithm, and usefulness of reports.

8.3 HARDWARE AND SOFTWARE CONTROLS

Modern computer hardware and software systems are equipped with a variety of built-in controls. The objectives of these controls are to:

1. Detect errors and malfunctions of the equipment.
2. Prevent unauthorized access to and use of data, programs, and equipment.
3. Support effective utilization of the computer.

HARDWARE CONTROLS

Hardware controls are built into computer equipment by the manufacturer to detect equipment failure. Particular attention should be paid to these control capabilities during installation and testing of the equipment and then utilized continually during operations. Failure to utilize available hardware controls could result in significant processing errors, and hardware faults should be recorded and investigated immediately. Some of the types of controls that computer manufacturers build into their equipment are:

1. *Boundary protection.* Protection is provided against unauthorized entry (read or write) to a tape, disk, or other storage device.
2. *Dual read.* Data are read twice during the input phase, and the two readings are compared.

3. *Dual circuitry.* Double wiring of key hardware elements and peripheral equipment ensures no malfunctioning. In addition, some manufacturers sell fail-safe systems that have duplex or triplex elements of key hardware.

4. *Echo check.* Data received by an output device is transmitted back to the source unit for comparison with the original data.

5. *Interlock.* This hardware device prevents more than one peripheral unit from communicating with the CPU at the same time.

6. *File protection ring.* A removable plastic or metal ring prevents improper use of a magnetic tape file.

7. *Parity check.* A bit (binary digit) of information is added to the data being processed in order to help ensure that no bits are lost in data transfers between input–process–output functions.

8. *Reverse multiplication.* The roles of the original multiplicand and multiplier are reversed, and the new product is compared with the original product.

9. *Validity check.* The bit pattern is checked to determine that the combination of the "on" and "off" bits is valid within the character set of the computer.

10. *Firmware.* A sequence of instructions (software) is substituted for hardware circuits and cannot be altered by applications programmers.

11. *Graceful degradation.* When certain hardware components malfunction, others can be programmed to continue processing, but on a less efficient basis.

12. *Overflow check.* Data are checked and a signal is activated when data are lost through arithmetic operations that exceed the planned capacity of receiving fields or registers.

13. *Uninterruptible power systems.* Battery and generator systems are provided for temporary backup in the event of power failure until normal electricity is restored.

In case of hardware failure or errors, the company should properly record, investigate, and take corrective actions to recover from hardware failure or errors.

As with other types of equipment, there are two types of maintenance for computer hardware: preventive and remedial. Remedial (or repair) maintenance is performed when the computer develops unexpected problems, such as an electronic component suddenly going bad. Preventive maintenance is designed to prevent problems. The maintenance engineer and computer operators should prepare regular maintenance reports. Operations logs should be established to account for normal processing time, downtime for preventive and remedial maintenance, abnormal job terminations, and job reruns. As a basic control, the operations manager should review and analyze the maintenance reports and operations logs periodically to identify causes of malfunctions and take corrective action as necessary.

SOFTWARE CONTROLS

The two major categories of software are systems software and application software. Systems software is a program or system of programs that can interconnect and control input, output, processing, data, and application programs. The most important systems software is the operating system, which is designed to schedule jobs, translate symbolic programs into machine code, and use the computer effectively. A control program called *supervisor* is an operating system program that schedules jobs and input/output, monitors programs, and issues appropriate error messages. Other types of systems software include system utilities, security software, program library systems, and file maintenance systems. Common system utilities are copy programs and sorts. Program library systems usually control access to, changes in, and conversion from source to object code for application programs. File maintenance systems are similar to program library systems but control tape and disk files rather than application programs. Application software is programs written specifically for individual applications, such as payroll, accounts receivable, and accounts payable.

Among the controls generally incorporated in operating systems are read or write check, record length check, label checking routines, and access control. The read or write check automatically halts a program when reading or writing is inhibited, such as when a printer runs out of paper. The record length check will screen input for proper record lengths so that all incoming data will be properly accepted. Label checking routines check internal tape or disk labels to ensure that the correct file has been mounted. Access control provides protection such as passwords to prevent unauthorized access to the program and/or data files.

Vendors often distribute patches for and updated versions of operating systems. In addition, systems analysts and programmers work on configurations and parameters to adapt the operating system to local requirements. A formal procedure should be established for requesting, authorizing, and approving all changes to systems programs. Systems documentation should indicate a chronological history of all changes made to operating system software. Included in this documentation should be the results of all testing of the system after each change.

Software for program maintenance, called program library software, is usually available from the manufacturer to maintain *source* (high-level language) code and *object* (compiled machine level) code programs on disk, with changes reported automatically. This software should be controlled and monitored by the independent control group. The security and control features of new releases or modifications of systems software and application software should be reviewed by EDP management before acceptance and installation, and all control features should be tested.

8.4 ACCESS CONTROLS

Access controls provide safeguards to ensure that EDP resources are properly utilized. In order to make unauthorized changes, an individual must have access to the data and programs. Thus the major objective of access controls is to allow only authorized personnel to have access to computer hardware, programs, program documentation, and data files. Many of the controls already discussed are related to access controls. For example, the segregation of user and EDP-department functions—and within the EDP department—augments access controls. The general guidelines for access controls are:

1. Access to the EDP department and computer hardware should be suitably restricted by the use of security guards, locks on entrances, electronic entry control procedures (such as magnetic cards) or similar methods. This type of control is called *physical access control.*
2. Within the EDP department, access to program documentation, data files, and programs should be controlled.
3. If on-line facilities are used, appropriate control procedures should be used to prevent or detect unauthorized access to terminals, programs, and data files.

PHYSICAL ACCESS

Access to computer operations area should be restricted to those personnel needed to operate equipment, supervise operations, deliver and pick up material in the area, and perform maintenance on the equipment. User personnel, programmers, systems analysts, and visitors should not be permitted in computer operations areas, except when authorized by the supervisor or manager of operations and appropriately escorted.

The physical layout and configuration of the computer system should prevent, to the greatest extent possible, unauthorized access to the system. Control of access can be accomplished effectively by enclosing the computer operations area with physical barriers, so that only those persons who need access in order to operate the computer system are permitted in the area. Locks, badges, alarms, keys, closed-circuit television monitors, or similar safeguards should be issued or installed. Additionally, physical access control procedures include:

1. Restricting access to terminals to authorized employees.
2. Recording the issuance and return of physical access devices, such as keys, magnetic coded cards, lock combinations, and identification badges.
3. Notifying the EDP manager and security personnel when an employee leaves his or her job.

All movements of personnel into and out of secured areas should be recorded by a security guard, if management is relying on physical control of the area. Logs should be maintained to identify the individual entering the area and the person who authorized access. The time and purpose of the activity, such as hardware maintenance, should also be recorded.

PROGRAM DOCUMENTATION

Program documentation is an extremely valuable asset that should be subjected to access control. With access to program documentation, a person may obtain the information necessary to change the programs, data file structures, programmed control criteria, and other elements of an application. To preclude misuse, it may be appropriate to keep documentation in a special library and maintain a log of its use.

Access to program documentation should be limited to those persons who require it in the performance of their duties. The computer operator's access to program documentation should be restricted to the basic outline needed to control operations, correct computer halts, and the like. Computer operators should not have access to the detailed logic diagrams or source programs, which could facilitate manipulation of the data being processed. The programmer should be allowed access to documentation for a particular program only when working on that particular application. Systems software support personnel should not have unsupervised access to any application program documentation. Access to systems software documentation should be restricted to authorized systems programmers.

DATA FILES AND PROGRAMS

Access to data files and programs should be limited to those individuals authorized to process or maintain particular systems. Access to data files should be restricted to the computer operator responsible for the scheduled application. Access to programs generally should be restricted to programmers authorized to make modifications. For example, access to systems software should be restricted to systems programmers, who usually have more sophisticated technical skills than application programmers. However, systems programmers should not be allowed to operate the computer to test or implement changes.

Storage and access to forms or documents such as blank checks, invoices, and purchase orders should be adequately controlled and restricted. These forms should be prenumbered and inventoried periodically. The destruction of these forms when incorrectly printed and the like, should also be adequately controlled and inventoried on destruction.

A librarian position should be established and given control over access to data files and programs. The librarian is responsible for (1) maintaining a library of all data files and programs; (2) ensuring that all data files and programs are properly labeled as to their contents; (3) checking out data files and programs to authorized personnel and storing the files and programs when they are returned; (4) maintaining a control log for the use of all data files and programs, which can be subsequently reviewed for unauthorized access; and (5) enforcement of the adequacy of retention procedures.

ON-LINE FACILITIES

If on-line facilities are used, several control procedures can be used to prevent and detect unauthorized access to data files and programs. The use of terminals should be restricted to selected types of transactions and certain terminal users. Thus certain terminal users can input only certain types of transactions while others can make only certain types of inquiries. An access control log can be used to record mode of entry, identification of terminal and user, data accessed, time of access, and identification of programs that opened and closed each file. This log should be reviewed by the management periodically.

A multilevel password scheme is most effective. It requires the user to input an identification code, an application system password, and the specific file access authorization code. All passwords should be stored in enciphered form, and passwords entered as input are enciphered before comparison to authorized passwords takes place. For sensitive files, passwords should be changed regularly. The access table of valid user and function codes that is stored in the computer's memory can be changed only by authorized personnel at certain times; changes must be documented, and the documentation should be physically controlled. Finally, an encryption scheme should be used to protect sensitive and confidential data files; that is, they should not be stored in a normal, clear data format.

The use of terminals at remote locations requires further control procedures, such as:

1. Location of terminals in supervised areas that are also secured by locks or by voice recognition or hand print analysis units.
2. Assurance of terminal security by key locks or badge readers.
3. Connection of terminals to the CPU during only certain periods of the day.
4. Automatic disabling of a terminal, sounding an alarm, or alerting security personnel after a specified number of unsuccessful attempts to gain access.

8.5 DATA AND PROCEDURAL CONTROLS

Data and procedural controls provide a framework for controlling daily operations and establishing safeguards against processing errors. Typical data and procedural controls include a control group, files and database controls, standard procedures, physical security, and the internal audit function.

CONTROL GROUP

A control group should be established as an independent unit within the EDP department. Control functions would be independent of EDP systems analysis, programming, and operations. The activities of the control group should include:

1. Receiving all input data to be processed.
2. Recording input data received in a control log.
3. Ensuring that each batch of input data is authorized, accurate, and complete.
4. Scrutinizing error listings.
5. Providing liaison with user(s) regarding errors and correction requests.
6. Supervising distribution of output.
7. Keeping track of work while it is in the EDP department for processing.

The control group logs input received, ensures that input is properly authorized, reviews input forms for accuracy and completeness, and reconciles input totals received to totals submitted by the user department computer. Operators process only input received from the control group. The control group subsequently verifies processing totals against input totals. The group also logs and checks computer-generated run-to-run totals and master file reconciliation and compares report totals with master file totals. Finally, the control group balances output totals and input totals. The group should use an error log to record processing errors and ensure that an error is forwarded to the proper source for correction and that the correction is entered into the system.

DATABASE AND FILE CONTROLS

Internal control in an EDP department involves the protection of files and the databases from unauthorized disclosure or accidental destruction.

Measures for Protecting Files. Operating procedures are needed to ensure that the correct files are mounted for processing, switches are correctly set, and output files are properly allocated. As mentioned previously, all computer files should be controlled by the library. Two devices available to prevent files from being inadvertently written over are the file protection ring and file labels.

A tape file protection ring is a plastic ring that, when inserted into a reel of magnetic tape, permits writing on the tape. When the ring is removed, the data on the tape are protected from accidental write-overs or erasure. Tape files should always be stored without the ring, forcing the operator to make a specific decision to write and preventing destruction of data through carelessness.

External and internal labels provide protection for reels of magnetic tape and disk packs. An external label attached to the outside of a magnetic tape reel or a magnetic disk pack indicates the name of the file, expiration date, and other pertinent information and can be read by the people handling the tape or disk. Internal labels are messages stored in machine-readable form inside the tape or disk. An internal header label appears at the beginning of the file and contains the file name, identification number, file creation date, and other data such as the tape reel number or volume number. The internal header label is read by the computer prior to processing and is checked against the program to ensure that the file is the correct one for the program. If not, the operating system alerts the computer operator through the computer console. An internal trailer label appears at the end of the file and contains end-of-file or end-of-volume code, record or block counts, and control totals. These record or block counts and control totals can be checked by the program to ensure that all data have been processed and that none has been lost.

If several user departments share a master file, control procedures should be provided to ensure that all these departments are aware of changes made to data used in common. When two or more files are simultaneously updated by on-line data entry, the control records maintained separately for each file should be balanced periodically.

Measures for Protecting the Database. A database is a collection of data used by several different applications. The control of data in the database (by a database administrator) should be separated from application program development and maintenance responsibilities. The database administrator should be responsible for the following:

1. defining and modifying the physical and logical database;
2. defining database documentation standards;
3. documenting database content and organization;
4. ensuring that controls are built into the database system to prevent or detect errors;
5. maintaining security by controlling access to database use;
6. designing and maintaining the data dictionary/directory;
7. controlling and reviewing the use of utility programs to amend records on the database;
8. approving and logging all changes to the database system library;
9. reviewing the operating system log and the database management system log; and
10. establishing backup and recovery procedures.

The database administrator should be the only person with both complete access to the database and the authority to change access levels for database users. However, the database administrator should not be allowed unsupervised access to the computer room and should not be allowed to operate the equipment. Since the database administrator knows the functions performed by all application programs, he or she should not be allowed to initiate transactions without user department approval.

Protection of the database system should include lock-out procedures to prevent the concurrent updating of an item of data by two programs. A utility program can be used to detect and report broken pointers and links between data elements, which would otherwise result in loss of data. Each user's subschema can be defined through password identification, which limits that user's ability to access the database to authorized functions. A log of all processing activity and periodic scans of database contents to accumulate individual records for agreement with a control record are also necessary.

STANDARD PROCEDURES

Computer operating procedures should ensure the prevention or detection of inaccurate, incomplete, or unauthorized recording of transactions. A written manual of standard procedures should be prepared and used for all computer operations and should provide for management's general or specific authorizations to process transactions. Operations should be reviewed periodically to ensure that these procedures are followed.

Efficient processing is possible only when all production is scheduled. All jobs should be authorized in advance by the operations supervisor or EDP-department manager, as should changes in the approved schedule. The reasons for changes in schedules and priorities should be documented. All variances from authorized schedules, as recorded in the console log and computer utilization reports, should be formally reviewed by the operations supervisor or the EDP-department manager.

Computer operating instructions (operator manuals) should clearly outline operational steps to be followed. The best instructions define the operator's duties from start to finish for each shift and for each job. The contents of the manuals should include (1) procedures for starting up and closing down the equipment; (2) instructions for initial data files and/or printer setup; (3) the designation of data files that should be left mounted on the drives and a requirement for the removal of file protection rings from magnetic tapes immediately upon dismounting an output file; (4) a description of actions required to respond to halts or error messages and restart procedures; (5) job-control specifications that may be required by the operating system; (6) disposition of input and output data and files; and (7) descriptions of prohibited activities.

PHYSICAL SECURITY

Physical security can ensure the separation of custody over computer equipment and data resources, prevent the accidental or intentional destruction of data, and provide for both the replacement of data that may be destroyed and the continuity of operations following a major hardware or software failure. The primary areas of concern for physical security are:

1. *Physical protection.* Computer hardware, programs, and files should be adequately protected against fire and other hazards.
2. *Backup files and programs.* Copies of all important files, systems software, application programs, and documentation should be stored off-premises.
3. *Contingency planning.* Detailed plans and recovery procedures for continuation of processing in the event of a major disaster should be prepared and a copy stored off-premises.

Physical Protection. Computer facilities should be environmentally controlled (temperature, humidity, lighting) and protected from disasters. For example, EDP facilities should not be located in hazardous or high-risk areas, such as an area subject to flooding. The computer center should be housed in a fire-resistant facility, and files should be stored in fireproof vaults or cabinets. Floors, walls, ceilings, and draperies should be made of noncombustible material. The fire protection system should be heat and smoke sensitive and emit a nonliquid fire extinguishing agent such as Halon.

Precautions should be taken against accidental water damage by providing, for example, a proper water drainage system under the floor of the computer room. The computer room should be air-conditioned and humidity-controlled, and air intakes and air-conditioning units should be protected from noxious substances. Uninterruptible power systems, or electrical backup devices, should be provided. Formal emergency procedures should be well-defined and tested, including hardware shutdown instructions.

Backup Files and Programs. Data files and programs are valuable assets, the destruction or loss of which would cause financial loss. Therefore their protection by means of backup copies and off-site storage is an important management responsibility. Backup copies of operating system programs, key master files and application programs, and documentation must be similarly stored off-site to enable timely reconstruction and recovery in the event that operational copies are destroyed. Off-site backup materials should be updated and tested periodically. The same level of security maintained at the main facility should be applied to off-site storage.

Backup for magnetic tape files is usually accomplished by using the grandfather-father-son concept of maintaining three generations of magnetic tape files, as illustrated in Figure 8.4. After updating today's transactions, today's updated master file is the son, yesterday's updated master file is the father, and the day-before-yesterday's updated master file is the grandfather. These three files are retained, along with today's and yesterday's transaction files. Furthermore, one generation would be stored off-site. If the son file were destroyed, it could be recreated by running the grandfather file with today's and yesterday's transaction files. When tomorrow's updating is completed, tomorrow's updated master file becomes the son, today's updated master file becomes the father, and yesterday's updated master file becomes the grandfather. At that time, the day-before-yesterday's updated master file (old grandfather) and yesterday's transaction file can be erased.

The contents of disk files should be duplicated (disk dump) on another machine-readable medium, such as a tape, or on another disk in case they are damaged or destroyed. If transactions are processed in batches, the duplicated tape serves as the father file in the event of destruction of data in

Figure 8.4   Three Generations of Magnetic Tape Files: (a) Grandfather (Day before Yesterday); (b) Father (Yesterday); (c) Son (Today)

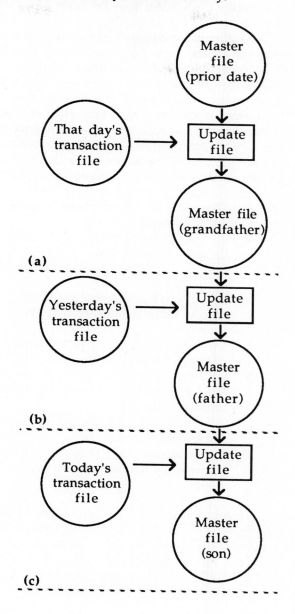

the updating process. If transactions are processed on-line, a log of all transactions may also be recorded on disk or tape which, together with the most recent copy of the tape file, could be used to re-create the current disk file.

For database management systems and sophisticated operating systems the backup procedures include (1) dual logging, which provides two transaction logs written simultaneously on two separate storage devices; and (2) before-image and after-image logs which provide "snapshots" of the database before and after each transaction.[4]

Contingency planning is important to ensure that an organization can respond rapidly to a disaster. A contingency plan should provide for continuing or starting up new operations in terms of hardware, software, communications, facilities, personnel, and electrical power. The major steps in implementing an effective contingency plan are:

1. Obtain top management concurrence with the need for contingency planning.
2. Assign appropriate key individuals to the analysis of various disaster possibilities.
3. Involve user departments in quantifying the impact of the loss of operations.
4. Perform risk assessment and disaster analysis functions that involve users, data processing management, and audit personnel.
5. Develop a contingency plan outline, including full consideration of implementation costs.
6. Obtain plan approval by senior management, even at the board level if necessary, to ensure that management backs the plan and its maintenance.
7. Assign implementation tasks to ensure that the plan will be implemented as designed.
8. Create an independent group to maintain the plan and test it periodically to ensure that users are prepared to implement the plan.[5]

An important aspect of contingency planning is to make formal arrangements for backup computer facilities at another location. These arrangements can be with other parts of the same organization or with a separate, but compatible, data center. In either case, to ensure that the backup facilities remain compatible, the arrangements should be tested periodically as part of contingency drills.[6]

INSURANCE

Despite precautions, disasters can occur, resulting in large economic loss (time and money). Insurance can insulate the firm against such losses. Major risks to be insured against include fire, flooding, severe weather, riots, theft, and sabotage. Insurance costs should be evaluated in terms of the risks involved and the potential consequences of those risks.

INTERNAL AUDIT

One of the most important EDP-center controls is the presence within the organization of an effective, well-trained internal audit group. Audit considerations cannot be considered independently of control in computer-based systems. This is supported by the following conclusion from a study conducted by the Institute of Internal Auditors, Inc.

> The changes in data processing have caused changes in the traditional role of the internal auditor. To understand this changing role, one must understand the changes occurring in internal control that are being brought about by increasing automation and new data processing technology. In addition, audit and control must be considered together, rather than separately, because they are completely interrelated. Internal controls in the data processing environment govern transaction processing, record keeping, reporting, and environmental security; internal auditing is the evaluation and verification of these controls and the records and reports produced by data processing are the objects of internal audit. Because of this interrelationship, one cannot consider internal audit without considering internal control.[7]

The following are examples of EDP-related activities performed by internal auditors:

1. Reviewing and evaluating proposed systems at critical stages of development, including feasibility study, system design, program design, testing, conversion, and implementation stages.
2. Reviewing EDP-department procedures to determine compliance with overall organizational policies and procedures.
3. Performing tests of computer programs and verification of transaction processing with computer-assisted techniques.

8.6 Summary

General controls relate to all parts of the EDP system. Weaknesses in these controls may seriously affect the effectiveness of the entire computerized information system. General controls include EDP-center controls and systems development controls. In this chapter we discussed the former, of which the major control areas are organization and operations, hardware and software, access, and data and procedures.

There are five types of controls in the organization and operations area: segregation of EDP-department and user functions, provision for general authorization of execution of transactions, segregation of functions within the EDP department, personnel controls, and planning, budget, and user billing systems.

Computer manufacturers and vendors usually supply a variety of built-in hardware and systems software controls. The EDP center should properly apply the available hardware controls and perform preventive maintenance on all hardware. The EDP manager should record the reasons and timing of hardware errors, as well as the corrective actions taken. The EDP personnel should review and test security and control features in systems and application software before using it. Adequate authorization and control should be exercised over changes to operating and other systems software.

Access controls provide safeguards to ensure that EDP resources are properly utilized. Access controls include limiting physical access to the computer operating area, program documentation, data files and programs, and computer hardware.

Data and procedural controls provide a framework for controlling daily operations and establishing safeguards against processing errors. These controls include an independent control group, file and database controls, standard procedures, physical security (physical protection of hardware, programs and files, backup files and programs, contingency planning, and insurance coverage), and the internal audit function.

Questions

1. Distinguish between general controls and application controls.
2. What are the major objectives of EDP-center controls?
3. What are the four categories of EDP-center general controls?

4. Describe some of the functions within an EDP center that can typically be segregated and some of the functions that can be given to non-EDP functions to improve the segregation of duties.
5. What kinds of control are required to ensure that all transactions processed by the EDP system are authorized?
6. Identify controls which would detect unauthorized transactions.
7. What personnel policies and procedures contribute to good internal control in EDP centers?
8. How do budgets and user billing systems contribute to good internal control?
9. What are the objectives of hardware and software controls?
10. Identify several commonly used hardware and software controls.
11. List some of the hardware controls that contribute to the reliability of the computer.
12. Describe each of the following access controls:
    a. Physical access
    b. Program documentation
    c. Data files
    d. Programs
13. What functions does a data processing librarian perform?
14. What kind of control procedures can be used to prevent and detect unauthorized access to data files and programs in an on- line system?
15. Identify two devices available to prevent files from being inadvertently written over.
16. How can security be established for remote computer terminals?
17. What functions are performed by a control group in an EDP department?
18. Why are contingency plans and backup files so important to an EDP center? How would you go about developing a disaster contingency plan?
19. Identify the primary areas of concern for physical security.
20. What role should internal auditors play in an EDP department's internal control system?

Problems

1. Briefly describe the following concepts
    a. Boundary protection
    b. Interlock
    c. Parity check
    d. Validity check

       e.   Graceful degradation

       f.   Overflow check

2. What level of understanding should be possessed by accountants concerning: (a) Computer hardware controls, (b) Organizational controls, (c) Data security measures, and (d) Physical security measures?

3. What sort of authorization lists do you think might exist at a typical EDP center? Try to determine how many you might need and who should approve and update each list.

4. What security measures should be used to:
   a. prevent the malicious destruction of data on magnetic disks?
   b. ensure the privacy of confidential files?
   c. ensure that data is being accessed and used with proper authorization?

5. How do you think the EDP department's budgeting process might be the same as that of any other department in an organization? How do you think it might vary?

6. Johnson, CPA, was engaged to examine the financial statements of Horizon Incorporated which has its own computer installation. During the preliminary review, Johnson found that Horizon lacked proper segregation of the programming and operating functions. As a result, Johnson intensified the study and evaluation of the systems of internal accounting control surrounding the computer and concluded that the existing compensating general controls provided reasonable assurance that the objectives of the system of internal control were being met.

   Required:
   a. In a properly functioning EDP environment, how is the separation of programming and operating functions achieved?
   b. What are the compensating general controls that Johnson most likely found? *Do not discuss hardware and application controls.*

                                         (AICPA adapted)

7. The Lakesedge Utility District is installing an electronic data processing system. The CPA who conducts the annual examination of the utility district's financial statements has been asked to recommend controls for the new system. Discuss recommended controls over
   a. EDP hardware
   b. tape files and software

                                         (AICPA adapted)

8. When auditing the financial statements of a client who utilizes electronic data processing, it is important for the CPA to understand the essential characteristics of the client's system and the controls that are built into it.

Required:
Describe how the client's EDP department should be organized to maximize internal control over processing activities. Include in your description how the EDP department should relate to the rest of the client's organization.

(AICPA adapted)

9. *Multiple Choice Questions from Professional Examinations:*

(1) So that the essential accounting control features of a client's electronic data processing system can be identified and evaluated, the auditor must, at a minimum, have

    (i) A basic familiarity with the computer's internal supervisory system.

    (ii) A sufficient understanding of the entire computer system.

    (iii) An expertise in computer systems analysis.

    (iv) A background in programming procedures.

(2) Which of the following best describes a fundamental control weakness often associated with electronic data processing systems?

    (i) Electronic data processing equipment is more subject to systems error than manual processing is subject to human error.

    (ii) Electronic data processing equipment processes and records similar transactions in a similar manner.

    (iii) Electronic data processing procedures for detection of invalid and unusual transactions are less effective than manual control procedures.

    (iv) Functions that would normally be separated in a manual system are combined in the electronic data processing system.

(3) A computer programmer has written a program for updating perpetual inventory records. Responsibility for initial testing (debugging) of the program should be assigned to the

    (i) EDP-department control group.

    (ii) Internal-audit control group.

    (iii) Programmer.

    (iv) Machine operator.

(4) Accounting functions that are normally considered incompatible in a manual system are often combined in an electronic data processing system by using an electronic data processing program or series of programs. This necessitates an accounting control that prevents unapproved

      (i) Access to the magnetic tape library.

      (ii) Revisions to existing computer programs.

      (iii) Usage of computer program tapes.

      (iv) Testing of modified computer programs.

(5) Which of the following employees in a company's electronic data processing department should be responsible for designing new or improved data processing procedures?

      (i) Flowchart editor

      (ii) Programmer

      (iii) Systems analyst

      (iv) Control-group supervisor

(6) An auditor's investigation of a company's electronic data processing control procedures has disclosed the following four circumstances. Indicate which circumstance constitutes a weakness in internal control.

      (i) Machine operators do not have access to the complete run manual.

      (ii) Machine operators are closely supervised by programmers.

      (iii) Programmers do not have the authorization to operate equipment.

      (iv) Only one generation of backup files is stored in an off-premises location.

(7) One of the major problems in an EDP system is that incompatible functions may be performed by the same individual. One compensating control for this is the use of

      (i) Echo checks.

      (ii) A self-checking digit system.

      (iii) Computer generated hash totals.

      (iv) A computer log.

(8) Which of the following constitutes a weakness in the internal control of an EDP system?

      (i) One generation of backup files is stored in an off-premises location.

      (ii) Machine operators distribute error messages to control log.

      (iii) Machine operators do not have access to the complete systems manual.

      (iv) Machine operators are supervised by the programmer.

(9) Which of the following activities would most likely be performed in the EDP department?

      (i) Initiation of the changes to master records.

      (ii) Conversion of information to machine-readable form.

      (iii) Correction of transactional errors.

      (iv) Initiation of changes to existing applications.

(AICPA adapted)

Notes

1. These four control areas correspond to four of the five control areas identified in Computer Services Executive Committee of the American Institute of Certified Public Accountants, *The Auditor's Study and Evaluation of Internal Control in EDP Systems.* New York: AICPA, 1977. The fifth general control area, systems development and documentation controls, is discussed in Chapter 11.

2. The accounting system should have clearly discriminated accounts for EDP supplies and services.

3. A typical Steering Committee is chaired by a high corporate officer, committee members represent key users, and the EDP department plays an advisory (nonvoting) role; see Francl, Thomas J., Lin, W. Thomas, and Vasarhelyi, Miklos A., *Planning, Budgeting, and Control for Data Processing,* New York: Van Nostrand Reinhold, 1984, p. 119.

4. Curtice, Robert M., "Integrity in Data Base Systems," *Datamation,* May 1977, pp. 65–66.

5. *Systems Auditability and Control: Control Practices.* Altamonte Springs, Fla.: Institute of Internal Auditors, 1977, pp. 96–97.

6. Large organizations sometimes pool resources to maintain "shell facilities" designed to serve as a backup computer center. Contracts covering these arrangements should contain a clear allocation of priorities for the potential users.

7. Ibid., p. 3.

Additional References

Burch, John G., Jr., and Joseph L. Sardinas, Jr., *Computer Control and Audit: A Total Systems Approach.* New York: John Wiley & Sons, 1978.

Computer Control Guidelines. Toronto: The Canadian Institute of Chartered Accountants, 1977.

Davis, Gordon B., D. L. Adams, and C. A. Schaller, *Auditing & EDP,* 2nd ed. New York: American Institute of Certified Public Accountants, 1983.

Fisher, Royal P., *Information Systems Security.* Englewood Cliffs, N.J.: Prentice-Hall, 1984.

Halper, Stanley D., Glenn C. Davis, P. Jarlath O'Neil-Dunne, and Pamela R. Pfau, *Handbook of EDP Auditing.* Boston: Warren, Gorham & Lamont, 1985.

Information Security. Delran, N.J.: Datapro Research Corporation, 1985.

Jancura, Elise G., and Robert Boos, *Establishing Controls and Auditing the Computerized Accounting System*. New York: Van Nostrand Reinhold, 1981.

Li, David H., *Control Objectives—Controls in a Computer Environment: Objectives, Guidelines, and Audit Procedures*. Carol Stream, Ill.: EDP Auditors Foundation, 1983.

Lord, Kenniston W., Jr., *The Data Center Disaster Consultant,* 2nd Ed. Englewood Cliffs, N.J.: Prentice-Hall, 1983.

Mair, William C., Donald R. Wood, and Keagle W. Davis, *Computer Control & Audit*, 2nd ed. Altamonte Springs, Fla.: The Institute of Internal Auditors, 1978.

Norris, Daniel M., "Compensating Controls," *The National Public Accountant,* May 1984, pp. 46–49.

Parker, Donn, *Computer Security Management*. Reston Publishing Company, Reston, Virginia, 1981.

Perry, William E., *EDP Administration and Control*. Englewood Cliffs, N.J.: Prentice-Hall, 1984.

Perry, William E., and Javier F. Kuong, *EDP Risk Analysis and Controls Justification*. Wellesley Hills, Md.: Management Advisory Publications, 1981.

Porter, W. Thomas, and William E. Perry, *EDP Controls and Auditing,* 4th ed. Boston: Kent, 1984.

Stanford Research Institute, *Systems Auditability & Control: Control Practices*. Altamonte Springs, Fla.: The Institute of Internal Auditors, 1977.

Watne, Donald A., and Peter B. B. Turney, *Auditing EDP Systems*, Englewood Cliffs, N.J.: Prentice-Hall, 1984.

Weber, Ron, *EDP Auditing: Conceptual Foundations and Practice*. New York: McGraw-Hill, 1982.

Chapter 9

Computer Application Controls

9.1 INTRODUCTION

Application controls relate to the specific control requirements of EDP accounting and business system applications. Application controls are designed to ensure that the recording and processing of authorized transactions and the updating of master files will produce accurate and complete output information on a timely basis. Specifically, the objectives of application controls are to ensure that:

1. All authorized transactions are completely processed once and only once.
2. Transaction data are complete and accurate.
3. Transaction processing is correct and appropriate to the circumstances.
4. Processing results are utilized for the intended benefits.
5. The application can continue to function.[1]

Application controls include three control areas: input, processing, and output.[2] These three areas and corresponding types of controls are summarized in Table 9.1. An application control system should incorporate most of the techniques and procedures that we discuss in this chapter. However, the absence of a particular control does not necessarily indicate a weakness in the system because there is some redundancy among controls. We conclude the chapter with an illustration of the relationship between application, preventive, detective, and corrective controls and their hypothetical application to selected computer fraud cases. We also present an on-line order entry control example in Appendix 9.A.

Much of the material in this chapter is based on AICPA audit guides and SAS No. 3 and SAS No. 48. The latter represented a significant improvement because it integrated the computer into the auditing literature more fully and reflected ten years of technological advance. These ad-

Table 9.1   Computer Application Controls

Control Area	Control Type
Input controls	Input authorization Data conversion Data movement/transmission Input validation Error handling
Processing controls	Maintaining data accuracy Programmed limit and reasonable- ness tests File controls
Output controls	Output control reconciliations Reviewing and testing processing results Distribution of output Record retention

vances had made the computer even more pervasive and important in accounting and auditing practice. With the increase in auditor sophistication in the use of computers, SAS No. 48 also became a more theoretical document. In effect, many of the specific techniques discussed in SAS No. 3 are now found in the audit guides.

LEARNING OBJECTIVES

By the time you complete this chapter, you should be able to:

1. Identify and describe input controls for computer applications.
2. Identify and describe processing controls for computer applications.
3. Identify and describe output controls for computer applications.
4. Describe preventive, detective, and corrective controls and how they could have been applied to prevent computer fraud in selected cases.

9.2 INPUT CONTROLS

Input controls provide reasonable assurance that data received for processing by the EDP department are free from error, complete, and have been properly authorized, converted into machine-readable form, identified, captured, and transmitted. There are four basic categories of input to EDP systems that should be subject to proper input controls:

1. Transaction entries involving large volumes of activity, such as sales, purchases, payroll, cash receipts, and cash disbursements, which usually account for the greatest number of errors.
2. File maintenance transactions, such as changing sales prices on a product master file. They usually involve a limited volume of data but have a cumulative effect on transactions and a long-term impact on the file or files that are updated.
3. Inquiry transactions, such as retrieving information on how many units of a particular inventory item are on hand. Although inquiry transactions do not alter the data in a file, the user of that information may make decisions having economic impacts on the company. For example, a credit check inquiry may cause a sales clerk to erroneously grant credit to a customer who has exceeded the credit limit.
4. Error correction transactions to correct errors in data files or errors resulting from the other three categories of transactions. They are more complex than the original transaction entries and should be properly controlled.[3]

INPUT AUTHORIZATION

Authorization procedures should be established for the four categories of transactions. Only properly authorized and approved input should be accepted for processing by the EDP department. Techniques used in the computer application system to help ensure that input is authorized include approval procedures, use of prenumbered and other specific types of forms, review by the control group, use of passwords and an authorization table, maintenance of system logs, and use of call-back procedures.

Approval procedures describe how data are to be entered on input documents and by whom. The input documents should show evidence of authorization, such as appropriate signatures, and should be reviewed by the EDP control group. Other procedures include requiring that batches of transactions be approved before processing, involving several persons in the preparation of each document, requiring that file maintenance transactions be approved by the supervisor of the originating department,

Table 9.2   Authorization Table

Users	Authorized to Communicate by:			Authorized Processing		Authorized Access to Information		
	Batch	Data Entry	Interactive	Read	Update	Transaction Data	History Data	Decision Criteria
Management	x	x	x	x	x	x	x	x
Operations	x	x		x	x	x	x	
Auditor	x	x	x	x		x	x	x
Application Programmer	x		x	x	x			
Systems Programmer	x		x	x	x			
EDP Control	x	x	x	x	x			
Computer Operators			x	x				

Source: From *Management, Control and Audit of Advanced EDP Systems*, New York: AICPA, 1977, p.33

and establishing limits on the approval of certain transactions, such as customer credit. If input transactions are not approved prior to processing, a review of output should be performed by someone not involved in the initiation or authorization of the transaction in the user department.

Input media should be designed to reduce and control errors. For example, forms should be concise and easily coded; instructions for completing forms should be clearly documented. Two common control techniques for source data preparation are using *prenumbered forms* and *turnaround documents*. Preprinted, sequentially prenumbered forms, such as sales orders, invoices, receiving reports, checks, and similar documents, provide a useful method of control over source documents that serve as input to the computer systems. The sequence of these forms is checked during processing. Missing-number reports should be reviewed by appropriate supervisory personnel in the originating department. Turnaround documents are computer-produced documents designed to eliminate all or part of the data to be recorded at the source. For example, utility bills normally include prepunched data for customer account numbers and the amount billed, so that they can be resubmitted to the computer system with greater reliability when they are returned by customers with their payments.

As we described it in Chapter 8, the *control group* is an independent unit in the EDP department. All transactions submitted for batch processing must be reviewed by the control group. The group accepts only properly authorized transactions and logs and checks batch control totals.

In an on-line system where on-line input devices such as terminals are used, *password and authorization table* controls ensure that specific files are accessed only by authorized personnel. Before a user can enter a transaction, he or she must provide one or more passwords, which are checked by the computer. Another type of control is the use of an authorization

Table 9.2   Authorization Table (continued)

Users	Application Software	General System Software	Systems Control Software	Audit Systems Software	Resource Data	Authorization Control Tables
Management						
Operations						
Auditor	x	x	x		x	
Application Programmer	x			x	x	x
Systems Programmer		x				
EDP Control			x		x	x
Computer Operators		x			x	

table, which identifies the users that are authorized to use various methods to communicate with the EDP system and process data and the types of data that the users can access. Table 9.2 shows the contents of a typical authorization table.[4]

Maintaining *system logs* is another type of on-line control. All terminal use is recorded on a tape or disk file. A review of the logs would reveal the frequency of security violations at terminals, frequency of sign-on errors at terminals, and other unusual occurrences.

One telecommunication control technique is the use of a *call-back procedure* to limit access to known, authorized terminals. As soon as a user signs on the terminal, the telecommunication line is disconnected automatically, and the location is called back by the computer. The user then has to answer one or several questions related to authorized identification or code numbers. This procedure detects the use of an unauthorized terminal to gain access to dial-up facilities and introduce fraudulent transactions. However, the technique is cumbersome; it requires additional sign-on complexity and predetermined input locations.

DATA CONVERSION

Data conversion is the process of converting data from source documents into machine-readable form on punched cards, magnetic tapes, disks, or diskettes. The most common data conversion errors are loss of data and keying mistakes. Techniques for controlling data conversion include visual verification, key verification, check-digit verification, batch control, and batch balancing and editing.

To help ensure that the information on source documents is complete and in the correct format, user departments should review or *visually verify* the transactions as they are batched. In on-line systems, the terminals may be equipped with a facility to provide automatic feedback for immediate visual checking by users.

A much more common technique for verifying the accuracy of the conversion process is a *key verification* of the data recorded on punched cards. Key verification usually consists of a second operator verifying the keying accuracy of the first operator on a special verifying keyboard. Differences between the data recorded by the first operator and the data entered in verification by the second operator trigger a mechanical signal. Key verification reduces the risk of significant undetected errors.

Use of a *check digit*, or self-checking digit, is another technique used to verify the accuracy of certain files. It checks the validity of the number itself. A digit determined according to a prespecified mathematical routine is added to the end of a string of data to permit the numeric data to be checked for accuracy during input, processing, or output. For example, using the customer account number 45679, the check-digit steps are:

1. Multiply each digit by a preselected weight. In this case the weight used will be 2–1–2–1–2, that is, multiplying every other digit by 2, which yields

$$4 \times 2 \ = \ 8$$

$$5 \times 1 \ = \ 5$$

$$6 \times 2 \ = \ 12$$

$$7 \times 1 \ = \ 7$$

$$9 \times 2 \ = \ 18.$$

2. Sum of the digits:

$$8 + 5 + 1 + 2 + 7 + 1 + 8 = 32.$$

3. Subtract the sum from the next highest multiple of 10:

$$40 - 32 = 8.$$

4. Add the check digit to the end of the original customer account number to form an account number with a check digit, or

$$456798.$$

The check digit can be recalculated after keypunching to detect a coding or keypunch error or when reading the data into the computer, through an edit routine. Assume that during keypunch the account number is transposed to 465798. The check digit would be recalculated as follows:

$$4 \times 2 \ = \ 8$$

Figure 9.1   A Systems Flowchart for Batch Control

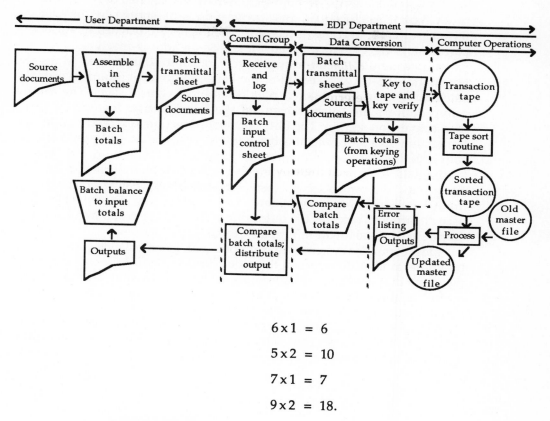

$$6 \times 1 = 6$$

$$5 \times 2 = 10$$

$$7 \times 1 = 7$$

$$9 \times 2 = 18.$$

Sum the digits:

$$8 + 6 + 1 + 0 + 7 + 1 + 8 = 31.$$

Subtract to get

$$40 - 31 = 9.$$

The check digit entered with the keypunch input was 8, but the recalculated check digit was 9. Since the two numbers do not match, the account number would be flagged as an error.

Input data should be batched close to the point of preparation and *batch control* totals prepared; batch transmittal sheets should contain a sequential batch number and record of the batch control total. Batch control totals can be used as input, processing, and output controls.

There are three types of batch control totals: (1) batch totals, such as total dollar amount of accounts receivable, total amount of gross pay, or total inventory quantities on hand; (2) hash totals, such as a total of the customer account number or a total of the employee identification number; and (3) record counts for the number of transactions entered or processed.

A typical batch control total application is illustrated by the systems flowchart shown in Figure 9.1. Source documents are batched in a user department. A clerk then runs batch totals on an adding-machine tape, prepares a sequential prenumbered batch transmittal sheet, and signs the transmittal sheet. Upon receipt of the batch, the control group records the batch number and batch totals on a batch input control sheet. The control group delivers the batch transmittal sheet and source documents to the data conversion section. The data conversion section keys and verifies the transaction data and generates batch totals. Then the control group or data conversion supervisor compares the new batch totals with the original batch totals. All outputs from computer processing are returned to the control group. The control group then compares output batch totals with the input batch totals and investigates and resolves any discrepancies. The user department receives the output from the control group and compares output batch totals with input batch totals.

Most computer systems are equipped with batch balancing and editing programs to identify errors in the input process. *Batch balancing* compares the items in documents actually processed against a predetermined input control total for those items. Table 9.3 shows an example of batch balancing for inventory storeroom transactions.

Computer editing programs or routines perform checks of a variety of conditions, such as data completeness, numeric field accuracy, code validity. Table 9.4 presents an example of edit criteria for inventory transactions.

DATA TRANSMISSION

Control over data transmission between departments and between processing steps is designed to prevent data from being lost, added, or altered. Such control should be established within user groups, the control group, and the EDP department. Data can be transmitted by mail, by messenger or over communication lines. Techniques for controlling data movement include logging and tracking of batches, verifying batch control totals and run-to-run totals by application programs, and on-line transmission verification techniques, such as echo checks, redundancy checks, and completeness tests.

Logging and tracking of batches involve calculating batch control totals, using batch serial numbers and transmittal sheet numbers, and logging the flow of transactions and/or batches. Incidentally, these are useful techniques for data conversion as well as data transmission control.

Table 9.3   An Example of Batch Balancing

Harvidell, Schakins & Co., Inc.
Storeroom Transactions
Batch Balancing

Batch Number	Document Number	Date	Quantity	Computed Quantity	Difference
1-1038			1243987	1243987	
1-1039			2486248	2486243	
2-1040	091435	1202XX	14525		
	091436	1202XX	18600		
	091437	1202XX	17720		
	091438	1202XX	9280		
	091439	1202XX	11435		
	091440	1202XX	10796		
	091441	1202XX	19700		
	091442	1302XX	12920		
	091443	1202XX	9061		
	091444	1202XX	21792		
	091445	1202XX	14729		
	091453	1202XX	13068		
	091454	1202XX	8096		
		1202XX	9762		
	091456	1202XX	14277		
	091457		12425		
	091458	1202XX	15390		
	091479	1202XX	9998		
	091480	1202XX	17975		
	091481	1202XX	11234		
	091482	1202XX	15853		
	091483	1202XX	16005		
	091484	1202XX	13740		
BATCH TOTALS			719285	709175	10110
1-1041			923724	923724	
3-1042			17125	17125	
4-1043			11475	11475	
2-1044			143927	143927	

Source: From *Audit Approaches for a Computerized Inventory.*
New York: AICPA, 1980, p. 16.

Table 9.4   Edit Criteria for Inventory Transactions

Transaction Type	Transaction Data Edited	Data Edited to Determine if		
		Present	Numeric	Validated to Master File
Receipt of	Receiving report number	X	X	
purchased	Date	X	X	X
material	Vendor number	X	X	X
	Material ID number	X	X	X
	Company order number	X	X	X
	Quantity	X	X	
	Unit of measure	X		X
Issuance of material	Document number	X	X	
for production	Date	X	X	X
(copy of factory's	Material ID number	X	X	X
receipt of material	Production order number	X	X	X
from storeroom)	Quantity	X	X	
	Unit of measure	X		X
Return of material	Document number	X	X	
to vendor	Date	X	X	X
	Vendor number	X	X	X
	Material ID number	X	X	X
	Quantity	X	X	
	Unit of measure	X		X
Return of material	Document number	X	X	
from production	Date	X	X	X
(copy of factory's	Material ID number	X	X	X
return of material	Production order number	X	X	X
to storeroom)	Quantity	X	X	
	Unit of measure	X		X
Receipt of material from storeroom	(See issuance of material for production above)			
Return of material to storeroom	(See return of material from production above)			

(continued on next page)

Table 9.4   Edit Criteria for Inventory Transactions (continued)

Transaction Type	Transaction Data Edited	Data Edited to Determine if		
		Present	Numeric	Validated to Master File
Transfer of produc- tion to warehouse (copy of warehouse's receipt of merchandise from production)	Document number	X	X	
	Date	X	X	X
	Production/rework order No.	X	X	X
	Finished goods style No.	X	X	X
	Quantity	X	X	
	Unit of measure (each)	X		X
Transfer of spoiled material to scrap	Document number	X	X	
	Date	X	X	X
	Production/rework order No.	X	X	X
	Quantity	X	X	
	Unit of measure	X		X
Merchandise receipt from warehouse for rework (copy of warehouse's transfer of merchandise to rework)	Document number	X	X	
	Date	X	X	X
	Finished goods style	X	X	X
	Quantity	X	X	
	Unit of measure (each)	X		X
Receipt of merchandise from production	(See transfer of production to warehouse above)			
Transfer of merchandise to rework	(See receipt of merchandise from warehouse for rework)			
Shipment of merchandise to customer	Document number	X	X	
	Date	X	X	X
	Finished goods style No.	X	X	X
	Quantity	X	X	
	Customer number	X	X	X
	Unit of measure (each)	X		X
	Method of delivery	X		

(continued on next page)

Table 9.4   Edit Criteria for Inventory Transactions (continued)

		Data Edited to Determine if		
Transaction Type	Transaction Data Edited	Present	Numeric	Validated to Master File
Removal of merchan-	Document number	X	X	
dise for samples or	Date	X	X	X
own use	Finished goods style No.	X	X	X
	Account to be charged	X	X	X
	Quantity	X	X	
	Unit of measure (each)	X		X
Return of	Document number	X	X	
merchandise from	Date	X	X	X
customer	Finished goods style No.	X	X	X
	Code for stock or rework	X	X	X
	Quantity	X	X	
	Customer number	X	X	X
	Unit of measure (each)	X		X
Physical inventory	Document number	X	X	
adjustment	Date	X	X	X
	Material ID or finished goods style number	X	X	X
	Quantity	X	X	
	Unit of measure	X		X

Source: From *Audit Approaches for a Computerized Inventory.*
New York: AICPA, 1980, p. 15.

Application programs should be used to verify batch control totals and run-to-run totals. *Run-to-run control totals* utilize output control totals resulting from one process as input control totals for subsequent processing. These control totals are carried as part of a transaction or master file and verified each time the file is processed.

When data are transmitted over communication lines from one location to another, there must be controls to ensure the accuracy of that transmission. One such control is the *echo check*, or closed loop verification, whereby data are transmitted back to the sending station for comparison with the initial data. For example, a purchase transaction just entered on the terminal would be displayed on the CRT screen for the sender to verify visually the description of each inventory item for which a number was entered.

Another technique to check data transmission is the *redundancy*, or matching, *check*. It requires the sender to enter a piece of data in addition to that being transmitted to enable the receiving station to check the accuracy of the transmitted data. For example, a purchasing records clerk enters the inventory item number and the first few letters of that inventory item description, so that the system can verify that the two data items match. If either of these elements does not match the master file, the transaction is rejected.

An on-line system should also perform a completeness test on each transaction input to verify that all required data have been entered. For example, the system should check for missing data, such as inventory item number, quantity, or unit cost in an inventory application.

INPUT VALIDATION

The objective of input validation is to ensure that all input data are accurate, complete, and reasonable. The input validation ability of the computer can be used to detect errors in input preparation that have not been detected by other control techniques. Computers can be programmed to perform the input validation function; hence the term program checks, or edit routines.

Program checks include the batch total, hash total, record count, completeness, and redundancy checks and self-checking digits discussed previously. The following are additional program input validation checks.

1. *Limit or reasonableness check:* A particular field of input transaction record is checked to see whether it is within reasonable limits. For example, hours worked on a payroll record may be checked to be sure they do not exceed 60 hours.
2. *Numeric and alphabetic checks:* Particular fields are checked to ascertain that numeric input record fields contain only numeric characters and alphabetic fields contain only alphabetic characters. For example, an inventory quantity field should not contain any alphabetic characters.
3. *Valid code check:* A particular input code is checked against the stored list of valid codes. Types of codes that might be checked include account number, job number, and transaction code. For example, customer numbers and inventory item numbers are checked against lists of valid numbers in a sales transaction processing system.
4. *Sequence check:* A key field of the input record is checked to see that it is in ascending or descending sequence. For example, the sales order numbers are checked to see that they are in ascending sequence. (This is normally handled through a utility sort before editing.)

5. *Sign check:* A particular field is checked to see whether it has the proper sign. For example, the net pay amount for each employee in the payroll system should have a positive sign.
6. *Logic check:* Logical relationships between input data and the file accessed are checked. For example, a closing entry for an accounting period that debits depreciation expense and credits cash is not a logical journal entry.
7. *Valid field size check:* A field size is checked to see that the input data contains a specific number of digits. For example, the Social Security number should have 9-digit field size.
8. *Anticipation control:* The programmed expectation that certain data will be inputted for a particular application. For example, a payroll application may be programmed to expect a time card input record for each worker.

ERROR HANDLING

Many input controls reject transactions that do not meet certain criteria. Proper controls for processing rejected transactions should include the identification of all rejects, review for the cause of rejection, correction of each reject, review and approval of the correction, and prompt reentry of the correction into the system. Techniques for error detection and correction include the use of error logs, suspended files, error reports and error correction and resubmission controls.

The control group should maintain an *error log* and record all rejected input data, investigate the errors, and clear all errors within a reasonable period of time. A supervisor should regularly review the error log.

Errors detected by batch balancing and program checks are recorded in a machine-readable *suspended file,* and a control total is generated. This technique is used to make sure that errors are corrected and returned to the EDP system for subsequent processing. Errors are written to a suspended file and held there until they are corrected. These files should be reviewed periodically for noncurrent errors.

An *error report* should be prepared to identify the record, the erroneous data, and the cause of the error. This error report should be sent to the originating department for correction and resubmission. Table 9.5 presents an example of an error report.

All *error corrections* that are entered into the system should flow through the same error detection and input validation control procedures as the original transactions. These include proper authorization, batching, logging, key verification, use of batch control totals, and rerunning of batch balancing and program tests.

Table 9.5   An Example of an Error Report

Harvidell, Schakins & Co., Inc.
Issuance of Material for Production
Error Report

BATCH NUMBER	DOCUMENT NUMBER	DATE	PRODUCTION ORDER NUMBER	MATERIAL ID NUMBER	UNIT OF MEASURE	QUANTITIES ITEM	QUANTITIES DOCU	REASON FOR ERROR
2-1040	091440	1202XX	061939	102064	YARDS	2200	10796	Unit of measure wrong for material ID
2-1040	09144D	1302XX	061952				12920	Document number is not numeric, month is greater than 12
2-1040	09144	122XX	06J954				21792	Document number does not contain 6 digits Date does not contain 6 digits, production order number is not numeric
2-1040		1202XX	01197				9762	Document number is missing, production order does not contain 6 digits
2-1040	091457						12425	Date is missing, production order is missing Quantity is missing
2-1040	091480	1202XX	061974	102376	YARDS			Material ID number is missing
	091480	1202XX	061974		YARDS	3500		Material ID is not numeric
	091480	1202XX	061974	10186C		1020		Unit of measure is missing
	091480	1202XX	061974	10769	EACH	K20	17975	Material ID number does not contain 6 digits
	TOTAL OF REJECTED TRANSACTIONS						85670	
	TOTAL OF ACCEPTED TRANSACTIONS						623505	
	BATCH TOTAL						709175	
2-1044	091496	1202XX	061988	106996	YARDS	2210	13405	Invalid material ID number
	TOTAL OF REJECTED TRANSACTIONS						13405	
	TOTAL OF ACCEPTED TRANSACTIONS						130522	
	BATCH TOTAL						143927	

Source: From *Audit Approaches for a Computerized Inventory.*
New York: AICPA, 1980, p. 17.

9.3 PROCESSING CONTROLS

Processing controls are designed to ensure the complete and accurate processing of the data through the system. These controls are applied after the data enter the system as application programs process the data. Processing controls are designed to prevent or detect the following types of errors:

1. Failure to process all input transactions or erroneous processing.
2. Processing and updating the wrong file or files.
3. Processing illogical or unreasonable input.
4. Loss or distortion of data during processing.[5]

Processing control techniques used include maintaining data accuracy throughout processing, programmed limit and reasonableness tests, and file controls.

MAINTAINING DATA ACCURACY

Data accuracy should be maintained throughout processing by using batch control totals, run-to-run control totals, transaction logs, and fallback, restart, and recovery controls. Batch control totals, such as batch totals, hash totals, and record counts should be produced and reconciled with input control totals. Run-to-run control totals should be reconciled at the conclusion of each processing step. For example, if 1000 transactions totaling $200,000 were just processed, and the prior open-item file contained 5000 transactions totaling $800,000, the updated output file should contain 6000 transactions totaling $1,000,000. Run-to-run control detect operator errors in mounting the wrong version of the master file because control totals will not balance.

In a real-time update processing system, a transaction log can be maintained to record transaction information such as function, operator, time, terminal identification and transaction control number. Transaction logs can be used as a control and balancing tool and serve as excellent audit trails.

In an on-line system, particularly a real-time update processing system, fallback, restart, and recovery procedures must be developed for use in case system failures occur. *Fallback procedures* are used to collect and control transactions that would otherwise be inputted during the time that the system is not operating. *Restart procedures* are used to restart the system following a shutdown. *Recovery* procedures restore the system and enter transactions that were canceled under fallback procedures.

PROGRAMMED LIMIT AND REASONABLENESS TESTS

Application programs generally include tests to edit data for completeness, accuracy, and reasonableness. The program checks described for input validation generally apply to the processing system as well, including updating computer files. Thus the following program checks can be used as processing controls: (1) sequence check, (2) check digit, (3) logic check, (4) limit and reasonableness checks, (5) sign check, (6) numeric and alphabetic checks, and (7) valid code check. Incorporation of these checks into programs provides further assurance that errors detected by input validation edit routines have actually been corrected.

Three additional techniques available for processing controls are the zero balancing check, overflow check, and crossfooting check. The *zero balancing check* is used to balance debits with credits, detail with summary, subsidiary ledger with general ledger control account, and the like. The *overflow check* is used to determine whether the size of the result of a computation exceeds the register size allocated to hold it. For example, if the register size is 4 positions and the product of a particular multiplication operation is 10985, it may be stored as 0985, with the 1 being lost to overflow. A *crossfooting check* involves the development of separate control totals for related fields and crossfoots at the end of a run. For example, in a payroll application, totals are developed for gross pay, net pay, and for each deduction. At the end of processing, net pay should equal gross pay less total deductions.

FILE CONTROLS

Adequate controls should be provided to prevent processing the wrong file, detect errors in file manipulation, and highlight errors caused by operators. The following file control techniques should be applied to batch processing systems.

1. Provide external labels on tape, disk, and card files, which should be checked by the operator to ensure that the correct files are being processed.
2. Use application programs to check internal header and trailer labels for data stored on tape and disk. Control totals should be maintained in the trailer labels on all files.
3. When several files or tables are stored on the same disk pack, all programs that read the disk or write on it should provide boundary protection. For example, if an accounts receivable master file is on disks 1–6, the payroll programs should be halted if an attempt is made to read from or write on disks 1–6.
4. To make sure that a magnetic tape input file is not used as an output file or accidentally written on, the magnetic tape reel's file-protection ring should be removed to place the reel in a "read-only" processing mode.
5. The number of records on the opening of a data file should be balanced against the changes made during the period and the closing balance. A report should be prepared to show master file contents before and after each change and be reviewed by the supervisory personnel.

In an on-line system, many transactions may be processed concurrently from a number of terminals. A lock-out technique should be provided to prevent simultaneous updating of a record; that is, the first arriving updating transaction should retain control of the master record until that updating function is completed. Also, the interface file should be operational. If a disabled file is detected, the on-line transaction should be aborted and a severe error message issued.

9.4 OUTPUT CONTROLS

Output controls are designed to verify that processed data are complete, accurate, and distributed to proper users. The basic output controls include: (1) output reconciliation; (2) processing result review and tests; (3) output distribution; and (4) record retention.

OUTPUT RECONCILIATION

The control group and user department should reconcile output with input and processing controls. This reconciliation may be performed with programmed reconciliation reports or by manually reconciling totals on output reports with input control totals. The system transaction log should be compared with a transaction log maintained at each output device on a regular basis.

PROCESSING RESULT REVIEW AND TESTS

Output should be reviewed and tested by comparing it to original source documents. The user department or control group should review the reasonableness of all the computer calculations and output formats. Lists of master file revisions should be reviewed carefully, which usually consists of a search for unusual or abnormal items.

The control group should review, investigate, and control exception or discrepancy reports. Discrepancy reports include a list of items that have violated controls and require further investigation. All error items are periodically printed on the discrepancy report and also recorded in the suspended error file. All errors stay in the file until they are corrected, to ensure that all errors are ultimately corrected.

OUTPUT DISTRIBUTION

Output reports should be distributed by the control group to authorized personnel on a timely basis. For each application, those persons receiving printed reports should be clearly identified and only the copies needed for those users should be produced. A cover sheet identifying the recipient is attached to each report, and a log is maintained showing when each output is distributed. The recipient should verify that all reports are promptly received by return of a special form.

For confidential output reports in an on-line system, a control can be ensured by restricting output printing at remote terminals. Special passwords, transaction codes, or central EDP supervisory approvals can be required before reports may be reprinted by remote printing terminals.

RECORD RETENTION

Retention periods should be formally specified for data files, computer output microfilm (COM), and printed output. The objectives are to maintain proper security over computer output, avoid unnecessary reconstruction of files, reduce EDP supply and material costs, and to control waste disposal. When reports are no longer useful they should be destroyed. Shredding out-of-date reports, and aborted computer runs provides one good way to control report destruction.

9.5 APPLICATION CONTROLS AND COMPUTER FRAUD CASES

The purpose of computer controls is to prevent, detect, and correct unintentional errors and intentional fraud.[6] A preventive control is one that serves to guide activities and to occur as planned. They are usually passive controls with little or no direct computer involvement. Examples of such controls are documentation standards, organization charts, and error correction and reentry procedures.

A detective control is one that indicates when an error occurs. It is a more active type of control than a preventive control because it might halt further processing until the error has been corrected. Examples of detective controls include console control messages, listing differences between various control totals, and alarms announcing that unauthorized entry to the system is being attempted.

A corrective control is one that helps in the investigation and resolution of errors that have been detected by detective controls. It is needed to determine the reason for the error and aid in its correction. Examples of

Table 9.6   Preventive, Detective, and Corrective Controls

Characteristics of Control Class	Type of Application Control
Preventive controls:	
These controls will reduce the frequency with which causes of exposure occur; they act as guides to help things happen as they should.	1. Input authorization 2. Data conversion 3. Distribution of output 4. Record retention.
Detective controls:	
These controls will detect the fact that a cause of exposure has already happened; they trigger an alarm after a cause of exposure has happened.	1. Input authorization 2. Data conversion 3. Data transmission 4. Input validation 5. Error handling 6. Maintaining data accuracy 7. Programmed limit and reasonableness tests 8. File controls 9. Output control reconciliation 10. Review and tests
Corrective controls:	
These controls will correct the effects of a cause of exposure after it has been detected; they assist in the investigation and correction of causes of exposures that have been detected.	1. Error handling 2. Maintaining data accuracy 3. Output control reconciliations 4. Review and tests of processing results

corrective controls include error source statistics, insurance coverage, or backup files.

Application controls are controls that relate to the specific control requirements of individual accounting and business system applications. Application controls include input controls, processing controls, and output controls. Table 9.6 summarizes specific controls within each of the three application control classes.

Table 9.7 shows those preventive, detective, and corrective application controls that might have been applied to avoid loss in the 15 largest computer fraud cases mentioned by Allen.[7]

Table 9.7   Application of Controls to Largest Computer Fraud Cases

Computer Fraud Case	Class and Type of Control (from Table 9.6)		
	Preventive	Detective	Corrective
Accountant at West Coast department store set up phoney vendors, purchase orders, and vouchers.	1, 3	1, 7, 10	4
Claims reviewer at insurance company prepared false claims payable to friends in a manner that would be paid automatically by the computer.	3	4, 7	
Clerk at storage facility falsified information entered into computerized inventory system to mask theft of inventory; shipments then made without billing.	3	1, 4, 7, 10	4
Warehouse employees manipulated computerized inventory system through unauthorized terminal entries to mask inventory thefts.	1	1, 4, 7, 10	4
Accountant at metal fabricating company padded payroll, thereby extracting funds for own use.	1, 3	1, 4, 8, 9, 10	3, 4
Officer in London bank stole funds from inactive customer accounts.	1, 3	1, 4, 6, 8, 9, 10	2, 3, 4
Bank employee misused on-line banking system to perpetrate large lapping fraud, including unrecorded transaction, altered transactions, and unauthorized account transfers.	1	1, 3, 4, 5, 10	1, 4
Manufacturing company manager who had designed and installed automated accounting system used it to steal company funds.	1	1	
Customer representatives of large public utility, together with an outside associate, erased customer receivables using computer error correction; received kickback from customer.	1, 3	1, 4, 5, 10	1, 4

(continued on next page)

Table 9.7   Application of Controls to Largest Computer Fraud Cases (continued)

Computer Fraud Case	Class and Type of Control (from Table 9.6)		
	Preventive	Detective	Corrective
Clerk in department store established phony purchases and vouchers for payment to friend's company.	1	1, 4, 10	4
Organized crime ring operated check-kiting fraud between two banks, using computer-room employee who altered deposit memos to record check deposits as available for immediate withdrawal.	1, 3	1, 3, 4, 8, 10	4
Accountant at large wholesaler established phony vendors through computerized accounting system that he operated.	1, 3	1, 3, 4, 8, 10	4
Officer of brokerage house misappropriated company funds through computer system that he controlled	1	1, 3, 4, 7, 8, 10	4
Partner at brokerage house transferred funds from firm's accounts to his own.	1	1, 4, 7, 8, 10	4
Director publishing subsidiary manipulated computer system to add false sales and block recording of accounts payable—all to improve operating results, thereby securing a position on board of directors.	1	1, 4, 7, 8, 9	3

9.6 Summary

Input controls provide reasonable assurance that data received for computer processing have been properly authorized, accurately recorded, and safely transmitted. Input controls include input authorization procedures, data conversion controls, data transmission controls, input validation procedures, and error handling procedures.

Processing controls provide reasonable assurance that the input data have been processed completely and accurately through the system.

Processing controls maintain data accuracy through batch control totals, run-to-run control totals, transaction logs, fallback, and restart and recovery controls, programmed limit and reasonableness tests; and file controls.

Output controls provide reasonable assurance that processed data are complete, accurate, and distributed to the user. Output controls include output control reconciliation, review and tests of processing results, control of output distribution, and record retention policies and procedures.

We concluded this chapter by applying appropriate controls to the situations in which the 15 largest computer fraud cases occurred.

Questions

1. What are the four basic objectives of applications controls?
2. What auditing standards deal with applications controls and how have these standards evolved?
3. What are input controls and what are they designed to do?
4. Describe the four basic categories of input controls. Which have the greater risk of errors?
5. Discuss some potential uses of turnaround documents.
6. What is the purpose of maintaining a transaction log?
7. Give a type of error that run-to-run control totals may identify.
8. How might authorization be a part of on-line computer systems?
9. Explain how batch control totals help to prevent the loss of data during the processing cycle of an application.
10. Why is error correction an important part of the input control process?
11. What four types of errors do processing controls prevent or detect?
12. How do file controls fit into processing control?
13. What are output controls and what are they designed to do?
14. Why should the control group review output before distributing it to users?
15. List the procedures which ensure that output will be distributed as authorized.
16. Describe and distinguish between preventive, detective, and corrective controls.
17. What is the relationship between fraud and the controls discussed in this chapter?

Problems

1. What is the meaning of each of the following terms?
    a. Visual verification
    b. Key verification
    c. Programmed checks
    d. Self-checking digit
    e. Redundancy check
2. The text described a check-digit algorithm. See if you can develop or find additional algorithms in the literature.
3. In an on-line system that presents the user with a format on a screen to fill in, how could completeness be assured?
4. How do you think user log books, control totals, and run-to-run totals might be combined in a system to improve controls?
5. What types of input validation could an on-line system provide for various accounting programs?
6. What application control(s) should be employed to detect and/or prevent each of the following occurrences?
    a. A $13.70 payment from a customer which is properly listed on a remittance advice is keyed onto tape by a data preparation clerk as $137.00.
    b. A salesman entering a sales order for 500 parts mistakenly keys in the product number for finished goods.
    c. The computer operator mounts the magnetic tape containing the cash receipts, rather than the cash payments, thereby incorrectly updating the accounts payable master file.
7. Big Deal Store processes its payroll by means of a small computer system. The following table presents the sorted payroll transaction data for the first week of June:

Employee number	Employee name	Department number	Wage rate	Hours worked
1254	Kadley Chris	1	$ 5	40
1367	Mansfield Linda	1	4	48
1348	Ong Richard	1	5	43
1706	Weber Michael	2	10	40
2192	Jones Craig	2	9	78
2428	Knudsen Sandy	2	11	40

Additional information:
  (1) The first digit of the employee number indicates the employee's department
  (2) An employee's hourly wage rate never exceeds $10.00
  (3) No more than 30 hours of overtime is allowed each week

Required:

    (a) Compute three types of batch control totals

    (b) Identify errors in the data and the specific type of programmed check that should detect each error

8. *Multiple Choice Questions from Professional Examinations*

  (1) The basic form of backup used in magnetic tape operations is called

    (i) Odd parity check

    (ii) Dual-head processing

    (iii) File-protection rings

    (iv) The son-father-grandfather concept

  (2) In designing a payroll system, it is known that no individual's paycheck can amount to more than $300 for a single week. As a result, the payroll program has been written to bypass writing a check and will print out an error message if any payroll calculation results in more than $300. This type of control is called

    (i) A limit or reasonableness test

    (ii) Error review

    (iii) Data validity test

    (iv) Logic sequence test

  (3) A customer payment recorded legibly on the remittance advice as $13.01 was entered into the computer from punched cards as #1,301.00. The best control procedure would be

    (i) A limit test

    (ii) A valid field test

    (iii) Keypunch verification

    (iv) A check digit

  (4) A weekly payroll check was issued to an hourly employee based on 98 hours worked instead of 38 hours. The time card was slightly illegible and the number looked somewhat like 98. The best control procedure would be

    (i) A hash total

    (ii) A code check

    (iii) Desk checking

    (iv) A limit test

  (5) A sales transaction document was coded with an invalid customer account code (seven digits rather than eight). The error was not detected until the updating run when it was found that there was no such account to which the transaction could be posted. The best control procedure would be

    (i) Parity checks

    (ii) Keypunch verification

    (iii) A hash total check

    (iv) A check digit

(6)   A customer inadvertently ordered part number 12368 rather
        than part number 12638. In processing this order, the error
        would be detected by the vendor with which of the following
        controls?
        (i) Batch total
        (ii) Key verifying
        (iii) Self-checking digit
        (iv) An internal consistency check

(7)   Totals of amounts in computer-record data fields which are not
        usually added but are used only for data processing control
        purposes are called
        (i) Record totals
        (ii) Hash totals
        (iii) Processing data totals
        (iv) Field totals

(8)   Which of the following is a computer test made to ascertain
        whether a given characteristic belongs to the group?
        (i) Parity check
        (ii) Validity check
        (iii) Echo check
        (iv) Limit check

(9)   If the last letter of a customer's name is erroneously entered in
        card column 31, which of the following is most likely to detect
        the error during an input edit run?
        (i) A logic check
        (ii) A combination check
        (iii) A valid character check
        (iv) A self-checking number

(10)   If a trailer label is used on a magnetic tape file, it is the last
        record and summarizes the file. Which of the following is
        information not typically found on a trailer label?
        (i) Record count
        (ii) Identification number
        (iii) Control totals for one or more fields
        (iv) End-of-file or end-of-reel code

(AICPA adapted)

Notes

1. Mair, William C., Wood, Donald R., and Davis, Keagle W., *Computer Control & Audit.* Altamonte, Fla.: The Institute of Internal Auditors, 1978, p. 82.

2. *The Auditor's Study and Evaluation of Internal Control in EDP Systems.* New York: AICPA, 1977, p. 13.

3. *Ibid.*, pp. 49–50.

4. *Management, Control and Audit of Advanced EDP Systems.* New York: AICPA, 1977, p. 33.

5. *The Auditor's Study. . .*, 1977, p. 56.

6. The classification of internal controls as preventive, detective, and corrective was developed by William C. Mair, Donald R. Wood and Keagle W. Davis, pp. 36–37.

7. Allen, Brandt, "The Biggest Computer Frauds: Lessons for CPAs," *The Journal of Accountancy*, May 1977, p. 63.

Additional References

Audit Approaches for a Computerized Inventory System. New York: American Institute of Certified Public Accountants, 1980.

Burch, John G., Jr., and Joseph L. Sardinas, Jr., *Computer Control and Audit: A Total Systems Approach.* New York: John Wiley & Sons, 1978.

Computer Control Guidelines. The Canadian Institute of Chartered Accountants, Toronto, 1970.

Davis, Gordon, D. L. Adams, and C. A. Schaller, *Auditing & EDP*, 2nd ed. New York: American Institute of Certified Public Accountants, 1983.

"The Effects of Computer Processing on the Examination of Financial Statements," *Statement on Auditing Standards*, No. 48, New York: American Institute of Certified Public Accountants, 1984.

Fisher, Royal P., *Information Systems Security.* Englewood Cliffs, N.J.: Prentice-Hall, 1984.

Information Security. Delran, N.J.: Datapro Research Corporation, 1985.

Jancura, Elise G., and Robert Boos, *Establishing Controls and Auditing the Computerized Accounting System.* New York: Van Nostrand Reinhold, 1981.

Li, David H., *Control Objectives—Controls in a Computer Environment: Objectives, Guidelines, and Audit Procedures.* Carol Stream, Ill.: EDP Auditors Foundation, 1983.

Parker, Donn, *Computer Security Management.* Reston, Va.: Reston Publishing Company, 1981.

Perry, William E., *EDP Administration and Control*. Englewood Cliffs, N.J.: Prentice-Hall, 1984.

Porter, W. Thomas, and William E. Perry, *EDP Controls and Auditing,* 4th ed. Boston: Kent, 1984.

Stanford Research Institute, *Systems Auditability & Control: Control Practices*. Altamonte Springs, Fla.: The Institute of Internal Auditors, 1977.

Vallabhaneni, S. Rao, *Information Systems Audit Process*. Carol Stream, Ill.: EDP Auditors Foundation, 1983.

Watne, Donald A., and Peter B. B. Turney, *Auditing EDP Systems*. Englewood Cliffs, N.J.: Prentice-Hall, 1984.

Weber, Ron, *EDP Auditing: Conceptual Foundations and Practice*. New York: McGraw-Hill, 1982.

Appendix 9.A ILLUSTRATION OF AN ON-LINE ORDER ENTRY CONTROL APPLICATION

In this appendix we present an illustration of an on-line entry control application. It was prepared for the Institute of Internal Auditors by the Stanford Research Institute and originally published in 1977 in *Systems Auditability and Control Study.* The purpose of this study was to investigate the then current data processing control practices. *The Data Processing Control Practice Report,* one of the three volumes that comprise the total study, contains four illustrative case studies, which are presented as examples of applications found in large organizations. The illustration in this appendix is one of these case studies and is reprinted with the permission of the Institute of Internal Auditors, Inc.

A.1 APPLICATION OVERVIEW

Order entry systems vary considerably; however, their basic objective is similar, namely, the accurate and timely completion of customer orders. The order entry system reviewed in this chapter is described as follows:

> The customer calls a customer order representative and places his order. A terminal operator enters the customer order into a central computer, where information files are checked on the customer's credit rating and on the availability of the product, bills of lading are calculated, and shipping points are assigned. Information is then sent to a warehouse in the form of "packing" and "shipping" papers,

and the materials are forwarded to the customer. The following control illustration describes the order entry segment of an order entry/inventory control system.

A.2 BACKGROUND

This control illustration describes an on-line entry system that is being used by a large continuous process manufacturer. The order entry system is operated on a large-scale computer that is used for the actual processing of customer orders, a medium-scale computer that is used for controlling the communication lines and terminals, and a small special purpose computer that is used as a connecting device or coupler between the two large computers. The order entry system, which is part of a system that includes inventory control, utilizes 15 high-speed hardwired leased lines that connect over 200 hard-copy and display-type terminals to the system. More than 4,000 customer orders, which represent approximately 16,000 order entry transactions, are processed weekly.

There are 15 control points in this system. These control points and the order entry system itself are illustrated in Figure 9.A.1.

A.3 APPLICATION DESCRIPTION AND CONTROL PRACTICES

To place an order, a customer calls toll free to a centralized order processing location. The call is routed to a customer order representative assigned to that customer's geographic region, who then completes a customer work order that includes the quantities and items ordered by the customer. The work order is then forwarded to a data entry operator within the order processing location for entry of the customer order data into the order entry system. The data entry operator, using a display type of terminal, requests the system to display the proper format for processing the specific type of order reflected on the customer work order (e.g., normal or consignment). The format request is made through the use of format codes.

CONTROL POINT 1—TRANSACTION CONTROL

A table of transaction codes that indicates which terminals are authorized to transmit certain data is maintained in the order entry system. The codes and terminals were preidentified by data processing and order entry management during the system's design. All terminal requests are checked

Figure 9.A.1   Order Entry Flowchart

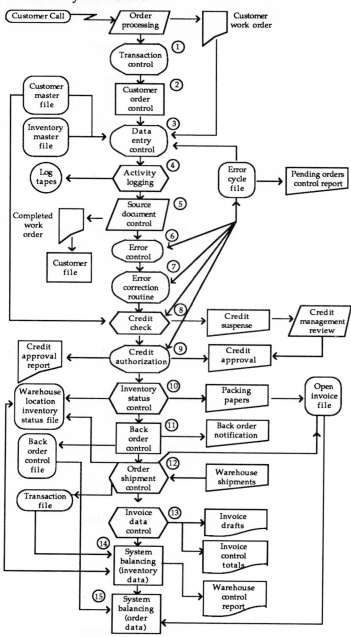

Source: From *Systems Auditability and Control: Control Practices.* Altimonte Springs, Fla.: Institute of Internal Auditors, 1977, p. 120A.

against this table and those transactions that do not match are rejected and the terminal does not have access to the data. As a further control, after five attempts by a terminal operator to access data that a terminal does not have clearance to access, the system will discontinue polling the terminal. The terminal can only be reinstated into the polling sequence by data processing operation personnel after having received a call from an authorized manager at the order processing location.

When a requested format is displayed, a computer-generated order control number is also displayed. This order control number consists of the terminal number, Julian date, the warehouse geographic location code, and serial number assigned by the computer.

CONTROL POINT 2—CUSTOMER ORDER CONTROL

The order control number is assigned by the computer to eliminate the possibility of duplicate order numbers being assigned to customer orders. All order entry transactions must reference an order control number or they are rejected. Order control numbers cannot be established or altered by terminal operator. This control establishes that the order entry system has a record of every customer work order entered into the system. The order control number also serves as a means of follow-up if something goes wrong during order entry processing.

The data entry operator then enters the data from the customer work order into the terminal. After entering all the items on the order, the operator enters a summary total of the quantity ordered, which was originally totaled by the customer order representative.

CONTROL POINT 3—DATA ENTRY CONTROL

The order entry system validates against customer and inventory master records the customer number and the items being ordered to ensure that the data entry operator is entering valid customer and product data into the system. The system also totals the quantities ordered and compares this total with the hash total entered by the data entry operator. If there are any discrepancies in this validation process, the system records all the data on an Error Cycle File and redisplays all the order entry data to the terminal operator (see Control Point 6).

All data transmitted to and from the order entry system are first recorded on a customer log tape on the message switching computer. All transactions that update an order entry system data base are also recorded on a computer log tape on the order entry processing computer.

CONTROL POINT 4—ACTIVITY LOGGING

The data recorded on the computer log tape of the message switching computer are used primarily for monitoring terminal and system transaction activity. Listings reflecting, by terminal, the date and number of transactions processed are prepared upon request. As an example, the Internal Auditing Department at times requests terminal activity at warehouses.

The computer log tape for the order entry processing computer is maintained primarily for file and system recovery purposes. The computer log tape is only printed out when difficulties are experienced in file recovery.

After the data entry operator has correctly entered all of the customer's order into the system, the operator posts the order control number on the customer's work order and the work order is filed.

CONTROL POINT 5—SOURCE DOCUMENT CONTROL

The customer's work order, which now has the order control number posted to it, is filed in the customer's order file. The order control number serves as a cross-reference between the customer's work order and the processing of the customer's order through the order processing system. The filed work order is used for answering customer inquiries relative to items ordered.

If, in the order entry processing cycle, an error is detected (e.g., an invalid item number, an invalid terminal transaction, reference to a nonexistent customer), the entire order is displayed to the order entry operator with an asterisk and an error code beside the line item as an indicator of the type of error detected (e.g., not on the master file, data entry procedural error). These codes assist the data entry operator to isolate and correct the error.

CONTROL POINT 6—ERROR CONTROL

When an error is detected by the order entry system, the entire customer order is recorded on an Error Cycle File and an error control number is assigned by the computer and associated with the order control number. An order cannot be processed if any part of it is in error. Daily, a report is prepared on the terminals at the order processing locations reflecting all pending error control numbers and associated order control numbers on the Error Cycle File. This report is reviewed by the sales services superior at the order processing location to ensure that action is being taken on all pending error items.

When an error has been corrected at the order processing location, the data entry operator requests the pending customer order from the Error Cycle File by referencing the error control number.

CONTROL POINT 7—ERROR CORRECTION ROUTINE

Access to the Error Cycle File can be made only by referencing the error control number. Upon identification of an error control number, the customer's order data will be released from the Error Cycle File for display to the data entry operator. When the data in error are corrected, the pending order data are deleted from the Error Cycle File and the entire customer order is again processed through the validation procedure of the order entry system.

Once the order entry system has determined that all the data entered for a customer's order are valid, then the actual processing of the customer's order data takes place. First, the customer master file is accessed to determine the terms and conditions for this customer (e.g., type of account, warehouse location, shipping instructions). Next, the value of the customer's order is calculated and a customer credit limitation check is performed.

CONTROL POINT 8—CREDIT CHECK

This control point is to ensure that the customer's order does not exceed the credit limitations established for this customer by the credit department. The credit limitation check is performed by calculating the value of this order and adding it to the sum of the customer's unpaid invoices. The new sum is then compared to the established credit limit. Should the customer's credit limitation check fail, then the entire customer order is recorded on the Error Cycle File (in a credit suspense category) and the regional credit location management is notified by terminal output that this customer order is being held in suspense. The terminal output includes customer name, credit terms, unpaid invoices dollar value, and current order dollar value.

To release a customer order that has been held in the Error Cycle File for credit limitation approval, the data entry operator at the order processing location must first receive authorization from the regional credit manager. The data entry operator then requests a display of the suspended order by referencing the order control number. The operator then enters on the terminal a credit authorization override code that deletes the order from the Error Cycle File and releases the customer order data for normal processing by the order entry systems.

CONTROL POINT 9—CREDIT AUTHORIZATION

The credit manager at the regional credit location must phone or wire the order processing location with approval to proceed with the processing of a customer order that has exceeded the customer's credit limitation. As a further control of this authorization procedure, a terminal printout is prepared daily for the regional credit managers and corporate headquarters, indicating all the previous day's credit approvals, as well as a list of all customer orders and order dates still being held pending credit authorization. These reports are reviewed by regional and corporate credit management to ensure that timely credit reviews are being initiated by the regional credit managers.

The next step in the order entry processing cycle is for the system to check the inventory status of the items on the customer's order to determine if sufficient quantity is on hand to fill the order. For those customer order items that have inventory on hand, the shipping weight for the items is calculated by the system, and a customer invoice number is automatically assigned by the computer. At this time, a set of packing and shipping papers is transmitted to a hard-copy terminal at the warehouse location. All the customer and shipment data included on the shipping papers are also updated on an Open Invoice File by invoice number.

CONTROL POINT 10—INVENTORY STATUS CONTROL

The order entry system checks the Warehouse Location Inventory Status File to determine if the items are available, and if so, to reserve the items and reduce the available inventory for subsequent orders. If there is insufficient quantity of an item, the customer's coded instructions are checked to determine whether this customer desires unfilled quantities to be back ordered or whether the unfilled quantity is to be canceled.

If the out-of-stock items are to be back ordered, a Back- Order File is updated with the customer's order reference data, the back-ordered item(s), and the quantities.

CONTROL POINT 11—BACK-ORDER CONTROL

A back-order control number is assigned by the system to the items back ordered on the customer's order. The back-order control number, customer number, order number, items, and quantities are also printed on the terminal at the order processing location. This is the customer's order representative's notification that all items ordered were not shipped, but were back ordered. The order representatives are responsible for releasing items from the Back-Order File. They do this by assigning inventory from another warehouse location that is under their control or by ultimately applying inventory from the original warehouse once that warehouse's inventory has been replenished.

After the warehouse personnel have shipped the items identified on the packing papers, a warehouse terminal operator transmits to the order entry system the invoice number, date shipped, and total quantity of all items shipped on this invoice number.

If there are any discrepancies in the quantity shipped and the quantities originally listed on the packing papers, the warehouse terminal operator also transmits the item number and quantity shipped for the item that was under- or overshipped.

CONTROL POINT 12—ORDER SHIPMENT CONTROL

The Warehouse Location Inventory Status File is updated for the items shipped. For each item, the quantity shipped, which is the ordered quantity unless otherwise indicated by the terminal operator, is subtracted from the inventory on-hand balance; then the open order balance and the shipped-to-date balance are updated by the quantity shipped. The items and quantities shipped are also recorded on a Transaction File. The Transaction File consists of a record for every item that has had an inventory transaction (i.e., shipment, inventory receipt, or inventory adjustment) processed through the entry system during the daily processing. Each inventory item record reflects the on-hand balance of the item prior to the transaction, the quantity of the transaction, the new on-hand inventory balance, and the invoice number of the transaction. The Transaction File data are maintained for at least seven years and are retrieved by the Internal Auditing Department when reviewing inventory activity related to a customer's shipment.

At the close of each business day, the order entry system prepares a draft of the customer invoices. The invoices are then forwarded to the Billing Department. The billing data include all customer shipping information, customer number, order number, items shipped, quantity shipped, and so on.

CONTROL POINT 13—INVOICE DATA CONTROL

For control purposes, the order entry system also prepares two summary control totals for the Billing Department. One total indicates the total number of invoices forwarded, and the other is a total of all the items shipped. Upon receipt of the invoices, the Billing Department counts the invoices and prepares an adding machine tape to verify the quantity shipped and to ensure that invoice data have been forwarded. If there is a discrepancy, the Billing Department contacts the Data Processing Department and the differences are reconciled. As required, new draft invoices are prepared. The preparation of the actual customer invoices is accomplished by the organization's billing application system.

At the close of each business day, the order entry system prepares a daily Warehouse Control Report for Warehouse Administration management. Each warehouse location is separately listed on this report, showing total warehouse inventory, inventory in-transit, inventory adjustments, orders shipped, and order backlogged.

CONTROL POINT 14—SYSTEM BALANCING (INVENTORY DATA)

Daily, the Transaction File is balanced by item, by adding and/or subtracting the day's inventory transactions to the previous day's ending balance to determine if the total equals the item's new on-hand balance. If the totals do not balance, then the Transaction File is printed out for the out-of-balance items and the individual transactions are reviewed by the data processing systems personnel to determine the error in systems processing and to initiate the appropriate adjustment. In addition, the Transaction File is sorted into items within location sequence and is processed against the Warehouse Location Inventory Status File. The ending on-hand balance for an item on the Transaction File should balance to the on-hand balance on the Warehouse Location Inventory Status File. If these balances agree, then it has been verified that all items identified as having been shipped from a warehouse have, in fact, been deducted from the on-hand inventory for that warehouse on the Warehouse Location Inventory Status File. If the two files do not balance, then the Transaction File is printed out and reviewed as above. A Warehouse Control Report is prepared as a by-product of the system balancing procedure. This report is forwarded to the Warehouse Administration group at the headquarters location, where it is reviewed as a control report to monitor overall daily warehouse activity and to reflect overall inventory status.

CONTROL POINT 15—SYSTEM BALANCING (ORDER DATA)

Also, daily the Open Invoice File and the Back-Order File are balanced by warehouse location for total units added to those files during the day's order entry processing, with the total units, by warehouse, that were entered into the order entry system that day. This balancing ensures that all valid order entry items that entered the order entry system have been accounted for either as shipment items or as a back-ordered item. Again, if the files do not balance, the data processing system personnel review a listing of the items within the warehouse that are out of balance to determine the processing error and initiate the appropriate adjustment.

Chapter 10

Auditing EDP Centers and Applications

10.1 INTRODUCTION

Auditing electronic data processing centers and applications is essentially an audit of the EDP organization and its policies, procedures, and applications to determine the extent to which the controls outlined in Chapters 8 and 9 are implemented. Every audit process starts with the development of the audit objectives and an audit plan. The American Institute of Certified Public Accountants has stated that

> The objective of the ordinary examination of financial statements by the independent auditor is the expression of an opinion on the fairness with which they present the financial position, results of operations, and changes in financial position in conformity with generally accepted accounting principles.[1]

Although specific audit procedures may differ, the auditor's objective does not change when EDP is utilized in the accounting process. Additional factors such as the EDP-related risk, potential for computer fraud, and computer-assisted audit techniques must be included in the overall planning of audit scope, staffing, scheduling, and budgeting.[2]

The sequence of audit procedures involved in the study and evaluation of EDP-based applications in a financial audit is outlined in Figure 10.1. The first step in an EDP audit is the preliminary review of the computer installation. The second step is the assessment of the preliminary review to decide whether to rely on the existing EDP accounting controls. If the auditor decides to rely on the system of internal control, the auditor should perform a detailed review of that system. Otherwise, the auditor has to rely more on compensating controls applied by the user and proceed to review and test these controls instead.

The objective of detailed review is necessary to give the auditor an in-depth understanding of the controls used in the EDP system. At the conclusion of the detailed review, the auditor should again decide whether to

Figure 10.1   Study and Evaluation of EDP-based Applications

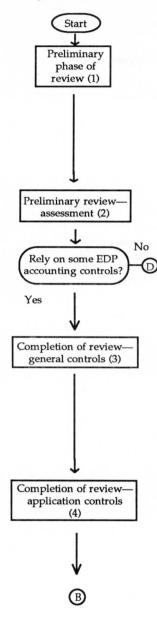

(1) Preliminary Phase of the Review
Purpose
Understand accounting system including both EDP and non-EDP segments:
- Flow of transactions and significance of output.
- Extent to which EDP is used in significant accounting applications.
- Basic structure of accounting control, including both EDP and user controls.

Methods
Inquiry and discussion; observation; review of documentation; tracing of transactions; control questionnaires and checklists.

(2) Preliminary Phase of the Review—Assessment
Purpose
- Assess significance of EDP and non-EDP accounting controls.
- Determine extent of additional review within EDP.

Method
Judgment.

(3) Completion of Review—General Controls
Purpose
- Identify general controls on which reliance is planned and determine how they operate.
- Determine the effect of strengths and weaknesses on application controls.
- Consider tests of compliance that may be performed.

Methods
Detailed examination of documentation; interviewing internal auditors, EDP and user department personnel; observing operation of general controls.

(4) Completion of Review—Application Controls
Purpose
- Identify application controls on which reliance is planned, and determine how the controls operate.
- Consider tests of compliance that may be performed.
- Consider the potential effect of identified strengths and weaknesses on tests of compliance.

Methods
Detailed examination of documentation; interviewing internal auditors, EDP, and user department personnel; observing operation of application controls.

(continued on next page)

Figure 10.1 Study and Evaluation of EDP-based Applications (continued)

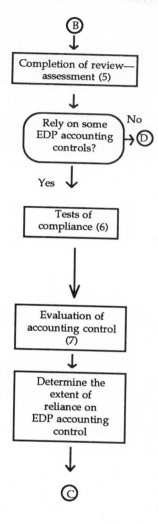

(5) Completion of Review—Assessment
Purpose
For each significant accounting application
•Consider the types of errors or irregularities that could occur.
•Determine the accounting control procedures that prevent or detect such errors and irregularities.
•Assess effectiveness of EDP and non-EDP accounting controls.

Method
Judgment.

(6) Tests of Compliance
Purpose
•Determine whether the necessary control procedures are prescribed and followed satisfactorily.
•Provide reasonable assurance that controls are functioning properly.
•Consider and, to the extent appropriate, document when, how, and by whom controls are provided.

Methods
Examination of records; test of control procedures; inquiry; observation.

(7) Evaluation of Accounting Control
Purpose
For each significant accounting application
•Consider the types of errors or irregularities that could occur.
•Determine the accounting control procedures that prevent or detect such errors and irregularities.
•Determine whether the necessary control procedures are prescribed and followed satisfactorily.
•Evaluate weaknesses and assess their effect on the nature, timing, and extent of auditing procedures to be applied.

(continued on next page)

Figure 10.1 Study and Evaluation of EDP-based Applications (continued)

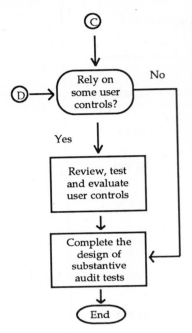

Method
Judgment.

NOTE: At any point after the preliminary phase of the review, the auditor may decide not to rely on EDP accounting controls for all or some applications (see SAS No. 3, paragraph 26). The auditor would then complete the design of the substantive audit tests. According to SAS No. 1, Section 320.70, substantive tests consist of the following classes of audit procedures: (1) tests of details of transactions and balances and (2) analytical review of significant ratios and trends and resulting investigation of unusual fluctuations and questionable items.

Note: This chart is a simplified illustration and does not portray all possible decision paths.

Source: From *The Auditor's Study and Evaluation of Internal Control in EDP Systems.* New York: AICPA, 1977, pp. 21–24. Reprinted by permission of the American Institute of Certified Public Accountants.

rely on any or all of the EDP accounting controls. If the auditor decides to rely on the system of internal control, the auditor must perform sufficient tests of compliance to establish with a reasonable degree of assurance that the accounting control procedures are functioning as intended.

The final step of financial audit field work is the substantive testing that helps the auditor formulate an opinion about the validity and reasonableness of the transactions and the propriety of the accounting treatment of the transactions and balances. Although the fundamental process of substantive testing is similar for both computerized and manual systems, many of the substantive test procedures require the use of computer-assisted audit techniques.

In this chapter, for purposes of discussion, we divided the EDP-audit process into two parts: (1) The study and review of internal controls; and

(2) compliance and substantive testing. The first part includes a preliminary review, an assessment of the preliminary review, detailed reviews of general controls and application controls, and an assessment of these detailed reviews. The second part includes compliance testing, an assessment of the compliance testing, testing and assessment of user controls, and substantive testing. In the last two sections of this chapter, we discuss computer-assisted audit techniques and the audit of records produced by service centers.

LEARNING OBJECTIVES

By the time you have completed this chapter, you should be able to:

1. Describe the basic approach to the audit of a data processing center and to the application controls in a computer-based system.
2. State the purposes and methods used in the preliminary phase of the audit review.
3. State the purposes and methods used in the detailed phase of the audit review.
4. Describe the compliance testing procedures for auditing a data processing center and for application controls.
5. Utilize substantive testing procedures.
6. Explain the applicability of computer-assisted audit techniques and their advantages and disadvantages.
7. List guidelines for auditing records produced by service centers.

10.2 STUDY AND REVIEW OF INTERNAL CONTROLS

When the computer is used in significant accounting applications, that is, those that relate to accounting information that can materially affect the financial statements, the auditor should include the EDP activity when performing the following tasks: (1) a preliminary review; (2) an assessment of the preliminary review; (3) a detailed review of general controls; (4) a detailed review of application controls; and (5) an assessment of the detailed reviews.

PRELIMINARY REVIEW

The objective of the preliminary review is to enable the auditor to understand the accounting system, including both the EDP and the non-EDP segments, in order to conduct the control evaluation effectively. This understanding should include:

1. The flow of transactions and the significance of the output.
2. The extent to which EDP is used in significant accounting applications.
3. The basic structure of the accounting controls, including both EDP and user controls.

A logical first step in conducting a preliminary review is to obtain general information relating to the extent that the client's accounting system is supported by EDP. Frequently, it is useful to prepare a "client EDP profile." This profile typically includes the following information: EDP-center organization chart, computer and peripheral equipment utilized, available software, a diagram of the physical facilities and communication networks, and a summary of computer applications.

Flow of Transactions. According to AICPA Statement on Auditing Standards No. 3, the auditor needs to understand the flow of transactions in order to design and apply appropriate procedures to review and evaluate accounting controls. During the preliminary review the auditor may obtain the following information for each application by a system walk-through or by the use of system flowcharts.

1. The various types of transactions and how they originate (sales, credit, bad debts, and the like).
2. The method of recording each type of transaction in the accounting records (invoices, credit memos, journal entries, and the like).
3. The significant processing steps performed (either manually or by EDP) on these transactions (extend price times quantity, prepare invoice register, and the like).
4. The accounting information maintained from one processing cycle to the next (open accounts receivable, credit limits, and the like).
5. Records and output listings that may be significant for audit purposes (invoice register, error listings, change notices, and the like).

6. The ways in which information from one application interface with that from another (how does accounts receivable information flow into the general ledger application and so on).[3]

Extent of EDP Utilization. In order to understand the extent of EDP utilization in each significant accounting application, the auditor should consider:

1. The number and types of transactions processed.
2. The total dollar value of each type of transaction.
3. The extent and nature of the processing accomplished within EDP, including that performed by computer programs.
4. The division of the flow of transactions between EDP and non-EDP activities.[4]

Accounting Control Structure. In order to understand the basic structure of accounting controls, the auditor should consider, but not necessarily limit his or her attention to:

1. The controls that are provided.
2. The division of control responsibility between the EDP and non-EDP portions of the system.
3. The relationship between manual and EDP-based controls.
4. The nature, extent, and availability of the information that provides a management or audit trail.[5]

During the preliminary review, the auditor should investigate potential access and operational vulnerabilities, inadequate division of responsibilities, inadequate documentation, potential problems revealed during interviews with the data center personnel, and similar conditions.

GENERAL AND APPLICATION CONTROL REVIEW

The preliminary review must encompass both general and application controls and should be performed early in the field-work phase of the audit. During the review of general controls, the auditor attempts to understand EDP-center controls, including organization and operation controls, hardware and software controls, access controls, and data procedure controls. During the review of application controls the auditor attempts to understand the controls exercised over the major types of transaction applications, such as input, processing, and output controls.

A preliminary understanding of the accounting system is usually obtained by inquiry, but it also may be obtained by observing client personnel and reviewing documentation. For example, the primary method of determining policies and practices in the EDP-center review is the examination of informal documentation. However, all policies and practices may not be documented. Therefore the auditor may have to interview personnel (EDP department, users, management, and internal audit) to obtain a complete understanding of the policies and practices applied in the data processing center.

The application controls review also includes reviewing existing documentation and interviewing personnel. Information about each application system should include documentation of system and application logic flowcharts, descriptions of programs and files, a summary of input and output forms, and a schedule of exception reports.

ASSESSMENT OF THE PRELIMINARY REVIEW

After completing the preliminary review, the auditor should assess the significance of EDP accounting controls in relation to the entire system of accounting controls and determine the extent of the detailed review of the EDP accounting controls required. Options available are: (1) to test and rely on EDP control procedures; (2) not to test EDP controls but to test and rely on user controls; (3) not to test any controls but to carry out other audit tests to achieve audit satisfaction; and (4) to determine the impact of weaknesses on substantive testing.

The choice of an appropriate course of action is based primarily on the auditor's judgment. When making this choice, the auditor should consider the potential effects of controls, effectiveness of available alternative audit approaches, audit efficiency considerations, and client expectations in reaching his or her decision.

It should be clear at this point that the auditor usually prefers to rely on either computer or user controls. Because of their speed and resultant processing power, most computerized systems involve a large number of transactions. To audit them by substantive testing would be both inefficient and expensive. Therefore, although reliance on internal controls is often not vital in other facets of the audit, reliance on internal controls to limit substantive testing is critical. This fact should further reinforce the auditor's insistence on good systems of internal control in an EDP environment.

DETAILED REVIEW OF GENERAL CONTROLS

General controls include those that relate to more than one application, such as EDP-center controls and system development controls. In this chapter we discuss the review of EDP-center controls and defer the review of system development controls to the next chapter.

The primary purpose of reviewing EDP-center controls is to identify weaknesses that must be considered during subsequent application reviews and in designing audit procedures. This review usually involves examining documentation, interviewing data processing personnel and users, and observing the actual operation of EDP-center controls. The audit review procedures are grouped according to the 16 types of EDP-center controls described in Chapter 8 and summarized in Table 10.A.1 in the appendix of this chapter.

DETAILED REVIEW OF APPLICATION CONTROLS

Having obtained an understanding of the environment in which the significant accounting applications or transaction cycles are processed, the auditor should proceed to review each significant application supported by EDP. This detailed review should concentrate on the specific controls and procedures that are directly related to audit objectives.

The primary purpose of reviewing application controls is to identify weaknesses that must be considered in designing substantive audit procedures and in subsequent compliance testing. The depth of the application control review will depend on the degree to which the auditor plans to rely on the client's system of internal controls.

The primary source of information for the detailed review is application documentation. The auditor can start with a review of the client's application documentation, such as system flowcharts, narrative descriptions, input documents, error reports, detailed computer program documentation, recorded layouts of transactions being processed, master files being updated, systems and procedures manuals, operator instructions, and users' manuals. The auditor should then interview internal audit and EDP personnel about specific controls for the significant accounting and financial applications. If possible, the auditor should observe the actual operation of the specific application controls by a walk-through of transactions from the point of origin in the user's area, including all phases of both manual and computerized processing, error correction, and output distribution. Application control review procedures are grouped according to the types described in Chapter 9 and summarized in Table 10.A.2 at the end of this chapter.

Figure 10.2   Auditing Around the Computer

ASSESSMENT OF DETAILED REVIEW

Evaluations of internal controls are usually made throughout the audit process. At the conclusion of the detailed review, the auditor should assess the effectiveness of EDP and non-EDP accounting controls and determine whether to rely on any or all of them. The auditor should relate the control and risk evaluation to specific control techniques and procedures, which, in turn, should relate to control objectives. At the end of the detailed review the auditor may decide to rely on some EDP accounting controls and to proceed with compliance testing procedures, or the auditor may decide to rely on some user controls instead of EDP controls.

10.3 COMPLIANCE AND SUBSTANTIVE TESTING

COMPLIANCE TESTING

The purpose of compliance testing is to determine whether the system of internal controls is operating as intended. The auditor may be able to perform compliance tests without the use of the computer in simple or small computer operations. In large or complex computer processing operations, where part of the transaction is in machine readable form only, the auditor should use the computer when testing the system.

Figure 10.2 illustrates the example of auditing without using the computer, that is, auditing around the computer. In this process, the auditor merely proves the accuracy of transaction data inputs, demonstrates that those inputs actually result in the obtained outputs, and concludes that the processing system is correct. Input controls are examined and tested, and a sample of actual inputs is selected. The auditor calculates the results of processing the sample inputs and checks those results against the actual values obtained as computer output in the system. Advantages of this approach are (1) low cost; (2) minimal technical expertise required; and (3) ease of comprehension. Disadvantages include (1) the impracticality of the approach in large systems; and (2) inability to make inferences about unexamined data or processes.

Manual compliance testing methods include the examination of records, inquiry, observation, and manual testing of control procedures. Many of the audit review procedures listed in Table 10.A.1 and Table 10.A.2 can also be applied to compliance testing.

Separate lists of additional compliance testing procedures for EDP center and application controls are shown in Tables 10.A.3 and 10.A.4, respectively. Note that many EDP-center controls, such as the segregation of functions, produce no documentary evidence. Compliance with these controls can be tested primarily by direct visual observation at various times. On the other hand, many application controls, such as input validation routines or programmed limit and reasonable tests, require computer-assisted audit techniques to obtain persuasive evidence. When designing compliance tests of application controls, the auditor should consider the effectiveness of EDP-center controls. For example, if these controls are weak or nonexistent, compliance tests of application controls may have to be more extensive and performed more often during the audit.

ASSESSMENT OF COMPLIANCE TESTING

At the conclusion of compliance testing, the auditor should consider the strengths and weaknesses of the application controls for each significant accounting application. The auditor should also assess the effectiveness of EDP-center controls in evaluating accounting controls in order to determine the nature, timing, and extent of the substantive tests to be performed. If the auditor decides that a greater reliance can be placed on the results of compliance testing, the nature and extent of substantive testing may be reduced. On the other hand, if the auditor decides not to rely or to place a lesser reliance on the internal controls, the nature and extent of substantive testing may be increased.

TESTING AND ASSESSMENT OF USER CONTROLS

In some situations the auditor might decide not to rely on EDP-center internal controls because user controls compensate for the weaknesses in the EDP internal controls system. For example, one common EDP-center control is the segregation of duties among EDP personnel. When the segregation of duties is inadequate, the following compensating controls should be applied in user departments: user input/output reconciliations, user examination of detailed output and error reports, and user manual tests of computer-generated data. Another example involves one of the application controls, data entry key verification. Key verification may not be of primary concern to the auditor, if the user exerts strong control over the completeness and accuracy of the data being processed, such as requiring the user to sight verify the data before they are processed in an on-line system. Data entered appear on a terminal screen or on a printout but will not be processed until the terminal user indicates to the computer that the data have been entered correctly.

SUBSTANTIVE TESTING

Substantive tests of transaction details are designed to validate that individual transactions are properly authorized, supported, and recorded in the accounts and that items recorded in the accounts are the result of properly authorized, supported, and classified individual transactions. The ultimate purpose of substantive testing in a financial audit is to obtain sufficient evidence to enable the auditor to make a final judgment about whether the financial statement account has been materially misstated.

The nature, timing, and extent of substantive tests depend on the particular circumstances and on the results of compliance tests. For example, if greater reliance can be placed on the results of compliance testing, the nature and extent of substantive testing may be reduced and vice versa. The audit procedures for substantive testing include inspection, observations, inquiries, analysis, and confirmations. Inspection, observation, and inquiry are performed manually. Analysis and confirmation procedures can be more efficiently and effectively performed by computer-assisted audit techniques.

10.4 COMPUTER-ASSISTED AUDIT TECHNIQUES

Computer-assisted audit techniques (CAAT) enable the auditor to use a computer to perform, or assist in the performance of, compliance tests and substantive audit procedures. Specifically, computer-assisted audit techniques give the auditor the ability to access data that are in machine readable form and extract and manipulate the data; to review large volumes of data for exceptions; to test extensions and footings; to perform statistical samplings of audit populations; to select and print confirmations; to compare the same data maintained in separate files for correctness and consistency; and to perform analytical review procedures.

In this section, we discuss a wide variety of CAAT, but in a given audit situation, only a few will actually be used. The CAAT we present are generalized audit software, test data, integrated test facility, tracing, mapping, embedded audit modules, snapshot, base-case system evaluation, job accounting data analysis, and parallel simulation.

GENERALIZED AUDIT SOFTWARE

Generalized audit software is a computer program or series of programs specifically designed to perform certain EDP functions useful to auditors. These functions include reading computer files, selecting desired information, performing calculations, and printing reports in a format specified by the auditor. As described in Chapter 7, generalized audit software is the most widely used computer-assisted audit technique, and many such packages are available to auditors today.[6]

TEST DATA

The auditor can use **test data** or test decks of transactions, as shown in Figure 10.3, to test programmed controls and procedural operations of computerized applications for compliance. The test data are processed with the same client programs used to process live data at the selected control point in the transaction cycle. The test transactions should include both valid and invalid transactions; they can be selected from previously processed transactions or created by the auditor. The auditor then computes expected results of processing the test data and uses them to check the results obtained from a computer run of the same data. If the actual results match expected results, the test provides reasonable assurance that the program and programming controls are functioning as designed.

Advantages of the test data technique include:

1. Minimal technical expertise required.
2. May be used on a surprise basis.
3. Yields excellent results if the variety of possible transactions is limited.
4. Once established, the test data can be used in the future with only minor modifications.

The disadvantages of the test data technique are that it is often costly to develop, it cannot include all possible combinations of data in order to test a program fully, and it may not verify that the program being tested is the one the client uses regularly.

Figure 10.3 Test Data Approach

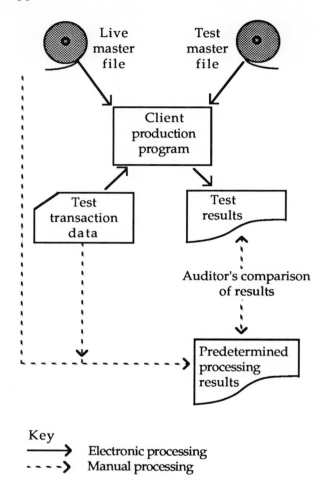

INTEGRATED TEST FACILITY

An **integrated test facility** (ITF) is an extension of the test data technique and is frequently referred to as the *minicompany* or *dummy company* technique. As shown in Fig. 10.4 a dummy entity (such as a fictitious division, subsidiary, or branch account) is established in the client's computer master file. Test data for the dummy entity are then processed through the client's system concurrently with the client's actual data, and the results of processing the test data are compared to the predetermined results. This technique ensures that test transactions are subjected to the same controls and procedures as live transactions. This technique is useful when the auditor wants to test a large number of varied and complex programs performing accounting computations.

Advantages of the integrated test facility include:

1. Minimal technical training required.
2. Low cost of test data as it is processed along with regular input.
3. Allows the auditor to check on a surprise basis and thereby provides a stronger deterrent to fraud.
4. Gives the auditor the ability to test the actual system as it routinely operates.

The disadvantages of the integrated test facility technique are that the test data transactions must be removed from the client's records with special care, it is difficult to consider all possible combinations of data in order to test a program fully, and there is a possibility of destroying a client's files because transactions can affect live data records.

Figure 10.4 Integrated Test Facility

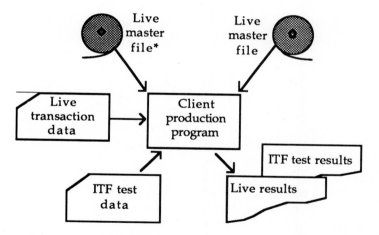

*Live master file contains dummy division, subsidiary, or branch account.

TRACING

Tracing is an audit technique that provides the auditor with the capability of performing a computer walk-through of an EDP application. It prints a listing of the program instructions (logical steps) that were executed in processing a transaction. By analyzing the results of the executed instructions, the auditor may be able to understand and evaluate the transaction flow, as in a manual processing system. Tracing can be used by the auditor to test programmed input validation routines for compliance.

Advantages of the tracing technique include:

1. Enables the auditor to identify whether the specific instructions or processing steps of a computer application were executed during the processing of a particular transaction. This evidence can be tested for compliance by comparing it with the client's policies and procedures.
2. Can be used with both live and test data.

The disadvantages of the tracing technique are that the auditor must be familiar with the programming language of the client's application program, and learning the details of a given program, performing the trace procedure, and analyzing the results may be time consuming.

MAPPING

Mapping is a technique that can be used to assess the degree of system testing obtained and to identify specific program logic that has not been tested. Mapping is performed by a software measurement procedure that monitors the execution of a program and produces a list of any program statements not executed, a list of the program statements consuming the most CPU time, and a list of source program statements, indicating the total number of times each was executed. By analyzing the output, the auditor can determine whether certain segments of the program were not used and investigate to find out whether this is appropriate. If the selected steps were performed properly, the auditor has some assurance that program controls are functioning as intended.

Advantages of the mapping technique include:

1. Refers the auditor to unexecuted program statements. These unexecuted program statements could be undesired codes such as unauthorized codes inserted by the programmer.
2. Can increase the efficiency of the computer operation through identification and subsequent elimination of unused code.
3. Once developed, easy to implement.

The disadvantages of the mapping technique are the cost of obtaining the necessary software and the time required to use it.

EMBEDDED AUDIT MODULES

Embedded audit modules are segments of a program code that have been written and complied into the system to perform audit functions. Such modules might consist of procedures that are activated by the auditor on a periodic basis. An example of this type of module is a confirmation selection module embedded in a monthly billing program. Others are audit modules that provide continuous monitoring at selected points in a program. An example is an audit module that monitors overrides of controls or errors that are outside established tolerances. The system control audit review file (SCARF) is a typical technique used. Still other audit modules use extended transaction records. An example is the accumulation of all transactions associated with specific customer accounts over a certain period of time to determine that invoices, credit, and cash collections are properly recorded and accumulated. Figure 10.5 shows a schematic representation of an embedded audit module system.

Figure 10.5 Embedded Audit Module

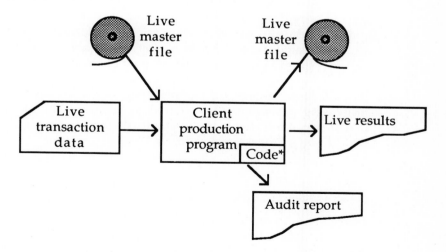

*Audit test embedded within production program, producing special audit report.

Advantages of embedded audit modules include:

1. They provide comprehensive transaction review.
2. Encourage auditor involvement while the system is being designed.

The disadvantages of embedded audit modules are that the auditor must build in controls to prevent unauthorized access to the embedded modules and that implementation is costly and time consuming and requires considerable skill.

SNAPSHOT

The **snapshot** is a technique that takes "pictures" of a transaction as it flows through the system. The auditor embeds software routines at different points within the system to print the contents of a transaction as it goes through the various processing stages. This technique allows the auditor to review the contents of computer memory and check, for example, different methods of depreciation computation for different types of assets.

Advantages of the snapshot technique include:

1. Limited printouts, concentrating on the needed data.
2. An invaluable aid to systems and programming personnel in debugging applications.
3. Very effective when used in conjunction with test data, integrated test facility, or tracing techniques to determine the results of processing for each type of test transaction entered.

The disadvantages of the snapshot technique are that a skilled data processing professional is required to use the technique effectively and that it may be difficult to anticipate all the conditions and logic points critical to the programming process.

BASE-CASE SYSTEM EVALUATION

Base-case system evaluation (BCSE) is a more comprehensive form of the test data and integrated test facility techniques. It uses a standardized body of data (input, parameters, and output) to test a computer application both before it is placed in a client's production program library and after its implementation. The term **base case** refers to a comprehensive set of test transactions (both valid and invalid) prepared by user personnel in conjunction with the auditor. This technique requires extremely heavy involvement of user personnel.

Advantages of base-case system evaluation include:

1. Because of the user's heavy participation in all phases of the development or modification process, the computer application more closely conforms to user requirements and therefore is more likely to function as prescribed.
2. Because of the built-in automatic file-to-file comparison and code comparison programs, less time and effort are needed for systems verification and greater accuracy results.
3. The use of a standardized body of data provides the auditor with an efficient means to test and verify the computer application.

The disadvantages of base-case system evaluation are the additional costs of system development and the need for heavy user involvement.

JOB ACCOUNTING DATA ANALYSIS

Most mainframe computer manufacturers provide the customer with a job accounting facility as an addition to their operating systems. *Job accounting* refers to collecting and maintaining a record of computer system activities and use. It provides the means for gathering and storing information to be used for billing users or for evaluating systems usage.

The auditor can use **job accounting data analysis** to test certain EDP-center controls, such as verifying that only authorized personnel used particular programs or data files, determining whether unauthorized uses, or attempts to use, remote terminals have occurred, and verifying that only authorized jobs have been processed and that proper tapes and disk files have been used.

Advantages of job accounting data analysis include:

1. Provides data on computer system activity and use of data processing resources.
2. Provides the auditor with information on how the data processing operation functions.

The major disadvantage of job accounting data analysis is that the auditor is unable to control the source of data through job accounting facilities, such as data or program manipulation.

Figure 10.6 Parallel Simulation

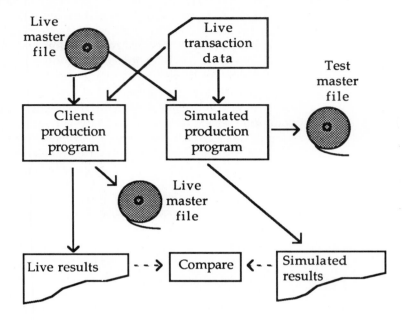

PARALLEL SIMULATION

Parallel simulation is illustrated in Figure 10.6. This method involves the use of one or more special computer programs to process live data files and simulate regular computer processing of applications. The same data are processed using the client's application program and the auditor's simulation program. The results are compared and discrepancies are investigated. In contrast to the test data and the integrated test facility methods, which process test data through live programs, the parallel simulation method processes live data through test programs. Generalized audit software can be used to improve the efficiency of the parallel simulation process.

Advantages of the parallel simulation include:

1. Auditor uses actual client data to examine a large number of comprehensive transactions.
2. Allows auditor to function independently from client personnel.
3. Only a moderate level of technical expertise required.
4. Audit tests can be performed at any time, subject only to the availability of computer time.

The disadvantages of parallel simulation are that it is time-consuming and costly to develop a complex simulation program and that the auditor has to update the simulation program whenever the client revises its application program.

SELECTING THE APPROPRIATE CAAT

Clearly, a number of techniques are available. By selecting and modifying them to fit the specific needs of different clients, the auditor can increase audit efficiency. At the same time, audit effectiveness will be increased because the auditor will invariably learn more about client EDP systems. This, in turn, leads to a better understanding of how the system functions and opens up additional opportunities for applying CAAT.

10.5 AUDITS OF RECORDS PRODUCED BY SERVICE CENTERS

NATURE OF SERVICE CENTERS

Service centers have taken on a major share of EDP activities for many companies. A **service center** is any organization that performs EDP functions for other organizations, including the actual processing of data.

Five major types of services are provided by service centers:

1. Renting computer time.
2. Providing time-shared computer services.
3. Providing computer facilities management.
4. Processing standard program packages.
5. Designing and processing tailored systems.[7]

The independent auditor can expect to encounter most frequently the last two types of services when auditing EDP-supported financial reporting systems. The use of a service center by the client does not in any way affect the auditor's objective and responsibilities when performing an audit.

EVALUATING CONTROLS AT SERVICE CENTERS

A review of the service center's controls is necessary when (1) the financial data processed by the service center have a material effect on the client's financial statements; (2) the auditor plans to rely to some extent on general and/or application controls exercised by the service center; and (3) user controls are not adequate to ensure prompt discovery of errors and irregularities. Reviews of the service center's operations should be similar in scope to those performed for a client-operated EDP center. In addition, they should include those factors unique to an off-premise service center operation, particularly the contractual agreement between the client and the service center.

Three major steps should be taken by the auditor when evaluating controls:

1. Gain an understanding of the system, including processing methods and controls used by the service center.
2. Perform compliance tests to ascertain that controls function as designed.
3. Obtain information needed to evaluate the client's control over the data processed at the service center.

ACCUMULATION OF EVIDENTIAL INFORMATION

The auditor can use several audit techniques, varying from traditional methods to CAAT applications, to collect evidential information. The CAAT programs could be those written by the service center, those written by or under the supervision of the auditor, and generalized computer audit programs.

Examples of applying CAAT applications include:

1. Examination of records for quality, completeness, consistency, and incorrect or unusual items.
2. Selecting and printing samples.
3. Testing calculations and making computations.
4. Summarizing data and performing analyses of the totals.
5. Comparing data maintained in separate files for correctness and consistency.
6. Comparing audit data with company records.[8]

THIRD-PARTY REVIEW OF SERVICE CENTERS

Duplication of effort resulting from an individual review of a service organization's general controls by the auditors of each of the center's customers can be avoided if the service center, its users, or their auditors engage a third-party auditor to review the service center's system and to issue an audit report. The following requirements are contained in the AICPA Audits of Service-Center-Produced Records, for an auditor's report to other CPAs on the internal controls of a service center:

1. A statement as to the scope of the examination and as to whether both a review of the system and tests of compliance were included.
2. A description of the service center's system, including controls, should either be included or incorporated by reference in the report.
3. The time period covered by the examination.
4. An opinion as to whether the system and system controls conform to the service center's description during the period under review.
5. A disclaimer of opinion as to the adequacy of accounting controls with respect to each user's application and with respect to the accounting controls of the service center itself. (Conclusions concerning these matters can be formulated only by the user auditor after consideration of both his client's internal accounting controls and those at the service center.)
6. Comments concerning unsatisfactory conditions in the system's accounting controls and recommendations for correction. This would include reporting the absence or nonoperation of the controls in the following categories:
    (a)   Controls that the service center's management have represented as being in existence but which are either not in existence or not in operation.
    (b)   Controls that the service center's management have not represented as being in existence but which, in the judgment of the third-party reviewer, are desirable.[9]

The client's auditor has the option of assuming or rejecting responsibility for the work of the other auditor. If the client's auditor is satisfied as to the independence and professional reputation of the other auditor, he or she may utilize the third-party auditor's report as a source of information in performing an evaluation of accounting control. Additionally the client's auditor may visit the third-party auditor and discuss the audit procedures followed and the results; review the audit programs of the third-party auditor; and review the working papers of the other auditor.

10.6 Summary

Auditing EDP centers and applications involves the study and review of internal controls, compliance testing, and substantive testing. The five major steps of internal control review are preliminary review, assessment of the preliminary review, detailed review of general controls, detailed review of application controls, and assessment of the detailed reviews. Compliance and substantive tests cover the four steps of compliance testing, compliance test assessment, testing and assessment of user controls, and substantive testing.

The objective of the preliminary review of internal controls is to understand the accounting systems in order to conduct the control evaluation effectively. During the preliminary review stage, the auditor should obtain information about the flow of transactions and the significance of output, the extent to which EDP is used in significant accounting applications, and the basic structure of accounting controls used. The preliminary review must encompass both general and application controls, including both EDP-center and user controls.

After completing the preliminary review, the auditor should assess the significance of the EDP accounting controls and determine the extent of the detailed review of the EDP accounting controls. The major objectives of the detailed review are to identify the general and application controls on which the auditor plans to rely, to determine how the controls operate, and to consider the effect of control strengths and weaknesses on tests of compliance. The auditor usually examines documentation; interviews internal auditors, EDP-center personnel, and user-department personnel; and observes the operation of accounting controls.

At the end of the detailed review the auditor should exercise audit judgment to decide whether to rely on EDP accounting controls, user controls, or a combination of the two and proceed with compliance testing. The purpose of compliance testing is to provide assurance that internal controls are functioning as intended and comply with the client's plans, policies, and procedures. The auditor usually applies both manual and computer-assisted audit techniques in performing compliance testing. Manual methods include the examination of records, inquiry, observation, and testing of control procedures.

In some situations the auditor may decide to rely on some user controls and reviews, tests, and evaluates them. At the conclusion of compliance testing, the auditor should exercise audit judgment to determine whether the necessary EDP- and user-control procedures are in place and are being followed satisfactorily. The auditor should also assess the effect of control strengths and weaknesses on the nature, timing, and extent of substantive testing to be applied. Substantive testing includes inspection, observation, inquiry, analysis, and confirmation. Inspection, observation, and inquiry procedures are manual. Analysis and confirmation procedures can be more efficiently and effectively performed by computer-assisted audit techniques, such as generalized audit software, test data, integrated test facility, tracing, mapping, embedded audit modules, snapshot, base-case system evaluation, job accounting data analysis, and parallel simulation.

Many companies use outside service centers to process their accounting and financial data. If possible, the auditor should conduct a review of the service center's controls and use several audit techniques to collect evidential information. Often, the service center, clients, or clients' auditors may engage a third-party auditor to review the service center's internal control system and to issue an audit report. In this situation the client's auditor should follow AICPA guidelines and prepare a report on third-party review of the service center.

Questions

1. If the auditor's objective of expressing an opinion on the financial statements does not change when the computer becomes part of a client's accounting system, what does change?
2. What are the objectives of the preliminary review of EDP internal controls?
3. What information will an application walk-through provide?
4. What conclusions should the auditor reach at the conclusion of the preliminary review of internal controls?
5. Why, when, and how would an auditor undertake a detailed review of an application's internal controls?
6. What is the purpose of compliance testing and how does it relate to substantive testing?
7. Describe each of the major computer-assisted audit techniques, when they would be used, and the evidence they would provide:
   - Generalized audit software.
   - Test data.
   - Integrated test facility.
   - Tracing.
   - Mapping.
   - Embedded audit modules.
   - Snapshot.
   - Base-case system evaluation.
   - Job accounting data analysis.
   - Parallel simulation.

8. Why should an auditor be concerned about records produced by a service center?
9. What evidence would the auditor collect for records produced by a service center?
10. What is a third-party review of a service center? How does it fit into the audit of records produced by a service center?

Problems

1. You are starting the audit of an EDP center. Whom would you interview and in what order? What questions would you ask these people?
2. Your client uses a service bureau to produce sales invoices and handle accounts receivable records. The client presents you with a third-party review of the service-center. What would you do to complete the audit of this sales and collection cycle?
3. A walk-through might be considered similar to the auditor's traditional plant tour. Compare and contrast these two auditing procedures.
4. Data processing departments are traditionally located in a number of different places in organizations. What are some of these places and how do you think they might affect your audit?
5. Classify the evidence obtained from the types of auditing procedures listed in Question 7 as compliance data, substantive data, or both. Develop a scheme for deciding how much of each type of evidence from the various tests you would need to satisfy the third standard of field work (sufficient competent evidential information).

Notes

1. Committee on Auditing Procedures, *Statement on Auditing Standards No. 1*. New York: AICPA, 1972, Paragraph 110.01.

2. For a detailed description of EDP audit planning, see Richard D. Webb, "Audit Planning—EDP Consideration," *The Journal of Accountancy*, May 1979, pp. 65–75.

3. Johnson, Everett C., Jr., "Applying SAS-3 in Your Audit Practice," *California CPA Quarterly*, December 1976, p. 27.

4. *The Auditor's Study and Evaluation of Internal Control in EDP Systems*. New York: AICPA, 1977, p. 11.

5. *Ibid.*, pp. 11–12.

6. *Computer-Assisted Audit Techniques.* New York: AICPA, 1979, p. 4.
7. *Audits of Service-Produced Records.* New York: AICPA, 1974, p. 4.
8. *Ibid.*, p. 33.
9. *Ibid.*, p. 43.

Additional References

Audit Approaches for a Computerized Inventory System. New York: American Institute of Certified Public Accountants, 1980.

Auditing in an EDP Environment: Partner/Manager Seminar—Participant's Guide. Chicago: Arthur Andersen & Co., 1981.

Audits of Service-Center-Produced Records. New York: American Institute of Certified Public Accountants, 1974.

Burch, John G., Jr., and Joseph L. Sardinas, Jr., *Computer Control and Audit: AT Total Systems Approach.* New York: John Wiley & Sons, 1978.

Cerullo, Michael J., and John C. Corless, "Auditing Computer Systems," *The CPA Journal,* September 1984, pp. 18–33.

Computer Audit Guidelines. Toronto: The Canadian Institute of Chartered Accountants, 1975.

Davis, Gordon, D. L. Adams, and C. A. Schaller, *Auditing and EDP,* 2nd ed. New York: American Institute of Certified Public Accountants, 1983.

Diesem, John, "EDP Auditing: A Team Effort," *Computer Decisions,* February 1985, pp. 42–45.

Efficient and Effective Use of CAAT. New York: Price Waterhouse, 1981.

"The Effects of Computer Processing on the Examination of Financial Statements," *Statement on Auditing Standards,* No. 48. New York: American Institute of Certified Public Accountants, 1984.

Halper, Stanley D., Glenn C. Davis, P. Jarlath O'Neill-Dunne, and Pamela R. Pfau, *Handbook of EDP Auditing.* Boston: Warren, Gorham & Lamont, 1985.

Information Security. Delran, N.J.: Datapro Research Corporation, 1985.

Jancura, Elise G., and Boos, Robert, *Establishing Controls and Auditing the Computerized Accounting System.* New York: Van Nostrand Reinhold, 1981.

Li, David H., *Control Objectives—Controls in a Computer Environment: Objectives, Guidelines, and Audit Procedures.* Carol Stream, Ill.: EDP Auditors Foundation, 1983.

Mair, William C., Donald R. Wood, and Keagle W. Davis, *Computer Control and Audit,* 2nd ed. Altamonte Springs, Fla.: Institute of Internal Auditors, 1978.

Molnar, Louie, "Disaster Recovery Testing," *EDPACS,* November 1984, pp. 1–6.

Perry, William E., *A Standard for Auditing Computer Applications.* Pennsauken, N.J.: Auerbach, 1985.

Pleier, Joseph R., "Computer-Assisted Auditing," *The EDP Auditor*, Vol. 2, 1984, pp. 13–20.

Porter, W., Thomas and William E. Perry, *EDP Controls and Auditing*, 4th ed. Boston: Kent, 1984.

Stanford Research Institute, *Systems Auditability and Control: Audit Practices.* Altamonte Springs, Fla.: Institute of Internal Auditors, 1977.

Vallabheneni, S. Rao, *Information Systems Audit Process.* Carol Stream, Ill.: EDP Auditors Foundation, 1983.

Watne, Donald A., and Peter B. B. Turney, *Auditing EDP Systems.* Englewood Cliffs, N.J.: Prentice-Hall, 1984.

Weber, Ron, *EDP Auditing: Conceptual Foundations and Practice.* New York: McGraw-Hill, 1982.

APPENDIX 10.A EDP CENTER AND APPLICATION AUDITING PROCEDURES *

Table 10.A.1   EDP Center Review Procedures

Control Type	Audit Review Procedures
1. Segregation of functions between the EDP department and users	1. Review organization charts and job descriptions for evidence of proper segregation of functions. 2. Interview EDP and user-department personnel to ascertain that the procedures designed to ensure organizational independence are clearly understood and adhered to.

(continued on next page)

---

* Most of the audit review procedures are based on *The Auditor's Study and Evaluation of Internal Control in EDP Systems.* New York: AICPA, 1977, Chapters 3 and 4.

Table 10.A.1   EDP Center Review Procedures (continued)

Control Type	Audit Review Procedures
	3. Observe actual operations on a surprise basis and note the degree of management supervision being exercised.
	4. Review top management's policy directives concerning the independence of the EDP department.
2. Authorization of transactions	1. Review input documents for authorization evidence.
	2. Review user-department approvals on output sent there for verification.
	3. Review the reconciliation of control totals maintained outside of EDP with the results of computer processing.
	4. Where feasible, examine available evidence indicating that such reconciliations take place in the normal course of operations.
	5. Review preprocessing, postprocessing, or programmed controls to determine whether processing is provided for in accordance with management authorization.
3. Segregation of functions within the EDP department	1. Review the EDP organization chart to ascertain that systems and programming functions are separated from computer operations.

(continued on next page)

Table 10.A.1   EDP Center Review Procedures (continued)

Control Type	Audit Review Procedures
	2. Observe EDP operations on a surprise basis to determine that systems analysts and programmers do not have unrestricted access to hardware, files, or programs.
	3. Observe the operation of the control group to determine whether it is independent of the systems, programming, and operations groups.
	4. Observe the operation of the librarian function, or review appropriate logs and records to determine that usage records are consistently maintained and that only authorized personnel are permitted to remove data files.
	5. Review alternate or back-up assignments to ascertain that segregation of functions is similarly maintained.
4. Personnel controls	1. Review documents such as job descriptions and employee selection criteria.
	2. Interview EDP personnel on proper employee selection and training.
	3. Interview EDP management and operating employees on the extent and effectiveness of management supervision.

(continued on next page)

Table 10.A.1   EDP Center Review Procedures (continued)

Control Type	Audit Review Procedures
	4. Examine time and job logs to determine that operators' responsibilities are rotated and that vacations are taken regularly by all EDP employees.
	5. Review screening policies in both employee relations and EDP for adequacy.
	6. Review recruitment policy documents to ascertain that security clearance procedures have been covered.
	7. Review employee manuals to determine whether new employees are provided with orientation programs on security and control requirements.
5. Planning, budget, and user billing systems	1. Review planning and budget documents.
	2. Review budget variance reports.
	3. Interview EDP and user-department personnel on the adequacy of the user billing system.
	4. Review job accounting reports.
	5. Interview top management and EDP management to identify and discuss long-range strategies, plans, and budgets related to EDP department goals.
	6. Review the description of responsibilities and functions of the steering committee.

(continued on next page)

Table 10.A.1   EDP Center Review Procedures (continued)

Control Type	Audit Review Procedures
6. Hardware controls	1. Interview users to determine their satisfaction level with equipment reliability. 2. Review the vendor's literature and systems documentation to determine the available control capabilities provided in the hardware. 3. Review preventive maintenance controls and records. 4. Review records for utilization, cleaning, and recertification of tapes and disks. 5. Review the maintenance logs for each hardware device to determine the needed frequency of nonscheduled maintenance.
7. System software controls	1. Review the vendor's literature to determine the available control features in system software. 2. Review the EDP department's control procedures for changes to system software. 3. Interview EDP personnel to determine whether significant changes have been made to the operating system during the period under review. 4. Review documentation supporting changes to system software. 5. Observe the console message to ascertain that the operating system is functioning properly.

(continued on next page)

Table 10.A.1   EDP Center Review Procedures (continued)

Control Type	Audit Review Procedures
	6. Review documentation related to system software maintenance.
8. Physical access controls	1. Interview appropriate personnel on proper physical access control devices. 2. Observe the presence of physical access control devices, such as keys, magnetic coded cards, badges, security guards, closed circuit TVs, and the like. 3. Review logs for EDP room sign-in and sign-out evidence. 4. Review the adequacy of procedures for escorting visitors during their stay in the EDP room. 5. Observe physical security procedures at remote locations.
9. Program documentation access	1. Review documented procedures for the existence of controls to prevent or detect unauthorized access to program documentation. 2. Interview the custodian of documentation and systems personnel about the procedures currently being followed. 3. Observe the operation of access controls. 4. Tour facilities used to store system software documentation.

(continued on next page)

Table 10.A.1   EDP Center Review Procedures (continued)

Control Type	Audit Review Procedures
10. Data files and program access	1. Review the librarian's method of controlling unauthorized access to programs and data files. 2. Review data files and program access records to test the librarian function as it applies to significant accounting applications. 3. If the librarian functions are a part-time duty of one or more employees, determine whether their other duties are incompatible with the control aspects of the librarian function. 4. Observe whether operators and programmers are denied access to the data files and programs in the computer library.
11. Computer hardware access	1. Perform an inquiry on and review the existence of data security provisions relating to system access from remote terminals. 2. Review the procedures for collecting and analyzing utilization data. Determine the extent and timing of management's review of these data. 3. Review, on a test basis, available console logs. Select questionable entries on the logs and make inquiries as to how they were resolved.

(continued on next page)

Table 10.A.1 EDP Center Review Procedures (continued)

Control Type	Audit Review Procedures
	4. On a test basis, compare utilization records to operations schedules and systems documentation to determine that processing is authorized and is performed in accordance with the established schedule. Determine whether run times appear reasonable, based on documentation estimates and prior experience. 5. Review procedures related to the location and use of terminals.
12. Control group	1. Review the organizational structure and relationships of the control function. 2. Obtain additional information about the application of controls by interviewing users, EDP personnel, and personnel involved in the control function.
13. Files and database controls	1. Review and interview EDP personnel about the organizational structure and relationships of the database administrator. 2. Review the vendor's literature to determine the available control features in the database management system.

(continued on next page)

Table 10.A.1   EDP Center Review Procedures (continued)

Control Type	Audit Review Procedures
	3. Review documentary evidence of the work of the database administrator, such as procedures manuals, periodic reports, and notes on meetings. 4. Review the types of information provided by the dictionary/directory and check to determine whether that security levels are appropriate. 5. Examine file protection rings and labels.
14. Standard procedures	1. Determine whether there are written procedures for preparation of input for processing and that input documents have been standardized where practicable. 2. Review operations manuals and determine whether they appear to provide the operator with an understanding of processing. 3. On a test basis observe operations to determine that those described in the manuals are being carried out. 4. Determine via inquiry, review, and observation that schedules for processing or output are prepared and utilized by appropriate personnel.

(continued on next page)

Table 10.A.1   EDP Center Review Procedures (continued)

Control Type	Audit Review Procedures
	5. Review systems and procedures manuals in user departments on quality and completeness.
	6. Interview user- and EDP-department personnel on their understanding and adherence to approved procedures.
15. Physical security	1. Review EDP department procedures with regard to:
	(a) Off-premises storage of important files, programs, and documentation, as well as a formal plan for record retention.
	(b) Environmental controls to prevent excess humidity, temperature variations, or other atmospheric conditions.
	(c) Protection of computer hardware, programs, and files against fire and other hazards.
	(d) Business interruption or special data-processing risk insurance to cover the costs of restoring EDP operations.
	2. Observe presence and use of temperature, fire, and humidity control devices.
	3. Observe off-premise back-up files and facilities.

(continued on next page)

Table 10.A.1   EDP Center Review Procedures (continued)

Control Type	Audit Review Procedures
	4. Examine recovery procedures to ascertain that they have been clearly defined, documented, and tested.
	5. Review monitoring logs and question EDP and user staff to determine the frequency of system failures and the level of user understanding of and satisfaction with recovery procedures.
	6. Interview EDP-department management to determine their functions in disaster recovery planning.
	7. Observe the results of disaster recovery tests.
16. Internal audit	1. Interview internal audit staff on their level of participation in systems design and findings in work performed.
	2. Interview internal audit staff to determine the nature and extent of independent review and test established controls.
	3. Review internal audit reports of work performed and working papers.
	4. Review the charter of the internal audit group to determine whether it has been accorded independence in its tasks and in reporting its audit findings.

Table 10.A.2 Application Control Review Procedures

Control Type	Sample Audit Review Procedures
1. Input authorization	1. Review a selection of processed input documents for proper approval in the user department. 2. Scan input control records to confirm that batch controls have been properly prepared and to identify unprocessed batches. 3. Inquire about and observe whether data control has accounted for all batch numbers. 4. Observe logging-on procedures and note the functioning of password verification. 5. Interview EDP manager to determine how often all passwords are changed and who has the authority to change them. 6. Observe input control processes. 7. Review user-department data preparation procedures. 8. Review source document retention procedures.
2. Data conversion	1. Discuss procedures with data entry personnel. 2. Review the procedures and techniques for controlling the conversion of input to machine-sensible form. 3. Observe the performance of verification procedures and the processing of edit or exception listings.

(continued on next page)

Table 10.A.2   Application Control Review Procedures (continued)

Control Type	Sample Audit Review Procedures
	4. Examine the cards sent to processing for evidence of key verification when data entry is performed by use of cards. 5. Review error reports to determine the types and extent of errors that have occurred. 6. Determine whether source documents used in data conversion are marked to protect against duplication.
3. Data movement: transmission	1. Review data movement control procedures. 2. Observe the procedures for issuing and verifying receipts used to control data movement and review procedures for batch total reconciliation. 3. Ascertain that the user department uses batch control totals generated by terminals to validate the completeness of batches received as input data.
4. Input validation	1. Review procedures for the application and verification of codes and determine that reasonably effective techniques are being used to check their accuracy. 2. Determine the existence of computer edit controls. 3. Examine evidence of various input validations.

(continued on next page)

Table 10.A.2 Application Control Review Procedures (continued)

Control Type	Sample Audit Review Procedures
	4. Determine whether intelligent terminals are in use for front-end validation and editing.
5. Error handling	1. Review error handling control procedures to determine their adequacy.
	2. Review the error log to determine whether any items have remained uncleared for an unreasonably long time.
	3. Observe the performance of error-handling procedures.
	4. Investigate old uncleared errors.
	5. Determine whether the suspense files have record counts to control the number of entries in the files.
6. Maintaining data accuracy during processing	1. Review procedures for generating and reconciling control totals.
	2. Observe the performance of the reconciliation process.
	3. Review whether control totals that are being generated to determine whether they provide a basis for establishing adequate run-to-run controls.
	4. Observe procedures for reconciling run-to-run controls.

(continued on next page)

Table 10.A.2   Application Control Review Procedures (continued)

Control Type	Sample Audit Review Procedures
	5. Through monitoring logs and discussion with EDP and user staff, determine the frequency of system failure and the level of user understanding of and satisfaction with recovery procedures.
	6. Determine whether audit trails exist to allow the reconstruction of data files when needed.
	7. When files are updated directly, determine whether the program generates a before-image and an after image of the record being updated.
	8. Determine that the application program includes file completion checks on both transaction file and master file.
7. Programmed limit and reasonableness tests	1. Review application documentation to determine what edit criteria have been provided within computer programs.
	2. Review data processing validation and editing procedures.
8. File controls	1. Review file and processing controls to determine their accuracy.
	2. Verify that external labels are observed and meaningful.

(continued on next page)

Table 10.A.2   Application Control Review Procedures (continued)

Control Type	Sample Audit Review Procedures
	3. Determine that the internal file trailer labels contain control totals.
	4. Determine that the application program includes routines to check internal file header labels before processing.
9. Output control reconciliations	1. Determine that a control group exists and has authority commensurate with tasks.
	2. Review procedures for reconciling output to other control totals.
	3. Observe the performance of reconciliations.
10. Reviewing and testing processing results	1. Review procedures for verifying changes that do not lend themselves to control by the balancing of totals.
	2. Observe the performance of verification procedures.
	3. Discuss with users the adequacy and adherence to controls.
	4. Review output error-handling procedures.
11. Distribution of output	1. Review procedures for controlling the distribution of output.
	2. Observe the distribution of output.

(continued on next page)

Table 10.A.2   Application Control Review Procedures (continued)

Control Type	Sample Audit Review Procedures
	3. Interview EDP users and output distribution personnel to obtain their opinion of the current system and their suggestions to improve it. 4. Determine whether distribution lists are updated properly.
12. Record retention	1. Interview EDP personnel about proper record retention policy and procedures.

Table 10.A.3   EDP-Center Control Compliance Testing Procedures

Control Type	Sample Compliance Testing Procedures
1. Segregation of functions between the EDP department and users	1. Direct visual observation at various times. 2. Vouch selected transactions related to EDP personnel. 3. For on-line systems, confirm through review of the list of authorized users that there is adequate segregation of duties between users and programmers.
2. Authorization of transactions	1. Trace flow of selected transactions to verify proper origination and authorization. 2. Examine logs and records.

(continued on next page)

Table 10.A.3 EDP-Center Control Compliance Testing Procedures (continued)

Control Type	Sample Compliance Testing Procedures
	3. Analyze system-generated job accounting statistics to identify persons submitting work, programs used, and whether an entry was a regular job or a test.
3. Segregation of functions within EDP department	1. Direct visual observation at various times. 2. Vouch selected transactions related to EDP personnel. 3. Examine the access capabilities of EDP management. 4. Examine console logs during operators' vacation periods.
4. Personnel controls	1. Examine personnel files and verify that adequate references were obtained and that each employee took his or her vacation entitlement during the preceding year. 2. Examine logs and attendance sheets for rotation of operator duties. 3. Verify that passwords or other control devices to gain access to terminals or other computer resources are changed immediately upon the termination of employees.
5. Planning, budget, and user billing systems	1. Review annual planning and budget documents prepared and approved by EDP management.

(continued on next page)

Table 10.A.3   EDP-Center Control Compliance Testing Procedures (continued)

Control Type	Sample Compliance Testing Procedures
	2. Trace billing statements back to job accounting records. 3. Test the reconciliation of monthly billing totals and total EDP costs.
6. Hardware controls	1. Review console printer and downtime logs. 2. Test compliance with the preventive maintenance schedule. 3. Verify that preventive maintenance is not scheduled during peak-load time.
7. Software controls	1. Review output of the job accounting system to determine proper authorization of the use of any utilities that enable programs or operating systems to be changed without leaving an audit trail. 2. Determine that system software installation activities were in compliance with the proper written procedures.
8. Physical access controls	1. Obtain lists of those having access to the computer area and confirm that these lists are authorized. 2. Observe and test specified procedures for compliance in actual practice.

(continued on next page)

Table 10.A.3   EDP-Center Control Compliance Testing Procedures (continued)

Control Type	Sample Compliance Testing Procedures
9. Program documentation access	1. Examine library records for checkout of program documentation to authorized personnel.
10. Data files and program access	1. Test library procedures for limiting access to data files and programs. 2. Trace file usage using a job accounting system to guard against exposure of confidential data. 3. Verify that authorizations are necessary to access restricted data files and programs.
11. Computer hardware access	1. Examine logs and records of hardware access. 2. Obtain lists of all terminals and verify that terminals are locked or inaccessible to unauthorized persons when not in use.
12. Control group	1. Trace data flow through the control group to determine adequacy of control and scheduling procedures. 2. Test the disposition of errors in significant accounting applications by tracing corrections to related records. 3. Observe and test specified procedures for compliance in actual practice.

(continued on next page)

Table 10.A.3   EDP-Center Control Compliance Testing Procedures (continued)

Control Type	Sample Compliance Testing Procedures
13. Files and database controls	1. Examine the approvals and approval procedures for access to the database and files. 2. Examine security procedures related to scheme data. 3. Verify the existence of a file-management system. 4. Perform a random sampling of inventoried files to ascertain that they have proper label identification.
14. Standard procedures	1. Verify that all standards are communicated and understood by the appropriate personnel. 2. Examine library records for checkout of manuals to authorized personnel.
15. Physical security	1. Examine insurance policies for adequate coverage and confirm coverage with insurers. 2. Review contractual agreements with back-up facilities. 3. Examine the records of performance reviews. 4. Observe and test specified procedures for compliance in actual practice.
16. Internal audit	1. Test internal audit work.

Table 10.A.4   Application Control Compliance Testing Procedures

Control Type	Sample Compliance Testing Procedures
1. Input authorization	1. Examine a selected sample of input documents for evidence that transactions were properly authorized. 2. Examine a sample of prenumbered forms and account for duplicated or missing documents. 3. Examine terminal access log and verify that failed access attempts of a suspicious nature were investigated. 4. Verify that approvals are granted by the responsible personnel. 5. Ascertain that passwords and authorization codes are non-printing, nondisplaying.
2. Data conversion	1. Trace a sample of batch totals to control logs. 2. Compare sample edited transactions to original input. 3. Select documents from those processed and examine for evidence of key verification.
3. Data movement: Transactions	1. Trace, on a test basis, a group of transactions through the system from initiation to completion of processing. 2. Test the reconciliation of key run-to-run controls.

(continued on next page)

Table 10.A.4   Application Control Compliance Testing Procedures (continued)

Control Type	Sample Compliance Testing Procedures
4. Input validation	1. Trace, on a test basis, code values on transaction files to supporting source documents to determine that codes are being properly verified. 2. Use a test deck to test the operation of specific control features or enter ambiguous or false data into the normal input processing flow to see whether errors are detected. 3. Review and test program coding. 4. Determine that no one is allowed to override or bypass input validation and editing procedures.
5. Error handling	1. Test for proper recording in the error log. 2. Test error clearance and the resulting corrected transaction. 3. Trace out-of-balance conditions for correction and reentry. 4. Test procedures for the cancellation of input documents. 5. Test that, before reentry, all corrections are reviewed and approved by supervisors.
6. Maintaining data accuracy during processing	1. Trace a sample of control totals to related input controls. 2. Test the reconciliation of selected run-to-run controls.

(continued on next page)

Table 10.A.4 Application Control Compliance Testing Procedures (continued)

Control Type	Sample Compliance Testing Procedures
	3. Use generalized audit software to check the accuracy of control records on the transaction log and master file.
	4. For selected days on which system failures occurred, verify that proper recovery procedures were followed.
	5. Verify that operations management reviews console logs for operator interventions, label overrides, and equipment checks.
7. Programmed limit and reasonableness tests	1. Use computer audit software to perform an after-the-fact edit and review of the data recorded on output files for significant accounting applications. This procedure may be utilized particularly in those cases where the output to be reviewed is only available in machine-readable form.
	2. Use test decks to test the limit and reasonableness checks in the system.
8. File controls	1. Examine, on a test basis, the console log for error messages caused by operator action or for indications that label processing and checking are being bypassed. Determine how errors were subsequently resolved.

(continued on next page)

Table 10.A.4   Application Control Compliance Testing Procedures (continued)

Control Type	Sample Compliance Testing Procedures
	2. Print header labels for selected files and check the information contained thereon. 3. Confirm, on a test basis, under audit control, master-file changes with the affected third parties.
9. Output control reconciliations	1. Test the reconciliations of output totals to input and cumulative data totals. 2. Test additions of final output and trace to the financial records.
10. Reviewing and testing processing results	1. Test the procedures used by user departments or independent groups to review output. 2. Test the comparison of output with source documents.
11. Distribution of output	1. Test the distribution of selected outputs to determine that the recipients are properly authorized. 2. Test the method of correcting output distribution errors.
12. Record retention	1. Trace file back-up and retention of a specific application. 2. Verify that the retention policies for output documents are being complied with.

Chapter **11**

System Development Controls and Auditing

11.1 INTRODUCTION

System development is the design, development, and implementation of new systems and modification or maintenance of existing systems, including user and EDP procedures, controls, and application programs. System development controls are concerned with designing and testing new systems, effective continuity of systems, program changes, operational efficiency and effectiveness, and auditability.

The investment in systems and programs frequently represents more than one-half of total EDP expenditures. Computerizing a major accounting system is a sizable undertaking. Often months, or even years, are required to design programs and implement a major system, so there are many opportunities for error and wasted effort. If a system is so poorly designed that it cannot prevent or detect intentional and unintentional errors or irregularities, it may be impossible to rely on system controls. In extreme cases, we might not even be able to use the output generated by the system.

The objectives of system development controls therefore are to

1. ensure that all system development activities are properly authorized, tested, reviewed, documented, approved, and implemented;
2. ensure that appropriate standards, policies, and procedures exist and are used to facilitate the management and control of systems and programming activities;
3. ensure that systems and programs are effectively maintained or modified; and
4. ensure that the system is auditable.

System development controls usually fall into one of three categories: new system development controls, system and program maintenance controls, and documentation. In this chapter, we discuss these three categories

Table 11.1   System Development Control Structure

Control Category	Control Type
New system development	Management and user participation and approvals Development standards and guidelines Project management System testing and conversion controls Post-installation review
System program maintenance controls	Authorization and approvals Standard procedures and documentation controls Programmer and operations personnel controls Testing of system and program changes
Documentation	Documentation standards System documentation Program documentation Operations and user documentation

and possible control techniques or procedures. They are summarized in Table 11.1 by control category and, within each category, by control type. In the final section of this chapter, we cover the internal auditor's role and steps in auditing the systems development process.

LEARNING OBJECTIVES

By the time you have completed this chapter, you should be able to:

1. Describe the three major areas of system development controls.
2. Identify specific system, program maintenance and documentation controls.

3. Explain the major phases in the system development process and the impact of each phase on the auditor's evaluation decision.
4. List the major steps in auditing the system development process.

11.2 SYSTEM DEVELOPMENT CONTROLS

System development controls should ensure a high level of accuracy and reliability in the development of new systems. In addition, they should help achieve the goals of developing quality systems within cost and on schedule. And, finally, they should include effective application controls and proper testing in order to preserve the integrity of application controls after the system has become operational. Five major types of controls govern the development of new systems: (1) management and user participation and approvals; (2) development standards and guidelines; (3) project management; (4) system testing and conversion controls; and (5) post-installation review.

MANAGEMENT AND USER PARTICIPATION AND APPROVALS

The procedures for system design, including the acquisition of software packages, should require active participation by representatives of the users and, as appropriate, the accounting department and internal auditors. Those who will use the new system generally know what they want the system to provide. Thus it is important that users be actively involved in the systems development process in the following ways to determine specifically the requirements for input data, calculations to be performed, and output data.

1. Definition of short-, medium-, and long-term objectives for use of the system.
2. Preparation of a formal statement of system requirements.
3. Approval of the feasibility study and outline of system proposals.
4. Participation in and approval of system design, including all report layouts, input forms, control reports, and the like.
5. Documentation of user controls.
6. System tests.
7. Approval of the results of testing the new system, training programs, and conversion plans prior to implementation.

8. Participation in the actual conversion to and implementation of the new system.
9. Selection of application software.
10. Post-implementation review of the actual operation of the system.
11. Acceptance of the new system for implementation.

Management approval at appropriate levels should be obtained after each major phase of system development. The following control techniques reflect the types of management participation needed.

1. Review and approval of the system proposal at the feasibility stage prior to system design.
2. Monitoring of the development process by comparing actual results to budgets and schedules at the conclusion of each major phase.
3. EDP-management supervision, review, and approval of new application programs.
4. User-management review and final approval of test results for the new system, training programs, and conversion plans prior to placing the new system in operation.

An internal auditor should be a member of the systems development team, review system specifications to ensure the adequacy of proposed controls, and participate in the development of specific controls. The external auditor is concerned primarily with the existing system of accounting control and would therefore be interested basically in the relationship between built-in controls and new applications implemented during the period under review. The internal auditor's working papers can provide valuable information about the participation of users, management, and internal auditors in the development of the new system for the external auditor's use.

When the new system has financial reporting or accounting significance, the accounting department should also be represented on the development team. The accountant should review system specifications to ensure the appropriateness of the accounting principles and controls proposed and participate in the actual development of accounting controls.

STANDARDS AND GUIDELINES

System development requires a coordinated effort among representatives of senior management, EDP-center managers, and user-department supervisory personnel. This coordination can best be accomplished with the use of formal standards and guidelines that describe the methodology to be followed from initial systems planning through final testing and conversion. System development standards and guidelines are important because they ensure that:

1. Appropriate general and application controls are considered, selected, and installed during the development process.
2. Adequate audit trails are provided to allow all transactions to be traced both forward and backward between their sources and final totals.
3. User and EDP personnel are familiar with the procedures, controls, and implementation of new applications.
4. Adequate testing is performed to verify all processing logic, computations, and control procedures.

Standards are necessary to ensure that all parts of a new system are developed on a consistent basis. Without standards, important system development activities may be omitted or performed incorrectly. Formal procedures provide EDP management with a means of evaluating and controlling performance. Organization-wide standards can also facilitate communication among the various groups responsible for a successful information system by providing a common vocabulary and methods of description. Improved communication can eliminate time-consuming and expensive misunderstandings.

System standards aid the auditing of computerized procedures because they assist the auditor in determining his or her role in the verification and attestation process. Documentation standards also provide a basis for both financial and operational audits. Typical system development standards and guidelines should include:

1. Identification of the necessary phases of system development and the approvals required at each phase.
2. Requirements for project planning and management, such as budgets, schedules, and staffing plans.
3. Standards for system controls.
4. Conventions to be used in system design and programming, such as required content and format of system design specifications, standard naming conventions for programs and files, programming languages to be used, program design conventions, and flowcharting.
5. Formal testing and implementation procedures.
6. Requirements for system and program documentation.
7. Guidelines for training EDP and user-department personnel.

System development standards and guidelines should be adequately documented and should be approved by senior management. System development activities should be closely supervised by EDP management to ensure adherence to the standards and guidelines.

PROJECT MANAGEMENT

Project management involves the planning and controlling of the system development process. The objectives of project management are to deliver a quality system on schedule and within budget and to communicate the status of each phase of the project to all participants. The main elements of project management include: (1) implementing a system development life cycle (SDLC); and (2) providing project time and budget status reports.

The SDLC is a systematic and structured approach to the development of a computerized system. This technique provides a model for management's use in determining the standard contents of each phase and controlling costs and schedules for the proposed system. Guidelines, communication channels, and back-up documents are developed for users and EDP personnel for use in planning and explaining the different phases of a project. Specific review points are established, at which management and users must make a decision to continue, modify, or terminate a project based on progressively refined benefit–cost analyses.

There are many variations of SDLC. Some organizations include as many as 15 phases; others as few as four. The 1977 Institute of Internal Auditors' report contained an example of SDLC that included five phases:

1. Project definition—that phase whose primary purpose is to define the user requirements and uses for the system.
2. System analysis and design—that phase in which an overall description of the system is prepared.
3. Detailed design and programming—that phase that focuses on the internal components of the system and the development of computer programs needed to form the system.
4. System test—that phase in which the system is exercised to determine the correctness and completeness of implementation to the user requirements as manifest in the design documents.
5. Conversion—that phase in which the tested system and operational procedures are initiated to move the system into a full operational mode.[1]

A number of activities comprise each phase of an SDLC. Figure 11.1 presents phases, activities, and control points for a typical SDLC. This SDLC is well-planned and contains sufficient detail to enable the auditor to perform distinct reviews of completed work. In addition, all requirements specified for each control point must be satisfied before that phase or the next phase can be continued.

There are 15 control points in the SDLC shown in Figure 11.1. These control points are internal auditor checkpoints; they are grouped in terms of general management controls and computer processing system quality controls. The six management controls discussed in the IIA report are:

- *Control point 1*—The EDP auditor, user, and the project leader review the project organization, the arrangements with the user for communications, and the plans and work program for the design. This central point helps the project leader to establish a good working relationship with the user to ensure that the system reflects user requirements.
- *Control point 2*—The user, EDP auditor, and project leader review the analysis and planned cost for completeness and accuracy. In addition, the project control and communications plan is discussed and changed if necessary. The user plays a major role at this control point in assuring himself that proper analysis has taken place.
- *Control point 3*—The user, EDP auditor, and project leader review the conceptual design documentation for accuracy, completeness, and any changes that may have occurred. A revised cost–benefit plan is developed, and the EDP auditor presents the findings to top management.
- *Control point 4*—The user, EDP auditor, and project leader review the project organization resulting from the first phase, the communication links established between team members, users, and EDP auditors, schedules and work plans, and other items germane to the specific project.
- *Control point 14*—The user, EDP auditor, computer operation personnel, and the project leader review the conversion plan for completeness of detail and personnel involved. Plans for communicating the production schedule to top management are discussed as well as other miscellaneous considerations germane to the specific project.
- *Control point 15*—The user, EDP auditor, and project leader review all problems not yet resolved, adequacy of documentation, and any incomplete activities identified. Final reports on the project status can then be written by the EDP auditor.[2]

Figure 11.1 System Development Life-Cycle Audit

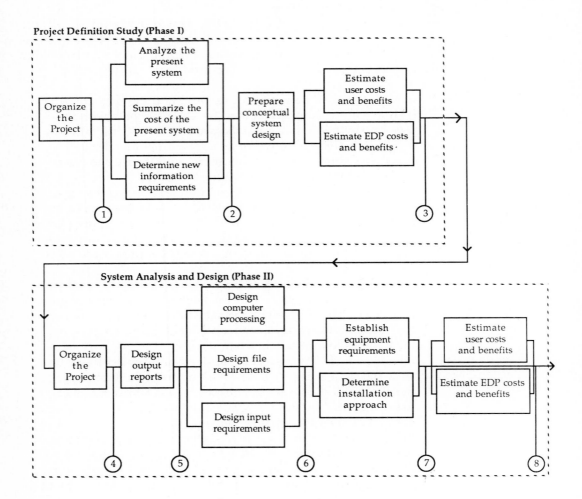

(continued on next page)

Source: Systems Auditability and Control: Control Practices. Al-tamonte Springs, Fla.: Institute of Internal Auditors, 1977, p. 104A.

Figure 11.1 System Development Life-Cycle Audit (continued)

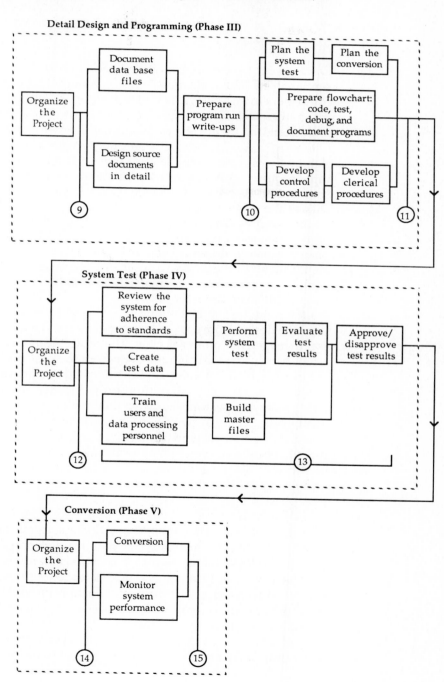

Eleven computer processing system quality controls are discussed in the IIA report. Control points 1 and 4 have already been discussed under management controls. The remaining nine control points are described as follows:

- *Control point 5*—The EDP auditor, user, project leader, and design analysts review the detailed design output reports for completeness and clarity. The EDP auditor attempts to ensure that sufficient design documentation exists to allow for a clear understanding by the test team and the EDP audit staff.
- *Control point 6*—The user, EDP auditor, project leader, and design analysts review the file requirement specifications and the input requirements associated with them. The user attempts to ensure that the file requirements do not implicitly or explicitly change the original system specifications.
- *Control point 7*—The user, project leader, EDP auditor and other data processing personnel responsible for hardware planning review the equipment requirements to meet the requirements of the designed systems. Completeness of the equipment requirement is important to avoid unanticipated equipment costs at a later date.
- *Control point 8*—The EDP auditor, user, and project leader review the design from cost, data processing standards, and general management points of view. The project leader is interested in ensuring that all loose ends from the past two phases are in place before moving into the detailed design phase.
- *Control point 9*—The EDP auditor, project leader, user, and data processing personnel make a final review of plans, equipment, costs, project organization, and communications channels to ensure that all participants have agreed upon the status and direction of the project. The project leader is primarily concerned with assuring top managment that sufficient systems analysis and design have taken place before the detailed design phase.
- *Control point 10*—The EDP auditor, user, and project leader review the documentation scheme and documents available describing the file systems, interface data handler programs, and program run documents for compliance to standards, completeness, accuracy, and clarity. The project leader is primarily concerned with ensuring that the project team is providing adequate documentation to meet data processing and user documentation standards.
- *Control point 11*—The EDP auditor, the project team members, testers, and user review the detailed system to ensure that it

follows from the general system design and still meets the user's requirements. In addition, the test plan is reviewed for completeness, timing, and cost. The conversion plan and associated paperwork are reviewed for reasonableness, completeness, and clarity. As this is the last checkpoint before the test phase, the project leader takes special care to ensure that the original design requirements are still intact or that a traceable trail exists that explains to top management and users why the system has changed.

- *Control point 12*—The EDP auditor, testers, user, and project leader review the test team organization to ensure that the proper people are present and that the project test plan is complete and consistent. The project leader is primarily concerned with assuring himself that the test plan will completely test the system and in particular will test internal controls designed in the system.
- *Control point 13*—The EDP auditor, user, and testers develop test data, build master files, review test results and monitor the test plan progress to ensure that it is adhered to throughout the test phase.[3]

SYSTEM TESTING AND CONVERSION CONTROLS

The purpose of the system testing activity is to test all aspects of the system as a unit, including programs, computer operations, user activities, and control group functions. Testing performed during the system development process can have a major impact on the subsequent reliability of that system. If adequate testing is not carried out, the system is not likely to function properly, and inadvertent application program errors or erroneous user procedures may not be detected. Thus, to ensure that a new system is operating satisfactorily before it is implemented, the user and EDP departments should together extensively test the system to see that it functions properly, that it satisfies the user's needs, and that its controls operate properly.

Systems and programs should generally be tested in three stages: (1) unit or program testing; (2) system testing; and (3) user-acceptance testing. In unit or program testing, each new program is tested individually with test data. Programmers who developed the programs test them to determine whether their logic is valid and whether the program consumes resources efficiently. This form of testing is oriented heavily toward the actual internal details of programs.

System testing is usually performed by systems analysts. It involves the testing of the various computer programs in the required sequence to ensure that related programs operate properly together. The general controls governing system testing include system testing standards and formalized guidelines or procedures for test-data preparation; test execution should be established, documented and enforced. System testing should be a joint effort of user and EDP personnel and should include both the manual and computerized phases of the system. Final approval should be obtained from appropriate levels of management, user personnel, and EDP personnel prior to placing a new system into operation.

User-acceptance testing is performed by or in conjunction with the user to reveal discrepancies between the total system and its original goals and objectives. It usually includes all phases of the system and involves the use of test transactions specifically designed to violate control procedures incorporated in the programs.

User-acceptance testing should include:

1. *Stress testing.* A determination of whether the system can process the maximum expected volume of data.
2. *Performance testing.* A determination that the system achieved the specified level of performance.
3. *Regression testing.* Determination that the system does not cause problems with existing systems and functions that currently work correctly.
4. *Error testing.* Determination that the system will reject erroneous conditions so that they will not adversely affect normal processing.
5. *Error handling.* Determination that errors uncovered in the system can be corrected and reentered on a timely basis.
6. *Operator testing.* Determination that the computer operators can adequately operate the system using operator documentation.
7. *Documentation testing.* Determination that there is sufficient written documentation to ensure that the system is understandable and maintainable.
8. *User training.* Determination that user personnel understand the system and can use it in the performance of their day-to-day activities.[4]

Adequate system testing will ensure that a system operates in conformity with its design specifications and that it satisfies user requirements. Test plans should include details of the scope of tests to be conducted and acceptance test criteria. The selection of test criteria and design of the data to carry out the tests should be as comprehensive as possible. The actual programs run on the computer are not the only part of the system that has to be tested. Procedures used by computer operators, the data control group, and source and user departments must also be tested. The final test will be done under actual operating conditions, using live data, supplemented by test data containing special error conditions and combinations of error conditions.

After the completed system has been fully tested and is ready for implementation, the data files must be converted from the old system to the new system. Conversion can be the most crucial part of system development. Conversion of master files to a machine-readable form should be carefully checked; soon the computerized file will be the only master file. Parallel operation of the old and new systems helps to ensure that the new system is functioning as designed and that critical master files are properly maintained.

All master file and transaction file conversion should be controlled to prevent unauthorized changes and to provide accurate and complete results. Appropriate personnel should establish control procedures such as record counts, hash totals, or amount totals on the old and new master files and balance or reconcile these totals. For critical master file information, such as employee pay rates, vendor names, and addresses, and similar data, the details of the new master file should be printed out for visual review and a test performed of selected master file records from the new file back to the old. In the case of particularly sensitive applications, confirmation requests may be sent to third parties to confirm data on the newly converted file.

POST-INSTALLATION REVIEW

Post-installation review is used to determine whether the system that has been developed and implemented satisfied the functional and internal control characteristics originally sought and specified. Performance affects those who were involved in system development, so management, users, and the EDP center should all participate in the review. It should focus on (1) verification of compliance with original user specifications to ensure that the system adequately performs its major activities and satisfies its basic purpose; (2) evaluation of adequacy of data security and application controls; and (3) verification of benefit–cost projections.

11.3 SYSTEM AND PROGRAM MAINTENANCE CONTROLS

For many organizations, the major programming effort is devoted to making maintenance changes in existing systems. These changes may result from user and EDP-center requests or external events, such as changes in tax laws. Controls exercised over changes should be similar to the controls used during the development of a new system and should include user involvement in acceptance testing and documentation updating.

Controlling system and program maintenance is necessary to preserve the integrity of the system, to prevent the accidental destruction or loss of programs, to prevent accidental introduction of errors into programs, and to prevent unauthorized intentional changes. The benefits originally gained by controlling development of a system can be eroded as subsequent changes are made. Thus the controls governing system and program maintenance are extremely important. Such controls can be grouped into four major types: (1) authorization and approvals; (2) standard procedures and documentation controls; (3) programmers and operations personnel controls; and (4) testing of system and program changes.

AUTHORIZATION AND APPROVALS

After a new system has been placed in operation, any proposed system or program change should first be authorized by the appropriate management, user, and EDP-center personnel. Management authorization helps to ensure that system objectives are maintained; user authorization helps to ensure that the system or application as changed will continue to meet their needs; and EDP-center authorization helps to ensure that the change is technically feasible. Approval and implementation should be granted only after an authorized change has been fully tested and documented.

Typical system and program change authorization and approval include the use of a formal change request and authorization form and procedure. Written authorization and approval are required for all system and program changes, except those required to eliminate programming errors. Operations personnel in the EDP center have the responsibility for ensuring that only properly approved programs are employed in actual processing.

STANDARD PROCEDURES AND DOCUMENTATION CONTROLS

Standard procedures should be developed and used to enforce adherence to established rules, standards, and conventions when system and program changes are made. Administrative procedures should ensure that all changes are documented in a consistent manner. Examples of standard procedures and documentation controls include:

1. Definition of who can initiate a change request and who can authorize it.

2. Requirement that the following listings are obtained before and after each change and retained as a permanent record: file directories, production library directories, program source listings, and production procedure listings.
3. Use of program library software to report all program changes to EDP management and user departments.
4. Reentry of a modified program into the production library.
5. Verification that authorized and approved changes are implemented.
6. Requirement that changes are adequately tested before they are implemented.
7. Documentation of adherence to standards for program changes.
8. Provision of an audit trail for changes implemented.
9. Updating of documentation for completed changes.
10. Retention of all significant documentation relating to testing program changes.

PROGRAMMER AND OPERATIONS PERSONNEL CONTROLS

When program changes are based on written authorization and approval by the user and an appropriate level of management, programmers should not be able to change production programs directly. In order to make a program change, a programmer should have to obtain a copy of the source program and program documentation from the librarian or use the access restriction mechanisms to access the source program and library in "read-only" mode for reviewing program logic. The procedures to be followed and controls applied within the system should prevent a programmer from accessing production data files, object programs, and automated procedures while making system changes. Program changes are made in a copy of the source program. After testing a change, the programmer submits job-control language, documentation, and the actual program change to a program change committee or program change coordinator for approval. The committee or coordinator verifies the authorization for the change, evaluates the technical accuracy and the programmer's testing of the change, and examines operating instructions and documentation before approving implementation.

The policies, procedures, and mechanisms controlling the system and program change process should ensure that no changes are made by personnel responsible for operations in the EDP center. Operations personnel may request changes to improve operational efficiency, but they should not have the authority to approve changes. If operations personnel were authorized to make even minor changes, the difficulty of controlling manipulation and of maintaining up-to-date documentation would increase greatly. Restricting access to detailed program logic should prevent operations personnel from obtaining the knowledge needed to make programming changes. Appropriate operational controls must be instituted to prevent unauthorized intervention from the computer console once the program is loaded for execution. However, operations personnel should have sole authority to elevate approved changed programs to production status and should act to preserve that authority.

TESTING SYSTEM AND PROGRAM CHANGES

All system and program changes should be thoroughly tested before implementation to ensure that each change has been properly made and that no other program logic has been accidentally altered. Changes should be tested independently, and test results should be reviewed by the user department. Test data and test criteria used in original system testing (modified where appropriate) should be utilized in testing subsequent changes. Test results should be compared to the original output of the system and significant differences reconciled. After completion of testing, the changes should be reviewed and approved by a supervisor who was not involved in either the revision or testing of the program.

11.4 DOCUMENTATION

System documentation is the record of methods and procedures used to develop a system and for performing various data processing tasks. It, collectively, describes what the system and applications do and how they do it. Documentation is not a control in itself, but it creates the framework for developing, maintaining, and using the system and for identifying needed application controls. Documentation generally provides:

1. An understanding of a system's objectives, concepts, and output.
2. A source of information for systems analysts and programmers who are responsible for maintaining and revising existing systems and programs.
3. Information necessary for supervisory review.
4. A basis for training new personnel.
5. A means of communicating common information to other systems analysts, programmers, and operators.
6. A source of information about accounting controls.
7. A source of information needed to provide continuity in the event of loss of experienced personnel.[5]

Control objectives with respect to documentation are:

1. To ensure that adequate documentation exists and is effectively controlled.
2. To ensure that all systems are adequately documented.
3. To ensure that all programs are adequately documented.
4. To ensure that instructions to all data processing and user personnel are adequately documented.[6]

In order to achieve these control objectives, a comprehensive documentation program should include documentation standards, system documentation, program documentation, and operations and user documentation.

DOCUMENTATION STANDARDS

Documentation standards should be established, published, and enforced. They specify consistent methods for systems analysts, programmers, computer operators, and other personnel involved with computer processing to use in their work and for recording the results of their work. Documentation standards should be applied to system development and maintenance activities, programming, operations, library or file controls, keypunching or other types of data conversion, and user and control personnel instructions. Documentation standards typically include flowcharting, decision-table, and coding conventions; a glossary of terms; reconstruction and restarting procedures; file numbering, dating, and storage methods; and methods of revising documentation. Management should require documentation and formal procedures levels of detail appropriate to various levels of activity.

SYSTEM DOCUMENTATION

In order to provide a comprehensive overview of the system, system documentation should include clear and accurate statements of the reasons for the system, how it works, and the procedures used to control it. At one level, management, users, and the auditor should be able to gain a general understanding of the system without having to become involved in its details. Therefore system documentation should include the reasons for implementing the system, its objectives, the types of operations performed, methods of authorizing and approving subsequent changes, and the assignment of responsibilities.

At another level, system documentation should include the specifications that governed the design and development of the system and provide sufficient information to trace data from their original entry to output. Usually, such documentation includes a flowchart, which shows the flow of information through the system and the interrelationships between manual and computer processing steps. Accompanying the flowchart should be input forms, record formats, output layouts, descriptions of each, report samples, and a processing narrative. Documentation should also describe controls, identify audit trails, and present the details of the system test plan. Finally, documentation should include copies of authorizations and approvals, showing their effective dates, for system changes that have been implemented.

With regard to controls, system documentation should include clear and complete statements of control functions, responsibilities, and procedures. The procedures should identify the persons (by position) responsible, the nature of the tasks to be performed, when each task is to be performed, a description of error conditions, and procedures for error correction.

PROGRAM DOCUMENTATION

Program documentation consists of the documents and layouts that explain all aspects of the programs used in a system. Used primarily by systems analysts and programmers, program documentation provides the information needed for and a control over program corrections and revisions. It may also be useful to the auditor in determining the current status of a program. Adequate program documentation should be prepared for each program, which includes:

1. Brief narrative description of the program.
2. Problem flowchart, decision table, or detailed logic narrative.
3. Source statements (such as a list of program instructions) or parameter lists.
4. List of control features.
5. Detailed description of file formats and record layouts.
6. Table of code values used to indicate processing requirements.
7. Record of program changes, authorizations, and effective dates.
8. Input and output formats.
9. Operating instructions.
10. Job-control language and other control instructions.
11. Program test data and a testing log.
12. Data and file retention instructions.
13. Sample core dump.

OPERATIONS AND USER DOCUMENTATION

Operations documentation provides EDP operations with the necessary instructions to run a computer-based application efficiently. Adequate operations documentation can help to ensure that the computer system is operated in a controlled manner. Operations documentation includes:

1. Computer equipment operation procedures, such as system start-up, shutdown, system back-up, and terminal operations.
2. Computer operations procedures, such as operating schedules, off-line file procedures, hardware maintenance, system change procedures, and recovery procedures.
3. Input transaction procedures, such as input receipt procedures, data entry procedures, error correction procedures, source document control, and permanent record retention.
4. Output procedures, such as output report generation, report balancing and reconciliation, report distribution, and system inquiries.
5. System-control procedures such as system balancing, access authorization, error response, system monitoring, and data verification.

User documentation describes required input and an output list. User documentation generally includes:

1. Narrative description of the system's operation accompanied by a general flow diagram.
2. Specific instructions governing the proper completion of input forms and transactions.
3. Report descriptions and examples.
4. List of control procedures and identification of who is responsible for enforcing those procedures.
5. Error correction procedures.
6. Cutoff procedures for submission of data to the EDP center.
7. Computer output balancing and checking procedures.

11.5 AUDITING SYSTEM DEVELOPMENT

Because system development is a time-consuming and expensive activity, it is much more practical and less expensive to include appropriate controls during the development stage. Auditors have an interest in ensuring that system design, development, and overall operations achieve the objectives of adequate internal control and effective auditability. The conventional viewpoint is that auditors should perform a review role only after completion of the system development process. The rationale is that independence and objectivity are lost through participation. However, early participation by the user, and particularly the internal auditor, is the key to ensuring that adequate controls are designed into a system; the rationale is that the internal auditor cannot affect adequacy without participating. Participation does not mean that the internal auditor actively develops or installs procedures. Rather, it means that the internal auditor should identify standards of control and auditability appropriate to the system under development and to recommend procedures that will meet those standards.

The auditor can become involved in the system development process in two ways: (1) as a member of the system development team, concurrently reviewing the system as it is developed; or (2) as a member of an annual audit team or post-installation audit team evaluating the quality of the system development process in general. Both approaches have a common objective: to ensure that the system development process is of high quality. When the auditor participates directly in the system development process, the auditor is concerned primarily with building adequate controls into the system. When the auditor assesses the system development process after installation, the auditor's main objective is to determine the extent to which substantive testing can be reduced by reliance on the internal control system.

AUDITOR PARTICIPATION IN SYSTEM DEVELOPMENT

In 1975, the Institute of Internal Auditors initiated a research project to study and document internal auditing in a computerized environment. The results, published by IIA in 1977, suggests that *internal* auditors participate in the systems development process to ensure that appropriate audit and control features are designed into new computer-based information systems.[7]

Standards published by the U.S. General Accounting Office suggest that participation by the auditor in the systems development process can accomplish six audit objectives:

OBJECTIVE 1: To provide assurance that the system/applications faithfully carry out the policies that management has prescribed for the system.

OBJECTIVE 2: To provide assurance that the system/applications provide the controls and audit trails needed for management, auditor, and operational review.

OBJECTIVE 3: To provide assurance to management that the system/applications include the controls necessary to protect against loss or serious error.

OBJECTIVE 4: To provide assurance that the system/applications will be efficient and economical in operation.

OBJECTIVE 5: To provide assurance that the system/applications conform to applicable legal requirements.

OBJECTIVE 6: To provide assurance that the system/applications are documented in a manner that will provide the understanding of the system required for appropriate maintenance and auditing.[8]

Internal auditors are generally concerned with two audit questions during the design of new computer applications: Have adequate controls been built into the system? and Is the system development process well-controlled? In 1977, Rittenberg and Davis surveyed internal audit departments of 39 major corporations concerning EDP audit activities during the system design phase. The survey results showed that the most commonly performed design-phase audit activity consisted of identifying audit trail and control requirements. Other audit activities frequently performed by the companies that responded concentrated on control standards for the development process, such as reviewing documentation for compliance to company policy, assessing and reporting potential risks of the proposed system to management, reviewing design activities for compliance to company policy, and indicating approval or specifying deficiencies at the end of each major phase.[9]

The typical SDLC illustrated in Figure 11.1 and discussed in Section 11.2 contains five major systems development phases and 15 control points. During the SDLC, the internal auditor should:

1. Review the adequacy of controls.
2. Assist in developing additional controls.
3. Determine whether the system meets user needs.
4. Test compliance with system development standards.
5. Test compliance with standards for system testing, programming, operations, and documentation.
6. Evaluate performance.

Halper et al. also suggest that the following activities be performed by the auditor during the SDLC:

1. Review the feasibility study.
2. Review the process used to select any new hardware or software.

3. Monitor compliance with system development standards.
4. Review the controls being designed into the new system.
5. Evaluate reporting, input, and processing features to ensure the adequacy of controls over completeness, accuracy, and authorization.
6. Review the system design to ensure an adequate audit or information trail.
7. Review and possibly reperform the testing plans and procedures.
8. Evaluate the system at a test site or during parallel processing.
9. Review and possibly test the conversion procedures.
10. Review the adequacy of documentation.
11. Perform a post-implementation review to help identify areas for future improvement.[10]

AUDITING THE SYSTEM DEVELOPMENT PROCESS

Internal auditors can serve as a member of an annual audit team or post-installation system audit team to evaluate the quality of the system development process. The main focus of this type of audit is to review the controls governing the process because these controls can directly affect the accuracy and reliability of the resulting computer applications. The purpose of auditing the system development process is to ensure that the new system is developed and maintained in a controlled environment. The external auditor normally treats the audit of the system development process as part of the regular audit, under review and evaluation of general controls. The four major steps performed by an external auditor in auditing the system development process are preliminary review, assessment of preliminary review, detailed review and testing compliance, and evaluate findings and issue a report.

Preliminary Review. The auditor gathers background information on standards, procedures, and applications in existence and in process. This information indicates the level of activity and scope of the system and programming functions.

Assessment of Preliminary Review. This assessment is based on the auditor's experience and judgment. If there are few applications in the process of development, or if the applications under development have no financial impact, a limited review may be sufficient. On the other hand, if major new applications have been implemented or major changes have been made in significant or critical applications, a review of all aspects of system and programming activities may be required.

Detailed Review and Testing Compliance. The auditor should examine existing documentation and interview user, management, EDP, and internal audit staff personnel. The sample audit review and test procedures are grouped according to type of system development controls and summarized in Table 11.2.[11]

Evaluate Findings and Issue a Report. The auditor should evaluate the detailed review and compliance testing results with respect to the adequacy of the planned scope of substantive testing. If the system development audit is performed prior to the audit of applications, modification of the scope of the application audit is necessary. If the system development audit is performed independently of the installation and applications examinations, the results must also be evaluated. With either approach, the auditor should prepare a written report that contains conclusions and recommendations.

11.6 Summary

System development controls usually address the three control areas of new system development, system and program maintenance, and documentation. Effective system and program controls will help ensure that all system development activities are properly authorized, tested, reviewed, documented, approved, and implemented.

Five major types of controls are applicable to new system development: management and user participation and approvals, development standards and guidelines, project management, system testing and conversion controls, and post-installation review. The typical system and program maintenance controls include authorization and approvals, standard procedures and documentation controls, programmer and operations personnel controls, and testing of system and program changes. Adequate documentation is essential to the development and maintenance of a well-controlled system. A comprehensive documentation program should include documentation standards and system, program, operations, and user documentation.

The auditor can be involved in the system development process in two ways. First, the auditor can serve as a member of the system development team and concurrently review the system as it is developed. That is, the auditor participates in the process to ensure that adequate controls are built into it. Second, the auditor can serve as a member of an annual audit team or post-installation system audit team to evaluate the quality of the system development process in general. Both approaches have the common objective of ensuring a system development process of high quality. The internal auditors usually participate in reviewing system development controls by serving in the system development team. The external auditors usually conduct a post-installation system audit as part of their annual audit tasks.

Table 11.2   System Development Audit Procedures

Control Type/Category	Audit Review and Test Procedures
Management and user participation and approvals	Interview representatives of user depts. for evidence of the level of participation in system definition.
	Review the specifications for new applications and look for evidence of their reviews and approvals.
	Review appropriate documents and related approvals for evidence that user departments have an adequate understanding of inputs, processing requirements, control procedures, and system outputs.
	Review the extent of internal auditor involvement in the definition of the system and review their related working papers.
	Review evidence of approval of significant accounting applications.
	Interview user and EDP personnel involved in approval process, inquire about their understanding and satisfaction with the system.
Development standards and guidelines	Review the installation's standards and guidelines for system design.
	Perform an initial survey to determine the adequacy of development standards and guidelines.
	Interview users to identify problems traceable to lack of development standards or compliance with existing standards.

(continued on next page)

Table 11.2   System Development Audit Procedures (continued)

Control Type/Category	Audit Review and Test Procedures
Project management	Review project plan and look for system development life-cycle approach.
	Review and evaluate system design documentation and installation procedures.
	Check the existence and content of project status reports.
System testing and conversion controls	Review testing standards, test data and resulting output to determine whether they are reasonably comprehensive.
	Interview both user and EDP department personnel to determine what test procedures are used during implementation.
	Review procedures for reconciliation of output produced during parallel testing.
	Review plans for controlling the conversion from one system to another. In particular, evaluate the reconciliation procedures that will be used between the files of each system.
	Review or observe the use of conversion procedures and controls.
	Test the conversion by tracing detailed records from the old files to the new. Trace selected records from the new files back to the old.

(continued on next page)

Table 11.2   System Development Audit Procedures (continued)

Control Type/Category	Audit Review and Test Procedures
Post-installation review	Interview appropriate personnel involved in the post-installation review to determine what procedures are used and the degree of satisfaction with the new system.
	Assess post-installation review documentation.
System and program maintenance controls	Interview operations and systems personnel to determine the procedures for controlling system and program changes.
	Review documentation in support of system and program changes to determine whether the procedures are being followed.
	Trace selected system and program changes to the appropriate supporting records to determine whether the changes have been properly approved.
	Review the results of tests that were made to verify the correctness of system changes.
	Review selected changes for proper approval.

(continued on next page)

Table 11.2   System Development Audit Procedures (continued)

Control Type/Category	Audit Review and Test Procedures
System and program maintenance controls *(continued)*	If extended testing seems warranted, in significant accounting applications, compare the original program source code and applicable changes to the current operational version. Reconcile any differences.
	Review program modifications, testing procedures, and the preparation of supporting documentation to obtain evidence of control over these activities.
Documentation	Review documentation standards to determine whether they appear to provide for adequate documentation.
	Review selected documentation to verify its compliance with the documentation standards.
	Note in workpapers how program listings and systems and programming documentation are physically secured, as well as who has access to them.
	Request a volume table of contents in a system resident disk listing of the system and private libraries and compare this listing to client documentation. Investigate test and other unidentified or unknown programs.

Questions

1. What is system development? Why should the auditor become involved in the development process?
2. What are some examples of user involvement in system development? Why is this involvement important?
3. What are some examples of management involvement in system development? Why is this involvement important?
4. Describe development standards and guidelines and their importance to the auditor.
5. Why is the system development life cycle (SDLC) important to an understanding of system development?
6. What are the major phases of the SDLC? How do they relate to control points in system development?
7. What are the three stages of system testing?
8. What is post-installation review?
9. What controls should be established over program maintenance? Why are these controls important?
10. What benefits does system documentation provide to system developers? System users? Auditors?
11. What are system documentation standards? Why are they important?
12. What are major objectives of system development?
13. Briefly describe three categories of system development controls.
14. Describe three types of user acceptance testing.
15. What general controls are required during system testing?
16. Describe two control procedures required during system conversion.
17. Why should the authorization and approval be necessary for system and program changes?
18. What are two ways the auditor can become involved in the system development process?
19. What major activities are performed by the auditor during the SDLC?
20. What are four major steps in auditing the system development process?

Problems

1. From research of the available literature and your own analysis:
   (a) Prepare a set of system development guidelines.
   (b) Develop a project management schedule.
   (c) Write a set of documentation standards.

2. A client has asked your audit firm to help develop a new EDP accounting system. What are some of the problems and benefits involved in performing this work?

3. Review the System Development Life Cycle (SDLC) and identify the more critical stages for auditor involvement. Explain why.

4. This is the third year you have audited a computerized system. What aspects of the system's maintenance documentation would you want to audit?

5. While a complete set of system documentation should be available from the librarian, who else might you ask to provide you with such documentation?

6. *Multiple Choice Questions from Professional Examinations*

   (1) EDP operating control is enhanced when
   a. A tape librarian is employed.
   b. There are experienced machine operators.
   c. All programs are tested before they are put into production.
   d. Access to the computer room is limited to programmers and computer operators.
   e. Machine operators have access to source programs.

   (2) Within an electronic data processing facility, the primary objective of establishing standards for documentation is to
   a. Set forth the appropriate separation of duties for the application being documented.
   b. Provide reasonable assurance that an application is automated only if other methods cannot produce equal benefits at a lower cost.
   c. Ensure the proper and timely reentry of rejected data.
   d. Discourage the improper manipulation of data.
   e. Provide for continuity and consistency of the data processing services provided to users.

   (3) EDP documentation standards are necessary to
   a. Provide continuity despite personnel changes.
   b. Enhance internal control.
   c. Assist review through standardization.
   d. Aid system evolution by providing a centralized record of system design and testing.
   e. Accomplish all of the above.

   (4) The internal auditor should recommend the use of a high-level language such as COBOL for an EDP business application in order to
   a. Minimize core storage requirements.
   b. Facilitate multiprogramming.
   c. Permit more rapid processing of data within the computer.

     d. Improve documentation of the application.
     e. All of the above.

(5) The technique of computer program comparison can be used by the internal auditor to
     a. Verify that the computer program performs the required functions.
     b. Test the efficiency of the computer program coding.
     c. Disclose unauthorized changes in the computer program coding.
     d. Determine that data produced by the computer program are reliable.
     e. All of the above.

(6) The internal auditor is reviewing the adequacy of application controls in a data processing system under development. What must be in place for that auditor to interface successfully with the systems and development programming team?
     a. Standards for systems development.
     b. Integrated test facility.
     c. System test plan.
     d. Post-audit review procedures.
     e. Program documentation standards.

(7) You were assigned to review the development of an EDP system for updating demand deposit accounts in a bank. In which of the following phases would you be concerned with general controls?
     a. Feasibility assessment.
     b. Information analysis.
     c. Program and procedures development.
     d. All of the above.

(8) What information would the internal auditor expect to find in the data dictionary which would assist in the preliminary survey phase of a payroll application audit?
     a. Programs that access the data.
     b. Type of operating system.
     c. System flowcharts.
     d. Online user identification.
     e. System network architecture.

(IIA adapted)

7. *Bank Holding Corporation: System Development Controls*
Introduction

Early this year, Bank Holding Corporation (BHC) of Cleveland, Ohio acquired its 25th affiliate by purchasing the stock of the First National Bank of Lordstown. Since the late 1950s, BHC has been expanding its assets and geographic area through the acquisition of small independent banks in several counties. The holding company's assets have increased from $1.2 billion in 1959 to $5.3 billion today, and continued growth, by acquisition, is forecasted. Local banks are allowed to manage themselves as long as operating results are satisfactory to the management of the holding company. Consequently, top management of BHC rarely get involved with the internal operations of the affiliates, except at the policy level.

One such policy was to implement on-line processing for all subsidiary banks and their branches. The on-line system was centralized at the BHC computer center just outside Cleveland. Previously, each subsidiary had performed its own data processing. They had developed a variety of different systems, ranging from manual processing to small computer operations in a batch mode. When the on-line system was instituted by the BHC data center, the affiliates ceased processing their own data except for minor applications.

BHC's centralized Data Center consists of two large CPU's, 28 disk drives, 22 tape drives, and related peripheral equipment. It currently provides the branches with all the data processing required for the following applications:

- Demand Deposit (checking)
- Passbook Savings
- Certificates of Deposit
- Commercial Loans
- Personal and Auto Loans
- General Ledger

The major components of the BHC on-line system are:

- The main computers, which accept data, apply prescribed processing to the data, and output the results. The computer hardware consists of two communication-oriented computers comparable to an IBM 370/168 mainframe. Each central processor contains 2.0 million characters of main memory (two megabytes).
- The on-line files, which provide direct access to the large store of information necessary for processing daily transactions. An average of 50,000 on-line transactions are processed daily.
- The terminals, which are attached to the communication network. There are 170 terminals at the 25 subsidiaries and their branch locations. The terminals, manufactured by NCR, are application-oriented with self-contained logic and memory.
- The communication network, which links the remote terminals to the computer. The communication network is composed of 18 dedicated lines leased from the telephone company.

- The software, which is the collection of computer programs and program segments or subroutines which enable the system to logically process entered transactions against stored data.

The four major objectives of the centralized Data Center are to provide and maintain for all affiliates:

1. Computer services to strengthen the financial security of affiliates.
2. Computer services to assist in the decision-making processes of affiliate management.
3. Computer services to improve the efficiency of the day-to-day operations of affiliates.
4. Research and development programs to improve existing systems and innovate new services for the affiliates.

Operation Committee Request

At the annual meeting of the corporate-wide operations committee in February, the vice-presidents of operations from several affiliate banks voiced a growing concern over the centralized data center concept. They were concerned about the cost and competitive disadvantage of an interruption in business activity that might be caused by the loss of data or the ability to process it. The centralized processing made them especially sensitive as they no longer had control over their own data. Even short processing interruptions could have negative effects on customer good will and any extended period of down time could severely hamper the business activity of affiliates. As a result of these concerns, the operations committee sent a request to the BHC internal audit staff to perform an internal control review of the Data Center.

The request for a review of the Data Center went to the newly appointed head of BHC's internal audit department, Ms. Margaret Johnson. Ms. Johnson, in light of the importance of this review, chose to undertake the project herself. She discovered that the internal audit department had not performed such a review before, and decided to begin with systems maintenance and development activities.

The committee felt that it was important for changes to the processing and reporting capabilities of the system to be made on a timely basis and that they be implemented as intended. They wondered if changes to the computer system were effectively managed and controlled. Ms. Johnson sensed that the operating vice-presidents had little faith in the system maintenance and development activities in particular and shared reservations about the quality of the center's management in general. She felt the report on her first study probably hadn't helped to improve this.

Ms. Johnson found that the Data Center considered system development to include all activities and standards for planning, designing, programming, and testing new systems. System maintenance, on the other hand, included project initiation, programming, and testing of any change to an existing system or program.

She inquired of Michael Heckman, head of Data Center operations, about the initiation of development and maintenance projects. He explained that until a few years ago subsidiary banks initiated most of the changes and a corporate-side steering committee reviewed them. This steering committee provided direction to the overall data processing and system development effort by resolving conflicts and giving guidance for the orderly evolution of data processing services. It had not met in over two years, however. Currently all maintenance and development activities were either initiated by one of the subsidiaries of BHC or by Mr. Heckman himself. "Since I am most familiar with the real strengths and weaknesses of the system, however, I probably initiate 90% of all projects," he said.

Ms. Johnson could not find any formal documentation or standard procedures for identifying, defining and evaluating projects, or for determining priorities, defining schedules, assigning responsibilities or allocating resources by a cost/benefit analysis. As a consequence, she questioned Mr. Heckman further on how he went about initiating a change in the system. "Well, I constantly monitor systems looking for trouble areas and ways to improve them," he replied. He pointed out that a software program produces certain reports such as:

- Work Flow Language Log
- CPU Usage Per Application
- Files Accessed/Changes Made
- Down-time Log
- Systems Log

"These reports review all activity on the computer and monitor the processing and recording, and any abnormal use or improper run procedures. But to tell you the truth, these reports were developed by a very technical software expert and I really do not use them. They are too lengthy and hard to understand. Besides, by listening to my operators and generally being aware of day-to-day problems, I get a very good intuitive feel for what needs to be done. You know, even though this is a very sophisticated operation, technically, managing its development and maintenance is really an art, not a science."

Ms. Johnson found out that not all system development and maintenance activities were performed in-house. Due to the rapid growth of BHC the Data Center has been unable to implement all changes by itself. Some system changes were contracted out to a programming company. These findings led her to expand her scope and review a system change conducted by the programming company as well as one conducted by the in-house group. Since one project was currently being performed by the programming company she decided to investigate that immediately. Mr. Heckman said, "I am very satisfied with the work they do. Once we give them the system specifications they do everything from coding to running system tests with historical data."

The programming company was currently involved with updating the banks' interest system. This was one of several programs that the banks use which is written in the Autocoder programming language. The documentation of these programs is minimal, runs are slow and cumbersome, and programmers at the Data Center understand only COBOL. The programming company was recoding the present interest system in COBOL. Ms. Johnson was informed that the system was just being recoded and no attention was being given to basic system redesign because of the time and cost involved. "First things first," said Mr. Heckman.

Ms. Johnson then decided to investigate the in-house procedures for system development and maintenance. She saw that all requests for system changes were reviewed by Heckman and at least one technical support person to see if the change was economically feasible. The system change request was then sent to the systems and programming group. It was their responsibility to actually define system specifications, and to program and test the system changes. Once a manager in the system and programming group decided what existing programs needed to be altered, the change was assigned to a programmer. Whenever possible, the programmer assigned had had prior responsibility over the area of the application or the specific programs to be changed. The programmer was then totally responsible for performing the necessary maintenance to the production program files and the related job control language. The programmer also tested the finished programs with historical data, on the operating equipment, to see if the system change was working properly.

By talking to a programmer, Ms. Johnson discovered the maintenance of the present system was very difficult because of a lack of flowcharts and program listings as well as the use of Autocoder for some systems. The programmer also pointed out that very few new system development and maintenance projects were well documented because of the severe time limitation put on the Data Center personnel.

After a system change has been completed by a programmer, a supervisor in the Data Center briefly reviews the test results and change is implemented. The only interaction with the subsidiary bank users occurred when the change was originally initiated and later when the change was finally implemented. Once each year the internal audit group usually reviewed the changes that affected each branch.

In concluding her investigation, Ms. Johnson felt that there was a lack of involvement by users and internal auditors in the system life cycle. Because of this she wrote a memo to the operating vice-presidents of the subsidiaries and pointed out where she felt involvement was necessary.

MEMO

To: Operating Vice-Presidents of Subsidiary Banks
From: Margaret Johnson, Head of Internal Auditing

As BHC continues to implement more extensive and sophisticated computer systems, the internal audit department needs to become an active participant in the design and testing of any new applications and in the maintenance of existing systems. The internal audit department's primary objective will be to assure management that newly implemented, as well as established, computer applications include sound and reliable control features.

I feel that the following guidelines set forth the minimum level of audit and user involvement necessary for implementing new applications and maintaining existing systems. The internal auditor needs to be involved in the critical phases of the system life cycle as follows:

System Life Cycle (Development Life Cycle)
System Planning
In this phase, the project's scope, objectives, costs, benefits, technical and economic feasibility are defined and determined. The internal auditors should be involved in this phase so they can anticipate future systems developments which may require them to gain the necessary knowledge to deal with any new technical concepts that are planned.

User Specification
This is the most important phase because basic functional concepts of the new system are defined from the user's perspective. In this phase, the auditor should define the controls by which the system can be monitored and regulated. The auditors should review the potential exposures and related controls. Internal auditing may also be a user of a new system.

Technical Specifications
Within this phase, the system analyist translates the user specifications into technical concepts at the level necessary to communicate with programmers. With appropriate technical knowledge and computer experience, the auditor can review this phase to ascertain if a reasonable translation has been made with adequate provision for any technical constraints.

Implementation Planning

This phase involves even closer coordination between the user and the EDP department in preparation for conversion. The auditor should be vitally interested in the controls planned over the conversion process, for problems in implementation can be costly.

Programming

The conversion of the technical specifications defined by the system analyst to computer operating instructions is completed in this phase.

User Procedures and Training

This phase includes the preparation of procedures for the conversion to, and the operation of, the new system. Auditors should check to see if the user has adequate procedure manuals and related job descriptions which serve to increase user awareness and control over the system.

System Test

The system test is an acceptance test conducted by the system group and the user. Internal audit participation is essential, for it is the last line of defense before implementation. Tests performed should be recorded and test checks retained with their results to indicate the adequacy and success of the testing. User approvals should be the last step of this phase.

Conversion

This is the phase in which the conversion of data, equipment, procedures, and personnel to the new system takes place. It should occur in a carefully planned and controlled environment. The auditor should be concerned about file integrity and the consistency of data affecting accounting reports.

Postimplementation

A review should be made by the auditor sometime after implementation to assure that all areas of the system are operating as intended.

Required:

(a)   Why is it important to control systems development and systems maintenance? What are some possible consequences if control over these procedures is lacking?

(b)   Evaluate Ms. Johnson's report on the system life cycle. Do you agree with her characterization of the role of the internal auditor? What changes would you suggest?

(c)   What weaknesses are there in the existing system?

(Prepared by Frederick Neumann, Richard Boland, and Jeffrey Johnson, with funding from the Touche Ross Foundation. Used and adapted with permission of the authors.)

8.   *Rayo Corporation: Program Change Controls*

Mike Kess, a senior auditor for the regional accounting firm Sanders and McDonald, was assigned to audit the Rayo Corporation. He was to conduct a preliminary review of the general controls over systems and programming. He had already identified the current applications and the equipment used in the data processing system, and is about to start on system maintenance.

Mike contacted Jim Stram, the manager of systems and programming in the EDP department. A summary of their conversation is presented below:

Mike: How are system maintenance projects initiated and developed?

Jim: All potential projects are sent to a member of my staff called an Applications Coordinator, for analysis. We do all our systems and programming work in-house. If a programming change is required for a project, the Applications Coordinator prepares a revision request form. These revision request forms must be approved by both the Manager of Operations and myself. The Director of Data Processing and the Internal Auditor receive copies of each revision request form for information purposes.

Mike: How does the Applications Coordinator keep track of the revision request form and any change that might be made to it?

Jim: The revision request forms are numbered in different series depending on the nature of the change requested. The Applications Coordinator assigns the next number in the sequence and records in a master log each request he prepares. Changes in revision requests, from whatever source, are prepared on request forms just as initial requests are. Each change request is given the same basic number with a suffix indicating it is an amendment, and there is a place for recording amendments in the master log.

Mike: What is the distribution of an approved request form?

Jim: It goes to one of my systems supervisors for design, programming, and testing. The primary effort is usually performed by a programmer who has responsibility over the area of the application or the specific programs to be changed.

Mike: But how are projects controlled?

Jim: At the beginning of each programming project, an estimated start and completion date are assigned and entered on the request form and the master log. The system supervisor keeps on top of the projects assigned to him, and the Applications Coordinator also monitors the open requests. The system supervisor files a written status report with the Applications Coordinator twice a month, and he briefs me on any problems. However, I'm usually aware of any difficulties long before then.

During the programming and testing phase, I think we have good control over the project. None of the compilations made during this phase changes any production source code for the existing computer programs. Also, all test object programs are identified by a strictly enforced naming convention that clearly distinguishes them from production programs. So far this has been successful in inhibiting their use in production processing. If a programmer has specific questions or problems on a project, his systems supervisor is generally available to give advice.

Mike: Are there written guidelines to direct this activity? If so, how detailed are they?

Jim: Only informal procedures exist to provide any uniformity to the programs and the coding changes which are made to a program. But, formal standards do exist which define what documentation should be present for a system and for the programs within a system. These apply to program changes as well, and again are strictly enforced. There is a periodic review to see we comply. We just had one about a month ago and got a clean bill of health.

Mike: Are adequate tests and reviews made of changes before they are implemented?

Jim: The Applications Coordinator, the systems supervisor and the individual programmer informally discuss the necessary tests for a specific project. Sometimes I get involved too, but our guidelines are pretty good in this area and provide a fairly thorough approach to test design. After the tests have been completed to the systems supervisor's satisfaction, the Applications Coordinator reviews and approves the test results. This must be done on all revision requests before they are implemented into production. I usually review the programmer's work to see that all authorized changes are made correctly and are adequately tested and documented.

Mike: How does implementation take place and what controls are exercised over it?

Jim: After the test results for a revision request have been approved by the Applications Coordinator, it is the responsibility of the programmer to implement the changes into production. In order for a programmer to put a program change into production, he must update the source code of the production program version. The programmer is required to provide program name and compile data information for all changed programs to his systems supervisor. The programmer also has the responsibility of updating the systems and programming documentation. His systems supervisor is supposed to review this and certify completion to the Applications Coordinator who then completes the log entry.

Mike: Are postimplementation reviews undertaken on system maintenance projects?

Jim: Once the project is implemented the Applications Coordinator reviews the output from the first few production runs of the changed program. He also questions users to see if any problem areas can be identified.

A documented audit trail is provided by a completed project file that is maintained by the Applications Coordinator for each request number. This file contains all the required documentation, including test results. A copy of the final summary goes to the department which originally submitted the request. A table in the computer is updated to provide listings of the most current compile dates for each set of production object code within the system. Before any program is implemented it is checked against this table.

Mike: Well, that seems to be it. I think I have all that I need for now, but I'll probably be back to take a look at the files and records. I may have more questions for you then. Thanks very much for your time and thoughtful answers. I really appreciate your help.

Jim: That's quite all right. If I can be of any more help, just let me know.

Required:

(a)   Keeping in mind that this is part of the preliminary phase of the review, are there any additional questions you would have asked Jim if you had been in Mike's place?

(b)   Make a list of weaknesses that you feel should be considered in the preliminary assessment of the internal control in this area.

(Prepared by Frederick Neumann, Richard Boland, and Jeffrey Johnson, with funding from the Touche Ross Foundation. Used and adapted with permission of the authors.)

Notes

1. Stanford Research Institute, *Systems Auditability and Control: Control Practices.* Altamonte Springs, Fla.: Institute of Internal Auditors, 1977, pp. 99–101.

2. *Ibid.,* pp. 101–102.

3. *Ibid.,* p. 101.

4. William E. Perry, *The Accountant's Guide to Computer Systems*. New York: John Wiley & Sons, 1982, pp. 190–191.

5. *The Auditor's Study and Evaluation of Internal Control in EDP Systems*. New York: AICPA, 1977, pp. 63–64.

6. *Computer Control Guidelines*. Toronto: The Canadian Institute of Chartered Accountants, 1970, p. 86.

7. *Systems Auditability and Control: Control Practices*, p. 5.

8. *Additional GAO Audit Standards: Auditing Computer-Based Systems*. Washington, D.C.: U.S. General Accounting Office, March 1979, pp. 5–8.

9. Rittenberg, Larry E., and Davis, Gordon B., "The Roles of Internal and External Auditors in Auditing EDP Systems," *The Journal of Accountancy*, December 1977, pp. 164–171.

10. Halper, Stanley D., Davis, Glenn C., O'Neil-Dunne, P. Jarla, and Pfau, Pamela R., *Handbook of EDP Auditing*. Boston: Warren, Gorham & Lamont, 1985, p. 7.

11. Most of the audit review procedures are based on *The Auditor's Study and Evaluation of Internal Control in EDP Systems*. New York: AICPA, 1977; and Li, David H., *Control Objectives*. Carol Stream, Ill.: EDP Auditors Foundation, 1983.

Additional References

Burch, John G., Jr., and Joseph L. Sardinas, Jr., *Computer Control and Audit: A Total Systems Approach*. New York: John Wiley & Sons, 1978.

Davis, Gordon B., D. L. Adams, and C. A. Schaller, *Auditing & EDP*, 2nd ed. New York: American Institute of Certified Public Accountants, 1983.

"The Effects of Computer Processing on the Examination of Financial Statements," *Statement on Auditing Standards*, No. 48, American Institute of Certified Public Accountants, New York, 1984.

Fisher, Royal P., *Information Systems Security*, Englewood Cliffs, N.J.: Prentice-Hall, 1984.

Information Security. Delran, N.J.: Datapro Research Corporation, 1985.

Jancura, Elise G., and Robert Boos, *Establishing Controls and Auditing the Computerized Accounting System*. New York: Van Nostrand Reinhold, 1981.

Li, David H., *Control Objectives—Controls in a Computer Environment: Objectives, Guidelines, and Audit Procedures*. Carol Stream, Ill.: EDP Auditors Foundation, 1983.

Mair, William C., Donald R. Wood, and Keagle W. Davis, *Computer Control & Audit,* 2nd ed. Altamonte Springs, Fla.: Institute of Internal Auditors, 1978.

Parker, Donn, *Computer Security Management.* Reston, Va.: Reston Publishing Company, 1981.

Perry, William E., *EDP Administration and Control.* Englewood Cliffs, N.J.: Prentice-Hall, 1984.

Porter, W. Thomas, and William E. Perry, *EDP Controls and Auditing,* 4th ed. Boston: Kent, 1984.

Vallabhaneni, S. Rao, *Information Systems Audit Process.* Carol Stream, Ill.: EDP Auditors Foundation, 1983.

Watne, Donald A., and Peter B. B. Turney, *Auditing EDP Systems.* Englewood Cliffs, N.J.: Prentice-Hall, 1984.

Weber, Ron, *EDP Auditing: Conceptual Foundations and Practice.* New York: McGraw-Hill, 1982.

Chapter 12

Risk Assessment and Analytical Review

12.1 INTRODUCTION

In this chapter, we deal with the concept of risk and the use of analytical review in the audit process. Audit risk, as defined in SAS No. 47 (AU § 312.02), "is the risk that the auditor may unknowingly fail to appropriately modify his opinion on financial statements that are materially misstated."

Analytical review (AR) has been used by accountants for at least a century, primarily in the form of *ratio analysis*. Analytical review is a general tool, utilizing evidence generation and/or evidence analysis, and is often used in connection with risk assessment and risk reduction.

Analytical review involves the utilization of analytical techniques (quantitative or qualitative) for the evaluation of accounting numbers. Among the quantitative techniques available for such use are regression analysis, discriminant analysis, and the Box–Jenkins time series model.

In 1983, the AICPA issued SAS No. 23, which discusses various analytical review procedures but allows for different methods of applying them based on professional judgment. More recently, research has focused on four general methods: ratio analysis, time series analysis, structural modeling, and subjective evaluation. In this chapter, we emphasize the first two of these methods.

Despite the fact that analytical review procedures are used by most practitioners as a routine part of their work, these procedures have remained an elective part of the audit engagement. The audit significance of analytical review procedures was recognized in SAS No. 1 and later emphasized in SAS No. 23, which focused on them.

In February 1987, the Auditing Standards Board issued an exposure draft that if enacted would supersede SAS No. 23, and would:

- Require the auditor to apply analytical procedures in the planning and final review stages of an audit engagement, wherein SAS No. 23 has no such requirement.
- Provide additional guidance on the development, use, and evolution of analytical procedures.

According to SAS No. 1, "substantive tests" involve two general classes of audit procedures: (1) tests of details of transactions and balances; and (2) analytical review. In the same statement, the AICPA emphasized the elective nature of analytical reviews by stating that "the auditor's reliance on substantive tests may be derived from tests of detail, from analytical review procedures, or from *any combination from both* that he considers appropriate in the circumstances." (Emphasis added.)

In this chapter, we initially discuss the general concept of risk. We devote the remainder of the chapter to analytical review, beginning with a theoretical framework for analytical review. We then demonstrate the use of regression analysis as a tool of analytical review. In the next section, we focus on the actual use of analytical review procedures (ARPs) in practice. Then we discuss ratio analysis and its potential as an analytical review tool. In the final section of this chapter, we touch briefly on the unrealized potential of analytical review as an audit tool.

LEARNING OBJECTIVES

By the time you have completed this chapter, you should be able to:

1. Discuss the concept of risk.
2. Describe a theoretical framework for analytical review.
3. Explain the use of regression analysis as a tool of analytical review.
4. Identify the main analytical review procedures used in practice.
5. Describe ratio analysis and its uses.
6. Identify other analytical review techniques and their potential applications.

12.2 RISK AND AUDIT RISK

Mock and Vertinsky state: "Definitions of risk abound. There is, however, a common notion that risk is associated with the chance of something undesirable happening."[1] They illustrate risk assessment in accounting by summarizing for nine areas of demand for risk assessment the objective of this assessment, the techniques to be used, and the potential results. This summary is shown in Table 12.1 and is self-explanatory. Mock and Vertinsky also break business risk into components, as shown in Figure 12.1. The main components of risk are:

- **Audit (ultimate) risk**

  Audit risk is the risk that audit procedures will fail to detect material errors. (CICA, 1980.)[2]

  The risk that the auditor may unknowingly fail to appropriately modify his opinion on financial statements that are materially misstated. (SAS 47.)

- **Information system risks**

  Inherent risk: The susceptibility of an account balance or class of transactions to error that could be material . . . assuming that there were no related internal accounting controls. (SAS 47.)

  Control risk: The risk that error[3] that could occur . . . will not be prevented or detected on a timely basis by the system of internal accounting control. (SAS 47.)

- **Compliance test risks**

  Sampling risk: The possibility that, when a compliance test is restricted to a sample, the auditor's conclusions may be different from the conclusion he would reach if the test were applied to all items in the population. (SAS 39.)

  Nonsampling risk: All aspects of ultimate risk that are not due to sampling. (SAS 39.)

  Risk of overreliance: Risk that the evidence supports the auditor's planned degree of reliance on the control when the true compliance rate does not justify such reliance.

  Risk of underreliance: Risk that the evidence does not support reliance when it should.

- **Substantive test (detection) risks**

  "Detection risk is the risk that an auditor's procedures will lead him to conclude that an error does not exist when in fact such an error does exist." (SAS 47.)

  Sampling risk: The possibility that, when a substantive test is restricted to a sample, the auditor's conclusion may be different from the conclusions he would reach if the test were applied . . . to all items. (SAS 39.)

  Nonsampling risk: All aspects of ultimate risk that are not due to sampling error. (SAS 39.)

Table 12.1   Risk Assessment in Accounting

Demand for Risk Assessment	Assessment Objective(s)	Assessment Techinque(s)	Assessment Results, Alternatives, or Actions
1. Cash management	Maintain vendor relations Maximize discounts Minimize discounts lost	Probability assessment Cash flow forecasts (probabilistic)	Estimated cash requirements Liquidity risk estimates Likelihood of bond indenture violations
2. General budgeting	Assess resource allocation problems	Probability assessment Multiple scenarios Probabilistic budgets Sensitivity analysis	Pro forma financial statements (probabilities) Indicators of projected cost and profit center difficulties Probabilistic cost/volume/profit analysis Estimated margin of safety
3. Capital budgeting	Assess risk/return options	Cash flow analysis Various risk indicators Portfolio analysis Statistical simulation	Cash flow projections Risk indicators (projection mean, variance, standard deviation) Market risk indicators (e.g., *beta*)
4. Accounting control systems	Provide risk signals for management	Accounting analysis of variance Statistical control modeling	Exception reports Likelihood estimates of system failures
5. Accounting system evaluation	Assess reliability of information system	Internal accounting control analysis Exposure assessments Statistical analysis (sampling) Subjective probability assessment	Error reports and estimates Control risk assessment
6. Bankruptcy and going-concern analysis	Predict chance of bankruptcy Loan assessment	Credit scoring models applied to accounting data Ratio analysis Statistical modeling Subjective probabilities	Default and bankruptcy likelihoods Various liquidity ratios and indicators Credit indicators Safety indicators

(continued on next page)

Source: From T. J. Mock and I. Vertinsky, *Risk Assessment in Accounting and Auditing.* Vancouver, B.C.: Canadian Certified General Accountant's Research Foundation, 1985, p. 18.

Table 12.1   Risk Assessment in Accounting (continued)

Demand for Risk Assessment	Assessment Objective(s)	Assessment Techinque(s)	Assessment Results, Alternatives, or Actions
7. Financial statement preparation	Provide relevant information Meet reporting standards	Subjective probabilities Techniques used in 1, 2, and 6.	Various financial reporting of uncertainties, risks, and contingencies Financial forecasts
8. External audits of financial statements	Provide independent auditor's report	Audit risk model Analytical review Internal control analysis Statistical sampling and modeling Subjective assessments (scanning, probability estimates, etc.)	Variance reports and ratio analyses Sampling results (balance estimates and confidences) Ratio analyses Inputs for going-concern and uncertainty judgments Internal control reliability estimates Estimates of audit risk components (control and procedures risk)
9. External auditor business decisions	Assess business risk (client selection, etc.)	See techniques in 2, 4, 5, 6, and 8.	Estimates of business risk components

Risk of incorrect acceptance: Risk that the evidence supports the acceptance (not materially misstated) conclusion . . . when it is materially misstated.

Risk of incorrect rejection: Risk that the evidence supports the rejection (materially misstated) conclusion . . . when it is not materially misstated.

• **Audit business risk**

"Business risk is the probability that an auditor will suffer a loss or injury to his professional practice."[4]

Within this general framework of audit risk, analytical review is often used in numerical assessment. Mock & Vertinsky[5] display a set of selected risk formulas linking several items, among which are:

$$\text{Ultimate risk} = (IR)(IC)(AR)(TD),$$

where:

IR	=	Inherent risk.
IC	=	Internal control.
AR	=	Analytical review.
TD	=	Test of details.

Figure 12.1   Components of Business Risk

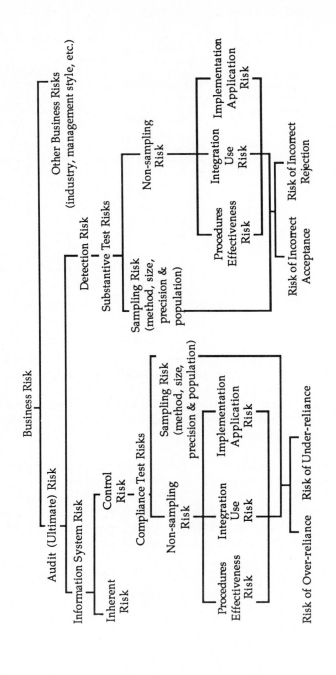

Source: From T. J. Mock and I. Vertinsky, *Risk Assessment in Accounting and Auditing.* Vancouver, B.C.: Canadian Certified General Accountant's Research Foundation, 1985, p. 116.

This type of formula is presented in subsequent chapters when applicable to different aspects of auditing.

12.3 A THEORETICAL FRAMEWORK FOR ANALYTICAL REVIEW

Analytical review involves an examination of the client's financial information in order to improve the focus and broaden the scope of the audit process. In SAS No. 23, the AICPA defines **analytical review procedures** (ARPs) as substantive tests of financial information made by a study and comparison of relationships among the data. In addition, SAS No. 23 states:

> A basic premise underlying the application of analytical review procedures is that relationships among data may reasonably be expected by the auditor to exist and continue in the absence of conditions to the contrary. The presence of those relationships provides the auditor with evidential matter required by the third standard to field work. The application of analytical review procedures may indicate the need for additional procedures or may indicate that the extent of other auditing procedures may be reduced.[6]

The standard further indicates that if patterns different from those expected are found, the auditor should follow up on them.

Analytical review may be used at different stages of an audit, depending on the objectives of the auditor. During the *initial stages* of the audit, it can identify problems, aid risk assessment, and support risk planning. *During* the audit it can serve to complement other procedures that are being used. At the *end* of the audit it can be used for overall review and checking the consistency of audit results.

According to SAS No. 23, the auditor should consider a series of factors when using analytical review procedures:

1. **Nature of the entity:** Analytical review may be used to examine a diversified entity both from the perspective of a consolidated firm and from the perspective of its individual components. The use of time series analysis in examination of the consolidated firm may be more appropriate, whereas intraindustry comparisons are easier to derive for specialized sectors of the company. For example, AT&T could be examined using financial ratios and compared to the competitors in its industry (such as MCI), but this comparison may not be very meaningful

because the companies are very different in nature. On the other hand, AT&TIS, a subsidiary of AT&T dedicated to the manufacture of computers, may be very comparable to the second echelon of computer firms. This type of analysis, although difficult for outside sources to do (owing to data confidentiality), can be particularly useful at the beginning of an audit when some choice of entities to be audited may be desirable.

2. **Scope of the engagement:** Analytical review may be used in many different ways, depending on the scope of the audit examination. Examining the entire financial statement may require the use of a much larger set of ARPs than might be necessary when examining a particular account or an element of a particular account. For example, the examination of a company's Accounts Receivables may encompass a time-series analysis of the data adjusted for seasonality and its comparison with sales figures. An audit plan for the entire corporation may require the breakdown of receivables by subentity and cross-sectional analysis.

3. **The availability of financial information about the entity's financial position and results of operations:** The auditor may be privy to a large amount of internal management accounting information that may serve AR purposes. This information includes budgets, forecasts, operation of subsidiaries, market data, litigation, patents, and other relevant aspects of company operations. This information should be used for analytical review purposes. For example, product plans for the prior year may be used as the referential for product sales analysis.

4. **The availability of relevant nonfinancial information:** Traditionally, auditors have tended to focus mainly on financial information. This information, however, is linked to nonfinancial data, which may be evaluated for consistency and homogeneity. For example, sales and inventory relate to levels of production and number of labor hours. Legal fees relate to potential litigation and regulatory issues. Research and development costs relate to patents and R&D equipment.

5. **The reliability of financial and nonfinancial information:** Over the duration of the relationship with the client, the auditor will gain substantial insight into the reliability of the client's data. This knowledge allows the auditor to determine the reliability of the client's information system, procedures, and data. Consequently, preliminary AR may be valid at any time for data that are deemed to be reliable over the audit period, but other data may be usable only after substantial adjustment. SAS No. 23 states that the auditor "may decide to make only

limited comparisons of actual and budgeted income and expense when the entity's budget is a motivational tool and not an estimate of the most probable financial position, results of operations, and changes in financial position."[7]

6. **The availability and comparability of financial information regarding the industry in which the entity operates:** In this time of empirical databases (such as Standard & Poor's COMPUSTAT), a large amount of information about other companies and specific industries is available. This information allows subentity cross-sectional comparison, as well as the com-parison of a large number of similar entities. This same advantage is also potentially a problem because companies often are not actually comparable and the results of financial comparisons usually reflect the substantial consolidation of data from dissimilar entities.

12.4 USING REGRESSION ANALYSIS FOR ANALYTICAL REVIEW

In SAS No. 1, the AICPA discusses the relationship of analytical review to tests of details:

Regardless of the extent of reliance on internal accounting control, the auditor's reliance on substantive tests may be derived from tests of details, from analytical review procedures, or from any combination of both that he considers appropriate in the circumstances.[8]

The relationship of risks is expressed in SAS No. 1 as follows:

$$S = 1 - [(1 - R)/(1-C)] \text{ or } (1 - R) = (1 - C)(1 - S),$$

where:

S = Reliability level for substantive tests.
R = Combined reliability level desired.
C = Reliance assigned to internal accounting control and other relevant factors.

We can expand this formula to include analytical review as a separate component of risk:

$$(1 - R) = (1 - C)(1 - D)(1 - AR),$$

where:

D   = Reliability level for detail testing.
AR = Reliability level for analytical review procedures.

We will explain this formula in more detail in Chapters 13 and 15.

Analytical review, as with all model-based performance analysis techniques, requires both a model and actual data. The comparison of actual data with the model yields variances and fluctuations. Analysis of these variances provides the results that constitute analytical review.

This process is analogous to that of budgeting. Corporations adopt budgets to quantify short-run plans in financial terms. The budget is used as a model for comparative purposes during the budget period to limit expenditures and evaluate corporate performance. Corporate controllers always face departures from budgeted amounts because expenses are not uniform throughout the year and economic events cannot be determined precisely in advance. Controllers must look at the nature of budget variances and decide whether the variances are significant and, if so, whether the budget is realistic.

However, there are many differences between budgeting and analytical review. Budgeting is an anticipatory technique, whereby a model is created in expectation of economic events. Budget control entails a certain degree of self-fulfilling prophecy because management strives to attain the budgeted amounts. On the other hand, analytical review relates to examining data after the fact, fitting it to some appropriate model (in this case, regression) and examining the variances and fluctuations from the model.

Regression analysis is a statistical technique that is widely used in many fields.[9] In its simplest form it entails the fitting of a straight line to a set of points in the x–y plane, using a least-squares solution. In simple regression analysis, the dependent variable, y, is related to the independent variable, x, by the equation

$$y = a + bx,$$

where:

a is the intercept of the straight line with the y axis.
b is the slope of the line.

Figure 12.2 shows the fitting of a straight line to several points, which is sufficient for an understanding of the use of regression analysis as discussed later in this chapter. A residual (r) is the difference between the

Figure 12.2   Basics of Regression Analysis

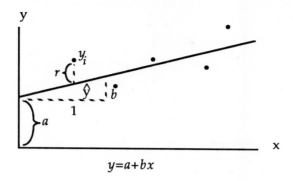

$$y=a+bx$$

Least Squares Solution

Calculation of the slope b:

$$b = \frac{\displaystyle\sum_{i=1}^{n} x_i\, y_i}{\sum x_i^{\,2}}$$

Calculation of the intercept constant a:

$$a = \overline{Y}$$

Residuals:

$$r = y_i - \hat{y}$$

Where

$\overline{Y}$ = mean of the y scores
$\overline{X}$ = mean of the x scores

actual value of any y and the calculated value y for each corresponding x on the line of best fit (or regression line). Residuals are either positive or negative, depending on whether they fall above or below the line of best fit. Because these positive and negative residuals cancel when added, we square each residual and then add them. The minimum value of Σr^2 indicates the line of best fit (hence the name *least squares*) and the greatest predictive accuracy. The maximum value of Σr^2 indicates the extreme dispersion from the trend line and the least predictive accuracy. However, the signs of the residuals should not be neglected if the auditor is looking for overstatement or understatement of audited values.

The use of regression analysis in auditing proposed by Stringer[10] was implemented by Deloitte, Haskins & Sells in its STAR program package. The steps involved in using the STAR method are:

1. Design application. Choose basic reference variables, time period, context of use, frequency of use, etc.
2. Complete specifications. Fill in parameters in STAR specification forms, fine-tune design.
3. Gather idea. Collect the necessary data, verifying its accuracy, make it available.
4. Execute programs.
5. Interpret results.
6. Investigate excesses.
7. Perform related audit work.

Let's turn to an example to illustrate the use of regression analysis. Table 12.2 shows data for sales and cost of goods sold for a particular business entity. These two sets of data are plotted in Figure 12.3.

A cursory examination of Figure 12.3 shows a reasonably good linear fit, with a few points out of the general range. However, we need to determine whether any of the points are far enough from the regression line to warrant (or require) examination. The question is: "What level of error can we tolerate and in what direction?" We can use materiality considerations to help us make this decision. Materiality is a general guideline for overall error in statements. Errors in specific accounts and/or periods may become material on an aggregate basis.

Let's examine the same data further and in more detail. Figure 12.4(a) and (b) display sales and costs of goods separately. This visual technique allows for some additional discrimination. In Figure 12.4(a), sales for period 20 seem to be unusually high; in Figure 12.4(b), we can easily see apparently significant deviations for periods 13, 20, and 32. Note that sales and cost both show substantial deviations in period 20, but both deviations are in the same direction. Consequently, we may find it useful at a later stage to examine profit = sales − cost of sales. Figure 12.4(c) and (d) show a *smoothed fit*[11] regression line for the data. This technique permits a better approximation of the trend and, in practice, requires the use of an exponential curve rather than a straight line.

We now want to examine the difference (residual) between each actual number and its calculated value for the corresponding period on the regression line. The residuals (in $) are shown in Figure 12.5(a) and (b). Each residual is labeled by its period number to facilitate identification. The residuals in Figure 12.5(a) indicate that periods 1, 13, 20, and 32 warrant further examination, as does the residual for period 21 in Figure 12.5(b).

Table 12.2   Sales and Cost-of-Goods-Data

Period	Sales (1)	Cost (2)	Period	Sales (1)	Cost (2)
1	$10,398	$ 1,002	19	$17,361	$11,412
2	9,723	6,606	20	16,055	16,518
3	11,193	7,704	21	20,794	14,220
4	11,942	8,460	22	17,981	12,549
5	9,734	7,258	23	14,389	8,768
6	13,616	9,499	24	14,856	11,084
7	10,198	7,485	25	18,399	10,944
8	12,912	7,225	26	14,882	10,841
9	11,444	8,351	27	17,387	12,324
10	12,084	8,381	28	19,525	14,133
11	12,074	7,844	29	18,781	15,312
12	14,179	9,129	30	20,303	14,176
13	12,509	1,739	31	18,462	13,474
14	14,138	9,489	32	18,709	3,242
15	16,084	12,185	33	18,538	13,270
16	17,331	10,505	34	16,819	11,554
17	12,951	8,527	35	16,596	11,234
18	16,700	11,551			

Source: Adapted from material at Deloitte, Haskins & Sells Auditscope seminar.

Figure 12.3   Regression of Sales and Cost of Goods

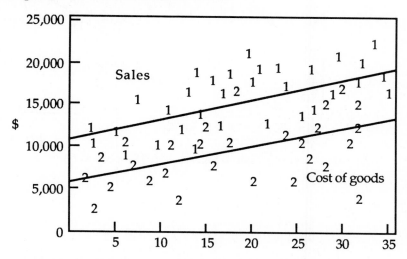

Source: Adapted from material at Deloitte, Haskins & Sells Auditscope seminar.

Figure 12.4   Linear and Smoothed Regression Lines for Sales and Cost of Goods

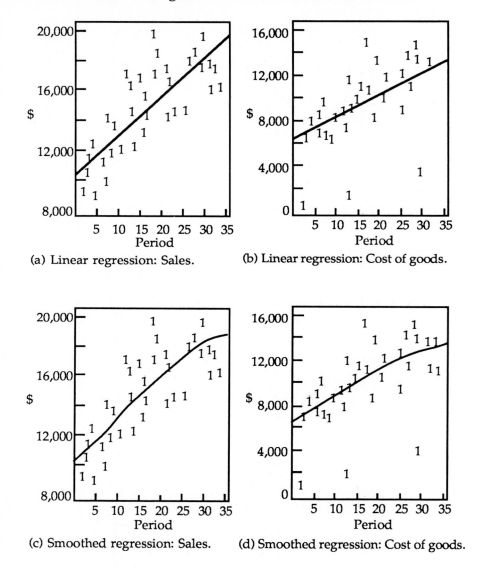

(a) Linear regression: Sales.   (b) Linear regression: Cost of goods.

(c) Smoothed regression: Sales.   (d) Smoothed regression: Cost of goods.

Figure 12.5   Residuals and Logarithmic Plotting of Data

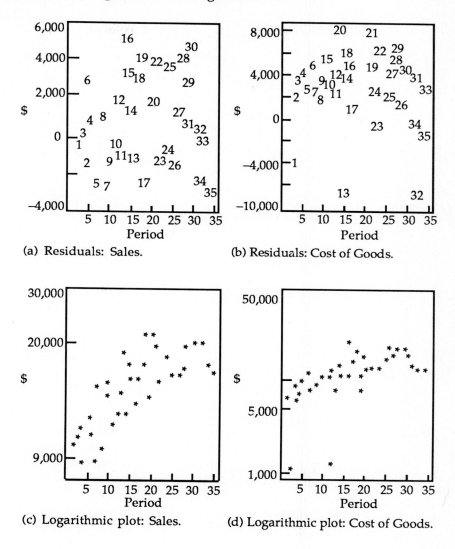

(a) Residuals: Sales.   (b) Residuals: Cost of Goods.

(c) Logarithmic plot: Sales.   (d) Logarithmic plot: Cost of Goods.

Figure 12.6 Comparative Boxplots

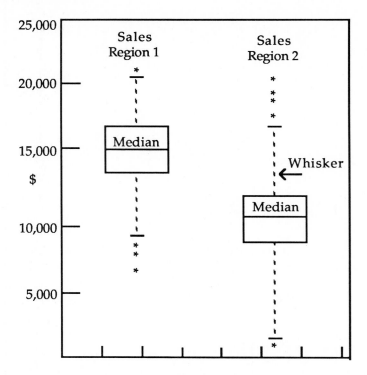

We can also examine the data by transforming the graph. Figure 12.5(c) and (d) show the data when a logarithmic scale is used for the y axis. The sales figures appear rather smooth, whereas the variations in cost for periods 1, 13, and 32 are immediately apparent.

Figure 12.6 shows a *boxplot*[12] of the sales and cost data. Such plots provide a good way to identify and compare the dispersion of data. The horizontal line in the box is the median value of the data, the upper and lower portions of the box represent the quartiles, and the dashed lines extending above and below the box (called *whiskers*) show the range of the data except for *outlyers,* which are shown as separate points.[13]

Figure 12.7(a) shows the results of combining the same data to obtain net income (sales – cost of goods). The two estimator lines represent a straight-line best fit and a smoothed fit. Figure 12.7(b) shows a plot of the absolute value of residuals. Use of an exaggerated scale on the y axis dramatically isolates outlyers in the data. The mix of Explanatory Data Analysis (graphic, visual, and tabulatory) and the more formal regression techniques allow in this example increased understanding of the data.

Figure 12.7   Presentation of Combined Data As Net Income

(a) Regression lines: Net income.   (b) Absolute values of residuals:
                                                Net income.

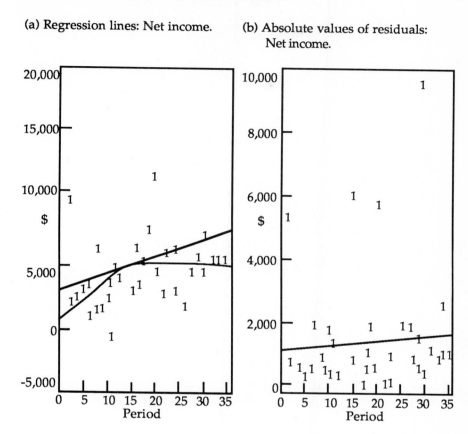

12.5 ANALYTICAL REVIEW IN PRACTICE

Daroca and Holder in 1985 surveyed 1600 member firms of the Private Companies Practice Section of the AICPA and obtained 269 usable responses.[14] Their survey investigated the applicability of particular analytical review techniques and the frequency of actual use. Tables 12.3 and 12.4 contain selected results from the survey.

Table 12.3 shows Analytical Review Procedures (ARPs) that are used most often and least often in audit (AUD) and review (RVW) engagements. Several ratio analysis procedures, particularly turnover analysis, lead the list. More sophisticated procedures such as regression analysis and Box–Jenkins analysis (a decomposition technique) are still not used frequently. Table 12.4 indicates that trend analysis is applicable to about

Table 12.3   Applicability and Use of Selected Analytical Review Procedures

			Often-Used Analytical Procedures			
	Engagement		Frequency of Applications			
Procedure	(% applicable)	Always	Usually	Sometimes	Rarely	Never
Receivable	AUD (69.1)	32.0	32.4	22.1	9.4	4.1
turnover	RVW (67.9)	26.2	32.0	23.8	12.7	5.3
Inventory	AUD (64.6)	32.4	35.7	19.0	7.3	33.6
turnover	RVW (63.2)	29.6	32.5	22.2	9.9	5.8
Day's sales in	AUD (61.8)	22.8	27.0	26.6	13.5	10.1
accounts	RVW (60.9)	19.6	25.9	24.3	14.5	15.7
receivable						
Debt to total assets	AUD (60.8)	15.1	18.9	32.0	21.0	13.0
	RVW (63.7)	13.2	19.6	27.6	20.9	18.7
Quick or acid test	AUD (60.6)	18.6	16.9	27.6	25.0	11.9
	RVW (62.5)	16.6	14.9	28.0	22.6	17.9
Rate of return on	AUD (56.0)	12.4	12.0	24.8	32.0	18.8
stockholders'	RVW (58.3)	10.8	12.1	20.7	32.3	24.1
equity						
Book value per	AUD (49.5)	11.4	15.3	31.0	18.3	24.0
share	RVW (50.2)	10.3	14.8	26.9	19.3	28.7
Rate of return on	AUD (52.8)	10.1	8.8	26.8	33.2	21.1
assets	RVW (53.7)	8.8	5.3	25.9	32.8	27.2
Asset turnover	AUD (43.5)	9.2	7.0	18.0	31.1	34.7
	RVW (45.4)	6.2	4.0	17.7	33.2	38.9

(continued on next page)

Source: Adapted from F. P. Daroca and W. W. Holder, "The Use of
Analytical Procedures in Review and Audit Engagements," *Auditing: A
Journal of Practice and Theory,* Spring 1985, p. 88.

one-half of all audit and review engagements and that scan analysis is
applicable to more than 40 percent of all audit and review engagements.
Table 12.4 also shows that other procedures are rated as moderately
applicable (30–50 percent range) and extensively used or often applicable
(30–40 percent) but infrequently used. Daroca and Holder concluded that

1. auditors apply ARPs to a similar extent regardless of the type
    of engagement;

Table 12.3   Applicability and Use of Selected Analytical Review Procedures (continued)

Procedure		Engagement (% applicable)	Always	Usually	Sometimes	Rarely	Never
				Frequency of Applications			
Current receivables daily	AUD	(34.2)	1.8	1.3	8.4	24.2	63.9
expenditures	RVW	(36.6)	1.3	2.7	6.3	21.0	68.3
Cash flow per share	AUD	(29.2)	1.8	2.3	8.1	26.7	61.1
	RVW	(31.0)	0.9	2.3	4.6	25.8	66.4
Price-earnings ratio	AUD	(16.3)	2.4	2.4	8.5	24.2	62.5
	RVW	(14.4)	1.0	3.4	4.3	22.1	69.2
Payout ratio	AUD	(14.3)	1.9	2.4	3.4	17.8	73.6
	RVW	(13.4)	0.5	3.4	2.5	19.1	73.5
Regression analysis	AUD	(16.1	0.0	1.0	4.3	12.0	80.4
	RVW	(14.6)	0.0	1.0	2.0	9.8	84.9
Box-Jenkins analysis	AUD	(9.0)	0.0	0.0	0.0	3.4	92.2
	RVW	(8.1)	0.0	0.0	0.0	3.5	92.0

Infrequently Used Analytical Procedures

2. several ARPs are applicable to most engagements and are applied extensively; and

3. procedures requiring extensive mathematical manipulation or additional data generation rarely are employed.[15]

Tabor and Willis obtained the cooperation of a Big Eight CPA firm in a large southwestern city to study ARPs. Seven audit managers and 14 clients were studied in terms of (1) procedures used; (2) stage of the audit process at which ARPs were used; and (3) changes in the use of ARPs from 1978 to 1982.[16] This study, despite its bias and sample limitations, provides a valuable glimpse into the use of ARPs in practice.

For purposes of the study, the following techniques were described to the firm's auditors.

Nonquantitative procedures—consist of a variety of methods which involve the application of accounting and business knowledge to judge the completeness, validity, and accuracy of an account balance or relationship. Examples include reviewing external information such as external databases or economic indices; or reviewing internal information such as personnel files, minutes of important meetings, correspondence files, production records, etc.

Table 12.4   Applicability and Use of Selected AR Techniques and Procedures

Use of Trend Analysis and Scan Analysis Techniques

Procedure	Engagement (% applicable)		Always	Usually	Sometimes	Rarely	Never
Trend analysis	AUD	(52.7)	12.5	22.8	25.4	13.4	25.9
	RVW	(49.8)	10.5	20.5	22.4	16.2	30.4
Scan analysis	AUD	(44.6)	19.5	13.6	8.2	8.2	47.3
	RVW	(42.5)	18.5	13.0	8.4	7.0	49.8

Moderately Applicable but Extensively Used Analytical Procedures

Procedure	Engagement (% applicable)		Always	Usually	Sometimes	Rarely	Never
Comparison of financial and budgeted information	AUD	(42.8)	25.9	23.9	32.4	10.5	7.3
	RVW	(31.1)	16.0	21.2	29.5	19.0	14.3
Comparison of interim and year-end data	AUD	(52.4)	18.4	27.4	28.6	12.0	12.8
	RVW	(45.5)	14.9	22.8	28.9	13.6	18.9

Often Applicable but Infrequently Applied Analytical Procedures

Procedure	Engagement (% applicable)		Always	Usually	Sometimes	Rarely	Never
Earnings per share	AUD	(39.6)	23.2	6.7	12.5	25.4	32.2
	RVW	(39.0)	15.8	8.6	11.7	20.7	43.2
Times interest earned	AUD	(31.1)	4.1	3.6	17.2	28.1	46.5
	RVW	(33.5)	3.2	4.1	11.9	30.1	50.2

Source: Adapted from F. P. Daroca and W. W. Holder, "The Use of Analytical Procedures in Review and Audit Engagements," *Auditing: A Journal of Practice and Theory*, Spring 1985, pp. 87–88.

Simple quantitative procedures—consist of a variety of simplified quantitative procedures used to highlight or identify relationships, reasonableness, etc., of account balances. Examples include ratio analysis, judgmental time-trend analysis, variance analysis, and predictive testing.

Advanced quantitative procedures—consist of a variety of techniques using economic or statistical models to relate an account balance to environmental variables that theoretically cause the account balance to vary. The most notable example in this category is regression analysis. Others would be any type of structural modeling procedures.[17]

The study showed that the auditors tended to use ARPs either intensively or not at all in audit planning. A more consistent but lower utilization rate emerged for detailed substantive testing. During final review, ARPs were utilized sparingly. Table 12.5 shows the role of ARPs in the audit engagements for the 14 clients and the mean percentage of use in each phase for all engagements.

Table 12.6 shows the utilization of three types of ARPs: nonquantitative, simple quantitative, and advanced quantitative. During the 14 audit engagements, simple quantitative procedures (SQPs) were used 37 percent, nonquantitative procedures (NQPs) 33 percent, and advanced quantitative procedures (AQPs) only 2 percent of the time.

Tabor and Willis concluded that ARP use increased between 1978 and 1982. Their results also showed clearly that financial ratio analysis ARPs were the most frequently used group of procedures.

12.6 RATIO ANALYSIS

Ratio analysis is one of the most popular techniques of financial analysis. It is often used for analytical review at the planning stage or at the evidence evaluation and opinion formulation stage of an audit. Ratio analysis can be performed either on a cross-sectional or a time-series basis. The objectives of this type of analysis are to develop a norm that the entity should achieve, compare actual results to this norm, and investigate variances from the norm—within the risk profile obtained for the entity.

In this section we initially define several key ratios and illustrate their use as building blocks in traditional financial statement analysis. We then present briefly several types of comparison and trend analysis that can be applied to these building blocks.

Table 12.5   Role of ARPs in Audit Engagements, 1982

Client	Planning Audit Hours	Planning ARPs (%)	Detailed Substantive Testing Audit Hours	Detailed Substantive Testing ARPs (%)	Final Review Audit Hours	Final Review ARPs (%)
1	30	90	667	44	380	10
2	35	91	289	33	47	0
3	80	9	474	18	100	0
4	21	0	311	31	120	0
5	60	90	137	34	39	0
6	65	55	1023	27	124	0
7	67	22	627	20	200	5
8	64	11	337	15	195	5
9	410	30	1460	29	560	15
10	50	26	425	25	100	10
11	78	0	404	65	252	0
12	145	0	784	43	391	0
13	20	80	125	58	40	0
14	115	87	102	63	23	0
Mean	1140	42	7165	35	2571	3.2

Note: ARPs (%) refers to the percentage of audit hours for the respective audit phase for which ARPs were used.

Source: Adapted from R. H. Tabor and J. T. Willis, "Empirical Evidence on the Changing Role of Analytical Review Procedures," *Auditing: A Journal of Practice and Theory*, Spring 1985, p. 101.

Although Foster[18] divides financial ratios into four major classes, we prefer to use five groups of traditional ratios, which are based on combining financial statement information and market-related data:

1. Liquidity ratios.
2. Financial leverage ratios.
3. Profitability ratios.
4. Turnover, or asset management, ratios.
5. Market-value ratios.

Table 12.6   Role of ARP Types in Audit Engagements, 1982

Client	Planning NQP (%)	Planning SQP (%)	Planning AQP (%)	Detailed Substantive Testing NQP (%)	Detailed Substantive Testing SQP (%)	Detailed Substantive Testing AQP (%)	Final Review NQP (%)	Final Review SQP (%)	Final Review AQP (%)
1	82	18	0	90	10	0	89	11	0
2	78	22	0	83	17	0	0	0	0
3	100	0	0	20	80	0	0	0	0
4	0	0	0	9	76	15	0	0	0
5	41	59	0	15	85	0	0	0	0
6	50	50	0	22	78	0	0	0	0
7	40	60	0	17	83	0	20	80	0
8	43	57	0	16	84	0	20	80	0
9	66	34	0	37	63	0	50	50	0
10	69	31	0	45	55	0	80	20	0
11	0	0	0	64	36	0	0	0	0
12	0	0	0	44	56	0	0	0	0
13	44	56	0	7	67	26	0	0	0
14	46	54	0	8	69	23	0	0	0
Mean	47	32	0	34	61	5	18	17	0

Note: NQP: Nonquantitative procedure (Overall mean for three phases = 33%.)
SQP: Simple quantitative procedure (Overall mean for three phases = 37%.)
AQP: Advanced quantitative procedure (Overall mean for three phases = 2%.)

Source: Adapted from R. H. Tabor and J. T. Willis, "Empirical Evidence on the Changing Role of Analytical Review Procedures," *Auditing: A Journal of Practice and Theory*, Spring 1985, p. 102.

We selected 12 of the most commonly used and significant ratios for illustrative purposes, with at least one ratio from each of these five groups. A word of caution about the use of financial ratios: There is a wide disparity in the nature and content of financial statements. Unlike the closely watched and often standardized treatment of items in financial disclosures there is no widespread agreement on the specific items to include in a particular ratio. Several of these inclusion issues are raised in this section.

    In order to make the key-ratio examples more meaningful, we use actual figures for the General Mills, Inc., 1985 annual statements. Table 12.7 is a simplified version of the consolidated income statement and Table 12.8 is a simplified version of the balance sheet for General Mills for the year ended May 26, 1985. Table 12.9 presents a five-year comparison of results

Table 12.7   General Mills, Inc., Consolidated Statement of Earnings for the Year Ended
May 26, 1985 (Amounts Are in Millions of Dollars, Except Per Share Data)

	1985	1984
Sales	4285	4118
Cost of Sales	2475	2433
Selling, General, & Administrative Expense	1368	1252
Depreciation & Amortization	110	99
Interest Expense	60	32
Earnings—Pretax	272	302
Gains from Redeployment	−76	53
Earnings after Redeployment	196	355
Income Taxes	81	154
Earnings after Taxes & Redeployment	115	201
Discontinued Operations after Taxes	−188	31
NET EARNINGS	−73	232
Net Earnings per share	−1.6	4.98

for selected information, which has been partially adjusted for inflation
(as required by SFAS No. 33 for inflation accounting).

LIQUIDITY RATIOS

Liquidity refers to the ability of an entity to meet its short-term financial
obligations. Auditors pay particular attention to these ratios when making a going-concern evaluation.

Current Ratio. General Mills includes an item called *net assets of discontinued operations and redeployments* in current assets. This item is not
usually found in this general category, which generally consists of cash,
short-term marketable securities, accounts receivable, inventories, and
prepaid items. Current liabilities typically include most items due within
one year.

Table 12.8   General Mills, Inc., Consolidated Balance Sheet for the Year Ended May 26, 1985 (Amounts Are in Millions of Dollars)

	1985	1984
Current Assets		
Cash & Short-Term Investments	67	66
Receivables less Allowances	285	551
Inventories	378	662
Investments in Tax Leases		50
Prepaid Expenses	40	44
Net Assets of Discontinued Operations	518	18
Total Current Assets	1288	1391
Land, Buildings, & Equipment	1486	1829
Less: Accumulated Depreciation	530	600
Net Land, Buildings, & Equipment	956	1229
Other Assets	420	239
TOTAL ASSETS	2664	2859
Current Liabilities		
Accounts Payable	360	478
Current Portion of Long-Term Debt	59	60
Notes Payable	380	251
Accrued Taxes & Payroll	93	193
Other Current Liabilities	164	163
Total Current Liabilities	1056	1145
Long-Term Debt	450	363
Deferred Income Taxes	30	77
Deferred Income Taxes—Tax Leases	61	
Other Liabilities	43	50
TOTAL LIABILITIES	1640	1635

(continued on next page)

Table 12.8   General Mills, Inc., Consolidated Balance Sheet for the Year Ended May 26, 1985 (Amounts Are in Millions of Dollars) (continued)

	1985	1984
Stockholders' Equity		
Common Stock	214	215
Retained Earnings	1202	1375
Less: Stock in Treasury	−334	−292
Cumulative Foreign Currency Adjustments	−58	−74
Total Stockholders' Equity	1024	1224
TOTAL LIABILITIES & EQUITIES	2664	2859

$$\frac{\text{Current assets}}{\text{Current liabilities}} = \frac{1288}{1056} = 1.22.$$

Quick Ratio. Inventories are not necessarily as liquid as cash or net receivables. Therefore the quick ratio was derived to provide a numerator that represents greater liquidity; these assets are often called *quick assets.* For General Mills, the quick ratio is the following:

$$\frac{\text{Cash + Short-term marketable securities + Accounts receivable}}{\text{Current liabilities}} =$$

$$\frac{67 + 285}{1056} = 0.33.$$

LEVERAGE RATIOS

Leverage ratios examine (1) the extent that nonequity funding (debt) is used by a firm; and (2) the long-term ability of the firm to meet its debt-service payments.

Debt to Equity Ratio. When calculating the debt to equity ratio, we try to assess the fair value of the firm's liabilities to third parties. General Mills' liabilities, as is the case with many other firms, include deferred taxes, which, it may be argued, are a liability to the government that will never actually have to be paid. Consequently, the definition of the debt to

Table 12.9 General Mills, Inc., Supplementary Information Years 1981–1985 (Amounts Are in Millions of Dollars, Except Per Share and CPI Data)

	Fiscal Year				
	1985	1984	1983	1982	1981
Sales					
Historical amounts	4285	4118	4082	3861	3466
Constant purchasing power	4285	4279	4394	4350	4251
Earnings from continuing operations					
Historical cost	115	203	162	142	128
Current costs	94	179	119	106	108
Earnings per share from continuing operations					
Historical cost	2.58	4.32	3.24	2.81	2.54
Current costs	2.10	3.82	2.38	2.09	2.14
Net assets at year-end					
Historical cost	1023	1225	1227	1232	1132
Current costs	1481	1910	2011	2167	2137
Current cost translation adjustment	(9)	(19)	(35)	(42)	
Market price per share at year-end					
Historical cost	58.13	50.13	56.38	39.88	34.62
Constant purchasing power	57.13	51.12	59.93	44.08	40.56
Dividends per share					
Historical cost	2.24	2.04	1.84	1.64	1.44
Constant purchasing power	2.24	2.12	1.98	1.85	1.77
Unrealized "gains" from decline in purchasing power of average net amounts owed	38	48	47	55	82

(continued on next page)

equity ratio restricts the numerator to current liabilities plus long-term debt. The denominator, on the other hand, may sometimes include preferred stock, which, some argue, is more like long-term debt than equity.

$$\frac{\text{Current liabilities} + \text{Long-term debt}}{\text{Shareholders' equity}} = \frac{1056 + 450}{1024} = 1.47.$$

Table 12.9   General Mills, Inc., Supplementary Information Years 1981–1985
(continued)

Increases in current cost of fixed assets (land, buildings and equipment, and inventories):					
Pro forma increase, due to general inflation as measured by the U.S. Urban Consumer Price Index	64	107	104	148	239
Compare to: estimated actual increases in specific prices of assets held by General Mills	18	125	70	212	195
Difference: excess (deficiency) of pro forma general inflationary increase over estimated actual specific increase	46	(18)	34	(64)	44
Average consumer price index for fiscal year (calendar 1967 = 100)	315.8	303.9	293.4	280.3	257.5

As you can see, we have adopted a less conservative approach by not including deferred income taxes due to leases in the numerator. In certain industries, these lease obligations may materially affect the results of ratio analysis.

Long-term Debt to Equity Ratio. Unfortunately, as in the preceding ratio, the financial accounting literature does not clearly distinguish between liabilities and equity. For General Mills,

$$\frac{\text{Long-term debt}}{\text{Shareholders' equity}} = \frac{450}{1024} = 0.43.$$

Times Interest Earned. Times interest earned indicates the relative ability of a firm to pay the interest on its debt. For General Mills, it is

$$\frac{\text{Operating income}}{\text{Annual interest payments}} = \frac{159}{60} = 2.65.$$

In a chart presented in the financial review section, General Mills disclosed *continuing operations earnings after tax,* prior to redeployment, of $159 million. You cannot extract this figure from the primary financial statements presented in Tables 12.8 and 12.9, but it is probably a better number to use than the 196, 115, or –73 that we could have used from Table 12.8. This emphasis on revenue and expenses for continuing operations is typical of a forward-looking financial analysis. Extraordinary and nonrecurring gains or losses are of little interest in terms of the forecast of long-term well-being of the corporation.

PROFITABILITY RATIOS

Profitability ratios provide a summary view of the company's relative earnings for the period in question. They typically relate a measure of earnings to a normalizing measure of size.

Return on Assets. If we use the income after taxes of continuing operations from the preceding ratio, add back interest expense, subtract the tax benefit from this interest expense and use the resulting number as the numerator, we can obtain a crude measure of profitability by dividing by total assets.

$$\frac{\text{Net income after tax + Interest expense} - \text{Tax benefit of interest expense}}{\text{Total assets}}$$

$$= \frac{159 + 60 - (81/146)(60)}{2664} = 0.09.$$

Because of the lack of other numbers, we divided earnings after redeployment into tax payments to obtain a tax-rate estimate of 41 percent.

Return on Equity. We took an "after everything" view of the General Mills situation, which shows that redeployment and discontinued operations caused a one-time negative return on equity to common shareholders, or

$$\frac{\text{Net income available to common shareholders}}{\text{Common shareholders' equity}} =$$

$$\frac{-73}{1024} = -0.07.$$

When using this ratio in practice, we would most likely exclude preferred stock from shareholders' equity and treat preferred stock dividends as long-term debt-interest payments.

The comparison of these two profitability ratios indicates that the company has good prospects for a positive return of assets on continuing operations but major costs related to disposing of less desirable operations.

TURNOVER RATIOS

Turnover ratios are measures of the dynamics of the entity. They will relate sales to items or total assets, inventory and accounts receivable to evaluate the utilization/measurement of these items. These ratios measure the dynamics of the financial operations of the firm.

Total Asset Turnover. This ratio indicates the number of times that annual sales covers total assets. Other turnover ratios complement this indicator.

$$\frac{\text{Sales}}{\text{Average total assets}} = \frac{4285}{(2664 + 2859)/2} = 1.55.$$

Inventory Turnover. Inventories at General Mills dropped significantly between 1984 and 1985. The decrease in inventories probably were related to redeployments and discontinued operations, making this ratio suspect for 1985.

$$\frac{\text{Sales}}{\text{Average inventory}} = \frac{4285}{(378 + 662)/2} = 8.24.$$

Accounts Receivable Turnover. The same 1984–1985 actions noted for the preceding ratio affect this ratio. The numbers used here for the denominator are net of allowance for bad debts.

$$\frac{\text{Sales}}{\text{Average (net) accounts receivable}} = \frac{4285}{(285 + 551)/2} = 10.25.$$

MARKET-VALUE RATIOS

Price-earnings Ratio. We calculated this ratio using the market value of a share of common stock at the end of the year (not the average for the year) and earnings per share from continuing operations. We have to interpret this ratio carefully in light of the major restructuring of General Mills in 1984–1985. The **P/E ratio** is one of the most frequently used ratios in the marketplace.

$$\frac{\text{Market price per share}}{\text{Earnings per share}} = \frac{58.13}{22.53} = 2.58.$$

Market to Book Ratio. A less commonly used ratio relates the market value of the stock to the company's book value. The numerator is the market value of the stock at the end of the year, and the denominator represents total shareholders' equity divided by the number of outstanding shares.

$$\frac{\text{Market value of stock}}{\text{Book value of stock}} = \frac{58.13}{1023/44.7} = 2.54.$$

This ratio gives the relationship between the market value of the stock and the company's assets, measured at the historical cost level. Interesting extensions of this calculation may be performed with figures adjusted for inflation.

TRENDS AND COMPARISONS

The 12 ratios discussed in this section can provide the auditor with valuable insights into the financial well-being of a company. Further, the auditor can use these ratios and qualitative evaluations of them to obtain trends and comparisons to established internal benchmarks, other comparable firms, or the industry as a whole. Three of the simple techniques used to facilitate this type of analysis are common size statements, comparison with industry ratios, and segment comparison.

Common Size Statements. The key in financial statements is set at a base of, say, 100 and the other accounts are factored to that base. In the income statement, the sales entry becomes the base of 100; in the balance sheet, total assets and liabilities and shareholders' equity become bases of 100. Common size numbers for the General Mills statements are provided in Tables 12.10 and 12.11.

Comparison with Industry Ratios. Table 12.12 displays a set of selected industry ratios adopted from Robert Morris Associates. These ratios can be used to compare a particular firm with others in its industry and with the industry as a whole.

Segment Comparison. Segment reporting is required by SFAS No. 14. It specifies that companies have to report specific information for their various lines of business. These lines of business are not fully comparable, and the data disclosed do not fully cover the scope of disclosure. However, used with caution, these data provide a rich source of prior-to-consolidation information about firms.

Table 12.10 Common Size Comparisons for General Mills, Inc., Income Statement.

	1985	1984
Sales	100.00	100.00
Cost of Sales	57.76	59.08
Selling, General, & Administrative Expense	31.93	30.40
Depreciation & Amortization	2.57	2.40
Interest Expense	1.40	0.78
Earnings—Pretax	6.35	7.33
Gains from Redeployment	−1.77	1.29
Earnings after Redeployment	4.57	8.62
Income Taxes	1.89	3.74
Earnings after Taxes & Redeployment	2.68	4.88
Discontinued Operations after Taxes	−4.39	0.75
NET EARNINGS	−1.70	5.63

Note: See Table 12.8 for the dollar amounts on which the proportions shown are based.

Trend Identification and Forecasting. Calculation and comparison of financial ratios over a period of several years can permit the discovery of variances, determination of the level of integrity among ratios, and identification of trends. Trends can then be used to forecast expected ratio values.

12.7 FUTURE OF ANALYTICAL REVIEW

Financial statement analysis is an extremely important part of the auditor's task, and extensive literature on the subject is available to guide the auditor in its utilization.[19] The examination of financial statements that have described and the procedures that we have applied to the statements of General Mills are merely representative of the auditor's work in analytical review.

Table 12.11 Common Size Comparisons for General Mills, Inc., Balance Sheet

	1985	1984
Current Assets		
Cash & Short-Term Investments	2.52	2.31
Receivables less Allowances	10.70	19.27
Inventories	14.19	23.15
Investments in Tax Leases	0.00	1.75
Prepaid Expenses	1.50	1.54
Net Assets of Discontinued Operations	19.44	0.63
Total Current Assets	48.35	48.65
Land, Buildings, & Equipment	55.78	63.97
Less: Accumulated Depreciation	−19.89	−20.99
Net Land, Buildings, & Equipment	35.89	42.99
Other Assets	15.77	8.36
TOTAL ASSETS	100.00	100.00
Current Liabilities		
Accounts Payable	13.51	16.72
Current Portion of Long-Term Debt	2.21	2.10
Notes Payable	14.26	8.78
Accrued Taxes & Payroll	3.49	6.75
Other Current Liabilities	6.16	5.70
Total Current Liabilities	39.64	40.05
Long-Term Debt	16.89	12.70
Deferred Income Taxes	1.13	2.69
Deferred Income Taxes—Tax Leases	2.29	0.00
Other Liabilities	1.61	1.75
TOTAL LIABILITIES	61.56	57.19

(continued on next page)

Note: See Table 12.9 for the dollar amounts on which the proportions shown are based.

Table 12.11 Common Size Comparisons for General Mills, Inc., Balance Sheet
(continued)

	1985	1984
Stockholders' Equity	8.03	7.52
Retained Earnings	45.12	48.09
Less: Stock in Treasury	−12.54	−10.21
Cumulative Foreign Currency Adjustments	−2.18	−2.59
Total Stockholders' Equity	38.44	42.81
TOTAL LIABILITIES & EQUITIES	100.00	100.00

The use of AR in the future is expected to increase and to become more sophisticated. In the Tabor and Willis survey discussed in Section 12.5, the seven auditors were asked to state their views concerning the future of AR. They expressed the opinion that the use of ARPs will increase in the future because:

1. The use of microcomputers will become easier and less costly.
2. Increased fee pressures will continue to require more efficient audit procedures.
3. Better internal control environments particularly among larger clients, will allow for the more efficient use of ARPs.
4. ARPs often are more efficient than additional compliance testing. Therefore, with a decrease in compliance testing, analytical review work could increase.
5. Regression analysis and/or predictive testing will begin to play a greater role in future audits.
6. The use of industry databases (nonquantitative techniques) to compare a client with its industry will increase.
7. Other techniques, such as trend analysis and variance analysis will be used increasingly.

The economics of auditing and the evolution of auditing procedures for EDP systems will make the analytic part of the audit one of its most important components.

Table 12.12
Distribution Statistics for Financial Ratios of Selected Industries

Industry and SIC Code	Number of Firms	Quick Ratio			Sales Receivables			% Profit Before Taxes to Tangible Net Worth		
		LQ	M	UQ	LQ	M	UQ	LQ	M	UQ
1. Paint, varnish, and lacquer (2851)	136	.8	1.1	1.7	6.8	8.1	10.7	3.2	11.0	23.6
2. Plastic materials (2821)	126	.6	.9	1.3	7.0	8.3	10.7	6.4	15.4	30.7
3. Bread and bakery products (2051)	108	.5	.8	1.3	13.1	17.0	27.0	8.0	22.1	47.3
4. Dairy products (2021)	124	.5	.8	1.1	12.9	16.9	22.5	6.8	17.3	31.2
5. Meat packing (2011)	134	.6	1.0	1.6	19.0	24.7	29.1	2.9	13.0	29.1
6. Wood furniture (2511)	129	.5	.8	1.4	7.0	8.9	13.9	.1	13.3	28.5
7. Millwork (2431)	142	.5	.8	1.7	7.0	9.3	12.6	-7.1	11.1	22.8
8. Sawmills (2421)	167	.2	.5	1.0	10.6	14.6	23.9	-18.8	3.5	10.7
9. Radio and TV transmitting equipment (3662)	166	.7	1.0	1.8	5.0	6.2	8.6	8.8	22.1	46.0
10. Construction equipment (3531)	117	.4	.7	1.7	6.0	8.3	13.6	-13.5	5.1	14.1
11. Electronic computing equipment (3573)	178	.7	1.1	1.9	4.6	5.6	7.2	3.8	21.3	39.7
12. General industrial equipment (3561)	411	.6	1.0	1.6	5.7	7.4	10.2	1.3	13.9	29.1
13. Machine shop repair (3599)	550	.6	.9	1.5	6.7	8.7	11.8	-5.5	12.3	28.1
14. Iron and steel foundries (3321)	147	.6	1.1	1.9	7.4	9.6	13.3	-13.5	4.0	18.3
15. Nonferrous fabricated products (3499)	183	.6	1.0	1.6	6.4	8.2	10.9	-3.6	11.6	27.7

LQ — Lower quartile (.25 percentile).
M — Median (.5 percentile).
UQ — Upper quartile (.75 percentile).

Source: Reprinted with permission from Robert Morris Associates (1983). Copyright © 1983.

12.8 Summary

In this chapter, we examined the general features of SAS No. 23 in relation to the role of analytical review. Analytical review is considered to be an important part of the process of substantive testing (complementing tests of details), as well as audit risk evaluation.

Risk may be divided into several components, which affect both accounting and overall business operations. These components are described in Figure 12.1 which breaks Business Risk into two main components: audit risk and other business risks.

SAS No. 23 suggests the consideration of the following factors when using AR procedures: nature of the entity, scope of the engagement, availability of financial and nonfinancial information, the reliability of this information and the availability of comparable information.

These factors are to be weighted in qualitatively into auditor judgments that may or may not take also into consideration financial statement analysis, regression techniques and graphical observation of data. Current auditing practices were found to previously rely on the analysis of ratios as quantitative techniques with the recent emergence of other more advanced AR techniques.

The new proposed standard of AR increases the importance and need for these techniques in the overall attestation process.

Questions

1. What is analytical review? What authoritative standards govern its use in auditing?
2. What functions do analytical review serve in an audit?
3. How do each of the following factors affect the use of analytical review?
   (a) Nature of the entity.
   (b) Scope of the engagement.
   (c) Availability of financial information.
   (d) Availability of nonfinancial information.
   (e) Reliability of information.
   (f) Availability of comparative information.
4. What is regression analysis? How can it be used as an analytical review technique?
5. What are the key questions that must be asked when analytical review procedures are used to examine a fluctuation?

6. Describe all ratios examined in this chapter and in your own words describe their functions and interrelationships.
7. What are common size statements? How can they be used in analytical review?
8. Based on common size statements, how would you rate General Mills' performance in 1985?
9. Examining Table 12.12, choose the industry with the best profitability. How does this industry rate in terms of the other ratios?
10. What are the expected developments in analytical review for the future?

Problems

1. At what points in the audit process might you use analytical review? Do you think you would rely on it equally at each point you use it? What factors might affect the level of reliance?
2. Refer to an elementary auditing text and compare the types of analytical review suggested in it with regression analysis and the ratio techniques presented in this chapter.
3. Would you rely on analytical review as the sole substantive test performed on an account? If so what are some of the circumstances that would affect your decision?
4. What level of mathematical sophistication do you think you need in order to use some of the statistical techniques introduced in this chapter? How might you acquire those skills?
5. What types of accounts would be most amenable to analytical review? Least amenable? Why?
6. Find the financial statements of a firm and:
   a) calculate the financial ratios prescribed in this chapter.
   b) prepare common size statements for this firm.
   c) compare this firm's ratios with the ratios of other firms in this industry.
   d) based on the analysis above, which accounts and time-periods would you emphasize in an audit? Justify.
7. Plot the data of Table 12.2 on graph paper. Try to visually fit a straight line to it. Next, calculate the linear regression line that would provide the best "least-squares" fit. Calculate residuals. Plot these residuals on the same graph paper. Evaluate your findings.

Notes

1. Mock, T. J., and Vertinsky, I., *Risk Assessment in Accounting and Auditing.* Vancouver, B.C.: Canadian Certified General Accountant's Research Foundation, 1985, p. 5.

2. Mock and Vertinsky, *op. cit.*, p. 18.

3. In these definitions, the term error usually refers to a material error or irregularity.

4. Brumfield, C. A., Elliott, R. K., and Jacobson, P. D., "Business Risk and the Audit Process," *Journal of Accountancy*, April 1983, pp. 60–68.

5. Mock and Vertinsky, p. 42.

6. AICPA, SAS No. 23, "Analytical Review Procedures," section 318 of the Codification of Auditing Standards, New York: AICPA, October 1978.

7. — SAS No. 23, section 318.07.f.

8. SAS No. 1 (section 320) was substantially modified by SAS No. 48 which measured the consideration of the effect of EDP systems on internal controls.

9. See Wonnacott, T. H., and Wonnacott, R. J., *Introductory Statistics for Business and Economics.* New York: John Wiley & Sons, 1972 and Ewart, P. J., Ford, J. S., and Lin, C. Y., *Applied Managerial Statistics.* Englewood Cliffs, N.J.: Prentice-Hall, 1982.

10. Stringer, K. W., "A Statistical Technique for Analytical Review," *Journal of Accounting Research,* Supplement 1975, pp. 1, 9.

11. Cleveland, W. S., "Robust Locally Weighted Regression and Smoothing Scatterplots," *Journal of American Statistical Association,* 74(368): 829–836, 1979.

12. See Tukey, J. W., *Exploratory Data Analysis.* Reading, Mass.: Addison-Wesley, 1977.

13. Becker, R. A., and Chambers, J. M., *"S": An Interactive Environment for Data Analysis and Graphics.* Belmont, Calif.: Wadsworth, 1984.

14. Daroca, F. P., and Holder, W. W., "The Use of Analytical Procedures in Review and Audit Engagements," *Auditing: A Journal of Practice and Theory,* Spring 1985, pp. 80–92.

15. *Ibid.*, p. 80.

16. Tabor, R. H., and Willis, J. T., "Empirical Evidence on the Changing Role of Analytical Review Procedures," *Auditing: A Journal of Practice and Theory,* Spring 1985, pp. 93–103.

17. *Ibid.*, p. 96.

18. Foster, G., *Financial Statement Analysis.* Englewood Cliffs, N.J.: Prentice-Hall, 1985.

19. An excellent compendium is Foster, *op cit.*

Additional References

AICPA Professional Standards, American Institute of Certified Public Accountants, Commerce Clearing House, 1983.

Bo, G. E. P., and G. M. Jenkins, *Time Series Analysis*, San Francisco: Holden Day, 1970.

Biggs, S. C., Jr., "Perspectives in Auditing for the 1980s and Beyond—Statements in Quotes," *Journal of Accountancy*, May 1982, pp. 93–104.

Biggs, S. F., and J. J. Wild, "A Note on the Practice of Analytical Review," *Auditing: A Journal of Practice and Theory*, Spring 1984, pp. 68–79.

Blocher, E., "Approaching Analytical Review," *The CPA Journal*, March 1983, pp. 24–32.

Graham, L. E., "Analytical Review Techniques: Some Neglected Tools," *The CPA Journal*, October 1981, pp. 18–24.

Holder, W. W., "Analytical Review Procedures in Planning the Audit: An Application Study," *Auditing: A Journal of Practice and Theory*, Spring 1983, pp. 100–107.

Holder, W. W., and S. Collmer, "Analytical Review Procedures: New Relevance," *The CPA Journal*, November 1980, pp. 29–35.

Kinney, W. R., Jr., "The Predictive Power of Limited Information in Preliminary Analytical Review: An Empirical Study," *Journal of Accounting Research*, 17(Suppl): 148–165, 1979.

Kinney, W. R., Jr., and W. L. Felix, Jr., "Analytical Review Procedures," *Journal of Accountancy*, October 1980, pp. 98–103.

Lev, B., "On the Use of Index Models in Analytical Review by Auditors," *Journal of Accounting Research*, Autumn 1980, pp. 524–545.

Wallace, W. A., "Analytical Review Misconceptions, Potential Applications and Experience—Part I," *The CPA Journal*, January 1983(a), pp. 24–37.

Wallace, W. A., "Analytical Review Misconceptions, Potential Applications and Experience—Part II," *The CPA Journal*, February 1983(b), pp. 18–27.

Chapter 13

Statistical Sampling: Basic Concepts

13.1 INTRODUCTION

Auditors normally use sampling procedures during the audit process to obtain evidence. Statement on Auditing Standards No. 39, *Audit Sampling,* provides guidance on the use of sampling in an audit of financial statements. According to SAS No. 39, "audit sampling is the application of an audit procedure to less than 100 percent of the items within an account balance or class of transactions for the purpose of evaluating some characteristic of the balance or class."[1] That is, audit sampling involves selecting a portion of a population of items being audited and using characteristics of that portion to draw inferences about the entire population.

Two general approaches to audit sampling are used: nonstatistical and statistical. Until SAS No. 39 was issued, nonstatistical sampling was called *judgmental sampling,* because it is based only on auditor judgment and does not quantify sampling risk. Statistical sampling, on the other hand, uses the mathematical laws of probability to aid the auditor in designing a sampling plan. Statistical sampling also requires that the sample be randomly selected and that the results be evaluated using mathematical statistics. Since both approaches require audit judgment in planning and performing a sampling procedure and evaluating the results, use of the term judgmental sampling has been discontinued.

This is the first of four chapters devoted to statistical sampling. In this chapter, we present the basic concepts of statistical sampling. In the following three chapters, we will discuss procedures and uses of the three major statistical sampling methods: (1) attribute sampling; (2) variable sampling; and (3) probability–proportional-to-size sampling.

We begin this chapter with definitions of audit sampling, nonstatistical sampling, and statistical sampling. Then we discuss the role of statistical sampling in the audit process and its advantages and disadvantages. Next, we review some basic statistical and sampling concepts, such as probability, population, precision, reliability, and sampling risk. We then turn to the major sample selection techniques and sampling plans. Finally, we present the uses of statistical sampling in auditing.

LEARNING OBJECTIVES

By the time you have completed this chapter, you should be able to:

1. Define and distinguish among audit sampling, nonstatistical sampling, and statistical sampling.
2. Explain the role of sampling in the audit process.
3. State the advantages and disadvantages of statistical sampling relative to nonstatistical sampling.
4. Explain basic statistical and sampling concepts.
5. Utilize different sample selection techniques.
6. List and define different sampling plans.
7. Identify the uses of statistical sampling in auditing.

13.2 STATISTICAL SAMPLING IN THE AUDIT PROCESS

Since uncertainty is inherent in auditing, an auditor designs and selects auditing procedures to reduce that uncertainty to a tolerable level. A tolerable level of error is one that is less than a material amount. Audit risk is defined as the probability that material errors or irregularities will not be detected. The auditor uses statistical sampling to help ensure that sufficient evidence is gathered to detect these material errors and irregularities. Thus statistical sampling is directly related to the *extent* of the audit evidence collected and evaluated. The auditor's decision to utilize statistical sampling affects the approach taken to (1) system review and preliminary evaluation of internal accounting control; (2) audit program design; and (3) application of audit procedures, evaluation of evidence, and refinement of the audit program, as required.[2]

Statistical sampling is not used to review the system of internal accounting control. However, the results of system review and preliminary evaluation directly affect the decision to use statistical sampling in tests of details. During audit program design, the auditor can use statistical sampling to select audit procedures for (1) compliance tests of internal accounting controls; (2) tests of details of transactions and balances; and (3) analytical review of significant ratios and trends and the investigation of unusual fluctuations and questionable items. An auditor generally selects attribute sampling plans for compliance testing of internal accounting controls and variable sampling plans for substantive testing purposes. The auditor can also apply probability–proportional-to-size sampling to conduct dual purpose tests. Proper application of statistical procedures is necessary to ensure the statistical validity of sampling results. We discuss in some detail the theoretical concepts of and procedures for major statistical sampling plans in Chapters 14, 15, and 16.

AUDIT RISK FORMULA

According to SAS No. 47, audit risk is the risk that auditors incur if they express an unqualified opinion on materially misstated financial statements. The following audit-risk formula is presented in SAS No. 47 and SAS No. 39. It shows the audit risk is a combination of four risks: inherent risk, internal control risk, analytical review procedure risk, and test of details risk.[3]

$$UR = (IR)(IC)(AR)(TD)$$

where

UR = Allowable ultimate audit risk.

IR = Inherent risk, i.e., auditor's assessment of the susceptibility of a material error occurs in the financial statement.

IC = Auditor's assessment of risk of internal accounting control failure.

AR = Auditor's assessment of risk of analytical review procedure and other supplemental procedure failure.

TD = Allowable risk of incorrect acceptance of results of substantive test of details.

The ultimate audit risk, of course, is that errors greater than tolerable error might remain undetected in an account balance or class of transactions after all audit procedures have been completed. Such errors can occur because the system of internal accounting controls fails to detect them, owing to either poorly designed controls or lack of compliance. If errors greater than tolerable error occur and the system of internal accounting control does not detect them, there is also a possibility that audit procedures and tests will not detect them. And, finally, if such errors occur and are not detected by controls, procedures, and tests, the auditor may incorrectly accept the results of detailed testing.

For audit sampling purposes, we can restate the formula as

$$TD = \frac{UR}{(IC)(AR)}.$$

In this formula inherent risk is assumed to be at the maximum (100 percent). This approach is suggested in SAS No. 39, due to a controversial issue of separate assessment of inherent risk at levels below the maximum. An auditor planning a statistical sample can use this form of the equation in making a decision about the allowable risk for incorrect acceptance of a specific substantive test of details.

Ultimate Audit Risk. The auditor starts by specifying the ultimate audit risk with respect to a particular account balance or class of transactions. The auditor considers such factors as the risk of material misstatement in the financial statements, the expense of reducing the risk, and the effect of the potential misstatement on the use and understanding of the financial statements.

Ultimate audit risk (*UR*) includes both sampling and nonsampling risk. Sampling risk is the risk that an auditor may fail to detect a material error simply because a 100 percent audit of all the entity's transactions is not feasible. Nonsampling risk includes all other aspects of ultimate audit risk, including the risk of a failure to detect a material error because of inherent problems associated with the interpretation or accumulation of data or test results.

Quantifying Risk. For purposes of using the basic risk formula, we can assume that the nonsampling risk aspect of ultimate risk is negligible. This assumption is based on the belief that adequate levels of audit quality control, including adequate staff training and supervision, will eliminate nonsampling errors. Most auditors consider nonsampling errors by increasing statistically determined sample size subjectively.

Quantification of the risk that the system of accounting internal control fails to detect an error (*IC*) is based on professional judgment, that is, the auditor's evaluation of the overall effectiveness of one or more internal accounting controls. Note that *IC* is not the same as the risk of overreliance on internal accounting control. The quantification of risk of undetected error because of analytical review procedures failure (*AR*) also requires the application of professional judgment.

For example, assume that an auditor is planning to test an entity's inventory balance by sampling. The auditor may subjectively quantify the risk of undetected error owing to internal accounting control failure as 20 percent and the risk of undetected error owing to analytical review failure as 70 percent. The auditor may also have decided to accept a 5 percent level of ultimate audit risk. The auditor can then use the formula to gain some understanding of the appropriate level of risk of incorrect acceptance for the sampling application being designed. In this case,

$$TD = UR/(IC)(AR)$$
$$= 0.05/(0.20)(0.70)$$
$$= 0.36.$$

Thus, by planning all the tests relating to a particular account balance or class of transactions at the same time, the auditor can control total sampling risk.

Formula Limitations. Before leaving this basic audit risk formula, we should point out, as SAS No. 39 does, that the formula does not represent a true mathematical formula that can be evaluated as we did in the preceding example. Instead, the formula is designed for comparative purposes to show that as one risk increases, it can be offset by decreasing another risk.

One obvious problem with using this formula as a mathematical formula is that it is based on the assumption that the variables are independent. This assumption is incorrect, and some sort of conditional probability formula would be appropriate. Another inadequacy relates to the assignment of values. Even if accurate values could be assigned, one simple formula is not sufficient to encompass all pieces of accounting information; each piece involves a number of assertions and has a different degree of risk associated with it.

ADVANTAGES AND DISADVANTAGES OF STATISTICAL SAMPLING

Statistical sampling helps auditors to understand the significance of discovered errors. The auditor can use statistical sampling to plan, document, and evaluate audit tests, thereby improving his or her judgment—but not replacing it. Although statistical sampling may involve the additional costs of training auditors and designing individual samples to meet statistical requirements, the benefits far outweigh the costs.

Advantages. Statistical sampling can provide several distinct advantages over nonstatistical sampling. It provides the auditor with a more objective method of determining sample risks and sample size and evaluating the sample. By using statistical sampling, the auditor can minimize sample bias. Statistical sampling allows the auditor to specify and control sampling risks by estimating the degree of precision and reliability that can be attained, that is, the range of values within which the true value is expected to fall and the degree of confidence that the true value is contained within that range. The auditor can obtain better results from the sampling process by specifying statistically the expected error rate, the required reliability, the maximum limit of acceptable error, the appropriate method of selection to avoid bias, and the best means of evaluating the sample and by determining whether all areas that should be tested will be. Statistical sampling may also save time and money because an efficient sampling plan can result in a smaller sample size than might be used in a nonstatistical sampling approach.

A survey by Rittenberg and Schweiger showed that the major benefits of statistical sampling, as perceived by practicing internal auditors, relate to (1) the characteristics of objectivity and defensibility associated with statistical sampling; and (2) the uniformity in audit approach and result interpretation inherent in statistical methodology.[4] Another survey, which was conducted by Bedingfield, also showed that objectivity is the major reason that external auditors use statistical sampling. Test aspects of objectivity are significant: one is the ability to provide proof of objectivity if necessary; the other is the ability to evaluate and state the results of audit tests.[5]

Disadvantages. The use of statistical sampling can involve additional costs for training auditors, designing individual samples to meet statistical requirements, and selecting items to be examined. Nonstatistical sampling is more appropriate than statistical sampling for (1) footing journals; (2) selecting client personnel to be interviewed; and (3) testing compliance with internal control procedures that do not leave an audit trail of documentary evidence.

The Rittenberg and Schweiger survey showed that the majority of internal auditors believed that (1) many audit areas were not extensive enough to warrant the use of statistical sampling; (2) much of internal auditing was not suited to its use; and (3) the background of the audit staff was inadequate.[6] Bedingfield's survey of the external auditors reported three major drawbacks to the use of statistical sampling: (1) lack of adequate training; (2) difficulties involved in sample selection; and (3) difficulty in interpreting the impact of the results of a statistical sample of some audit staff members.[7] Clearly, the results of these two surveys are similar and identify the same problems: auditor training and technical difficulties.

STEPS IN STATISTICAL SAMPLING

The use of statistical sampling involves three basic steps: design, selection, and evaluation. During sample design, the auditor defines the objective of sampling and the type of sampling to be used. The auditor then determines sampling criteria, such as reliability and precision, and chooses sampling evaluation and selection methods. Sample design ends with the calculation of the sample size, based on the sample type and criteria. Sample selection involves identifying the items to be examined individually and applying auditing procedures to those items. Sample evaluation entails forming conclusions about the data from the examination of individual sample items in terms of audit objectives.

13.3 BASIC STATISTICAL AND SAMPLING CONCEPTS

In this section, we discuss statistical and sampling concepts that are fundamental to an understanding of statistical sampling as applied to auditing. We use the term *statistical concepts* to refer to descriptive statistics, which can be used to reduce a large amount of data to a few descriptive figures. We use the term *sampling concepts* in relation to inferential statistics, which can be used to make inferences about a population from sample data.

STATISTICAL CONCEPTS

The basic statistical concepts normally include population, sample, measures of central tendency, measures of dispersion, normal distribution, skewed distribution, central limit theorem, and distribution of sample means. The population is the total of all items or elements about which information is desired. Typical elements of interest to auditors are documents, transactions, individual account balances, and the like, which comprise cash disbursement, accounts receivable, inventory, and similar audit populations. The parameters of a population give auditors information about its shape and size. Two commonly used population parameters are the *mean* and *variance,* which measure the central tendency and dispersion of observations or data, respectively. The population size is expressed symbolically as N. A **sample** is a collection of items or elements drawn from a population. For example, auditors may select 50 invoices from a population of 200 unpaid invoices for accounts receivable confirmation purposes. The sample size is expressed symbolically as n.

Three measures of central tendency can be calculated for data:

1. Mean—the average value of the observations. It is obtained by totaling all the values and dividing by the number of items. The mean of a population is expressed symbolically as (μ). The mean of a sample is expressed symbolically as x.
2. Median—the value of the midpoint item(s) when the data are arranged in ascending or descending sequence. One-half of the observations lie above and one-half lie below the median value.
3. Mode—the value that occurs most frequently in the data.

For example, a sample of five invoice items have values of $4, $10, $15, $18, and $18. We calculate the mean as follows:

$$x = \frac{\sum_{i=1}^{n} x_i}{n} = \frac{\$4 + \$10 + \$15 + \$18 + \$18}{5} = \$13.$$

Looking at the five data values, you can easily see that $15 is the median. Similarly, the mode is $18.

Auditors may use different techniques when items or accounts within a population differ substantially. An auditor may simply scan a small item or account for reasonableness but vouch extensively a large item or account in order to confirm it. In either case, the size of the difference between elements is important. The common measures of dispersion or variability of sample observations are range, variance, and standard deviation.

1. Range—the difference between the largest observed value and the smallest observed value.
2. Variance—a measure of the extent to which the values of the items are dispersed around the mean. It is the average of the squared deviations of each observation from the mean. The variance of a population is expressed symbolically as σ^2. The variance of a sample is represented as s^2.
3. Standard deviation—the most frequently used measure of variability. It is the square root of the variance. The population standard deviation is expressed symbolically as σ. The sample standard deviation is expressed as s.

We calculate the population variance using

$$\sigma^2 = \frac{\sum_{i=1}^{N} (x_i - \mu)^2}{N} = \frac{\sum_{i=1}^{N} x_i^2 - N\bar{x}^2}{N}$$

and the sample variance using

$$s^2 = \frac{\sum_{i=1}^{n} (x_i - \bar{x})^2}{n - 1}.$$

Returning to the five-item invoice example, we calculate the variance of each value as follows:

Observation	Invoice value	Mean	Deviation squared
(i)	(x_i)	(x)	$(x_i - x)^2$
1	$ 4	$13	$ 81
2	10	13	9
3	15	13	4
4	18	13	25
5	18	13	25
	—		—
	65		144

We can now calculate the sample variance as follows:

$$s^2 = \sum_{i=1}^{n} \frac{(x_i - x)^2}{(n-1)} = \frac{\$ 144}{4} = \$ 36.$$

The standard deviation for the sample is the square root of the sample variance, or $6.

The *normal distribution* is a unimodal distribution that is continuous and symmetric about its mean. The curve of the normal distribution is bell-shaped; that is, the right side is a mirror image of the left side. The mean, median, and mode of a normally distributed set of observations or data are equal, as shown in Figure 13.1. An important feature of the normal distribution is that the relative frequency of any interval can be determined from only the mean (μ) and the standard deviation (σ). The interval $\mu \pm \sigma$ contains 68 percent of the items, that from $\mu \pm 2\sigma$ contains 95 percent of the items, and that from $\mu \pm 3\sigma$ contains 99 percent of the items.

Many audit populations are not normally distributed. Instead, they are *skewed distributions* in which the mean, median, and mode are not the same. Figure 13.2 shows two skewed distributions, namely, a positively skewed distribution and a negatively skewed distribution. A positively skewed distribution has a large number of small-value items and an increasingly smaller number of high-value items. In practice, a company may have many small customer account balances and only a few large customer account balances. Conversely, negatively skewed distributions have a few items with very small values and relatively more items with high values.

Figure 13.1   A Normal Distribution (Bell Curve)

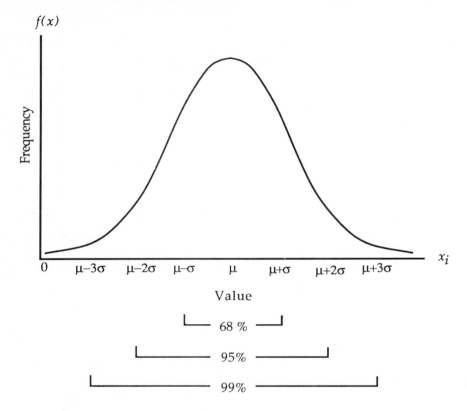

Traditional statistical sampling methods are applicable to auditing, even though most accounting data are not normally distributed. This situation is possible because the **central limit theorem** states that when the mean of a large sample is calculated, the distribution of sampling means calculated from all possible samples of size n tend to be distributed normally, regardless of the shape of the true population distribution. A **distribution of sample means** has three properties:

1. The distribution is centered at the population mean.
2. The shape of the distribution will approach a normal distribution as the sample size becomes larger.
3. The standard error of the mean equals the estimated population standard deviation divided by the square root of the sample size. This statistic is often referred to as the standard deviation of the sampling distribution or the standard error of estimate.

Figure 13.2   Skewed Distributions

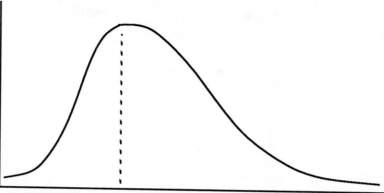

A. Positively skewed distribution

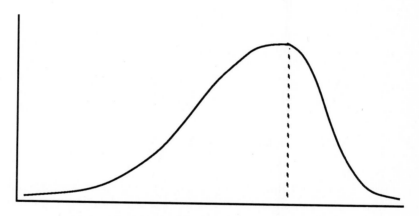

B. Negatively skewed distribution

SAMPLING CONCEPTS

Sampling is the process of obtaining information about an entire population by examining only a part of the population. Before sampling can be properly used, certain sampling fundamentals and terms must be clearly understood. Sampling concepts include sampling unit, random, attribute, stratification, sampling risk, precision, and reliability.

A **sampling unit** is the element in a population having the char-acteristics that are to be measured in order to estimate those charac-teristics for the entire population. For example, if an auditor wants to verify the total balance of accounts receivable by confirmation, any of the following could be specified as the sampling unit: (1) a particular sales branch; (2) total customer balances; (3) open invoices; and (4) line items on open invoices.

Random is the condition of being without bias or pattern. A *random sample* is one selected from a population in such a way that all elements of the population have an equal chance of being selected.

An **attribute** is any characteristic that an element of a population either possesses or does not possess. When an attribute is measurable quantitatively it is called a *variable*.

If a population is composed of distinct subpopulations, an efficient procedure may be to divide the population into separate populations and then sample from each, rather than sample from the overall population. This process is called **stratification**. A *stratum* is a section of a population that differs in some respect from the rest of the population.

Sampling risk arises from the possibility that a test applied to a sample will result in a conclusion that may be different from the conclusion that the auditor would reach if the test were applied in the same way to all elements in the population. Sampling risk is determined and controlled in a statistical sample. Statisticians refer to two types of sampling risk: alpha risk, which is called Type I error, and beta risk, which is also called Type II error. *Alpha risk* is the probability that an auditor will reject a correct or true population or book value. *Beta risk* is the probability that an auditor will accept a materially misstated book value.

In SAS No. 39, the terms *risk of overreliance on internal accounting control* and *risk of incorrect acceptance* are used instead of beta risk. **Risk of overreliance on internal accounting control** is the risk that the sample supports the auditor's planned degree of reliance on the control, even though the true compliance rate does not justify such reliance. **Risk of incorrect acceptance** is the risk that the sample supports the conclusion that the population is not materially misstated, even though, in fact, the population is materially misstated. In SAS No. 39, also, the terms *risk of underreliance on internal accounting control* and *risk of incorrect rejection* are used instead of alpha risk. **Risk of underreliance on internal accounting control** is the risk that the sample does not support the auditor's planned degree of reliance on the control, even though the true compliance rate supports such reliance. **Risk of incorrect rejection** is the risk that the sample supports the conclusion that the population is materially misstated, even though it is not.

Precision is a measure of the closeness between the sample estimate and the true population value. Actually, the term is used to refer to the amount of imprecision an auditor is willing to accept. Precision is expressed as a range of values, plus and minus, around the sample estimate and may be used in planning for audit sampling. In SAS No. 39, the term *tolerable error* is used in preference to *precision* in the sample planning stage. Precision may also be used in audit sampling as an evaluation concept. In SAS No. 39, the term *allowance for sampling risk* is used in place of precision in the sample-result evaluation stage.

Reliability, or confidence level, is the percentage of the time the sample estimate differs from the actual population value by the precision value or less. Reliability may be viewed as the confidence level or degree of assurance that an auditor can place on the sample estimate. In SAS No. 39, the concept of risk, instead of reliability or confidence level, is used. **Risk** is the complement of reliability or the confidence level. For example, if an auditor specifies a reliability or confidence level as 95 percent, the auditor is willing to accept a 5 percent risk.

13.4 SAMPLE SELECTION TECHNIQUES

Selection of a **statistical sample** usually involves the use of random numbers. They can be obtained from various numbers tables of random or by using a generalized computer program that will create random numbers according to user specifications.

A random sample is one in which all items in the population have an equal chance of being selected for the sample. The laws of probability can be used to evaluate a sample only if it is randomly selected and thus free from sampling bias. Some commonly used techniques for selecting a random sample are simple (or unrestricted) random selection, systematic selection, stratified selection, and cluster sample selection.

SIMPLE RANDOM SELECTION

In **simple random selection,** the auditor relies on tables of random numbers or computer-generated random numbers to select population items for sampling. The use of random-number tables is facilitated when the items in a population are numbered consecutively.[8] Tables of random numbers contain columns and rows of randomly generated digits, as shown in Table 13.1.

To illustrate the use of a table of random numbers, let's assume that an auditor wants to take a random sample from a population of 800 vouchers. The vouchers are in ascending numerical sequence, starting with 001 and ending with 800. The auditor starts by establishing a relationship between a table of random numbers and the population being sampled. There are only three digits in the voucher numbers, so the auditor decides to use the last three digits having values within the limits of 001 to 800 from Table

Table 13.1   Partial Table of Random Numbers

Row	Column					
	1	2	3	4	5	6
1	6767	0125	7936	2894	9619	5365
2	2782	7091	4297	0456	9087	5861
3	8050	2858	2544	6581	1054	5715
4	1488	1023	6543	7547	8735	6682
5	6771	9975	9357	0963	2347	8784
6	4058	8270	3216	3996	5380	2264
7	9387	6783	4143	4175	1818	2616
8	1652	9984	1285	3266	8680	5391
9	4026	4152	3990	6590	3819	4485
10	3946	9010	4040	0079	5784	2413

13.1. The auditor may begin at any number, say, row 8 of column 2. The first number (984) is ignored because it falls outside the limits. Reading down the column, the auditor next comes to the numbers 152 and 010, which become the numbers of the first two vouchers selected for the sample. The auditor then moves to row 1 of column 3, reads down the column, goes on to column 4, and so on, until the desired number of items have been selected.

SYSTEMATIC SELECTION

In **systematic selection**, the auditor calculates a sampling interval (i) by dividing the total number of items in the population by the required sample size and rounding down. The auditor next selects a random number between 1 and the sampling interval i as a starting point and then selects every ith item. For example, if the auditor needs to select a sample of size 20 from a population of 400 accounts, the sampling interval is 20 (400/20), or every 20th item. Any number between 1 and 20 can be selected as the first item in the sample.

Systematic selection often is easier than simple random selection, especially when the sampling unit is stored on magnetic tape, a computer printout, or a file of ledger cards or vouchers. Random numbers are required only to designate the starting point. The items in the sampling unit do not need to be numbered consecutively for use with a random number table.

However, systematic selection may produce a biased sample because it is valid only when it approximates a random selection. Systematic selection therefore requires a relatively homogeneous population and a fairly uniform error pattern. To ensure randomness in systematic selection, an auditor should use multiple random starting points for the selection process. It is preferable that the population elements be arranged in random order instead of placing them in sequential order.

When multiple random starting points are used, the auditors should multiply the sampling interval calculated for systematic selection by the number of random starts to keep the total sample size the same. For example, if five multiple starts are desired for the preceding example, the new sampling interval is $100 = (20)(5)$. Five random numbers between 1 and 100 should be selected from a random number table as the first five sample items. Then, every 100th item from the five numbers is selected, and so on.

STRATIFIED SELECTION

Stratified selection involves subdividing a population into homogeneous groups, called strata, and selecting separate samples for each strata using the simple random selection technique. For example, an auditor may divide a client's trade receivables accounts into three strata: (1) account balances of more than $10,000; (2) account balances of between $1,000 and $10,000; and (3) account balances of less than $1,000. The auditor might positively confirm all of the accounts, positively confirm a random sample of the medium-sized accounts, and negatively confirm a random sample of the smaller accounts. The principal advantage of stratified sampling is that it produces subpopulations that are individually more homogeneous, thus decreasing the sample size required to accomplish audit objectives.

CLUSTER SAMPLE SELECTION

Cluster sample selection permits the selection of more than one item at a time. It involves selecting groups of items, rather than individual items, at randomly selected points in the population. For example, an auditor may want to select ten groups of five consecutively numbered vouchers, starting with each of ten randomly selected vouchers. Cluster sample selection is not widely used in auditing because it is more likely to be biased. For example, the ten vouchers selected may not be representative of the transactions that occurred throughout the entire year.

13.5 SAMPLING METHODS

The types of statistical sampling methods used by auditors may be grouped into three categories: attribute sampling, variable sampling, and probability–proportional-to-size sampling. Attribute sampling is used primarily in tests of internal accounting controls. Variable sampling is used most frequently to test the monetary value of accounting balances, that is, substantive testing. Probability–proportional-to-size sampling, combining attribute and variable sampling, is a dual purpose testing plan.

ATTRIBUTE SAMPLING

Attribute sampling is used to reach a conclusion about rate of occurrence in a population. It is normally used to test the rate of compliance with a prescribed internal accounting control procedure to determine whether planned reliance on that control is appropriate. An auditor concerned with estimating the percentage of vouchers that do not have proper supporting documents and/or signatures could use one of three types of attribute sampling: fixed-sample-size, stop-or-go sampling, and discovery sampling. We mention these techniques only briefly here and discuss them fully in Chapter 14.

Fixed-sample-size attribute sampling is used to estimate the occurrence rate of a certain attribute or characteristic of a population. It is one of the most widely used statistical sampling techniques in auditing.

Stop-or-go sampling is used when the audit objective is acceptance. In that case, an auditor wants to determine whether a population characteristic, such as an error rate, is less than some predetermined value. The auditor would accept the population if there were less than a predetermined number of errors. For example, based on sample results, an auditor may determine at a 95 percent confidence level that the actual error rate in controls over voucher processing does not exceed 3 percent.

Discovery sampling is a special case of attribute sampling. In a typical discovery sampling application, the attribute is defined as an irregularity, for which the expected occurrence rate is zero or near zero. This technique is used in searches for fraud and can be very efficient because disclosure of only one irregularity may be sufficient to spur further action or investigation.

VARIABLE SAMPLING

Variable sampling is used if an auditor wants to reach a conclusion about a dollar amount of a population. The principal use of variable sampling is for substantive tests of details to determine the reasonableness of recorded amounts. At least five different variable sampling techniques are used currently in practice: unstratified mean-per-unit, stratified mean-per-unit, difference estimation, ratio estimation, and regression estimation. We discuss these techniques fully in Chapter 15.

Unstratified mean-per-unit sampling or simple extension, is a method by which the auditor calculates a sample mean and then estimates the population value by multiplying the sample mean by the size of the population. For example, if the mean audited value of a sample of 100 inventory items is $1,000 and there are 2,000 inventory items in the population, the auditor would estimate the total value of the 2,000 inventory items to be $2,000,000,

Stratified mean-per-unit sampling is a variation of unstratified mean-per-unit sampling that requires the auditor to take samples from various segments or groups of the population and determine the value of the samples selected from each group. Stratified mean-per-unit sampling usually produces a smaller overall sample size than does unstratified mean-per-unit sampling.

Difference estimation is used to estimate the difference between audited value and book value. An auditor first calculates the average difference between the audited value and the book value of the items in the sample selected and then multiplies this average difference by the size of the population. For example, if the average difference between book value and audited value for each inventory item in a sample of 100 inventory items is $20 and if there are 2,000 inventory items in the population, an auditor will estimate that there is a $40,000 difference between book value and the actual value of the population.

In **ratio estimation**, the ratio of the audited value of the sample items to their book value is applied to the population. The auditor first uses sample results to calculate the ratio of audited value to book value and then multiplies this ratio by the size of the population to estimate its actual value. For example, if the average ratio of audited value to book value for a sample of 100 inventory items is 1.06 and if the book value for the population is $2,000,000, the estimated actual value of the population would be $2,120,000.

In **regression estimation**, linear regression is used to determine the functional relationship between audit value and book value. That relationship is then used to estimate the actual value of the population.

Difference, ratio, and regression estimators are generally called *auxiliary information estimators* because they are based on auxiliary information, such as book value, to estimate the variable of interest: actual or audit value. Since auxiliary information is usually available, these methods are generally more efficient because the auditor focuses on the area of greatest concern: the estimation and control of errors.

PROBABILITY–PROPORTIONAL-TO-SIZE SAMPLING

Probability–proportional-to-size (PPS) sampling is a relatively new technique, specifically designed for audit sampling. It is also called *cumulative monetary amount sampling* or *dollar unit sampling*. In PPS sampling, attribute sampling theory is used to express a conclusion in dollar amounts. Therefore it is a hybrid method, combining the characteristics of both attribute and variable sampling. We discuss this method fully in Chapter 16.

The population is viewed as individual dollar units rather than account book values. A random sample is selected and audited from a population of dollar units such as invoice amounts. A sales invoice with a $5,000 total would have a five times greater chance of being selected than an invoice with a $1,000 total. Each sampling unit has a probability of being selected that is proportionate to its book value. This method is most useful for testing one-direction, overstatement errors.

13.6 USES OF STATISTICAL SAMPLING

Three studies involving surveys of practitioners have examined the uses of statistical sampling in auditing. In this section, we present the results of these studies regarding application areas and sampling methods.

APPLICATION AREAS

In 1975, Bedingfield surveyed public accounting practitioners and found that statistical sampling is used in the following areas.

1. Internal control tests: Cash disbursements, sales, payroll, cash receipts, voucher systems, and purchasing.
2. Account balance tests: Accounts and notes receivable, inventory, revenues and expenses, accounts and notes payable, property, plant and equipment, and cash.[9]

In 1978, Rittenberg and Schweiger found that statistical sampling is used by internal auditors for (1) confirmations; (2) inventories; (3) transactions testing; (4) accounts payable and other disbursements work; (5) payroll tests; (6) insurance claims and procurement analysis; (7) tests of billing process and sales analysis; (8) adequacy of documentation; and (9) fixed asset work.[10]

In 1980, the AICPA Statistical Sampling Subcommittee task force also conducted a survey of the profession's use of statistical sampling and identified the following areas of application: (1) revenue systems; (2) cash receipts systems; (3) cash disbursements systems; (4) purchasing and accounts payable systems; (5) payroll systems; (6) inventory valuation; (7) accounts receivables; (8) repair and maintenance expenditures; (9) cost of goods sold; and (10) warranty reserves.[11]

SAMPLING METHODS

Bedingfield's survey of CPAs identified the three most widely used statistical sampling methods as: (1) estimation sampling for attributes; (2) estimation sampling for variables; and (3) stratified sampling of variables.[12] Rittenberg and Schweiger's survey of internal auditors also identified the four most widely used statistical sampling methods as: (1) attribute sampling; (2) discovery sampling; (3) stop-or-go sampling; and (4) probability–proportional-to-size sampling.[13]

The AICPA Statistical Sampling Subcommittee task force arrived at the following findings.

1. Use of statistical sampling is increasing. More CPA firms began using it in the early 1970s.
2. Most firms that use statistical sampling are using attribute sampling primarily.
3. Variable sampling is not often used by most CPA firms, and most of its use is by the largest firms.[14]

13.7 Summary

Audit-risk models show the relationships among risks associated with the auditor's evaluation of internal accounting controls, substantive tests of details, and analytical review procedures and other relevant substantive tests. In this chapter, we used a simple audit-risk formula to show those relationships quantitatively and to emphasize the comparative nature of the quantities utilized.

Auditors normally use sampling procedures to obtain audit evidence. Statistical sampling uses the mathematical laws of probability to aid the auditor in designing a sampling plan and evaluating sample results. In this chapter, we introduced basic statistical sampling concepts and techniques as a prelude to the in-depth discussions contained in Chapters 14–16.

We defined and presented examples of population, sample, measures of central tendency, measures of dispersion, normal distribution, skewed distribution, central limit theorem, distribution of sample means, sampling unit, random sample, attribute, sampling risk, stratification, precision/tolerable error, and reliability/confidence level. We also presented and discussed four sample selection techniques: simple random selection, systematic selection, stratified selection, and cluster sample selection.

Attribute sampling is used by an auditor primarily to test the rate of compliance for a specific internal accounting control procedure. The principal use of variable sampling is for substantive tests of details to determine the reasonableness of recorded amounts. Probability–proportional-to-size sampling is a hybrid method, combining the characteristics of both attribute and variable sampling, and has become popular in recent years.

Questions

1. What is the difference between statistical and nonstatistical sampling?
2. What are the advantages and disadvantages of using statistical sampling?
3. Define the following terms, both mathematically and in relation to their practical application and meaning.
   (a) Mean.
   (b) Median.
   (c) Mode.
   (d) Range.
   (e) Variance.
4. What is the relationship among the normal distribution, the central limit theorem, and the distribution of sample means?
5. Why is selection of a random sample important in performing statistical sampling?
6. What is alpha risk? Beta risk? How do these concepts relate to internal control risk?
7. What are some of the differences among a simple random sample, a systematic sample, and a stratified sample?
8. When and why would an auditor use
   (a) attribute sampling?
   (b) variable sampling?
9. What are some of the most common uses of statistical sampling?
10. Is the use of statistical sampling generally increasing or decreasing? Why?
11. Define audit risk, inherent risk, and internal control risk.

12. List three types of attribute sampling methods.
13. List five types of variable sampling methods.
14. What precautions must be taken by an auditor when using systematic sampling to produce a random sample?
15. What does it mean to say that internal control risk is 15 percent?
16. Define the following sampling concepts:
    (a) Sampling unit.
    (b) Sampling risk.
    (c) Tolerable error.
    (d) Reliability.

Problems

1. In your opinion, which of the following factors will lead to a general increase in the use of statistical sampling?
   (a) The microcomputer.
   (b) Client computerization.
   (c) Staff sophistication.
   (d) Quantification of risk.
   (e) Litigation.
2. Review the material presented in this chapter and identify those concepts that were not presented in your college statistics course, that is, those statistical concepts that are unique to auditing.
3. The basic audit-risk formula presented in this chapter is based on SAS No. 39. A number of more sophisticated models are available in the auditing literature. Find those models and use them to develop one of your own.
4. There was a delay of one year between the issuance of SAS No. 39 and its effective date. See if you can find out why by reading some of the accounting journals of that time. What problems do you think practitioners would have had initially with SAS No. 39?
5. When do you think statistical concepts should be introduced into an audit? When would you actually decide to use statistical auditing procedures? How would this relate to a firm's audit philosophy?
6. In the risk of incorrect acceptance formula, $TD = UR/(IC \times AR)$, which risk factors are guided by authoritative auditing literature and which are determined by professional judgment?
7. Calculate TD for the following situations:

	UR	IC	AR
a.	5%	5%	50%
b.	5%	10%	50%
c.	5%	10%	70%
d.	5%	20%	60%
e.	5%	30%	80%

8. Identify the first five random numbers for a population numbered 3001 to 7999. Use Table 1, Partial Table of Random Number. The starting point is row 3, column 2. The route is down the table reading from left to right.

9. Calculate the sampling interval using systematic selection methods for a sample size of 30 from a population of 900 accounts. What is the sampling interval if four multiple starts are desired?

10. *Multiple Choice Questions from Professional Examinations*
   (1) Which of the following is an advantage of systematic sampling over random number sampling?
      a. It provides a stronger basis for statistical conclusions.
      b. It enables the auditor to use the more efficient "sampling with replacement" tables.
      c. There may be correlation between the location of items in the population, the feature of sampling interest, and the sampling interval.
      d. It does not require establishment of correspondence between random numbers and items in the population.
   2) When performing a compliance test with respect to control over cash disbursements, a CPA may use a systematic sampling technique with a start at any randomly selected item. The biggest disadvantage of this type of sampling is that the items in the population
      a. Must be recorded in a systematic pattern before the sample can be drawn.
      b. May occur in a systematic pattern, thus destroying the sample randomness.
      c. May systematically occur more than once in the sample.
      d. Must be systematically replaced in the population after sampling.
   (3) What is the primary objective of using stratification as a sampling method in auditing?
      a. To increase the confidence level at which a decision will be reached from the results of the sample selected.
      b. To determine the occurrence rate for a given characteristic in the population being studied.

      c. To decrease the effect of variance in the total population.

      d. To determine the precision range of the sample selected.

(4) Which of the following statistical selection techniques is least desirable for use by an auditor?

      a. Systematic selection.

      b. Stratified selection.

      c. Block selection.

      d. Sequential selection.

(5) Which of the following best describes the distinguishing feature of statistical sampling?

      a. It requires the examination of a smaller number of supporting documents.

      b. It provides a means for measuring mathematically the degree of uncertainty that results from examining only part of a population.

      c. It reduces the problems associated with the auditor's judgment concerning materiality.

      d. It is evaluated in terms of two parameters: statistical mean and random selection.

(6) An important statistic to consider when using a statistical sampling audit plan is the population variability. The population variability is measured by the

      a. Sample means.

      b. Standard deviation.

      c. Standard error of the sample mean.

      d. Estimated population total minus the actual population total.

(7) The auditor's failure to recognize an error in an amount or an error in an internal control data processing procedure is described as a

      a. Statistical error.

      b. Sampling error.

      c. Standard error of the mean.

      d. Nonsampling error.

(8) There are many kinds of statistical estimates that an auditor may find useful, but basically every accounting estimate is either of a quantity or of an error rate. The statistical terms that roughly correspond to "quantities" and "error rate," respectively, are

      a. Attribute and variables.

      b. Variables and attribute.

     c. Constants and attribute.

     d. Constants and variables.

(9) Auditors often utilize sampling methods when performing tests of compliance. Which of the following sampling methods is most useful when testing for compliance?

     a. Attribute sampling.

     b. Variable sampling.

     c. Unrestricted random sampling with replacement.

     d. Stratified random sampling.

(10) In connection with a test of the accuracy of inventory counts, a CPA decides to use discovery sampling. Discovery sampling may be considered a special case of

     a. Judgmental sampling.

     b. Sampling for variables.

     c. Stratified sampling.

     d. Sampling for attributes.

(AICPA adapted)

Notes

1. Auditing Standards Board of the American Institute of Certified Public Accountants, *Statement on Auditing Standards No. 39—Audit Sampling.* New York: AICPA, 1981, p. 1.

2. Roberts, Donald M., *Statistical Auditing.* New York: AICPA, 1978, p. 2.

3. Auditing Standards Board of the American Institute of Certified Public Accountants, *Statement on Auditing Standards No. 47—Audit Risk and Materiality in Conducting an Audit.* New York: AICPA, 1984, p. 2.

4. Rittenberg, Larry E. and Schweiger, Bradley J., "The Use of Statistical Sampling Tools—Parts I and II," *The Internal Auditor*, August 1978, p. 37.

5. Bedingfield, James P., "The Current State of Statistical Sampling and Auditing," *The Journal of Accountancy*, December 1975, p. 50.

6. Rittenberg and Schweiger, p. 35.

7. Bedingfield, pp. 51–52.

8. For a comprehensive table of random numbers, see Arkin, Herbert, *Handbook of Sampling for Auditing and Accounting*, 2nd ed. New York: McGraw-Hill, 1974, pp. 219–279.

9. Bedingfield, p. 51.

10. Rittenberg and Schweiger, p. 31.

11. Akresh, Abraham D., "Statistical Sampling in Public Accounting," *The CPA Journal*, July 1980, pp. 24–25.

12. Bedingfield, p. 52.

13. Rittenberg and Schweiger, p. 36.

14. Akresh, p. 22.

Additional References

Elliott, Robert K. and John R. Rogers, "Relating Statistical Sampling to Audit Objectives," *The Journal of Accountancy*, July 1972, pp. 46–55.

Guy, Dan M., *An Introduction to Statistical Sampling in Auditing*. New York: John Wiley & Sons, 1981.

Ijiri, Yuji, and Robert S. Kaplan, "The Four Objectives of Sampling in Auditing: Representative, Corrective, Protective and Preventive," *Management Accounting*, December 1970, pp. 42–44.

Stringer, Kenneth W., "Statistical Sampling in Auditing: The State of the Art," *Annual Accounting Review*, 1979, 1:113–127.

Vagge, Richard, "Toward Understanding Statistical Sampling," *The CPA Journal*, May 1980, pp. 13–19.

Chapter 14

Statistical Sampling: Attribute Sampling

14.1 INTRODUCTION

Attribute sampling is used primarily to test the rate of deviation from a prescribed internal accounting control procedure to determine whether reliance on that control is appropriate. For example, approval of a sales order by a credit manager may require a signature or initials; thus a sample of sales orders could be examined to verify that this form of approval was used. This example is typical of compliance tests for those controls having an audit trail or documentary evidence. Other types of controls, such as the segregation of duties between computer operator and programmer, leave no audit trail. Those types of controls are tested by other techniques, such as observation and inquiry.

We begin this chapter with a discussion of the uses of attribute sampling in auditing. We then describe the application of audit judgment to compliance testing. Next, we discuss attribute sampling theory and its relationship to attribute sampling tables. Finally, we describe and illustrate three types of attribute sampling: fixed-sample-size, stop-or-go, and discovery.

LEARNING OBJECTIVES

By the time you have completed this chapter, you should be able to:

1. Describe the uses of attribute sampling in auditing.
2. Define the concepts of deviation, expected population deviation rate, risk of overreliance, risk of underreliance, tolerable rate, and maximum population deviation rate.
3. Identify areas of audit judgment required in performing compliance testing.
4. Explain attribute sampling theory and its relationship to attribute sampling tables.

5. Explain the effect of changing factor quantities on sample size.
6. Plan, execute, and evaluate fixed-sample-size, stop-or-go, and discovery attribute sampling applications.
7. Explain how stop-or-go sampling and discovery sampling are special cases of fixed-sample-size attribute sampling.

14.2 THE USE OF ATTRIBUTE SAMPLING

Attribute sampling is applicable to almost every type of audit engagement and has been used frequently in audit practice. The AICPA Audit Sampling Guide lists the following uses of attribute sampling.[1]

1. Tests of controls for voucher processing.
2. Tests of controls for billing systems.
3. Tests of controls for payroll and related personnel policy systems.
4. Tests of controls for inventory pricing.
5. Tests of controls for fixed-asset additions.
6. Tests of controls for depreciation computations.

Bedingfield's 1975 survey also showed that auditors who use attribute sampling consider the most likely areas of application to be tests of cash disbursements, sales, payroll, and cash receipts.[2]

When testing cash disbursement transactions, the auditor usually performs the following functions: (1) test for the existence of compliance items, such as vendor's invoices and purchasing and receiving documents; (2) check for computations, clerical accuracy, price and payment approvals, proper account classification, and validity of transactions; (3) examine the related canceled checks for proper payees and amounts, authorized signatures, and proper endorsements.

When testing sales transactions, the auditor usually traces a sample of sales orders to shipping, billing, and cash receipts documents. Such checking includes verification of proper supporting documents, clerical accuracy, proper approvals, and correct account classifications.

When testing payroll transactions, the auditor usually checks for clerical accuracy in recording time worked from time cards, use of appropriate rates of pay, accurate computations of gross and net pay and approvals of hiring, change in employee status, overtime, leave time, and the like. The tests also involve examination of canceled checks for proper payees and amounts, authorized signatures, and proper endorsements.

Cash receipts testing is usually conducted along with sales transaction testing. The auditor selects a sample of cash receipts records, checks to determine whether payment has been received and, if it has, that it agrees with the sales order, invoice, or other contract, and that the cash has been properly recorded and deposited.

In addition to tests of compliance with prescribed control procedures, attribute sampling may be used for substantive tests. However, auditors generally use variable sampling to conduct substantive testing because the audit objective is to estimate total dollar amounts for various account balances.

14.3 AUDIT JUDGMENT IN COMPLIANCE TESTING

The study and evaluation of internal control is a process that depends heavily on an auditor's experience and judgment. For example, in order to determine sample size the auditor must specify the expected population deviation rate, the risk of overreliance on controls, and the tolerable rate. The auditor must therefore assign quantities to these factors *in advance* of performing an audit. These quantities represent acceptable levels of performance, as determined by the auditor, rather than mathematical certainty.

Thus the auditor is interested in determining the differences between (deviations from) norms or anticipated performance and actual performance. In this context, a *deviation* is a departure from a prescribed internal accounting control procedure. For example, if the prescribed procedure requires that each paid invoice be stamped *Paid*, the deviation may be defined as *a paid invoice that has not been stamped Paid.*[3] An **expected population deviation rate** is the deviation rate anticipated for an entire population. This rate is used in determining the appropriate sample size for an attribute sample. It is also called *likely rate of deviation, expected rate of occurrence,* or *expected error rate.*

We have already defined and discussed the risks of overreliance and underreliance on internal accounting control in Chapter 13. Recall that the former is also called beta risk or Type II error, the latter alpha risk or Type I error.

The **tolerable rate** is the maximum rate of deviation for a population from a prescribed control procedure that the auditor will tolerate before altering planned reliance on the control. This rate is also called the *maximum rate of deviation, desired upper precision limit,* or *acceptable upper precision limit.*

The **maximum population deviation rate** is the worst likely rate of deviation for a population from a prescribed control procedure and is calculated at the conclusion of compliance testing. This rate is also called *computed upper deviation rate, computed upper precision limit, achieved upper precision limit,* or *upper limit.*

SAMPLE DESIGN

As we have stressed before, statistical sampling does not eliminate professional judgment; rather, statistical sampling requires the exercise of considerable professional judgment. The auditor's judgment is applied first to the design of particular audit sample for a compliance test of details and involves considerations such as:

1. The relationship of the sample to the objective of the compliance test.
2. The maximum rate of deviation from prescribed control procedures that would support the auditor's planned reliance on the controls.
3. The auditor's allowable risk of overreliance.
4. Characteristics of the population, that is, the items comprising the account balance or class of transactions of interest.[4]

The objective of compliance tests is to provide reasonable assurance that internal accounting control procedures are being applied as prescribed. That is, the attribute sampling objective is usually to test the reliability of controls over cash disbursements, sales, payroll, or cash receipts transactions. It is important for the auditor to define the proper population and attributes, which means that they should be appropriate for the specific audit objective. For example, if the auditor wants to test compliance with a control procedure designed to ensure that all shipments are billed, the auditor would not detect deviations by sampling billed items because some orders might have been shipped but not billed. An appropriate population for detecting such deviations is usually the population of all shipped items.[5] Attributes should be defined so that each sample item can be easily classified as possessing or not possessing that particular quality. For example, for cash disbursements transactions one attribute can be defined as "a canceled check with proper supporting documents, such as a receiving report, rent agreement, or service contract.

When determining the tolerable rate, the auditor should consider the relationship of procedural deviations to (1) the attributes being tested; (2) any related internal accounting control procedures; and (3) the purpose of the auditor's evaluation. Different tolerable rates are commonly used for different attributes. For example, if one attribute is important, the auditor may decide to assign a tolerable rate of 5 percent or less; if another attribute is less important, the auditor may decide that a tolerable rate of 10 percent is reasonable.

The tolerable rate also depends on the auditor's planned degree of reliance on specific internal accounting controls. Auditors generally use tolerable rates no larger than 12 percent and no smaller than 2 percent. The following overlapping ranges of tolerable rates were adapted from the AICPA Audit Sampling Guide.[6]

Planned Degree of Reliance	Tolerable Rate
Substantial reliance	2–7%
Moderate reliance	6–12%
Little reliance	11–20%
No reliance	Omit test

The auditor is concerned with two aspects of sampling risk in attribute sampling. First, the risk of overreliance on internal accounting control relates to the effectiveness of the audit; it can lead to an inadequate number of scope tests. Second, the risk of underreliance relates to the efficiency of the audit; it can lead to an unnecessarily large number of substantive tests. While the risk of underreliance is important, the risk of overreliance is crucial. Thus the risk of overreliance typically is the sampling risk selected for attention in attribute sampling.[7] The risk of overreliance is the beta risk, and its complement is the reliability, or confidence, level. Specifying reliability is a matter of professional judgment and depends on the importance of attributes and the auditor's planned degree of reliance on the internal accounting control. In practice, the minimum reliability level often selected is 90 percent. However, 95 percent reliability is used if an attribute is critical and/or the auditor intends to place substantial reliance on the internal accounting control.

Using professional judgment, the auditor estimates the expected population deviation rate by considering factors such as results of testing the identical control attribute the preceding year and the overall control environment. The prior year's deviation rate can be used only if the client's system of internal accounting control and personnel have not changed. If prior-year results are not available, or are inapplicable, the auditor can take a small preliminary sample of approximately 50 randomly selected items of the current year's population for this purpose. For example, if two errors are discovered for a given attribute in a sample of 50 items, the expected population deviation rate is $(2/50)(100) = 4$ percent.

In order to determine the sample size for a compliance test, the auditor first selects the allowable risk of overreliance on internal accounting procedures. The auditor can then use an attribute sampling table to select the tolerable rate of deviation from the internal accounting control procedures being tested and the expected population deviation rate. Tables 14.1 and 14.2 show the relationships between the two factors for beta risks of 5 percent and 10 percent, respectively.

Table 14.1   Statistical Sample Sizes for Compliance Testing: 5 Percent Risk of Overreliance (with number of expected errors in parentheses)

Expected Population Deviation Rate (%)	Tolerable Rate of Deviation from Internal Accounting Control												
	2%	3%	4%	5%	6%	7%	8%	9%	10%	15%	20%
0.00	149(0)	99(0)	74(0)	59(0)	49(0)	42(0)	36(0)	32(0)	29(0)	19(0)	14(0)
0.25	236(1)	157(1)	117(1)	93(1)	78(1)	66(1)	58(1)	51(1)	46(1)	30(1)	22(1)
0.50	*	157(1)	117(1)	93(1)	78(1)	66(1)	58(1)	51(1)	46(1)	30(1)	22(1)
0.75	*	208(2)	117(1)	93(1)	78(1)	66(1)	58(1)	51(1)	46(1)	30(1)	22(1)
1.00	*	*	156(2)	93(1)	78(1)	66(1)	58(1)	51(1)	46(1)	30(1)	22(1)
1.25	*	*	156(2)	124(2)	78(1)	66(1)	58(1)	51(1)	46(1)	30(1)	22(1)
1.50	*	*	192(3)	124(2)	103(2)	66(1)	58(1)	51(1)	46(1)	30(1)	22(1)
1.75	*	*	227(4)	153(3)	103(2)	88(2)	77(2)	51(1)	46(1)	30(1)	22(1)

(continued on next page)

Table 14.1   Statistical Sample Sizes for Compliance Testing: 5 Percent Risk of Overreliance (with number of expected errors in parentheses) (continued)

2.00	*	*	181(4)	127(3)	88(2)	77(2)	68(2)	46(1)	30(1)	22(1)
2.25	*	*	208(5)	127(3)	88(2)	77(2)	68(2)	61(2)	30(1)	22(1)
2.50	*	*	*	150(4)	109(3)	77(2)	68(2)	61(2)	30(1)	22(1)
2.75	*	*	*	173(5)	109(3)	95(3)	68(2)	61(2)	30(1)	22(1)
3.00	*	*	*	195(6)	129(4)	95(3)	84(3)	61(2)	30(1)	22(1)
3.25	*	*	*	*	148(5)	112(4)	84(3)	61(2)	30(1)	22(1)
3.50	*	*	*	*	167(6)	112(4)	84(3)	76(3)	40(2)	22(1)
3.75	*	*	*	*	185(7)	129(5)	100(4)	76(3)	40(2)	22(1)
4.00	*	*	*	*	*	146(6)	100(4)	89(4)	40(2)	22(1)
5.00	*	*	*	*	*	*	158(8)	116(6)	40(2)	30(2)
6.00	*	*	*	*	*	*	*	179(11)	50(3)	30(2)
7.00	*	*	*	*	*	*	*	*	68(5)	37(3)

*Sample size is too large to be cost effective for most audit applications.

Note: This table is to be used for large populations. For the discussion of the effect of population size on sample size, see   Chapter 14.

Source: From *Audit Sampling.* New York: AICPA, 1983, p. 106

Table 14.2 Statistical Sample Sizes for Compliance Testing; 10 percent Risk of Overreliance (with number of expected errors in parentheses)

Expected Population Deviation Rate (%)	Tolerable Rate of Deviation from Internal Accounting Control										
	2%	3%	4%	5%	6%	7%	8%	9%	10%	15%	20%
0.00	114(0)	76(0)	57(0)	45(0)	38(0)	32(0)	28(0)	25(0)	22(0)	15(0)	11(0)
0.25	194(1)	129(1)	96(1)	77(1)	64(1)	55(1)	48(1)	42(1)	38(1)	25(1)	18(1)
0.50	194(1)	129(1)	96(1)	77(1)	64(1)	55(1)	48(1)	42(1)	38(1)	25(1)	18(1)
0.75	265(2)	129(2)	96(1)	77(1)	64(1)	55(1)	48(1)	42(1)	38(1)	25(1)	18(1)
1.00	*	176(2)	96(1)	77(1)	64(1)	55(1)	48(1)	42(1)	38(1)	25(1)	18(1)
1.25	*	221(3)	132(2)	77(1)	64(1)	55(1)	48(1)	42(1)	38(1)	25(1)	18(1)
1.50	*	*	132(2)	105(2)	64(1)	55(1)	48(1)	42(1)	38(1)	25(1)	18(1)
1.75	*	*	166(3)	105(2)	88(2)	55(1)	48(1)	42(1)	38(1)	25(1)	18(1)
2.00	*	*	198(4)	132(3)	88(2)	75(2)	48(1)	42(1)	38(1)	25(1)	18(1)
2.25	*	*	*	132(3)	88(2)	75(2)	65(2)	42(1)	38(1)	25(1)	18(1)
2.50	*	*	*	158(4)	110(3)	75(2)	65(2)	58(2)	38(1)	25(1)	18(1)
2.75	*	*	*	209(6)	132(4)	94(3)	65(2)	58(2)	52(2)	25(1)	18(1)

(continued on next page)

Table 14.2 Statistical Sample Sizes for Compliance Testing: 10 percent Risk of Overreliance (with number of expected errors in parentheses) (continued)

3.00	*	*	*	*	132(4)	94(3)	65(2)	58(2)	52(2)	25(1)	18(1)
3.25	*	*	*	*	153(5)	113(4)	82(3)	58(2)	52(2)	25(1)	18(1)
3.50	*	*	*	*	194(7)	113(4)	82(3)	73(3)	52(2)	25(1)	18(1)
3.75	*	*	*	*	*	131(5)	98(4)	73(3)	52(2)	25(1)	18(1)
4.00	*	*	*	*	*	149(6)	98(4)	73(3)	65(3)	25(1)	18(1)
4.50	*	*	*	*	*	218(10)	130(6)	87(4)	65(3)	34(2)	18(1)
5.00	*	*	*	*	*	*	160(8)	115(6)	78(4)	34(2)	18(1)
5.50	*	*	*	*	*	*	*	142(8)	103(6)	34(2)	18(1)
6.00	*	*	*	*	*	*	*	182(11)	116(7)	45(3)	25(2)
7.00	*	*	*	*	*	*	*	*	199(14)	52(4)	25(2)
7.50	*	*	*	*	*	*	*	*	*	52(4)	25(2)
8.00	*	*	*	*	*	*	*	*	*	60(5)	25(2)
8.50	*	*	*	*	*	*	*	*	*	68(6)	32(3)

*Sample size is too large to be cost effective for most audit applications.

Note: This table is to be used for large populations. For the discussion of the effect of population size on sample size, see   Chapter 14.

Source: From *Audit Sampling*, New York: AICPA, 1983, p. 107.

SAMPLE SELECTION

After selecting the sample size for the attribute sampling application, the auditor must select sample items in such a way that the sample can be expected to be representative of the population; that is, sample items must be selected at random. This step is accomplished by using tables of random numbers, computers, or systematic sampling, as discussed in Chapter 13.

EVALUATION OF SAMPLE RESULTS

The auditor must analyze the results obtained from the sample in order to make an inference about the population deviation rate and to reach conclusions about the extent to which reliance can be placed on the prescribed internal accounting control procedures. The auditor can begin to evaluate sample results by using statistical sampling tables that show the maximum population deviation rate (that is, an estimate of the upper limit of the possible deviation rate) for a specified level of beta risk. Tables 14.3 and 14.4 can be used to evaluate sample results at 5 percent and 10 percent risks of overreliance, respectively, for various sample sizes and the actual number of deviations found.[8]

Let's assume that an auditor planned a 5 percent risk of overreliance, with a tolerable rate of 5 percent, and found 2 deviations in the 150 sample items. In Table 14.3 the intersection of the column for 2 deviations with the row for a sample size of 150 gives the maximum population deviation rate of 4.1 percent. Since the maximum deviation rate is less than the tolerable rate for the population, the auditor would conclude that the test supports the planned reliance on internal accounting control, with a 5 percent risk of overreliance.

The auditor then uses professional judgment in evaluating the results and reaching an overall conclusion.[9] Part of the auditor's considerations include the qualitative aspects of the deviations, which include: (1) the nature and cause of the deviations, such as whether they are errors or irregularities or were caused by misunderstanding of instructions or carelessness, and whether they have resulted in monetary errors; and (2) the possible relationship of the deviations to other phases of the audit, such as whether the deviations represent a temporary or permanent breakdown of a specific control or a collapse of the entire system of internal accounting controls.

If the maximum deviation rate is greater than the tolerable rate for the population, the auditor may choose one of the following alternatives.

Table 14.3   Evaluation of Statistical Sample Results for Compliance Tests: 5 Percent Risk of Overreliance

Sample Size	Actual Number of Deviations Found										
	Maximum Population Deviation Rate (%)										
	0	1	2	3	4	5	6	7	8	9	10
25	11.3	17.6	*	*	*	*	*	*	*	*	*
30	9.5	14.9	19.5	*	*	*	*	*	*	*	*
35	8.2	12.9	16.9	*	*	*	*	*	*	*	*
40	7.2	11.3	14.9	18.3	*	*	*	*	*	*	*
45	6.4	10.1	13.3	16.3	19.2	*	*	*	*	*	*
50	5.8	9.1	12.1	14.8	17.4	19.9	*	*	*	*	*
55	5.3	8.3	11.0	13.5	15.9	18.1	*	*	*	*	*

(continued on next page)

Table 14.3 Evaluation of Statistical Sample Results for Compliance Tests: 5 Percent Risk of Overreliance (continued)

60	4.9	7.7	10.1	12.4	14.6	16.7	18.8	*	*	*	*
65	4.5	7.1	9.4	11.5	13.5	15.5	17.4	19.3	*	*	*
70	4.2	6.6	8.7	10.7	12.6	14.4	16.2	18.0	19.7	*	*
75	3.9	6.2	8.2	10.0	11.8	13.5	15.2	16.9	18.4	20.0	*
80	3.7	5.8	7.7	9.4	11.1	12.7	14.3	15.8	17.3	18.8	*
90	3.3	5.2	6.8	8.4	9.9	11.3	12.7	14.1	15.5	16.8	18.1
100	3.0	4.7	6.2	7.6	8.9	10.2	11.5	12.7	14.0	15.2	16.4
125	2.4	3.7	4.9	6.1	7.2	8.2	9.3	10.3	11.3	12.2	13.2
150	2.0	3.1	4.1	5.1	6.0	6.9	7.7	8.6	9.4	10.2	11.0
200	1.5	2.3	3.1	3.8	4.5	5.2	5.8	6.5	7.1	7.7	8.3

*Greater than 20 percent.

Note: This table is to be used for large populations.

Source: Adapted from *Audit Sampling*. New York: AICPA, 1983, p. 108.

Table 14.4 Evaluation of Statistical Sample Results for Compliance Tests: 10 Percent Risk of Overreliance

Sample Size	Actual Number of Deviations Found										
	Maximum Population Deviation Rate (%)										
	0	1	2	3	4	5	6	7	8	9	10
20	10.9	18.1	*	*	*	*	*	*	*	*	*
25	8.8	14.7	19.9	*	*	*	*	*	*	*	*
30	7.4	12.4	16.8	*	*	*	*	*	*	*	*
35	6.4	10.7	14.5	18.1	*	*	*	*	*	*	*
40	5.6	9.4	12.8	15.9	19.0	*	*	*	*	*	*
45	5.0	8.4	11.4	14.2	17.0	19.6	*	*	*	*	*
50	4.5	7.6	10.3	12.9	15.4	17.8	*	*	*	*	*

(continued on next page)

Table 14.4 Evaluation of Statistical Sample Results for Compliance Tests: 10 Percent Risk of Overreliance (continued)

55	4.1	6.9	9.4	11.7	14.0	16.2	18.4	*	*	*	*
60	3.8	6.3	8.6	10.8	12.9	14.9	16.9	18.8	*	*	*
70	3.2	5.4	7.4	9.3	11.1	12.8	14.6	16.2	17.9	19.5	*
80	2.8	4.8	6.5	8.3	9.7	11.3	12.8	14.3	15.7	17.2	18.6
90	2.5	4.3	5.8	7.3	8.7	10.1	11.4	12.7	14.0	15.3	16.6
100	2.3	3.8	5.2	6.6	7.8	9.1	10.3	11.5	12.7	13.8	15.0
120	1.9	3.2	4.4	5.5	6.6	7.6	8.6	9.6	10.6	11.6	12.5
160	1.4	2.4	3.3	4.1	4.9	5.7	6.5	7.2	8.0	8.7	9.5
200	1.1	1.9	2.6	3.3	4.0	4.6	5.2	5.8	6.4	7.0	7.6

*Greater than 20 percent..

Note: This table is to be used for large populations.

Source: Adapted from *Audit Sampling*. New York: AICPA, 1983, p. 109.

1. Increase the tolerable rate or the allowable risk of overreliance. This action would be extremely difficult to defend. This alternative would be chosen only if the auditor finds other compensating control(s) to rely on partially and expands audit tests in related areas.

2. Increase the sample size. Assume that 4 rather than 2 deviations were found in the preceding example, yielding an unacceptable 6.0 percent maximum population deviation rate (Table 14.3). Then the required sample size for a 5 percent tolerable rate with 4 deviations found is approximately 200, instead of the original 150. In deciding whether to increase the sample size, the auditor must weigh the cost of taking an additional sample against the possible savings of avoiding extensive follow-up substantive testing, which will be necessary if the population is rejected.

3. Modify the related substantive tests to reflect reduced or no reliance on internal accounting controls. For example, if the sample results indicated that the client failed to internally verify prices, extensions, and footings on vendor's invoices, the auditor could extend substantive testing of vouching these invoices.

14.4 ATTRIBUTE SAMPLING THEORY

In this section, we present a theoretical explanation of attribute sampling using the cumulative binomial distribution. We show how attribute sampling tables are developed and how risk of overreliance (beta risk), tolerable rate, expected population deviation rate, and population size affect sample size.[10]

THE CUMULATIVE BINOMIAL DISTRIBUTION AND SAMPLING TABLES

The theory of attribute sampling is explained in terms of a cumulative binomial distribution.[11] For a population of infinite size, if we select a sample of n items with replacement, the binomial distribution for the probability that k deviations will occur in the sample is mathematically described as

$$p(k; n, p) = \binom{n}{k} p^k (1-p)^{n-k} = \frac{n!}{k!(n-k)!} p^k (1-p)^{n-k}$$

The cumulative binomial distribution for the probability of selecting x or fewer items with deviations in a sample of n for an assumed population deviation rate p, is

$$P(x \text{ or fewer deviations; } n, p) \quad = \quad \sum_{k=0}^{x} p(k; n, p)$$

$$\Sigma P \quad = \quad \sum_{k=0}^{x} \binom{n}{k} p^{k} (1-p)^{n-k}$$

where

$\quad n \quad = \quad$ Sample size.

$\quad x \quad = \quad$ Number of deviations in the sample.

$\quad k \quad = \quad$ Counter from 0 to x.

$\quad p \quad = \quad$ Probability that an item has a deviation.

$\quad \binom{n}{k} \quad = \quad$ Number of combinations of n items taken k at a time (that is, the number of unique ways in which k deviations could appear in a sample of n items).

$\quad \binom{n}{k} \quad = \quad \dfrac{n!}{k!(n-k)!} .$ *

$\quad P(x; n, p) \quad = \quad$ $P(x$ or fewer deviations; $n, p) = $ Probability of selecting x or fewer items with deviations in a sample of n, for an assumed population deviation rate p.

In compliance testing, p is the tolerable rate, or the maximum rate of deviations in a population that the auditor will tolerate. $P(x$ or fewer deviations; $n, p)$ is risk of overreliance or beta risk.

Example 1. Let's assume that $n = 124$, $x = 2$, and $p = 0.05$. The probability of selecting two or less sample items (such as invoices containing a deviation) in a sample of 124 with a 5 percent tolerable rate is

$$P(2 \text{ or fewer deviations}) \quad = \quad \sum_{k=0}^{2} \binom{124}{k} (0.05)^{k} (0.95)^{124-k} .$$

---

* The term (!) represents *factorial*, meaning the product of all whole numbers from 1 to the number represented. For example, 3! = (3)(2)(1) = 6.

For k = 0,

$$P(0; 124; 0.05) = \frac{124!}{(0!)(124!)}(0.05)^0(0.95)^{124} = 0.00047.$$

For k = 1,

$$P(1; 124; 0.05) = \frac{124!}{(1!)(123!)}(0.05)^1(0.95)^{123} = 0.01128.$$

For k = 2,

$$P(2; 124; 0.05) = \frac{124!}{(2!)(122!)}(0.05)^2(0.95)^{122} = 0.03652.$$

Thus the cumulative probability is

$$\Sigma P = 0.00047 + 0.01128 + 0.03652 = 0.04827,$$

and the estimated deviation rate is

$$P = \left(\frac{2}{124}\right)(100) = 1.61\%$$

Therefore the probability is 0.04827 (or 4.827%) that a population with a 5 percent deviation rate will produce 2 or fewer deviations in a sample of 124. It is the beta risk that in concluding that the population deviation rate is 5 percent or lower, the auditor will be wrong.

Example 2. Now, let's find out what happens when we are willing to accept a beta risk greater than 4.827%. By accepting greater risk, we can decrease the sample size n, say, to 105. However, if we hold x to 2 or fewer deviations and p to 0.05, we get

$$P(2 \text{ or fewer deviations}) = \sum_{k=0}^{2} \binom{105}{k}(0.05)^k(0.95)^{105-k}.$$

For k = 0,

$$P(0; 105; 0.05) = \frac{105!}{(0!)(105!)}(0.05)^0(0.95)^{105} = 0.00458.$$

For k = 1,

For k = 1,

$$P(1; 105; 0.05) = \frac{105!}{(1!)(104!)}(0.05)^1(0.95)^{104} = 0.02532.$$

For k = 2,

$$P(2; 105; 0.05) = \frac{105!}{(2!)(103!)}(0.05)^2(0.95)^{103} = 0.06929.$$

Thus the new cumulative probability is

$$\Sigma P = 0.00458 + 0.02532 + 0.06929 = 0.09919,$$

and the estimated deviation rate is

$$P = \left(\frac{2}{105}\right)(100) \doteq 1.90\%$$

Comparison of Calculations and Tables. Auditors seldom use the binomial distribution equation to calculate sample size because a wide range of possible combinations of p, x, and n values have already been put in table form. In Example 1, we calculated a cumulative probability of 4.827 percent, which we can approximate at 5 percent risk of overreliance. The estimated deviation rate, 1.61 percent, is close to the 1.50 percent in Table 14.1. The intersection of the 5 percent tolerable rate (p) and the 1.50 percent expected population deviation rate yields a sample size of 124, which is the sample size we used in the calculations. Similarly, the expected number of deviations to be found in the sample, 2, is the same in Table 14.1 and in our example.

We find similar relationships between the numbers used in Example 2 and those in Table 14.2. In Example 2, the new cumulative probability is 9.919 percent, which we can approximate at 10 percent risk of overreliance. The estimated deviation rate is 1.90 percent, which is close to 1.75 percent. In Table 14.2, we find that the intersection of the 5 percent tolerable rate and the 1.75 percent expected population deviation rate has an expected number of deviations of 2 and yields a sample size of 105.

In practice, an auditor will select the table corresponding to the acceptable level of risk of overreliance to be used. The auditor then reads down the expected population deviation rate and across to the column for the tolerable rate to find the corresponding sample size.

When auditing an actual sample, if the auditor finds that the number of deviations in the sample is the same or fewer than the number shown in parentheses in the table the auditor can conclude that, at the desired risk of overreliance, the projected deviation rate for the population (and an allowance for sampling risk) is not more than the tolerable rate. To illustrate, in Example 1 if the auditor finds 2 or fewer deviations in the sample of 124 items, he or she can conclude that at 5 percent risk of overreliance the projected deviation rate for the population (and an allowance for sampling risk) is not more than a 5 percent tolerable rate.

If the auditor finds more than the expected number of deviations in the sample, he or she cannot conclude that the population deviation rate is less than the tolerable rate. Thus the test would not support the auditor's planned reliance on internal accounting control. In this situation, the maximum population deviation rate may be greater than the tolerable rate. For example, since the chance of finding 2 or fewer deviations in a sample of 105 with 5 percent tolerable rate is 9.919 percent, as shown in Example 2, the chance of finding 3 or more deviations is 90.081 percent. Likewise, the chance of finding 2 or fewer deviations for a maximum population deviation rate p = 0.06 is 4.517 percent, which is calculated as follows:

$$P(0; 105; 0.06) = \frac{105!}{(0!)(105!)} (0.06)^0 (0.94)^{105} = 0.00151.$$

$$P(1; 105; 0.06) = \frac{105!}{(1!)(104!)} (0.06)^1 (0.94)^{104} = 0.01011.$$

$$P(2; 105; 0.06) = \frac{105!}{(2!)(103!)} (0.06)^2 (0.94)^{103} = 0.003355.$$

$$\text{Cumulative probability } (\Sigma P) = 0.04517.$$

Thus the chance of finding 3 or more deviations is 95.483 percent, a higher probability for the higher maximum population deviation rate.

If the number of deviations found in the sample is not equal to the expected number of deviations shown in the table being used, and the auditor wants to calculate the maximum population deviation rate, the auditor can evaluate the sample results using either Table 14.3 for a 5 percent allowable risk of overreliance or Table 14.4 for a 10 percent allowable risk of overreliance.

EFFECT OF CHANGING FACTOR QUANTITIES ON SAMPLE SIZE

There is an inverse relationship between the tolerable rate and sample size. From Table 14.1 you can easily see the relative effect of different tolerable rates on sample size for a large population with a 5 percent risk of overreliance. For example, a 0 percent expected population deviation rate shows a rapidly decreasing sample size as the tolerable rate increases, as follows:

Tolerable Rate	Sample Size
2%	149
5%	59
10%	29
15%	19
20%	14

There is also an inverse relationship between the risk of overreliance on internal accounting control and sample size. For a large population, a tolerable rate of 5 percent, and a 2 percent expected population deviation rate, we can obtain the following relationship from Tables 14.1 and 14.2.

Risk of Overreliance	Sample Size
5%	181
10%	132

There is a direct relationship between the expected population deviation rate and sample size. For a large population, a 5 percent tolerable rate, and a 5 percent risk of overreliance, we can obtain the following relationships from Table 14.1.

Expected Population Deviation Rate	Sample Size
0.00%	59
1.00%	93
1.50%	124
2.00%	181
2.25%	208

Population size has little or no effect on sample size determination, except for very small populations. The following tabulation illustrates the limited effect of population size on sample size for a 5 percent tolerable rate, a 5 percent risk of overreliance, and a 1 percent expected population deviation rate.[12]

Population Size	Sample Size
50	45
100	64
500	87
1,000	90
2,000	92
5,000	93
100,000	93

Tables 14.1–14.4 are based on a large population. For a small population, especially when the sample size is more than 10 percent of the population, the following adjustment called the finite correction factor should be applied.

$$n = \frac{n'}{1 + \left(\dfrac{n'}{N}\right)}$$

where

n' = Sample size before considering the effect of population size.
n = Revised sample size.
N = Population size.

For example, if $n' = 100$ and population size = 500, we calculate the revised sample size as follows:

$$n = \frac{100}{1 + \dfrac{100}{500}} = 84.$$

However, if the population size is 5000 rather than 500, the revised sample size is 98, which is not much lower than the sample size of 100 shown in the table. Because the sample size is less than 10 percent of the population, we would not apply the finite correction factor in this case.

The following tabulation summarizes the effects of changing factor quantities on sample size.

Factor	General Effect on Sample Size
Tolerable rate increase (decrease)	Smaller (larger)
Risk of overreliance increase (decrease)	Smaller (larger)
Expected population deviation rate increase (decrease)	Larger (smaller)
Population size increase (decrease)	No effect for large population size; slightly larger (smaller) otherwise

14.5 FIXED-SAMPLE-SIZE ATTRIBUTE SAMPLING

The concepts discussed so far in this chapter relate to attribute sampling in which a fixed sample size is used. Let's now apply those concepts to a hypothetical detail test of shipping.

OBJECTIVES, POPULATION, AND ATTRIBUTES

The audit objectives are to determine whether internal controls over shipping are operating effectively, whether shipments are made in accordance with approved sales orders, and whether all shipments have been billed and recorded properly. The auditor first conducts a preliminary review of the client's internal accounting control procedures over shipping and finds the following:

1. When goods are shipped, the shipping clerk enters the shipment in the shipping log in numerical sequence.
2. The shipping clerk matches the bill of lading, shipping report, and sales order and batches them, attaching a sequentially numbered batch ticket.
3. The shipping supervisor reviews the shipping log and batches. Batches are then sent to the accounting clerk.
4. The batch control log is maintained by the accounting clerk, who lists the record count, hash total of customer numbers and part numbers, and batch totals of quantity shipped.
5. The accounting clerk ensures numerical sequence of batches.
6. The accounting clerk checks the daily sales-tape report against the batches processed for quantities, hash totals of customer numbers and part numbers, as recorded in the batch control log.

7. The daily sales computer program edits sales data for validity of part numbers, customer, reasonableness of extensions, and the like.

The auditor then decides to apply inquiry and observation techniques to control procedures 1, 3, 4, and 5 and to test the rest of control procedures (2, 6, and 7), using the fixed-sample- size attribute sampling technique.

There are two populations: (1) shipping reports for the period 1/1/8X to 12/31/8X; and (2) batch control numbers for the period 1/1/8X to 12/31/8X. The sampling units are the shipping report numbers in the shipping log and the batch numbers in the batch control log. The auditor defines the following attributes.

Attribute	Definition of Deviation
1. Sales order and sales invoice attached to shipping report.	1. Sales order or sales invoice is missing.
2. Sales order agrees with shipping report details of part number, customer number, and quantity.	2. Number or quantity does not agree.
3. Sales invoice agrees with sales order details of part number, customer, and quantity.	3. Number or quantity does not agree.
4. Each batch total in daily sales tape equals the batch/hash total in the batch control log.	4. Batch/hash total does not agree.
5. Accounting clerk initials each batch after checking totals with daily sales tape.	5. Initials are missing.
6. Sales invoice price agrees with price list.	6. Price does not agree.

To test attributes 1, 2, 3, and 6, the auditor selects samples from the shipping log. To test attributes 4 and 5, the auditor selects samples from the batch control log.

DETERMINATION OF SAMPLE SIZE

The auditor determines sample sizes with the aid of attribute sampling tables. Using a 10 percent risk of overreliance, the auditor obtains the sample sizes from Table 14.2 for selected tolerable rates and expected population deviation rates.

Attribute Number	Tolerable Rate	Expected Population Deviation Rate	Sample Size
1	3%	0%	76
2	5	1	77
3	5	1	77
4	4	1	96
5	7	1	55
6	7	1	55

EVALUATION OF SAMPLE RESULTS

The auditor finds two deviations for attribute 3 and one deviation for attribute 5. Therefore the maximum population deviation rates for all attributes, from Table 14.4, are as follows:

Attribute Number	Sample Size	Actual Number of Deviations	Maximum Population Deviation Rate
1	76	0	3.0%
2	77	0	3.0
3	77	2	6.8
4	96	0	2.4
5	55	1	6.9
6	55	0	4.1

Evaluation of the sample shows that the maximum population deviation rate is less than tolerable rate for all but attribute 3. For attribute 3, additional confirmation is needed in the form of an accounts receivable substantive test. For the other attributes, statistical sampling showed that the internal accounting control procedures for shipping can be relied on.

14.6 STOP-OR-GO SAMPLING

Use of the fixed-sample-size attribute sampling approach may require examination of a fairly large sample. Through the use of the stop-or-go sampling method, similar results can be achieved with a smaller sample size. This method is also called *sequential sampling.* Stop-or-go sampling should be used when the audit objective is acceptance, such as achieving a maximum population deviation rate of 2 percent or 5 percent risk of overreliance in testing a payroll control procedure, and it can also be used when there is no reasonable basis for estimating an expected population deviation rate.

DETERMINATION OF SAMPLE SIZE

Let's say that an auditor wants to test the correctness of coding on a certain type of document, such as accounts payable invoices. Let's assume that the population size is 3000, the risk of overreliance is 5 percent, and the tolerable rate is 6 percent. From Table 14.1 for a fixed sample size, and an expected population deviation rate of 2 percent, the sample size is 127. If the auditor decides to use stop-or-go sampling, takes an initial sample of 50 items and finds no deviation, further sampling is unnecessary. From Table 14.5, the auditor knows that for a sample size of 50 and a tolerable rate of 6 percent, there is a 95.47 percent probability that the population deviation rate is 6 percent or less. Table 14.5 shows different reliability or confidence levels (complement of the risk of overreliance) at specified tolerable rates for a particular sample size and the number of deviations found in that sample. Although the auditor does not know the actual deviation rate, the table shows that if no errors are found in a sample of 50, there is a 39.50 percent probability (confidence level) that the actual population deviation rate is less than 1 percent (tolerable rate); there is a 63.58 percent probability that the actual population deviation rate is less than 2 percent; and so on. If the auditor had found 1 error in the sample, there is a 26.42 percent probability that the actual population deviation rate is less than 2 percent.

EVALUATION OF SAMPLE RESULTS

Basically, stop-or-go sampling allows the auditor to stop sampling after examining a selected number of items and evaluating the results. Depending on the findings, the auditor may decide to accept the population, reject the population (that is, to conclude the testing and pursue another course of action), or to continue sampling.[13]

Table 14.5 Stop-or-Go Attribute Sampling Confidence Levels (population size > 2000)

Sample Size	Number of Deviations	Tolerable Rate									
		1%	2%	3%	4%	5%	6%	7%	8%	9%	10%
50	0	39.50	63.58	78.19	87.01	92.31	95.47	97.34	98.45	99.10	99.49
	1	8.94	26.42	44.47	59.95	72.06	81.00	87.35	91.73	94.68	96.62
	2	1.38	7.84	18.92	32.33	45.95	58.38	68.92	77.40	83.95	88.83
70	0	50.52	75.69	88.14	94.26	97.24	98.69	99.38	99.71	99.86	99.94
	1	15.53	40.96	62.47	77.51	87.03	92.81	96.10	97.93	98.92	99.45
	2	3.34	16.50	35.08	53.44	68.63	79.87	87.59	92.60	95.72	97.58
	3	0.54	5.19	15.87	30.71	46.61	61.15	73.07	82.10	88.53	92.88
	4	0.07	1.32	5.93	14.85	27.21	41.13	54.77	66.80	76.61	84.12
100	0	63.40	86.74	95.25	98.31	99.41	99.80	99.93	99.98	99.99	100.00
	1	26.42	59.67	80.54	91.28	96.29	98.48	99.40	99.77	99.91	99.97
	2	7.94	32.33	58.02	76.79	88.17	94.34	97.42	98.87	99.52	99.81
	3	1.84	14.10	35.28	57.05	74.22	85.70	92.56	96.33	98.27	99.22
	4	0.34	5.08	18.22	37.11	56.40	72.32	83.68	90.97	95.26	97.63
	5	0.05	1.55	8.08	21.16	38.40	55.93	70.86	82.01	89.55	94.24
	6	0.01	0.41	3.12	10.64	23.40	39.37	55.57	69.68	80.60	88.28

(continued on next page)

Table 14.5 Stop-or-Go Attribute Sampling Confidence Levels (population size > 2000) (continued)

120										
0	70.06	91.15	97.41	99.25	99.79	99.94	99.98	100.00	100.00	100.00
1	33.77	69.46	87.82	95.53	98.45	99.48	99.83	99.95	99.98	100.00
2	11.96	43.13	70.16	86.28	94.25	97.75	99.17	99.71	99.90	99.97
3	3.30	22.00	48.67	71.13	85.56	93.40	97.19	98.87	99.60	99.84
4	0.74	9.38	29.24	52.67	72.18	85.27	92.83	96.75	98.61	99.44
5	0.14	3.41	15.29	34.83	55.85	73.23	85.23	92.47	96.42	98.40
6	0.02	1.07	7.03	20.57	39.37	58.50	74.26	85.35	92.26	96.18
7		0.30	2.86	10.90	25.24	43.20	60.81	75.25	85.57	92.16
8		0.07	1.04	5.21	14.74	29.39	46.51	62.85	76.21	85.86

150										
0	77.86	95.17	98.96	99.78	99.95	99.99	100.00	100.00	100.00	100.00
1	44.30	80.39	94.15	98.41	99.60	99.90	99.98	100.00	100.00	100.00
2	19.05	57.91	83.07	94.16	98.19	99.48	99.86	99.96	99.99	100.00
3	6.47	35.28	66.16	85.42	94.52	98.14	99.42	99.83	99.95	99.99
4	1.80	18.30	46.93	72.04	87.44	95.01	98.20	99.40	99.81	99.95
5	0.42	8.19	29.57	55.76	76.56	89.17	95.52	98.31	99.41	99.81
6	0.08	3.20	16.60	39.37	62.71	80.16	90.66	96.03	98.45	99.44
7	0.02	1.11	8.34	25.32	47.72	68.34	83.12	91.94	96.50	98.60
8		0.34	3.78	14.85	33.62	54.84	72.98	85.58	93.04	96.93
9		0.10	1.55	7.97	21.91	41.26	60.93	76.85	87.65	94.00
10		0.02	0.58	3.93	13.22	29.03	48.15	66.16	80.13	89.40

Source: Adapted from *Audit Sampling.* Cleveland, Ohio: Ernst & Whinney, 1979, pp. 186–187.

Returning to the coding example, with no deviations in the 50 sample items, the auditor concludes that the actual population deviation rate is less than 6 percent, with 95.47 percent probability and decides to accept the population. However, if the auditor finds 5 deviations in the initial 50 sample items, the sample size required to achieve a 5 percent risk of overreliance (95 percent confidence level) with 6 percent maximum population deviation rate is at least 150 (Table 14.3). Since 5 deviations were found in a sample of 50 items, it is highly improbable that the 100 additional items will contain no errors. After analyzing the nature and causes of the deviations, the auditor may decide to reject the population and not to rely on this internal accounting control procedure.

If the auditor had found one deviation in the initial sample of 50 items, he or she would have continued sampling. As a general rule, however, stop-or-go sampling should be discontinued when the sample size reaches three times the initial sample size.[14] The stop-or-go sampling procedure is illustrated in Table 14.6. It is based on the sample sizes shown in Table 14.5 for a 6 percent tolerable rate and a 5 percent risk of overreliance.

14.7 DISCOVERY SAMPLING

Discovery sampling is a special application of attribute sampling that is used when the expected population deviation rate is near zero and the attribute being tested is critical. Some examples of critical attributes are payroll padding, unauthorized shipment of goods, illegal payments, and circumvented controls. In discovery sampling, one deviation in a sample is sufficient to conclude that the true population rate of deviation is greater than the critical tolerable rate of deviation.

DETERMINATION OF SAMPLE SIZE

The discovery sampling function is a hypergeometric distribution which is similar to the binomial distribution, except that sampling is made without replacement. In practice, the auditor uses tables such as Tables 14.7 and 14.8 to determine the appropriate sample size. These two tables are used for population sizes between 2000 and 5000 and between 5000 and 10,000, respectively.[15]

Determining sample size in discovery sampling requires that the auditor specify population size, a critical tolerable rate of deviation, and probability of discovery at least one deviation in a sample (the reliability or confidence level). Selecting the critical tolerable rate of deviation

Table 14.6   Stop-or-Go Sampling Procedure

Step	Cumulative Sample size	Stop if Deviations Are Less Than	If Deviations Are	Go to Step
1	50	1	1	2
			2	4
			3 or 4	5
			5 or more	6
2	70	1	1	3
			2	4
			3 or 4	5
			5 or more	6
3	100	2	2	4
			3 or 4	5
			5 or more	6
4	120	3	3 or 4	5
			5 or more	6
5	150	5	5 or more	6
6	Evaluate the sample results using Table 14.3 to determine the maximum population error rate.			

and the probability of discovering at least one deviation in a sample requires professional judgment and depends partly on planned reliance and partly on the importance of the attribute. Note that in Tables 14.7 and 14.8, the maximum critical tolerable rate is 2 percent.

Let's assume for purposes of illustration that we are examining a population of 4000 payroll checks. We want to find at least one instance of payroll padding (such as checks payable to fictitious employees) with a 0.5 percent critical tolerable rate and a 95 percent confidence level. Using Table 14.7, we read down the 0.5 percent column to the row that contains the 95 percent probability (or the next greater probability, if the specified one is not in the table). Reading left across this row to the sample size column, we find that the required sample is 600.

EVALUATION OF SAMPLE RESULTS

If we do not discover any deviations in the 600 items examined, we can state that there is a 95 percent probability that the population rate of deviation in payroll checks is less than or equal to 0.5 percent. If one or more deviations appear, we could use fixed-sample-size attribute sampling to calculate the maximum population deviation rate and take an appropriate next step, such as expanding the investigation.

Table 14.7   Probability of Discovering at Least One Deviation in a Sample (for population sizes of 2000–5000)

	Tolerable Rate							
Sample Size	0.3%	0.4%	0.5%	0.6%	0.8%	1.0%	1.5%	2.0%
50	14%	18%	22%	26%	33%	40%	53%	64%
60	17	21	26	30	38	45	60	70
70	19	25	30	35	43	51	66	76
80	22	28	33	38	48	56	70	80
90	24	31	37	42	52	60	75	84
100	26	33	40	46	56	64	78	87
120	31	39	46	52	62	70	84	91
140	35	43	51	57	68	76	88	94
160	39	48	56	62	73	80	91	96
200	46	56	64	71	81	87	95	98
240	52	63	71	77	86	92	98	99
300	61	71	79	84	92	96	99	99+
340	65	76	83	88	94	97	99+	99+
400	71	81	88	92	96	98	99+	99+
460	77	86	91	95	98	99	99+	99+
500	79	88	93	96	99	99	99+	99+
600	85	92	96	98	99	99+	99+	99+
700	90	95	98	99	99+	99+	99+	99+
800	93	97	99	99	99+	99+	99+	99+
900	95	98	99	99+	99+	99+	99+	99+
1000	97	99	99+	99+	99+	99+	99+	99+

Note: 99+ indicates a probability of 99.5% or greater because probabilities in this table are rounded to the nearest 1%.

Source: Audit Sampling. Cleveland, Ohio: Ernst & Whinney, 1979, p. 168.

Table 14.8   Probability of Discovering at Least One Deviation in a Sample (for population sizes of 5000–10,000)

Sample Size	\multicolumn{8}{c}{Tolerable Rate}

Sample Size	0.1%	0.2%	0.3%	0.4%	0.5%	0.75%	1.0%	2.0%
50	5%	10%	14%	18%	33%	31%	40%	64%
60	6	11	17	21	38	36	45	70
70	7	13	19	25	43	41	51	76
80	8	15	21	28	48	45	55	80
90	9	17	24	30	52	49	60	84
100	10	18	26	33	56	53	64	87
120	11	21	30	38	62	60	70	91
140	13	25	35	43	51	65	76	94
160	15	28	38	48	55	70	80	96
200	18	33	45	56	64	78	87	98
240	22	39	52	62	70	84	91	99
300	26	46	60	70	78	90	95	99+
340	29	50	65	75	82	93	97	99+
400	34	56	71	81	87	95	98	99+
460	38	61	76	85	91	97	99	99+
500	40	64	79	87	92	98	99	99+
600	46	71	84	92	96	99	99+	99+
700	52	77	89	95	97	99+	99+	99+
800	57	81	92	96	98	99+	99+	99+
900	61	85	94	98	99	99+	99+	99+
1000	65	88	96	99	99	99+	99+	99+
1500	80	96	99	99+	99+	99+	99+	99+
2000	89	99	99+	99+	99+	99+	99+	99+

Note: 99+ indicates a probability of 99.5% or greater because probabilities in this table are rounded to the nearest 1%.

Source: Audit Sampling. Cleveland, Ohio: Ernst & Whinney, 1979, p. 169.

14.8 Summary

Attribute sampling is used primarily to test the rate of deviation from a prescribed internal accounting control procedure in order to determine whether planned reliance on that control is appropriate. We explained the theory of attribute sampling using the cumulative binomial distribution and showed its relationship to attribute sampling tables.

Three major factors affect the sample size in attribute sampling, namely, tolerable rate, risk of overreliance, and expected population deviation rate. The tolerable rate and risk of overreliance are inversely related to sample size, whereas the expected population deviation rate is directly related to sample size. Population size has little or no effect on the determination of sample size, except for very small populations.

Audit judgment plays a key role in compliance testing. The auditor has to use professional judgment throughout the attribute sampling process, including sample design, sample selection, and sample evaluation.

The auditor usually will use the fixed-sample-size approach for audit compliance testing. If the auditor expects a very low population deviation rate, the stop-or-go sampling approach can be used with a small sample. Discovery sampling is a special application of attribute sampling and is used when the auditor expects zero or near zero population deviation rate and the attribute being tested is critical.

Questions

1. When would an auditor use attribute sampling? Give three examples.
2. What is a *deviation* and a *deviation rate*?
3. What is the relationship between overreliance, underreliance, and types I and II errors?
4. What factors might an auditor consider to estimate the expected population deviation rate?
5. What three factors need to be quantified in order to determine sample size?
6. After sampling, how does an auditor evaluate the results?
7. How does the cumulative binomial distribution aid in understanding attribute sampling?
8. What is the effect of sample size on tolerable error rate? On allowable risk?
9. How does the auditor tie audit objectives to attribute sampling?

10. What are the differences between stop-or-go sampling and ordinary attribute sampling?
11. Describe the role of audit judgment in a typical attribute sampling application.
12. Define tolerable rate and maximum population deviation rate.
13. What preliminary sample size should be used by an auditor to estimate an expected population deviation rate if the prior year's deviation rate is not available or is inapplicable?
14. What qualitative aspects of the deviations should an auditor consider in evaluating the sample test results?
15. If the maximum deviation rate is greater than the tolerable rate for the population, what course of action should the auditor pursue?
16. In what types of situations will an auditor use discovery sampling?

Problems

1. What are some factors that would affect your decision to use attribute sampling?
2. Given the following factors, determine the sample size using Table 14.1 and Table 14.2.

Case	Tolerable Error Rate	Expected Error Rate	Risk of Overreliance	n
1	5%	2%	10%	_____
2	5%	0.25%	10%	_____
3	10%	5%	5%	_____
4	10%	1%	5%	_____
5	10%	3%	5%	_____

3. If you have taken an attribute sample and the achieved risk of overreliance is not as high as you had wanted, what would you do?
4. Generally, more than one attribute will be sampled at a time. While this may be efficient, what effect will it have on sample size? What problems, if any, do you see with this approach?
5. Given the following factors, use Table 14.3 and Table 14.4 to determine the maximum population error rate.

Case	Numbers of Errors Found	Sample Size	Risk of Overreliance	Maximum Population Error Rate
1	5	100	10%	_____
2	5	200	10%	_____
3	10	100	5%	_____
4	10	200	5%	_____
5	5	200	5%	_____

Describe what you would do in each case.

6. Paula Horne, an accountant with Hopkins and Manegold, a CPA firm, is currently on an audit assignment at Carlton Products, Inc., a plastics product manufacturer. One of her assignments involves testing sales transactions to determine compliance with internal control policies and procedures. One of the attributes to be tested is whether or not credit sales have been properly approved. Credit sales which have not been properly approved will be treated as compliance deviations. Paula has gathered information which indicated that 15,000 credit sales invoices were processed during the year under review. Since Carlton Products is a first time client of Hopkins and Manegold, Paula decided to take a preliminary sample of 50 sales invoices in order to estimate the population deviation rate. This sample yielded 1 error. To avoid the risk of unwarranted reliance, Paula specified a 10% risk of overreliance (i.e., a 90% reliability level) and a tolerable deviation rate of 5%.
   (a) Using fixed-sample-size method, what is the required sample size?
   (b) Assuming that the preliminary sample produced no deviation, what sample size would Paula obtain?
   (c) Assume Paula obtained a sample size of 160 and found a total of two errors, how should she evaluate this sample result?

7. Construct a stop-or-go decision table like Table 14.6 for 8 percent risk of overreliance and 5 percent tolerable rate.

8. In stop-or-go sampling, if a sample of 100 produced 3 deviations what is the probability that the population deviation rate is 8 percent or less?

9. Determine discovery sample sizes for each of the following situations.

Case	Population Size	Tolerable Rate	Confidence Level
1	2,000	0.3%	90%
2	3,000	1%	99%
3	4,000	2%	95%
4	6,000	0.5%	90%
5	8,000	1%	95%

10. Smith, CPA, has decided to rely on an audit client's internal accounting controls affecting receivables. Smith plans to use sampling to obtain substantive evidence concerning the reasonableness of the client's accounts receivable balances. Smith has identified the first few steps in an outline of the sampling plan as follows:
   1. Determine the audit objectives of the test.
   2. Define the population.
   3. Define the sampling unit.
   4. Consider the completeness of the population.
   5. Identify individually significant items.
   Required:
   Identify the remaining steps which Smith should include in the outline of the sampling plan. Illustrations and examples need not be provided.

   (AICPA adapted)

11. Jiblum, CPA, is planning to use attribute sampling in order to determine the degree of reliance to be placed on an audit client's system of internal accounting control over sales. Jiblum has begun to develop an outline of the main steps in the sampling plan as follows:
   1. State the objective(s) of the audit test (e.g. to test the reliability of internal accounting controls over sales).
   2. Define the population (define the period covered by the test; define the completeness of the population).
   3. Define the sampling unit (e.g. client copies of sales invoices).
   Required:
   (a) What are the remaining steps in the above outline which Jiblum should include in the statistical test of sales invoices? Do not present a detailed analysis of tasks which must be performed to carry out the objectives of each step. Parenthetical examples need not be provided.
   (b) How does statistical methodology help the auditor to develop a satisfactory sampling plan?

   (AICPA adapted)

12. *Multiple Choice Questions from Professional Examinations*
   (1) Which of the following statistical sampling methods is most useful to auditors when testing for compliance?
      a. Ratio estimation.
      b. Variable sampling.
      c. Difference estimation.
      d. Discovery sampling.
   (2) In the examination of the financial statements of Delta Company, the auditor determines that in performing a compliance test of internal accounting control, the compliance rate in the sample does not support the planned degree of reliance on

the control when, in fact, the compliance rate in the population does not justify such reliance. This situation illustrates the risk of

a.   Overreliance.
b.   Underreliance.
c.   Incorrect rejection.
d.   Incorrect acceptance.

(3) Jones, CPA, believes the industry-wide occurrence rate of client billing errors is 3% and has established a maximum acceptable occurrence rate of 5%. In the review of client invoices Jones should use

a.   Discovery sampling.
b.   Attribute sampling.
c.   Stratified sampling.
d.   Variable sampling.

(4) In performing compliance testing, the auditor will normally find that

a.   The level of risk is directly proportionate to the rate of error.
b.   The rate of deviations in the sample exceeds the rate of error in the accounting records.
c.   The rate of error in the sample exceeds the rate of deviations.
d.   All unexamined items result in errors in the accounting records.

(5) In assessing sampling risk, the risk of incorrect rejection and the risk of underreliance on internal accounting control relate to the

a.   Efficiency of the audit.
b.   Effectiveness of the audit.
c.   Selection of the sample.
d.   Audit quality controls.

(6) Given random selection, the same sample size, and the same precision (tolerable rate) requirement for the testing of two unequal populations, the risk of overreliance on the smaller population is

a.   The same as the risk of overreliance on the larger population.
b.   Higher than the risk of overreliance on the larger population.
c.   Lower than the risk of overreliance on the larger population.
d.   Indeterminate relative to the risk of overreliance on the larger population.

(7) At times a sample may indicate that the auditor's planned degree of reliance on a given control is reasonable when, in fact, the true compliance rate does not justify such reliance. This situation illustrates the risk of
   a. Overreliance.
   b. Underreliance.
   c. Incorrect precision.
   d. Incorrect rejection.

(8) An auditor examining inventory may appropriately apply sampling for attributes in order to estimate the
   a. Average price of inventory items.
   b. Percentage of slow-moving inventory items.
   c. Dollar value of inventory.
   d. Physical quantity of inventory items.

(9) The tolerable rate of deviations for a compliance test is generally
   a. Lower than the expected rate of errors in the related accounting records.
   b. Higher than the expected rate of errors in the related accounting records.
   c. Identical to the expected rate of errors in the related accounting records.
   d. Unrelated to the expected rate of errors in the related accounting records.

(10) An auditor plans to examine a sample of 20 checks for countersignatures as prescribed by the client's internal control procedures. One of the checks in the chosen sample of 20 cannot be found. The auditor should consider the reasons for this limitation and
   a. Evaluate the results as if the sample size had been 19.
   b. Treat the missing check as a deviation for the purpose of evaluating the sample.
   c. Treat the missing check in the same manner as the majority of the other 19 checks, i.e., countersigned or not.
   d. Choose another check to replace the missing check in the sample.

(AICPA adapted)

Notes

1. Statistical Sampling Subcommittee of the American Institute of Certified Public Accountants, *Audit Sampling.* New York: AICPA, 1983, p. 16.

2. Bedingfield, James P., "The Current State of Statistical Sampling and Auditing," *The Journal of Accountancy,* December 1975, p. 51.

3. AICPA, 1983, p. 23.

4. Auditing Standards Board of the American Institute of Certified Public Accountants, *Statement on Auditing Standards No. 39—Audit Sampling.* New York: AICPA, 1981, p. 10.

5. AICPA, 1983, p. 23.

6. *Ibid.,* p. 32.

7. Finley, David R., "Controlling Compliance Testing with Acceptance Sampling," *CPA Journal,* December 1978, pp. 30–35. For a discussion of how to control the risk of underreliance, see Roberts, Donald M., *Statistical Auditing.* New York: AICPA, 1978, pp. 55–57.

8. Tables 14.3 and 14.4 are based on the one-tailed, upper-limit approach. For a discussion of two-tailed interval estimates, see Roberts, *op. cit.,* p. 53.

9. For a detailed discussion of sample evaluation, see Warren, Carl S., "Interpreting and Evaluating Attribute Sampling," *Internal Auditor,* July/August 1975, pp. 45–56.

10. Some accounting firms use operating characteristic curves instead of tables to obtain sample size. For a discussion of operating characteristic curves, see Bamber, E. Michael, and Bylinski, Joseph H., "Attribute Sampling: A Review in Light of SAS No. 39," *Journal of Accounting Education,* Spring 1984, pp. 83–97.

11. This section is based primarily on the work of Professor James K. Loebbecke at the University of Utah, and Appendix A of the AICPA *Audit Sampling Guide.* Tables 14.1 to 14.2 are based on the binomial distribution and are exact only when sampling with replacement is used. When sampling without replacement is used, the hypergeometric distribution is theoretically superior to binomial distribution but leads to difficulties in constructing sample-size tables. In practice, auditors use the binomial tables to obtain valid but conservative (larger) sample sizes.

12. AICPA, 1983, p. 35.

13. Janell, Paul A., "Stop or Go Sampling: A Tool for Reducing Audit Costs," *Practical Accountant,* July/August 1978, pp. 53–59.

14. *Audit Sampling.* New York: Ernst &Whinney, 1979, p. 26.

Additional References

Akresh, Abraham D., "Statistical Sampling in Public Accounting," *CPA Journal*, July 1980, pp. 20–26.

Akresh, Abraham D., and David R. Finely, "Two-Step Attributes Sampling in Auditing," *CPA Journal*, December 1979, pp. 19–24.

Arens, Alvin, and James K. Loebbecke, *Applications of Statistical Sampling to Auditing.* Englewood Cliffs, N.J.: Prentice-Hall, 1981.

Bailey, Andrew D., Jr., *Statistical Auditing: Review, Concepts and Problems,* New York: Harcourt Brace Jovanovich, 1981.

Guy, Dan M., *An Introduction to Statistical Sampling in Auditing.* New York: John Wiley & Sons, 1981.

Guy, Dan M., William C. Dent, and Frederick A. Hancock, "Some Practical Guidelines for Using Attribute Sampling," *Practical Accountant,* April/May 1979, pp. 34–40.

Naus, James H., "Effective Uses of Statistical Sampling in the Audit of a Small Company," *Practical Accountant,* March/April 1978, pp. 33–45.

Reneau, James Hal, "Guidelines for Selecting Sampling Procedures," *Internal Auditor,* June 1980, pp. 77–82.

Warren, Carl S., Steven V. N. Yates, and George R. Zuber, "Audit Sampling: A Practical Approach," *Journal of Accountancy,* January 1982, pp. 62–72.

Chapter 15

Statistical Sampling: Variable Sampling

15.1 INTRODUCTION

Variable sampling is a statistical technique that auditors use to reach conclusions about the monetary value of accounts. For example, an auditor would use a variable sampling plan to determine whether the book value of a particular account, such as inventory or accounts receivable, is fairly stated. The principal use of variable sampling in auditing is for substantive tests of details to determine the reasonableness of recorded book values. That is, the auditor is interested in answering the question: "Is the account materially correct?" Variable sampling may also be used to estimate the dollar value of an account balance or a class of related transactions, such as the estimated accounts receivable balance or the estimated total sales revenue for a particular period.

There are two basic choices in variable sampling methods: classical variable sampling and probability–proportional-to-size (PPS) sampling. Classical variable sampling requires an estimate of the population standard deviation, whereas PPS sampling does not. Classical variable sampling depends on statistical characteristics of the normal distribution, whereas PPS sampling theory is based upon Poisson distribution. In this chapter we focus on the five classical variable sampling methods that we introduced and defined in Chapter 13: unstratified mean-per-unit estimation, difference estimation, ratio estimation, regression estimation, and stratified sampling. We discuss PPS sampling in Chapter 16.

We begin this chapter by presenting the types of variable sampling plans used in auditing and when they should be used. Next, we build on the statistical and sampling concepts introduced in Chapters 13 and 14 to develop variable sampling theory; new concepts presented include the standard error of the mean, precision interval, and normal distribution theory as it relates to variable sampling tables and formulas. Then we review the audit judgments involved in substantive testing. Finally, we examine five types of variable sampling: unstratified mean-per-unit estimation, difference estimation, ratio estimation, regression estimation, and stratified sampling.

LEARNING OBJECTIVES

By the time you have completed this chapter, you should be able to:

1. Describe the uses of variable sampling in auditing.
2. Explain variable sampling theory and its relationship to variable sampling tables.
3. Explain the effect of changing factor quantities on sample size.
4. Identify areas of audit judgment required in performing substantive testing.
5. Plan, execute, and evaluate unstratified mean-per-unit estimation variable sampling applications.
6. Describe procedures for calculating sample sizes, point estimates, precision intervals, and reliability levels for difference, ratio, regression estimation, and stratified sampling.

15.2 THE USE OF VARIABLE SAMPLING

Variable sampling is applicable primarily to substantive testing of transactions and account balances. The AICPA suggests that classical variable sampling may be especially useful in the following circumstances.

1. Tests of accounts receivable when a large number of unapplied credits exist.
2. Inventory test counts and price tests where the auditor anticipates a significant number of audit differences.
3. Conversion of inventory from FIFO to LIFO.
4. Applications for which the objective is to estimate independently the amount of a class of transactions or account balance.[1]

The AICPA Audit Sampling Guide also lists the following specific examples of uses for variable sampling.

1. Tests of the amount of receivables.
2. Tests of inventory quantities and amounts.
3. Tests of recorded payroll expense.
4. Test of the amount of fixed-asset additions.

5. Tests of transactions to determine the amount that is not supported by proper approval.[2]

15.3 VARIABLE SAMPLING THEORY

Before using any of the classical variable sampling methods, the auditor should be familiar with the basic statistical and sampling concepts and definitions presented in Chapter 13, the relationship of variable sampling to the normal distribution theory, and the relationship of sampling tables to sample size formulas.

The basic statistical and sampling concepts involved in variable sampling include the mean, standard deviation, normal distribution, standard error of the mean, allowance for sampling risk (precision or tolerable error), reliability, risk of incorrect acceptance (beta risk), risk of incorrect rejection (alpha risk), and precision interval. All of these concepts were defined, explained, and illustrated in Chapter 13 and do not need to be discussed further here.

THE NORMAL DISTRIBUTION AND SAMPLING TABLES

In this section, we present a theoretical explanation of classical variable sampling using the normal distribution. We also show how the sample size formulas are derived and variable sampling tables are developed.

In a typical variable sampling situation the auditor does not know the shape of the population distribution curve. However, the central limit theorem gives the auditor the means to determine some special properties of the distribution of sample means and the distribution of sample estimates.[3]

Recall that the central limit theorem states: Regardless of the nature of the original population, the distribution of sample means tends to become normal as the sample size increases, and that when the estimate is unbiased, the mean of the sampling distribution is the mean of the unknown population. This implies that the difference between the sample estimate and the population audited amount is approximately normal, but with a mean of zero.

Further, the central limit theorem indicates that the standard deviation of the distribution of the sample means, that is, the standard error of the mean ($S_{\bar{x}}$), is the standard deviation of the population (σ) divided by the square root of the sample size (n), or

$$S_{\bar{x}} = \frac{\sigma}{\sqrt{n}}.$$

Not knowing the standard deviation of the population (σ), the auditor uses the standard deviation of the sample mean (s) as an estimate of σ. The formula for the estimated standard error of the mean thus becomes

$$S_{\bar{x}} = \frac{s}{\sqrt{n}}.$$

The distribution of the population estimates from all possible samples of a particular size is called the **distribution of sample estimates**. The central limit theorem also states that the distribution of sample estimates is approximately normally distributed. Therefore the mean of the distribution of sample estimates is equal to the mean of the population.

The standard deviation of the distribution of sample estimates is called the **standard error of the estimate** (S_e). It is equal to the number of items in the population (N) multiplied by the standard error of the mean (S_x), or

$$S_e = (N)(S_{\bar{x}}).$$

In an actual audit situation, the auditor would take only one sample of a predetermined size; however, knowledge of the distribution of population estimates provides information about the relation of the population estimate based on the sample to the actual population value. For example, assume that an auditor decides to use the unstratified mean-per-unit estimation technique. The auditor would first take a sample of, say, 49 from population of 500. Finding its means to be $30, the auditor would then use $30 as an estimate of the mean of the population and multiply by the population size in order to make an inference about the total value of the population. That is, $(N)(x) = 500(\$30) = \$15,000$.

Let's further assume that the auditor set the acceptable levels of precision at $1640 and reliability at 90 percent. These levels mean that the auditor wants to be able to infer with 90 percent confidence that the mean of the sample will yield a value within $1640 of the actual population value. In our example, there would be a 90 percent chance of selecting a sample that would provide an estimated total value between $13,360 ($15,000 − $1640) and $16,640 ($15,000 + $1640), which is called the precision interval. Thus the precision interval is a function of the reliability level and the standard error of the estimate. Figure 15.1 shows the distribution of sample estimates and precision intervals.

Figure 15.1 Distribution of Sample Estimates and Precision Intervals

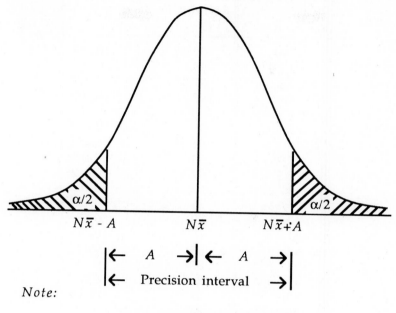

Note:

α =	Risk of incorrect rejection.
N =	Number of items in the population.
$\bar{x}$ =	Sample mean.
A =	Precision (allowance for sampling risk).

Mathematically, the relationship between the precision (A), the reliability level ($z_{\alpha/2}$), and the standard error of the estimate (S_e) can be shown as follows:

$$A = (z_{\alpha/2})(S_e) = (z_{\alpha/2})(N)(S_{\bar{x}})$$

$$= (z_{\alpha/2})(N)\left(\frac{s}{\sqrt{n}}\right)$$

Solving for n, we get the sample-size formula:

$$n = \left(\frac{Nz_{\alpha/2}s}{A}\right)^2,$$

15.1

Table 15.1   Risk of Incorrect Rejection and Reliability Factor

Risk of Incorrect Rejection (α)	Reliability $(1 - \alpha)$	Normal Curve Area $(0.5 - \alpha/2)$	Reliability Factor $(z_{\alpha/2})$
1%	99%	0.495	2.58
2	98	0.49	2.33
2.5	97.5	0.4875	2.24
3	97	0.485	2.17
4	96	0.48	2.06
5	95	0.475	1.96
6	94	0.47	1.89
7	93	0.465	1.82
7.5	92.5	0.4625	1.78
8	92	0.46	1.76
9	91	0.455	1.70
10	90	0.45	1.64
11	89	0.445	1.60
12	88	0.44	1.56
13	87	0.435	1.52
14	86	0.43	1.48
15	85	0.425	1.44
16	84	0.42	1.41
17	83	0.415	1.38
18	82	0.41	1.35
19	81	0.405	1.32
20	80	0.40	1.28
25	75	0.375	1.16
30	70	0.35	1.04
35	65	0.325	0.94
40	60	0.30	0.84
45	55	0.275	0.76
50	50	0.25	0.68

where

N = Number of items in the population.
s = Standard deviation of the sample.
$z_{\alpha/2}$ = Reliability factor for risk of incorrect rejection.
A = Precision (allowance for sampling risk).
n = Number of items in the sample.

   In Eq. (15.1), $z_{\alpha/2}$ is the standard normal deviate, or the number of standard errors of the mean; its value is obtained from a table such as

Table 15.1, which presents $z_{\alpha/2}$ values for two-sided estimates. The z value is based on the normal table value of $0.5000 - \alpha/2$, which leaves an area of $\alpha/2$ in each tail of the curve. For example, when $\alpha = 0.05$, the reliability level is 95 percent, and $z_{\alpha/2}$ is 1.96. When $\alpha = 0.01$, the reliability level is 99 percent, and $z_{\alpha/2}$ is 2.58.

The auditor can also determine the sample size by relating the precision to the risk of incorrect acceptance (beta risk) and tolerable error. Tolerable error (E_t) is the minimum amount of error considered material. In terms of the beta risk, an auditor would want, for example, to detect an understatement by the amount (at least) of tolerable error. Tolerable error can be stated mathematically as

$$E_t = z_{\alpha/2}S_e + z_\beta S_e.$$

Substituting

$$S_e = N\left(\frac{s}{\sqrt{n}}\right),$$

we get

$$E_t = (z_{\alpha/2} + z_\beta)(N)\left(\frac{s}{\sqrt{n}}\right).$$

Solving for n, we obtain the sample-size formula:

$$n = \left(\frac{Ns(z_{\alpha/2} + z_\beta)}{E_t}\right)^2,$$

(15.2)

where

N = Number of items in the population.
s = Standard deviation of the sample.
$z_{\alpha/2}$ = Reliability factor for risk of incorrect rejection.
z_β = Risk factor for risk of incorrect acceptance.
E_t = Tolerable error.
n = Number of items in the sample.

In Eq. (15.2), z_β is the normal deviate for a one-tailed estimate; its value is obtained from tables such as Table 15.2. If the auditor is willing to accept a 5 percent risk of incorrect acceptance, the appropriate risk factor (z_β) is 1.64.

Table 15.2 Risk of Incorrect Acceptance and Beta Risk Factor

Risk of Incorrect Acceptance (β)	Normal Curve Area ($0.5 - \beta$)	Beta Risk Factor (z_β)
1%	0.49	2.33
2	0.48	2.06
2.5	0.475	1.96
3	0.47	1.89
4	0.46	1.76
5	0.45	1.64
6	0.44	1.56
7	0.43	1.48
7.5	0.425	1.44
8	0.42	1.41
9	0.41	1.35
10	0.40	1.28
11	0.39	1.23
12	0.38	1.18
13	0.37	1.13
14	0.36	1.09
15	0.35	1.04
16	0.34	1.00
17	0.33	0.96
18	0.32	0.92
19	0.31	0.88
20	0.30	0.84
25	0.25	0.68
30	0.20	0.53
35	0.15	0.39
40	0.10	0.26
45	0.05	0.13
50	0.00	0.00

In practice, the auditor has some feeling about the direction of the risk of incorrect acceptance (β risk). Therefore the auditor calculates the sample size to protect against the risk of incorrect acceptance in only one direction. For example, if a recorded book value (V_B) is understated by the amount of the tolerable error (E_t), the true book value will be the recorded book value plus the tolerable error, or $V_B + E_t$, and the probability of rejecting the recorded book value as acceptable (not materially misstated) is $1 - \beta$.

Figure 15.2 shows the relationships for the book-value example. The relationship between the precision (allowance for sampling risk) and tolerable error (materiality) can be stated mathematically as

$$A = z_{\alpha/2} S_e \text{ and } E_t = z_{\alpha/2} S_e + z_\beta S_e$$

Therefore

$$A = E_t - z_\beta S_e$$

$$= E_t \left(1 - \frac{z_\beta S_e}{E_t} \right)$$

$$= E_t \left(1 - \frac{z_\beta S_e}{z_{\alpha/2} S_e + z_\beta S_e} \right)$$

$$= E_t \left(1 - \frac{z_\beta}{z_{\alpha/2} + z_\beta} \right)$$

$$= E_t \left(\frac{z_{\alpha/2}}{z_{\alpha/2} + z_\beta} \right)$$

(15.3)

and

$$E_t = A \left(\frac{z_{\alpha/2} + z_\beta}{z_{\alpha/2}} \right).$$

(15.4)

If we substitute Eq. (15.4) for E_t into Eq. (15.2), we get

$$n = \left(\frac{NS(z_{\alpha/2} + z_\beta)}{A(z_{\alpha/2} + z_\beta) / z_{\alpha/2}} \right)^2$$

$$= \left(\frac{NS z_{\alpha/2}}{A} \right)^2,$$

Figure 15.2 Relationships among Statistical Sampling Risks

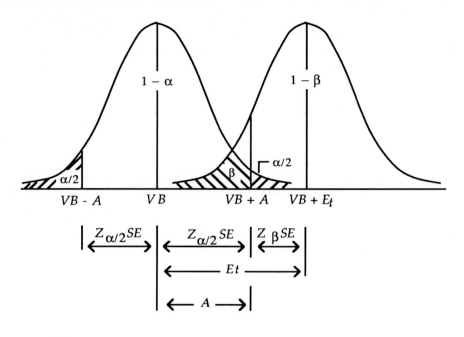

Note: V_B = Recorded book value.
               A = Precision (allowance for sampling risk).
               α = Risk of incorrect rejection.
               β = Risk of incorrect acceptance.
               E_t = Tolerable error (materiality).
               $z_{\alpha/2}$ = Reliability factor.
               s_e = Standard error of the estimate.

which is Eq. (15.1). Therefore the auditor can use either the first or the second sample-size formula to determine the sample size.[4]

From Eq. (15.3), the relationship between the precision and tolerable error can also be represented by the ratio:

$$\frac{A}{E_t} = \frac{z_{\alpha/2}}{z_{\alpha/2} + z_\beta}.$$

(15.5)

Table 15.3 shows different values for the ratio in Eq. 15.5, which can be used to calculate precision (allowance for sampling risk) when risk of incorrect acceptance, risk of incorrect rejection, and tolerable error have been determined. We can use Table 15.3 to select the precision (A) to control the risk of incorrect acceptance (β) for a given value of E_t and the appropriate risk of incorrect rejection (α). For example, if E_t equals $10,000 and the auditor is willing to accept a 5 percent α risk and a 20 percent β risk, he or she should specify the precision (A) at $7000, or (0.7000)($10,000), when calculating sample size. Note that Table 15.3 shows an A/E_t ratio of 0.7000 for a 5 percent risk of incorrect rejection and a 20 percent risk of incorrect acceptance.

If either the risk of incorrect rejection or the risk of incorrect acceptance calculated does not appear in Table 15.3, we can use Tables 15.1 or 15.2 to get $z_{\alpha/2}$ and z_β and then substitute into Eq. (15.3) to calculate the precision (A). For example, from Table 15.1, a 5 percent risk of incorrect rejection shows that $z_{\alpha/2} = 1.96$. From Table 15.2, $z_\beta = 0.84$ for a 20 percent risk of incorrect acceptance. We then use Eq. (15.3) to calculate the allowance for sampling risk:

$$A = \$10,000 \left(\frac{1.96}{1.96 + 0.84} \right)$$

$$= \$10,000 \, (0.70) = \$7000 \, .$$

Equations 15.1 and 15.2 are based on the premise that the population has an infinite number of items. If sampling is done without replacement (a finite population), the sample size can be smaller. We simply divide either equation by a correction factor to reduce the sample size from n to n'. This factor is $1 + n/N$. The additional calculation to obtain the sample size without replacement is

$$n' = \frac{n}{1 + (n/N)}$$

(15.6)

When the sample size with replacement is 5 percent or more of the population size, the sample size should be adjusted to reflect sampling without replacement. That is, when $n/N > 5$ percent, use Eq. 15.6 to make the adjustment. As a practical matter, if n/N is less than 5 percent, the effect of the adjustment is insignificant and can be ignored.

HYPOTHESIS TESTING

In statistical terms, the auditor's decision to accept or reject a value is referred to as hypothesis testing. With regard to a recorded book value, the

Table 15.3   Ratio of Desired Allowance for Sampling Risk to Tolerable Error

Risk of Incorrect Acceptance	Risk of Incorrect Rejection			
	20%	10%	5%	1%
1%	0.355	0.413	0.457	0.525
2.5	0.395	0.456	0.500	0.568
5	0.437	0.500	0.543	0.609
7.5	0.471	0.532	0.576	0.641
10	0.500	0.561	0.605	0.668
15	0.511	0.612	0.653	0.712
20	0.603	0.661	0.700	0.753
25	0.653	0.708	0.742	0.791
30	0.707	0.756	0.787	0.829
35	0.766	0.808	0.834	0.868
40	0.831	0.863	0.883	0.908
45	0.907	0.926	0.937	0.952
50	1.000	1.000	1.000	1.000

Sources: Statistical Sampling Subcommittee of the American Institute of Certified Public Accountants, *Audit Sampling Guide*. New York: AICPA, 1983, p. 115; Donald M. Roberts, *Statistical Auditing*. New York: AICPA, 1978, p. 247.

auditor actually tests the null hypothesis that the book value is materially correct. There are four possible outcomes from this test:

1. The auditor can accept the book value when it is, in fact, not materially misstated. This is the correct decision.
2. The auditor can reject the book value as materially in error when it is, in fact, not materially misstated, committing the alpha error. This possibility is called the risk of incorrect rejection.
3. The auditor can accept the book value when it is, in fact, materially misstated, committing the beta error. This possibility is called the risk of incorrect acceptance.
4. The auditor can reject the book value as materially in error when the book value is, in fact, materially misstated. This is the correct decision.

Figure 15.3   Possible Audit Decisions Regarding an Account Balance

	True State of the Population	
	Not Materially	Materially
Audit Decision	Misstated	Misstated
Accept Book Value	Correct Decision	Incorrect Decision: Risk of Incorrect Acceptance (β)
Reject Book Value	Incorrect Decision: Risk of Incorrect Rejection (α)	Correct Decision

Figure 15.3 summarizes these outcomes, which can arise from testing sample evidence of account balances. Figure 15.3 also emphasizes the point that the auditor should try to hold both the risk of incorrect rejection (α risk) and the risk of incorrect acceptance (β risk) to acceptable levels.

EFFECT OF CHANGING FACTOR QUANTITIES ON SAMPLE SIZE

From Eq. 15.1 we can easily see that as the alpha risk decreases, $z_{\alpha/2}$ increases, and the sample size increases. Similarly, as the number of items in the population (N) increases, the sample size increases. Since s is the standard deviation of the sample and is used to estimate the population standard deviation, as the variability of a population increases, both the standard deviation and the sample size increase.

From Eq. 15.2 we can also easily see that the population size, estimated standard deviation of the population, desired reliability factor, and beta risk factor vary *directly* with the sample size. The larger they are, the larger the sample size.

The beta risk factor is inversely related to the risk of incorrect acceptance. In Chapter 13, we presented one integrated audit-risk formula. It shows that the risk of incorrect acceptance is inversely related to the risks of internal accounting control, analytical review procedures, and other related substantive tests of details. Since the beta-risk factor varies directly with sample size, we can conclude that both the risk of internal accounting control and the risk of analytical review procedures and other relevant substantive tests of details vary directly with the sample size. The greater these two risks, the larger should be the sample size. When an auditor expects one of these two risks to be high, greater reliance, and therefore less risk, would be taken with the other. Thus there is an *inverse* relationship between the degree of reliance on internal accounting controls or other relevant substantive tests and sample size.

Precision (allowance for sampling risk) and tolerable error vary *inversely* with sample size. Precision appears in the denominator of Eq. 15.1, and tolerable error appears in the denominator of Eq. 15.2. When precision or tolerable error increases, the sample size decreases.

Since both sample-size formulas contain squared terms, the relationships between sample size and the various factors are not linear. That is, doubling N, s, or $z_{\alpha/2}$ will not double the required sample size, and doubling A or E_t will not cut it in half. The following tabulation summarizes the effects of changing factor quantities on sample size.

Factor	General Effect on Sample Size
Population size increases (decreases)	Larger (smaller)
Estimated standard deviation of the population increases (decreases)	Larger (smaller)
Desired reliability factor increases (decreases)	Larger (smaller)
Desired precision widens (narrows)	Smaller (larger)
Tolerable error increases (decreases)	Smaller (larger)
Beta risk factor increases (decreases)	Larger (smaller)
Greater (lesser) reliance on internal accounting controls	Smaller (larger)
Greater (lesser) reliance on analytical review procedures and other relevant substantive tests of details	Smaller (larger)

15.4 AUDIT JUDGMENT IN SUBSTANTIVE TESTING

The use of audit sampling for substantive tests of details depends heavily on the auditor's experience and judgment. For example, in order to determine the size of a sample the auditor must specify the risk of incorrect rejection, the degree of reliance on internal accounting controls, the degree of reliance on analytical review procedure and other relevant substantive tests of details, the degree of population variation, and the amount of tolerable error.

PLANNING SAMPLES AND ASSESSING RISK

When planning a particular sample for a substantive test of details, the auditor should consider:

1. The relationship of the sample to the relevant audit objective.
2. Preliminary estimates of materiality levels.
3. The auditor's allowable risk of incorrect acceptance.
4. Characteristics of the population, that is, the items comprising the account balance or class of transactions of interest.[5]

Specifying the Objective. A sampling plan for substantive tests of details is usually designed to test the reasonableness of an amount. For example in testing accounts receivable balances, the specific audit objective is to determine the fairness of the book value as to existence, rights, and valuation. This approach is referred as the hypothesis testing objective. In this case, the auditor desires to accept the book value if it is reasonably correct. Sometimes, the auditor may want to make an independent estimate of some amount, such as the value of LIFO inventory, that was previously recorded on a FIFO basis. This approach is called the dollar-value estimation objective.

Defining the Population. The population consists of the items constituting the account balance or class of transactions of interest. In accounts receivable testing, the auditor usually defines the population as the recorded amounts receivable balances, including debit balances, credit balances, and zero balances. If the amount of credit balances is significant, the auditor might find it more effective and efficient to perform separate tests of the debit balances and the credit balances. In that case, the debit and credit balances would be defined as separate populations in order to achieve different audit objectives.[6]

In accounts receivable testing, a sampling unit (element) might be a customer account balance, an individual invoice, or an individual line item in an invoice. The auditor must use professional judgment when choosing the sampling unit. For example, since most computerized accounting systems keep track of individual invoices by customer, the auditor may select a sample of invoices, instead of account balances, for positive confirmation purposes.

Choosing a Sampling Method. The most common variable sampling methods are classical variable sampling plans (such as unstratified mean-per-unit estimation, difference estimation, ratio estimation, regression estimation, and stratified sampling) and probability–proportional-to-size (PPS) sampling. Evaluation of results of classical variable sampling is based on normal distribution theory; attributes sampling theory is used to evaluate the results of PPS sampling (Chapter 16). The auditor must use professional judgment when choosing a particular sampling method in order to achieve the specific audit objective. The appropriate uses of different variable sampling methods are discussed in sections 5 to 7.

In determining the sample size, an auditor must exercise professional judgment to establish decision criteria related to the tolerable error, the risk of incorrect acceptance, and the risk of incorrect rejection. Also, the auditor needs to consider the variation within the population.

Estimating Tolerable Error. The auditor should consider the amount of monetary error that can be present in an account balance or class of transactions without causing the financial statements to be materially misstated. This amount is the tolerable error, and the auditor must use professional judgment to decide on the amount that is material in the circumstances.[7]

Assessing the Risk of Incorrect Acceptance. Recall from Chapter 13 that, in assessing the risk of incorrect acceptance, the auditor should consider the acceptable level of ultimate risk, the effectiveness of the internal accounting controls, and the probability that analytical review procedures and other relevant substantive tests of details will fail to detect a material misstatement of the account under investigation. Subject to the limitations presented in Chapter 13, we can view the overall ultimate risk (UR) as the product of the risk of undetected error owing to internal accounting control failure (IC), the risk that the analytical review procedures and other relevant substantive tests of details will not detect misstatements (AR), and the risk of incorrect acceptance associated with the tests of details (TD), or

$$UR = (IC)\,(AR)\,(TD)$$

and

$$TD = \frac{UR}{(IC)(AR)}.$$

$$(15.7)$$

The primary audit judgment required is the degree of reliance to be placed on internal accounting controls. If the system is properly designed and compliance tests indicate that controls are operating effectively, the auditor may conclude that it is an excellent internal accounting control system and that substantial reliance is warranted. The following tabulation indicates the ranges of IC applicable to degrees of reliance on internal accounting controls.[8]

Subjective Evaluation	IC Range
Substantial reliance is warranted.	10–30%
Moderate reliance is warranted.	20–70%
Limited or no reliance is warranted.	60–100%

The analytical review procedures risk (AR) is difficult to quantify and is generally treated conservatively by assigning a high value: 40–100%. The following tabulation indicates the ranges of AR applicable to the effectiveness of analytical review procedures and other relevant tests of details.[9]

Subjective Evaluation	AR Range
Very effective	10–40%
Moderately effective	30–60%
Marginally effective or ineffective	50–100%

In summary, if we assume that $UR = 5\%$, $IC = 20\%$, and $AR = 80\%$, we can use Eq. (15.7) to calculate the risk of incorrect acceptance:

$$TD = \frac{UR}{(IC)(AR)} = \frac{0.05}{(0.2)(0.8)} = 0.31 = 31\%.$$

Assessing the Risk of Incorrect Rejection. The risk of incorrect rejection selected has a bearing on the efficiency of the audit. Since sample size varies inversely with the risk of incorrect rejection, the lower the risk, the higher will be the level of reliability, the greater the sample size, and the higher the cost of additional evidence. Generally, the risk of incorrect rejection for substantive tests should be set at 5% or less.

Considering Variation within a Population. When determining sample size, the auditor must estimate the population deviation, which is a measure of the variation within the population. Sample size generally decreases as the population variation becomes smaller. In practice, the auditor often uses a computer to estimate the population variation by measuring the variation in recorded book amounts. If the client's records are manually stored, the auditor may select a pilot sample of 30–50 sampling units and use the sample standard deviation as an estimated population standard deviation to calculate sample size.

SAMPLE SELECTION

After calculating the sample size for the variable sampling method to be used, the auditor must select sample items in such a way that the sample can be expected to be representative of the population. That is, the sample items must be selected at random, which is done by using a table of random numbers, computers, or systematic sampling, as discussed in Chapter 13.

SAMPLE EVALUATION

According to SAS No. 39, the auditor should project the errors found in the sample to the population from which the sample was selected and add that projection to errors discovered in any items that were examined 100 percent. The auditor should then compare this total projected error with the predetermined tolerable error for the account balance or class of transactions and give appropriate consideration to sampling risk.

Note that the projection of results required by SAS No. 39 must be done whether or not statistical sampling is used. The clear advantage of using statistical sampling is that it allows the auditor to quantify reliability levels for test results and thus control alpha and beta risk.

If the book value of a class of accounts is within the precision interval of the audit estimate of the population plus or minus an allowance for sampling risk, the auditor would accept the book value as not materially misstated. If the book value is not within the precision interval but the difference between the book value and the tail end of the precision interval is less than tolerable error, the sample results might still suggest that the book value is not materially misstated. If the book value is not within the precision interval and the difference between the book value and the tail end of the precision interval is greater than tolerable error, the auditor may choose one of the following alternatives.

1. If the allowance for sampling risk has not been adequately limited, that is, the achieved sampling risk (reliability level, alpha or type I error) is larger than the specified sampling risk and there is reason to believe that the sample is not representative of the population, the auditor may examine additional sampling units or perform alternative procedures to assist in determining whether the book value is misstated.

2. If the auditor believes that the book value may be misstated, he or she should consider the error along with other quantitative and qualitative audit evidence when evaluating whether the financial statements are in fact materially misstated. The auditor generally would suggest that the client investigate the errors and, if appropriate, adjust the book value.

15.5 UNSTRATIFIED MEAN-PER-UNIT ESTIMATION

One method of variable sampling that is widely used for substantive testing is mean-per-unit estimation, sometimes called *direct extension* or *simple extension estimation*. The auditor first takes a sample from the population and calculates its mean value and then multiplies this mean value by the number of items in the population to obtain an estimate of the total population value.

The auditor also uses normal distribution theory to calculate an allowance for sampling risk based on the variation of the audited values in the sample.

DETERMINATION OF SAMPLE SIZE

Let's assume that an auditor decides to design a mean-per-unit estimation plan to test the pricing of inventory as part of the examination of Socal Toy Company's December 31, 198X financial statements. The auditor takes the following steps to determine the sample size.

Step 1: Specifying the audit objective. The audit objective is to determine whether the book value of the Socal Toy Company's inventory is fairly stated.

Step 2: Defining the population. The population includes all Socal Toy Company inventory as of December 31, 198X. The auditor finds that the company has a recorded amount (V_B) of $100,000 and consists of approximately 2000 different items (N).

Step 3: Estimating tolerable error. The auditor decides that a misstatement of $3000 ($E_t$) or more in the inventory balance, when combined with error in other accounts, would result in the financial statements being materially misstated.

Step 4: Assessing the risk of incorrect acceptance. Based on a study and evaluation of the company's internal accounting controls, the auditor decides that a substantial degree of reliance can be placed on those controls in determining the scope of substantive testing of the inventory balance. The auditor decides to assign a 2 percent internal accounting control risk (IC).

By physically observing the inventory and applying appropriate cutoff procedures, the auditor obtains reasonable assurance that inventory quantities are recorded properly as of December 31, 198X. The auditor also plans to use some ARPs to obtain further assurance that both inventory quantities and pricing are reasonable. The auditor decides to assign a 5 percent risk to analytical review procedure and other relevant tests of details (AR). The auditor also decides to use a 3 percent ultimate risk (UR) for the inventory accounts balance.

Using Eq. (15.6), the auditor calculates the risk of incorrect acceptance (β, or TD) as follows:

$$TD = \frac{UR}{(IC)(AR)}$$

$$= \frac{0.03}{(0.02)(0.05)} = 0.30.$$

From Table 15.2, the auditor finds the beta risk factor (z_β) of 0.53 for a 30 percent risk of incorrect acceptance.

Step 5: Assessing the risk of incorrect rejection. The auditor is willing to tolerate a 5 percent chance of the risk of incorrect rejection and uses Table 15.1 to obtain the reliability factor ($z_{\alpha/2}$) of 1.96.

Step 6: Considering variation within the population. The auditor decides not to rely on the standard deviation from the prior year. Instead, the auditor selects a random sample of 50 items, calculates the sample standard deviation (s) to be $10, and uses this value as an estimate of the population variation.

Step 7: Calculating sample size. The auditor decides to use Eq. (15.1), to calculate sample size but first estimates precision (allowance for sampling risk) (A), using Eq. (15.3).

$$A = E_t \left(\frac{z_{\alpha/2}}{z_{\alpha/2} + z_\beta} \right)$$

$$= \$3000 \left(\frac{1.96}{1.96 + 0.53} \right) = \$3000(0.787) = \$2361.$$

Note that Table 15.3 also shows that the ratio of desired allowance for sampling risk to tolerable error (A/E_t) at 30 percent risk of incorrect and 5 percent risk of incorrect rejection is also equal to 0.787.

Now, the auditor can use Eq. (15.1) to obtain the sample size for sampling with replacement.

$$n = \left[\frac{2000(1.96)(10)}{2361} \right]^2 = 275.66 \text{ or } 276.$$

The resulting sample size of 276 is greater than 5 percent of the population, audit time can be saved by sampling without replacement. The auditor obtains the new sample size (n') by substituting into Eq. (15.6):

$$n' = \frac{n}{1 + (n/N)}$$

$$= \frac{276}{1 + (276/2000)} = 243.$$

EVALUATION OF SAMPLE RESULTS

After calculating the sample size, the auditor proceeds to evaluate the sample results.

Step 8: Drawing remaining sample items. The auditor now selects the remainder of the sample. Having already selected 50 items (in step 6), the auditor selects 193 more for the required total of 243. After performing the proper audit testing procedures for all 243 sample items, the auditor calculates their total value to be $12,271.50 and their standard deviation (s) to be $9.50. Note that s is slightly smaller than the original estimate of $10.00, based on 50 items.

Step 9: Estimating population value and precision interval. The auditor calculates the mean value of the sample items ($\bar{x}$) as

$$\bar{x} = \frac{\$12,271.50}{243} = \$50.50,$$

and then estimates total population value (V_P) by multiplying the mean value by the population size, or

$$V_P = \bar{x}N$$

$$= \$50.50(2000) = \$101,000.$$

Since the standard deviation of the sample differs from the standard deviation of the initial estimate, it is necessary to calculate an achieved precision (A'), based on the standard deviation. The auditor calculates the achieved precision as follows:

$$A' = \frac{N z_{\alpha/2}\, s}{\sqrt{n}}$$

$$= \frac{2000(1.96)(\$9.50)}{\sqrt{243}} = \$2389.$$

However, since the auditor samples without replacement, the achieved precision must also reflect the finite population correct factor, $\sqrt{1 - n/N}$. Hence, A' becomes

$$A' = \$2389\ \sqrt{1 - (243/2000)}$$

$$= \$2389(0.9373) = \$2239.$$

The achieved precision (A') differs from the planned precision (A) that the auditor calculated in step 7. Since the auditor desires to evaluate the sample results using the risk of incorrect acceptance calculated in step 4, the achieved precision must be adjusted.[10] The auditor uses the following formula to compute the achieved precision (A'').

$$A'' = A' + E_t \left(1 - \frac{A'}{A}\right)$$

$$= \$2239 + \$3000 \left(1 - \frac{\$2239}{\$2361}\right) = \$2394.$$

The auditor then uses the following formula to calculate the precision interval (PI) that corresponds to a 30 percent risk of incorrect acceptance.

$$PI = V_p \pm A''$$

$$= \$101,000 \pm \$2394$$

$$= \$98,606 \ \text{to} \ \$103,394.$$

Step 10: Interpreting sample results. Since the client's book value, $100,000, falls within the precision interval, the audit evidence supports a conclusion that the book value of the inventory is fairly stated, at the levels of risk specified by the auditor.

APPROPRIATE USES OF MEAN-PER-UNIT ESTIMATION

The unstratified mean-per-unit estimation method can provide a highly reliable estimate of the population value when the population values are not highly skewed. However, in most auditing situations, the population values tend to be skewed and have large standard deviations, which makes the unstratified mean-per-unit method inefficient and costly because of the large sample size required.

A principal use of the unstratified mean-per-unit estimation is to make an estimate of a population total when there are no recorded book values for individual population items. For example, an auditor may need to estimate an inventory value for supplies when the dollar amount in the general ledger is kept constant and all supplies purchased are charged to expense. Other examples include estimating the amount of obsolete inventory written off and estimating an allowance for uncollectible accounts. Also, when few or no differences are expected, the auditor may use unstratified mean-per-unit estimation with confidence.

15.6 DIFFERENCE, RATIO, AND REGRESSION ESTIMATION

Difference, ratio, and regression estimators are generally called auxiliary information estimators because they are based on auxiliary data (that is, book value of each sample item) and assumptions about the relationship between the audited value and the book value of sample items. They can be used only when book values are available for each sample item and thus require more information than does mean-per-unit estimation. In many audit situations, they tend to require a smaller sample for the same level of risk of incorrect acceptance as that of mean-per-unit estimation.

DIFFERENCE ESTIMATION

Difference estimation is used by the auditor to estimate the total error amount in an audit population. The auditor calculates the average difference between audited values and book values of the sample items and then projects that average difference to the population. Difference estimation is relatively easy to apply and is used extensively by practitioners.

The sample size formulas for the unstratified mean-per-unit estimation and difference estimation are the same, except for the method used to obtain the sample standard deviation. In unstratified mean-per-unit estimation, the sample standard deviation is based on audited values; in difference estimation the sample standard deviation is based on the differences between the audited values and the book values of the sample items.

Again, let's follow an auditor through the steps of the application. This time, difference estimation is used to determine the correctness of the Roland Company's accounts receivable balance.

Step 1: Specifying the audit objective. The audit objective is to determine whether the Roland Company's book value for accounts receivable is fairly stated. The auditor decides that book value will be accepted as fairly stated if it falls within the precision interval computed from a random sample.

Step 2: Defining the population. The auditor defines the population as the recorded accounts receivable balances. The 3000 accounts receivable listed on the aged trial balance have a recorded book value of $100,000. The sampling unit is each account in the accounts receivable subsidiary ledger recorded in a magnetic tape file of customer accounts.

Step 3: Estimating tolerable error. The amount of error that the auditor is willing to accept is a materiality question. After discussing the situation at Roland Company with his supervisors, the auditor decides (on the basis of professional judgment) to accept a tolerable error of $6000.

Step 4: Assessing the risk of incorrect acceptance. The auditor assesses a 20 percent risk of incorrect acceptance of internal control (*IC*), a 50 percent risk of incorrect acceptance from analytical review procedures (*AR*), and a 4 percent ultimate risk (*UR*). The auditor then calculates the desired beta risk for tests of details (*TD*) as follows:

$$TD = \frac{UR}{(IC)(AR)}$$

$$= \frac{0.04}{(0.20)(0.50)} = 0.40.$$

and obtains the beta risk factor (z_β) of 0.84 for the 40 percent risk of incorrect acceptance from Table 15.2.

Step 5: Assessing the risk of incorrect rejection. In order to determine the risk of incorrect rejection, the auditor considers the cost of resampling, should the results be rejected. It is costly to confirm accounts receivable a second time, so the auditor uses an α risk of 5 percent. From Table 15.1, the auditor determines that the reliability factor ($z_{\alpha/2}$) at 5 percent risk of incorrect rejection is 1.96.

Step 6: Considering variation within the population. The auditor decides to obtain the estimate of the population standard deviation by randomly drawing an initial sample of 30 items and uses the following formula to calculate the sample standard deviation.

$$s_d = \sqrt{\frac{\sum\limits_{i=1}^{n} (d_i - \bar{d})^2}{n-1}} \, ,$$

where

s_d = Sample standard deviation for the difference estimation.
$\bar{d}$ = Average difference in sample, or difference sample mean.
d_i = Difference between the audited value and the book value of the ith sample item.
n = Sample size.

Let's assume that the auditor obtains the following results from the initial sample.

Account Sampled	Book Value (V_B)	Audited Value (V_A)	Difference (d_i)	$d_i - d$	$d_i - d^2$
1	$ 48	$ 50	$ -2	$-5	$ 25
2	35	30	+5	+2	4
3	95	100	-5	-8	64
4	75	80	-5	-8	64
5	205	200	+5	+2	4
6	2010	2000	+10	+7	49
.	.	.	.	.	.
.	.	.	.	.	.
.	.	.	.	.	.
30	1010	1000	+10	+7	49
			$+90		$2900

$$\bar{d} = \frac{\$90}{30} = \$3 \quad \text{and} \quad s_d = \sqrt{\frac{2900}{30-1}} = \$10.$$

The desired allowance for precision (or sampling risk) (A) is

$$A = E_t \left(\frac{z_{\alpha/2}}{z_{\alpha/2} + z_\beta} \right) = \$6000 \left(\frac{1.96}{1.96 + 0.84} \right) = \$5298.$$

Step 7: Calculating sample size. The auditor uses the following formula to calculate the sample size.[11]

$$n = \left[\frac{N s_d (z_{\alpha/2} + z_\beta)}{E_t} \right]^2$$

$$= \left[\frac{3000(10)(1.96 + 0.84)}{6000} \right]^2 = 196.$$

Since 196/3000 is greater than 5 percent, the auditor calculates the sample size for sampling without replacement, or

$$n' = \frac{196}{1 + (196/3000)} = 184.$$

Step 8: Drawing remaining sample items. The auditor next selects an additional 154 (184 − 30) items at random. After receiving customer confirmations, the auditor calculates the new average difference (for the entire sample of 184 items) to be $1.70 and the new sample standard deviation to be $9.00.

Step 9: Estimating population value and precision interval. The auditor uses the new average difference to calculate the projected population error (E_p) as follows:

$$E_p = \bar{D} N$$

$$= \$1.70(3000) = \$5100.$$

The auditor also calculates the difference estimate value (V_d) of the accounts receivable as:

$$V_d = V_B - E_p$$

$$= \$100,000 - \$5100 = \$94,900.$$

Since the standard deviation of the sample differed from the standard deviation of the initial estimate, the auditor calculates the achieved precision, using the new sample standard deviation.

$$A' = \frac{1.96(\$9)(3000)}{\sqrt{184}}\sqrt{1 - \frac{184}{3000}} = \$3780.$$

To maintain the same risk of incorrect acceptance at 0.40, the auditor then calculates the adjusted precision (A''),

$$A'' = A' + E_t\left(1 - \frac{A'}{A}\right)$$

$$= \$3780 + \$6000\left(1 - \frac{\$3780}{\$5298}\right) = \$5500.$$

and the precision interval (PI),

$$PI = V_d \pm A''$$

$$= \$94{,}900 \pm \$5500 = \$89{,}400 \text{ to } \$100{,}400.$$

Step 10: Interpreting sample results. The Roland Company's book value for accounts receivable of $100,000 falls within the calculated precision interval. The auditor concludes that the book value is fairly stated.

RATIO ESTIMATION

An alternative for increasing accuracy of inference without increasing the sample size is the ratio estimation method. In ratio estimation, the auditor calculates the ratio between the sum of the audited values and the sum of the book values of the sample items and then projects that ratio to the population.

Sample size is calculated in basically the same way as it is for unstratified mean-per-unit estimation and difference estimation. However, the estimated standard deviation is now that of the ratios of the population, not of the population itself or the differences in the population. The formula for the standard deviation of sample ratios is

$$s_r = \sqrt{\frac{\sum\limits_{i=1}^{n} a_i^2 + R^2 \sum\limits_{i=1}^{n} b_i^2 - 2R \sum\limits_{i=1}^{n} a_i b_i}{n - 1}}$$

where

s_r = Sample standard deviation for the ratio estimation.
a_i = Audited value of the ith sample item.
b_i = Book value of the ith sample item.
n = Number of sample items.
r = Sample ratio, that is, the sum of the audited values of sample items divided by the sum of their book values.

A basic assumption in ratio estimation is that the book values are all positive. Ratio estimates have smaller sampling errors than difference estimates, when the audited values are approximately proportional to the book values. However, more calculations are required for ratio estimation, and they can be made most easily with the aid of a computer.[12]

The sample ratio (r) is the sum of the audited values of sample items divided by the sum of their book values, or

$$r = \frac{\displaystyle\sum_{i=1}^{n} a_i}{\displaystyle\sum_{i=1}^{n} b_i}.$$

The ratio estimate of the total population value (V_r) is

$$V_r = r V_B.$$

For example, if we select a sample of 50 inventory items from a population of 3000 items that have a total book value (V_B) of $500,000, a total sample audited value of $99,950, and a total sample book value of $100,000, we can calculate the estimated total audited value of the inventory as follows:

$$V_r = \frac{\$99,950}{\$100,000} (\$500,000) = \$499,750.$$

REGRESSION ESTIMATION

In regression estimation, we use linear regression first to determine the functional relationship between audit value and book value and then use that relationship to estimate the actual value for the population. We can use regression estimation when book values are available for each sample item and their distribution is not highly skewed.

The regression estimate of the total audited value can be expressed as

$$V_g = N\bar{a} + g(V_B - N\bar{b}) \,,$$

where

V_g = Regression estimate of the population value.
N = Population size.
$\bar{a}$ = Sample mean audited value.
g = Estimated regression coefficient.
V_B = Total book value.
$\bar{b}$ = Sample mean book value.

The equation for estimating the regression coefficient (g) is

$$g = \frac{\sum\limits_{i=1}^{n} a_i - b_i - n\bar{a}\bar{b}}{\sum\limits_{i=1}^{n} b_i^2 - n\bar{b}^2}$$

where

a_i = Audited value of the ith sample item.
b_i = Book value of the ith sample item.

When $g = 0$, V_g equals the unstratified mean-per-unit estimate of the total audited value. When $g = 1$, V_g equals the difference estimate of the total audited value. When $g = \bar{a}/\bar{b}$, V_g equals the ratio estimate of the total audited value.[13]

Sample size is calculated in basically the same way as it is for difference estimation. However, the formula for the estimated standard deviation becomes

$$s_g + \sqrt{\frac{1}{n-2}\left[\sum_{i=1}^{n} a_i^2 - n\bar{a}^2 - \frac{\left(\sum_{i=1}^{n} a_i b_i - n\bar{a}\bar{b}\right)^2}{\sum_{i=1}^{n} b_i^2 - n\bar{b}^2}\right]}.$$

The equations and concepts of regression estimation are extremely complicated. In practice, auditors use computer programs for regression estimation.[14]

APPROPRIATE USES OF DIFFERENCE, RATIO, AND REGRESSION ESTIMATION

The principal reason for using difference, ratio, or regression estimation is efficiency. A smaller sample size than that required for the unstratified mean-per-unit estimation achieves the same results at the same risk of incorrect acceptance and tolerable error, as specified by the auditor. However the auditor should consider the following constraints when considering the use of difference, ratio, or regression estimation.

1. The book value for each item in the population, the total number of items, and total book value must be known.
2. Differences between audited and book values must not be too rare in the sample.[15]
3. The auditor needs to obtain reasonable assurance that the client has properly accumulated the book values of the items in the population without compilation errors such as footing errors and errors arising from duplicating sampling units or omitting sampling units.

Unstratified difference estimation can be used effectively when the population data are not in computer-readable form, the population contains a large number of small differences or errors, the distribution of differences is not highly skewed, and difference or error amounts are fairly constant. Difference estimation is more efficient than mean-per-unit estimation when book and audited values have a high positive correlation. Difference estimation is also more efficient than ratio estimation when the magnitudes of differences are not proportional to book values.

Unstratified ratio estimation can be used effectively when the population data are not in computer-readable form, the population contains a large number of small differences or errors, the distribution of ratios is not highly skewed, and audited values are approximately proportional to book values. The ideal situation for the use of ratio estimation is for each audited value to be proportional to the book value. Ratio estimation is more efficient than the mean-per-unit estimation when book and audited values have a high positive correlation. Ratio estimation is also more efficient than difference estimation when the differences are proportional to the book values. Before ratio estimation can be used, the book value of each sampling unit must be positive.

Unstratified regression estimation can be used effectively when the population contains a large number of small differences or errors, the distribution of book values is not highly skewed, the relationship between book value and audited value is not proportional or difference amounts are not fairly constant. Regression estimation is more efficient than the mean-per-unit estimation when the correlation between book and audited values is anything but zero, which is nearly always the case. Regression estimation is almost as (or more) efficient as difference estimation and ratio estimation. Regression estimation should be used with the aid of the computer.

15.7 STRATIFIED SAMPLING

Our discussion of variable estimation sampling thus far has focused on unstratified sampling methods. When a population is highly variable and has a large standard deviation, unstratified sampling may produce excessively large sample sizes. Stratified sampling is a sample selection method that can be used to increase efficiency in variable sampling by subdividing the population into two or more strata. Efficiency is achieved by means of smaller sample sizes for given levels of allowance for sampling risk and tolerable error or by lower sampling risk for a given sample size.

PURPOSE OF STRATIFICATION

An auditor rarely deals with a population of variable items that have a narrow range of individual values. The purpose of stratification is to subdivide a wide-range, heterogeneous population into relatively homogeneous strata. This technique decreases the skew of subpopulation samples, thereby improving efficiency and reliability.

Each subpopulation of relatively homogeneous groups of items, or stratum, is then independently audited. After estimating the average value and variability in each stratum, the auditor can combine sample results for the individual strata to obtain an overall population estimate.

Because all items in a particular stratum are relatively homogeneous, the standard deviation for that stratum will be relatively small, leading to a smaller sample size.

Stratification is applicable to mean-per-unit, difference, ratio, and regression estimation. In this section, we illustrate an application of stratified mean-per-unit estimation. Stratified difference, ratio, and regression estimation require far more complicated equations, and these topics are beyond the scope of this text.[16]

DETERMINATION OF SAMPLE SIZE

In order to use stratified sampling, the auditor must determine the number of strata, stratum boundaries, total sample size, and sample size for each stratum. Let's consider the following illustrative audit situation.

Audit objective: To determine whether the client's inventory book value is fairly stated.

Population: 1000 inventory items, with a total book value of $3,003,000.

Desired reliability: 95 percent, that is, a 5 percent risk of incorrect rejection, with $z_{\alpha/2} = 1.96$.

Tolerable error: $15,000.

Risk of incorrect acceptance: 5 percent, that is, $z_\beta = 1.28$.

Sampling method: Stratified random sampling without replacement.

Let's say that the auditor decides to use recorded values as the basis for stratifying the population. Determining the number of strata requires professional judgment, although, if the population is in computer-readable form, there are mathematical formulas that can be applied to suggest an optimal number of strata. The creation of more strata usually improves the accuracy of the estimate and reduces the required sample size to achieve a specific level of precision, but diminishing returns and other factors usually lead to selection of 3–10 strata for most audit situations. Assume in this case that the auditor decides to use three strata after considering cost and the range of recorded book values.

When determining stratum boundaries, an auditor should be aware that every population element must be associated with only one stratum. There are several techniques for locating stratum boundaries from which to choose. The auditor in this case decides to use a simple method: a frequency analysis computer program to stratify items so that each stratum contains an approximately equal recorded total amount. The following tabulation presents the result of the analysis.

Stratum	Book Value	Number of Items	Total Dollar Amount	Standard Deviation
1	$1500–$5000	100	$1,000,000	$250
2	$500–$1500	500	1,002,000	50
3	Under $500	1000	1,001,000	20
Total population		1600	$3,003,000	

The auditor decides to apply a widely used method to allocate the sample to the strata: the Neyman (optimum) allocation method. This method allocates sample elements to strata in proportion to the product of the number of stratum population items times the stratum standard deviation. Strata with many items and/or large standard deviations are assigned more items than those with few items and/or small standard deviations. This method of allocation leads to the smallest possible standard error. The following sample size formulas are derived from the Neyman allocation method.

$$ n = \frac{\left(\sum_{i=1}^{k} N_i s_i\right)^2}{\left(\dfrac{A}{z_{\alpha/2}}\right)^2 + \sum_{i=1}^{k} N_i s_i^2} \quad \text{and} \quad n_i = \frac{n N_i s_i}{\sum_{i=1}^{k} N_i s_i} = \frac{(N_i s_i)\left(\sum_{i=1}^{k} N_i s_i\right)}{\left(\dfrac{A}{z_{\alpha/2}}\right)^2 + \sum_{i=1}^{k} N_i s_i^2} $$

where

n = Total sample size.

n_i = Sample size for the ith stratum, when the total sample size is known.

N_i = Population size for the ith stratum.

s_i = Standard deviation for the ith stratum.

A = Allowance for sampling risk (or precision).

$z_{\alpha/2}$ = Reliability factor for a selected risk of incorrect rejection.

The auditor calculates the desired precision, using Eq. (15.3).

$$A = E_t \left(\frac{z_{\alpha/2}}{z_{\alpha/2} + z_\beta} \right)$$

$$= \$15,000 \left(\frac{1.96}{1.96 + 1.28} \right) = \$15,000(0.605) = \$9075.$$

The auditor then calculates the sample sizes for three strata as follows:

$$n_1 = \frac{100(250)[(100)(250) + (500)(50) + (1000)(20)]}{\left(\frac{9,075}{1.96} \right)^2 + [(100)(250)^2 + (500)(50)^2 + (1000)(20)^2]} = 59.6 \text{ or } 60;$$

$$n_2 = \frac{500(50)[(100)(250) + (500)(50) + (1000)(20)]}{\left(\frac{9,075}{1.96} \right)^2 + [(100)(250)^2 + (500)(50)^2 + (1000)(20)^2]} = 59.6 \text{ or } 60;$$

$$n_3 = \frac{1000(20)[(100)(250) + (500)(50) + (1000)(20)]}{\left(\frac{9,075}{1.96} \right)^2 + [(100)(250)^2 + (500)(50)^2 + (1000)(20)^2]} = 47.7 \text{ or } 48.$$

Thus the total required sample size is

$$n = n_1 + n_2 + n_3$$

$$= 60 + 60 + 48 = 168.$$

EVALUATION OF SAMPLE RESULTS

The auditor then selects at random 60 items from stratum 1, 60 items from stratum 2, and 48 items from stratum 3. After performing the proper audit tests, the auditor has the following sample results:

Stratum	Sample Items	Sample Mean	Sample Standard Deviation
1	60	$9900	$250
2	60	2050	40
3	48	990	20

The sample standard deviation amounts were calculated by using the formula:

$$s_i = \sqrt{\frac{\sum\limits_{j=1}^{n_i} x_{i,j}^2 - n_i x_i^2}{n_i - 1}}$$

where

s_i = Sample standard deviation for stratum i.
$x_{i,j}$ = Sample value of jth item in stratum i.
x_i = Sample mean for stratum i.

The estimated population total value (V_P) is

$$V_P = \sum_{i=1}^{k}(N_i x_i)$$

$$= \ 100(\$9900) + 500(\$2050) + 1000(\$990) = \$3,005,000.$$

The auditor then calculates the achieved precision:

$$A' = z_{\alpha/2} \sqrt{\sum_{i=1}^{k} N_i (N_i - n_i)\left(\frac{s_i^2}{n_i}\right)}$$

$$= \ 1.96 \sqrt{\frac{100(40)(250)^2}{60} + \frac{500(440)(40)^2}{60} + \frac{1000(952)(20)^2}{48}}$$

$$= \$8,308.$$

To maintain the risk of incorrect acceptances at the original 10 percent level, the auditor calculates the adjusted precision as follows:

$$A'' = A' + E_t\left(1 - \frac{A'}{A}\right)$$

$$= \$8308 + \$15,000\left(1 - \frac{\$8308}{\$9075}\right) = \$9576.$$

The precision interval is

$$PI = V_P \pm A''$$

$$= \$3,005,000 \pm \$9576 = \$2,995,424 \text{ to } \$3,014,576.$$

Since the client's book value of $3,003,000 falls within the precision interval, the auditor concludes that the book value of the inventory is fairly stated.

APPROPRIATE USES OF STRATIFIED SAMPLING

Most actual sampling applications make use of stratified sampling. Stratified mean-per-unit estimation is useful when the client's data are in computer-readable form and the auditor uses the computer as an audit tool. This sampling method can be used in suspected low-error and high-error circumstances and, with the use of a sufficient number of strata, can often result in relatively efficient sample sizes. Since stratified mean-per-unit estimation requires a random selection of population items, zero-value items have a chance to be selected. This method can be equally effective for evaluating overstatements or understatements of recorded values or net error amounts; it is used primarily in inventory and accounts receivable applications.

The auditor who decides to use mean-per-unit estimation will generally use stratified rather than unstratified sampling, unless the population is highly homogeneous or when a computer is not available. However, stratified sampling cannot be used effectively unless the number of items in each stratum is known precisely, and there is an identifiable means of subdividing a heterogeneous population into strata with more homogeneous characteristics. Specialists can help the auditor to specify the number of strata, determine an appropriate sample size, and ensure that the results are properly analyzed.

15.8 Summary

Variable sampling is used primarily in substantive tests of details to determine the reasonableness of recorded book values. Classical variable sampling theory was explained in this chapter in terms of the normal distribution theory and its relationship to variable sampling tables.

Six major factors affect sample size: population size, estimated population standard deviation, desired reliability factor, desired precision, beta-risk factor, and tolerable error. The population size, estimated population standard deviation, desired reliability factor, and beta-risk factor vary directly with the sample size. When precision (or tolerable error) increases, the sample size decreases.

Audit judgment also plays a key role in substantive testing. The auditor has to use professional judgment throughout the variable sampling process when planning samples, assessing risk, selecting the sample, and evaluating sample results.

We discussed five classical variable sampling methods in this chapter: (1) unstratified mean-per-unit sampling; (2) difference estimation; (3) ratio estimation; (4) regression estimation; and (5) stratified sampling. Most applications of sampling involve the use of stratified sampling. Stratification is applicable to mean-per-unit, difference, ratio, and regression estimation. Difference estimation can be used efficiently when the population contains a large number of fairly constant small differences or errors and the distribution of errors is not highly skewed. Ratio estimation can be used efficiently when the population contains a large number of small errors and the audited values are approximately proportional to book values. Regression estimation is more efficient than mean-per-unit estimation. It is almost as (or more) efficient as difference estimation and ratio estimation and should be used with the aid of a computer. Unstratified mean-per-unit sampling is the least efficient variable sampling method. It is used when there is no computer software available and when few or no differences are expected in the audit population.

Questions

1. What is variable sampling? When is it generally used in an audit?
2. Define the mean and standard deviation of a sample and describe their relationships to the normal distribution.
3. What is the relationship between reliability and type I and type II error?
4. What is the relationship between sample size and
   (a) population size.
   (b) reliability.
   (c) precision.
   (d) reliance on internal control.
   (e) reliance on other procedures.

5. How do auditors generally select a tolerable error or precision amount?
6. What should be the relationship between the precision interval of the sample and the book value?
7. What steps would you take to determine sample size in an unstratified mean-per-unit estimation method?
8. When would you use mean-per-unit sampling as opposed to difference, ratio, or regression estimation?
9. What factors affect the use of stratified sampling but do not affect simple single-strata sampling?
10. How can you determine the number of strata to use in a stratified sample?

Problems

1. Using the ultimate risk formula, determine how you could set a tolerable error level for various internal control reliance and analytical review procedures?
2. For a population size = 5,000, sample size = 400, sample mean = $96, and standard deviation = $28, risk of incorrect rejection = 5%, calculate the achieved precision using the mean-per-unit estimation.
3. How can you use a computer to help you perform some of the statistical analyses presented in this chapter?
4. What are the alternatives available to you when a value falls outside the audited precision interval? How would you explain the situation to a client when you want to make an audit adjustment?
5. What are the relationships, if any, between the size of a client's operations or the size of an account balance and the decision to use variable sampling?
6. If the auditor determines a tolerable error of $20,000, a 5% risk of incorrect rejection, and a 10% risk of incorrect acceptance, what is the allowance for sampling risk (precision)?
7. Calculate the sample size using the following information:
   Number of items in the population—1000
   Standard deviation of the sample—$10
   Reliability factor for risk of incorrect rejection—1.96
   Precision or allowance for sampling risk—$1200
8. If a population of size 500 is footed and yields $15,000 and the average difference is $2, what is the projected population error? What is the estimated value?
9. If the auditor selects a sample of 50 inventory items from a population of 2000 items that have a total book value of $400,000. The

auditor determines a total sample audited value of $10,000 and a total sample book value of $10,500. Using the ratio estimation method, what is the estimated total value of the inventory?

10. If the precision or allowance for sampling risk is 9800 and the reliability factor for a risk of incorrect rejection is 1.96, determine the sample size for each of the following strata:

Stratum	Size	Standard Deviation
1	1,000	20
2	500	40

Notes

1. Statistical Sampling Subcommittee of the American Institute of Certified Public Accountants, *Audit Sampling*. New York: AICPA, 1983, p. 88.

2. *Ibid.*, pp. 16–17.

3. Sample estimates can be derived by using one of the variable estimation techniques: unstratified mean-per-unit estimation, difference estimation, ratio estimation, regression estimation, or stratified sampling. These techniques are discussed and illustrated later in this chapter.

4. Other formulas in the auditing literature should produce the same sample size as our two formulas. For additional information, see Roberts, Donald M., *Statistical Auditing*. New York: AICPA, 1978, pp. 45–48. Also see Dykxhoorn, Hans J., and Sinning, Kathleen E., "The Lack of Uniformity in Statistical Audit Sampling," *Journal of Accounting Education*, Fall 1984, pp. 153–161.

5. Auditing Standards Board of the American Institute of Certified Public Accountants, *Statement of Auditing Standards No. 39—Audit Sampling*. New York: AICPA, 1981, p. 5.

6. AICPA, 1983, p. 43.

7. For an expanded discussion of materiality allocation, see Elliot, Robert K., and Rogers, John R., "Relating Statistical Sampling to Audit Objectives," *Journal of Accountancy*, July 1972, pp. 52–53.

8. AICPA, 1983, p. 124.

9. AICPA, 1983, p. 125.

10. For a detailed explanation of the rationale for adjusted precision, see Roberts, *op. cit.*, p. 43.

11. Some auditors also consider the expected point estimate of the population error (Ep) in calculating sample size. For a detailed description

of this approach, see Arens, Alvin A., and Loebbecke, James K., *Application of Statistical Sampling to Auditing.* Englewood Cliffs, N.J.: Prentice-Hall, 1981, Chapter 5.

12. See volumes 4 and 6, *An Auditor's Approach to Statistical Sampling.* New York: AICPA, 1974, for methods of calculating the standard deviation of ratios.

13. Roberts, *op. cit.,* p. 86.

14. For an advanced discussion of regression estimation, see Deakin, M. F., and Granof, M. H., "Regression Analysis as a Means of Determining Audit Sample Size," *The Accounting Review,* October 1974, pp. 764–771; Kinney, Jr., William R., and Bailey, Jr., Andrew D., "Regression Analysis as a Means of Determining Audit Sample Size: A Comment," *The Accounting Review,* April 1976, pp. 396–401; and Kaplan, Robert S., "Statistical Sampling in Auditing with Auxiliary Information Estimation," *Journal of Accounting Research,* Autumn 1973, pp. 238–258.

15. For the minimum number of differences, see Roberts, *op. cit.,* p. 74; McCray, J. J., "Ratio and Difference Estimation in Auditing," *Management Accounting,* December 1973, p. 47.

16. For an advanced discussion of these methods of stratified sampling, see Cochran, William G., *Sampling Techniques,* 3rd ed. New York: John Wiley & Sons, 1977; Neter, John, and Loebbecke, James K., *Behavior of Major Statistical Estimators in Sampling Accounting Populations.* New York: AICPA, 1975.

Additional References

Akresh, Abraham D., "Statistical Sampling in Public Accounting," *CPA Journal,* July 1980, pp. 20–26.

Audit Sampling. New York: Ernst & Whinney, 1979.

Baggett, Walter, "Using Time-Sharing Facilities for Statistical Sampling," *CPA Journal,* October 1977, pp. 85–86.

Bailey, Andrew D., Jr., *Statistical Auditing: Review, Concepts, and Problems.* New York: Harcourt Brace Jovanovich, 1981.

Baker, Robert L., and Ronald M. Copeland, "Evaluation of the Stratified Regression Estimator for Auditing Accounting Populations," *Journal of Accounting Research,* Autumn 1979, pp. 606–617.

Garstka, Stanley J., and Philip A. Ohlson, "Ratio Estimation in Accounting Populations with Probabilities of Sample Selection Proportional to Size of Book Values," *Journal of Accounting Research,* Spring 1979, pp. 23–59.

Guy, Dan M., *An Introduction to Statistical Sampling in Auditing*. New York: John Wiley & Sons, 1981.

Kinney, William R., Jr., "A Note on Compounding Probabilities in Auditing," *Auditing: A Journal of Practice & Theory*, Spring 1983, pp. 13–22.

McCray, John H., "Ratio and Difference Estimation in Auditing," *Management Accounting*, December 1973, pp. 43–48.

Nanus, James H., "Effective Uses of Statistical Sampling in the Audit of a Small Company," *Practical Accountant*, March/April 1978, pp. 33–45.

Reneau, James Hal, "Guidelines for Selecting Sampling Procedures," *Internal Auditor*, June 1980, pp. 77–82.

Stringer, Kenneth W., "Statistical Sampling in Auditing: The State of the Art," *Annual Accounting Review*, 1979, 1:113–127.

Vagge, Richard, "Toward Understanding Statistical Sampling," *CPA Journal*, May 1980, pp. 13–19.

Van Martre, Joseph, and Ellis Loudell, "The Ratio Estimate—Conceptual Review and a Case Illustration," *Woman CPA*, April 1978, pp. 12–15.

Zuber, George R., Robert K. Elliott, William R. Kinney, Jr., and James L. Leisenring, "Using Materiality in Audit Planning," *Journal of Accountancy*, March 1983, pp. 42–55.

Chapter 16

Statistical Sampling: PPS Sampling

16.1 INTRODUCTION

Probability–proportional-to-size (PPS) sampling is a recent innovation in audit sampling methods. We discussed two classical statistical sampling methods in Chapters 14 and 15: attribute sampling for compliance testing and variable sampling for substantive testing. A hybrid method, PPS sampling involves the use of attribute sampling theory to express conclusions in dollar amounts, rather than as rates of occurrence. This method can be used for both compliance and substantive testing, but in this chapter we limit the discussion of PPS sampling to substantive testing.

The name *PPS sampling* relates to the concept that each transaction or balance in account population has a probability of selection proportional to its recorded dollar amount. The key to PPS sampling is defining the sampling unit as one dollar. Accordingly, PPS sampling is also known as *dollar-unit sampling* (DUS). Other variations of PPS sampling are called *combined attributes–variables* (CAV) *sampling* and *cumulative monetary amount* (CMA) *sampling*.

We begin this chapter with a discussion of the characteristics of PPS sampling. We then present the basic concepts underlying PPS sampling theory and their relationships to sampling tables. Next, we describe the basic steps in PPS sampling and follow that with discussions, in some detail, of the determination of sample size, sample selection procedures, and evaluation of sample results. Finally, we state the advantages, disadvantages, and uses of PPS sampling.

LEARNING OBJECTIVES

By the time you have completed this chapter you should be able to:

1. Describe the major characteristics and assumptions of probability–proportional-to-size (PPS) sampling.

483

2. Define PPS sampling concepts such as expansion factor, tainting, upper error limit, basic precision, and incremental allowance.
3. Explain the PPS sampling theory and its relationship to PPS sampling tables.
4. Determine sample size, select a sample, and evaluate sample results for PPS sampling applications.
5. Identify the advantages, disadvantages, and uses of PPS sampling.

16.2 CHARACTERISTICS OF PPS SAMPLING

A modified form of attribute sampling, PPS sampling permits an auditor to reach conclusions about the total dollar amount of error in the population being sampled. Thus one major PPS sampling objective is to estimate the monetary amount of errors (overstatements) in the population.

Recall that, in variable sampling (such as mean-per-unit, difference, and ratio estimation), the sampling unit is a physical unit (account balance, invoice, inventory item, and the like). However, in PPS sampling, each individual dollar in the audit population is treated as a separate sampling unit, and each dollar has an equal chance of being selected. In order to illustrate this difference, let's assume that an auditor is verifying an accounts receivable file having total of $100,000 and consisting of 1000 customer accounts. Using variable sampling methods, we would define the population as 1000 units, whereas in PPS sampling, we would consider the population to be 100,000 sampling units (dollars).

When an individual sampling unit (dollar) is selected, an auditor does not directly test that particular dollar. Instead, that dollar acts as a hook, which is used to pull the entire physical unit (such as a customer account) out for examination. In the accounts receivable example, if a dollar of customer A's account balance of $100 is selected, the sample item becomes the entire $100. The balance or transaction that the auditor examines is called a *logical unit*.

Because each dollar in the file has an equal chance of being selected, the accounts containing larger dollar balances have a higher probability of being selected and audited. For example, a $1000 customer account contains 1000 sampling units and has a better chance of being selected than a $100 customer account, which contains only 100 sampling units. In fact, the chances of selecting a dollar from the $1000 customer account are ten times better than the chances of selecting a dollar from a $100 account.

The PPS sampling method is based on two assumptions:

1. The error rate in the population should be small, say less than 10 percent.[1]
2. The amount of error in any item cannot exceed 100 percent of the book value of the item.

The auditor should be aware of these two assumptions before deciding to use PPS sampling. In PPS sampling, the auditor follows the same basic steps as in attribute and variable sampling. And, again, the auditor must use professional judgment in determining the acceptable level of risk, tolerable error, and expected amount of error, along with the population size, in calculating the sample size.

16.3 PPS SAMPLING THEORY

Before attempting to use PPS sampling, the auditor should be familiar with basic PPS concepts, the relationship of the Poisson distribution to PPS sampling tables, and audit steps in PPS sampling. The basic concepts involved in PPS sampling include tolerable error, projected error, risk of incorrect acceptance, risk of incorrect rejection, and sampling interval, all of which we have previously defined and discussed in relation to attribute and variable sampling. The reliability factor used in PPS sampling is different from that used in the sampling methods presented so far. New concepts introduced for PPS sampling are tainting, upper error limit, basic precision, and incremental allowance.

The **reliability factor** (RF) is a Poisson factor in the PPS sampling table, representing a one-tailed value for each risk and number of errors allowed in a sample. The reliability factor is one of the major factors in determining sample size. The **expansion factor** (EF) is a factor used in the calculation of sample size if errors are expected. **Tainting** (t) is the ratio of the amount of error in the sample item to the item's recorded amount. For example, if Customer A's account balance is $1000 and the audit amount is $900, tainting is ($1000 − $900)/$1000 = 10%.

The **upper error limit** (E_{UL}) is the maximum dollar amount of overstatement. It is equal to the projected error plus an allowance for sampling risk. Upper error limit is also called *upper limit on error, achieved upper monetary bound, maximum dollar amount of error,* and *upper error bound.* The **basic precision** (P_b) is the minimum allowance for sampling risk inherent in the sample. It is also called *basic bound,* and *basic risk.* The **incremental allowance** (A_I) is that part of the allowance for sampling risk affected by errors found in the sample, which cause incremental changes in the reliability factor.

Table 16.1   Reliability Factors for Errors of Overstatement

Number of Overstatement Errors (k)	Risk of Incorrect Acceptance (B)								
	1%	5%	10%	15%	20%	25%	30%	37%	50%
0	4.61	3.00	2.31	1.90	1.61	1.39	1.21	1.00	0.70
1	6.64	4.75	3.89	3.38	3.00	2.70	2.44	2.14	1.68
2	8.41	6.30	5.33	4.72	4.28	3.93	3.62	3.25	2.68
3	10.05	7.76	6.69	6.02	5.52	5.11	4.77	4.34	3.68
4	11.61	9.16	8.00	7.27	6.73	6.28	5.90	5.43	4.68
5	13.11	10.52	9.25	8.50	7.91	7.43	7.01	6.49	5.68
6	14.57	11.85	10.54	9.71	9.06	8.56	8.12	7.56	6.67
7	16.00	13.15	11.76	10.90	10.24	9.69	9.21	8.63	7.67
8	17.41	14.44	13.00	12.06	11.38	10.81	10.31	9.68	8.67
9	18.79	15.71	14.21	13.25	12.52	11.92	11.39	10.74	9.67
10	20.15	16.97	15.41	14.42	13.66	13.02	12.47	11.79	10.67
11	21.49	18.21	16.60	15.57	14.78	14.13	13.55	12.84	11.67
12	22.83	19.45	17.79	16.72	15.90	15.22	14.63	13.89	12.67
13	24.14	20.67	18.96	17.86	17.02	16.32	15.70	14.93	13.67
14	25.45	21.89	20.13	19.00	18.13	17.40	16.77	15.97	14.67
15	26.75	23.10	21.30	20.13	19.24	18.49	17.84	17.02	15.67
16	28.03	24.31	22.46	21.26	20.34	19.58	18.90	18.06	16.67
17	29.31	25.50	23.61	22.39	21.44	20.66	19.97	19.10	17.67
18	30.59	26.70	24.76	23.51	22.54	21.74	21.03	20.14	18.67
19	31.85	27.88	25.91	24.63	23.64	22.81	22.09	21.18	19.67
20	33.11	29.07	27.05	25.74	24.73	23.89	23.15	22.22	20.67

Source: Statistical Sampling Subcommittee of the American Institute of Certified Public Accountants, *Audit Sampling Guide.* New York: AICPA, 1983, p. 117.

THE POISSON DISTRIBUTION AND SAMPLING TABLES

In this section, we present a theoretical explanation of PPS sampling, using the Poisson distribution, and show how PPS sampling tables are developed. The Poisson distribution is a continuous, unimodal, nonsymmetric distribution. It is specified by the mean of λ, which is equal to the number of trials, that is, the sample size (n), multiplied by the probability of an occurrence of error for one trial (p), or

$$\lambda = np.$$

(16.1)

The Poisson distribution allows an auditor to state with a specified risk (β) the tolerable error (E_t) per sample size (n) of the population when the sample contains k errors. In practice, auditors use reliability factor and expansion factor tables rather than Poisson distribution tables to calculate sample size. Table 16.1 shows the relationship of the number of over-statement errors (k) to the risk of incorrect acceptance (β) and reliability factors (RF).

Let's look at the relationship between Poisson distribution tables and Table 16.1. In a typical Poisson distribution table, the left-hand column shows the potential number of occurrences (errors), k, and the top row shows selected values of $\lambda = np$. The body of the table contains the probabilities of k or more errors for each value of λ. The following tabulation is taken from a Poisson distribution table.

						λ				
Row	k	0.70	1.00	1.21	1.39	1.61	1.90	2.31	3.00	4.61
(1)	0	1.00	1.00	1.00	1.00	1.00	1.00	1.00	1.00	1.00
(2)	1	0.50	0.63	0.70	0.75	0.80	0.85	0.90	0.95	0.99

Since the body of the Poisson distribution table contains the probabilities of k or more errors for selected λ values, we can show the probabilities of 0 errors by subtracting the values in row (2) from those in row (1).

Number					λ				
of Errors	0.70	1.00	1.21	1.39	1.61	1.90	2.31	3.00	4.61
0	0.50	0.37	0.30	0.25	0.20	0.15	0.10	0.05	0.01

The result is the risk of incorrect acceptance (β), or the decimal equivalent of the percentages (in reverse order) at the top of Table 16.1. The λ values, then, are equivalent to the reliability factors (RF). The remaining rows of Table 16.1 are derived from the Poisson distribution table with different combinations of k and λ.

16.4 DETERMINATION OF SAMPLE SIZE

Sample size (n) calculations are based on the reliability factor (RF), tolerable error (E_t), recorded book value (V_B) (also called *recorded amount of the population*), and expected error, (E_e). It is important to remember that the reliability factor corresponds to the risk of incorrect acceptance and is also equivalent to the Poisson factor λ.

NO ERRORS EXPECTED

The $k = 0$ row of Table 16.1 shows the relationship between various β-risk values and reliability factors when no errors are expected. We obtain the sample-size formula by substituting into Eq. (16.1).

$$\lambda = np \text{ and } \lambda = RF;$$

thus

$$RF = np.$$

Since p is equivalent to E_t/V_B, the tolerable rate (or maximum allowance error rate),

$$RF = n\left(\frac{E_t}{V_B}\right),$$

(16.2)

and

$$n = RF\left(\frac{V_B}{E_t}\right),$$

or

$$n = \frac{RF}{(E_t/V_B)}$$

(16.3)

which is the sample-size formula when no errors are expected.

Note that the calculation of sample size for PPS sampling is different from that for the other variable sampling methods. Recall the calculation of sample size for mean-per-unit, difference, and ratio estimation requires an estimate of the population standard deviation of error or absolute amount, whereas PPS sampling requires only an estimate of β risk and tolerable error.

Let's suppose that Western Furniture, Inc., has debit balances totaling $250,000 in its accounts receivable file. We plan to use PPS sampling to evaluate customer confirmation requests. Our objective is to determine whether the recorded book value is materially overstated. Based on our audit experience and professional judgment, we choose $E_t = \$15,000$, β =

10%, and $k = 0$. We use Eq. (16.3) and values from Table 16.1 to calculate sample size.

$$n = \frac{RF}{(E_t/V_B)}$$

$$= \frac{2.31}{(15,000/\$250,000)} = 39 \text{ (rounded up).}$$

ERRORS EXPECTED

If an auditor expects to find errors, the reliability factor must be modified and one of two methods used to calculate sample size: (1) subtract the combined effect of expected error (E_e) and an expansion factor (EF)—see Table 16.2—from tolerable error (E_t) and calculate the sample size as when no error is expected; or (2) convert E_t and E_e to percentages of the total recorded book value and obtain the sample size for the equivalent rates shown in Table 14.1 or Table 14.2, which is based on attribute sampling theory.[2]

Method 1. Returning to our accounts receivable example, let's say that we expect a total error (E_e) of \$4500 in the accounts receivable file. The new sample-size formula will be

$$n = \frac{RF}{[E_t - (E_e)(EF)]/V_B}$$

or

$$n = \frac{(RF)(V_B)}{[E_t - (E_e)(EF)]}$$

(16.4)

Table 16.2 Expansion Factors for Expected Errors

	Risk of Incorrect Acceptance (β)							
1%	5%	10%	15%	20%	25%	30%	37%	50%
1.9	1.6	1.5	1.4	1.3	1.25	1.2	1.15	1.0

Source: Statistical Sampling Subcommittee of the American Institute of Certified Public Accountants, *Audit Sampling Guide.* New York: AICPA, 1983, p. 118.

where *EF* is the expansion factor. Referring to Table 16.2, we see that $EF = 1.5$ for our β of 10 percent. Substituting into Eq. (16.4), we get

$$n = \frac{(2.31)(\$250{,}000)}{\$15{,}000 - (\$4500)(1.5)} = 70.$$

Note that the sample size increases from 39 (no errors expected) to 70 ($4500 total error amount expected). One further comment about method 1: It tends to overstate the required sample size when the expected error approaches the tolerable error.

Method 2. Method 2 relies directly on the statistical sample-size tables for compliance testing in Chapter 14, resulting in a more exact sample-size calculation than does method 1. Using the same accounts receivable audit example, we first convert the tolerable error of $15,000 and the expected amount of error of $4500 to percentages of the recorded book value of $250,000, or

$$TR = \frac{\$15{,}000}{\$250{,}000} = 6\% \text{ and } s = \frac{\$4500}{\$250{,}000} = 1.8\%.$$

We then obtain the sample size from Table 14.2 for a 10% risk. If the calculated tolerable rate is not shown in the table, we select the sample size for the next smallest tolerable rate shown. Similarly, if the calculated expected population deviation rate is not shown in the table, we select the sample size for the next highest deviation rate shown. In our example, the calculated population deviation rate of 1.8 percent is not shown in Table 14.2, so we use the next highest rate, or 2.00 percent, to obtain a sample size of 88.

When using PPS sampling, auditors usually try to control both risk of incorrect acceptance (β) and risk of incorrect rejection (α) simultaneously. The sample-size formulas presented in this section include only β risk. We can add 10 percent to the calculated sample size to implicitly recognize α risk.

16.5 SAMPLE-SELECTION PROCEDURES

In order to obtain a PPS sample, the auditor can use either random or systematic selection techniques. Table 16.3 presents book-value data for Western Furniture, Inc.'s accounts receivables. Also shown are cumulative totals, associated dollar units, and corresponding numbers for the two selection techniques. We use these data to illustrate PPS sample selection for both random and systematic selection procedures.

RANDOM SELECTION

If we use unrestricted, random sampling and expect zero errors in the accounts receivable, the calculated sample size is 39 (from Section 16.4). Our use of the random-sample selection procedure then involves the following steps.

Step 1. Select 39 random numbers, using a table of random numbers or a computer program.

Step 2. Arrange these random numbers in ascending order.

Step 3. Prepare a list of cumulative recorded book-value amounts, as shown in the cumulative total column of Table 16.3.

Step 4. Match the random numbers with the corresponding sampling unit, as shown in the ordered random number column in Table 16.3.

We select the 39 random numbers from a range of 1 to 250,000, or the total book value of the accounts receivable. Note that, in Table 16.3, account number 009 has a ($13,000/$250,000)(100) = 5.2% chance of being included in the sample, whereas account number 010 has only a ($1000/$250,000)(100) = 0.4% chance of being included. Since account number 009 is 13 times as large as account number 010, its chance of being selected is 13 times greater. Although account number 009 is selected twice, it will be audited only once.

Table 16.3 Accounts Receivable and Sample Selection Data

Account Number	Book Value	Cumulative Total	Associated Dollar Units	Ordered Random Number	Systematic Selection Value
001	$5,000	$5,000	1–5,000	2,801	1,000
002	250	5,250	5,001–5,250	—	—
003	2,700	7,950	5,251–7,950	7,064	—
004	6,500	14,450	7,951–14,450	8,475	7,410
					13,820
005	700	15,150	14,451–15,150	—	—
006	1,500	16,650	15,151–16,650	15,793	—
007	4,300	20,950	16,651–20,950	17,248	20,230
008	100	21,050	20,951–21,050	—	—
009	13,000	34,050	21,051–34,050	21,079	26,640
				34,028	33,050
010	1,000	35,050	34,051–35,050	—	—
.	.	.	.	.	.
.	.	.	.	.	.
.	.	.	.	.	.
Total	$250,000				

SYSTEMATIC SELECTION

The selection procedure for systematic sampling is closely related to that for random selection. We proceed as follows:

Step 1. Calculate sampling interval (*SI*) for using the formula

$$SI = \frac{V_B}{n} = \frac{\$250,000}{39} = \$6410 \text{ (rounded down)}.$$

That is, every 6410th dollar is to be selected from the cumulative total.

Step 2. Select a random number between 1 and 6410 as a random start (*RS*), say, 1000.

Step 3. Prepare a list of cumulative recorded book-value amounts, as shown in the cumulative total column of Table 16.3.

Step 4. Select every 6410th dollar, starting with 1000 (that is, *RS*, *SI* + *RS*, 2*SI* + *RS* ...) and match it with the corresponding sampling unit, as shown in the systematic selection value column in Table 16.3.

Account values should not be arranged in an obvious pattern, such as ascending or descending sequence. Note that all accounts with balances of $6410 or more are selected when we use a sampling interval of $6410. Many auditors like to use this procedure because it selects large balances automatically, and these large amounts are more likely to contain large overstatements.

16.6 EVALUATION OF SAMPLE RESULTS

After selecting the sample, the auditor follows the planned substantive audit procedures, testing each sample item and noting any errors discovered. The auditor then projects the error results of the sample to the population and calculates an allowance for sampling risk. In this section, we describe the evaluation of three possible sample results: (1) no errors; (2) errors of 100 percent; and (3) errors of less than 100 percent. We will continue to use Western Furniture, Inc.'s accounts receivable and sampling data to illustrate the evaluation procedures. Recall that the total book value and tolerable error are $250,000 and $15,000, respectively.

NO ERRORS

When we assumed that $E_e = 0$ and set $\beta = 10\%$, our sample size was 39 items. In order to evaluate the actual result of no errors, estimate the maximum dollar amount of overstatement, or the upper error limit (E_{UL}).

$$E_{UL} = \left(\frac{V_B}{n}\right) RF_{k=0}$$

$$= \left(\frac{\$250,000}{39}\right)(2.31) = \$6410\ (2.31) = \$14,807.$$

$$(16.5)$$

For this case, note that $V_B/n = SI$, and the upper error limit should be equivalent to the tolerable error. Our calculation yielded an E_{UL} of 14,807 instead of 15,000 because of rounding in calculating the sampling interval and reliability factor.

As a result of testing the sample items, we found no errors and can conclude that the total recorded book value is not overstated by more than the tolerable error for our specified risk of incorrect acceptance. Thus we are 90 percent confident that the dollar amount of overstatement error in the total recorded book value does not exceed $15,000.

ERRORS OF 100 PERCENT

Let's now assume that we found an error of 100 percent in one account balance, say, the account for which the recorded book balance of $4500 actually has a balance of zero. In this case we calculate the upper error limit by multiplying the reliability factor for the actual number of errors found ($RF_{k=1}$) for the specified risk of incorrect acceptance by the sample interval, or

$$E_{UL} = (SI)(RF_{k=1}).$$

$$(16.6)$$

From Table 16.1, we find that the RF with 1 error for a 10 percent β risk is 3.89. Substituting into Eq. (16.1), we obtain

$$E_{UL} = \$6410(3.89) = \$24,935,$$

which represents a projected error of $(1)(100\%)(\$6410) = \$6410$ and an allowance for sampling risk of $\$24,935 - \$6410 = \$18,525$.

Thus the upper error limit increased from $15,000 for no errors to $24,935 for one error. The impact of this one error on the results is $24,935 − $15,000 = $9,935. The sample results are not acceptable because the tolerable error is only $15,000. We expected no error in the sample in the planning stage but actually found one error: a $4500 overstatement. We need to increase our sample size by using $4500 as an expected error amount. In Section 16.4 we determined that the sample size for a $4500 expected error amount, using method 1, is 70.

If we take an additional sample of 31 items (70 − 39) and find no additional errors, the revised upper error limit is

$$E_{UL} = \frac{V_B}{n} RF_{k=1}.$$

(16.7)

Substituting, we get

$$E'_{UL} = \frac{\$250,000}{70}(3.89) = \$13,893.$$

Thus the sampling results are acceptable because the upper error limit is less than the tolerable error.

ERRORS OF LESS THAN 100 PERCENT

In practice, an auditor may identify an error of less than 100 percent in a sampling unit. In order to calculate the upper error limit in this case, the auditor adds three components: (1) the basic precision; (2) the projected error; and (3) the incremental allowance based on the projected errors. To illustrate this procedure, let's consider the following summary of errors found in the sample of 39 for Western Furniture, Inc.'s accounts receivable (V_B = book value, V_A = audited value, E = error or difference, t = tainting, SI = sampling interval, E_p = projected error).

V_B	V_A	E	t	SI	E_p
$ 5000	$ 0	$5000	100%	$6410	$ 6410
3200	3000	200	6.25	6410	401
200	100	100	50	6410	3205
10000	9000	1000	NA*	6410	1000
				ΣE_p	$11016

*The sampling unit is greater than the sampling interval, so the projected error equals the actual error.

In general, we classify errors in recorded book values at or above the sampling interval of $6410 ($250,000/39) as projected errors (E_P). Thus we classify the $1000 overstatement in $10,000 as a projected error of $1000. Errors in recorded book values that are less than the sampling interval of $6410 have a tainting factor (the ratio of the error amount to the recorded book value).

We calculate the basic precision (P_b) as follows:

$$P_b = (SI)(RF_{k=0})$$

$$= \$6410(2.31) = \$14,807.$$

In order to calculate the incremental allowance, we have to divide the errors into two groups: (1) those occurring in sampling units having values less than the sampling interval; and (2) those occurring in sampling units having values equal to or greater than the sampling interval.[3] We next obtain the incremental changes in the reliability factor (ΔRF) from the k and 10% β columns in Table 16.1; ΔRF is simply the difference between consecutive values of RF, as shown in the following tabulation.

k	RF	ΔRF
0	2.31	—
1	3.89	1.58
2	5.33	1.44
3	6.69	1.36

We now rank the projected errors (E_P) for sampling units that are less than the sampling interval (excluding the sampling units having values equal to or greater than the sampling interval) in descending sequence. We multiply each projected error by ΔRF to obtain the adjusted projected error (E_P), as shown in the following tabulation.

E_P	ΔRF	E'_P
$ 6,410	1.58	$10,128
3,205	1.44	4,615
401	1.36	545
$10,016		$15,288

We then subtract the total for the first column ($10,016) from the total of the third column ($15,288) to obtain the incremental allowance for sampling risk ΔA_t: $5272.

Thus, from our series of calculations,

$$E_{UL} = P_b + E_p + \Delta A_t$$

$$= \$14{,}807 + \$11{,}016 + \$5272 = \$31{,}095,$$

and we can summarize the sample results as follows:

1. The sample contains an actual error of $6300 (total sample book value minus total audit value).
2. The total projected error is $11,016.
3. The basic precision is $14,807.
4. The incremental allowance is $5272.
5. The total allowance for sample risk is $20,079 (basic precision plus incremental allowance).
6. Consequently, there is a 10 percent risk that the total recorded book value of the company's accounts receivable is overstated by more than $31,095.

Alternatively, we can calculate the upper error limit using the following formula:

$$E_{UL_e} = SI\ [RF_{k=0} + (RF_{k=1} - RF_{k=0})\ t_{k=1} + \ldots + (RF_e - RF_{e-1})\ t_e] + E$$

$$(16.8)$$

where

E = Error amount in sampling units that are equal to or greater than the sampling interval.

e = number of error amounts in sampling units that are less than the sampling interval.

Substituting into Eq. (16.8),

$$E_{UL_3} = \$6410[2.31 + (3.89 - 2.31)(100\%) + (5.33 - 3.89)(50\%)$$
$$+ (6.69 - 5.33)(6.25\%)] + \$1000$$

$$= \$6410(4.695) + \$1000 = \$31{,}095.$$

Since the upper error limit of $31,095 is larger than the tolerable error of $15,000, we can either examine an additional representative sample from the population or perform additional substantive tests directed toward the same audit objective.

In this section we limited the discussion of sample- evaluation methods to overstatements because PPS sampling is designed primarily for use with overstatements. If understatements are a significant consideration, the auditor should refer to the advanced audit sampling and select an appropriate method.[4]

16.7 USES OF PPS SAMPLING

Developed in recent years, PPS sampling combines certain features of both attribute and variable sampling. Auditors use PPS sampling primarily when they expect zero or very few errors and desire a dollar result. This method can be used to test transactions for compliance purposes and to test the details of year-end asset account balances.

In practice, PPS sampling is used extensively in auditing accounts receivable, inventory, fixed assets, expense accounts, and cash disbursements. In auditing accounts receivable, auditors frequently use PPS sampling to sample account balances and open items for confirmation purposes, estimate aging of accounts, and estimate the allowance for doubtful accounts. In auditing cash disbursements, auditors frequently use PPS sampling to test authorizations of cash disbursements and to estimate the maximum probable dollar value of disbursements that are not supported by vendor invoices or other supporting documents. In fact, PPS sampling has become a major audit tool for both external and internal auditors.

ADVANTAGES

The use of PPS sampling has a number of advantages over other sampling methods. Because it is easy to use, PPS sampling is appealing. Its use requires only one table, based on the Poisson probability distribution, to evaluate sample results. Sample selection can be performed using a computer program or an adding machine. Since PPS sampling does not depend on normal distribution theory, the sample size determination does not require direct consideration of the standard deviation. If the auditor expects no errors, the PPS sampling size is usually smaller than that required using classical variable sampling techniques.

The sampling process is more efficient because PPS sampling automatically results in a stratified sample. The chance of selection is proportional to book value, which increases the probability of detecting large errors in large dollar values. The systematic sample-selection procedure automatically identifies any significant item, if its value exceeds the sampling interval.

The auditor can use PPS sampling simultaneously for both attribute sampling (used to judge the reliability of internal control) and variable sampling (used to reach a conclusion about the fairness of account balances presentations). This approach can also improve audit efficiency.

DISADVANTAGES

However, the use of PPS sampling also has several major disadvantages. With PPS sampling, understated accounts have a smaller probability for selection than they should because they contain fewer dollar units. If the auditor identifies understatements in a PPS sampling, special considerations are required to evaluate the sample. Zero balances or missing accounts will not be sampled. Further, accounts with negative balances (such as accounts receivable credit balances) should be excluded from PPS sampling tests and tested separately.

Several errors in the recorded values of sample items can easily lead to an upper error limit of overstatement that exceeds the tolerable error. As a result, the auditor may be more likely to reject an acceptable recorded population book value. As the expected number of errors increases the sample size needed becomes much greater for PPS sampling than for other variable sampling techniques.

16.8 Summary

Probability–proportional-to-size sampling can be used for both compliance and substantive testing. One major objective in the use of PPS sampling is to estimate the monetary amount of errors in a class of accounts. It treats each individual dollar in the audit population as a separate sampling unit. Because each dollar in the population has an equal chance of being selected, the accounts containing larger dollar balances have a higher probability of being selected and audited.

In this chapter, we presented, discussed, and illustrated the following PPS sampling concepts: tolerable error, projected error, risk of incorrect acceptance, risk of incorrect rejection, sampling interval, reliability factor, tainting, upper error limit, basic precision, and incremental allowance. We also developed the relationship between the Poisson distribution and PPS sampling tables.

A typical PPS sampling plan would include six basic steps: determining the audit objective, defining the population and sampling unit, calculating the sample size, selecting the sample, applying the sampling techniques, and evaluating sample results. The auditor should consider the acceptable level of risk, tolerable error, expected amount of error, and population size when calculating sample size. The auditor should also project sample errors to the population and calculate an allowance for sampling risk before reaching a conclusion about the results.

Auditors use PPS sampling extensively in auditing accounts receivable, inventory, fixed assets, expense accounts, and cash disbursements. The auditor should carefully consider the advantages and limitations of PPS sampling before deciding to use this method.

Questions

1. How does PPS sampling differ from variable sampling?
2. Define
    (a) Tolerable error.
    (b) Projected error.
    (c) Sampling interval.
    (d) Reliability factor.
    (e) Expansion factor.
    (f) Tainting.
    (g) Upper error limit.
    (h) Basic precision.
    (i) Incremental allowance.
3. Describe both mathematically and in words the Poisson distribution.
4. What are the six steps in PPS sampling?
5. What factors must an auditor estimate in order to determine the PPS sample size?
6. How does the expectation of some errors rather than no errors affect the calculation of sample size?
7. Describe the PPS sample-selection procedure for both random sampling and systematic sampling.
8. Describe the sample-evaluation procedures used when there are no errors, errors of 100 percent and errors of less than 100 percent.
9. What does *total allowance for risk* mean?
10. What are the advantages and disadvantages of using PPS sampling? When would you use it?

Problems

1. Does PPS sampling differ from attribute sampling? Variable sampling? If so, how? Are there factors other than the sampling method itself that would affect your selection of PPS sampling?
2. Why was PPS sampling developed? Try to find some historical references to who developed it and where it was developed.
3. As with other statistical methods, the auditor must make a number of estimates when planning for sampling. Review the estimates required for PPS sampling and describe how you might make them.
4. Do you think that PPS sampling is more responsive to auditors' needs than other forms of variable sampling? Why or why not?
5. Read (or review) *Behavior of Major Statistical Estimators in Sampling Accounting Population* by Neter and Loebbecke (AICPA, 1975) and determine what the authors concluded when they compared PPS sampling with other variable sampling methods.
6. You are planning accounts receivable confirmation procedures using PPS sampling with no errors expected. You have determined that 3% of the total accounts receivable balance would be the tolerable rate (E_t/V_B). If the following risks of acceptance are desired, what is the required sample size?
    (a) 1%
    (b) 5%
    (c) 10%
    (d) 15%
7. An auditor plans to use PPS sampling to test the client's inventory with the population of 2000 inventory items valued at $600,000. The tolerable error is $30,000 at 5% risk of incorrect acceptance. No errors are expected in the population.
    Required:
    (a) What is the required sample size?
    (b) The auditor has selected a sample of 60 items and discovered the following three exceptions:

Book Value	Audited Value
$ 5,000	$ 0
2,500	2,000
12,000	11,000

    Calculate the basic precision, total projected error, incremental allowance for sampling risk, and upper error limit.
    (c) What conclusion can be drawn from this test?

Notes

1. For a PPS sampling model that includes high-error rate situations, see Roberts, Donald M., *Statistical Auditing.* New York: AICPA, 1978, pp. 116-119.

2. Statistical Sampling Subcommittee of the American Institute of Certified Public Accountants, *Audit Sampling.* New York: AICPA, 1983, p. 75.

3. *Ibid.,* p. 80.

4. For discussions of methods for evaluating understatements, see Roberts, *op. cit.,* p. 124; Bailey, Jr., Andrew D., *Statistical Auditing.* New York: Harcourt Brace Jovanovich, 1981, Chapter 9; Guy, Dan M., *An Introduction to Statistical Sampling in Auditing.* New York: John Wiley & Sons, 1981, pp. 181–183; Arens, Alvin A., and Loebbecke, James K., *Application of Statistical Sampling To Auditing.* Englewood Cliffs, N.J.: Prentice-Hall, 1981, Chapter 9; Anderson, Rodney J., Leslie, Donald A., and Teitlebaum, Albert D., *Dollar Unit Sampling.* Chicago: Commerce Clearing House, 1979.

Additional References

An Auditor's Approach to Statistical Sampling, AICPA New York, 1974.

Andrews, W. T., Jr., and Alan G. Mayper, "Dollar-Unit Sampling," *The Internal Auditor,* April 1983, pp. 31–34.

Arkin, Herbert, *Sampling Methods for the Auditors: An Advanced Treatment.* New York: McGraw-Hill, 1982.

Audit Sampling. New York: Ernst & Whinney, 1979.

Crum, Robert P., "Using Combined Attributes-Variables Tests," *The CPA Journal,* July 1981, pp. 38–45.

Gafford, W. W., and D. R. Carmichael, "Materiality, Audit Risk and Sampling: A Nuts-and-Bolts Approach," *The Journal of Accountancy,* October 1984, pp. 109–118; November 1984, pp. 125–138.

Garstka, Stanley J., "Models for Computing Upper Errors Limits in Dollar-Unit Sampling," *Journal of Accounting Research,* Autumn 1977, pp. 179–192.

Harwood, Gordon B., Ronald E. Shiffler, and James M. Wood, Jr., "Putting Dollar-Unit Sampling to Work," *The Internal Auditor,* February 1982, pp. 50–55.

Kaplan, Robert S., "Sample Size Computations for Dollar-Unit Sampling." *Journal of Accounting Research: Studies on Statistical Methodology in Auditing,* 1975 Suppl., pp. 126–133.

Neter, John, Robert A. Leitch, and Stephen E. Fienberg, "Dollar-Unit Sampling: Multinomial Bounds for Total Overstatement and Understatement Errors," *The Accounting Review,* January 1978, pp. 77–93.

Reneau, J. Hal, "Guidelines for Selecting Sampling Procedures," *Internal Auditor,* June 1980, pp. 77–82.

Stringer, Kenneth W., "Statistical Sampling in Auditing: The State of the Art," *Annual Accounting Review,* 1979, 1:113–127.

Vagge, Richard, "Toward Understanding Statistical Sampling," *CPA Journal,* May 1980, pp. 13–19.

Chapter 17

Advanced EDP Concepts

17.1 INTRODUCTION

In this chapter, we extend the discussion in Chapter 2 regarding the basic concepts of data processing. The additional concepts presented here are intended to provide sufficient knowledge of data processing to permit the understanding of a wide range of EDP-based systems. We first define and discuss microcomputers and their main elements. We then focus on telecommunication networks. We next deal with databases in organizations. We conclude the chapter with a discussion of basic concepts in artificial intelligence (AI) and expert systems (ES).

The field of databases and database management is extensive and an in-depth treatment of DBMS is beyond the scope of this chapter. However, we present sufficient background material in this chapter to provide a foundation for the discussion of database auditing in Chapter 18.

LEARNING OBJECTIVES

By the time you have completed this chapter, you should be able to:

1. Describe microcomputer hardware elements and types of software.
2. Explain telecommunication and network concepts.
3. Identify the hierarchy of data.
4. Discuss database concepts such as schema, subschema, data dictionary, logical structure, and database management systems.
5. State some of the relevant concepts of artificial intelligence and expert systems.

Table 17.1   Computer Classification by Price

| | Price | |
Type	Low	High
Microcomputer	$ 50	$ 20,000
Workstations	10,000	30,000
Minicomputer	30,000	100,000
Medium (size)	100,000	1,000,000
Large (size)	1,000,000	5,000,000

17.2 MICROCOMPUTERS

Despite major changes in price and marketing of computers, price is still the best criterion for classifying computers of different sizes. Thus, for purposes of discussion in this chapter, we classify computer types on the basis of the purchase price of an entire system. Table 17.1 shows this classification.

The microcomputer market has been the most volatile, particularly in terms of price. Much of the instability in prices has been driven by an exponential decrease in memory and other chip prices. For example, the price of a 256-kilobit RAM chip plummeted from $38.00 to $2.10 from 1984 to 1985. Price stability may be some years away and may not be attained until machines that we can hardly visualize today come into existence.

Within the microcomputer market, there are several subdivisions: (1) home and hobby; (2) education; (3) technical; (4) business; and (5) workstations. Workstations may not fall within the microcomputer price range because a full workstation configuration can cost as much as $30,000. Workstations for professionals (such as the IBM PC RT or the IBM PS/2 Model 80) will eventually drop substantially in price; they often have the power of current models of minicomputers and even some medium-size computers.

SYSTEM CONFIGURATION AND DATA STORAGE

Figure 17.1 shows the basic system configuration for the microcomputer (personal computer, or PC).[1] The central processing unit (CPU) is supported by random access memory (RAM) and read only memory (ROM) storage. Random access memory is used to store part of the operating system and the user programs that are currently being accessed; ROM usually contains often-accessed parts of the operating system and may be a resident inter-preter such as BASIC. Some lap-top computers (such as the HP 110) are now supplied with software in the form of word processors and spread-sheets on a chip.

The main hardware elements of the microcomputer are linked by a *data bus,* which serves as the main conduit for data between the CPU, main memory, and other devices. When data travels in this common bus, it reaches the different hardware elements that identify which data flows are to be received and which are to be ignored.

The operating system (typically CP/M, DOS or UNIX) controls the main functions of the microcomputer. The operating system monitors the different hardware elements, provides a language for the performance of certain *utility* functions, helps in system management, provides some ac-counting functions, limits user access, and so on. Many hardware and data transfer functions that are now performed by external operating systems are progressively being incorporated into the microprocessor.

When a micro is started ("booted"), its wired-in intelligence typically checks its memory, looks for the operating system and passes control to this system that loads itself partially into the main memory.

Figure 17.1   Microcomputer System Configuration

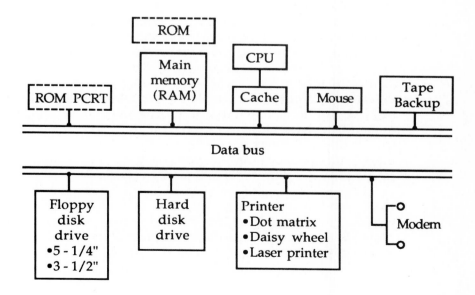

Table 17.2   Personal Computer Sales in 1981 and 1982 (revenues in $ millions)

Company	1982 PC Revenues	1981 PC Revenues	Percent Increase
Apple Computer	664	401	65.5
IBM	500	N/A	N/A
Tandy	466	293	59.1
Commodore	368	184	99.4
Hewlett-Packard	235	195	20.6
Texas Instruments	233	144	61.4
Digital Equipment	200	N/A	N/A

The basic classification of CPU chips is currently divided between 8- (e.g., Z-80, 6502), 16- (e.g., Intel 8088, Motorola 6800) and 32-bit (e.g., Motorola 68010, 68020, Intel 80386 and IBM 801) machines. The generation of 32-bit supermicros is rapidly expanding. Typically a 32-bit machine is more powerful and has the possibility of larger direct access space than a 16 bit machine and so on.

Programs and data are kept in floppy disk (diskette) devices that can typically store 200K–1.2M bytes of information. Recall from Chapter 2 that a *bit* of information typically relates to the existence (or nonexistence) of a magnetic mark in a particular position (logical *yes* or *no*) and that a *byte* is typically composed of 8 bits, allowing for the storage of $2^8 = 256$ (or $2^7 = 128$ if a bit is held for parity control) different potential combinations of bits. In practical terms, a byte contains a character. Therefore an 8 1/2" x 11" page with 60 characters per line and 50 lines will contain (60)(50) = 3000, or 3K, characters (bytes). Consequently, a 386K diskette (for an IBM PC) can store more than 126 pages of data, and 60 diskettes can store enough data to fully back up a 20 megabyte (20M), or 20 million byte, hard disk.

There is a growing popularity of direct address magnetic Winchester disks (hard disks) that can store something between 10 to 140 megabytes of information. An IBM PC XT is typically very similar to an IBM PC but instead of two floppy disk units, it will have a floppy disk drive and a 10M hard disk. The price of these hard disk devices has been decreasing very rapidly. The new family of IBM PS2 systems, ranging from model 30 to 80, is rapidly becoming the new industry standard. It now uses a new operating system, OS/2.

Figure 17.2 The Business Segment of the Personal Computer Market

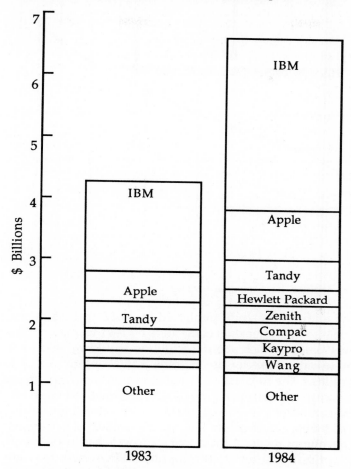

Source: Adapted from Infoworld, Future Computing and Data Analysis.

GROWTH IN MICROCOMPUTER UTILIZATION

The growth in the microcomputer market from 1981 to 1982 was about 61 percent. The entry of IBM into the market in mid-1981 prompted speculation that the company would become dominant in the PC market as it is in the mainframe market, which is now a reality, particularly in the business segment of the PC market. Table 17.2 shows sales by the major manufacturers of microcomputers in 1981 and 1982; Figure 17.2 shows sales in the business segment of the market in 1983 and 1984. By 1985, IBM's share of this segment topped 50 percent.

Figure 17.3   Projection of Microcomputer Purchases

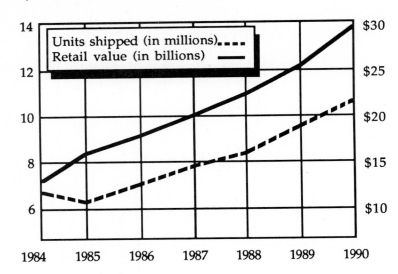

Source: Adapted from multiple reviews.

The author of a study published in *BYTE* in 1983 predicted the shipment of 11 million personal computers by 1991 (compared to about 2.2 million in 1983), of which about 2.5 million would be sold to businesses, 2.2 million to individuals for use at home, and about 0.5 million to educational institutions.[2] The forecast of 11 million units compares favorably with the 1985 forecast shown in Figure 17.3. The trend is toward highly decentralized computer power and many decentralized applications. Auditors must add these conditions to the concerns indicated in Chapters 1 and 2.

The microprocessor industry's growth has been surpassed by the growth of software for microcomputers. Microcomputers are used extensively as word processing stations in small businesses. The use of word processors and other software accelerated the need for printed outputs; the three basic types of printers marketed are the dot printer, letter quality (daisy wheel) printer, and laser printer. The increasing number of business applications available for microcomputers and used in small businesses requires special auditing attention, and care controls. Microcomputers are also valuable auditing tools, which we discuss in Chapter 20.

ADVANCES IN TECHNOLOGY

The video-game market, once heralded as an area of major growth for the future, was rapidly engulfed by aggressive development of home computers, which now can even be programmed for applications ranging from the control of a variety of home devices to videotext and telecommunications. A number of computer games found their way into corporate mainframes, often creating distractions and wasting resources. However, a new generation of management games and simulation software is evolving from computer games and is providing valid management training applications.

At the beginning of 1983, APPLE announced its revolutionary LISA system, featuring a 16-bit machine, and integrated software that calculated, stored data, edited text, drew graphs, and allowed interactive programming. The LISA system was quickly replaced by the next generation of microcomputers having user-friendly features and a wide range of software at the user's fingertips. The Amiga and Atari dominate the market for smaller systems; the Macintosh and IBM PCs dominate the middle range; and the IBM PS/2 Model 80, Apollo, and Sun III workstations dominate the higher range.

In 1987 IBM announced an entire new line of microcomputers (IBM Personal Systems/2, models 30, 50, 60, and 80) which are expected to determine universal standards for the ensuing 3–5 years. Figure 17.4 displays the main characteristics of these machines. They continue the DOS operating system dominance with version 3.3, and add multitasking and windowing capabilities. Their speed ranges from 1.9 to 7.6 times the speed of the traditional IBM PC/XT. Furthermore, the IBM PS/2 series presents greatly enhanced graphics, greater memories and the optional use of optical disk drives for large storage capacity. The optical drive uses WORM (Write Once Read Many times) technology, each disk can store 200 megabytes of information, and the Model 80 can take up to 8 of such disks.

Another important development is the advent of a full generation of portable (15–30 lb.) and lap-top (5–10 lb.) microcomputers, featuring integrated software, a full-fledged configuration (except for printers), and different degrees of portability. The 1986 IRS award to Zenith of a $27 million contract to supply 15,000–18,000 Z-171 portables that weigh 15 pounds, are IBM-compatible and have 2 floppy-disk drives, built-in modem, 512K of memory, and green backlit screens with liquid crystal display (LCD) technology,[3] is expected to spur market acceptance of portables.

The most popular operating systems are CP/M (nearly the standard for non-APPLE 8-bit machines), DOS (IBM PC), and UNIX (developed by Bell Laboratories and expected to be the standard for 32-bit machines). These operating systems usually are accompanied by a modest version of the BASIC language. Other programming languages often purchased by microcomputer users are the C language and Pascal. In addition to the demand for general purpose programming languages, microcomputer users have insatiable appetites for public domain and certain proprietary software.

Figure 17.4 Characteristics of the IBM Personal System/2

	Model 30	Model 50	Model 60	Model 80
Potential system speed	Up to 2.5 times PC XT	Up to 2 times PC AT	Up to 2 times PC AT	Up to 3.5 times PC AT
Microprocessor	8088	80286	80286	80388
Standard memory Expandable to	640KB[1]	1MB[1] 7MB	1MB 15MB	Up to 2MB 16MB
Diskettes used	3.5–inch, 720KB	3.5–inch, 1.44MB	3.5–inch, 1.44MB	3.5–inch, 1.44MB
Fixed disk[2]	20MB	20MB	44, 70MB	44, 70, 115MB
Additional options			44, 70, 115MB	44, 70, 115MB
Maximum configuration[3]	20MB	20MB	185MB	230MB
Expansion slots	3	3	7	7
Operating system(s)	PC DOS 3.3	PC DOS 3.3 and Operating System/2	PC DOS 3.3 and Operating System/2	PC DOS 3.3 and Operating 2 System/2
Availability	now	now	now	July–Dec. '87
Price	$1,695–$2,295	$3,595	$5,295–$6,295	$6,995–10,995

[1] KB = kilobyte; MB = megabyte

[2] Model 30 also comes in a diskette-based configuration.

[3] Models with 44MB fixed disk are expandable to 88MB.

Source: International Business Machines Corporation.

Three types of software of major interest are *word processors* (such as Wordstar and Microsoft's Word), *spreadsheets* (such as Visicalc, Supercalc, and Lotus 1-2-3), and *databases* (such as Dbase III). A 1985 survey of PC users in business indicated that about 80 percent utilized spreadsheets, 75 percent used PCs for other types of financial analysis, 70 percent utilized word processing, 55 percent generated graphics, 50 percent used databases, and 20 percent made use of other applications. In addition, memory-resident software (such as Borland's SIDEKICK)[4] represent an increasingly large share of the software market. This type of software reduces available memory but serves a variety of important functions. Among these functions we find expansions to the DOS procedures, resident dictionaries and run-time spreadsheets.

The rapid evolution toward workstations and office automation brought about by the explosion in microprocessor and software technology has created a great need for compatibility and adequate communication. In the future, auditors will use memory-resident software as data and system integrity evaluation devices in self-contained computing machines, along with further technological advances that we are not even aware of today. Thus microcomputers (in conjunction with telecommunications) are changing the entire auditing process.[5]

17.3 TELECOMMUNICATION NETWORKS

In 1980, more than 200 billion data transactions were transmitted over telecommunication lines in the United States. That is a staggering number, but the frequency of data communication undoubtedly has grown and will probably continue to grow dramatically over the next decade. The advent of microcomputers, LANs, IBM's SNA architecture, cable TV, and videotext impose an unprecedented set of requirements on communication media. For example, an office can now have a LAN (local area network), which allows independent stations to send mail, transfer files, and share a common database. The exponential growth projected for the use of LANs is expected to be spurred, in part, by a similar decline in price, as shown in Figure 17.5. By 1990, more than 1.5 million workstations are expected to be connected to a LAN, with the average price per connection decreasing to about one-fifth the current cost.

Typical communication needs of businesses include

- computer terminal communication;
- monitoring of production devices;
- remote transmission of data gathered locally;
- transfer of data to different locations;
- computer-to-computer communication;
- inquiry systems;
- facsimile transmission; and
- electronic mail.

Auditors generally rely on the integrity of communication links because the technological investment necessary to intercept communications usually makes committing this type of fraud uneconomical. However, auditors should be aware of the basic principles, the potential capabilities, and issues involved in telecommunication and networks.

There are two categories of data transmission: on-line and off-line. On-line data transmission may entail the monitoring of EDP devices, interactive use of computers, and prompt updating of databases. Off-line data transmission takes advantage of idle communication routes during periods

Figure 17.5   Projected LAN Use and Connection Cost

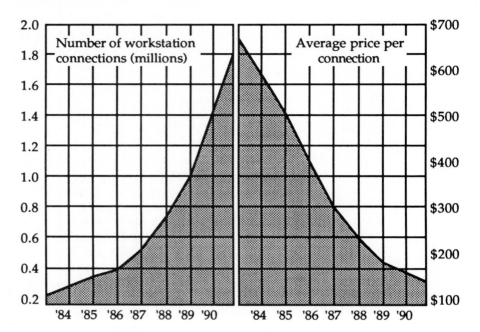

of slack communication demand. Most transmission is either duplex (sending and receiving at the same time) or half-duplex. Communication links are either synchronous (continuous data transmission) or asynchronous (also called stop and go) for communication by terminals or other applications.

The transmission speed is typically 120 cps (cycles per second, or bauds in two state lines) for teletypes, 300 bauds for hard copy terminals and higher at baud rates of 1200, 2400, 4800 or even 9600 for screen displays or computer to computer communication.

The need for communication between computers and between terminals and computers generated major research and commercial interest in the EDP community. Major networks, such as ARPANET and BITNET, were developed to link educational institutions. Network software and de facto standards, such as SNA and Ethernet, represent further advances. Two basic communication codes are currently used in the computer industry: the ASCII code of the standard-setting group of mainframe manufacturers and the PC industry (excluding IBM); and the EBCDIC code used in IBM mainframes and IBM-compatible machines.

Auditors will be increasingly concerned about the effect of telecommunication on system security. Most large organizational systems allow remote access to computers containing sensitive information. Protection is effected by user accounts (with selective access to applications and data), passwords, and intrinsic knowledge about the systems in question. In addition, large systems often keep logs on data access and path for all users.

In a network users can access most types of computers from a remote location. For this purpose, a personal computer with a modem (and its indigenous software) can emulate a computer terminal. The user must specify an acceptable transmission speed, echo (duplex or half-duplex), parity, handshake, and the like. The user can find these parameters if he or she knows the type of hardware at the other end or by judicious trial and error.

When connected to the computer, the user types in his or her identification number and the password, which give access to the system application desired. The user may transfer information from a file by simply logging the PC user's communication or by more sophisticated means involving resident software on the mainframe that communicate and transfer information to the microcomputer. Kermit is one such communication software package that is relatively inexpensive and very popular.[6] In addition, UNIX systems have UUCPs (UNIX to UNIX communication protocols) that allow automatic machine communication and file updates. In addition, within the UNIX environment, the CU protocol allows terminal emulation.

17.4 DATABASES

Traditionally, EDP systems were designed with a set of programs acting on a series of independent files. Different systems were often developed independently; systems analysts and programmers might use similar data, fields, records and files—usually in different formats—but store them on different recording media. Rapidly increasing complexity, cost, and technological change led to the development of databases, in which most files and records are fully compatible and are centrally created, tested, managed, updated, and purged. The database approach offers major advantages to organizations but also involves some perils and costs.

The fundamental characteristics of databases are:

- Physical and logical data independence.
- Rapid response to queries.
- Controlled redundancy.
- Versatility in data representation.
- Protection of data against undue access.
- Security of data against mishaps.

Table 17.3   Data Hierarchy

Designation	Representation	Example
Element	x	L
Field	xxxx	Linn
Record	!xxxx!yyyy!zzzzzzzz!	Linn 8350 12/01/47
File	A set of records	Payroll
Segment	A subset of records	Employees of Division A
Database	A set of files	Personnel records
Database cluster	A set of databases	Corporate records

DEFINITIONS AND CONCEPTS

We define a **database** as a collection of data stored together, with controlled redundancy, to serve one or more applications in an efficient manner. A **database cluster** is a set of databases that contain different types of data but typically relate to the same organizational entity. Data are stored in such a way that they are independent of the programs that make use of them. A standard, controlled method is used to change, add, recover, and eliminate database items. Table 17.3 is an elaboration of the different levels of data aggregation that we presented in Chapter 2.

The two basic concepts in databanks are **entities** and **attributes**. An entity is the person, object, or class of items about which data are collected. Attributes are the characteristics of an entity that define the types of data to be collected. For example, an employee is an entity in this context, and the employee's attributes include his or her name, employee number, date of employment, title, salary level, department, and similar information. A product held in inventory is also an entity, and its attributes encompass inventory stock number, location, quantity, extended cost, and other relevant information.

Database software for mainframe computers is typically called a **database management system** (DBMS). The most popular of these systems are IBM's IMS and Cincom's Total and Adabas. A DBMS typically provides the interface between an application and the data. Figure 17.6 illustrates the DBMS process. Application programs address data by a name that is known by the data dictionary (DD). The data dictionary typically entails a matrix that relates field names, aliases, format, physical location, schema, and subschema. These are defined later in this section. The DBMS finds this name and relates it to data structures, data format and an indication of the location of the data. Data is retrieved by the DBMS and delivered to the application program.

Figure 17.6   Steps in the DBMS Process

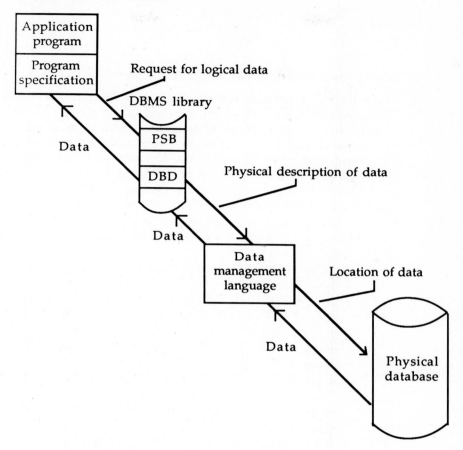

Data are defined in two ways: logically and physically. Logical definition of data corresponds to the particular attributes of the data. Physical definition of data corresponds to the physical location and recorded values of the data. In databases, records are identified by **keys**. A primary key is a singular field that identifies a particular record (such as employee number or inventory item number). A **direct file** contains the primary key and all the attributes of each record. An **indirect file** contains the identifiers of each entity that possess a certain attribute. For example, a direct file may hold all the attributes of employee Jane Savage, while an indirect file may hold all the employee numbers of personnel assigned to the management consulting services department.

A **schema** is the logical description of a database, which summarizes the type and relationships of the data being used. It gives the names of the entities and their attributes and specifies their relationships. A **sub-**

schema is a further breakdown or classification of those same characteristics. A schema and a subschema can be thought of as *logical views* of the system.

AN EXAMPLE OF DATABASE DEVELOPMENT

Let's turn to a hypothetical description of the development of a traditional system as a means of illustrating database concepts. You should recognize that this description, of necessity, is an oversimplification.

A small university in a northeastern state, Emanon University (EU) has existed for more than 50 years. The administration acquired the university's first medium-size computer in order to manage administrative functions more effectively. The first system included an application, programmed in COBOL, for the registrar's office and consisted of (1) a master student file; (2) posting of grades to the master file; and (3) updating the master file with changes in students' names, grade-point averages, admissions, transfers, and the like.

This system proved to be reliable and cost-effective, so the bursar's office decided to implement a student tuition-control system. This system utilizes a different student master file because some students have tuition waivers or are not dormitory residents. After experimental runs of the new system the EDP staff realized that its system design creates major updating problems and potential inconsistencies. In addition, other planned applications will require information from both the registrar and bursar's systems (such as student records, class lists, faculty course coverage, and so on).

A meeting involving administrative and academic department heads and EDP staff leads to a decision to establish an integrated management information system for EU. The registrar and bursar's systems are to be converted to two independent, but related, systems using the same database. The first step is to set up a database dictionary that will progressively allow full development of a database cluster for the university's EDP systems. The initial DD is a simple matrix, as shown in Table 17.4.

This data dictionary (DD) allows data independence if it is properly used. Changes in the format or location of the data will be entered directly in the DD, and programs used to read the data will always call up the table to access the data. Some fields, such as amount, present a certain degree of controlled redundancy, since Amt, for example, is defined as the sum of Tuitd - Payrec over time.

Table 17.4 Emanon University's Initial Data Dictionary

Field Name	Field Description	Format	Location*
ID	Student ID	f4.0	TSi
Name	Student Name	x20	DSi
Address	Student Address	x60	DSi
Addrho	Home Address	x60	TBi
Stat	Student status	f1.0	DSi
Amt	Amount Due	f8.2	DSi
Grds	Grades	20x10	TSit
Blg	Billing Instructions	x100	TBi
Payrec	Payment Records	20F8.2	TSit
Tuitd	Tuition Due	20F8.2	TSit
Other	Observations	x2000	TSit

*Where location defines the storage device (or logical location) of the field. For example disk ITCH01 or tape TS53.

The logical structure of student files could be designed hierarchically, relating students to their respective colleges and specialties, as shown in Figure 17.7 for the College of Engineering, Department of Mechanical Engineering.

After utilizing the DD for a few years, the university acquired a database management system (DBMS) to facilitate the use of common files. Some of the basic functions of this DBMS are listed, along with examples in Table 17.5.

Figure 17.6 showed in detail the steps in DBMS usage: (1) an application program submits a data request to the DBMS; (2) the DBMS assumes control and accesses its schema and/or subschema, searching for the variable, format, and relationships; (3) it finds the logical description and also provides the corresponding physical description of the data, which is transmitted to the computer's operating system for use in retrieval; (4) the operating system searches for the physical location and finds the data; (5) the data are retrieved and transferred to temporary storage for use by the application program; (6) the data are called up to the working area of the application program; and (7) the DBMS returns control to the application program.

Figure 17.7   Hierarchical Logical Structure for Student Files: College of Engineering,
Emanon University

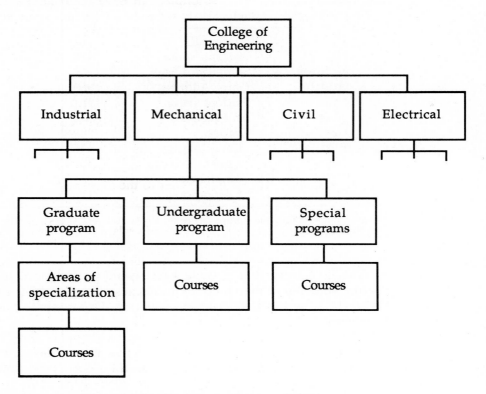

Table 17.5   Selected Functions of the Emanon University DBMS

Function	Example
Query	Student record retrieval
	Student payment record retrieval
Selective query	Search for students with GPA of less than 2.0 and on scholarship
Updating	Adding new students, grades
Purging	Deleting payment records after 3 years
Primary key	Student ID number
Secondary keys	Department code
	Probationary status
Summarization	Total outstanding tuition (aged)
Data independence	Programs containing only symbolic names for variables (no format, no location)

MICROCOMPUTER DATABASES

Databases have become commonplace in the age of the microcomputer, and a large number of database software packages for microcomputers are available. In 1984, Bond catalogued 47 of these systems, comparing hardware requirements, price, operating systems, allowed data structures, limitations, and other characteristics.[7] Krojewski classified microcomputer databases as six overlapping types,[8] of which the following is a modification.

1. **File management system:** Allows the storage of data in records and fields. These records and fields are analogous to a card file in which the cards may be organized in primary-key order but lists may be based on secondary keys.
2. **Relational database:** Similar to the file management system but allows the combination of different files based on a common field.
3. **Hierarchical database:** Records related in preset hierarchies.
4. **Network database:** Like a relational database but does not require one-to-one relationships. Records may relate to each other on a many-to-many basis. (See Figure 17.8.)
5. **Free-format database:** Information stored in any potential format. Knowledge about data characteristics used for retrieval and management purposes.

In addition to these structural considerations, databases can be classified according to the accessibility and use of the data. Thus databases may also be classified as single-user, cluster-user, and multiple-user systems. Use of an IBM PC with DOS and dBASE III to control inventory at a particular location is an example of a single-user system. Cluster users can be several typists in a typing pool who access and store information on common disk drives.

17.5 ARTIFICIAL INTELLIGENCE AND EXPERT SYSTEMS

Artificial Intelligence is a widely used expression with many different meanings to different publics. Typically the public understood it as the ability to develop some form of "intelligent" behavior through artificial (human made) devices.

Figure 17.8   Illustration of a Network Database Structure

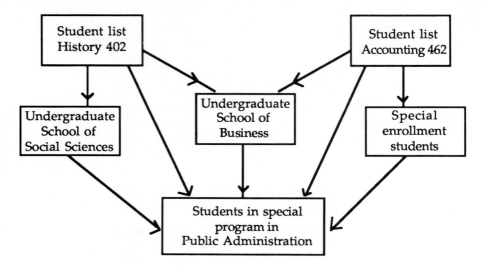

The evolution of the field of "Artificial Intelligence" (AI) can be better understood by the discussion of its subfields. In a 1965 paper, Dreyfus complained about "stagnation" in the field of artificial intelligence (AI). He divided the field into four major subareas

1. Game playing.
2. Problem solving.
3. Language translation.
4. Pattern recognition.

Few major advances in AI were made until the late 1970s, when new developments in both hardware and software and some major conceptual leaps resulted in substantial progress. Research in AI evolved from the search for generalizable solutions and algorithms based on the concept of partial solution of problems by means of expertise. This opened the way to examination of problems having no clearcut solution but for which the application of expert knowledge could improve the quality of outcomes. In 1985 the field of AI can be now divided into four principal areas that portray the state-of-the-art: 1) expert systems, 2) visualization systems, 3) natural languages, and 4) robotics. Of particular interest to auditors was the development of expert systems (ES) in several application areas.[9] These systems showed that available human expertise could model systems for solving complex problems to aid the decision-making process.

Expertise consists of knowledge about a particular domain (area of knowledge) an understanding of **domain** problems, and the skills needed to solve, or at least partially solve, some of these problems.

We can define knowledge as descriptions, relationships, and procedures in some domain of interest. For example, an auditor has knowledge about a series of facts relative to accounting rules (as prescribed in GAAP and GAAS) and data. Among these rules, for example, are how to compute depreciation and methods to measure inventory. On the other hand, auditors have an intuitive feeling for certain data relationships, such as when a company is in financial distress, it may have cash flow problems; that is, a company preparing to file for Chapter 11 reorganization may hoard cash, which is reflected in the company's statement of sources and uses of funds. In addition, the auditor knows that the controller is responsible for accounting practices and the treasurer for cash flow management. These relationships, descriptions, and procedures comprise the auditor's **knowledge base.**

Knowledge in most domains is either public or private. **Public knowledge** is knowledge that is articulated, disseminated, and propagated through technical literature, professional journals, and formal education. **Private knowledge** is the knowledge that an individual possesses, either consciously or unconsciously. For example, an auditor who is an expert in internal control system evaluation develops a set of rules to identify a single indicator that would tell the auditor that further investigation of a particular item is required. These rules may not be in the accounting firm's formal audit rules but are clear in the mind of the auditor. The auditor applies these heuristic rules consciously and, when asked, can easily state them.

On the other hand, an auditor may have some internal control cues, each of which indicates some trouble but does not necessarily determine the need for further action. By combining these cues, the auditor can determine the need for further audit examination. However, the auditor may have difficulty in articulating these rules when asked to do so. This unconscious rule combination process is a product of experience and may lead to a method for determining how computer software should perform these functions. **Knowledge engineers** often use a series of techniques when trying to get experts to articulate their unconscious processes. Among these techniques are the use of real-life examples as cases, think-aloud problem solving, panels of experts who evaluate outcomes, problems having a known outcome to evaluate problem-solving approaches, and the like. The idea of using rules to represent expert knowledge has permeated expert systems work.

DEVELOPMENTS IN ES APPLICATIONS

The DENDRAL program[10] involved translating—and, ultimately, encoding for EDP use—the heuristic knowledge of expert chemists into rules that controlled the search for possible molecular structures, making it possible to obtain satisfactory answers with a fraction of the effort. CASNET[11] was developed to aid in the diagnosis and therapy of glaucoma and has been rated by professionals as having a performance level close to that of human experts. It led to a methodology for modeling diseases, in general, and to the development of the software package EXPERT, a tool that has been applied in the diagnosis of rheumatology and endocrinology, specifically.

The MACSYMA program[12] has achieved a high level of competence in handling the symbolic computations associated with applied analysis. CADUCEUS[13] and MYCIN[14] address different medical diagnosis problems. CADUCEUS (also known as INTERNIST–1) handles a large semantic network of relationships (some 100,000 associations) between diseases and symptoms in internal medicine. About 400 rules comprise MYCIN, which deals with the diagnosis and treatment of infectious blood diseases.

Efforts of researchers at Carnegie-Mellon University, in conjunction with Digital Equipment Corporation, led to the development of R1,[15] an expert system used to configure DEC VAX computer systems. Another interesting application of expert systems is speech–understanding systems. HEARSAY–II incorporates a 1000-word vocabulary, and "its skill rivals that of a ten-year-old child."[16]

Figure 17.9 shows the evolution of selected expert systems during the past 20 years. Generic languages for expert systems emerged as important by-products of initial ES efforts. The MYCIN effort led to EMYCIN; Rand Corporation's efforts led to ROSIE;[17] the work at Carnegie-Mellon University led to the development of the OPS series of production system languages;[18] and the HEARSAY work led to AGE.

Traditionally, AI-oriented systems were programmed in LISP,[19] a symbol manipulation language. A wide variety of LISP dialects is now used in AI/ES applications, including some versions for microcomputers. Another popular AI programming language is PROLOG.[20] All of these programming languages are complemented in the arsenal of AI/ES designers by a set of **knowledge engineering languages** (ES shells), such as ART, KEE, EMYCIN, and ROSIE. In addition, owing to the intensive computing environment required for AI/ES, some special hardware (such as SYMBOLICS and Xerox machines) are emerging for use in such work.

These efforts have shaped much of today's work in expert systems. Recent noteworthy efforts include applications in interpreting oil drilling data (Schlumberger), diagnosing equipment failures, assessing military threats, targeting for weapons systems, designing VLSI, and managing crises. Efforts in the areas of accounting and auditing applications have been less successful.

Figure 17.9 Evolution of Selected Expert Systems and Expert System Building Languages

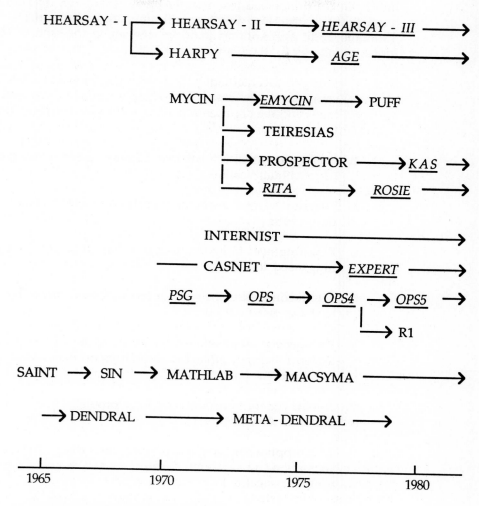

Note: Italics indicate system building languages.

Source: Adapted from Frederick Hayes-Roth, Donald A. Waterman, and Douglas B. Lenat (Eds.), *Building Expert Systems.* Reading, Mass.: Addison-Wesley, 1983.

AI/ES, ACCOUNTING, AND AUDITING

Expert systems have been applied to EDP problems such as (1) design; (2) prediction; (3) diagnosis; (4) monitoring; (5) planning; (6) debugging; (7) repair; (8) instruction; (9) interpretation; and (10) control functions. Potential audit applications could be developed for each of these functions, as follows:

1. **Design**—reconstructing the path of data flow in an integrated computer system based on client documentation, some program logic, and the organization's procedures for approval and authorization.

2. **Prediction**—examining relevant figures and issuing a going-concern qualification.

3. **Diagnosis**—inferring breakdown in controls from patterns in daily sales.

4. **Planning**—planning the steps in the audit process (audit planning).

5. **Monitoring**—keeping track of transactions in an on-line system to detect potential problems.

6. **Debugging**—evaluating the integrity of particular computer systems that may affect the accounting process and identifying problems.

7. **Repair**—identifying software logic problems and their automatic correction.

8. **Instruction**—resolving real problems and using ES self-documentation and justification features for training new accountants (or auditors).

9. **Interpretation**—examining variances in compliance with internal control standards and interpreting them as relevant or meaningless.

10. **Control**—interpreting, predicting, repairing, and monitoring system behavior.

In addition to these generic audit areas, some accounting-related areas also deserve ES consideration: providing tax advice, estimating insurance coverage, preparing and analyzing consolidation models, examining the existing body of precedents (legal, audit) and indexing the standards in GAAP and GAAS.

In 1984, 1986, and 1988, the School of Accountancy of the University of Southern California sponsored three symposia on "Decision Support Systems and Expert Systems" in auditing. During these symposia several researchers presented papers on their work in expert systems applications, particularly in the evaluation of internal controls and audit planning.

Many CPA firms are committed to programs of audit automation, and some of these efforts involve ES technology. Coopers & Lybrand's EXPERT-TAX aids in the process of tax-accrual assessment. Arthur Andersen has been working in the areas of audit planning and risk assessment. Peat, Marwick, Mitchell & Co. has developed an expert system for evaluating bank loan-loss reserves.

17.6 Summary

In this chapter, we added to the basic data processing concepts introduced in Chapter 2. The chapter covered basic principles and practice in the rapidly expanding fields of microcomputers, telecommunications, databases, and an introduction to artificial intelligence (AI) and expert systems (ES).

Microcomputers (personal computers) can be classified according to primary use: home and hobby, education, technical, business, and workstations. Their main hardware elements are similar to those of mainframe computers and include the CPU, main memory (ROM and RAM), disk storage devices, printers, keyboard and screen. The most commonly used software are operating systems, interpreters, word processors, and spreadsheet calculators. The capabilities of PCs can be expanded by the addition of communications software and a communications modem.

The rapid growth of EDP and widespread use of remote access devices, databases and computer-to-computer communication, generated a demand for communication technology that expanded exponentially. This demand was met by development of a wide range of products and still the absence of an accepted communication standard.

The rapid emergence of databases was supported by the use of DBMSs and/or DBDs. The scope of such systems is expanding, allowing for greater recognition of organization-wide data interrelationships and definition of flexible data. These systems represent a major breakthrough in physical and logical EDP design and will be used widely in the home and by organizations in the years ahead. Auditors will have to become proficient in the utilization of DBMS and DBD technical capabilities and personally be able to design and examine their interfaces, as well as access data directly, without third-party assistance.

In the last part of the chapter, we discussed briefly the emerging fields of artificial intelligence and expert systems. Expert systems were identified as an area of major interest to auditors. Audit planning, audit judgment, internal control evaluation and attestations are areas where ES may prove to have major impact.

In a brief overview of ES, we described some of the original efforts, their conceptual contributions, and some current work in ES applications. In the concluding part of that section, we examined potential ES applications to auditing.

Questions

1. State the method used to distinguish among microcomputers, mini-computers, medium-sized computers, and large computers.
2. What are the major categories of microcomputers?
3. What are the major elements of a microcomputer system?
4. What is a Local Area Network (LAN)? What kind of benefits can it provide to microcomputer users?
5. What are some of the major features of communications software? Describe functions, parameters, and difficulties.
6. Define schema and subschema. Why do they make databases such powerful programming tools?
7. What is a data dictionary?
8. Describe the operation of a DBMS in relation to an application program.
9. What is artificial intelligence? How does it relate to expert systems?
10. What are the main characteristics of expert systems?
11. Describe one of the early applications of ES and its main contribution to the field.
12. Describe five areas of auditing that may be a prime target for ES application.

Problems

1. What are some of the problems with the distinction made among various types of computers in this chapter? Do you think that these distinctions will continue?
2. Survey the various uses to which the microcomputer is put on your campus. How do they compare with those identified in the text? Do you think that this range of use will change in the future? If so, why and how?
3. Find out from your campus computer center if it utilizes dial-up telephone equipment. Obtain the technical specification to set up a modem to use this service. Identify all the steps you have to take to sign on through a remote line.
4. Locate a written description of one of the popular PC database packages. Compare the documentation for that package to the descriptions provided in this chapter and relate the two.
5. What audit applications can you envision for microcomputer communication devices and databases? Talk to a representative of a local or national accounting firm to determine whether it uses any of this new computer technology.
6. Search through the computer literature for a recent (and successful) application of ES. Describe the problem, objectives, software, and hardware used; any implementation problems of interest; and your assessment of the value of the application.
7. Obtain the use of a simple expert system shell. Examine its manual, features, and potential use. Flowchart the process by which an auditor chooses the size of a sample in a receivables audit. Prepare ten rules that should be followed under certain contingencies. Program the shell with those roles. Test your system. Write up your findings and evaluate your results.

Notes

1. For further information about microcomputers, see Loebbecke, J., and Vasarhelyi, M. A., *Microcomputers: Applications to Business Problems.* Homewood, Illinois: Richard D. Irwin, 1986.

2. Blundell, G. S., "Personal Computers in the Eighties," *BYTE,* January 1983, pp. 166–182.

3. *INFOWORLD*, "IRS Awards Contract to Zenith," March 3, 1986, pp. 1–4.

4. Bannister, Hank, "RAM-Resident Programs Establish Their Space," INFOWORLD, December 9, 1985, pp. 1–14.

5. For further information on the subject, see Vasarhelyi, M. A., "Automation and Changes in the Audit Process," *Auditing: A Journal of Theory and Practice*, Fall 1984, (1):100–106.

6. DaCruz, F., and Catchings, B., "Kermit: A File-Transfer Protocol for Universities, Part 1: Design Considerations and Specifications," *BYTE*, June 1984, pp. 255–78.

7. Bond, George, "A Database Catalog," *BYTE*, October 1984, pp. 227–238.

8. Krojewski, Rich, "Database Types," *BYTE*, October 1984, pp. 137–42.

9. See Hayes-Roth, Frederick, Waterman, Donald A., and Lenat, Douglas B. (Eds.), *Building Expert Systems*. Reading, Mass.: Addison-Wesley, 1983.

10. Buchanan, B. G., and Feigenbaum, E. A., "DENDRAL and Meta-DENDRAL: Their Applications Dimension," *Artificial Intelligence*, 1978, 11:5–24.

11. Weiss, S. M., Kulikowski, C. A., and Safir, A., "A Model-Based Consultation System for the Long-Term Management of Glaucoma," IFCAI, 1977, 5:826–832.

12. Martin, W. A., and Fateman, R. J., "The MACSIMA System." *Proceedings of the Second Symposium on Symbolic and Algebraic Manipulation*, Los Angeles, 1971, pp. 59–71.

13. Pople, Jr., H. E., "Heuristic Methods for Imposing Structure on Ill-Structured Problems: The Structuring of Medical Diagnostics." In P. Szolovitz (Ed.), *Artificial Intelligence in Medicine*. American Association for the Advancement of Science. Boulder, Colo.: Westview Press, pp. 119–185.

14. "Computer-Based Medical Decision Making: From MYCIN to VM." In Shortliffe, II, W. J., and Hance, E. (Eds.), *Readings in Medical Artificial Intelligence*. Reading, Mass: Addison-Wesley, 1984.

15. McDermott, J., "R1: A Rule-Based Configurer of Computer Systems," *Technical Report CMU-CS-80-119*. Pittsburgh: Carnegie-Mellon University, Department of Computer Science, 1980.

16. Hayes-Roth, Waterman, and Lenat, p. 11.

17. ROSIE is a registered trademark of the Rand Corporation.

18. Forgy, C. L., "The OPS5 User's Manual," *Technical Report CMU-CS-81-135*. Pittsburgh: Carnegie-Mellon University, Computer Science Department.

19. Winston, P. H., and Horn, B. K. P., *LISP*. Reading, Mass.: Addison-Wesley, 1981.

20. Clocksin, W. F., and Mellish, C. S., *Programming in Prolog*. New York: Springer-Verlag, 1981.

Additional References

Cardenas, A. F. *Database Management Systems*. Boston: Allyn and Bacon, 1979.

Date, C. J. *An Introduction to Database Systems*. Reading, Mass.: Addison-Wesley, 1975.

Davis, G. B., and Cushing, Barry E. & Romney, Marshall B. Olson, *Accounting Information Systems and Business Organizations*. Reading, Mass: Addison-Wesley Publishing Company, 1987.

Chapter 18

Auditing Advanced Computer Systems

18.1 INTRODUCTION

*Advanced computer systems will have a direct impact
on the information used by management to establish
systems, strategies and policies. Specifically, advanced
systems will affect the internal processing of data, the
processing of data between firms and the user
orientation of the system.*[1]

As indicated by this quotation, advanced computer systems have several
unique implications for auditors because of the decreased applicability of
traditional audit techniques. As reliance and emphasis on the reliability
and integrity of computer systems increases, the auditor must take a more
active role in planning and controlling computerized facilities. Whereas
direct physical verification of control adequacy was once possible, the auditor must now ensure that the computer system itself is designed to provide the required level of many types of controls.

The effectiveness and integrity of the audit process depend on the integrity of the EDP system in an advanced computer environment. Therefore
the auditor must understand the implications for auditing of these advanced systems and take the initiative in designing controls and using the
computer for auditing purposes.

In this chapter, we deal first with auditing one-site/one-facility centralized EDP systems, both large and small. We then discuss auditing decentralized EDP systems, including electronic fund transfer (EFTS) systems,

telecommunications, and distributed data processing (DDP). Finally, we analyze the related areas of auditing hardware and software contracts.

LEARNING OBJECTIVES

By the time you have completed this chapter, you should be able to:

1. Identify the controls used in a centralized on-line, real-time EDP system.
2. Describe the relationship of database controls to audit procedures.
3. Evaluate control problems in the operation of small-business computer systems and auditing techniques required.
4. Explain control implications of electronic funds transfer systems.
5. Discuss the controls and audit concerns that are unique to minicomputer networks and distributed data processing systems.
6. State the audit issues involved in hardware and software contracts.

18.2 CENTRALIZED SYSTEMS

A centralized computer system has only one main processing site. Any large system can accommodate remote terminals, but the critical factor for control and auditing of centralized systems is the concentration of EDP personnel and functions in one location. Since all users of the system interact with the mainframe computer for all processing, the need for data security is great, whereas the need for redundant controls is not so important.

In this section we specifically discuss database management issues for large, integrated facilities and the growing use of minicomputers and microcomputers by small businesses. While these two topics represent the extremes of the computer-size spectrum, they raise many of the same issues, but also have some distinctly different aspects, with regard to controlling and auditing EDP systems. The capabilities of computers are changing so rapidly that defining what is a maxicomputer, a minicomputer, and a microcomputer is very difficult. In Chapter 17, we made the distinction based on relative costs. However, with regard to characteristics, many of the capabilities of yesterday's mainframe computers are embodied in today's small computers. Figure 18.1 shows the primary use characteristics of the three types of systems; note the system overlapping that is indicated.

Figure 18.1 System-use Characteristics

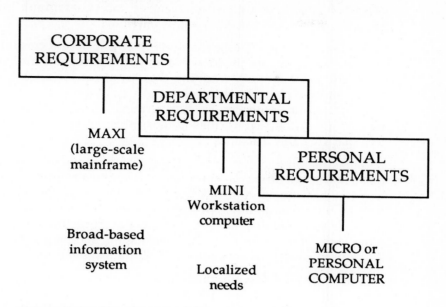

Source: William E. Perry, *Auditing the Small Business Computer,* p. 20.

LARGE-SCALE SYSTEMS

The basic steps in auditing a large-scale, centralized EDP facility are:

1. Gain a good understanding of the control system.
2. Identify control weaknesses and their likely effects.
3. Examine the processing of a few transactions to establish how well the controls are functioning.
4. Test system procedures on the basis of the control evaluation.
5. Determine the timing, nature, and extent of the audit.[2]

Thus the key to auditing a large-scale system lies in identifying and evaluating system controls. The five main points of control in a centralized real-time system are access controls, terminal controls, transmission-line controls (from remote terminals), the audit trail, and database controls.

Access Controls. Designed to decrease the exposure of the system to unauthorized access or use, access control is usually accomplished by means of identifying codes, identification/access magnetic cards, and passwords.

Access controls also encompass hardware, software, and data-protection procedures, such as authorization tables and program-use limits, which are usually based on a need-to-know determination.

Terminal Controls. Designed to supplement access controls, terminal controls focus on the physical protection of terminals and the areas in which they are located. Auditing these controls includes review of the administrative control over procedural steps followed by users, random observation and inspection tours of terminal areas, and review of the terminal-code check that verifies authorization of the user's access to the terminal area and machines.

Transmission-line Controls. Designed to prevent wiretapping and/or distortion of data transmissions, transmission-line controls include encryption (the basic method of protecting sensitive data) checks, and error-detecting codes. The auditor's primary concern is prevention of unauthorized access to data and that all such attempts be recorded in the system's operating logs. Dual transmission, retransmission, and alternative routing can all be used to test the reliability of data-transmission lines.

The Audit Trail. Usually thought of as a visible record of evidence, the audit trail enables the auditor to trace figures contained in statements or reports back to the point of processing and from processing back to the point of input. Real-time EDP systems substantially decrease or even eliminate the traditional audit trail of direct entry of data, decrease the availability of hard copy back-up lists and reports, allow for the random arrival and processing of data, as well as multiple access to and use of the system. These features require the creation of a new form of audit trail to ensure data integrity, without interfering with the efficiency of the system. Single-transaction control, such as serial numbering and completeness checks, combined with group transaction controls, such as time-control totals and a log of all incoming transactions, are replacing the more traditional audit trail documents. Such continuous monitoring can be combined with test-deck procedures to aid the auditor in detecting control weaknesses and verifying system processing.

Database Controls. In a large-scale, centralized EDP facility, efficient processing and data consistency entail the sharing of data files by several users. Additionally, several data files may contain cross-referenced material that must be updated each time related data elements are changed in other files. This joint use and data interdependence create unique problems for control and auditing. Therefore database controls must be more intricate than the other types of controls that we have mentioned.

Data files are designed for specific applications, so there are no logical relationships among the files. Within an integrated database system, each program has a unique logical link to the database, but the data themselves are shared by all applications. Although the database approach brings many advantages, it also creates new problems in terms of security and data integrity. In a database environment, many users with different security requirements, some online, have access to a common pool of data of varying degrees of sensitivity. Therefore, access to the data must be controlled.

Three interlinked methods of controlling database systems and ensuring their integrity are an on-line control system, the use of a data dictionary, and the appointment of a database administrator. Each of these solutions creates its own unique auditing problems, though.

In most on-line systems, a control program will reside in one partition, or segment, of the system's memory and control all on-line operations that interface with the operating system. Such control software is necessary to ensure the integrity of the operating system by denying access to systems development software and program debugging aids to users of an on-line production program. The purpose is to prevent concurrent access to programs and data that would enable a user to commit computer fraud. However, the integrity of the system is threatened whenever these control programs share a memory partition with application programs because the control program can be accessed without knowledge of the operating system. Auditors should therefore ensure that all access to control programs are monitored by the operating system.

Another important database control mechanism is the data dictionary. (See Chapter 17.) This documentation tool is designed to provide a standard definition for all data elements and segments of the database. It contains narrative and technical descriptions of the data and information pertaining to security, edit considerations, structure, and application use of the database system. The DD is a critical feature of proper management of a database system and, as such, must be closely controlled. Updated authority should reside jointly with the user and the database administrator, and the auditor should verify all such changes to ensure compliance with internal controls. Distribution of the data dictionary should be on a need-to-know basis only, and the auditor should make inquiries in order to make sure that no one, with perhaps the exception of the database administrator, has access to all the details of the entire DD. Finally, the DD is a high-cost asset that requires maintenance of duplicate back-up copies, the security of which must be ensured. Properly developed, maintained, and controlled, the data dictionary provides an invaluable documentation and audit tool.

The role of the database administrator (DBA) is to administer the database management system (DBMS). Some of the administrator's functions are to control access to the DBMS library by utility programs, devise procedures to prevent access to the DBMS when it is not being controlled by DBMS software, approve and log all changes in the DBMS library, and review the written documentation standards for all application programs before they are actually used. Because the database administrator has the sole authority to modify the DBMS library, the auditor must be concerned with controls over the administrator's actions. The control weaknesses here relate to inadequate separation of duties and the concentrated knowledge and access to utilities necessary to override database integrity safeguards. The auditor should ensure that the DBA's performance is controlled and that the DBA is required to take time off during the year. The system should be continuously monitored in order to detect all transactions initiated by the DBA. Finally, a back-up employee should always be available to replace the DBA to ensure the continuous processing and monitoring of DBMS transactions.

Table 18.1 presents a summary of control techniques and related functions for a database system. An auditor should consider using the following procedures for auditing a database system.

1. Review and test security requirements and procedures.
2. Review and test compliance with standards, procedures, and controls for system design, operations (including accessing and updating the system), and database administration.
3. Examine data definitions, language specifications, access logs, application program codes, job descriptions, storage-structure analysis reports and documentation for subschema generation to determine whether authorization and other control procedures are being followed properly.
4. Process actual transactions to determine whether the security mechanism is operating as it should.
5. Review the contents and determine the accuracy of the DD with respect to edit and validation rules, security measures, and maintenance procedures.
6. Review and test DD update and change procedures. Reconcile transaction trails to actual database controls.
7. Sample some logical views (subschema) containing data elements of accounting significance and ensure there is an owner identified and that the owner has approved any other use or access of the data elements.
8. Observe modifications made to the logical views (subschema) of database with proper authorization procedures.
9. Observe individuals as they work on database design, development, and modification and review written evidence that they submit about following proper procedures.

Table 18.1   Control Techniques and Related Control Functions

Techniques	Functions		
	Access/ Update	Coordination of Activities	Concentration of Resources
Access/Update Controls			
Restrict data resources and update functions to authorized users by passwords	X		
Restrict data resources and update functions to authorized users by sub-schema	X		
System Design Controls			
Implement application systems using a systems development life cycle tailored to consider the use of a DBMS		X	X
Implement a standardized approach for making modifications to application systems		X	X
Automatically generate data base description by the DD/DS		X	
Develop adequate transaction trails		X	
Consider the DBMS return codes during the detailed design phase	X	X	X
Data Base Administration Controls			
Assign responsibility for data ownership	X	X	
Centralize administration of schema/ sub-schema	X	X	
Maintain adequate segregation of duties	X		X
Operational Control			
Analyze internal storage structures (pointers)			X

Source: From *Report of the Joint Data Base Task Force.* New York: AICPA, 1983, p. 26. Reprinted by permission of the American Institute of Public Accountants.

SMALL-SCALE SYSTEMS

Although we can describe both large-scale and small-scale EDP systems as one-site, one-facility operations, we need to consider the unique characteristics of small businesses when auditing their EDP systems. The following are the main characteristics that distinguish the operation of an EDP system in a small business from that of a large business.

1. *People responsible for the system:* Staffing is limited, as are separation of duties and detailed systems knowledge.
2. *Lack of resources:* Most small businesses cannot afford high security costs or losses resulting from computer fraud.
3. *Attitude of personnel:* The size of a small company creates a family type of atmosphere, in which management trust often translates into lax controls.
4. *Inadequate control procedures:* Lax controls result in poor or nonexistent back-up policies, audit trails, and documentation.

The dilemma for the auditor of small-business computer systems is that while audit tools and techniques are geared to large computer systems, the real growth in computer use is in the minicomputer and microcomputer segments of the market.[3] For brevity, we will refer to a minicomputer or microcomputer as a small business computer (SBC) when one or the other is used as a stand-alone computer "system." When auditing an SBC installation, the auditor is likely to encounter copyrighted software with source code that cannot be obtained, programs stored in read-only memory that cannot be reviewed, and audit trails that cannot be traced.

Since the SBC is primarily a tool for processing information, the auditor needs to assess the risk associated with its use and make a judgment about the extent of auditing required.[4] The auditor's role includes alerting management to significant changes occurring in the use of the system, being involved at the outset in the introduction of new technology in order to ensure adequate controls, and evaluating the effectiveness of controls after they have been implemented. As for any EDP system, controls can be divided into general and application controls.

General controls for an SBC installation are normally established as management strategies rather than by means of formalized general control policies. These strategies entail methods of software acquisition and use, methods of hardware acquisition, and decisions concerning level of technical sophistication. The auditor's role is to verify the completeness of the controls, to ensure that they have been followed properly, and to help monitor the translation of the management strategies into system configuration and efficiency.

Since SBC sites are not normally control-oriented, the auditor should approach the audit of general controls from a risk perspective. The key risks and related control options are (1) loss of continuity of processing, which is controllable through back-up procedures, hardware and software contracts, and minimum levels of documentation; (2) circumventing of standards, which can be countered by standardized hardware and SBC justification procedures prior to purchase; (3) SBC mismanagement and/or abuse, which entails increased supervision of employees and their use of SBC procedures; (4) uncontrolled access, which calls for supervisory action, physical security of hardware and media, and user access responsibilities; and (5) uneconomical operations, which can be controlled by means of error/complaint logs and good communication between users.[5]

At the SBC installation, an important part of application controls is the person who prepares the input and operates the system because many application controls are performed manually. Although manual controls can be adequate, confounding factors, such as the infeasibility of proper separation of duties, unsupported application programs, loss of data integrity, and lack of a clear audit trail, come into play. The auditor should focus efforts on decreasing these risk exposures by promoting dual programming responsibility (when applicable), requiring input retention and creation of an internal audit trail, and enforcing the use of external control totals and other simple accounting proofs. Techniques for auditing an SBC installation include:

1. Auditing through the system, using simulation modeling, test data, parallel operations, parallel simulation, general audit software (where possible), terminal audit software, and special purpose audit programs (such as ITF).[6]
2. Using a special audit minicomputer that interfaces with the SBC. The advantages of its use are increased auditor independence from the SBC staff, the ease of interface with the SBC because of similarities in size, and decreased impact on other users of the system.
3. Testing system interface, requiring the transfer of floppy disks between computers; direct connection between computers via a common bus; or the use of test peripherals to emulate component operations.

Auditing through the SBC is harder than auditing around it. The method used and the tests performed by the auditor must be based on the relative risks versus costs of the different methods available.

18.3 DECENTRALIZED SYSTEMS

An increasing number of companies are linking their minicomputers and microcomputers into networks, to form decentralized computer systems, pursue various forms of distributed processing, and enter the world of electronic funds transfers. In the following discussion, we progress through increasing levels of complexity in decentralized systems, noting the unique audit problems at each level.

ELECTRONIC FUNDS TRANSFER SYSTEM

An **electronic funds transfer system** (EFTS) is a computer-based network that enables payment-system transfers to be initiated, approved, executed, and recorded by means of electronic impulses and machine-sensible data. A physical audit trail is practically nonexistent because of the lack of hard-copy documentation of the funds transactions. The three main types of EFTS are remote banking services, retail point-of-sale services, and direct deposit/preauthorized payment services.

In an EFTS, many of the general controls that were useful under a batch system are no longer applicable. They have to be changed significantly or totally replaced by new types of control systems. The most obvious modifications in general controls required are in the area of organizational/operational controls and system-development controls. Since the primary objective of organizational/operational controls is to ensure the segregation of incompatible functions among individuals, several unique control problems are created by an EFTS. First, it is imperative that computer personnel not have access to the plastic cards or personal identification numbers (PINs) issued to customers. The reason for this is obvious: Fraud could easily be perpetrated if the physical access to these cards is inadequately controlled. Additionally, it is important to prevent computer personnel from being involved in the customer-service function. Finally, systems-development work must be done on a team basis, with adequate segregation of responsibility to guarantee that no one programmer has complete knowledge of the system. The importance of separation of duties in an EFTS cannot be overstated because of the liquidity of the assets being protected and the great potential for computer fraud.

Systems-development and documentation controls should ensure that systems are designed, modified, and tested only under proper authorization and are adequately documented. It becomes crucial for the auditor to verify that program modification controls are adequate and enforced because these controls are essential to the system's integrity. Similarly, it is important for the auditor to follow routine systems-testing procedures in an EFTS, especially of all system interfaces with users and developers. Once again, the auditor's focus must be on preventing and detecting computer fraud.

Hardware and software controls can be used to generate an electronic audit trail of individual transactions. This is a critical feature of a reliable EFTS and entails the identification of each transaction by time and date, transaction sequence number, terminal identification number, and the merchant/employee identification code. This combination of identification procedures allows the auditor to track a series of transactions through the system in order to verify that internal controls are functioning properly. Many EFTSs issue hard-copy receipts to customers and thereby provide another source of verification and system integrity.

Access controls in an EFTS are linked to the integrity of the controls on identification cards and PIN assignments. It is important for the auditor to verify that each customer's data is isolated, that joint access to several accounts is not possible within the system.

The final type of general control problem unique to an EFTS revolves around data and procedural controls. These controls provide for the proper operation of the system on a day-to-day basis and thereby ensure the reliability of the processed data. Transactions take place in a very short time frame, which increases the importance of having an independent control group to detect errors, inconsistencies, and irregularities in transaction processing. Unsuccessful access attempts should be logged, and the card used in such attempts should be retained by the system. The design and implementation of back-up procedures are extremely important in an EFTS because of the time frame and the possibility of fraud.

General controls alone are not adequate to ensure the integrity of an EFTS. Both physical security controls and application controls are also essential. The objective of application controls is to ensure that all data are recorded and processed correctly and that the output of the processing is accurate. Access and use controls, such as transaction logs, help the auditor to verify the completeness and integrity of all data input elements. Process controls are used to provide assurance that processing is performed only as intended. Finally, output controls take the form of printed receipts and limited data responses.

The Securities and Exchange Commission currently regulates seven areas of EFTS operations: (1) terminal and operator identification codes; (2) control of PIN numbers and access cards; (3) "bad-card" identification procedures for off-line systems; (4) segregation of duties among EDP personnel; (5) documentation; (6) encryption of data transmission; and (7) insurance against fraud and computer crime.[7]

Under present audit standards, the auditor must review and comprehend both the internal controls of an EDP system and the flow of transactions through that system. This entails identifying the boundaries of the client's system, which are the points at which transactions begin and end.

In an EFTS, the point at which authorization for the transaction occurs and at which assets or services are exchanged will be the outer boundary of the system's flow of transactions.[8] The auditor's task is to ensure the integrity of the funds flowing through this system in order to prevent fraud and protect the assets of the organization and its customers. The complexity of this task is illustrated by the following forecast.

> The future holds the prospect of situations in which one company's computer arrives at decisions and, potentially, also initiates trigger actions in the computer of another company, thus committing resources and affecting the company's financial position. Since such transactions will occur through an electronic dialogue so compressed in time that measurement can be made in microseconds, specific management authorization and approval of transactions will not take place as transactions are originated; rather, they must be carefully considered by management and then preprogrammed into the financial system itself.[9]

NETWORKS OF MINICOMPUTERS

A natural extension of stand-alone SBCs and EFTSs is the networking of these systems. The EFTS provides the potential for connecting many different organizations to one vast system. Typically, the SBC installation begins as a stand-alone computer, but within a short period of time it may become desirable for an organization to connect its computer to others in order to access and transmit common data. The audit implications of such shared resources include the need to verify that controls are compatible between systems and that the integrity of the component systems is maintained. Figure 18.2 shows the continuum of development from stand-alone to fully distributed systems.

DISTRIBUTED EDP SYSTEM

Distributed data processing (DDP) is an approach to business data processing in which emphasis is placed on the use of multiple small computers (having stand-alone capabilities) concurrently with use of the mainframe processing unit. As such, a DDP system is based on the premise of isolated, yet partially supervised, processing sites (or nodes) interconnected in a pyramid (or tree) structure.[10]

Figure 18.2 Continuum of EDP-system Distribution

Unsophisticated   Sophisticated
Use   Use

Stand-alone SBC with adequate hard-copy audit evidence	SBC in a distributed environment with heavy use of electronic evidence

(Little or no audit   (Heavy audit involvement)
involvement, except
data security and
back up)

Source: Everett C. Johnson (Chairman, AICPA Computer Auditing Subcommittee), "Advanced EDP Systems and the Auditor's Concern," *Journal of Accountancy*, January 1975, p. 72.

The auditing concerns unique to DDP are the increased exposure of hardware, software, and data to abuse and fraud, owing to multiple processing sites. Related to these concerns is the possibility that acquisition of software and subsequent modifications are no longer a centralized function. Further, as the number of sites increases, the number of employees at each particular site usually decreases, resulting in inadequate separation of duties. Finally, nonstandard policies and reduced back up make data storage, retention, and recovery more difficult.

Current audit standards are not applicable to DDP because of the nature of data storage, access restrictions, processing segmentation and management philosophy in these systems.

Audit problems with respect to DDP can best be thought of in terms of increased exposure to potential losses of capital, information, or inventories. Because of the multiple-site, file-storage characteristic of a DDP system, data-file losses are the auditor's main concern. Limited main storage at the distributed sites prevents the use of elaborate logging and password schemes. Dispersed data files increase the probability that identical data elements are not consistently and accurately maintained throughout the system. Such weaknesses have the potential for making the system unauditable.

Several network exposure risks are important to the auditor and represent the unique problems associated with DDP. Routing priorities must be established for system messages and data or program transmissions. Network failure is one of the greatest threats posed by DDP, and, when combined with decreased capability to recover the system, it presents a critical audit problem. The potential danger of distortion or loss of messages as they pass through the system increases as the number of possible intermediary relay modes grows and related controls deteriorate.

Other exposures of concern to the auditor when working with a DDP system relate to input/output, audit trails, and application software modifications, to name a few. The increased number of processing sites combines with a lack of well-tested DDP-system software to create a potentially uncontrollable and unauditable system. The key is for the auditor to focus on preventive controls, rather than to rely on local EDP staff to detect and correct errors, and to move toward the best back-up system possible to ensure that data can be retrieved.[11]

Some types of controls that are useful in a DDP environment are data-file controls, recovery-oriented controls, network and transmission controls, and personnel and procedures controls. The purpose of data-file controls is to safeguard access to the data, whereas recovery-oriented controls create an interactive audit trail that stores transactions and allows for the reconstruction of the files in case of interruption. Algorithmic coding schemes and networking software can help the auditor to ensure message integrity. Centralizing software and structuring adequate uploading and downloading controls (that is, parity and/or bit checks) further reduces exposure to fraud. Duties should be segregated where feasible and supervised carefully where not feasible. In conclusion, we can only agree with the statement that:

> "As more advanced design concepts have been implemented, the auditor has been forced not only to augment and modify audit approaches but also begin an introspective process of anticipating sweeping new dimensions in technology and systems design."[12]

18.4 OTHER AUDIT ISSUES

We need to examine two additional issues before we leave the topic of auditing advanced EDP systems. One is an ancillary issue—involving hardware and software contracts—and the other—expert systems—a look to the future. For both, we emphasize that the auditor will have more control in the future over auditability of advanced EDP systems at the design stage than after implementation. As with the auditing of all advanced EDP systems, it is becoming imperative that the auditor plays a proactive role, rather than the more traditional, reactive one.

HARDWARE AND SOFTWARE CONTRACTS

The best place for the auditor to focus control efforts in contracting is from the beginning. The auditor can serve as an independent third party to ensure that the contracting process is adequately controlled and that the client will acquire a highly useful and effective product. In this type of situation, the auditor examines compliance to organizational standards and evaluates the contract from an operational perspective in order to determine whether the product will meet the user's needs.

In the contractual process, the auditor is evaluating something that has not yet happened, thus is involved in a process that is concurrent with the audit process.[13] The benefits of having the auditor involved at this stage are decreased contract cost, subsequent enforcement of contract provisions, and decreased exposure to fraud, to name a few. By having a voice in the adequacy of the contract and reasonableness of the product—and by verifying that the product will meet the organization's needs, the auditor can perform a valuable service for the client and, at the same time, ensure the future auditability of the system.

EXPERT SYSTEMS

Replacing human expertise at some levels is proving to be feasible in manufacturing, as robots assume menial, repetitive tasks that people find so hard to perform consistently. Artificial intelligence systems have evolved over the last 25 years from devices capable of playing chess to those that can now mimic human expertise in such complex fields as assembly-line scheduling, advanced missile-guidance systems, and computer-aided design.[14] Computer-aided diagnosis of diseases and design of buildings are among the tools that are complementing and adding to human expertise. (See Chapter 17.)

Unlike human beings, computers do not have good peripheral comprehension of related problems. Consequently, despite very good judgment in a particular domain, expert-system software may produce absurdities with regard to the analysis or projection of peripheral events. The ability to learn from trial and error, to understand the nuances of human language, and the weeding out and forgetting of nonessential information are effortless skills for the individual that are currently still not within reach of computer logic and design.

The implications of AI and ES for auditing are staggering: The auditor will have to verify the integrity of these systems and also use the technology in performing audit tasks. The auditor must approach AI and ES methodologically, basically assessing the quality of inputs and their corresponding outcomes. Validation of expert systems is an unexplored field, which will become a major concern to auditors as organizations progressively place more emphasis on expert systems.[15] As they did with the advent of computers, auditors will have to develop methods to cope with these new systems. Early involvement of the auditor in this rapidly evolving field will help to ensure the auditability of such advanced systems.

18.5 Summary

We began this chapter with a discussion of centralized EDP systems and related database integrity concerns. The controls necessary to maintain and/or attest to this integrity were noted and the audit implications discussed.

We discussed the key issues related to database audit and control with particular emphasis on the role and function of the DBA.

We examined the concept of SBC and the audit implications of small businesses using these computers, their control environment and the methods that are preferable for their auditing.

Decentralized systems were discussed with focus on: EFTSs, minicomputer networks and distributed data processing systems. Their control and audit procedures were highlighted and discussed.

Questions

1. Why must auditors become more involved in computer-facility planning and control as computer systems become more sophisticated?
2. Differentiate among general controls, applications controls, and system-integrity controls.
3. Differentiate between centralized and decentralized computer systems and describe the impact decentralization has on the auditor.
4. Describe the elements of each of the five types of controls for a centralized, real-time system:
    (a) Access controls.
    (b) Terminal controls.
    (c) Transmission-line controls.
    (d) Audit-trail controls.
    (e) Database controls.

5. What are some of the differences between a centralized small-scale business computer system and a centralized large-scale business computer system?

6. What are some of the problems an auditor encounters when auditing an installation?

7. In the EFTS discussion, what segregation of duties, systems-development, hardware, software, and access controls related specifically to the resolution of control problems for decentralized systems?

8. What are some of the unique audit problems associated with mini-computer networks and distributed data processing?

9. What are the audit implications of a contract for acquiring computer hardware and software?

10. Will artificial intelligence and expert systems affect the auditor? If so, how?

Problems

1. Draft an audit program for a centralized, large-scale business computer system, a centralized small-scale business computer system, and a decentralized computer system. What elements are similar? What elements are different?

2. Electronic funds transfer systems are vital to the U.S. and free-world economy. Why? Are their auditability and control vital? Why?

3. Many small-business minicomputer systems use copyrighted software. Other than actual simulation of test data and tracing transactions through the system, what other ways do you think you could verify the programs? How do you think you might use vendor software?

4. Database administrators and file-control measures become increasingly important in decentralized systems. Why? What other methods can be used to decrease this dependency?

5. As the distinction between large and small systems becomes more blurred, in what ways will the distinction between minicomputer networks and distributed data processing become blurred? What will be the implications for the auditor?

6. Examine the issues concerning controls and audit of EFTSs and DDP in a comparative mode. Draw a table of four columns where the first column is an issue, the second and the third relate to the systems and the fourth highlights the differences.

Notes

1. Johnson, Everett C. (Chairman, AICPA Computer Auditing Committee), "Advanced EDP Systems and the Auditor's Concern," *Journal of Accountancy*, January 1975, pp. 72–85.

2. Okkesse, Paul, "Computers: The Audit Challenge," *The Australian Accountant*, July 1980, p. 387.

3. Perry, William E., *Auditing the Small Business Computer*, Carol Stream, Ill.: EDP Auditors Foundation, 1983.

4. Ibid., p. 5.

5. Ibid., p. 48.

6. ITF stands for *integrated test facility* and involves establishing the capability to introduce selected input into a system simultaneously with live data, thereby tracing the flow of transactions through the various functions in the system. For further information, see Chaiken, Barry, and Perry, William E., "ITF—A Promising Audit Technique," *Journal of Accountancy*, February 1973, p. 74.

7. *Audit Considerations in EFTS.* New York: AICPA, 1978.

8. Richardson, Dana R., "Auditing EFTS," *Journal of Accountancy*, October 1978, p. 81.

9. Ibid., p. 82.

10. Kneer, Dan C., and Lampe, James C., "Distributed Data Processing: Internal Control Issues and Safeguards," *EDPACS*, June 1983, p. 1.

11. Ibid., p. 10.

12. Richardson, p. 81.

13. Perry, William E., *Auditing Hardware and Software Contracts.* Carol Stream, Ill.: EDP Auditors Foundation, 1983, p. 19.

14. "Machines That Think: They're Brewing a Revolution," *U.S. News and World Report*, December 5, 1983, p. 60.

15. See O'Leary, D. E., "Validation of Business Expert Systems." *Proceedings of the USC Symposium on Expert Systems in Auditing*, Los Angeles, Calif.: 1986.

Additional References

Adams, Donald L., "Systems and Audit Aspects of the Data Dictionary," *EDPACS*, May 1976, pp. 1–14.

Barkat, Shulamit, "Using DBMS and TP Software in the Audit of Large Data Files," *EDPACS*, May 1982, pp. 1–14.

Cerullo, Michael J., "Controls for On-Line Real-Time Computer Systems," Part I, *CA Magazine*, March 1980, pp. 58–61.

Cerullo, Michael J., "Controls for On-Line Real-Time Computer Systems," Part II, *CA Magazine*, May 1980, pp. 54–58.

Gilhooley, Ian A., "Auditing Computerized Systems," *EDPACS*, February 1982, pp. 1–8.

Grihalva, Richard A., "Control Characteristics of On-Line Systems," *EDPACS*, February 1978, pp. 1–8.

Hodge, Robert D., "Auditing Micro Systems," *EDPACS*, March 1980, pp. 1–5.

Hubbert, James F., "An Audit of a Realtime System—A Case Study," *EDPACS*, December 1979, pp. 1–15.

Management Control and Audit of Advanced EDP Systems. New York: American Institute of Certified Public Accountants, 1977.

Patrick, Robert L., "Integrity Considerations in Distributed Systems," *EDPACS*, August 1980, pp. 1–6.

Report of the Joint Data Base Task Force (of the AICPA, CICA, and IIA). New York: American Institute of Certifed Public Accountants, 1983.

St. Clair, Linda, "Security for Small Computer Systems," *EDPACS*, November 1983, pp. 1–10.

Weber, Ron, and Gordon C. Everest, "Database Administration: Functional, Organizational and Control Perspectives," *EDPACS*, January 1979, pp. 1–10.

Wood, C., E. B. Fernandez, and R. C. Summers, "Database Security: Requirements, Policies and Models," *IBM Systems Journal*, 1980, pp. 229–251.

Chapter **19**

A Career in EDP-Systems Auditing

19.1 INTRODUCTION

The most frequent definition of the term "audit" is the examination of financial records. Thus, auditors must of necessity thoroughly understand the various systems and procedures used by an entity to generate accounting, financial and operating information.[1]

Few practicing auditors or accounting professors would disagree with the assertion that auditing a system requires a thorough understanding both of the client's system and its related procedures. Yet, when EDP-systems auditing is discussed, disagreements arise as to what a thorough understanding of the client's system encompasses. This controversy forms the backdrop for this chapter on educational and career choices related to EDP-systems auditing.

This chapter discusses the main issues related to careers in EDP audit. It starts by presenting the tradeoffs between EDP and accounting in the audit career, then the role of the auditor, then the EDP auditor, and various backgrounds and career paths. The chapter is concluded by considerations relative to EDP audit as a profession and its future.

LEARNING OBJECTIVES

By the time you have completed this chapter, you should be able to:

1. Distinguish between EDP auditors and other types of auditors.
2. Assess the career opportunities and educational requirements of the EDP auditor.
3. Explain the difference between auditing EDP systems and the use of computers to perform financial audits.
4. Identify the job dimensions of the EDP-system auditor.

19.2 THE CONTROVERSY

There is considerable disagreement among auditing professionals regarding the degree of understanding, or computer proficiency, necessary for effectively performing an audit in a computerized environment. At one extreme is the position that a staff auditor, armed with one or two general computer classes and a good generalized audit software package, can properly and effectively review a client's system. This viewpoint reflects the perception of competence required to use EDP to conduct financial audits. However, Bariff argues that this approach is not equivalent to auditing an EDP system.[2] This dichotomy of viewpoints can be used to clarify the arguments surrounding the EDP auditing professional.

From the use perspective, the computer is simply another tool for the auditor to use when examining the financial records of an entity. Generalized audit software does represent one effective, cost-efficient way to perform a financial audit. Vasarhelyi and Pabst found that most accounting firms utilize standardized facility review questionnaires and generally use the computer in auditing a client's records to perform analytical reviews, for sampling purposes, and to prepare confirmations.[3] That study underscored an increasing use of computers for performing financial audits. In recent years, many accounting firms have begun to use microcomputers to perform many audit tasks. Obviously, the depth of actual data processing knowledge required to use the computer in making a financial audit is far less than that necessary to audit an EDP system.

Auditing an EDP system requires far different skills and perspectives than does the use of the computer as an audit tool. The EDP auditor is not primarily concerned that the financial output of the system be consistent with generally accepted accounting principles. Instead, the EDP auditor is interested in ensuring that the processing software is consistent with user specifications and that custodial programs and data are secure from unauthorized intervention.[4] The EDP-system audit includes reviews of system practices and controls, including system development, data files, operating procedures, management policies, system security and privacy, system software, and application programs.

When approaching the question of auditing in a computerized environment, you should keep in mind the implications of that dichotomy. We use it throughout the rest of this chapter to examine more fully the educational and professional differences of the two perspectives.

19.3 COMPUTERS AND THE STAFF AUDITOR

As mentioned in Section 19.2, most accounting firms use the computer in their examination of client records and for other audit procedures. Capitalizing on the efficiency of the computer to perform these tasks is increasingly important because of greater price competition among accounting firms. These firms are concerned, therefore, with improving the performance of the general staff auditor.

Because of the increasing importance of automated data processing systems in the United States, in-charge general staff auditors are being required to expand both the depth of their technical knowledge of computers, as well as the breadth of their understanding of many data processing techniques, in order to adequately and efficiently perform audits in a computer-oriented environment.[5]

In order for the staff auditor to use the computer in analyzing and testing an organization's records, he or she should have:

1. A basic understanding of computer systems.
2. A basic understanding of the most commonly used computer operating systems and software.
3. General familiarity with file-processing techniques and data structures.
4. A working knowledge of computer audit software.
5. An ability to review system documentation.
6. A working knowledge of EDP-system controls.
7. Sufficient working knowledge of EDP systems to develop, execute, and supervise audit plans.
8. A familiarity with methods used in developing and modifying programs and systems.[6]

This list reflects the minimum EDP-skill levels needed to audit financial records in a computerized environment. However, few auditors get this necessary level of understanding from their basic EDP course or in continuing education courses. Inadequate basic EDP knowledge is compounded dramatically by the impact of rapid technological change in the computer field.

To date, the accounting profession's response to this problem has been to advocate an increased number of EDP courses in the basic accounting curriculum and to note the need for EDP-audit specialists. The current view holds that hands-on experience with audit software should be emphasized, along with an understanding of the implications of the computer for internal control at all levels of the client's organization.

At issue are the skills needed for conducting an audit with the aid of the computer. The key point in this regard is that the general staff auditor needs to be familiar with basic computer concepts, audit software, and the implications of using the computer to evaluate internal controls. Gaining this knowledge entails increasing the number and intensity of computer courses in the accounting curriculum. The major question that remains is: Who should assume responsibility for auditing the EDP system itself?

19.4 THE EDP AUDITOR

The three major influences on EDP auditing are systems technology, business demands, and the Foreign Corrupt Practices Act. With regard to the technological influence, it is important to note the impact of the AICPA. In 1974, it adopted SAS No. 3, which stated that in a complex EDP environment, EDP expertise is necessary to perform audit procedures. This and subsequent standards are continuing to modify the required EDP skills for entry-level accountants. Competitive pressures are also forcing public accounting firms to utilize EDP professionals in audits of computer systems. Since passage of the Foreign Corrupt Practices Act in 1977 by Congress, business executives have begun to recognize the importance of EDP-system security and the role of the EDP auditors. A number of companies have established a separate EDP audit group in their internal audit departments. A major New York bank has an EDP audit group with more than 100 professionals, comprising approximately one third of the entire audit staff.

Since the EDP auditor is not as concerned with the output of the financial system as with the integrity of the EDP processes and programs that produce financial reports and records, EDP auditing can be thought of as an integral, but separate, part of the total audit function. There are several reasons for having a specialized EDP auditor (or computer audit specialist) function in an audit organization. One reason is the need to retain the independence of the external audit staff. Having a technically proficient person on the staff to conduct the EDP audit increases the accounting firm's independence, hence improving the value and reliability of the analysis. Also, an auditor who can converse with the client's EDP staff in their own jargon is much more likely to gain their acceptance and access to inside information, both of which are invaluable in the evaluation of internal controls. Finally, having an EDP auditor perform the system review increases both the efficiency and the effectiveness of the audit. This translates into increased competence of the firm and decreased exposure to litigation owing to inadequate procedures. The same arguments apply to EDP auditors in internal audit organizations.

Besides the basic skills delineated for the general staff auditor, the EDP audit specialist should have a good understanding of operating, file-processing, and database management systems. The specialist should understand the most widely used computer languages at the level of an experienced programmer. Additionally, the EDP auditor needs to be familiar with state-of-the-art technologies in networking, electronic funds transfer systems, distributed data processing systems, and other advanced EDP concepts. Lin has proposed that EDP auditors must have a working knowledge of

1. data processing;
2. programming;
3. flowcharting;
4. file organization;
5. microcomputers;
6. business and accounting information systems;
7. systems design concepts and techniques;
8. data processing control techniques;
9. general auditing concepts and techniques; and
10. computer audit approaches and techniques.[7]

In a study conducted by the Educational Testing Service, it identified the following job dimensions for EDP auditing.[8]

Application systems control review: Review of installed application system controls in order to determine that the system produces information in a timely, accurate, and complete manner.

Security review: Review of security methods and procedures in order to ensure the appropriate protection of programs, data, and the EDP installation.

Data integrity review: Review of data for completeness, consistency, and correctness in order to determine data integrity.

General operational procedure control review: To determine that applications are processed in a controlled environment.

Application development review: To determine the adequacy and completeness of planned controls and, if necessary, to recommend additional controls.

Information system audit management: To organize, set priorities, and assume responsibility for the EDP-system audit function in order to effectively utilize the available resources of the system and to fulfill the audit requirements of the organization.

System development life-cycle review: To determine adherence to generally accepted standards in the life-cycle development of the system.

Systems software review: To determine compliance with the organization's policies.

Data processing resource management review: To determine the adequacy in this area in fulfilling the organization's goals.

Maintenance review: To ensure that existing system modifications are performed in accordance with organizational policies.

Acquisition review: Review of the process of acquiring services, hardware, and software in order to determine that organizational resources are being used in an economical manner.

EDUCATIONAL AND TRAINING REQUIREMENTS

Because the level of technical proficiency necessary for conducting an EDP audit surpasses that required to use the computer in financial audits, the issue of educational and training requirements for the EDP audit specialist becomes important. In a study they conducted, Vasarhelyi and Pabst asked representatives of accounting firms to indicate the preferred major field of study, and related degree requirements, for EDP auditors. Of those responding, 85 percent indicated that a bachelor's degree was the basic degree required at any level, while 7 percent indicated that a master's

Table 19.1   Major-Field Desirability

	Accounting	Business	Computer Science
Joint major	69%	59%	41%
Exclusive major	24	0	7
Desirability quotient	93	59	48

Source: Vasarhelyi, Pabst & Daley, page 40.

degree was desirable and 7 percent indicated that their expectation increased from a bachelor's to a master's degree for positions at the supervisory level and above. None of the respondents indicated that a Ph.D. is required at any level. With respect to the preferred major field of study, Vasarhelyi and Pabst used the results of the survey to derive a desirability quotient for purposes of comparison. Table 19.1 shows the percentage of respondents who expect an EDP auditor to have joint majors or an exclusive major. The totals represent the relative desirability of each major field.

It is not surprising to find that preference for the accounting degree predominates. However, the results do indicate that computer science is a desirable degree for the EDP audit specialist. Since this study did not utilize the specialist/generalist dichotomy, we cannot draw any firm conclusions from the results. The fact that 7 percent of those responding felt that an exclusive major in computer science and 41 percent felt that a joint major in computer science and another field are appropriate for an EDP auditor indicates that data processing capabilities play a key role in the recruiting decisions of public accounting firms.

CAREER PATHS

Whether the EDP auditor majored in accounting and then received additional training in EDP, or instead began as an EDP professional and was subsequently trained in basic accounting and control procedures, he or she often faces a career path that is significantly different from the general staff auditor. The first concern of the EDP auditor is whether the position will be regarded as advisory or an integral part of the overall audit team. The arguments for treating the EDP auditor as part of the audit team are as follows:

1. Promotes greater congruence with overall audit objectives.
2. Facilitates communication between the general auditor and the EDP auditor.
3. Improves the EDP expertise of the audit team. Since all members of the team are involved in the final audit results, there is generally greater sharing of knowledge resulting in better overall auditing and training.[9]

There are also several convincing arguments for having the EDP auditor play an advisory role:

1. Better utilization of EDP audit resources because the advisory role improves the utilization of a scarce resource.
2. Greater work satisfaction for the EDP auditor.
3. Increased organizational commitment to EDP auditing.
4. Improved coordination and control of EDP audits.
5. Increased specialization enables the EDP auditor to cope with complex technologies and keep abreast of technological changes.

In their study, Vasarhelyi and Pabst found that some 41 percent of the accounting firms contacted tended to use regular audit staff to perform computer audit functions. Although a substantial number of firms treat the EDP auditor as a general staff auditor, 28 percent of the respondents indicated that they maintained a core of computer audit specialists, while 27 percent replied that they used management advisory services (MAS) consulting personnel to support this effort. Further, 26 percent of the respondents maintained separate EDP audit departments, and 71 percent did not. Therefore, while approximately 56 percent of the accounting firms regarded EDP auditing as an advisory role, only 26 percent actually maintained a separate career path for the EDP auditor within the firm. Thus, if the accounting firm treats its EDP auditors as part of the general audit staff, their career development will parallel that of a general auditor. Table 19.2 shows the relationship of background to job level found by the study.

Note that the percentage of full-time EDP audit specialists in partner positions is substantially less than that of either the part-time specialist or the generalist. This result can be interpreted in two ways. First, the data may reflect the fact that, although hiring EDP auditors as specialists is becoming more prevalent, the small proportion who are partners reflects the length of time it takes for a staff auditor to rise to that level. The relatively large proportions of EDP specialists (full-time and part-time) at the manager and senior auditor levels indicates a growing com-

Table 19.2   Background of Personnel at Various Job Levels

Background	Partner	Manager	Senior Auditor	Staff Auditor	Other
Full-time EDP specialist	3%	33%	61%	1%	3%
Part-time EDP specialist	10	30	48	6	6
Generalist doing EDP audits	14	19	23	43	0
All categories	9	27	43	19	2

Source: Results adapted from the data on the Vasarhelyi & Pabst survey.

mitment to EDP auditing that should be reflected in partner statistics in the future as promotions occur.

Second, the skills of the EDP specialist may be more useful at the manager and senior auditor levels and may not transfer well to the partner level. This interpretation reflects the career-path problems facing any specialist in most organizations. Further, employees who play advisory roles are seldom promoted to upper management because of a general perception that they do not possess the requisite management skills that nonspecialists acquire.

Vasarhelyi and Pabst found that 55 percent of the respondents in the study felt that opportunities for the EDP auditor to advance to the partner-in-charge level were equal to those of other professional personnel, but a significant group (35 percent) indicated that such opportunities were greater for the specialist. For the partner-principal level, 48 percent indicated an equal opportunity, while 26 percent felt that the EDP audit specialist faced better than average career-advancement potential.

Alternative paths are developing within the auditing profession as the impact of increased computerization in the business world continues to change the scope and character of auditing. Within an EDP audit group of a large company or financial institution one such career path would be:

1. Audit trainee—EDP.
2. Internal audit specialist—EDP.
3. Internal audit analyst—EDP.
4. Assistant internal auditor—EDP.

5. Internal auditor—EDP.
6. Associate internal audit manager—EDP.
7. Consultant for internal audit—EDP.
8. Internal audit manager—EDP.

In a public accounting firm, a similar career path here would be from EDP audit trainee to EDP auditor, to supervisor, EDP audit, to audit manager, EDP audit, partner, and finally to director of EDP auditing.

If an EDP auditor decides to pursue a different career path, he or she can accept positions in information systems or business. Examples of such positions include database administrator, data processing consultant, data processing manager, and investments manager. Regardless of the career path the EDP audit specialist pursues, it is evident that the increasing complexity of computer systems being utilized by business will be reflected in increasing demands for EDP auditors and auditors with EDP training.

19.5 EDP AUDITING AS A PROFESSION

Under the Taft-Hartley Act, five criteria determine whether a particular occupation qualifies as a profession:

1. Common body of knowledge.
2. Standards of competence.
3. Examination of competence.
4. Developed code of ethics.
5. A disciplinary mechanism.

With regard to the first requirement, in 1976 the EDP Auditors Association established the EDP Auditors Foundation (EDPAF), Inc., to engage in education and research to qualify EDP auditing as a profession. One of the first projects undertaken by this group was to identify a common body of knowledge for the EDP auditing field. The EDPAF identified 10 key EDP audit tasks, in decreasing order of importance: general operational controls review, security review, production systems control review, application development review, financial audit support, systems development and acquisition management review, data quality assurance review, system software review, data processing resource management review, and benefit and usage review.[10]

After identifying these tasks, the EDPAF undertook a survey of EDP auditors concerning the level of knowledge necessary in areas such as internal control requirements and evaluation, processing and audit trails, data security, and error and exception recovery. There was considerable agreement among those who responded regarding the knowledge and expertise required for establishing EDP-auditor competence. Based on this study, and one sponsored by the Educational Testing System, it can be concluded that EDP auditing meets the first requirement for being recognized as a profession.

The second and third requirements are closely related, for if competence is to be tested, standards on which to base the examination must exist. In June 1978, EDPAF instituted a certification program for information-system auditors. Its initial phase included a grandfather clause whereby EDP specialists with five or more years of experience in EDP audits could apply for and receive certification. This phase terminated in June 1979. Currently, certification is granted by examination only. The first test was conducted April 10, 1981, and 417 of the 659 people taking the exam passed and became certified information system auditors (CISAs).

In 1980, the nation's first graduate program in EDP auditing was introduced at California State University in Pomona. The establishment of this program, along with others (such as the certificate program at New York University) and the certification movement indicate that EDP auditing has successfully met the second and third requirements for becoming a profession.

The EDPAF's continuing work should make achievement of the fourth and fifth criteria possible. The code of ethics and general policing procedures for auditors in general apply to EDP auditors. Nevertheless, a high degree of technical proficiency is needed for supervision of a code of ethics and disciplinary mechanism. As certification becomes synonymous with competence, self-policing will become possible and desirable.

There are still several shortcomings in standards for reporting and for professional conduct. There is no standard form for reporting the results of an EDP audit. Standardization clarifies the message conveyed by a report and thus is desirable for any public attestation document. Also, there is no equivalent to GAAP or GAS for the EDP auditor. Professional standards decrease the ambiguity and increase the reliability and comparability of audit results.

Rapid changes in computer hardware and software create continuance problems for consecutive EDP audits. There is no reliable way at present to use past control evaluations for an audited system in order to reduce current review tasks. Hence, costs of repeat EDP audits do not decrease, and an accounting firm must recover all its EDP-audit expenses from the client each year. Modern audit technology may change this state of affairs by automating the examination of access controls (passwords, access restrictions) and data structures that reside in a DBMS. This would allow substantial decrease in EDP audit effort in the years following the initial definition of the DBMS structures.

Since there is no such thing as an absolutely secure data processing system, accounting firms, in conjunction with the SEC, will have to establish *reasonable-assurance* criteria for EDP audits. The inherent weaknesses of all EDP systems suggest that the risk of undetected fraud and errors is quite large, and the EDP auditor must be protected by limitations on exposure to liability in those areas.

19.6 THE FUTURE OF EDP AUDITING

The advancement of EDP auditors to the higher management levels of major CPA firms is an emerging trend. This trend will further facilitate career progress by EDP auditors and their acceptance as bonafide audit professionals.

Constantly changing technology and the rapid increase in use of computerized systems in small- and medium-sized businesses are forcing change in traditional auditing approaches. The most likely audit approach for the late 1980s and into the 1990s will be for a general staff auditor with increased data processing skills to perform the preliminary systems review, use a microcomputer-based "toolchest" for traditional audit tasks, and call in an EDP auditor for more specialized reviews. The EDP auditor would assist with database, telecommunication, and microcomputer problems. The EDP auditor would also work on the development of audit-related tools and consult with general staff auditors on internal control design at system specification time.

Training requirements for general staff auditors, EDP auditors, statistical specialists, and others are in a state of flux and will continue to evolve. However, we can state with confidence that substantial knowledge of computer capabilities and computer literacy will be expected for future accounting graduates.[11] Auditors will extend their backgrounds with extensive use of computer-aided education tools for self-instruction. Gallegos has noted that by the year 2000, EDP auditing skills may require extensive knowledge in telecommunications, teleprocessing, microcircuitry, embedded systems technology, and the laws regarding privacy, security, fraud, interstate data transfer, and international data transfer.[12] Whether or not these projections are accurate, it is obvious that rapid technological change and the increased use of computerized systems in business will provide ever greater challenges and opportunities for the EDP audit professional.

19.7 Summary

In this chapter, we examined career opportunities and educational requirements for the EDP auditor. Throughout, we stressed that auditing EDP systems is not equivalent to using a computer to perform financial audits. At the least, the depth of knowledge required for auditing EDP systems is much greater than that involved in using computer-aided audit techniques. We can say that EDP auditing is on its way to becoming a recognized profession that requires expertise in all areas of computer technology and the related areas of internal control and data security. Furthermore, with the recent emphasis on technology in the audit process, the role of specialized audit/EDP consultant will offer a needed outlet to highly technical EDP auditors that do not opt and/or may not be able to pursue audit management careers.

Questions

1. What are the minimum skills that an auditor must have in order to audit a computerized system?
2. What are two approaches to providing auditors with those minimum skills?
3. What additional skills and capabilities should an EDP-audit specialist have?
4. What major factors affect the skills of an EDP auditor? How have they been reflected in the EDP auditor's general educational background?
5. What are the arguments for using EDP auditors as part of the auditing team versus using them only to advise other auditors?
6. Why are EDP auditors not often found at the partner level of an accounting firm? Do you expect this to change? If so, in what way?
7. What are some of the nonpublic-accounting careers an EDP auditor might pursue?
8. Describe the certified information system auditor program and its origins.
9. What are some of the problems facing the future of EDP auditing?
10. What are the options for a highly specialized EDP auditor not desiring to pursue a managerial career?

Problems

1. Based on what you have read in this chapter, would you choose EDP auditing as a career? Why? Why not?
2. Using local and national publications, such as the *Wall Street Journal*, various accounting magazines, and classified ads in newspapers, compare the job listings and descriptions for general staff auditors and EDP auditors. What are the key differences?
3. If you were to decide to go into EDP auditing, how would you pursue such a career from your current position?
4. What are some of the problems you might encounter if you select a career in EDP auditing?
5. Do you think EDP auditors can have successful careers within traditional CPA firms? Would they be more successful in a separate unit of the CPA firm or as a separate entity hired as specialists by CPA firms? Can you identify any CPA firms that specialize in EDP auditing in your local area?

Notes

1. Verschoor, Curtis C., and McEnroe, John E., "Perceptions of the Importance of Computer-Related Competencies of General Staff Auditors," *The EDP Auditor*, 1984, 2:45.

2. Bariff, Martin L., "Increasing Responsibilities and Professionalism for EDP Auditing in the 1980's," *The EDP Auditor*, Spring 1982, p. 23.

3. Vasarhelyi, Miklos A., and Pabst, Carl A., "Practices, Standards, Involvement, the Usage of the Computer in EDP Audit: A Survey," *The EDP Auditor*, Summer 1981, p. 30.

4. Bariff, p. 23.

5. Verschoor and McEnroe, p. 46.

6. Cheney, Paul H., and Lyons, Norman R., "Educating the Computer Audit Specialist," *The EDP Auditor*, Fall 1980, p. 12.

7. Lin, W. Thomas, "Computer Security and EDP Auditor Education," *The EDP Auditor*, 1986, 1:38–39.

8. Weiss, Ira R., "The Certified Information Systems Auditor Examination: A Description of Examination Development and Analysis of Results," *The EDP Auditor*, Spring 1982, pp. 18–19.

9. Weber, Ron, *EDP Auditing.* New York: McGraw-Hill, 1982, p. 49.

10. Li, David H., "Common Body of Knowledge for EDP Auditing: A Summary Report," *The EDP Auditor,* Summer 1983, p. 4.

11. Theodore J. Mock, chairman, "Committee on Contemporary Approaches for Teaching the Accounting Information Systems," Sarasota, Fl.: American Auditing Association, 1986.

12. Gallegos, Frederich, "The Need for a Better Trained EDP Auditor," *The EDP Auditor,* Fall 1981, p. 2.

Additional References

Hall, Kenneth D., "The Changing Role of the EDP Auditor," *The EDP Auditor,* Spring 1982, pp. 1–12.

Vasarhelyi, Miklos A., Carl A. Pabst, and Ian Daley, "Organizational and Career Aspects of the EDP Audit Function: A Survey," *The EDP Auditor,* Spring 1981, pp. 35–43.

Chapter 20

The Future of Auditing: Evolution and Automation

20.1 INTRODUCTION

Throughout this book we have discussed the evolution of audit processes and the impact of technology on those processes, as applied in practice and as proposed in the academic literature. In this chapter, we leave this normative basis and venture into a more speculative vision of auditing in the 1980s and 1990s.

As we discussed in earlier chapters, the auditing profession has been affected substantially by the automation of corporate (and nonprofit organization) information processing. Auditors face the task of applying this technology to auditing procedures in order to facilitate the audit process and make it more effective and economical. The use of mainframe or minicomputer sampling plans, management science models, on-line technology, communication networks, and microcomputers in auditing leads directly to the automation of standardized documentation, comparative analysis, scheduling, embedded audit routines, and various other audit procedures.

The audit process will be affected to the extent that location, timing, access, procedure, and working papers, among others, are changed. These factors will be influenced by changes in the six major steps of the audit process, that is, engagement definition, engagement planning, internal-control evaluation, compliance testing, substantive testing, and attestation. Substantial investment and research are needed over the next decade to determine the extent and direction of such changes required by further advances in technology.

In this chapter, we initially examine state-of-the art EDP auditing. Next, we discuss the impact of automation on the audit process and resulting changes in that process. In the concluding section, we present some of the ways in which further advances in EDP technology are likely to aid auditors in their work and further change the audit process itself.

LEARNING OBJECTIVES

By the time you have completed this chapter, you should be able to:

1. Explain state-of-the-art EDP auditing and the potential for further automation.
2. Describe some potential automation tools and their relationships to the further automation of audit tasks.
3. Identify the impact of automation on auditing in terms of changes required in the audit process.
4. Discuss what the future holds for automated auditing.

20.2 STATE-OF-THE-ART AUDITING

The traditional audit process has been highly manual and labor intensive, with many audit procedures done on an ad-hoc basis. Auditors often find themselves still using manual methods to examine and comprehend highly automated accounting systems, the designers of which have used technology extensively to improve the reporting function. Thus most major U.S. organizations now use databases to store substantial amounts of their accounting data. Accountants grew concerned about the increasing use of databases and set up a task force to examine and issue a report on its impact on the audit process.[1] Another major development affecting accounting is the use of minicomputers and microcomputers, which decreases the impact of general controls and places greater emphasis on application-specific controls. Databases and minicomputer/microcomputer systems represent two distinct sets of problems for the auditor. Networks and communication links bring these two sets of audit problems together in an environment that is even more complex and exposed to risk.

Manual audit processes cannot adequately monitor this increasingly complex environment. The technological lag in the audit process is a natural consequence of reliance on methods that have survived experimental and legal testing over the years and an environment that is highly resistant to change. Current computer-aided audit techniques tend to reflect the computerization and manual audit methods, rather than being the product of a reanalysis and redesign of the entire audit process. For example, in the late 1960s and early 1970s, most of the major accounting firms experimented with application-specific software, leading to the development and use of generalized audit software. (See Chapter 7.) The integration of some audit sampling plans into generalized audit software, and the development of independent software for sampling purposes followed. These applications are currently used by many corporations and large accounting firms, but their use is not as widespread in small accounting firms. In addition, some general descriptive statistical features are commonly part of sampling and generalized audit software. Typically, these features provide counts, means, standard deviations, and strata of distinct population samples.

Another important audit aid is the use of regression analysis in analytical review. Deloitte Haskins & Sells has recently publicized its STAR package, which performs these functions. (See Chapter 10.) And, finally, the efforts of two other Big-Eight accounting firms illustrate the extent to which the audit process has been automated to date.

COOPERS & LYBRAND APPLICATIONS

Coopers and Lybrand has approached audit automation on a modular basis, offering a series of microcomputer-based software packages for accounting and audit applications. These packages include:

- Pre-audit.
- Field pack.
- A series of tax packages (1120 tax, 1065 tax, and so on).
- A series of spreadsheet templates to interface with pre-audit.
- Specific accounting procedures for recording lease, real-estate, and other transactions.
- Communication with and data extraction from client files.
- A tax-accrual expert system.
- Many audit-support tools for internal use.

ARTHUR ANDERSEN & CO. APPLICATIONS

Arthur Andersen & Co. has used a similar approach. It has developed modules for:

- Microcomputer trial balance.
- Data transfer.
- Statistical sampling computations.
- Random-number generation.
- Foreign currency translation.
- Debt analysis.
- Tax-accrual work papers.
- LIFO work papers.
- Audit software application development aids.

CURRENT LIMITATIONS AND WIDESPREAD USE OF AUTOMATION FOR AUDITING

At present, the automation of audit tasks and the widespread use of state-of-the-art audit automation are restricted by the limitations of the individual auditor as an information processor. The audit process as a whole is often too detailed and complex for assimilation by an auditor. Identification of multiple interrelationships is difficult, and, even when they can be identified, many of their consequences are counterintuitive and difficult to ascertain. In addition, the auditor must make a series of judgments concerning the adequacy of evidential information, which may exceed his or her human information processing capabilities.[2] Furthermore, audit decisions are often linked to a process of successive review by different auditors. These reviewers often work exclusively from archival audit evidence and lack direct personal observation. This process adds homogeneity to audit quality but often hides informal but important evidence from the eyes of the more experienced auditors. Thus it appears that structural changes in the audit process itself are needed in order to utilize the untapped capabilities of automation.

20.3 AUTOMATION AND AUDIT-PROCESS CHANGE

The adoption of radically different technologies requires modifications in the processes to which these technologies are applied. In fact, studies indicate that the full impact of technological change cannot be absorbed unless the process is also changed. One of the most important technological changes that impacts auditing is on-line EDP capability. Five aspects of the auditing process are affected by this capability: (1) physical location of the auditor; (2) time required to access data; (3) audit timing; (4) treatment of working papers; and (5) technological dependence.

PHYSICAL LOCATION OF THE AUDITOR

With on-line EDP capabilities, the auditor will not work at the client's EDP site but at the location where source documents or their equivalents can be directly accessed (such as the accounting department). At the client's site auditors, using on-line terminals, will access client databases and query for exceptions as well as sample for random or stratified samples. The result of these queries will determine the source documents to be examined, including variables such as filecabinet location of microfiche unit. Furthermore, functions such as "continuous process auditing" can be developed where auditors, at their audit firm site, monitor transactions flowing through the client's main systems.

TIME REQUIRED TO ACCESS DATA

Auditors will be able to use random-number generators when choosing the source documents to be examined. Results obtained from accessing these documents can be entered immediately on a spreadsheet working paper and tests can be run to determine the need for and location of additional sample documents. On-line auditing and recording allows quicker sampling of subpopulations and identification of sources of systematic discrepancies.

The use of an optical scanning device to read source documents can substantially reduce information recording and examination time. The use of voice recognition devices in the future may further enhance the interfacing of auditor and machine. The advent of optical-disks and other forms of inexpensive, large-scale data storage will substantially expand microcomputer capabilities and usefulness in the audit process.

Large CD databases can be used, even at an auditor's microcomputer, containing: (1) audit manuals, (2) audit procedures, (3) post audit work papers, and (4) related audit and accounting standards.

AUDIT TIMING

Currently, audits are planned for specific time intervals and usually begin on an announced date. This procedure is based primarily on the traditional auditing of year-end financial statements, it has little, if any, deterrent value. If client source documents are kept in computer-readable code, available auditor time (such as a day) can be used to make unannounced compliance and substantive tests. Furthermore, "continuous auditing" can provide a higher level of assurance that large/important transactions are being monitored.

TREATMENT OF WORKING PAPERS

The preparation of working papers currently follows general accounting-firm guidelines but vary substantially from office to office, engagement to engagement, and year to year. These differences increase the difficulties of peer review, staff integration, and recall of events in a particular situation. The development of event databases to facilitate research and avoid rediscovering solutions within firms is also made difficult by working-paper variability.

On-line technology can lead to standardized, but flexible, formatting of working papers and substantially increased indexing. Automatic reindexing and updating of secondary and tertiary indexes at different sites will logically follow. Additionally, word processing software will be used for preparation of working papers, spelling checks, and standardized footnote comments; arithmetical and mathematical aids will ease footing and subtotaling tasks. It is somewhat more difficult to access changes in working-paper techniques per se. However, a trend toward more voluminous documentation is expected, which implies more extensive support of evidential matter and additional supporting schedules.

Cross-indexing (tying) of numbers in schedules will be substantially aided by computer-based search procedures that allow for finding relationships without considerable page flipping and the use of colored pencils and various symbols. Of course, current technology also allows for multicolored displays and symbols but, most likely, the complexity and cost introduced by using these media will not immediately compensate for its advantages.

Internal audit departments benefit from substantially less variability in working-paper standards within the firm. On the other hand, substantial differences can be found from firm to firm, which may result in difficulties in the development of standardized working-paper management systems. Consequently, for internal audit departments, working-paper management systems should be highly modular and flexible, allowing both corporate definition of working-paper formats and easy interface with corporate databases and communication systems.

TECHNOLOGICAL DEPENDENCE

Although auditors currently depend on client computer availability for part of their audit work, they are still mainly self-reliant and use manual auditing methods. The evolution of more advanced forms of auditing will depend on (1) audit-aid access; (2) communication lines; (3) database access; and (4) above all, technical competence.

Technical competence, in particular, may cause substantial changes in the audit process and the careers of auditors. Studies such as those by Vasarhelyi and Pabst indicate that EDP auditors are, on average, more experienced and better trained than their traditional counterparts.[3] This finding supports the argument that EDP training and experience is not as available and EDP auditors require more time to become proficient and useful in audit engagements than do traditional auditors. Current career paths must be adjusted if audit staffs are to include technologically proficient auditors. Furthermore, alterations in the present curricula for college accounting training will be required.

20.4 POTENTIAL TECHNOLOGICAL AIDS FOR AUDITING

In addition to the applications mentioned in Section 20.2, Arthur Andersen & Co. has also been working on an audit system for the future, which it calls the *auditor's workbench*. In the words of an Arthur Andersen partner:

> We began with the promise that a computer environment should support and enhance all aspects of the audit process. We defined an environment that would allow our auditors to *literally put aside their stocks of yellow workpapers, forms and pencils* and use the micro as an extensive, professional audit tool.[4]

The system provides for a microcomputer to be fully integrated with a database. Its main functions are:

1. Risk analysis and scope-determination assistance.
2. Work-paper creation.
3. Engagement administration.
4. Work-paper preparation and organization.
5. Review assistance.
6. Financial reporting.

These technologically aided audit procedures are related to several of the main steps in the audit process, which, as you will recall are:

1. Engagement (audit) definition.
2. Engagement (audit) planning.
3. Internal-control evaluation.
4. Compliance testing.
5. Substantive testing.
6. Attestation.

Let's now examine some of the potential automation tasks and/or impacts for each of these steps.

ENGAGEMENT DEFINITION

Engagement definition includes two major tasks: contract preparation and client investigation. The use of technological aids can increase the efficiency with which both tasks are performed.

Contract Preparation. Large law firms often prepare repetitive types of contracts and have stored contract-clause databases for accessing through compatible word processors. Thus the actual preparation of a contract usually entails paragraph selection from a database and minimizes the rewriting and retyping of applicable paragraphs. The same approach can easily be extended to audit contracts, engagement letters, and other engagement definition documents. In the contemporary audit environment, the frequency of public bidding for audit engagements has increased substantially, particularly in the public sector. These processes are expensive but very repetitive. Many larger organizations have a basic bid, which they tailor to the specific requirements of bidding on a particular engagement. These specific changes in the basic bid document can be made easily using word processors.

Client Investigation (Analytical Review, Database Queries). Database availability results in a wider scope of analytical reviews. A substantial number of databases are currently available for the examination of financial statements (such as NAARS), stock prices (such as CRSP), legal precedents and rulings (LEXIS), and other purposes. These applications can be used for analytical review both for time-series and comparative analysis. When discussing the use of on-line databases in an accounting practice, Gale identified a series of databases in addition to the ones mentioned above. They include NEXIS (current and recent news articles), CD DISCLOSURE (SEC filings as 10K, 4K, 10Q, proxy statements and initial registrations), and general database indexes such as DIALOG and ORBIT.[5]

Microcomputers have facilitated the use of external databases at either the audit firm or client's location. Database services such as THE SOURCE and the Dow Jones News Retrieval Service cater directly to the microcomputer market and allow rapid, easy, and relatively inexpensive access to a broad range of information.

ENGAGEMENT PLANNING

Engagement planning includes the four major tasks of analytical review, risk assessment, planning matrix preparation, personnel scheduling, and multiyear engagement planning. All can benefit from greater use of technological aids.

Analytical Review. During the analytical review process, the need to compare a firm with others in its industry may arise.

Auditor specialization has allowed the development of comparative standards and the detection of discrepancies across an industry. The utilization of financial databases allows for the formalization and expansion of these efforts. This type of analysis can be facilitated by using financial accounting databases (such as COMPUSTAT or Value Line) as sources for comparative analysis. The scope can then be expanded to include linear and multiple regression. The same data can also be used for financial-ratio calculations or cluster analysis. Auditors can also use databases to examine, unit by unit, historical ratios for a company that may not be available from manual examination of file systems. The use of expert systems and advanced statistical techniques will substantially change analytical review.

Risk Assessment. A series of different methodologies have been proposed for the assessment of audit risk. Automation would permit the use of simulation "what if" models and sensitivity analysis in risk assessment. Corporate risk is typically measured by the so-called Betas, which are numbers that measure the variance of the stock price or the accounting Beta, the variance of income figures. These risk measures, however, are not the most appropriate for audit risk assessment. New technology will allow the auditor to break down the client's system into subunits, for which risk could be quantified. Actually, the quantification of audit-related variables (such as risk or internal-control quality) is one of the major challenges to management scientists interested in auditing. Spreadsheet software such as Lotus 1-2-3 can be used to facilitate risk assessment.

Planning Matrix (Spreadsheet Software Utilization). Audit planning is among the most complex and judgment-rich areas of auditing. In this stage, audit risks and audit needs must be balanced against audit resources, timing issues and auditor competence issues. For such a purpose auditors often resort to preposing a "planning matrix" where areas and sub-areas of the audit are defined in terms of risks found, resources required and history of former audits.

These matrices, which may contain quantitative and qualitative assessments, may be laid-out onto spreadsheet software for formalization as well as quantification purposes. There, audit planners may measure, quantify, weight, and summarize all content to reach audit emphasis decisions.

Spreadsheet software (such as Lotus 1-2-3) can be used for engagement planning and scheduling. These plans may be incorporated into actual budgets and serve as audit-control mechanisms.

Personnel Scheduling. Traditionally, a major problem in managing a large audit practice has been the assignment of staff to audit engagements.[6] Typically this problem has two dimensions: (1) a long-term assignment plan, and (2) a short-term, engagement-management plan.

The approaches to long-term assignments and short-term scheduling/management are substantially different. Long-term staff assignments can be made by formalizing corporate policies as constraints in a linear programming formulation.[7] The optimal staff assignment can be made using a microcomputer and spreadsheet software. Engagement and auditor characteristics can be matched and optimized in terms of skills required and team composition. Combinations that would maximize staff utilization can be obtained.

The short-term scheduling/management plan can be devised using the query/update mode with the same database. Inherent in the process is unplanned rescheduling (to increase or decrease the size of the audit staff for a particular engagement; to replace a particular staff auditor because of illness, incompatibility, or turnover; and the like).

The value of timely and up-to-date information is clearly evident in short-term scheduling and management. On-line reservation systems furthered the art of resource-utilization management. These systems, if transferred to auditing, could provide timely information on the progress of different engagements, allowing for prompt attention to variances and evaluation of the adequacy of personnel and physical resource utilization and task completion estimation.

Multiyear Engagement Planning. Multiyear models can be used for personnel assignments in order to improve audit management and decrease multiyear risk. The annual choice of areas to be audited should be part of this risk-minimization process. The first year of an engagement is typically the most expensive, both to the auditor and the client. Multiyear contracts for engagements can be used to decrease the annual cost of audit and, combined with technological aids, can produce other substantial benefits.

The following are some of the advantages of this approach. Office automation techniques, or automatic document retrieval, may help alleviate the problems of document organization, storage, and retrieval. Current working papers can be stored in an orderly fashion, while older documents can be microfiched and magnetically encoded for later retrieval. These techniques permit the auditor to cross-tabulate and integrate entire sets of working papers into master catalogs of audit data, precedents, industry comparisons, and auditor tendencies. In addition, the auditor may be able to develop audit subschemas that are more directly connected to the attestation process. Further, the substantial potential that exists for the integration of interactive (on-line) technology into the audit process may be explored. Interactive audit program development, testing, and implementation, as well as potential on-line data queries, may become valuable ancillary audit tools. And, finally, embedded audit routines and other new methods that have great potential become more feasible.

EVALUATION OF INTERNAL CONTROLS

Automated techniques for evaluating internal controls include computerized internal control questionnaires (ICQs), automated flowcharting, critical-control combination analysis, and audit-trail sampling.

Computerized ICQs. Internal controls are complex and interrelated. The evaluation of internal control design and compliance is usually performed manually from a set of ICQs. The system is evaluated in terms of the importance of internal control procedures and their combinations.[8] The combination of procedures may involve a large number of variations, which can be easily evaluated by using EDP.

The automation of the ICQ technique may provide a basis for ICQs that are tailored to industry type, company size, and company error experience. Of the 11 audit firms that responded to the Loebbecke and Cushing survey (Chapter 5), only six used preprinted questionnaires. This may be attributed to philosophical objectives to the ICQ approach or, more likely, to company size and industry differences that pose difficult questionnaire transferability problems. Word-processing technology applied to a well-conceived classification of industries, size, and other factors may allow for properly tailored ICQs, thus decreasing the prohibitively expensive process of tailoring them individually to the evaluation of internal controls for each client. This approach may also yield benefits in terms of efforts to standardize working-paper preparation and, potentially, to automatic quality monitoring.

Automated Flowcharting. Software can be developed that will read the responses to ICQs and generate a document-flow, procedure-performed, and control-prescribed flowchart. These ICQ flowcharts can be used in relation to actual document flows to evaluate system integrity.

Critical-Control Combination Analysis. Computerized ICQs and automated flowcharting can be combined into a semiautomatic procedure for evaluating the design of and compliance with internal control systems. This procedure involves comparing the tailored ICQ (which would contain a maximum set of controls) with the responses obtained from the survey. The overlap between the maximum and the existing would show the extent to which controls are provided. Critical combinations of internal weaknesses would be identified and written up in a working document that would precede the management letter. Compliance would be examined by tying the ICQ responses to data obtained from the use of tagging and tracing (T & T) techniques or other forms of documented internal control compliance.

Audit Trail Sampling. Recall that SAS No. 3 requires a preliminary review of EDP-based systems in order to identify document flows. Tagging and tracing techniques can be used to automate the linkage between accounting events and the evaluation of internal controls and compliance testing. The number of potential combinations of transaction characteristics is so great that it is virtually impossible to prepare test decks that will cover all potential events. At present, T & T allows for ad-hoc examination of document flow through manual procedures through the invisible paths of computer logic. Therefore trail formation, and transaction characteristics monitoring can notably change the nature of interim and year-end work.

The audit of on-line systems poses a new range of problems to the auditor, including: (1) operations with system-generated (as opposed to user-generated) source documents; (2) transactions flowing through highly integrated systems; (3) data stored and accessed in multiple data-storage media; and (4) multiple simultaneous access by users. These requirements may lead in the future to substantially different audit procedures, particularly with respect to audit trails. One possibility is the use of passive devices that examine the flow of automated transactions and that are activated by a particular event, which may be the parameters of a transaction, a random choice, or a systematic data-collection heuristic. Such techniques (self-activation) require substantial changes in existing software and/or the integration in the path of the flow of data of audit/monitoring devices (hardware, software, or firmware). Self activation algorithms must be based on auditor expertise impounded into software.

COMPLIANCE TESTING

Two computerized audit methods can be used in compliance testing: (1) multiple sampling plans; and (2) over-the-shoulder supervision of compliance.

Multiple Sampling Plans. Complex sampling plans become menial computation tasks when used with state-of-the-art data processing. They can be directly linked to both the internal-control compliance testing and the substantive sample-selection processes.

Let's consider the operation of multiple sampling plans in an automatic teller machine (ATM) system. A unique sequence number is assigned to each banking transaction initiated. Each ATM keeps a magnetic trace of all daily transactions, as well as updating continuously master files in a central EDP facility. An auditor's compliance evaluation plan for the system would involve:

1. Random drawing of transactions for direct confirmation. The confirmations are automatically produced from customer records in conjunction with transactions found.
2. Surprise audits, which are linked to stratified sampling models that predict levels of cash at each ATM, at each cashier, and at the entire branch or entity.
3. Variance-monitoring algorithms that call for major differences between recorded transactions and the predictions.
4. Authorizations are entered by some type of electronic imprint, such as an approval key or a password.
5. These imprints are changed often and are uniquely identified to an individual. Location and individual controls are strictly enforced.
6. Sophisticated sampling plans are used for balance extrapolation and control.
7. Records are automatically drawn for source-document or characteristic-validity checks. Auditors simply serve as examiners, rather than having to select the transactions and documents.

Over-the-shoulder Supervision. Most interactive computer systems provide the option of an operator (or someone else with proper authority) to visibly or invisibly link with another terminal and monitor the user-system interaction being performed. This feature can be used for auditing the alertness of users in interactive systems and their compliance to internal control rules. Communication features (such as a verbal or written mode) can make such supervision a deterrent or intervention procedure.

SUBSTANTIVE TESTING

Three major audit tasks can be automated in substantive testing: (1) preparation of confirmations; (2) generation of random numbers; and (3) retrieval of source documents.

Preparation of Confirmations. The combination of word processing, EDP-data files, and effective (perhaps automatic) sampling plans can generate audit economies. This traditional use of computer-assisted auditing can be substantially improved to gather further evidential information at lower cost. We have already discussed some of these features in connection with compliance testing.

Despite the great benefits that may be obtained from the automation of manual audit procedures these are not a panacea. Some manual procedures make little or no sense in an integrated EDP environment. Individual extensions and footing, a common concern in manual audits, tend to lose some of their meaning when systems are automated. For example, consider a department store with point-of-sales cash registers and optical scanning for tags. Computers do most of the arithmetic operations, which are seldom found to be in error. Master tables of per-unit prices and inventory numbers verify the validity of the entered (or optically read) item number. Physical counts are used to reconcile cash register and prescribed inventory totals. In this situation, the auditor must emphasize validation of the master lists, actual utilization of these lists (as opposed to tampered lists), and totals of different types. An auditor who previously handled written sales tickets and invoices, verified the correctness of extensions, checked for the existence of source documents, and then reconciled overall levels of cash, receipts and inventory will now utilize master lists (or electronically interrogate them), will worry about the integrity of the point-of-sales device, and so on.

Another interesting possibility is the automation of standardized working papers. If working papers are standardized and their format is flexible enough for generic allocations and variable data gathering (in terms of format and size), the appropriate data can be automatically entered in working papers, extended, cross-tabulated, footed, and so on, without any manual intervention. The automatic procedures for generating random numbers already discussed can be used to draw numbers of invoices based on their stated amounts, retrieve magnetically encoded source documents, retrieve magnetically indexed source documents, retrieve the location of the source documents, merge these documents with name and address files, and automatically issue confirmations. The confirmations could go directly into an electronic work sheet. In addition, traditional confirmations can be marked and then read by a mark-sensing device and posted to confirmation work sheets.

Generation of Random Numbers. We have already discussed techniques such as multiple sampling methods, revised sampling schedules, and verifiable sample plans (See Chapters 13 to 16). Advances in mathematics and simulation are creating ways to achieve simple audit objectives with maximum efficiency. These methods, combined with self-starting mechanisms, will change the nature of the search for evidence and documentary support, expand the scope of audits, and help to decrease audit costs and increase audit reliability.

Source-document Retrieval. New data-storage technologies at lower cost may substantially increase the amount of source-document storage in EDP media. Recently, electronic storage costs have decreased exponentially, paralleling those of raw data-processing power over the past two decades. This type of data storage, in which most information is digitized, is useful for written text and numbers. However, the most dramatic changes will occur when pictures and sounds can be stored effectively and economically as part of EDP systems. Visual scanners that can input information directly from printed pages will revolutionize methods of data collection and storage costs. Emphasis will then be given to the information identification and indexing systems needed for massive data-retrieval purposes.

In the near future, it is difficult to visualize systems that can, for example, directly record and save magnetically addressable data for a medium-sized bank that processes three million transactions each night. However, intermediate procedures involving magnetic addressing and indexing, associated with mechanical retrieval and image storage, are already widely available.

The implications for auditing are immense. The grueling process of searching for, examining, and validating source documents will be simplified and less costly. Software can be designed to retrieve automatically a sample of these data. This software may also be used to automatically generate tables with document availability, content, location, and update data. These tables can be associated with or directly incorporated in working papers. Consequently, tradeoffs among different stages of the auditing process will change.

ATTESTATION

We interpret the process of attestation as the aggregation of evidence and formulation of judgments in addition to the issuance of an audit opinion.

Evaluation of Audit Evidence. The most likely change in the audit process will be the proliferation of decision-making and computational aids used by auditors.[9] Some methods of directly affecting the process of decision making are bound to be developed. Audit research has shown substantial differences in the quality of decisions within CPA firms, as well as disagreement among auditors about the many judgment decisions that they have to make during the course of an audit.

Expert systems may be used in the future to supplement audit judgment.[10] The use of ES in auditing is analogous to that for medical diagnoses.[11] In both cases there is a set of objectives (attestation; recovery of health), a set of symptoms (errors found, high blood pressure), and, potentially, the diagnosis of a pathology (poor input controls, cardiac disease) the linkages are not a one-to-one but many-to-many relationships, involving probabilistic associations and best guesses. Medical systems have been developed by having experts (such as the internist) replicate their heuristics and diagnostic reasoning. A series of intermediate decisions have to be made about the need for additional measurements (search for evidence; medical tests), their cost, the degree of their interference (for example requesting dangerous medical diagnostic procedures) in the situation, and the like. Finally most pathologies (errors) are at least somewhat interrelated and often, even with positive results, the clinician (auditor) is not quite sure whether he or she has made the correct diagnosis (interpretation).

In order to apply ES broadly in auditing, knowledge engineers must work with experienced accountants and auditors to identify (1) evidence being gathered; (2) areas being examined; (3) rules for evidence gathering; (4) rules for auditor and client relationships; (5) subsystem-evaluation heuristics; (6) evidence costs; (7) methods of assessing subjective risks; (8) rules for inference; (9) rules relied on setting boundaries where adjustments are required from clients; and finally (10) heuristics for final opinion formulation. These factors would be used to develop software and a database, creating the *auditor's helper* to support audit field efforts. This system would be used regularly to help the auditor make judgment decisions and to forcefully remind the auditor of the need to consider particular audit factors.

Issuance of Opinions and Management Letters. Dictionaries of types of opinions, qualifications, restrictions of scope, and the like can be used to decrease the expense of creating new wording on an ad hoc basis or searching for similar precedents and established disclosure wording. A CPA firm could have a series of disclaimers and "subject to" paragraphs to include in opinions, as well as for use in characterizing or categorizing situations. These considerations are as applicable to management letters as they are to the issuance of opinions.

A somewhat less likely, but possible, change would be the natural step of segmenting opinions for organizational units and systems. These opinions could be stated in terms of probabilities (such as: "We are 93 percent sure that . . . "), along with disclosure of materiality thresholds (such as: "We used a materiality threshold of $100,000.") and observed variances.

20.5 Summary

This chapter examined the future of the process and the automation of audit procedures. We first positioned some problems found in traditional audit practice. We then identified some progressive audit automation approaches currently being developed by major accounting firms.

The following section identified five major aspects of auditing where process changes can be identified: (1) physical location of the auditor, (2) data access time, (3) audit timing, (4) working papers, and (5) technological dependence by the auditor.

The ensuing section examined the potential automation tools and procedural changes that will affect each major step of the audit process. Many of these tools and procedural elements may be applicable to other areas of the audit that were not discussed in this chapter.

In conclusion, this chapter raised a series of questions to challenge students, researchers and practitioners in the search of better quality auditing.

Questions

1. Auditing is still primarily a manual, labor-intensive process. Why does this make audit automation imperative?
2. Besides solving some basic audit problems what are some other benefits that audit automation will provide?
3. Describe each of the following forms of audit automation.
    (a) Standardized documentation.
    (b) Comparative analysis.
    (c) Scheduling.
    (d) Internal control evaluation.
    (e) Audit planning.
    (f) Self-starting audit procedures.
4. How will new audit technology affect each of the following?
    (a) Physical location of the auditor.
    (b) Time required to access data.
    (c) Audit timing.
    (d) Working papers.
5. How can the assessment of audit risk be improved through the use of new technologies?
6. Describe tagging and tracing (T & T) techniques.
7. How does over-the-shoulder supervision and compliance work in an on-line situation?

8. How can new technologies aid the auditor in evaluating evidence?
9. What possible changes could occur in the form of the auditor's opinion as a result of new technologies?
10. How could the preparation of management letters be improved by new technologies? Consider automated working papers, internal-control questionnaires, and critical combinations.
11. How do the efforts of the two major CPA firms described in Section 20.2 relate to the general framework of audit automation?
12. Prepare a table that compares the expert system formulation of audit and medical systems as discussed in this chapter.

Problems

1. Based on the changes in the audit process suggested in this chapter, do you think the structure of CPA firms will change?
2. What skills will new technologies require the auditor to learn? Will this have an impact on your education? How will auditors now in the field acquire these skills?
3. Besides economic efficiency, what improvements in actual audit quality are these new technologies likely to generate?
4. Given the ability of audit automation to provide immediate access to working papers as they are generated, do you think these technologies will change the style of audit supervision?
5. If you were the managing partner of a CPA firm today, how would you prepare your firm to adapt to the changes suggested in this chapter? How would you deal with resistance from your partners?
6. Prepare a chart illustrating an audit-decision support system encompassing most of the audit and automation functions described in this chapter.

Notes

1. *Report of the Joint Data Base Task Force* (of the AICPA, CICA and IIA). New York: The American Institute of Certified Public Accountants, 1983.

2. Libby, Robert, *Behavioral Decision Theory Research in Accounting*, Prentice-Hall, 1982, p. 1.

3. Vasarhelyi, Miklos A., and Pabst, Carl A., "Practices, Standards, Involvement, the Usage of the Computer in EDP Audit: A Survey," *The EDP Auditor*, Summer, 1981, pp. 29–35.

4. Roussey, Robert S., "Automating the Auditor." Presentation to Beta Alpha Psi, Honolulu, 1986, p. 35.

5. Gale, A. P., "Computerized Research: An Advanced Tool," *Journal of Accountancy*, January 1982, pp. 73–84.

6. Vasarhelyi, Miklos A., "Staff Assignment in Accounting Firms," *Journal of Accountancy*, 1981, p. 42.

7. Summers, E. L., "The Audit Staff Assignment Problem: A Linear Programming Analysis," *Accounting Review*, July 1972, p. 443–453.

8. Vasarhelyi, Miklos A., "A Taxonomization of Internal Controls, and Errors for Audit Research," Touche Ross Audit Symposium, U. of Kansas, 1980.

9. Bedard, J., Gray, G. L., and Mock, T. J., "Decision Support Systems and Auditing," *Advances in Accounting*, 1984, 1: pp. 239–66.

10. Elliott, Robert K., and Kielich, John A., "Expert Systems for Accountants," *Journal of Accountancy*, September 1985, pp. 127–134; Hansen, J. V., and Messier, W. F., "Expert Systems for Decision Support in EDP Auditing," *International Journal of Computer and Information Sciences*, 1982, pp. 357–379; Messier, W. F., and Hansen, J. V., "Expert Systems in Accounting and Auditing: A Framework and Review." In Joyce, E., and Moriarity, S. (Eds.), *Decision Making and Accounting: Current Research*, Norman: University of Oklahoma, 1984.

11. Gallegos, Frederick, "The Need for a Better Trained Auditor," *EDP Auditor*, Spring 1985.

Additional References

Argyris, C., "Management Information Systems: The Dialogue to Rationality and Emotionality," *Management Science*, February 1971.

Audit Sampling. Cleveland: Ernst & Whinney, 1979.

Audit SCOPE Manual. Deloitte, Haskins & Sells, New York: 1978.

Balachandran, Bala V., and Andris A. Zoltners, "An Interactive Audit-Staff Scheduling Decision Support System," *The Accounting Review*, October 1981, pp. 801–812.

Balachandran, K. R., and R. E. Steuer, "An Interactive Model for the CPA Firm Audit Staff Planning Problem with Multiple Objectives," *The Accounting Review*, January 1982, pp. 125–140.

"Conference on EDP Audit," *Proceedings*. New York: Institute of Internal Auditors, February 1983.

"The Effects of EDP on the Auditor's Study and Evaluation of Internal Control," *Statement on Auditing Standards No. 3*, New York: American Institute of Certified Public Accountants, December 1973.

"The Effects of Computer Processing on the Examination of Financial Statements," *Statement on Auditing Standards, No. 48*, New York: American Institute of Certified Public Accountants, July 1984.

"Innovations in Auditing." A brochure that describes audit tools and software available at Arthur Andersen & Co. Chicago, Illinois, 1986.

Sigma Users Guide. Cleveland: Ernst & Whinney, 1976.

Stringer, K. W., "A Statistical Technique for Analytical Review." Proceedings of the Conference on Statistical Methodology in Auditing at the Graduate School of Business, University of Chicago, 1975.

Vasarhelyi, Miklos A., "Audit Automation: Online Technology and Auditing," *The CPA Journal*, April 1985, pp. 10–17.

Vasarhelyi, Miklos A., "Automation and Changes in the Audit Process," *Auditing: A Journal of Theory and Practice*, Fall 1984, pp. 100–105.

Vasarhelyi, Miklos A., Carl A. Pabst, and Ian Daley, "Organizational and Career Aspects of the EDP Audit Function: A Survey," *The EDP Auditor*, Spring 1981.

Appendix: Applications of the Terminal Related Education Audit Tool (TREAT)

A.1 INTRODUCTION

In this appendix, we describe the general features of the Terminal Related Educational Audit Tool (TREAT)[*], a generalized audit software, oriented to the instructional process. We also present a walkthrough of an inventory audit (Magic Desk Company) and present three additional cases with all necessary information to specify a TREAT application. This section provides a nontechnical introduction to the main features of the TREAT system and its applications. It is designed to allow a rapid grasp of the system without requiring an in-depth understanding of its mechanics.

TREAT is a generalized audit software (GAS) system, designed particularly for audit instruction purposes. However, because of its state-of-the-art features, it can also serve as a useful tool for certain specific noneducational audit applications. It emulates the Touche Ross STRATA system by replicating most of its features and using similar coding forms. However, TREAT is terminal-based (interactive), whereas STRATA is batch-oriented.

MINIMUM REQUIREMENTS FOR SYSTEM USE

The TREAT system is programmed in APL language, so the computer system to be used must have an APL language interpreter available. Most computers that support the APL language can be used for the TREAT system, including IBM, UNIVAC, HP, DEC, Burroughs, and CDC equipment. In addition a few minicomputers and microcomputers support APL and, consequently, TREAT.[1] Most time sharing terminals may be used for student–TREAT interaction and do *not* have to be APL terminals.

---

[*] Copyright by Miklos A. Vasarhelyi and W. Thomas Lin, 1979; all rights reserved. The Terminal Related Educational Audit Tool (TREAT) was developed under a project sponsored by The Touche Ross Program to Support Accounting Education. To obtain further information about the system, or to obtain the software itself, write to Dr. Miklos A. Vasarhelyi, 30-G-014 Bell Laboratories, 600 Mountain Ave., Murray Hill, NJ 07974.

In addition to the instructor, one systems person, knowledgeable in APL and in systems procedures, should be available to help install the system. The system can be installed, in most instances, by simply loading a tape onto the host computer with the data sets named in an APL compatible notation. Then, in most cases, one of the developers would call up the installation over the telephone and test the system remotely.

Student data storage requirements vary according to the way TREAT is to be used in the classroom. The TREAT system itself occupies about 70 pages (2K each) but may be segmented into smaller work spaces. An additional work space with supplemental test data and programs is supplied with the system and occupies about 30 pages. Each student (or student group) should be allotted from 20 to 50 pages to store their own programs and a master routine that calls up the TREAT system.

SYSTEM FEATURES

The system is interactive in question-and-answer and menu-selection modes, whereby users sign on to the APL system in the usual manner and invoke the TREAT system. In utilizing the system they may use the

1. *definition mode* to specify TREAT programs by following TREAT specification forms;
2. *modification mode* to change TREAT programs or to define parts of a TREAT program;
3. *list mode* to prepare detailed documentation of their program;
4. *execution mode* to test and execute the TREAT programs defined earlier.

In addition users may utilize the TREAT system as front-end software to prepare and test TREAT programs, which can then be dumped onto cards or tape and executed using the batch version, or STRATA.

Figure A.1 shows the main features of system utilization. A large number of students may use the system simultaneously; each student is connected to a different time-sharing terminal, but all use the same computer, TREAT system, and student libraries.

Figure A.2 displays the main elements of the system's internal structure. The TREAT system is activated by calling the TREAT master. The student's library will contain only this short TREAT master and the student's own TREAT programs, called programmer's source code matrices (PSCMs). Further information concerning system structure, and in particular the programs and files used, is contained in the TREAT systems manual.

Figure A.1   TREAT Usage

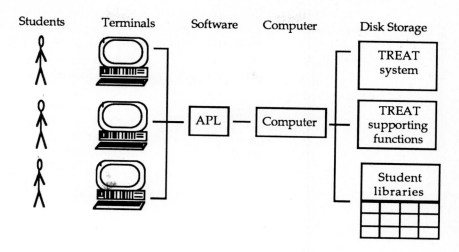

Figure A.2   TREAT System Structure

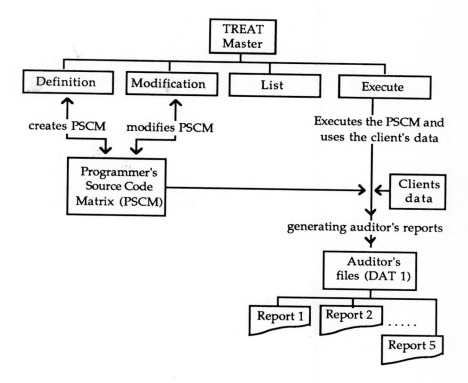

SYSTEM USE

The TREAT system may be used for both instruction and actual audit applications. The user will use the definition and modification modes to create a TREAT program, the list mode to document it, and the execute mode to run the program.

Instructional Use. Typical student use of the TREAT system involves the following:

1. Program definition.
2. Program list.
3. Execution.   } Several
4. Modification.   iterations
5. Final report run.
6. Documentation.

Contingent on storage availability at the EDP facility, students may be permitted to keep copies of several of their applications after they complete their final reports. An extensive discussion of approaches for using TREAT for instructional purposes is contained in the TREAT instructor's manual.

Audit-practice Use. The TREAT system is interpreter-based because of its APL language structure, with line-by-line execution. This type of execution is less efficient than that for a compiler-based language, where execution follows the compilation of the entire program.[2] Because of this feature, use of TREAT for auditing large files may not be effective. However, there are several instances in which the use of TREAT may be warranted in practice:

1. When TREAT is used as a front-end system to generate a STRATA program.
2. When the computer system is too small for another generalized audit software or when no other GAS is available but an APL interpreter is available.
3. When files are small and applications complex.
4. When the economics of the audit process warrant inefficient audit software execution with savings in personnel and transportation and from the avoidance of location work.
5. In exotic systems where GAS is not available or not of good quality.

For expanded use of the TREAT system in audit practice, some of the features that were eliminated to simplify it for educational purposes would have to be reinstated, requiring additional developmental work.

A.2 CASE STUDY WALKTHROUGH: MAGIC DESK COMPANY INVENTORY AUDIT

The Magic Desk Company is located in the northeast and is a large manufacturer of office desks. Mr. Clever, the company's founder, had captured a major portion of that market by building production facilities close to each major market area; hence the company has numerous warehouses, which stock only items unique to local market demand.

The end of the company's fiscal year is approaching, and Mr. Clever has asked your firm, Big & Co., to perform a comprehensive audit. Harold Bummer, your boss, has asked you and a co-worker to perform the inventory audit; that is, to verify the accuracy of the computer inventory files. Harold informs you of Mr. Clever's concern about rising inventory costs: "In this period of tight money, with the Feds raising interest rates and all, our company has been trying to reduce the amount of money tied up in inventory. We would like your firm, Harold, to look into this matter and come up with some suggestions in the management letter."

Harold directs the two of you to the company's data library, where the files are stored. Your assistant, just out of Columbia Business School, questions the possibility of the two of you accomplishing this task: "After all, there are thousands of items stocked in those warehouses." You confidently respond that only a small sample (1 percent of the population) needs to be tested because your firm determined that such a sample size fairly represents the population before accepting the assignment. With the data files containing the 1% sample in hand, you proceed to the computer room to tackle the assignment.

AUDIT OBJECTIVES

The first objective is to select items to be physically counted. Choose those items with an extended cost of more than $1000.00. Sort and print these items by location in ascending order of extended cost.

The second objective is to select items for which the unit price is to be checked against purchase invoices or standard-cost sheets. Choose those items with a unit cost greater than $5.00. Sort and print these items by part number in ascending order.

APPLICATION AND LOGIC FLOWCHARTS; LAYOUT WORKSHEETS

An application flowchart, in standard flowchart symbols, describes the interaction between the client's file and the firm's software, the resequencing of the files, and the output points in the application. Figure A.3 presents such a flowchart.

Figure A.3 TREAT Application Flowchart

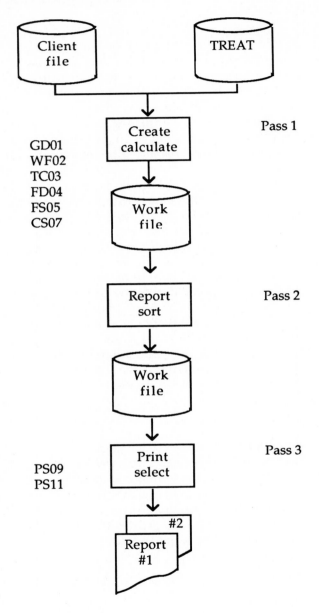

Two important worksheets must be completed before the STRATA–TREAT specification forms can be filled out:

1. A record layout worksheet, which specifies input (client's) record format and is shown in Fig. A.4.
2. A report layout worksheet, which specifies output report format (for each report to be printed). This report is shown in Figure A.5.

The logic flowchart (Figure A.6) details the step-by-step operations performed in processing the data. It is the next step after the objectives have been chosen and input and output requirements have been set.

SPECIFICATION FORMS

With the completion of the application flowchart, record layout worksheet, report layout worksheet, and the logic flowchart, you are now ready to fill out the following specification forms.

1. **General description (GD) page:** Describes the user environment and gives a description of the type of recording media (disc or tape) used by the system.

2. **Working file (WF) page:** Allows you to create your own work file, which will receive the parts of the client's file specified by the field selection (FS) page.

3. **Temporary core storage (TC) page:** An optional page, it allows the use of working (w), temporary numeric (t), and temporary alphanumeric (a) fields.

4. **File definition (FD) page:** Used to define the client's data medium.

5. **Field selection (FS) page:** Selects fields to be drawn from the client's file and copied into your working file, as set up by the WF page.

6. **Calculate stratify (CS) page:** Performs the main computations as described in the logic flowchart.

7. **Print select (PS) page:** Allows comprehensive comparison, analysis, and calculation with TC fields and prints the records in the file as selected.[3]

Figure A.4   Record Layout Worksheet with Input Record Format

TREAT RECORD LAYOUT WORKSHEET
WITH INPUT RECORD FORMAT

FILE DESCRIPTION   _Inventory Master File_

FILE LABEL | S | T | R | A | T | I | N | V | | | | | | | | | | | | | | | | | |

VOLUME SER. NO. | I | T | C | H | 0 | 3 |

DEVICE TYPE   T9 2311 (3330) Card   DISK FILE
T7 2314   Data Call   ORGANIZATION   (SD)   DA   IS HIERARCH-ICAL FILE   YES (NO)

BYTES PER RECORD   80   RECORDS PER BLOCK   10   BYTES PER BLOCK   800   FIXED OR VARIABLE   (F) T

O/S UNIT JCL PARAMETER | | | | | | | | O/S 7 TRACK TRTCH | | | C - Convert ET - Even/Translate   O/S TAPE DEN PARAMETER | |
E - Even T - Odd/Translate

O = T7-200   2 = T7/T9-800
1 = T7-556   3 = T9-1600

	LOCATION 5											
To work field												
Client field name	CONTROL FIELD	DESCRIPTION	ISSUES YTD	ISSUES LAST YEAR BLANK	QTY BOM	PURCHASES	ISSUES	ADJUST-MENTS	LAST UNIT	DATE LAST PURCH	VNDOR CODE	DATE LAST ISSUE
Storage format	C	C	P+	P+	C	P+	P+	P-	P+	P+	C	C	C
Decimal position			0	0		0	0	0	0	2			

* BYTES 1-4 ARE PART NUMBER
√ BEGINNING OF MONTH QUANTITY
√ YEAR TO DATE
Ø WAREHOUSE 6-9

To work field					
Client field name					
Storage format					
Decimal position					

Checked by: (Client Signature)

Character - C; Packed Decimal (Signed) - P; Binary - B; Unsigned Packed - U; Unsigned
Packed Right - R; Unsigned Packed Left - X; Unsigned Packed all - A; Bit field - H (Show Detail);
Variable length field - V or D. Indicate positive or negative on numeric fields.

Figure A.5   Record Layout Worksheet with Output Record Format

TREAT **RECORD LAYOUT WORKSHEET
WITH OUTPUT RECORD FORMAT**

Page PS __09__ - Report No./Title __Report No. 1__ TEST COUNT ITEMS

Strata field	W14	W02	W09	W08	W10	W13	W17
Column heading	PART NO.	DESCRIPTION	VENDOR CODE	DATE LAST PURCHASE	DATE LAST ISSUE	QUANTITY EOM	EXTENDED
Print Position							

Strata field	SIM	LOCA- TION					
Column heading		COST					
Print Position							

Page PS __11__ - Report No./Title __Report No. 2__ SELECT ITEMS FOR PRICE CHECK

Strata field	W14	W15	W02	W09	W08	W10	W13	W17
Column heading	PART NO.	LOCA- TION	DESCRIPTION	VENDOR CODE	DATE LAST PURCHASE	DATE LAST ISSUE	QUANTITY EOM	EXTENDED
Print Position								

Strata field		W07						
Column heading	COST	LAST UNIT COST						
Print Position								

Page PS ____ - Report No./Title ____

Strata field							
Column heading							
Print Position							

Strata field							
Column heading							
Print Position							

Figure A.6   Logic Flowchart

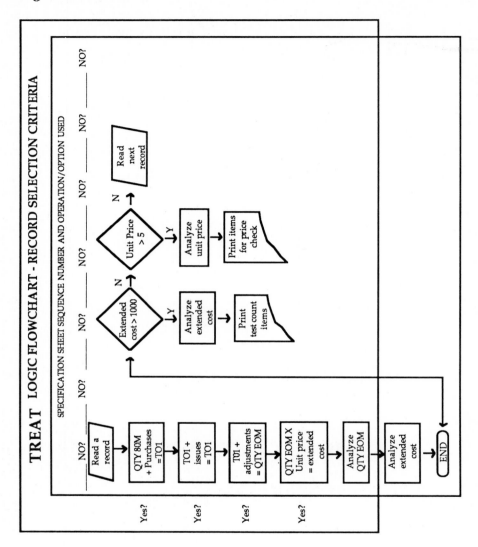

USING THE DEFINITION MODE

After you have completed the specification forms, go to the computer terminal. First, follow the sign-on procedures in the user's manual. Then type TREAT and the computer will respond with [CHOOSE THE MODE OF OPERATION: D, M, E, L, OR O] (definition, modification, execution, list, or out). Start by typing [D] for definition mode. Figure A.7 shows an example of how to use the definition mode.

Figure A.7   Example of a Definition from the GD Page Specification Form

```
        TREAT
CHOOSE THE MODE OF OPERATION: DEFINITION (D),
MODIFICATION (M), EXECUTION (E), LIST (L), OR OUT (O)
D
IS THIS THE DEFINITION OF A NEW PROGRAM? (YES (Y) OR
NO (N))
Y
ARE YOU SURE THAT YOU WANT TO DELETE YOUR OLD PROGRAM?
(Y OR N)
Y
YOUR PROGRAM AREA IS CLEAR, YOU MUST BEGIN WITH GD AND
WF PAGES
ENTER PAGE AND NUMBER TO BE DEFINED (E.G., GD01)
TYPE EXIT TO LEAVE THE DEFINITION MODE
GD01
ENTER DATE, EXIT WITH BLANK: 110578
COMPANY HEADING: MAGIC DESK COMPANY
APPLICATION HEADING: INVENTORY CASE
DATA RECORDED: GD011110578   TREAT COMPANY    INVENTORY
CASE
FILE ASSIGNMENT — NON SAVED WORK FILES
A. ENTER FILE CODE
D4
ENTER INSTALLATIONS WITH JCL PARAMETER OR SORT FILES:
DATA RECORDED: GD012D4
```

Figure A.8   Example of a List from the FS Page Specification Form

```
CHOOSE   THE   MODE   OF   OPERATION;   DEFINITION   (D),
MODIFICATION  (M),  EXECUTION  (E),  LIST  (L),  OR  OUT  (O)
L
TCE  29


COMPLETE  (C),  PARTIAL  (P)  LIST  OR  OUT  (O)?
P
ENTER  PAGE  TO  BE  LISTED
FS05
DO  YOU  WANT  TO  PAGE  SKIP  (Y  OR  N)?  N
PLACE  PAGE  IN  PRINTING  POSITION  AND  PRESS  RETURN
```

The entire TREAT system is designed using a *dialogue* style. For example, after you type [D], the computer asks you whether this is the definition of a new program. You type [Y] for yes. If there is an old program in the system, the computer asks you whether you want to delete the old program. In this case, you type [Y] for yes. Then the computer asks you to enter page and number to be defined. You type in [GD01] page. Then you continue to go through the first card in GD page. When you finish the first card, the computer responds with [DATA RECORDED : GD12D4.]

USING THE LIST MODE

After you have finished using definition mode, you may want to see a list of the input program. The list mode will provide you with this documentation. Figure A.8 presents a typical output resulting from the use of the list mode.

The computer first requests the desired mode of operation. Since the list mode is wanted, you enter [L]. The computer responds to this input with a request for the type of listing, [C, P, OR O] (complete, partial list or out). Because you need only a partial listing of a particular page, you enter [P]. Next, the computer requests the desired page number, and your response is [FS05]. You then have the option of using either special output formatting, which provides for only one report to be printed on each page, or continuous printing of reports without spaces between reports. In Figure A.6, the response typed in, [N], means no request for special formatting.

Finally, place the paper in printing position and press the [RETURN] key. The resulting output is shown in Fig. A.9.

USING THE MODIFICATION MODE

With the modification mode, you may (1) redefine a particular page; (2) delete a page; (3) correct a particular line on a page; (4) insert a line on a page; or (5) delete a line from any page. Figure A.10 shows how to correct a line. Note that the line correction is a combination of two operations: deleting a line and inserting a new line in its place.

As soon as you type in [M], the computer asks you to select one of the following alternatives: (1) to enter the page number to be modified [(NUMBER)]; (2) to examine a list of pages [(PALI)]; (3) to examine a card list and its contents [(CARD)]; and (4) to renumber the page sequence [(RENU)]. The purpose of the page list command [(PALI)] is to obtain a list of page numbers and starting line numbers for each page. The card list [(CARD)] will show the sequence number and content of each card.

Figure A.9   Example of Output of the List Mode

```
Treat—Version 78.01—VS    Columbia University    10/7/86

              LISTING OF DATA FIELD SELECTION    PAGE—FSO5

COMPANY—STRATA INVENTORY              APPLICATION—INVENTORY WALKTHROUGH

     FIELD          LEFTMOST                      WORK
     NAME           LOCATION     SIZE   DECIMAL   FORMAT FIELD   FIELD

     CONTROL FIELD     0           4               C  W01  PART NUMBER
     LOCATION          4           1               C  W02  LOCATION
     DESCRIPTION       5          12               C  W03  DESCRIPTION
     QUANTY BOM       17           6       0       P  W04  QUANTY BOM
     PURCHASE         23           6       0       P  W05  PURCHASE
     ISSUES           29           6       0       P  W06  ISSUES
     ADJUSTMENTS      35           6       0       P  W07  ADJUSTMENTS
     LAST UN COST     41           6       0       P  W08  LAST UN COST
     MONTH DAY PURC   47           4       2       C  W09  MONTH DAY PURC
     YEAR L PURC      51           2               C  W010 YEAR L PURC
     VENDOR CODE      53           5               C  W011 VENDOR CODE
     MONTH DAY LA I   58           4               C  W012 MONTH DAY LA I
     YEAR L ISSUE     62           2               C  W013 YEAR L ISSUE
     ISSUES           64           6       0       P  W014 ISSUES
     ISSUES L YEAR    70           6       0       P  W015 ISSUES L YEAR
     BLANK            76           4               C  W016 BLANK

COMPLETE (C), PARTIAL (P) LIST OR OUT (O)?
```

Figure A.10 Example of Line Correction Using the Modification Mode

```
CHOOSE THE MODE OF OPERATION: DEFINITION (D),

MODIFICATION (M), EXECUTION (E), LIST (L), OR WORD (W)

M

WFE 5

TCE 29

ENTER PAGE NUMBER (E.G., CS20) TO BE MODIFIED, PALI

FOR A LIST OF DEFINED PAGES, CARD FOR A CARD LIST,

RENU FOR PAGE RENUMBERING OR OUT

PS08

PAGE ALREADY DEFINED: ENTER RE FOR PAGE REDEFINITION,

DE FOR PAGE DELETION, CO FOR CARD CORRECTION, IN FOR

CARD INSERTION, DC FOR CARD DELETION, OR OUT

CO

ENTER CARD NUMBER IN YOUR MAIN CARD LIST, EXIT WITH

ZERO

[]:

      100

CARD NUMBER OUT OF RANGE, TRY AGAIN

ENTER CARD NUMBER IN YOUR MAIN CARD LIST, EXIT WITH

ZERO

[]:

      46

WAS THE CARD THE FOLLOWING?

FS052 47    4C MONTH DAY PURCW10

(YES(Y), NO(N) OR OUT(O))

N
```

(continued on next page)

Figure A.10 Example of Line Correction Using the Modification Mode (continued)

```
DO YOU WANT TO LIST PAGE PS08'S CARDS TO FIND THE
DESIRED CARD?
(YES(Y) OR NO(N))
N
ENTER CARD NUMBER IN YOUR MAIN CARD LIST, EXIT WITH
ZERO
[]:
     54
WAS THE CARD THE FOLLOWING?
PS08110W13L       10
(YES(Y), NO(N) OR OUT (O))
Y
CARD DELETED
ENTER NEW PS081 DEFINITION
ENTER LINE NUMBER, EXIT THIS MODE WITH 100
[]:
     110
ENTER OPERATION
G
ENTER FIELD A
W13
ENTER FIELD B

ENTER A FOR ALPHANUMERIC AND N FOR NUMERIC CONSTANTS:
A
```

(continued on next page)

Figure A.10 Example of Line Correction Using the Modification Mode (continued)

```
ENTER ALPHANUMERIC CONSTANT: 10

INSERTED CARDS

PS08110W13G        10

ENTER PAGE NUMBER (E.G., CS20) TO BE MODIFIED, PALI

FOR A LIST OF DEFINED PAGES, CARD FOR A CARD LIST,

RENU FOR PAGE RENUMBERING OR OUT
```

Assume that you want to correct a PS page. First, you type in [PS08] and then [CO]. The computer then asks which card you want to correct. Since you aren't sure, you guess [100]. The computer responds with [CARD NUMBER OUT OF RANGE, TRY AGAIN.] So you try [46]. The computer answers with a question:

```
'WAS THE CARD THE FOLLOWING?
FS052 47 4C MONTH DAY PURCW10
(YES(Y), NO(N), OR OUT(O))'.
```

Since it isn't, you type [N]. The computer then offers you the opportunity to list card numbers and contents so that you may find the one you want. Your response is [N]. Instead, you again try to enter the correct card number by typing [54]. After your confirmation, the computer tells you that this card has been deleted and that you should enter a new definition for this card.

USING THE EXECUTE MODE

If you want the computer to process your program, just type [E] for execution. Figure A.11 shows execution of the TREAT program, with the output omitted. After the [E] response to the prompt, the computer's response is [GDE 1], meaning page GD was executed and was card equivalent number 1. Then the computer prints [WFE 5], which means that page GD, starting at card equivalent number 5, was executed, while [TCE 29] means that page TC starting at card equivalent 29 (or line 29 of the PSCM) was executed.

Figure A.11 Example of Program Execution

```
CHOOSE THE MODE OF OPERATION: DEFINITION (D),

MODIFICATION (M), EXECUTION (E), LIST (L), OR OUT (O)

E

GDE 1

WFE 5

TCE 29

FDE 35

FSE 38

PASS STARTS AT CARD 54 AND ENDS AT CARD 67

PAGE: CS10   LINE 125 VARIABLE: W25

SAMPLE SIZE 20 MAXIMUM 10938.99 MINIMUM -432.9

MEAN 2070.947 VARIANCE 9272853.699 RANGE 11371.89

POSITIVE VALUES: 17 NEGATIVES 3 ZEROS 0


PAGE: CS10   LINE: 160 VARIABLE: W25

SAMPLE SIZE 8 MAXIMUM 10938.99 MINIMUM 1007.6

MEAN 4752.265 VARIANCE 11253045.16 RANGE 9931.39

POSITIVE VALUES: 9 NEGATIVES 3 ZEROS 0


PAGE CS15   LINE: 105 VARIABLE: W25

SAMPLE SIZE 12 MAXIMUM 869.22 MINIMUM -432.9

MEAN 283.402 VARIANCE 141214.054 RANGE 1302.12

POSITIVE VALUES: 9 NEGATIVES 3 ZEROS 0
```

(continued on next page)

Figure A.11 Example of Program Execution (continued)

```
PAGE CS15   LINE: 120 VARIABLE: W25

SAMPLE SIZE 1 MAXIMUM -432.9 MINIMUM -432.9

MEAN -432.9 VARIANCE 1 RANGE 0

POSITIVE VALUES: 0 NEGATIVES 1 ZEROS 0


SSE 68

PASS STARTS AT CARD 69 AND ENDS AT CARD 75

PAGE" PS25 LINE: 110 VARIABLE: W25

SAMPLE SIZE 20 MAXIMUM 10938.99 MINIMUM -432.9

MEAN 2070.947 VARIANCE 9272853.699 RANGE 11371.89

POSITIVE VALUES: 17 NEGATIVES 3 ZEROS 0


PAGE: CS 27 LINE: 110 VARIABLE: W25

NO RECORDS FOUND TO ANALYZE


REPORT NUMBER 01 PRINTING

 SET THE PAPER IN THE BEGINNING OF A NEW PAGE.

 AND PRESS THE RETURN KEY:
```

The comment [PASS STARTS AT CARD 54 AND ENDS AT CARD 67] means that a pass relates to those specific lines of the PSCM. The ensuing blocks give statistics required by an [ANL] command in a CS page relating to the total number of records that (after the pass is completed) had passed through that point. This is a valuable aid for the auditor who may be losing records or not be quite sure of the logic of his or her TREAT program. After you confirm the request for a printout by pressing the carriage return key, the output is provided.

TREAT CODING FORMS

Figure A.12 shows the filled-in TREAT coding forms for this application.

Figure A.12 TREAT Forms for Magic Desk Company Inventory Audit

(a) General System Specification

TREAT General System Specification

SEQUENCE
NUMBER

| G | D | 0 | 1 | 1 |

1. DATE

MO DAY YR

| 1 | 1 | 0 | 7 | 7 | 9 |

2. COMPANY HEADING

| M | A | G | I | C | | D | E | S | K | , | | I | N | C |

3. APPLICATION HEADING

| I | N | V | E | N | T | O | R | Y | | C | A | S | E |

Card 2

6. FILE ASSIGNMENT - NON-SAVED WORK FILES

| G | D | 0 | 1 | 2 |

    A. ENTER STRATA FILE CODE OF NOT-SAVED
    WORK FILES

| D | 4 |

    T9 for 9 Track Tape   D1 for 2311 Disk
    T7 for 7 Track Tape   D2 for 2314, 3340 & 3344 Disk
    D4 for 3330 & 3350 Disk

Card 3

| G | D | 0 | 1 | 3 |

8. ENTER A STARTING NUMBER FOR
    RANDOM SELECT

| | | | | 3 |

9. ENTER THE SYSOUT INFORMATION (1)
    A. Enter strata file code for sysout unit, or 19 for
    9 Track Tape, T7 for 7 Track Tape

| T | 9 |

    B. ENTER SYSOUT BLOCK SIZE

| | | 1 | 3 | 2 |

10. ENTER THE PROCEDURE NAME FOR THE
    APPLICATION

| T | R | O | S | 0 | 0 | 3 | 1 |

11. ENTER THE NUMBER OF RECORDS TO BE
    PROCESSED FOR A "TEST"

| | | | | 1 | 0 |

(b) Work Record Layout

1. WORK TOTAL FIELD
   Enter numeric non-indicative WORK field for pass control totals - for DOS or OS

TREAT
WORK RECORD LAYOUT

SEQUENCE NUMBER

W	F	0	2

1   4

1

5

W	/	/	

6   8

4. WORK FIELD CHARACTERISTICS

WORK FIELD NUMBER	WORK FIELD NAME (2)	STORAGE FORMAT (3) ALPHA-NUMERIC LENGTH	NUMERIC (4) Decimal Places	Indicative Y - Yes	REDEFINITION (5) STARTING WORK FIELD	STARTING LOCATION	DO NOT PUNCH LEFT-MOST BYTE LOCATION MEMO ONLY
5 6 8	9 22	23 25	26	27	28 30	31 33	
W01	CONTROL	5					
W02	DESCRIPTION	12					
W03	QUANTITY BOM		0				
W04	PURCHASES		0				
W05	ISSUES		0				
W06	ADJUSTMENTS		0				
W07	LAST UNIT COST		2				
W08	DATE LAST PUR	6					
W09	VENDOR CODE	5					
W10	DATE LAST ISSU	6					
W11	ISSUE YTD		0				
W12	ISSUE LAST YR		0				
W13	QUANTITY EOM				W01	0	
W14	PART NO	4			W01	4	
W15	LOCATION	1					
W16	FLAG	1	2				
W17	EXTENDED COST		2				
W							
W							
W							
W							
W							
W							
W							
W							

NOTES: (1) Enter form extant file WF02 and SVnn DIAGNOSTIC
(2) Name is used for column heading by SELECT & PRINT
(3) Either an alpha-numeric length or a numeric decimal place must be speified for each WORK field.
(4) Numeric fields designated as indicative will not be summarized.
(5) Only alpha-numeric fields may be redefined.
(6) T7, T9, D1, D2 or D4

(c) Temporary Core Storage

TREAT

SEQUENCE NUMBER

| T | C | O | 3 |

TEMPORARY CORE STORAGE

☐

	NUMERIC TEMPORARY STORAGE FIELD	ASSIGNED NAME	DECIMAL PLACES
5	6 8	9 22	23
1	T 0 1	C O M P U T A T I O M	2
1	T 0 2		
1	T 0 3		
1	T 0 4		
1	T 0 5		
1	T 0 6		
1	T 0 7		
1	T 0 8		
1	T 0 9		
1	T 1 0		
1	T 1 1		
1	T 1 2		
1	T 1 3		
1	T 1 4		
1	T 1 5		

	ALPHA-NUMERIC TEMPORARY STORAGE FIELD	ASSIGNED NAME	ALPHA-NUMERIC LENGTH
5	6 8	9 22	23 25
2	A 0 1		
2	A 0 2		
2	A 0 3		
2	A 0 4		
2	A 0 5		
2	A 0 6		
2	A 0 7		
2	A 0 8		
2	A 0 9		
2	A 1 0		
2	A 1 1		
2	A 1 2		
2	A 1 3		
2	A 1 4		
2	A 1 5		

(d) Data File Definition

TREAT Data File Definition

SEQUENCE NUMBER

`F` `D` `0` `4`

Card `1`

1. DATA SET NAME `S T R A T I N V`

2. VOLUME SERIAL NUMBER `I T C H 0 3`

3. STRATA FILE CODE: `□`
   CD for Card   T7 for 7 Track Tape
   T9 for 9 Track Tape Leave Blank for Disk

4. DISK FILE OR DATA CELL `S D` 5. BLOCK SIZE `8 0 0`
   ORGANIZATION SD for Sequential
   Disk file and partitioned data sets (Enter maximum block size)
   IS for Index Sequential Disk files
   DA for Direct Access files

6. RECORD TYPE `F` 7. RECORD SIZE (Enter length `8 0`
   F for fixed length records of type F records or maximum
   V for variable length records record size for type V records

8. ENTER H for Hierarchical file `□`
   (Hierarchical files cannot be used in updates)

10. FUNCTION OF THE DATA FILE `C R`
    CR Creates a WORK file from the DATA file.

12. BYPASS AUTOMATIC SORT `Y`
    (Enter Y to By pass)

16. NUMBER OF DATA RECORDS PROCESSED `1 0`
    FOR A TEST RUN ON THIS DATA FILE

Card `3`

19. MULTI-VOLUME SERIAL NUMBERS
    Enter additional volume serial numbers of input DATA file

6   11 12   17 18   23 24   29
30   35 36   41 42   47 48   53
54   59 60   65 66   71

(e) Data Field Selection

TREAT DATA FIELD SELECTION

FIXED SECTION OR REPEATING SECTION

SEQUENCE NUMBER

| F | S | 0 | 5 |

1

RECORD ID   SELECTION

1. RECORD ID'S TO BE SELECTED. Enter right justified 1 to 3 Record ID specifications. All criteria must be met for a record to be selected.

ID 1
ID 2
ID 3

3.   DATA FIELD DEFINITION

2	LOCATION (1) OF DATA FIELD		SIZE OF DATA FIELD	FOR-MAT	DEC. PL. IN NUMERIC FIELDS	DATA FIELD NAME (3) ALPHA-NUMERIC CONSTANT	NUMERIC CONSTANT	RECEIVING WORK FIELD (4)
5	6	9	10 12	13	14	15 21	28	29 31
2		0	5	C		CONTROL		W01
2		5	12	C		DESCRIPTION		W02
2		17	6	P	0	QUANTITY BOM		W03
2		23	6	P	0	PURCHASES		W04
2		29	6	P	0	ISSUES		W05
2		35	6	P	0	ADJUSTMENTS		W06
2		41	6	P	2	LAST UNIT COST		W07
2		47	6	C		DATE LAST PUR		W08
2		53	5	C		VENDOR CODE		W09
2		58	6	C		DATE LAST ISSU		W10
2		64	6	P	0	ISSUES YTD		W11
2		70	6	P	0	ISSUES LAST YR		W12
2								W
2								W
2								W
2								W
2								W
2								W
2								W
2								W
2								W
2								W
2								W
2								W
2								W
2								W
2								W

(1) Number of bytes preceeding the left-most byte of the DATA field

(2) C for character
B for binary
P for packed (signed)
L for constant
U for unsigned packed
R for unsigned packed right
X for unsigned packed left

A for unsigned packed all
H for addressing bits

V for variable length fields preceded by 1 byte
D for variable length fields preceded by 2 bytes
*Do not use on RS

(3) Constants can be entered into a WORK field by entering constant value here.
Alpha-Numeric Constant will be moved to work field from left, and Numeric Constant from right.

(4) Do not specify a numeric indicative WORK field as the receiving WORK field for more than one DATA field. Indicative fields are not summarized

(5) If using more than one FSnn sheet to describe one DATA record the FSnn sequence numbers on each sheet are to be the same.

(f) Calculate-Stratify

SEQUENCE NUMBER
C S 0 7

TREAT   CALCULATE - STRATIFY

LINE NO. (5 7)	FIELD A (8 10)	OPERATION (11 13)	FIELD B (14 16)	CONSTANT VALUE — NUMERIC (17 21) / ALPHA-NUMERIC (24)	DEC. PL (25)	FIELD C RESULT (26 28)	GO TO (1) (29 32)
1 0 5	W 0 3	A D D	W 0 4			T 0 1	
1 1 0	T 0 1	A D D	W 0 5			T 0 1	
1 1 5	T 0 1	A D D	W 0 6			W 1 3	
1 2 0	W 1 3	M U L	W 0 7			W 1 7	
1 2 5		A W L	W 1 3				
1 3 0		A N L	W 1 7				E N D
1 3 5							
1 4 0							
1 4 5							
1 5 0							
1 5 5							
1 6 0							
1 6 5							
1 7 0							
1 7 5							
1 8 0							
1 8 5							
1 9 0							
1 9 5							

CONDITIONAL OPERATIONS (1)

L - A less than B
E - A equal to B
G - A greater than B
RS - Random Selection of nn%
   nn is a numeric constant
   from 01 to 99. For nn% of
   the records chosen at
   random, the condition
   is met. (3)

LE - A less than or Equal to B
NE - A not equal to B
GE - A greater than or equal
   to B
SC - Tests STRATA Code
   field of the WORK record.
   If equal to the two-digit
   Alpha-Numeric constant,
   the condition is met. (4)

EXIT ROUTINE - AVAILABLE IN O/S ONLY

XIT - EXTPROG3 - Allows exiting from STRATA to a user coded subroutine to act upon STRATA Work record. Enter "XIT" in Operation column and user exit member name in the constant value field.

MATHEMATICAL AND OTHER OPERATIONS (2)

ADD   A + B = C
SUB   A - B = C
ANL   Analyze Field B
      Optional - To obtain "Variance" of
      Field B with Analyze results enter
      ANL in "Operation" column and "V"
      in column 17
      Available in 65K STRATA only.
MOV   B → A, Moves Alpha-Numeric field
      B or Constant to field A.
COD   Enters any two digit Alpha-Numeric
      Constant in the STRATA code field
      of the WORK record. (4)
EQP   Enter EOP to stop all processing in
      that STRATA Pass.

GO TO OPTIONS (1)

END   Pass curent WORK
      record to next STRATA
      function. (After Calculate/
      Stratify.)
READ Reject current WORK
      record from any
      further STRATA function
      by getting the next record.
CSnn Branch to page number nn.
EX   CSnn. Perform steps on page
      nn and return. Put EX in
      "Operation Field" and CSnn
      in "Go To" field.
Blank If any conditional
      operation fails, a blank
      "Go To" will cause a
      branch to the next page.

(1) In Conditional Operations
   • if the tested condition is met the next sequential
     operation is performed.
   • if the tested condition fails, STRATA takes "Go
     To" option.
(2) After performing a mathematical or other operation (except
   for EOP) STRATA performs the next sequential operation
   unless the "Go To" field is non-blank.

(3) Enter Numeric Constants and Random Selection percent
   right justified in Constant Value field.
(4) Enter Alpha-Numeric Constants and two digit STRATA
   Codes left justified in Constant Value field.

(g) Select and Print I

TREAT   SELECT & PRINT

SEQUENCE NUMBER

P	S	0	9

REPORT SELECTION CRITERIA (1)

LINE NO.	FIELD A	OPERATION	FIELD B	CONSTANT VALUE NUMERIC / ALPHA-NUMERIC	DEC. PL	FIELD C RESULT	ALLOWED OPERATIONS
5 7	8 10	11 13	14 16	17 21 24	25	26 28	
1 1 0	W / 7	G		/	0 0 0	0		Conditional
1 1 5		A N L	W / 7					L Less Than
1 2 0								LE Less Than or Equal to
1 2 5								E Equal to
1 3 0								NE Not Equal to
1 3 5								G Greater Than
1 4 0								GE Greater Than or Equal to
1 4 5								RS Random Select
1 5 0								SC Test Strata Code Field
1 5 5								

ALLOWED OPERATIONS

Conditional
- L   Less Than
- LE   Less Than or Equal to
- E   Equal to
- NE   Not Equal to
- G   Greater Than
- GE   Greater Than or Equal to
- RS   Random Select
- SC   Test Strata Code Field

Mathematical
- ADD   Add
- SUB   Subtract
- MUL   Multiply
- DIV   Divide

Other
- ANL   Analyze
- MOV   Move
- COD   Fill Strata Code Field

PRINT SPECIFICATIONS

REPORT NO.   REPORT NAME

2	0 1	T E S T C O U N T I T E M S
5	6 7	8 35

SORT CONTROL FIELDS FOR RECORDS SELECTED

Major ————————————► Minor

3	W / 5	W / 7	W
5	6 8	9 11	12 14

LINES TO BE PRINTED - (Enter Y for Yes)

	Details	Major Totals	Intermediate Totals	Minor Totals	Page Totals	Grand Totals
4	Y	Y	☐	☐	☐	Y
5	6	7	8	9	10	11

Totals, spacing and breaks are controlled by the corresponding WORK fields specified in Columns 1, 2, and 3 below.

SPACING BETWEEN LINES AND PAGE BREAKS

Details	Major Breaks	Intermediate Breaks	Minor Breaks	Omit Dashed Lines on Totals (Enter Y for Yes)
☐ (2)	☐ (3)	☐ (3)	☐ (3)	☐
12	13	14	15	16

CONTENTS OF COLUMN (4)

CONTROL FIELD FOR MAJOR TOTALS BREAKS			CONTROL FIELD FOR INTERMED. TOTALS BREAKS			CONTROL FIELD FOR MINOR TOTALS BREAKS					
Col. No.	Field	Low-order position	Col. No.	Field	Low-order position	Col. No.	Field	Low-order position	Col. No.	Field	Low-order position
0 1	W / 5		0 2	W / 4		0 3	W 0 2		0 4	W 0 9	
0 1	W 0 8		0 6	W / 0		0 7	W / 3		0 8	W / 7	
0 1			1 0			1 1			1 2		

(row labels at left: 5, 5, 5)

(h) Select and Print II

TREAT SELECT & PRINT

SEQUENCE NUMBER
| P | S | 1 | 1 |

REPORT SELECTION CRITERIA (1)

LINE NO.	FIELD A	OPERATION	FIELD B	CONSTANT VALUE NUMERIC / ALPHA-NUMERIC	DEC. PL	FIELD C RESULT	ALLOWED OPERATIONS
5 7	8 10	11 13	14 16	17 21 24	25	26 28	Conditional
1 1 0	W 0 7	G			5 0		L Less Than
1 1 5		A N L	W 1 7				LE Less Than or Equal to
1 2 0							E Equal to
1 2 5							NE Not Equal to
1 3 0							G Greater Than
1 3 5							GE Greater Than or Equal to
1 4 0							RS Random Select
1 4 5							SC Test Strata Code Field
1 5 0							Mathematical
1 5 5							ADD Add / SUB Subtract / MUL Multiply / DIV Divide

Other: ANL Analyze, MOV Move, COD Fill Strata Code Field

PRINT SPECIFICATIONS

REPORT NO. REPORT NAME
| 2 | 0 2 | S E L E C T   I T E M S   F O R   P R I C E   C H E C K |

SORT CONTROL FIELDS FOR RECORDS SELECTED (Major → Minor)
| 3 | W 1 4 | W | W |

LINES TO BE PRINTED - (Enter Y for Yes)
| 4 | Details Y | Major Totals ☐ | Intermediate Totals ☐ | Minor Totals ☐ | Page Totals ☐ | Grand Totals Y |

Totals, spacing and breaks are controlled by the corresponding WORK fields specified in Columns 1, 2, and 3 below.

SPACING BETWEEN LINES AND PAGE BREAKS
Details (2) ☐ Major Breaks (3) ☐ Intermediate Breaks (3) ☐ Minor Breaks (3) ☐ Omit Dashed Lines on Totals (Enter Y for Yes) ☐

CONTENTS OF COLUMN (4)

CONTROL FIELD FOR MAJOR TOTALS BREAKS			CONTROL FIELD FOR INTERMED. TOTALS BREAKS			CONTROL FIELD FOR MINOR TOTALS BREAKS					
Col. No.	Field	Low-order position	Col. No.	Field	Low-order position	Col. No.	Field	Low-order position	Col. No.	Field	Low-order position
0 1	W 1 4		0 2	W 1 5		0 3	W 0 2		0 4	W 0 4	
0 1	W 0 8		0 6	W 1 0		0 7	W 1 3		0 8	W 1 7	
0 1	W 0 7		1 0			1 1			1 2		

Exercise. Performing the above assignments allowed you to go through an example of a TREAT application. Now, using the Magic Desk file and initial walkthrough specification sheets extend this work by

1. Choosing three or more objectives which will lead to recommendations concerning Mr. Clever's problem; one of these objectives must include the task of verifying the accuracy of the client's records.
2. Preparing all necessary flowcharts, worksheets and specification sheets necessary to program TREAT.
3. Setting-up budget sheet (remember, your firm has to bill the client for your work) which lists your estimates and actual time spent on each section of the job. (Setting objectives, filling-out forms, programming, debugging programs, printing, analysis, etc.)
4. The finished product should include a print-out of each specification page, a print-out of the results of your run, all flowcharts and worksheets, your objectives and your analysis and recommendation.

A.3 CASE STUDY: TROJAN COMPANY PROPERTY, PLANT, AND EQUIPMENT AUDIT

Located in the greater Los Angeles area, the Trojan Company is a well-established distributor of sporting goods. The firm was established in 1964 by the Henbenger brothers, who initially worked out of the backyard of their house and catered to the sports equipment needs of the University of Southern California. The nature of their business gradually changed, becoming more and more oriented toward the distribution of sports equipment for a group of small manufacturers (including their own manufacturing operation) to many independent sporting goods stores located nationwide. In spite of this increasing emphasis on wholesale operations, Trojan still operated its original Los Angeles retail store profitably and maintained its small manufacturing facility that produced USC Trojan memorabilia. Mr. Brendon Henbenger, the founder, stated that "Our store allows us to keep better track of the trends in our business."

Trojan Company sales grew from about $1 million in 1969 to $105 million in 1979. In 1975 the Henbenger brothers decided to issue shares to the public in the over-the-counter (OTC) market. Trojan Company shares were issued at $1.00, were trading at $2.65 in early 1980, and had earnings per share of $0.60 in 1979. The firm has consistently paid dividends of about 40 percent of earnings since it went public. The company is reputed to

be sound and to have conservative management. Daley and Paine, a local
CPA firm, has been the company's auditor since it went public and has
consistently issued unqualified audit statements.

Fiscal year 1979 was one of solid growth for Trojan, but growth pains
were evident. The Henbengers had to bring in a computer consultant, David
Tomlin, who advised them on the purchase of an IBM system/3, which
had been installed in March 1979. Many of the application systems that
were implemented were purchased as software packages from IBM and
other suppliers. In 1980, the company had an EDP staff of three, with Mr.
Tomlin spending about 50 percent of his time to supervising their efforts.

Daley and Paine concluded that the EDP system required additional
attention as part of the audit process, particularly with respect to recently
issued audit standards. Fortunately, they had just hired a new auditor,
Sherry Snodgress, who had extensive training in EDP from a well-known
eastern university. The partner in charge, Cynthia Paine, was also
concerned that Gertrude Stein, the long-time bookkeeper at Trojan, now in
semiretirement, worked only 20 hours per week and that she, in spite of
attempting to be helpful, had little contact with the company's EDP staff.

Ms. Snodgress, after interviewing the Henbengers, Mr. Tomlin, and Ms.
Stein, came to the conclusion that computer applications at the Trojan
Company had barely scratched the surface and that the only operational
system of importance was the PPE management system. She decided to
begin by examining it, but unfortunately, the documentation of the package
was not available to her. However, the EDP staff indicated that the
totals for fixed assets, depreciation, and accumulated depreciation in the
financial statements were derived directly from the PPE file. Under Ms.
Snodgress's supervision, the EDP staff drew a 10 percent sample of all
items for audit purposes and named this file STRATPPE. Ms. Snodgress
will use the TREAT package to analyze the file's contents.

AUDIT OBJECTIVES

Ms. Snodgress's task is to test Trojan Company's depreciation calculations
for the year ended December 31, 1979. She establishes the following audit
objectives.

Objective 1: Print a report with a list of all acquisitions and
dispositions.

Objective 2: Determine differences between her calculations and the
company's depreciation book figures.

Objective 3: Identify status codes other than current status for further investigation.

Objective 4: Investigate the reasons for variances in the tax depreciation figures obtained.

Objective 5: Determine whether any depreciation was applied to land.

Objective 6: Prepare an aggregate summary list of all items where exceptions were found.

Objective 7: Prepare a documentation report, including conclusions based on an analysis of findings.

RELEVANT INFORMATION

The EDP staff provided Ms. Snodgress with the following description of the data file used for determining depreciation book values.

Bytes	Field Name	Format	Decimal
1–5	Asset number	C	
6–17	Description	C	
18–19	Type	C	
20–22	Location	C	
23–28	Year acquired	P	0
29–34	Cost	P	0
35–40	Accumulated depreciation—book—end of year	P	0
41–46	Depreciation—book—year to date	P	0
47–48	Life	C	
52–57	Accumulated depreciation—tax—end of year	P	0
58–63	Depreciation—tax—year to date	P	0
64	Status code	C	
65–68	Blank	C	

The company determines book depreciation by the straight-line method, with a 10 percent scrap value. The company takes a full year's depreciation in the year of acquisition. Additional first-year depreciation and investment credit are not considered to be applicable.

The formula for computing depreciation based on the straight-line method, as outlined in the Internal Revenue Code, is

$$Cost - Scrap\ value = Basis.$$

$$\frac{Basis}{Life} = Annual\ depreciation.$$

The company uses the following codes for various types of assets.

Land	10
Office building	20
Warehouses	30
Production equipment and vehicles	41
Office equipment	42
Sales vehicles	43

The company's status codes are:

A = Current.
B = Disposed of in current period (no depreciation taken for the current year).
C = Disposed of in prior periods (useful life = 00).
D = Land.

DOCUMENTATION REQUIREMENTS

As a competent EDP auditor, Ms. Snodgress plans to document her work carefully in order to facilitate review by the partner in charge, as well as next year's work. She prepares the following list of documentation.

1. A cover page.
2. An outline with pages cross-referenced.
3. A budget, with expected and actual time for each member of the audit team.
4. A description of the audit process.
5. Client's file layouts.
6. Application flowchart.
7. Work-file layout.
8. TREAT program flowchart.
9. TREAT list.
10. Report layouts.
11. Reports obtained—annotated.
12. Analysis of results, cross-referenced to the annotations.
13. Analysis of conclusions and about internal controls and other considerations.

When preparing the documentation report, she makes sure that topics are tied together and presented clearly and that it won't be necessary for Ms. Paine to disassemble or flip back and forth in the report in order to review it. Ms. Snodgress's conclusions will also contain a list of items for the partner in charge to examine with particular care.

A.4 CASE STUDY: TREATCO, INC., ACCOUNTS RECEIVABLE AUDIT

You have just been promoted to senior EDP auditor because of the outstanding work you did on the audit of Magic Desk Company's inventory. Because of that success and your strong EDP audit background, your next assignment is to make the computer audit examination of TREATCO Inc.'s accounts receivable system.

TREATCO, Inc., is a small manufacturer of wizbizes which, in spite of their price, have become quite popular among college students, particularly MBA candidates. The supervisor in charge of the overall audit of TREATCO, Bill Knox, tells you that

> TREATCO will provide you with a complete description of its accounts receivable transactions file. At my request, Ms. Smith, the company's internal auditor, has dumped 5 percent of their transaction records onto a disk file called STRATAR1. As far as we know, there are source documents to substantiate all transactions. The company's total book value for the transactions is $750,200. At your request I am assigning Jim Peterson [a junior staff auditor] to assist you.

INFORMATION GATHERING

When you arrive at TREATCO's offices, you begin by examining all the documentation you can get your hands on. You soon conclude that the company's EDP installation is well-organized and run smoothly by a small staff consisting of the EDP manager (who is also the systems analyst), two programmers, and three operators who alternate hours to run the computer six days a week from 8 A.M. to 6 P.M.

You learn that a client transaction data file for accounts receivable consists of two types of records: 3 and 4. The following file layout is for type 4 records.

Bytes	Field Name
1–15	Customer number.
16	Record type.
17–21	Document number.
22	Transaction type.
23–31	Blank.
32–37	Date.
38–45	Amount.
46–50	Batch number.
51–60	Blank.

1. CREATE a Work File consisting *solely* of type 4 records, and omitting the last 5 bytes of the record from the Data file.
2. The transactions of the Data File are for the period 040177 to 033178.
3. Analyze (ANL) the amount field as the first instruction of your initial CS page.
4. The first 3 characters of the customer number are a division number. Redefine into two fields on your Work File.
5. The random number for random select should be 3.
6. To enhance the quality of your audit objectives you may want to explore further some of the findings in objectives 1 through 4.
7. As you will be on your own at the client's location you must be sure to carefully record your computer usage to later report it to the client. Remember that the quality of your documentation is of utmost importance for a successful audit and for return engagement efficiency.

You also determine that the codes for transaction types are as follows:

1	Invoices.
2	Credit memos.
4–9, A–N	Cash receipts by source.

Other relevant information is that all data are stored in character format; the amount field has an implied two decimal places; the order of records in the data file is not known; records other than type 4 have a fixed length of 60 characters and the record type is in character 16; and the blocking factor is 20, file name is STRATAR1.

AUDIT OBJECTIVES

Following your initial information gathering assessment work, you prepare a set of audit objectives for Mr. Knox's approval.

AUDIT PROCEDURES

1. Select all account balances over $100.00 and random select 30 percent of the remaining positive (debit balance) accounts from the data file. Print a report of these items with a subtotal between sections. Assign a sequential confirmation number to each account balance selection after the account balances are listed in ascending amounts. ANALYZE the account balances before and after the above selection criteria are applied.

    This report will be used to prepare confirmation letters and to control confirmation replies. The confirmation letters will be prepared in a separate application of TREAT for which you are not responsible.

    Any account balances not selected for any of the other groups should be listed as the last group on the report in the form of a summarized record. There should be a major total after each group on the record and a grand total for the report as a whole.

2. List any credit or zero account balances from the Data File in descending order. These accounts will be investigated and reclassified as accounts payable on the financial statements.

3. Make the following tests on the records of the file:

    a. Set up a one byte alpha-numeric field. If any type 1 transactions have a negative amount, place a "-" in the alpha-numeric field.

    b. Set up a second alpha-numeric field. If any type 2 transactions have a positive amount, place a ";" in the second alpha-numeric field.

    c. Set up a third alpha-numeric field. If any type 4-9 or A-N transactions have a positive amount, place a "D" in the third A/N field.

    d. Set up a fourth alpha-numeric field. If there are any unauthorized transactions (a type other than 1, 2, 4-9, or A-N) place a "U" in the fourth alpha-numeric field.

    e. If batch number is blank, place a "B" in the fifth alpha-numeric field.

    f. If the blank field (bytes 23-31) is not blank, place a "NB" in a sixth alpha-numeric field.

g.   If any of the transactions has a zero amount, place an "A" in a seventh alpha-numeric field.

h.   Create a numeric field and place in it a count of the anomalous occurrences for each of the records registered in items a to g.

From the sample, list in the report only those transactions for which at least 1 of the above types of errors were found. Show the sequence number of the record as it appeared in the original file, the division number, customer number, and the seven alpha-numeric fields. Show a grand total of the amount field for these items.

4. Age the accounts receivable transaction file into the following mutually exclusive categories:

(a)   Not more than 1 month old.

(b)   Not more than 3 months old.

(c)   All others.

(d)   Show the total balance for each account as well. Apply cash receipts and other credits to the account charges on a FIFO basis for accounts with a positive or zero balance. For accounts with negative balances, show the age of the net credits after the charges to the accounts have been offset by the credits.

5. As a competent auditor you may want to look into any other factors that come to your attention throughout the audit.

A.5 CASE STUDY: TREATCO, INC., ACCOUNTS RECEIVABLE AUDIT WITH FILE MERGE

Treatco Inc. is a small manufacturer of wizbizes which, in spite of their not inconsequential price, have become quite popular among college students, particularly MBA candidates.

You are a recently graduated MBA spending some time in the internal audit department of Treatco Inc. and the department head, noticing in your vita that you have just completed a course in computer auditing, says as he hands you a piece of paper (Attachment I):

This is a client's description of its accounts receivable transaction file. I have requested that Ms. Smith dump 5 percent of our transaction records onto a disk file denominated STRATAR1. As far as we could reasonably ascertain, there are source documents to substantiate these transactions. The book value for the transactions (which are represented by 5 percent sample) is $750,200.00. In addition you may use the Accounts Receivable Master File, the layout of which can be found in Attachment 2, and which is to be updated by these transactions. You may find it strange that there are some old transactions in this batch but remember that our control group is quite efficient and thorough and makes sure that transactions earlier rejected for some cause are entered if later found acceptable. I am concerned with the value of the updated balances as we seem to have been receiving an inordinately large number of complaints.

I would appreciate it if you could:

1. Prepare a list of the total transaction values for each of the clients with a debit total transaction value.
2. Prepare a list of all clients (using just the transaction file) with a zero transaction balance.
3. Prepare a list of all clients in the transaction file with a credit contribution to their master file balance.
4. Prepare a list of all clients with a final balance (transaction plus master file) larger than 100. This list should be in descending order and should contain all information necessary to prepare confirmation requests for balances in question.

As you start at the engagement you begin by examining all the documentation you can get your hands on. The installation seems very well organized—running smoothly under a small staff consisting of a manager (who is also the system analyst), two programmers and three operators who alternate hours to run the machine six days a week from 8 AM to 6 PM.

GENERAL INSTRUCTIONS

1. CREATE a Work File consisting *solely* of type 4 records, and omitting the last 5 bytes of the record from the Data File.
2. The transaction of the Data File are for the period 140177 to 033178.
3. Analyze (ANL) the amount field as the first instruction on your initial CS page.
4. The first 3 characters of the customer number are a division number. Redefine into two fields on your Work File.
5. The random number for random select should be 3.
6. To enhance the quality of your audit objectives you may want to explore further some of the findings in objectives 1 through 4.
7. As you will be on your own at the client's location you must be sure to carefully record your computer usage to later report it to the client. Remember that the quality of your documentation is of utmost importance for a successful audit and for return engagement efficiency.

8. The file layout of the account receivables transaction file is the same of the TREATCO I use. The master file layout follows.

ACCOUNTS RECEIVABLE MASTER FILE

Bytes	Field Name
1–15	Customer No.
16–34	Customer Name
35–49	Address
50–60	Customer Balance

The name of the file is STRATARO.

The file is sequential in nature, its logical record length is 60 bytes, and it has 10 records per block.

The client's balance field has an implied decimal place setting of 2.

Notes

1. An IBM/PC version of TREAT is available using IBM's APL.

2. STSC's new APL compiler may be the predecessor of a generation of PC software that allows compilation of APL source code.

3. Other, less important pages, are also listed in the TREAT user's manual.

Index